SCIENTISTS *and the* SEA
1650-1900
a study of marine science

IN MEMORY OF
MARGARET ELSA DEACON

SCIENTISTS *and the* SEA
1650-1900
a study of marine science

MARGARET DEACON

Ashgate

First edition   ©1971 by Academic Press Inc. (London) Ltd.
This edition   ©1997 by Margaret Deacon.

Published by   Ashgate Publishing Limited
Gower House, Croft Road,
Aldershot, Hampshire GU11 3HR
Great Britain

Ashgate Publishing Company
Old Post Road,
Brookfield, Vermont 05036–9704
USA

ISBN 1-85928-352-7

British Library CIP Data
Deacon, Margaret.
Scientists and the Sea, 1650–1900: a Study of Marine Science. - 2nd ed.
1. Marine sciences—History. 2. Oceanography—History.
I. Title.
551.4'6'09

US Library of Congress CIP Data
Deacon, Margaret.
Scientists and the Sea, 1650–1900: a Study of Marine Science/ Margaret Deacon–2nd ed.
    p. cm.   Includes bibliographical references and indexes.
ISBN 1-85928-352-7 (hb: acid-free).
1. Oceanography–History. 2. Marine biology–History. I. Title.
GC29.D38 1997   97-844
551.46'009–dc21   CIP

This volume is printed on acid-free paper.

Printed in Great Britain by Galliard (Printers) Ltd, Great Yarmouth

CONTENTS

Foreword to Second Edition vii
Preface to First Edition ix
Acknowledgements xv
Introduction to Second Edition xvii

THE BACKGROUND TO THE SEVENTEENTH CENTURY MOVEMENT

1. The Ancient World 3
2. The Middle Ages 20
3. The Renaissance 39

MARINE SCIENCE IN THE SEVENTEENTH CENTURY

4. The Seventeenth Century Movement towards a Science of the
   Sea 69
5. Theories and Observations of Tides 93
6. Marine Science in the Works of Robert Boyle . . . 117
7. The Currents in the Strait of Gibraltar 132
8. Robert Hooke and the Vanishing Harvest . . . 154

AN AGE OF PHILOSOPHY AND CURIOUS NAVIGATION

9. Reawakening Interest in the Sea, 1700–1800. . . 175
10. Widening Horizons: The Last Quarter of the Eighteenth Century 199
11. Marine Science in the Early Nineteenth Century: A Period of
    Growth 220

THE UNSATISFIED OCEAN

12. Wild-Meeting Oceans: the Study of Tides . . . 251
13. The Threshold of the Deep Ocean 276
14. The Magnificent Generalization 306
15. The Voyage of H.M.S. *Challenger* 333
16. Edinburgh and the Growth of Oceanography at the end of the
    Nineteenth Century 366

APPENDIX 1

    Propositions of some Experiments to be made by the Earl of
        Sandwich in his present Voyage   407

APPENDIX 2

    Experiments made by Captain Robert Holmes on 2 and 30 May
        1663 409

APPENDIX 3

    Other Inquiries Concerning the Sea   410

    Select Bibliography to First Edition   411
    Bibliography to Second Edition Introduction   .   .   . 417
    Index of Persons   431
    Subject Index 443

PUBLISHER'S NOTE

References to the Addenda et Corrigenda at the ends of chapters are indicated by asterisks next to the passages concerned.

FOREWORD TO SECOND EDITION

In 1978, Margaret Deacon wrote of the oceans that "what was thought, little over a hundred years ago, to be a dead world has turned out to be alive and continually changing". The responsibility for the first concerted study of that change of attitude, and for the origin of a new discipline, the history of oceanography, rests largely with Margaret Deacon. She was among the first and is still the pre-eminent scholar of this field. For the past twenty-five years the main reference source for anyone contemplating work on the history of oceanography has been her book *Scientists and the Sea*, first published in 1971 and long out of print. Now Ashgate has reprinted a revised version of this important work.

Scientists and the Sea was a pioneering work, unequalled since in its depth and breadth of coverage. It remains invaluable to anyone wanting to understand the origins of marine science in Antiquity, the Middle Ages, during the period of the Scientific Revolution, the great seventeenth- and eighteenth-century explorations, and during the nineteenth-century when the early work was transmuted into a modern science of the oceans. It has been the springboard for many of Margaret Deacon's more recent historical studies, dealing, for example, with the contributions of the early Fellows of the Royal Society (especially Robert Boyle and Robert Hooke) to the marine sciences and the reasons why their work did not develop further. It introduced the historical background of knowledge about currents in the Strait of Gibraltar (a subject still being studied today), showing how the early speculations arose and how difficult it was to put them to any definitive test. Additionally, it introduced many little-known aspects of early nineteenth-century marine science that had disappeared into the mists of time and the dust of library collections.

The background provided by *Scientists and the Sea* allowed Margaret Deacon to take unorthodox and fruitful approaches to the study of the voyage of H.M.S. *Challenger* (1872–1976), showing in a later publication how influential the work done on *Challenger* was for marine geology, and that the voyage was not (as is commonly stated) the origin of modern oceanography but an important waystation in its development. It also led to her outstanding work on other nineteenth-century marine investigations of the Mediterranean, of the seas north of Britain, and on early twentieth-century oceanography. Thus *Scientists and the Sea* helped to open up new areas of study of not only marine science itself, but of how it originated or evolved in political, economic and social contexts. Recently, in a subtle and penetrating way, she has shown how marine science institutions developed in the United Kingdom and how dependent they were upon the economic and political climates of their times.

The insights into the nature of science and its historical development first presented in *Scientists and the Sea* have been profound, and were in the vanguard of a new historiography of science in 1971. Margaret Deacon clearly recognized the episodic nature of scientific change, rather than linear or cumulative "progress". She identified the problems of professionalization in the marine sciences, especially the difficulty that early natural philosophers and scientists had in finding a suitable context for their work on the oceans. As well as this she pointed out an important difference between the marine sciences and other sciences: an early stage of non-professional investigation or experiment was hampered or made impossible by the magnitude and hostility of the marine environment. The keen eye for important historical problems shown then and in her later work has made these writings an inspiration to her colleagues in the history of science, and has made her publications, beginning especially with this book, essential to all who wish to understand the development of the marine sciences.

In 1971, *Scientists and the Sea* put the marine sciences in a new context – that of the social and scientific development of the basic sciences and technology. It asked questions that are still stimulating research as the 1990s close. After admiring its virtues and being invigorated by its originality, users of increasingly battered library copies of *Scientists and the Sea* now have a new edition for their shelves. I think that my brief remarks on the book and its consequences during the past twenty-five years will indicate why the reappearance of this book now is as important as its appearance was a quarter century ago.

September 1996   ERIC L. MILLS
Dalhousie University
Halifax, Canada

PREFACE TO FIRST EDITION

This book was originally planned as an outline of the development of physical oceanography in Britain. The idea of writing it took shape while my father and I were at work on a paper dealing with the interest in the sea shown by seventeenth-century scientists. There was clearly more to be learned about their activities. Then, the question arose, in what way were they linked to present day oceanography? For all we knew the one might slowly have evolved into the other. Though largely unsurveyed the two intervening centuries were not uncharted and historical summaries listed many contributions to man's knowledge of the sea made during this time. Outstanding among these was the work of the *Challenger* expedition, often held to be the foundation of modern oceanography.

The most pressing questions to be answered were, who were these people and what did they do? But almost at once more queries arose. What motives did these people have for pursuing the scientific study of the sea and did they vary from person to person or from one time to another? Did they think of themselves as contributing to a distinct "science of the sea"? To what extent were they representative of the scientific community of their time and what degree of recognition or support did it afford them? This book in no way provides complete answers to these questions, if indeed they all could be found, but the sources for marine science do contain some revealing insights along these lines.

Already the original purpose of the book had proved deceptively simple and further complications were soon to arise. Firstly, the intention, adopted purely for convenience, of restricting its scope to the British Isles, had soon to be abandoned. From quite early on there was evidence of contacts between scientists of different nationalities. Furthermore, the exchange of ideas and information was not limited to the diffusion of books and journals or even to correspondence. Of numerous examples two, by no means the most striking, may be given. In the early nineteenth century Russian explorers came to London to purchase thermometers for deep sea work and suggested a new idea to a British inventor. At about the same time Humboldt was planning a visit to this country partly in order to discuss with James Rennell their mutual interest in ocean currents.

Further on in the nineteenth century it proved impossible to go on writing about "physical oceanography", a term employed in its widest sense, without taking into account the development of marine biology. Until this time the physical and biological aspects of marine science had, with the exception of Marsigli's work, been pursued quite

ix

separately. Then, interest in marine biology came to play an important part in stimulating deep-sea exploration and a dominant role in the creation of marine stations.

Another problem was to know where to begin the book. The seventeenth century scientists who became interested in studying the sea did not start without any preconceived ideas. The information to be found in books, which as they not infrequently remarked was precious little, was adequately represented by the general scientific and geographical works of the time. From what source did these books derive their ideas? It appeared that they had been transmitted relatively unchanged, and with occasional injections of the original material, through generations of authors and thinkers from the work of the ancient Greeks and their successors. Inasmuch as this was mere copying it did little but keep alive the topics which they had debated but when, during the later Middle Ages, philosophers began a more critical discussion of the original works themselves they were, if perhaps indirectly, in this instance, preparing the way for the renewal of scientific study of the sea in the seventeenth century. A further element in their outlook can be seen developing in some of the Renaissance writers who reacted violently against the scholastic technique, as they conceived it, and insisted that true knowledge of natural phenomena would be attained only by studying the objects themselves.

The first part of this book is therefore a sketch of scientific thought about the sea up to the scientific revolution of the seventeenth century. The other three sections deal with marine science in the seventeenth century, in the eighteenth and early nineteenth centuries and in the middle and late nineteenth century.

The most far-reaching modification of the original plan occurred when it became plain that there was in fact no continuous development of marine science between the seventeenth century and the present day. What we were looking at were large-scale fluctuations of interest in which activity in the marine sciences built up, flourished for a while, and then declined. Though in each succeeding period of activity observations and ideas tended to become more sophisticated than in the one before, this change was allied more to the scientific climate of the time than to one generation "improving" the work of another. Areas of particular interest shifted between one period of expansion and the next. Generally the people involved in such a cycle had only a very partial appreciation of the work which had gone on in the previous ones. Their interest in it, if any, was largely antiquarian. There are few if any clear cut cases of work in one cycle being generated directly by work in the preceding one, though accounts of specific problems and, in a dilute form, of previous work were transmitted by textbooks and undoubtedly had an effect, as in the seventeenth century.

The last three sections of the book cover roughly three cycles of activity. We are in the fourth today.

What is the reason for this pattern of alternating outbursts of activity and periods of stagnation? Can one see any common feature to account for the succession of growth and decay? Perhaps the scientists in each period had some motive or stimulus in common which made them turn to the sea? However, when we look at the immediate reasons given for studying the sea, they seem to differ each time. The great upsurge of activity in the seventeenth century seems adequately explained by the circumstances of the scientific revolution and by the scientists' own words. They believed that the natural world was amenable to scientific study and that knowledge could be employed to better the condition of mankind. As far as the sea was concerned this was no vague hope but a well-founded expectation of humanitarian and economic benefits. They foresaw that improved understanding of waves, tides and currents would bring improved safety at sea and that knowledge of the properties of sea water would lead to better desalination processes and deep-sea diving techniques, as indeed they have.

In the eighteenth and early nineteenth centuries the principal reason for studying the sea seems to have lain in the belief that it would throw new light on subjects already engaging the attention of scientists, whether terrestrial physics and astronomy, or meteorology and geology. Later in the nineteenth century interest in a virtually unknown area which might provide answers to major questions at issue in the scientific community, the origin of species and of life itself, seems to have been the dominant motive.

Conscious motives do not, therefore, seem to provide the link. Nor, except in the last instance, do these waves of activity seem to have owed their existence to the force of a single paradigm, in the sense of a new scientific theory. They were not due either to the sudden provision of technical opportunities or facilities. The idea of the lineless sounding machine had apparently been in existence for hundreds of years before it was tried out. In the mid-nineteenth century improvements in methods of deep-sea sounding provided information and the means of obtaining more which aroused some interest among scientists but they did not lead to the emergence overnight of a science of the sea.

Yet perhaps the final explanation does include elements of all these, of opportunity, motive and of a paradigm in the broadest sense of an underlying attitude to science and its role. The mid-seventeenth and late eighteenth and nineteenth centuries were periods of expansion in the natural sciences generally. People became aware of the possibility of extending knowledge by diversifying scientific activity and extending it into fields hitherto neglected or ignored. Of these marine science was one. After the initial outburst was over a period of stabilization or even contraction set in when, the original vision having been lost sight of, those branches of science which had proved intractable and insufficiently rewarding to researchers were dropped in favour of the more successful— both in terms of obtaining usable results and of providing prospects of employment in the future. Marine science always came off badly here and, quite clearly in the late nineteenth century and probably in the early years of the century as well, one can see people abandoning hitherto fruitful projects, rarely if ever to revert to them.

Some resisted the general downward trend. For some scientists the study of the sea had become absorbing for its own sake and a few continued work long after most people had lost interest and sometimes, apparently, in complete isolation. Occasionally they crusaded to arouse new interest among their contemporaries, but without much success. Realization of his inability to do this lies behind Hooke's mood of depression in his 1691 lectures. Against their failure to win support one has to put the success enjoyed by the innovators who were successful in securing the interest and participation of others at times when science was expanding, people like Moray, Hales and Jameson.

These premature curtailments long delayed the development of marine science as we know it today. It meant that those who became involved in research often moved into other fields, or back to their original subjects, before they had time to consolidate new positions in knowledge or to acquire pupils who would propagate and continue their work. This must be the explanation for the sometimes quite extraordinary ignorance of basic discoveries in this field shown by scientists in general in between periods of activity and of the isolation of one period from another.

This has not answered the question of why interest in marine science should be generated at some times and not at others, except to suggest that it should be seen as part of the wider question of why science has developed and in the way that it has. Perhaps one can give a more positive answer to the question why, having begun, the study of the sea did not for so long establish itself as one of the recognized sciences. Yet even here difficulties arise. Lack of interest and lack of support were apparent in each period of decline. Which was the cause and which the effect? Had the stock of ideas been exhausted or were new theoretical developments impossible without further improvements in observations, brought about in their turn by fresh technical advances? It does not seem likely that such impasses, either theoretical or practical, were reached; if they were, this was certainly not a common occurrence. Those people who had developed a special interest in marine science never ceased to emphasize what advantages would accrue if people would make more observations with existing instruments. They never felt that interesting possibilities were lacking;

what were missing were the people and resources to provide the data necessary to exploit them.

The trouble was that, as even Marsigli found, the amount that any one person could do was severely limited. Making successful observations at sea entailed willing helpers, money for ships and instruments, and, an important consideration in the early days, security from attack. Only a person or body commanding wealth and power could fulfil these conditions and Marsigli envisaged some ruler becoming a patron of marine science. Rennell declared that it must be the work of government. During the nineteenth century a number of attempts were made to initiate schemes of voluntary co-operation among seamen for collecting data and to involve governments in furthering this kind of work. Some of these were successful, notably the Brussels conference on maritime meteorology in 1853 and the Scandinavian initiative which led to the formation of the International Council for the Exploration of the Sea. Yet government support for marine science, particularly in the United Kingdom, was not to be forthcoming on a large scale until the mid-twentieth century.

Without facilities for collecting observations, without opportunities for work on shore and without a recognized career structure, it was difficult if not impossible for people to make marine science their life's work. Marine biology became an exception in the late nineteenth century when academic zoologists could specialize in marine life and there were opportunities for full time research in the marine stations and the fisheries laboratories. In the other branches of marine science such opportunities were almost non-existent. H. R. Mill described how he had had to give up marine science to be able to earn his living and this dilemma faced most of his contemporaries as well. One can see the same forces at work in the 1820s and 1830s though it would be wrong to rule out here the possibly superior attractions of other subjects. The volume of research being done in mathematics and physics was presumably not so great as to overcrowd the more orthodox lines of approach. Some academics in Britain took up work on tidal theory but not, as Carpenter hoped, the theory of ocean circulation which Scandinavian scientists eventually developed in the 1890s.

Though oceanography had by this time acquired its own identity among the sciences, the position of those wishing to work on it was no better in this country. The development of a separate identity had in any case been a long slow process, not an overnight realization following a new theory or discovery. Various phrases had been used descriptively earlier in the century, maritime science, maritime geography, physical geography of the sea. Whewell introduced one of his less happy inventions—tidology—for his own subject but it did not catch on. Only in the 1880s was a name adopted for the whole science in a specific sense—oceanography—and it had to compete for some time with competitors like thalassography and oceanology.

At about the same time specialist organizations began to appear on a local, national and international level, the Liverpool Marine Biology Committee, the Marine Biological Association, the Challenger Society, the International Council for the Exploration of the Sea. The emphasis was strongly biological but physical oceanography was represented to some extent at all these levels. Nevertheless there was no comparable growth of public institutions to match these developments. Government funds were forthcoming only for fisheries work and research connected with it and with the I.C.E.S. at Plymouth and Lowestoft. Of the marine stations founded privately some fell by the wayside and schemes for separate research institutes and university departments came to nothing, except for Herdman's chair and the Tidal Observatory at Liverpool.

A paradoxical situation had now arisen. Oceanography by 1900 was a recognized science but it was about to enter yet another period of abeyance. It was perhaps no coincidence that, tides and biology apart, paradigms and institutions were both late to arrive. An established science needs paradigms, a framework of shared ideas and concepts in which new work may be carried out, but for this framework to be maintained it also requires some continuity of the people engaged in it. Yet people could not continue their work on problems which seemed relevant without financial and institutional resources and these resources tended to be monopolized by sciences which were already established. It was a vicious circle. Ideas were not lacking but long term work could not be carried out without the appropriate organizational background to support it.

This phase is, however, outside the scope of this book. Some reasons have been suggested why there was so long a gap between the first signs of scientific interest in the sea and the development of the modern science of oceanography. The intervening centuries saw several phases of intensified activity and many outstanding individual contributions. These are of interest both because they foreshadow modern work and illuminate the pattern of current trends and for what they reveal about the nature and development of science in general. It is hoped that this book will help in making better known the thought and work of those who pioneered the scientific study of the sea.

May 1971   MARGARET DEACON

ACKNOWLEDGEMENTS

It is difficult to know how to thank adequately all the people who have helped me in the work of preparing this book. My first acknowledgement must be to my father who first interested me in the history of marine science and without whose help the task could never have been undertaken.

I am most grateful to the Royal Society, and in particular to Sir Harold Hartley, for their kind interest and support and to the Goldsmiths' Company and the Natural Environment Research Council for providing grants for the research. My warmest thanks are also due to Dr D. O. Edge who has generously allowed me to complete the book while working in the Science Studies Unit at Edinburgh University.

Of the many people and institutions who have provided materials and facilities for research I would especially like to thank the Librarian of the Royal Society and his staff and the Librarian and staff of the National Institute of Oceanography for all their help. I am very grateful to Dr P. S. Laurie of the Royal Greenwich Observatory, David Bryden, formerly of the Royal Scottish Museum, Dr Wiseman of the Natural History Museum and Mr Finlayson of the University of Edinburgh Library for showing me the archives and collections in their care, to the Whitby Literary and Philosophical Society for permission to consult and quote from the Scoresby Papers and to the Master and Fellows of Magdalene College, Cambridge, for permitting me to use quotations and illustrations from the manuscripts in the Pepysian Library. I must also thank the Editor of *Nature*, the Royal Geographical Societies of England and Scotland and the Massachusetts Historical Society for permission to make extensive quotations from their periodicals.

I would like to thank all the oceanographers of the elder generation who have kindly told me of their experiences in the inter-war years, either informally or as part of the Science Studies Unit oral history survey, in particular Dr J. N. Carruthers, Sir Geoffrey Taylor, Sir Frederick Russell, Dr Sheina Marshall, Sir Maurice Yonge and Dr J. B. Tait. On the historical side I am very grateful to Dr H. L. Burstyn of Carnegie-Mellon University, Pittsburgh, for his interest and encouragement, and to colleagues in the Science Studies Unit for many helpful conversations. I should also like to thank Dr A. G. Keller of Leicester University for kindly showing me his unpublished work on the lineless sounding machine.

I am especially grateful to all those who have helped me in preparing the book: to my father; to Dr Edge and David Bloor of the Science

Studies Unit and Dr W. I. Jenkins of Loughborough University for reading portions of the typescript and suggesting improvements; to Miss Sylvia Harvey, Mrs Kathleen North, Mrs Jeverley Smith, Mrs Kay Clement and Mrs Corinne Robertson who kindly typed the manuscript; to Steve Richard who kindly compiled the indexes and to Miss Lorna Duffin and Mrs Fiona Bloor for their generous help with proof reading.

INTRODUCTION TO SECOND EDITION

Scientists and the Sea – twenty-five years on

THIS book is a reprint of the 1971 edition of *Scientists and the Sea*, with a new introduction and bibliography added, and misprints and minor errors corrected. When writing the 1971 preface, I used the opportunity to give a resumé of the book's aims and conclusions, rather than considering how the work fitted in to the wider context of historical writing on marine science. This new introduction gives me a chance to do this, and also to say something about more recent developments in the history of oceanography. These have been considerable, so last but not least, the reader is entitled to some explanation as to why *Scientists and the Sea* is still being read by scientists and historians and has been reprinted more than twenty-five years after its first appearance.

It should be emphasized that this is a reprint and not a full revision. Fully incorporating new work done on the history of oceanography during the intervening twenty-five years would have entailed lengthening an already long book, or cutting out some of the original material. Many of the more recent studies in the field deal with the late nineteenth and twentieth centuries and with events that are only touched on towards the end of this volume, or beyond its scope altogether. Comparatively little new work has been done on the earlier period which forms the bulk of this book. Since it first appeared *Scientists and the Sea* has been considered a useful resource by both scientists and historians interested in the history of oceanography, and continues to be in demand, so it seemed inappropriate to jettison information not readily available elsewhere and to transform the book into something less close to its original purpose. As it stands, the text is already very much compressed, giving a generally unelaborated account of events, with personal details and motivations and discussion of the influence of wider issues kept to a minimum. Ideally, it would be expanded rather than contracted; but that would make another book. The reprint therefore contains the original text, slightly modified, while this introduction looks at the book firstly in relation to earlier historical writing on marine science and then in the context of more recent developments in oceanography and its history. This gives me an opportunity to mention new contributions which bear on specific passages in this work. Full references to these and other items will be found in the new bibliography at the end of the volume.

Scientists and the Sea is an account of the development of marine science within the western scientific tradition from the earliest records up to the beginning of the twentieth century. In fact it might be more accurate to describe it as a prehistory rather than a history of oceanography, since the modern science only came into being right at the end of this period. But however one defines these terms there was no doubt that scientific interest in the sea was of great antiquity and could be traced back to the works of Aristotle and beyond. When I began my research in the mid-1960s there was already a considerable interest in the subject among oceanographers – which is why I was asked to undertake it – but little in the way of detailed investigation had been done. Existing summaries highlighted landmarks going back to the voyage of H.M.S. *Challenger* in the 1870s. Some looked back even further, to essays written by Robert Boyle in the seventeenth century and contemporary designs for apparatus by Robert Hooke, and beyond. But what were the connections, if any, between these events? They occupied the collective consciousness of oceanographers rather like coral atolls rising up to the sunlit surface of a blue and unplumbed sea. No one knew what lay beneath the surface, and myths and inconsistencies abounded.

My initial research was on seventeenth-century efforts to create the science of the sea. The work of Boyle and Hooke turned out to be part of a wider movement centred around the newly founded Royal Society of London. The appearance of people like Sir Robert Moray, already familiar in a more conventional historical context – the political turmoils of the middle years of the century – in this new, and at any rate to me, unfamiliar activity, was a prelude to uncovering an absorbing and little-known series of events featuring work on different aspects of what we now call oceanography. A preliminary account of the work by the early Royal Society (Deacon, 1965) was followed by a paper describing contemporary attempts by British travellers to the Mediterranean to explain the system of currents in the Strait of Gibraltar (Deacon, 1968). A revised version of this appeared as Chapter 7 in *Scientists and the Sea*. These two trial essays apart, the remainder of the contents appeared for the first time on the book's publication in 1971.

The starting point for the book was therefore not, as with some other accounts which appeared around the same time, the postwar expansion in marine science traced backwards from the perspective of the present day (i.e. the 1960s), but seventeenth-century activity and its aims and objectives. To explain these it was necessary to go back further still and look at early scientific and geographical literature on the sea since this had a considerable influence on later events. Then I went forward in time to examine why the movement substantially failed in its purpose and what impact it had, if any, on the scientific exploration of the sea in the eighteenth and nineteenth centuries. Was there any direct link with the great expansion of activity in the latter part of the nineteenth century, in which the *Challenger* expedition was an outstanding element, and the rise of the modern science of oceanography in the twentieth?

It has often been claimed, that the voyage of H.M.S. *Challenger* was itself the foundation of the modern science. This has the convenience of being able to assign that development to a particular event. Indeed one of the scientists who took part in the expedition, J. Y. Buchanan (1919, pp. xii-xiii) went further and specified the exact day, writing: "It may be taken that the Science of Oceanography was born at Sea, in Lat. 25° 45' N., Long. 20° 14' W., on 15th February 1873." This was the date of the first official station made by the expedition, west of Tenerife. However if one takes the view that a science depends on the existence of a community of workers in a particular field with shared aspirations and institutions, whether laboratories, societies or dedicated journals, then it was a little while longer before oceanography satisfied these criteria. I have always thought this happened in the 1880s and 1890s when the scientists in several countries who were working on the results of the *Challenger*, and of the other expeditions that took place about that time, felt that the various aspects of the science of the sea could no longer remain divided piecemeal between their parent disciplines, but should henceforth be regarded as part of a unified science of the ocean. However this is only one of a number of questions about the origin of oceanography which is still being debated. Helen Rozwadowski (1996) follows my dating of its emergence, but others (Mills, 1993b) put it later.

Clearly the *Challenger* expedition played a significant part in this process, partly through its scientific contribution but also as a result of the creation of a network of researchers during the subsequent work on the Report. Parallel developments in other countries were also significant (see for example Mörzer Bruyns, 1988) but the *Challenger Report* helped to synthesize the new knowledge, particularly on the biology of the deep sea, and acted as a rallying point for the new science. The personalities and international outlook of Wyville Thomson and John Murray played an important part in this process. More recently the expedition has continued to be a focus of attention. This is mainly because its work on deep-sea sediments and the deep-sea fauna in particular, formed the foundation of modern research in these areas, but it still holds a broader iconic significance for the marine science community.

Nevertheless, if one looks at events in Britain following the expedition, it is clear that by the turn of the century the scientific initiative had at least for the time being moved elsewhere. It was particularly in Germany and Scandinavia that new ideas were being developed, especially on plankton studies and the question of marine productivity (Mills, 1989) and on the dynamics of ocean circulation. This was partly due to lack of resources for new research in Britain (Deacon, 1993, 1994) but there had also been a failure there to engage in these basic and closely related fields of study which pointed the way to oceanography's future development, this in spite of the fact that interest in ocean circulation had played a crucial role in the origins of the *Challenger* expedition (see Chapter 14). Thus, it is generally agreed today that the expedition was perhaps not the unique event it once seemed, but an integral component of a wider process. The interest in the deep sea, of which it was a part, developed through the convergence of a number of independent lines of research in nineteenth-century science, some of which can tenuously be traced back to more distant origins. The establishment of oceanography as a science occurred somewhat later, and Eric Mills has suggested that this was not until the first decade of the twentieth century, and was a consequence of the later scientific developments referred to above (Mills 1993b, p. 11).

This book contributes only indirectly to the debate; its purpose was rather to throw light on the scientific interest in the sea in previous generations, to which the *Challenger* expedition and contemporary enterprises succeeded. What sort of links, if any, did they, let alone the modern science, have to earlier manifestations of interest in the science of the sea? What *Scientists and the Sea* did was to collect together the evidence available at the time, and try to look for patterns in how knowledge of the sea developed up to the end of the nineteenth century.

For the purposes of this book, the term "oceanography" is employed in a less specific sense to describe the science of the sea. This is done for convenience, as from what has already been said it will be clear that it is anachronistic to speak of it as an entity, or of its practitioners as oceanographers – or indeed even as scientists, since this word is itself a nineteenth-century concept that it is convenient to use retrospectively. Few of the people mentioned in these pages were professional scientists in the modern sense; up to the end of the nineteenth century such persons were rare. Most of the great and lesser scientists of the eighteenth and nineteenth century were amateurs, in the old-fashioned sense of the word with no connotations of dilettantism (see for example, Rudwick, 1985) or defective workmanship. The cast of *Scientists and the Sea* is extremely diverse, including courtiers, diplomats, virtuosi (Stoye, 1994), naval and army officers, geographers, academics, engineers, travellers and explorers, doctors, clergymen, and many others. Most of them worked in specific areas of marine science, such as chemistry or tides, and had little sense of contributing to a wider field. If they were aware of a wider context for their work it would be more likely to appear to them as part of their parent discipline, whether chemistry, astronomy or mathematics. However, there were exceptions to this, like Moray and Hales, where an individual interest progressed from the particular to a more general feeling for the subject, and this can be seen at virtually every stage.

I tried to range as widely as possible over the different aspects of oceanography. The principal omission is marine biology. For a long time this field developed largely in isolation from other branches of marine science, and *Scientists and the Sea* picks up the story only where it began to impinge on them in the early to mid-nineteenth century. Was it wrong, from the historian's point of view, to put together such varied scientific activities which often had no link at the time, apart from the common theme of their endeavours?

I was aware that it could be said there is an element of artificiality in doing this retrospectively. The justification as I saw it, was the need to redress the balance of existing accounts. General histories of science, except those dealing with tides (usually in relation to astronomy) often ignored scientific research on the sea. There were a number of reasons for this. One was unfamiliarity; the low profile of oceanography made it a rather esoteric activity well into the second half of the twentieth century. Another was the difficulties experienced by early would-be explorers of the sea, many of which are documented in these pages, including problems with ships, instruments and a hostile research environment, which meant that their results often appeared at best unimpressive, at least to the uninitiated. A third was that the history of science itself is still a relatively small speciality, which has only emerged this century and has lately undergone a maturation process in which methodology played a large part. In consequence it tended, at least until recently, to confine itself to the highlights of scientific discovery. These factors contributed to the lack of attention paid to the origins of marine science outside its own specialist literature. Conscientious biographers mentioned this aspect of their subjects' activities, but usually lacked the necessary background to put it in context.

In fact there was also a real element of continuity to be described. Though some ideas, more especially of eighteenth-century figures such as W. G. De Brahm (De Vorsey, 1976) and J. S. von Waitz (Deacon, 1985) (see pp. xxxv–xxxvi), made little impact on succeeding generations, in spite of the fact that their activities might have different origins and intentions, those coming later to the field were often aware, if only imperfectly, of previous work and influenced by it. Harold Burstyn too has defended the book against possible charges of being "tunnel history":[1]

Unlike electricity, for example, oceanography has a reality in the past more palpable than a set of details abstracted by the historian from the works of those who lived before the term acquired anything like its present meaning ... The ocean forms a distinct geographical province, and thus the history of man's understanding of the ocean's nature as a physical realm has an intrinsic validity that the history of the disparate phenomena we now call electricity lacks.

Nevertheless even while *Scientists and the Sea* was being written it was plain that it would not be a definitive study but rather a starting point for further inquiry, since research undertaken at that time showed how much there was still to learn. This was the reason why the phrase "history of oceanography", which had already been used rather optimistically elsewhere, was deliberately avoided when choosing a title. Even then no one really appreciated quite how rich and diverse the history of marine science would turn out to be – something that has become more fully apparent as interest in the area has grown and diversified, both geographically and in choice of topic area, during the last quarter of a century.

Even so, the project turned out to be much larger than envisaged. Early data collection at sea was restricted to a far greater extent than I at first appreciated, both by lack of opportunity and by the expense and non-standardization of early scientific instruments (see McConnell, 1982). This meant that at least until the end of the eighteenth century a little observation went a long way, giving the subject a deceptive air of simplicity. True, from the mid-nineteenth century onwards the quantity of data began to burgeon beyond what the practitioners of the age could readily cope with. Lord Kelvin's tide prediction machines were a clever answer to one problem of data handling in the pre-computer age. At all periods however, the amount of speculation and discussion on the sea was enormous. Where should the line be drawn? As Harold Burstyn (1968, p. 670) has remarked:

Most of the great scientists of the past have contributed directly or indirectly to the history of oceanography, so that our science, far from being on the fringes of scientific effort as our colleagues in other disciplines sometimes think, has from the very first been close to the center.

---

[1] Harold L. Burstyn, writing in "Book Reviews", *Isis* (1974) **65**, p. 95.

To embark on such a survey was therefore rash, but rewarding. As Mott Greene (1985) was later to write, encouraging students of the history of geology to be more adventurous in their choice of projects:

It makes little sense ... to pursue any project without first creating a context, however rudimentary into which it might fit. Moreover, the challenge and excitement of actually writing, rather than revising a field of history, is unparalleled and ought to be welcomed.

Scientists and the Sea was largely written in the 1960s, at a time when new approaches to the history of science were in their infancy. Few works today would undertake an entire discipline; it is now more usual to look at a particular field within a discipline, or a technique and its application, or the development of a single theory or controversy, in much greater depth and over a time scale of usually, no more than a century at most.

However, when the book appeared in 1971 it was welcomed by oceanographers, and historians interested in the field, as the first in-depth survey of the origins of the science. Harold Burstyn wrote:[2]

The chief danger in approaching the history of science from a broadly cultural viewpoint is superficiality. One has to understand the scientific details in considerable depth to penetrate beneath the glib generality, to replace mere temporal contiguity with genuine relationship. Though the sciences of the physical environment, with their long histories both of large-scale enterprise and of repeated questions asked in widely differing cultural contexts, might seem ideal subjects for a broader history of science, they have (except for geology) suffered almost total neglect ... Hitherto only a handful of persons ... have traced any pathways through the internal history of the environmental sciences for externally minded scholars to follow.

Margaret Deacon's pathbreaking monograph is thus especially welcome. In 400 pages she has magisterially surveyed the history of man's knowledge of the oceans from the beginnings to the turn of the twentieth century—the first time this has been done with depth and authority. She has brought together, in a single, largely chronological account, a horde of details gleaned from a careful survey of a vast and mainly unorganized literature.

Much work has been done on the history of oceanography since those days, but *Scientists and the Sea* remains the only work to cover the field in depth over the whole of its early history. Within its own terms of reference the book continues to give a useful account of the origins of scientific interest in the sea, and one that, while some of the details and conclusions have been modified by more recent work, has stood the test of time well. It was originally envisaged that *Scientists and the Sea* would be reprinted when the original version sold out, as it did within a few

---

[2] Book reviews, *Isis*, **65**, p. 92.

years, but it then transpired that the original publishers, Academic Press, were no longer able to produce a new edition, and economic problems in the early 1980s prevented attempts elsewhere. It seemed at that point that perhaps the moment had passed. However the book has continued to be in demand from both scientists and historians of science and remains a valuable introductory survey of the field. It is therefore gratifying to have the opportunity to reissue it after so many years.

Previous work on the history of oceanography

The absence of any detailed historiography in the original preface was not intended to suggest that there had been no previous interest in the history of oceanography, and earlier books and articles on the subject were referred to in the text and notes. Not surprisingly, these were mainly the work of scientists rather than historians, as the growth of the history of science as a separate discipline was still in its early stages in the first half of the twentieth century. A sense of history or at least of a historical perspective is intrinsic to work in many scientific fields where present-day activity has built upon previous ideas and observations. Awareness of past achievements, often felt to be remarkable in view of the difficult conditions, lack of resources and paucity of observations that had frequently to be overcome, has generated a natural curiosity about early discoveries, and about the people who made them.

The most common expression of this interest is to be found in the many historical introductions of oceanographic literature – in papers, monographs and textbooks. One of the earliest and best of these, from the *Report* of the voyage of H.M.S. *Challenger* (Murray, 1895; reprinted 1977), still well worth reading, traces the science of the sea back to classical times. Few succeeding articles of this kind were so wide-ranging, depending on the scope of the individual publication. However, while some were excellent, others were of more variable quality. Caveats made by Mott Greene (1985), on the use of historical writing for scientific purposes in geology, apply equally well here. He remarks, talking about celebratory writing, such as *Festschrifts* and obituaries (Greene, p. 98): "Criticism is minor, muted, oblique, and may often be entirely lacking." Similarly reviews of a particular field, undertaken as an aid to understanding its present state, may, he points out, overlook discoveries and ideas taken seriously by previous generations but since discounted. His major criticism, however, was that the authors had not always gone back to the originals for their earlier material and that errors were thereby perpetuated. This certainly happened in the history of oceanography.

The *Challenger Report* introduction was the first extensive piece of writing to give a well-researched overall view of the history of marine science. Earlier works, for example Wyville Thomson's *Depths of the Sea*, published in 1873 (see p. 317) and Kohl's (1868) history of the Gulf Stream, often contained substantial references to earlier discoveries and one could go back further, for example to the history of tidal observations compiled by the astronomer Lalande in the eighteenth century (see p. 252). However, like the collection of historic data on deep-sea temperatures published by Sir Joseph Prestwich in 1875 (see p. 345), and exercises of a similar kind by modern scientists, the primary purpose here was scientific. Nevertheless, in the years following Murray's introduction, a number of works on aspects of marine science that were more truly historical began to appear. Rollin A. Harris wrote a historical appendix to his *Manual of Tides*, issued by the U.S. Coast and Geodetic Survey in 1898 (see p. 271, note 3) and historical surveys of ideas about tides during the classical and mediaeval periods by Roberto Almagia and Pierre Duhem were published soon afterwards (see pp. 32-33, note 1).

During the first half of the twentieth century perhaps the outstanding work by an oceanographer on the history of his discipline is found in the opening chapters of W. A. Herdman's *Founders of Oceanography* (1923) (see p. 395, note 18). These biographical studies, of Edward Forbes, Wyville Thomson, Sir John Murray, Prince Albert of Monaco and Alexander Agassiz, formed part of his inaugural lecture course in oceanography at Liverpool in 1920, but they were originally undertaken during World War I when sea-going work was halted. However, with the exception of Edward Forbes who died in 1854, Herdman knew the people he was writing about so his accounts occupy a middle ground between history and reminiscence and the "life and letters" type of biographies common in the late nineteenth and early twentieth centuries. These were often written by family members, such as George Agassiz's memoir (1913) of his father Alexander, or by colleagues if no suitable relative was available, as in the case of Edward Forbes (Wilson & Geikie, 1861). Such works are extremely valuable sources for the history of science, often containing extensive verbatim quotations from correspondence long since vanished. However, the authors were always concerned to do full justice to the achievements of their subjects and while they might feel able to comment on scientific ideas that were no longer accepted, they generally avoided any reflection of the cut and thrust of competition for scientific influence and resources that undoubtedly existed. While some come into Mott Greene's third category (1985, p. 99) – the concealed "literature of attack and defense", where, as in Charles Lyell's work of the previous century, *Principles of*

Geology, a controversial position is concealed under a guise of reasonableness – one generally has to look elsewhere for this kind of information.

The history of science was in its infancy at this time so it is hardly surprising that the early practitioners and their journals paid little attention to the history of marine science, itself a struggling discipline during the early twentieth century. An occasional relevant article appeared, as for example an item on ichthyology (Gudger, 1934) in an early volume of *Isis*. Even Duhem's work on tides is not really an exception, as he dealt with them as an aspect of astronomy. The growth of interest in the history of marine science, evident in a small way by the middle years of this century, came mainly from scientists. It gathered momentum during the period of scientific expansion of the 1950s and 1960s in which oceanography shared. A number of semi-popular works with a historical bias appeared in the 1960s. Muriel Guberlet (1964) wrote on expeditions from the days of Maury onwards, but without mentioning the central contribution of Prince Albert of Monaco. This omission was remedied by Dean (1966). *Exploring the ocean world* (Idyll, 1969) was subtitled "a history of oceanography", but such books were to a greater or lesser extent concerned with modern research, and the past was seen merely as a prelude to the present. The history of oceanography was largely equated with the history of expeditions (Mills 1993b, pp. 7-8, 10) and little attempt was made to look beyond this, or to relate earlier events to their historical context.

The interest shown by scientists in the history of their science was generated by a number of considerations. Apart from a natural curiosity, the earth sciences are always to a certain extent historical as they search for data to reveal variation over time as part of their elucidation of the present and future. Similarly biologists refer to the work of their predecessors for information on taxonomy and distribution of organisms. However, this was only part of the explanation, which had much to do with how marine scientists perceived their discipline. There was perhaps a mixture of proper pride with a certain defensiveness, even an element of public relations, a desire to show the external world that oceanography was not a new science but had a past which could be compared with the better known histories of established sciences such as astronomy. The difficulty was that this past was hard to locate because oceanography as a recognized discipline was still quite new. As seen earlier, it only emerged in the period around 1900, even though scientific interest in the sea clearly went back much further. There was no ready-made route to investigate it except through citations but these were of limited use since the modern system of referencing in scientific papers did not come in until around the mid-nineteenth century.

The oceanographers' agenda (put crudely) was to show that their science was a recent creation only in name and that it in fact had a history as long and distinguished as other sciences. *Scientists and the Sea* can be seen as part of this endeavour; inasmuch as I was encouraged to write it by scientists and supported by scientific organizations, it was a commissioned history. As already noted, scientists have practical as well as personal reasons for being interested in the past. As part of the wider study of the Earth and its environment, oceanography is not dealing with something presumably static, like the laws of physics (even if our perception of them changes) but with a dynamic system which undergoes changes over time. The measurements of today may differ from those taken last week, or last century; thus the use and interpretation of historic data is a serious topic in oceanography, as in other earth sciences. However, the past could also be used, not only to perhaps redress a historical imbalance in the way the science of the sea was perceived by other sciences, but also in conjunction with other factors, to bring it more forcibly to the attention of the general public, lawmakers and grant-givers.

The historian has a somewhat different set of priorities, of which the overriding one is to advance understanding of the scientific process. Mere documentation however meticulous of the discoveries of the past is not enough; through seeing how those discoveries were made and ideas formulated and modified, using both published works and unpublished sources, the historian seeks to enter the mind of the scientist and to understand the creative process, the choices of ideas which may lead to new advances, and why others are rejected.

However, scientists, too, may take a more thoughtful approach and this can be seen already emerging in writings on both sides of the Atlantic in the mid-twentieth century. In America Daniel Merriman and Joel Hedgpeth produced scholarly studies on aspects of the history of oceanography, marine biology and ecology. In the 1960s, Harold Burstyn was the first historian of science to devote himself extensively to the field, writing valuable papers on seventeenth-century ideas on the circulation of the atmosphere amd oceans (Burstyn, 1971) before making the *Challenger* expedition his principal field of study (Burstyn, 1972; 1975).

However, it was European interest that led to the first conference devoted to the history of marine science – the *Colloque international sur l'histoire de la biologie marine, les grandes expéditions scientifiques et la création des laboratoires maritimes* was held in France in 1963, following a proposal made to the 10th International Congress of History of

Science by Jean Théodoridès. The following year the veteran German physical oceanographer Georg Wüst (1964) published a long paper on the history of expeditions in which he attempted to give a framework for the development of oceanography since the *Challenger* in terms of forcing by the demands of expeditions. This was perhaps the first time that any attempt had been made to investigate the internal dynamics of oceanography. Although Wüst's conclusions have since been challenged by historians, his attempt to analyse past events was a new departure. In 1966 these separate strands of activity were brought together at the First International Congress on the History of Oceanography, held suitably in Prince Albert I's already historic Musée Océanographique in Monaco. The history of oceanography as a discipline may be said to date from this time (Mills 1993b).

This was the context in which *Scientists and the Sea* appeared. One criticism often made of the book, in spite of its title, was that it did not carry the story of marine science up to the present time (i.e. the 1960s). The reason for this was that the principal aim was to explore the little-known work of previous centuries. To have continued it into the twentieth century, when the vast majority of oceanographic research has taken place, the sheer volume of material to be considered would have made it impossible to continue with the same level of coverage, and very probably have resulted in the kind of superficiality Harold Burstyn deplores. The account of the earlier work would have to have been similarly curtailed, and the whole enterprise would have exceeded the length of a manageable research project. It also centred to a large extent on work done in Britain and gave a rather limited picture of work elsewhere.

It was fortunate therefore that *Scientists and the Sea* was followed two years later by Susan Schlee's *The Edge of an Unfamiliar World: a History of Oceanography* (1973). The two books are complementary, both in style and content, and concentrate on different periods in the development of marine science. Whereas the main objective of *Scientists and the Sea* was to throw light on the early stages of scientific interest in the sea, from the seventeenth to the late nineteenth centuries, Schlee, based in the United States, charted the rise of the modern science from the middle of the nineteenth century, the time of Maury and the cable-laying explorations, onwards. Her book carries the story through the *Challenger* era, to the development of fisheries research and dynamical oceanography under the umbrella of the International Council of the Exploration of the Sea in the early twentieth century, the impact of World War II and oceanography's subsequent establishment as a major scientific discipline. However, the only post-war aspect of marine science of the 1960s to be described in detail is the field of marine geology, at the time when evidence of sea-floor spreading was beginning to appear,

Oceanography and the history of science

Eric Mills (1993b, p. 7) has written of *Scientists and the Sea* and Schlee's work: "Both opened – and continue to open – a host of worthwhile problems for historians of science." How far has the challenge been taken up? A further criticism of *Scientists and the Sea* was that it did not do enough to highlight external influences that were acting at different stages to promote, or retard, marine science, for example the mid-nineteenth century undertaking of laying submarine telegraph cables, which enabled scientific research in the depths of the ocean, or the ending of the wars against Napoleon in 1815 which left the Admiralty with unemployed ships and men who could then be sent on polar expeditions (Levere, 1993). There are many instances in which similar events had a decisive influence, and we now know much more about the social context in which early marine research took place, especially in the nineteenth and twentieth centuries. In many ways oceanography experienced influences in common with other sciences, but there are differences of degree. Funding of research was always a particular problem and this is brought out in a number of more recent publications (Burstyn, 1975; MacLeod, 1976; Alter, 1987; Deacon, 1994).

That we now know more about such things is due to changes under-gone in the intervening years not only by the history of oceanography, but also in its parent discipline, the history of science. Relations have not always been close. Historians of oceanography have often felt that their subject was neglected by the wider fraternity, in much the same way that oceanographers felt that other sciences were not taking the sea as seri-ously as they ought. Happily, the situation has altered considerably. One aspect of the problem was that traditionally historians of science concen-trated on the physical and mathematical sciences, to a lesser extent on biology, and in particular on a few key figures such as Newton and Darwin. It was these "industries" that Mott Greene (1985) was complain-ing about in the article already quoted.

Recently however, there has been more activity in the history of the earth sciences, and in environmental sciences and ecology. Some out-standing studies have resulted, for example, of particular episodes in the history of geology, such as Martin Rudwick's book *The great Devonian controversy* (1985), in which he shows how the social and institutional context of mid-nineteenth-century geology influenced the development of new ideas. Such writings often have a direct bearing on marine science.

For example, in David Oldroyd's new book *Thinking about geology* (1996), his overview of the development of ideas about the Earth also reflects much of the thinking about the sea in different periods, so this clearly is a work of potential interest to historians of oceanography. Similarly, in *Appropriating the weather*, Robert Marc Friedman (1989) writes about the foundation of modern, dynamic, meteorology which in turn would profoundly influence the study of the oceans. Historians of science are concerned to understand the scientific process rather than minutely documenting the past as an end in itself. In their discipline the interpretation of data, both past scientific and modern historical, has been influenced by parallel studies in the sociology and philosophy of science which since the 1960s have revolutionized the way historians think about science. Such work is not always easily accessible to the non-specialist but books like those mentioned above incorporate new approaches and use them to enable the reader to appreciate the work and ideas of the scientists involved and to understand why they thought as they did and how and why their ideas changed over time.

The aspect of oceanography that has most interested historians of science during the last two decades has been its involvement in the earth sciences revolution that has come about since 1960, when ideas of continental drift, leading to the theory of sea-floor spreading and plate tectonics began to obtain wider acceptance in the scientific community. Accounts of the origin of these ideas by Marvin (1973) and others, and of their experiences by some of the scientists involved, have been supplemented by investigative studies by historians and philosophers of science interested in the actual debate itself for what it could teach them about the nature of scientific knowledge and the mechanisms of change. Frankel (1982) and Oreskes (1986) examine aspects of the controversy, while a more general account, both of the scientists' ideas and those of the historians, may be found in Homer LeGrand's *Drifting Continents and Shifting Theories* (1988).

The only comparable body of work within marine science history, if not "oceanography" more narrowly interpreted, has been on the foundation of marine stations and their impact (e.g. Benson, 1988; Maienschein, 1988; Metz, 1985). However, there are many other aspects of marine science that deserve attention from historians, and it is good that recently there has been more diversity in publications by professional historians, with items dealing with aspects of biology (e.g. Mills, 1989), fisheries (Van Sittert, 1995), physical oceanography, and scientific institutions. Eric Mills (1993b, p. 11–12) issued a powerful challenge which is already bearing fruit in meetings such as an interdisciplinary symposium on the history of the Berlin Institut für Meereskunde held in 1996.

As seen earlier, scientists writing on the history of their subject may have different priorities, but here too perceptions have changed and some valuable contributions have recently appeared which rely on their specialist knowledge of scientific problems and source material. For example, couple of recent monographs (Hisard, 1993; Peterson, Stramma and Kortum, 1996) add considerably to our knowledge of the early recognition and charting of ocean currents. Much of the newer writing is on twentieth-century topics and too diverse to be covered here, ranging from ships and expeditions, such as the *Meteor*, the *Mabahiss* (Rice, 1986) and the *Atlantis* (Schlee, 1976), and the development and application of new techniques such as sonar, to the establishment of new research fields and institutions. For reasons that are partially dealt with in the final pages of this work, oceanography was still relatively small-scale during the first half of the twentieth century. The increased resources made available after World War II had already enabled important new areas of research to be established before the time when this book was written, and these have continued to develop, and new ones to open up in the intervening years.

Oceanography in the late twentieth century

Although *Scientists and the Sea* does not deal with the development of oceanography in the twentieth century, it is nevertheless a product of the 1960s when it was written, and reflects the state of the science at that time. The new approaches referred to above in the history of science were still in their early stages; I was more aware of them in writing the later portions of the book. Especially in the first three chapters, there are value judgements of early ideas which would be out of place in a modern study. Historians of science today seek to understand past ideas in the context of contemporary knowledge and possibilities, not to measure their accuracy by the standard of present-day thinking. Time has shown this to be a dangerous exercise; science is not static, and an idea which was dismissed on sound scientific grounds in one generation may, for equally compelling reasons, be revived by the next. The 1950s and 1960s saw the invention of important new techniques for exploring the seas and these and subsequent developments have radically altered our perception of the ocean.

When this book was taking shape, oceanography was still a small and little-known science, of which the general public knew nothing beyond the televised expeditions of Jacques Cousteau. Nor was there any general feeling that understanding the sea was important, apart from scientific curiosity, or economically useful, except possibly to certain minority groups whose livelihood depended on it. Since those days oceanography has come to figure prominently in the greater interest, awareness and knowledge of the Earth and its environment which has taken place in recent years, and its contribution is now more widely appreciated, both by the scientific community at large and by the general public. Though the rapid growth of scientific institutions during the 1950s and 1960s was followed by more variable fortunes in recent decades, the importance of the work being carried out by oceanographers in the late twentieth century has been reflected in the United Kingdom by the creation of the Southampton Oceanography Centre, successor to the Institute of Oceanographic Sciences, or National Institute of Oceanography as it was when the initial research on this book was carried out there in the mid-1960s.

When I began work the concept of continental drift and sea-floor spreading was only just beginning to be widely accepted. Since then these new ideas, allied to new techniques of exploration such as side-scan sonar, have revolutionized knowledge of the sea bed. Evidence from sediment cores obtained through the Ocean Drilling Programme shows how the present-day oceans have evolved and reveals how the Earth's climate has changed over time. One of the most dramatic discoveries associated with this area of work occurred as recently as 1979 when hydrothermal vents, found in association with mid-ocean ridge systems, were shown to support assemblages of creatures hitherto unknown to science, which rely on bacteria able to use the minerals in the discharge from the vents as an energy source. This has opened up an exciting new field of research for marine biologists, as well as geologists and physical oceanographers.

Significant advances have also been made in other branches of marine science. The 1950s also saw the start of a revolution in the understanding of the internal dynamics of the ocean. Though less well known than theories of plate tectonics, which fundamentally changed Earth sciences in general and not just oceanography, it showed that circulation in the ocean depths was not necessarily slow and gradual, as had been assumed since the time of the *Challenger*. To knowledge of the surface and upper-layer circulation, which had been charted gradually over several centuries (Peterson, Stramma & Kortum, 1996), oceanographers added new understanding of the effect of the earth's rotation in producing deep current systems and the discovery of short-term variations or eddies, resembling atmospheric weather systems within the body of the ocean.

Theoretical and and observational advances since then have been made possible by late twentieth-century technology. Information from current meters moored on the sea bed or from tracking floats has been supplemented by use of chemical tracers in sea water. Satellite observations now provide measurements of surface temperature, currents, and other features on a global scale. In the World Circulation Experiment (WOCE), part of the World Climate Research Programme, scientists from many countries have been making use of these methods during the 1990s to investigate how the ocean stores and distributes heat, through ocean currents, a subject of more than academic interest in view of fears about global warming.

The revolution in the earth sciences of the 1960s followed by environmental issues in the 1980s and 1990s, has meant that oceanography now occupies a much more central role in science than when this book was written. This development has been reinforced by the growing importance in recent decades of marine-based economic activities, such as the offshore oil and gas industries. In the 1990s oceanography, in spite of being vulnerable to difficulties experienced by science in general, no longer has to seek for additional ways of validating itself. It is very much a science of the present, with an atmosphere of discovery and excitement to equal that of fifty or a hundred years ago. The ocean, from being something widely regarded as peripheral both to the main thrust of science and to human endeavour, is now more properly appreciated as central to the understanding of the past, present and future environment and life of the earth we inhabit. It forms part of a dynamic system, subject to change from both natural and also, now, man-made forces. From the perspective of the 1990s some of the speculations of earlier eras, such as Kircher's subterranean channels, seem less outlandish than they did twenty-five years ago. But there is also a downside. In the 1960s, there was optimism that with good will problems of environmental pollution, overfishing etc., could be solved. Experience has shown that the problems are more wide-ranging and complex than they then appeared and agreed solutions hard to find.

New work in the history of oceanography

Since 1971 a great deal of new work has been published on the history of oceanography. Some of this is listed in the bibliography, and, since material is scattered, some suggestions have been made on how to find it. Contributions have come from a wide variety of people, mainly either scientists or professional and independent historians of science, but also including geographers, lawyers, maritime and economic historians, sociologists, journalists, and biographers. Not surprisingly there has been a considerable amount of variation in the approach taken, and sometimes in the quality of the product, but the net result has been that far more information is available now. Some key contributions are noted here. It is also important to consider developments in related fields which have assisted the historian of oceanography.

Some key aspects of the science of the sea were only lightly dealt with in *Scientists and the Sea*. One of these was the history of oceanographic instruments, of the utmost importance to scientists engaged in sampling and measuring the various properties of ocean waters, their inhabitants and the earth beneath the sea. Wolfgang Matthäus wrote on tide-gauges etc. during the 1960s and '70s, while Anita McConnell's book *No Sea too Deep* (1982) traced the development of the principal types of oceanographic apparatus up to the early twentieth century. Her central theme is how the first proposals for apparatus to explore the depths of the sea, by Hooke, Hales and others in the seventeenth and eighteenth centuries, were replaced in the nineteenth century by a range of different kinds of instruments capable of making accurate measurements in the greatest depths of the ocean. New aids to the study of this essential field have also been provided by Christian Carpine's meticulous catalogues of the apparatus collected early this century by Prince Albert of Monaco. Five of these have already been published (Carpine, 1987, 1991, 1993, 1996), on photometers, current meters, biological sampling, water sampling and sounding. The final volume deals with temperature measurement. As awareness of the history of oceanographic work increases, new discoveries of historic apparatus have been made in collections round the world. One that was not expected because of the nature of the medium was an example of an eighteenth-century glass sea gauge, of the type proposed by Desaguliers in 1728 (see this volume, p. 180) which was recently identified in the George III collection at the Science Museum in London.

Another essential aspect of marine technology too little explored in this work is the ship. The last twenty-five years has seen the publication of many contemporary accounts of expeditions, such as the *Challenger* letters of Joseph Matkin (Rehbock, 1992), as well as historical studies, but some writers have concentrated on the ships themselves, for example the Ray Society volume *British Oceanographic Vessels* (Rice, 1986), Reinke-Kunze (1986) on German vessels and Nelson (1971) on U.S. oceanographic ships.

There have been important contributions to the history of marine biology, only briefly dealt with in this volume. These range in time from the eighteenth-century controversy due to Marsigli's insistence that coral was a plant (McConnell, 1990) to Eric Mills's *Biological Oceanography* (1989), dealing with attempts to understand, and to measure, marine productivity of the oceans in the late nineteenth and early twentieth centuries. In this major study he shows not only how ideas developed but also why, for reasons that were largely non-scientific, the emphasis shifted from Germany to the United Kingdom in the 1920s and 1930s. The Victorians seaside craze, which both reflected and further stimulated a growing scientific interest in marine life, is described in D. E. Allen's *The naturalist in Britain* (1976). This enthusiasm underlay the dredging expeditions carried out by the British Association (Rice and Wilson, 1980), originally under the leadership of Edward Forbes (Rehbock, 1979). Rehbock (1983) has written on the philosphical ideas underlying Forbes' work. Both the development of marine biology and the surveying of the deep ocean from the 1850s onwards were key elements in the events leading to the *Challenger* expedition.

Geology and marine science have also been linked for a long time. During the seventeenth and eighteenth centuries much intellectual effort was expended in the quest for a unified theory of the earth, in which the relationship between land and sea was a crucial factor. This involved both great scientists like Leibniz (Pécaut, 1951) and Buffon (see this volume, p. 204) and lesser ones, like Marsigli, who envisaged his marine work as part of much wider studies (Stoye, 1994). The geology and geography of the seas and their relationship to oceanography have been treated in an extended essay by Pfannenstiel (1970) and monographs by Paffen and Kortum (1984) and Vanney (1986). Geological and astronomical considerations lay behind James Croll's vigorous defence of his theory of ocean currents which is extensively dealt with in chapters 14 and 15. He believed (Hamlin, 1982) that the Ice Ages were cyclical events, caused by perturbations in the Earth's orbit which reduced the amount of heat reaching the Earth from the sun. This altered the course of the trade winds, and this in turn changed the pattern of ocean currents which were chiefly responsible for the transport of heat from equatorial to polar regions. If winds were no longer allowed to be the driving force of ocean currents, his carefully elaborated theory fell to the ground. Croll's periodic changes in the earth's orbit, now known as Milankovitch cycles after a more recent exponent of the idea, are now taken seriously as suggesting a possible mechanism of climate channge.

During the past twenty-five years comparitively little attention has been paid to the history of marine science before 1800, but there are some exceptions to this. A major contribution to knowledge about the surface circulation of the North Atlantic, made during the middle decades of the eighteenth century (i.e. before Franklin's chart of the Gulf Stream) by William Gerard de Brahm has been described by Louis de Vorsey Jr

(1976). About the same time J. S. von Waitz was speculating about the existence of thermohaline circulation, half a century before those usually credited with the idea (Deacon, 1985). Anita McConnell has worked extensively on Marsigli's interest in the sea; her translation of the *Histoire Physique de la Mer*, and account of its writing and publication, should appear shortly. She has also edited the work of James Six (1980), whose deep-sea thermometer plays such a significant role in these pages. The contribution of Sir Henry Sheeres, who figures in chapter 7 of this book, has recently been the subject of a paper by C. Solis Santos (1992). Another interesting addition in piecing together the history of ideas on the currents in the Strait of Gibraltar was made when a commonplace book of Edmond Halley was published (Cohen & Ross, 1985), showing that he did indeed know Sheeres' paper, which was circulating in manuscript (see pp. 146-147). Little has been added to our knowledge of work before the seventeenth century; Laird (1990) is one of the few items dealing with topics discussed in the early part of the book.

However, the amount of material available for the study of the history of science in earlier periods has been greatly increased. This is particularly true for the scientific revolution of the seventeenth century. A much improved understanding of the early Royal Society (Piviver, 1967) and its circle has come about through the work of Michael Hunter (1989) and others, as well through individual studies of key figures like Boyle and Hooke. Partly as a result of this process new resources have become available for researchers, such as the microfilm of the Boyle papers (Hunter, 1992) and the papers of Samuel Hartlib, another important member of the Royal Society's circle, preserved at Sheffield University, now available on CD-ROM. The existence of a much more comprehensive body of work on the field, together with the enhanced accessibility of source material, provide the potential for a more thorough understanding of marine research at this time, and will hopefully yield new information on it.

There have already been many new contributions to our knowledge of marine science in the nineteenth and twentieth centuries which expand and sometimes correct the account given in this book. Trevor Levere (1993) has produced a valuable account of the expeditions to the Canadian Arctic in the nineteenth century, on which much oceanographic work was done. One of the most interesting of these, scientifically speaking, was the geographically unsuccessful voyage led by Sir John Ross (see p. 229) of which Tony Rice (1975) gives a fuller account. Towards the middle of the nineteenth century and again towards its end attention shifted to the southern hemisphere. Scientific work done on Antarctic expeditions is summarized by Fogg (1992), but there are also accounts of individual Antarctic expeditions in which oceanography played an important part, including Bellingshausen's voyage (Rubin, 1982), Sir James Clark Ross's voyage of 1839–43 (Ross, 1982), Speak (1992) on W.S. Bruce and the *Scotia*, and A.C. Hardy (1967) on the 1925–27 voyage of R.R.S. *Discovery*. The problems experienced by Sir James Clark Ross with temperature measurements are explained in McConnell (1978). When I was writing *Scientists and the Sea*, I felt that, in spite of the work being done by Antarctic voyages, the middle of the nineteenth century, between about 1830 and 1850, was not a very productive time for marine science. The exception was the tidal studies described in Chapter 13, for which more information has become available with publication of correspondence of early members of the British Association by Morrell & Thackray (1984). However, recent work in Germany has shown that there is more to say; a paper by Gerhard Kortum (1990) has shown that a key figure of the early part of the century, Alexander von Humboldt, continued to actively think and write about ocean currents, though his treatise was never published.

One of the areas of development responsible for the *Challenger*, and similar expeditions in the 1870s, was technological – the result of the industrial revolution which at sea led to the gradual replacement of sail by steam. Motor power made possible the exploration of deep sea, and the specialized techniques to achieve this were developed firstly in conjunction with survey work for, and then with the actual laying and retrieving of submarine telegraph cables, as shown by McConnell (1982). To this was linked the growing interest in life in the sea. In extending these discoveries to deeper water the work of the dredging committees of the British Association played an important role (Rehbock, 1979; Rice & Wilson, 1980). Edward Forbes (Rehbock, 1979; 1983) was a key figure in this enterprise but the information he and his contemporaries were seeking was not exclusively biological; they also wanted more information about the present-day inhabitants of British seas in order to compare them with recent fossil deposits on land, at a time when it was beginning to be realized that climate had changed through time and evidence of widespread glaciation was starting to be recognized.

Forbes's generalization from dredging in the Mediterranean, that marine life was probably absent in the deep sea, may have set back the realization of its existence for a generation. It is an interesting case of the strength of an idea which already had a body of evidence against it. G. C. Wallich (Rice, Burstyn & Jones, 1976) felt that he should have been given more credit for its eventual overturn but his work was somewhat overlooked in the general excitement of the discoveries which preceded the *Challenger* expedition (Chapter 14). The present volume showed the importance of the physical work in the events leading up to the voyage, for it was W. B. Carpenter's enthusiasm for his theory of currents which led him to undertake what Harold Burstyn (1972) has shown to be a key role in the realization of the expedition.

As well as several papers by Harold Burstyn (including 1972, 1975), there has been a popular account of the *Challenger* (Linklater, 1972) and publication of original accounts (Müller, 1984; Rehbock, 1992) but no survey of the expedition as a whole, of which the account given in chapter 15 of this volume remains a useful summary. One particular area of further development should be mentioned. The story of the protoplasmic organism *Bathybius* (pp. 352-3) has been told in greater detail by historians of science (see Rehbock, 1975) but what of the reports of its discovery by the *Porcupine*, or by Bessels? More recent observations by oceanographers in the North Atlantic shows that during the spring phytoplankton bloom productivity is so intense that the marine life forms that feed upon the microscopic plant life cannot keep pace with it. The remains may fall as detritus to the ocean floor in such quantities that there is a delay before it is scavenged by benthic organisms. This is the most likely explanation for the *"Bathybius"* found in newly-dredged samples last century.

One of the consequences of the *Challenger* voyage was a renewed interest in coral reefs (pp. 383-385). The story of the Christmas Island phosphates (p. 385) has been told in full by Harold Burstyn (1975) and Roy MacLeod (1988) has studied the background to the Funafuti expeditions. The *Challenger* was soon followed by expeditions from other countries, and accounts of their work may be found in the proceedings of the international congresses on the history of oceanography, and elsewhere. By the close of the nineteenth century, institutions dedicated to marine science were already appearing. Most of these were initially zoological laboratories located by the sea, but some went on to make a wider contribution to marine studies. These have received considerable coverage during the last twenty-five years, especially as the earlier foundations achieved their centenaries. The work of Anton Dohrn (Heuss, 1948; Groeben, 1982) and the influence of his foundation, the Stazione Zoologica at Naples (Benson, 1988; Metz, 1988) have received special attention. Of the British laboratories (Deacon, 1993), Plymouth (Southward & Roberts, 1987), Jersey (Heppel & West, 1989) and Millport (Marshall (1987) have received more extensive treatment. Government organizations (Pinsel, 1981) were already beginning to appear, especially in connection with fisheries research (Allard, 1978; Lee, 1992). The oceanographic laboratories in existence today are largely mid to late twentieth-century foundations, though some have evolved out of earlier institutions. For example, in America a marine biological station on the west coast was transformed in the 1920s into the Scripps Institution of Oceanography (Raitt & Moulton, 1967; Shor, 1978). Scientific societies dedicated to marine science also appeared about this time. The history of the short-lived Société d'Océanographie du Golfe du Gascogne has been pieced together by Jacqueline Carpine-Lancre (1995). The Challenger Society, founded in 1903 (p. 392), continues active. Its early history and the career of G. Herbert Fowler who was largely responsible for its foundation have been described by Deacon (1984; 1990). Its archives, referred to in notes 200, 206, 208 to chapter 16 (on p. 405), and the card catalogue mentioned in note 206, are now located in the National Oceanographic Library at the Southampton Oceanography Centre.

In the bibliography accompanying this introduction is listed a selection of works which may be helpful for anyone coming new to this subject area. Many people on becoming interested in the history of oceanography have felt that they were working on their own. Happily this no longer has to be the case. They will be welcomed to the community! During the last twenty-five years much important new work has been published, some of which has been referred to above. However, as so often happens in research, it has become apparent that the more we find, the more there is to know and much remains to be done. This includes not only finding out more about the different aspects of scientific interest in the sea, but how they may link in to wider developments in the history of science, and other disciplines. For example, the history of oceanography in recent years has not been solely concerned with recent scientific exploration of the sea. Knowledge of the sea can be traced in ancient and traditional cultures, as well as in the Western scientific tradition. A related theme that has interested historians of science in recent years is "scientific imperialism" or the export of western scientific ideas to other parts of the world, and the ensuing assertion of independence by native and colonial science. Oceanography, and more especially fisheries, are prime targets for such treatment and are beginning to receive attention (Harrison, 1988; Van Sittert, 1995).

In both the nineteenth and early twentieth centuries biographical and autobiographical writing has provided valuable accounts of the lives of key figures. T. R. R. Stebbing's biography of David Robertson, *The naturalist of Cumbrae* (Stebbing, 1891), H.R. Mill's *Autobiography* (1951) and a sympathetic biography of Matthew Fontaine Maury by Frances

Leigh Williams (1963) and similar works contain much information on the progress of marine science. Indeed so great is the potential interest of such accounts to historians that the Forbes memoir by Wilson and Geikie (1861) has itself been the subject of a historical investigation (Browne, 1981). More recently the scientific biography of individuals has been somewhat out of fashion, but the success of Adrian Desmond's life of T.H. Huxley (1994) has brought about a revival of interest. This book too has a place in the history of oceanography canon, because of its treatment of Huxley's time on the *Rattlesnake*, and its signifcance in his work. The *Dictionary of Scientific Biography* provides basic information on the more distinguished scientists of all periods, as do national biographical dictionaries. The problem comes in trying to find out about less important but still interesting figures. The *New Dictionary of National Biography* should make this easier, at least for the U.K.

More fundamental problems also remain. As Eric Mills (1993a, b) has pointed out, following on from Burstyn (1968), much is still to be done. In spite of the growth of interest and materials available over the last two decades, he argues (Mills, 1993b, p. 5) that "the history of oceanography is still in a primitive state", needing internal histories, critical biographies, studies of institutions and national contributions, but beyond this, discussion of what "oceanography" means in a historical context, how it was perceived and at what stage it became a science and a profession in the full sense. He suggests numerous important topics which, using the tools and methodologies of modern history of science, would advance the study of the subject. *Scientists and the Sea* was intended to provide a survey of the early development of oceanography that would serve as an introduction to a subject that was not well known, and encourage new work in the field. Hopefully as the history of marine science comes of age, it can still continue to do this.

Acknowledgements

To the gratitude and acknowledgements already expressed in 1971, I should like to add my warmest thanks to the Department of Oceanography, University of Southampton, for its hospitality to me over the last sixteen years, first as Hartley Research Fellow, and later as honorary research fellow. In 1992 Dalhousie University, Halifax, Nova Scotia, made a generous recognition of the work contained in this volume, for which I am very grateful. Finally, I thank my husband, David Seward, for much help and encouragement.

February 1997   MARGARET DEACON
University of Southampton

THE BACKGROUND TO THE SEVENTEENTH CENTURY MOVEMENT

1. THE ANCIENT WORLD

Let us explain the nature of winds, and all windy vapours, also of rivers and of the sea. But here, too, we must first discuss the difficulties involved: for, as in other matters, so in this no theory has been handed down to us that the most ordinary man could not have thought of.
Aristotle, *Meteorologica*, I, xiii.

OCEANOGRAPHY, like the other environmental sciences, is less of a science than an application of science in general to the study of a particular subject, the sea in this instance. It differs from geology, meteorology and biology in that whereas they can be studied to a considerable degree without having to be broken down into their component specialized branches, physical oceanography at any rate cannot now develop and never could beyond a very early stage without the assistance of the mathematical and physical sciences and a certain amount of technical skill.

Accurate measurement is a prerequisite of oceanography. The variations of temperature and salinity in the surface water are generally too small and too gradual to be detected by the unaided senses. Waves and tides are too ephemeral to be studied without a record while the movement of a current out of sight of land is imperceptible to the ship carried with it. When it is a question of investigating the characteristics of the great mass of the sea, below the surface, man's dependence on instrumentation becomes absolute.

The significance of measurement in studying the physical conditions of the sea was seen by the philosophers and scientists of Renaissance Europe. It was they who felt the need to introduce into the dialectical discussion, with which writers on geography and science were largely content, some factual knowledge and who investigated ways of obtaining it. They foresaw the possibility of measuring the depth of the sea with special machines, of using hydrometers to measure salinity and thermometers to measure temperature both at the surface and in the depths of the sea and of using gauges to measure the rise and fall of tides. This was not all. While many were content merely to indicate the possibility, a few people put these instruments to practical use.

Taking a more exact view some people say that the science of oceanography did not come into existence until the beginning of the twentieth century since it was only then that scientists began the task of progressing from the static picture of the ocean which their observations had built up to the formation of a dynamic theory which would take into account all the physical characteristics of the ocean and the external forces acting upon it. Whether the contributions of the years before 1900 amount to a science or should only be regarded as prescientific, it is certain that the modern science of oceanography has grown out of concepts which began to take shape in Europe during the Renaissance era. The development was a slow process, chequered by interruptions and reverses, but it is often possible to see an underlying continuity of ideas and methods. Yet man's interest in the sea is much older than this. As the perilous highway of ships and sailors, as a geographical entity, as an aspect of the natural world which had to be incorporated into cosmologies and accounted for by nascent science, the sea aroused much interest in earlier civilizations and it is among their surviving writings that the origins of knowledge about the sea are to be found.

Attempts to give a rational account of the origin and nature of the sea are as old as science itself. They go back at least to the Greek scientists of Asia Minor who, in the sixth century B.C., abandoned the mythological interpretations of the universe held by previous civilizations in favour of explanations based on the operation of natural causes. The sea naturally occupied a place in their cosmologies and Aristotle (384–322 B.C.) prefaced his own study of the origin of the sea in the *Meteorologica* with a summary of the views put forward in the two preceding centuries.

The old writers who invented theogonies say that the sea has springs, for they want earth and sea to have foundations and roots of their own. Presumably they thought that this view was grander and more impressive as implying that our earth was an important part of the universe. For they believed that the whole world had been built up round our earth and for its sake, and that the earth was the most important and primary part of it. Others, wiser in human knowledge, give an account of its origin. At first, they say, the earth was surrounded by moisture. Then the sun began to dry it up, part of it evaporated and is the cause of winds and the turnings back of the sun and the moon, while the remainder forms the sea. So the sea is being dried up and is growing less, and will end by being someday entirely dried up. Others say that the sea is a kind of sweat exuded by the earth when the sun heats it, and that this explains its saltness: for all sweat is salt. Others say that the saltness is due to the earth. Just as water strained through ashes becomes salt, so the sea owes its saltness to the admixture of earth with similar properties.[1]

The picture of the primitive earth surrounded by moisture which was evaporated by the sun was common to the scientists of Miletos-Thales, Anaximander and Anaximenes. The idea of the sea as the sweat of the earth was introduced by the fifth-century scientists, Empedocles and Democritos; the idea that the salt in sea water was due to the admixture of earth by, amongst others, Anaxagoras of Clazomenae (*c.* 500–428 B.C.).[2]

Aristotle did not accept these views as they stood. Nor did he approve of the description given by Plato (*c.* 427–347 B.C.) in the *Phaedo*.[3] Plato supposed that the origin of the water found in rivers and in the sea lay in a vast body of water oscillating to and fro in the centre of the earth. From this reservoir ran a network of tunnels carrying water into the rivers and the seas. This imaginative hypothesis seems to have had little in common with the more sober speculations of ancient scientists either before or after its appearance. It was perhaps closest to the idea of Xenophanes who said that springs and rivers derived their supplies from the sea underground, the salt being filtered out of the sea water during its passage through the earth.[4] During the Renaissance, such ideas were taken very seriously by scientific writers including Athanasius Kircher (1602–1680) in *Mundus Subterraneus* and John Woodward (1665–1728) in *An Essay towards a Natural History of the Earth*. As late as 1757 Joseph Mead published *An Essay on Currents at Sea* which contained an intricate description of the circulation of water through the centre of the earth.[5]

Aristotle himself thought that the sun evaporated water from the surface of the sea but he did not share the idea of the Milesian philosophers who thought that the sun consumed the vapour so produced and that the sea would therefore eventually dry up.[6] Instead he followed Anaxagoras in saying that the water vapour rose into the air where it was condensed by cold and fell as rain. It was this rain which supplied the springs and rivers. Anaxagoras thought that the rain collected in reservoirs under the hills which was why rivers continued to flow when it was not actually raining. Aristotle, on the other hand, thought that rain alone was insufficient and that it must be supplemented by water condensed by cold and gradually collecting in the ground.[7] In the second book of the *Meteorologica*, however, he is at pains to show that he regards the process of evaporation and precipitation as a cycle in which the sea and its sources, the rivers, are continually renewed. He stresses that while water is constantly changing its state from one stage in the cycle to another the total amount of water remains the same:

we always plainly see the water that has been carried up coming down again. Even if the same amount does not come back in a year or in a given country, yet in a certain period all that has been carried up is returned. This implies that the celestial bodies do not feed on it, and that we cannot distinguish between some air which preserves its character once it is generated and some other which is generated but becomes water again and so perishes; on the contrary, all the moisture alike is dissolved and all of it condensed back into water.[8]

This explanation of the relationship between the water in the sea and that in springs and rivers was generally regarded as an alternative only to the idea of the subterranean connection at least until the end of the seventeenth century (see Chapter 8). Robert Plot (1640–1696) tells us that among those who preferred it were Vitruvius, Peter Martyr, Cardano, Molina, Palissy, Gassendi and Hooke.[9] To these one might add Edmond Halley (1656–1742).[10] These writers commonly attributed the hypothesis of the exchange of water between the ocean and the atmosphere to Aristotle and that of the subterranean origin of springs to Plato for their works contained the earliest studies on these subjects to survive complete. Aristotle in particular dominated scientific thought until the seventeenth century and so wide was the range of his works and the influence of his opinion on all branches of learning that, until new work superseded his own, he was accredited with virtual omniscience. Any ideas about the sea were, true to this pattern, held to be of weight in the absence of more positive knowledge, if his name was attached to them, even if they were not in fact his own.

This was what happened with ideas about the saltness of the sea. Aristotle's own hypothesis was that the salt came from a dry exhalation from the earth analogous to the moist evaporation raised from the sea by the sun. The water vapour and the dry exhalation, which he likened to smoke, together constituted the air.[11] When the vapour was condensed by cold to form rain some of the dry exhalation mixed with it, giving the rain a salt content which, so he said, was great enough to be noticeable in rain from the south and in the first rain of autumn. It is of course true that wind and rain transport salt over the land so that Aristotle may not have been imagining the effects he described but the salt in the atmosphere is derived from the sea and not in the way he supposed.[12] He knew that if salt water is heated fresh water is evaporated and the salt remains behind but supposed that the amount of salt in the sea remains the same since

some part of its saltness is always being drawn up with the sweet water. This is less than the sweet water in the same ratio in which the salt and brackish element in rain is less than the sweet, and so the saltness of the sea remains constant on the whole. Salt water when it turns into vapour becomes sweet, and the vapour does not form salt water when it condenses again. This I know by experiment.[13]

However it was difficult to account for the occurrence of springs of salt and fresh water and this made it hard for him to sustain his own case or to give cogent reasons for dismissing the ideas of his predecessors. One of these was the suggestion made by Xenophanes and Anaxagoras that salt was washed from the earth into the sea by rivers. Aristotle replied to this that the rivers were not salt but this objection could be applied equally well to his own explanation. Nor did the properties of sea water favour either side. Aristotle held that the salt was a substance added to water. This could be deduced from, among other things, the weight of salt water which was greater than that of fresh. He also said that the salt could be separated from sea water by filtration into a closed wax bottle. Commentators have thrown doubts on Aristotle's veracity here, supposing such a result to be impossible. The matter is not really quite so simple. The salt can be separated out of sea water in certain circumstances, either by filtration or by a process of ion exchange. It is difficult to know whether this experiment really would have succeeded if Aristotle did make it but the possibility should not be dismissed.[14]

The explanation of the sea's saltness contained in the *Meteorologica* is not the one attributed to Aristotle by most Renaissance writers. In its place one finds the idea that the salt was residual, the part of the water left behind by evaporation, much as ashes are left behind after burning. This explanation was adopted by Pliny (A.D. 23–79) who specifically rejected Aristotle's idea and said that the sun evaporated only the sweet and mild water

while all the more acrid and thick matter is left behind; on which account the water of the sea is less salt at some depth than at the surface.[15]

From Pliny this explanation travelled into the Middle Ages and survived into the seventeenth century—where by a process of accretion it appeared as part of the Aristotelian tradition. Only one or two writers seem to have realized that his account actually differed from this. Bernhard Varen (1622–?1650) knew the distinction and Georges Fournier had a curious version which combines the two:

Ie reponds auec Aristote; que le Soleil attire du fond de la Mer, quantite d'exhalaisons grossieres & de vapeurs qui se meslent, qu'il cuit, & brusle lors qu'elles s'approchent de la surface de l'eau, & c'est cela qui engendre cette* salure.[16]

Most, like the Hon. Robert Boyle (1627–1691), were content to assume that the two were one and the same—

The Peripateticks do, after their master *Aristotle*, derive the saltness of the sea from the adustion of the water by the sun-beams.[17]

If Pliny's account was the origin of this confusion he must be equally responsible for the idea also common among seventeenth-century writers and wrongly attributed by them to Aristotle that the sea was salt on the surface only which was a corollary to the opinion that the salt was formed in the surface water. Aristotle, however, did not think that a layer of dense water would float on the surface of lighter water. He says in one place

The sea is there and some of it is continually being drawn up and becoming sweet; this returns from above with the rain. But it is now different from what it was when it was drawn up,* and its weight makes it sink below the sweet water.[13]

There is a passage in the *Problemata*, which, taken on its own, may have been misleading in both cases, which describes how the sun concentrates the water on the surface of the sea but it seems from the context that it refers neither to the creation of salt nor to a permanent difference from one layer to another but to the immediate effect of hot sun on the water, evaporating fresh water and leaving behind water slightly hotter and more salt than normal.[18]

The idea that the sea was salt only at the surface finally disappeared after the publication of Boyle's *Observations and Experiments about the Saltness of the Sea* in 1673.[17] By this time a number of philosophers, including Palissy, Gassendi and Boyle himself, had revived the idea that the saltness was due to minerals dissolved in water.[19] The pre-Aristotelian hypothesis had returned to favour after a lapse of two thousand years.

The *Meteorologica* is said to have been written during Aristotle's second stay in Athens between 334 and 323 B.C.[20] In common with his other works on natural science it was produced as a result of a change in emphasis in his thought during the middle period of his life. After the death of Plato in 347 B.C. he had gradually come to the conclusion that philosophical knowledge was to be found through the study of the world around him rather than in metaphysical thought. This conviction led him in particular to biological research, much of which was concentrated on creatures living in the sea. He described 180 different species of the fauna of the Aegean, the pioneer work of marine biology.[21]

If Aristotle was almost undoubtedly the earliest marine biologist, his position with regard to the physical side of marine science is a little less easy to define since it is not easy to know how many of the ideas and observations in the works ascribed to him were actually his. Observations attributed to him are to be found in the *Problemata* but this work is held to be a compilation based only in part on his works and mostly on those of his successors.[22] Book 23, "Problems Connected with Salt Water and the Sea", contains several passages dealing with the physical aspects of the sea, in particular with the properties of sea water and of waves. It would seem to be a useless task to try and discover the ultimate provenance of these ideas, but what is said about the density of sea water and its buoyancy follows on from the *Meteorologica* so that the explanations have an affinity with Aristotle's thought even if he did not make the observations himself. One thing is lacking; there is no mention of tides in this section. Aristotle himself makes little

* Because of mixing with the dry evaporation.

mention of them but in the years immediately before his death they became familiar to the Greek world and, from that time on, interested scientists much more than any other aspect of the sea.

Among the questions of interest in respect to oceanography is a group∗ dealing with waves. Why do waves begin to move before the wind reaches them? It is suggested that the original impulse of wind on the sea surface is transmitted through the water and that in this medium it travels more quickly than the wind itself.[23] Also, why are waves less pronounced in deep water than they are in the shallows? ∗

Another section deals with the saltness and temperature of the sea. In∗ answer to the question "Why is the sea less cold than drinking water, and salt water in general than fresh?" it is suggested that this might be because the sea water is denser and therefore able to retain heat better. Also, why should sea water be more transparent than fresh water in spite of being denser?

The most interesting part of this section begins with the question "Why is it that the upper parts of the sea are saltier and hotter than the depths?" Aristotle knew that salt water is heavier than fresh and, as we have seen in the *Meteorologica*, that it would sink below fresh water on account of its greater weight. This explained how it was that the water on the surface of the sea and, as was supposed, of wells became saltier than the water below:

Now water which is suitable for drinking is always lighter, and the sun can more easily attract it from the part of the water nearest to it. And so that which is left on the surface both of the sea and of drinking water is saltier (since the fresh element has been extracted) than that from which little or nothing has been withdrawn.

Near the shore, however, the sea was less salt. This might be because the water was moving about more or because it was shallower since

the salty element being heavy is carried down more into deep water.

Aristotle's final contribution to marine science seems to have been a consideration of tidal conditions in the Euripus, made during his last months which were spent in Euboea.[24] It is probable that the Greeks did not know enough about tides in the ocean at that date for Aristotle to have been aware that the complex movements in the Euripus had anything to do with them. In the *Meteorologica* he distinguished between standing water and flowing water. Rivers, among which he included the Mediterranean, flowed from a higher to a lower level but the ocean consisted of water which had collected at the lowest level to which it could go.

It is true that in straits, where the land on either side contracts an open sea into a small space, the sea appears to flow. But this is because it is swinging to and fro. In the open sea this motion is not observed, but where the land narrows and contracts the sea the motion that was imperceptible in the open necessarily strikes the attention.[25]

Understandably Aristotle failed to establish the cause of the very complicated tidal variations. Later writers, elaborating the story, said that this failure so frustrated him that he flung himself into the offending strait and was drowned. Such desperation struck an echoing chord in the minds of seventeenth-century students of tides, who accepted the legend as true, but fortunately none of them were tempted to make a similar demonstration. In 1675 Richard Bolland wrote

The great Master of Philosophy drowned himself, because he could not apprehend the Cause of Tydes; but his Example cannot be so prevalent with all, as to put a Period to other Mens Inquiries into this Subject.[26]

The scope of Aristotle's work on marine science, extending as it did to both the physical and biological aspects, is perhaps unique for any one person in ancient times though a true comparison with other scientists is impossible for his works have survived whereas theirs have not. His significance as a pioneer of marine biology has never been questioned. As a writer on physical oceanography one has to remember that the best ideas to be found in the *Meteorologica* were those of earlier scientists, in particular Anaxagoras. In spite of this both for his own work and for his influence on the later development of attitudes towards marine science Aristotle is an undeniably important figure in the history of oceanography. He might be a better candidate than some for the somewhat casually distributed honour of being the "father of oceanography."[27]

Aristotle does not seem to have inspired his successors to develop his work on the sea. As far as one can judge from what survives of their works their knowledge appears to have been of a more general kind, except where tides were concerned, depending more on reported information and its interpretation than on new discoveries of their own. This at any rate is the picture given by Strabo (63 B.C.–*c.* A.D. 24) whose *Geography* contains much of what is known about the work of scientists and geographers after Aristotle.[28]

As early as the time of Herodotus (fifth century B.C.) sailors were acquainted with the shoal water at the mouth of the Nile through soundings with lead and line which were already part of the routine of navigation.[29] It was generally recognized that the shoals here and in the Sea of Azov had been built up by the deposition of silt by the rivers. Scientists speculated that the process of erosion on land and silting at sea would continue, perhaps until the basins occupied by the sea had been filled in.[25, 29, 30]

Little, understandably, was known about the deeper parts of the Mediterranean or other seas. Aristotle knew of a deep place in the Black Sea where no one had been able to find the bottom by sounding.[31] He believed that this was where a subterranean channel from the Caspian entered the Black Sea and that this was the source of the fresh water to be found there. Considering what he has to say in the same work about the importance of evaporation it is strange that Aristotle found it necessary to resort to such an artifice to account for the fact that the Caspian remains at the same level although it has no outlet to the sea. Like so many of his statements this suggestion had a far-reaching effect. Kircher was among those who used it to lend an aura of respectability to even more complicated systems of the same kind.[32]

Aristotle put forward the idea that the oceans occupy the deepest parts in the surface of the earth, which he knew to be a globe. Later geographers, from their ideas on the possibility of the sea's silting up, would seem to have shared this view. They had no knowledge of the sea's actual depth. The sole piece of factual evidence, which appears comparatively late, was given by Posidonius (c. 135–50 B.C.), the Stoic philosopher, perhaps in his work on the ocean which has not survived. He said that the Sardinian Sea had been sounded to a depth of about a thousand fathoms and that this was the greatest depth known.[33]

The Mediterranean was thought to be in a separate category, however, from the ocean as a whole. This was because Aristotle had described it as a river flowing down an inclined bed from the Sea of Azov into the Mediterranean, accumulating at the western end.[25] In support of this view he cited the existence of the current which flows out of the Black Sea into the Mediterranean through the Bosporus but admitted that otherwise a westward flow was hard to detect. This idea was accepted and extended by Eratosthenes (c. 273–192 B.C.), the Alexandrian astronomer and geographer, and by Strato (fl. c. 288 B.C.).[34] Strato incorporated it into an account of the origin of the Mediterranean. He said that the Black Sea and the Mediterranean had originally been lakes with no outlet to the ocean. The rivers of eastern Europe raised the level of the Black Sea until it forced its way into the Mediterranean through what is now the Bosporus. The level of the Mediterranean then rose in the same way until it broke through the Strait of Gibraltar into the Atlantic. There was a submarine ridge running across the Strait, a relic of the former landbridge joining Europe with Africa. The comparative freshness of the water of the Black Sea was due to its lacustrine origin. A theory of this kind fitted in with evidence of changes in sea level which had been remarked upon even by the pre-Socratic scientists. Eratosthenes argued from the existence of marine fossils in Egypt that the Mediterranean might once have extended almost to the point of merging with the Red Sea. Strabo, on the other hand, thought that the changes of sea level were due not to alteration in the sea itself but in the relative height of the land through earth movements.[35]

Strabo's contribution to this hypothesis was to point out that the idea of a sloping sea floor, which Aristotle and later geographers had regarded as an essential part of it, was unnecessary. Whereas Aristotle had supposed that water would only flow down an inclined plane Strabo realized that the difference in level created by the rivers in the Black Sea was sufficient to maintain the outward flow through the Bosporus and that the shape of the sea floor was immaterial.[36] He knew of the existence of the current flowing into the Mediterranean from the Atlantic through the Strait of Gibraltar and realized that if the theory were admitted in the form in which Aristotle and the others had held it only an outward current would be possible.

Aristotle had supposed that the sea proper consisted of water which had accumulated at the lowest common level but Eratosthenes thought that different parts of the same sea might have different levels. When two areas of unequal height were juxtaposed a flow of water would take place from the higher to the lower level, and this was what produced tides and currents in straits, but, he believed, when they were separated as are the Adriatic and the Aegean, by a peninsula, no loss of equilibrium would follow. He based this opinion on the apparent discovery of engineers who, investigating the possibility of constructing a canal through the Isthmus of Corinth, had obtained measurements showing the sea to be higher on one side than the other.[37] Hipparchus (*fl. c.* 162–126 B.C.) criticized this opinion on the grounds that all confluent seas must have surfaces in equilibrium. Strabo pointed out that Archimedes (287–212 B.C.) had shown that the surface of a fluid at rest must adopt the form of the surface of a sphere with a centre the same as that of the earth.[38]

The ideas of ancient geographers about the Mediterranean were based on information which in general was accurate but when they came to consider the ocean what they said was of necessity almost entirely speculative. This is not the place to give an account of the development of general geographic theory which has been described by many authorities,[39] but the idea of the ocean as a single body of water surrounding the land survived from the tradition of Homeric geography into later times. It was impossible with their limited geographical knowledge for the Greeks to prove that the Atlantic and Indian Oceans were part of the same body of water by direct methods but Eratosthenes thought that this could be inferred from the fact that the two oceans were both subject to semi-diurnal tides. It could be argued that parts of the ocean which behaved in an identical manner must be linked.[40] Hipparchus challenged the validity of this argument. Contrasting the tides observed by Seleucus in the Indian Ocean (*see* p. 14) with the lack of tides in the Mediterranean, he reasoned that these two stretches of water could not be connected and that the supposed link between the two oceans to the south of the African continent might not exist.[41] Strabo himself, eager to vindicate the tenets of Homeric geography and in possession of more details about the tides in the Atlantic, thought that in spite of local variations an underlying similarity could be seen and that the argument of Eratosthenes was permissible.

The oceanic phenomenon which the early scientists found most striking was its tides. Although they were to be found in various parts of the Mediterranean, as had been mentioned by Herodotus,[42] Greek scientists do not seem to have been aware of them as a general feature of the ocean until about 320 B.C. when they were reported from the Indian Ocean by the army of Alexander the Great and from the Atlantic by the explorer Pytheas. In the succeeding centuries they attracted considerable attention until more was known about them than any other aspect of marine science and the work done then, as in more recent times, on this subject has been dealt with more fully by historians of science than any other part of oceanography, in particular by Pierre Duhem.[43]

The development of knowledge of oceanic tides as given by these authorities is as follows. Neither Aristotle nor Plato seem to have known of their existence though they were afterwards often supposed to have done so.[44] In point of time, the existence of tides was first noticed by Alexander's army as it descended the Indus[45] but not more than a few years later Pytheas of Marseilles brought back information on Atlantic tides from the voyage of discovery in which he circumnavigated the British Isles. Pytheas made the first recorded mention of the relationship between the tides and the movements of the moon. He is supposed to have said that the tide came in as the moon waxed and went out as it waned but his own report has not survived and one ancient author attributes this to another sailor who, Duhem suggests, may have preceded him.[46] Whatever the truth of this, it seems highly unlikely that a navigator as capable as Pytheas undoubtedly was could have explored the coasts of Europe without becoming aware of the semi-diurnal tide and its dependence on the moon and it is perhaps possible to think that his knowledge was really more accurate than this fragment suggests. According to Pliny he also reported that tides rose to a height of 120 feet on the coast of Britain.[47] This is far too high a figure even for the greatest variation if a perpendicular height is meant but as it must have been arrived at by estimation rather than measurement the exaggeration is only to be expected. Similar errors were still being made about the high tides of the English Channel in the seventeenth century.[48]

The next person who figures in the history of tides is Eratosthenes who was the first known person to record the law of the semi-diurnal tide in the ocean.[46] Strabo tells us how he described the tide starting to come in as the moon rose over the horizon and flowing until it reached the meridian.[37] When the moon began to set the tide ebbed until it disappeared below the horizon. The flood and ebb then repeated themselves for the second time in the twenty-four hours as the moon approached and left the meridian below the earth. Eratosthenes used Pytheas's determinations of latitude and may well have learned about the behaviour of tides from his account as well.[49]

Geographers before the time of Aristotle had tended to repeat the Homeric tradition of the ocean flowing round the flat inhabited earth. Aristotle, as we have seen, introduced a new concept of the ocean and though he supposed that by definition it was impossible for it to flow he did allow that it might oscillate to and fro.[50] As tides became better known it was apparent that the ocean was subject to regular movements and this concept superseded the earlier tradition.

The most interesting of the tidal studies made in the ancient world is undoubtedly that of Seleucus of Babylon (*fl. c.* 150 B.C.) who was apparently the only astronomer in ancient times to accept the idea of a heliocentric universe put forward by Aristarchus of Samos. Seleucus made his observations in the Persian Gulf, as far as is known, and they must have been both thorough and prolonged for him to have reached such a good understanding of the tides there. He discovered the existence, Strabo tells us,

of a certain irregularity in these phenomena, or regularity, according to the differences of the signs of the zodiac; that is, if the moon is in the equinoctial signs, the behaviour of the tides is regular, but, in the solstitial signs, irregular, in respect both to amount and to speed, while, in each of the other signs, the relation is in proportion to the nearness of the moon's approach.[51]

Sir George Darwin (1845–1912) recognized this as a description of the diurnal inequality of tides which is to be found in the Indian Ocean.[52] The difference between the tides increased in proportion to the moon's distance from the equator, being greatest when it was furthest away and disappearing when the moon crossed the equator at the equinoxes. Duhem adds to this the account of the eighth-century writer St John Damascene[53] who tells us that Seleucus believed that tides were caused by pressure on the sea surface. The moon rotating round the earth compressed the atmosphere and it in its turn communicated the disturbing force to the sea. It sounds as though he intended something not dissimilar to the mechanism suggested by Descartes (*see* p. 52).

The other early work on tides about which some detail is known is that of Posidonius. Strabo tells us how he travelled to Cadiz and made tidal observations both there and at other places on the Atlantic coast of Europe.[54] He discovered that the tides were not only coming in and going out alternately twice a day but also increased and decreased in size for alternate weeks. This monthly variation consisted of a regular pattern in which the greatest floods and ebbs occurred at the conjunction and at full moon. During the fortnight which separated these peaks the size of the tides grew smaller to reach a minimum at the quarters and then increased again.

Posidonius also described an annual variation. The inhabitants of Cadiz told him that the highest tides of the year arrived at the summer solstice.[55] From this information he drew the conclusion that there might be two such maxima, at the summer and winter solstices, with corresponding decreases and increases to and from the equinoxes. He spent some time at Cadiz at the time of the summer solstice hoping to obtain verification for this hypothesis but no such abnormality was to be seen. This was hardly surprising since the bi-annual high tides occur at the equinoxes and not at the solstices but they otherwise follow the pattern Posidonius suggested. The close resemblance between the real and supposed state of affairs led Duhem to suggest that Strabo might have accidentally transposed the times in giving his own version of Posidonius's account.[56]

Duhem, quoting from a sixth-century philosopher, Priscien of Lydia, tells us that Posidonius believed the tide-raising force to be the astrological power of the moon, possibly through the agency of the winds, and that this interpretation remained paramount throughout the Roman period and even afterwards because nothing else seemed to explain the obvious interdependence between the movement of the moon and the sea.[57] Practical knowledge of the behaviour of tides continued to improve, culminating in the account given by Pliny in his *Historia Naturalis*.[47]

Pliny followed the earlier writers in describing the diurnal and monthly cycles of the tide. He was correctly informed that the diurnal tides are geared to the lunar day and therefore progress in time relative to the solar day and knew that the annual springs occur about the equinoxes and the neaps at the solstices. Two of his ideas were less well founded, one that tides were less in summer because the moon was further from the earth when it was north of the equator, the other that the tides had a cycle of eight years.* What was an advance on Posidonius's ideas, as Strabo describes them, was the description of the lunitidal interval. Pliny tells us that the tides do not coincide exactly with the movement of the moon but follow it after a pause. When the moon rises over the horizon the flood does not begin immediately, as Erastosthenes had supposed, but two hours later. High tide and the ebb were similarly delayed. Proportionate delays occurred between the conjunction and opposition and the quadratures and

---

* There is a variation in the moon's motion with a cycle of just over eight years. More noticeable however, and with regard to its effect on tides, is the nineteen year cycle which was known to ancient astronomers but which Pliny does not mention in this connection.

the corresponding effects in the tides and between the equinoxes and the solstices and the annual springs and neaps. This was due, said Pliny, to "the effect of what is going on in the heavens being felt after a short interval". It is most unlikely that Pliny actually discovered this since his work was compiled of extracts from previous authors rather than on his own research.[58] It was the sort of information that sailors would have had and may well have been known to the earlier scientists who worked on tides and whose books have disappeared.

1. NOTES

1. Aristotle, *Meteorologica*, translated E. W. Webster, in *The Works of Aristotle* (ed. W. D. Ross), 12 vols, Oxford (1908–1952), Vol. 3 (1931), 2, i, 353*a–b*. Quotations are included by kind permission of the Clarendon Press, Oxford.

2. *Ibid.* 2, i, 353*b*, and footnotes to the above edition.
See also: Charles H. Kahn, *Anaximander and the Origins of Greek Cosmology*, New York (1960), pp. 100–102.
Jean Zafiropulo, *Anaxagore de Clazomène*, Paris (1948), p. 329 says that Anaxagoras explained the salt taste of the sea as the result of the solution by its water of minerals from the earth and their subsequent concentration by the action of the sun.

3. Aristotle, *Meteorologica*, in *The Works of Aristotle* (ed. W. D. Ross). Vol. **3**, 2, ii, 355*b*–356*a*.

4. *Ibid.* 2, ii, 354*b*, and footnote to the above edition.

5. Athanasius Kircher, *Mundus Subterraneus, in XII Libros Digestus*, 3rd edition, Amstelodami (1678). Vol. **1**, bk 3, part 3, ch. 2, pp. 169–171.
John Woodward, *An Essay towards a Natural History of the Earth*, London (1695), p. 117.
Joseph Mead, *An Essay on Currents at Sea*, London (1757).

6. Aristotle, *Meteorologica*, in *The Works of Aristotle* (ed. W. D. Ross). Vol. **3**, 2, ii, 355*a*.

7. *Ibid.* 1, xii–xiii. It is necessary to bear in mind Aristotle's theory of matter. He held that there was a scale of four elements—earth, water, air and fire—and that it was possible for them to transmute from one to another either up or down the scale.

8. *Ibid.* 2, ii, 355*a*. Compare 2, iii, 358*b*, "the parts neither of the earth nor of the sea remain constant but only their whole bulk".

9. Robert Plot, *De Origine Fontium, Tentamen Philosophicum*, Oxford (1685), p. 7.

10. Edmond Halley, "An account of the circulation of the watry vapours of the sea, and of the cause of springs", *Phil. Trans.* (1691–1693). Vol. **17**, pp. 468–473.

11. Aristotle, *Meteorologica*, in *The Works of Aristotle* (ed. W. D. Ross). Vol. **3**, 1, iv, 341*b*; 2, iii, 358*a*–358*b*.

12. A certain amount of salt enters the atmosphere from spray and is deposited on the land. In certain circumstances the quantity is great enough to be detected unaided. John Dalton described an instance of this kind after a storm in 1822, "On the saline impregnation of the rain, which fell during the late storm, December 5th, 1822", *Memoirs of the Literary and Philosophical Society of Manchester* (1824), 2nd series. Vol. **4**, pp. 324–331, 363–372.

13. Aristotle, *Meteorologica*, in *The Works of Aristotle* (ed. W. D. Ross). Vol. **3**, 2, iii, 358*b*.

14. *Ibid.* 2, iii, 359*a*.

15. Pliny, *The Natural History of Pliny*, translated by J. Bostock and H. T. Riley, 6 vols, London (1855–1857). Vol. **1**, bk 2, ch. 104.

16. Georges Fournier, *Hydrographie Contenant la Théorie et la Pratique de Toutes les Parties de la Navigation*, 2nd edition, Paris (1667), bk 9, ch. 24, p. 357. See pp. 56–57.

17. Robert Boyle, *Observations and Experiments about the Saltness of the Sea*, in *The Works of the Honourable Robert Boyle* (ed. T. Birch), 5 vols, London (1744). Vol. **3**, p. 378.

18. Aristotle (attrib.), *Problemata*, translated by E. S. Forster, in *The Works of Aristotle* (ed. W. D. Ross), 12 vols, Oxford (1908–1952) Vol. **7** (1927), bk. 23, no. 30. Quoted by kind permission of the Clarendon Press, Oxford.

19. Bernard Palissy, *Discours Admirables de la nature des eaux et fontaines*, in *Les Œuvres de Bernard Palissy* (ed. Anatole France), Paris (1880), p. 200.
Pierre Gassendi, "Syntagmatis Philosophici", *Opera Omnia*, 6 vols, Lugduni (1658). Vol. **2**, p. 53.
Robert Boyle, *op. cit.* Vol. **3**, pp. 381–382.

20. W. D. Ross, *Aristotle*, London (1923), p. 19.

21. Aristotle, *Historia Animalium*, translated by D'Arcy Wentworth Thompson, in *The Works of Aristotle* (ed. W. D. Ross), 12 vols (1908–1952). Vol. **4** (1910).
Sir John Murray, *Report on the Scientific Results of the Voyage of H.M.S. Challenger, Summary of the Scientific Results*, London (1895). Vol. **1**, p. 17.

22. Aristotle, *Problemata*, see ref. 18.
W. D. Ross, *Aristotle*, London (1923), p. 13.

23. Aristotle, *Physica*, in *The Works of Aristotle* (ed. W. D. Ross), 12 vols (1908– * 1952). Vol. **2** (1930), 267*a*, 4. Aristotle's concept of motion required that a projectile should receive a continuing impulse transmitted through the air.

24. H. F. Tozer, *A History of Ancient Geography*, 2nd edition, Cambridge (1955), pp. 185 and 192–193. Tozer thinks that Aristotle believed tides to be caused by the wind. In his discussion of earthquakes Aristotle attributes seismic surges to the action of the wind (*Meteorologica*, 2, viii, 368*a*, *b*) and describes vapour flowing into the earth "like a sort of ebb tide" (*Meteorologica*, 2, viii, 366*a*) but he does not seem to refer to anything resembling tidal motion except in *Meteorologica*, 2, i, 354*a*.

25. Aristotle, *Meteorologica*, in *The Works of Aristotle* (ed. W. D. Ross). Vol. **3**, 2, i, 354*a*.

26. Richard Bolland, *A Draught of the Streights of Gibraltar. With Some Observations upon the Currents thereunto Belonging*, in *A Collection of Voyages and Travels*, Awnsham and John Churchill, 4 vols, London (1704). Vol. **4**, p. 847.

27. The title of father or founder of oceanography has been bestowed on various people who figured significantly in the development of oceanography, including Count Marsigli, Major James Rennell and Matthew Fontaine Maury. But such a concept is always bound to be misleading. No one person can be said to have played a decisive role.

28. Strabo, *The Geography of Strabo*, translated by H. L. Jones and J. R. S. Sterrett, Loeb Classical Library, Harvard University Press, 8 vols, (1917–1932).

A modern work which covers the sea well is J. O. Thomson's *History of Ancient Geography*, Cambridge (1948).

29. Herodotus, *The History of Herodotus*, translated by G. C. Macaulay, 2 vols, London (1890), bk 2, ch. 5.

30. Strabo, *The Geography of Strabo*, I, 3, iv.
    J. O. Thomson, *op. cit.* p. 103.

31. Aristotle, *Meteorologica*, in *The Works of Aristotle* (ed. W. D. Ross). Vol. 3, 1, xiii, 351*a*.

32. Athanasius Kircher, *Mundus Subterraneus* in *XII Libros Digestus*, 3rd edition, Amstelodami (1678). Vol. 1, bk 3, part 2, ch. 10, pp. 157–163.

33. Aristotle, *Meteorologica*, in *The Works of Aristotle* (ed. W. D. Ross). Vol. 3, 2, ii, 355*b*.
    Strabo, *The Geography of Strabo*, I, 3, ix.

34. *Ibid.* I, 3, iv; I, 3, xii.

35. *Ibid.* I, 3, v.

36. *Ibid.* I, 3, v–vi; III, 2, iv.

37. *Ibid.* I, 3, xi.

38. *Ibid.* I, 3, xiii.
    Archimedes, *The Works of Archimedes* (ed. T. L. Heath), Cambridge (1897), p. 254.

39. E. H. Bunbury, *A History of Ancient Geography*, 2 vols, London (1879).
    J. O. Thomson, *op. cit.*

40. Strabo, *The Geography of Strabo*, I, 1, iii–x.

41. D. R. Dicks, *The Geographical Fragments of Hipparchus* London (1960), pp. 114–115.

42. Herodotus also mentioned tides in the Red Sea, *The History of Herodotus*, bk 2, ch. 11.

43. Pierre Duhem, *Le Système du Monde: Histoire des Doctrines Cosmologiques de Platon à Copernic*, 10 vols, Paris (1913–1959).
    Duhem refers extensively to Roberto Almagia, "La dottrina della marea nell'antichita classica et nel Medio Evo", *Atti Accad. naz. Lincei Memorie*, 5th series (1904). Vol. 5, pp. 377–513. *See also:*
    R. Almagia, "La conoscenza del fenomeno delle maree nell'antichita", *Archs int. Hist. Sci.* (1948–1949). Vol. 28, no. 8, pp. 887–899.

44. Among the early writers who thought Plato was describing tides when he spoke of water oscillating through the centre of the earth were Joannes Stobaeus and the author of *De placitis philosophorum* (Duhem. Vol. 2, p. 269). More recently the mistake was repeated by Fournier, pp. 341–342 *op. cit*:
    "Platon se persuadoit qu'au centre de la terre il y auoit des abismes d'eaux, qui de temps en temps se desgorgeoient en la Mer, & causoient ces flux & reflux."

45. Arrian, *Anabasis*, Loeb Classical Library, London (1954), bk 6, ch. 19.

46. Pierre Duhem, *op. cit.* Vol. 2, pp. 270–271.

47. Pliny, *The Natural History of Pliny*. Vol. 1, bk 2, ch. 99.

48. For example Sir Robert Moray writing to John Winthrop in 1669 referred to "the Coast of France where the tide rises 14. fathom upright", R. C. Winthrop, "Correspondence of Hartlib, Haak, Oldenburg, and others of the founders of the Royal Society, with Governor Winthrop of Connecticut", *Proceedings of the Massachusetts Historical Society* (1878). Vol. 16, pp. 206–251; p. 243.

49. J. O. Thomson, *op. cit.* pp. 143,146.
50. Strabo, *The Geography of Strabo*, I, i, iii.
    J. O. Thomson, pp. 97–98. Aristotle, *Meteorologica*, in *The Works of Aristotle* (ed. W. D. Ross). Vol. **3**, 2, i, 353*b*–354*a*.
51. Strabo, *The Geography of Strabo*, III, 5, ix. Quoted by kind permission of Harvard University Press.
52. G. H. Darwin, *The Tides and Kindred Phenomena in the Solar System*, 3rd edition, London (1911), p. 88.
53. Pierre Duhem, *op. cit.* Vol. **2**, pp. 273–274.
54. Strabo, *The Geography of Strabo*, III, 2, iv; III, 5, viii.
55. *Ibid.* III, 5, ix.
56. Pierre Duhem, *op. cit.* Vol. **2**, p. 282.
57. *Ibid.* Vol. **2**, pp. 280–285, pp. 460–462.
58. William H. Stahl, "Dominant traditions in early medieval Latin science", *Isis* (1959). Vol. **50**, part 2, no. 160, pp. 95–124.

Addenda et Corrigenda

p.7, 1.29: *before* c'est *insert* que

p.9, 1.4: *after* group *insert* (2)

p.9, 1.9: *after* shallows? *insert* (See also sections 28 and 29)

p.9, 1.10: *after* section *insert* (30-31)

p.17, n.23, 1.1: *before* Aristotle *inset: Cf.*

2. THE MIDDLE AGES

IN the fourteen hundred years which elapsed between the writing of Pliny's *Natural History* and the Renaissance, knowledge in the marine sciences scarcely advanced at all. Paradoxically it is the developments which took place during this time rather than later which have received more attention from historians of science. Although the net gain was small and the general standard of information mediocre in comparison to classical science, large numbers of medieval writers discussed problems connected with the sea. Phenomena such as ocean tides and the saltness of the sea never failed to arouse curiosity and whenever civilized life and thought had a chance to appear, even during the Dark Ages which followed the fall of the Roman Empire in Western Europe, scholars attempted to account for these and other aspects of the natural world.[1]

Pliny and his contemporaries, writing in the middle of the first century A.D., introduced a new era in the history of science.[2] The enquiring tradition of the Greeks gave way to the literary approach of the encyclopaedic writers who were content to give an account of natural phenomena which was a synthesis of the views to be found in previous works. They did not necessarily go back to original works or even to Pliny, from whom this type of work was ultimately derived, nor did they as a rule show any personal knowledge, except of a very general kind, of the subjects they were discussing.

Pliny, as we have seen, gave a more detailed and accurate account of tides than earlier writers.[3] He ascribed the saltness of the sea to the action of the sun on the surface water, evaporating the fresh particles and leaving the heavier, bitter, water behind, and rejected Aristotle's theory of the moist and dry exhalations.[4] The *Natural History* remained the principal authority on science available to scholars in Western Europe until the translation of Greek scientific writings into Latin in the twelfth century. None of the accounts given in later Roman authors or in theological and encyclopaedic works written after the fall of the Roman Empire succeeded in giving a more comprehensive account of tides than it contained.[5] Indeed the process by which these works were compiled gradually tended to dilute the factual content and weaken the arguments used.[2] Among the Roman writers who referred to tides, and sometimes at least, to other aspects of the sea, were Plutarch, Solinus and Ptolemy.[6] Post-Roman theological writers, who seem to have been reasonably well-informed on such matters, included St Augustine and St Ambrose.[5]

Isidore of Seville (A.D. 560?–636) seems to have been a typical example of the compiler. He included several chapters on the sea in his encyclopaedical work De Natura Rerum Liber.[7] He did not give a factual account of tides but merely offered explanations as to why they might occur. Some people supposed that there was some kind of exhalation of wind from the depths of the ocean, as though the earth had nostrils and breathed in and out, so causing the fall and rise of the tide. Other people thought that the moon was responsible.[8] In accounting for the saltness of the sea he quoted directly from St Ambrose the same explanation that Pliny had given.[9] He also explained how it was that the influx of rivers never raised the level of the sea.[10] A balance was maintained because the sea lost an equal quantity of water, partly through evaporation by the sun and wind and partly by a supposed outflow of water through channels in the earth which led from the sea floor to the sources of rivers on land.[11]

A little later on, in 655, the writer known as the Irish Augustin gave a more factual description of tides.[12] He mentioned the semi-diurnal tide and the twice monthly springs, malinae, and neaps, ledones.[13] The springs lasted three and a half days both before and after new moon and full moon and were highest at the equinoxes. During the springs the flood lasted five hours and the ebb seven but at the neaps both took six hours.

Pliny's authority was not always sufficient to guarantee unquestioned acceptance of his statements. Another Irish writer, Dicuil, who lived in the ninth century and described the Atlantic voyages of monks from Ireland, criticized the passage where Pliny quotes Fabianus as saying that the greatest depth of the sea was fifteen stadia.[14] How, asked Dicuil, could Fabianus know the depth of the sea?[15]

The outstanding figure in Western Europe during the Dark Ages, both in the history of marine science and in the history of science in general, is the Venerable Bede (A.D. 673–735), whose repuation in this field is founded * largely on the chapter on tides in his computistical work, De Temporum Ratione, which he wrote in about 730.[16] In this chapter he improved on Pliny's description of tides in general and illustrated his account with information about tides on the coast of Britain, particularly in his native Northumbria.

The first work in which Bede dealt with questions of marine science was his De Natura Rerum Liber, written about 703.[17] This book is in the tradition of Pliny and Isidore of Seville and illustrates the degree of standardization to which the encyclopaedic tradition had led. In it Bede mainly follows Pliny's description of tides and quotes the ideas peculiar

to him of an eight-year tidal cycle and of tides being smaller in summer
* than in winter.[18] In describing the alteration of spring and neap tides in the
month, *malinae* and *ledones*, and in saying that at the springs the ebb lasts
longer than the flood he was echoing more recent authors, possibly
Augustin who gave a similar account.[19]

Bede followed Isidore of Seville, whose works he knew,[20] in describing
how the sea comes to be salt and why rivers do not increase its level.[21] In
one respect though, he seems to have left the pattern of argument on these
subjects, which Pliny had established and Isidore reproduced, and described how fresh water spreads over the surface of the sea because it is
lighter than the salt sea water.[22]

De Temporum Ratione is, as its name suggests, a work on the calendar and
the subject of tides is introduced because of the close connection between
the moon's movements and the different phases of the tides, familiar to
Bede both through written authorities and his own experience.[23] He dealt
first with the daily retardation which moon and tides have in common.
In an earlier chapter he had referred to an estimate of three-quarters of an
hour[24] given in a commentary on Job by Philippus, a fifth-century
author,[25] as the interval by which the passage of the moon and the arrival
of high waters grows later in the 24 hours. In *De Natura Rerum* Bede gave
a figure of 50 minutes for the retardation[26] but in *De Temporum Ratione* he
altered it to 48 minutes. This figure was less close to the one now accepted
of 52 minutes 24 seconds than his first estimate but it was the value used in
the St Albans tide-table (*see* p. 29) and by sailors until the seventeenth
century. Bede called attention to the effect of strong on or offshore winds
which could alter both the height and time of high water, either impelling
the water forward or holding it back.[27]

Modern knowledge does not seem to support Bede's belief that during
the springs either the morning or evening tide was higher for the duration
of each spell of high tides, depending on what time of day it was when the
spring tides began. It does, however, confirm the observation that high
flood tides are followed by proportionately low ebbs. Some people, Bede
wrote, followed Philippus in believing that high water was caused everywhere simultaneously by an outrush of water into the sea. However

we know, we who live on the many sided shore of the British Sea, that when
this sea begins to flow, in the same hour another will begin to ebb.

From this fact and from the associated pattern of high tides and low ebbs
other people had come to the conclusion that the rise and fall of the tide
was caused by the transfer of water from one place to another so that when
there was a higher tide than usual in one place there would be a lower ebb
in compensation somewhere else.[28] This was a very much clearer explana-

tion of the mechanism of tides than the often clumsy ideas put forward by medieval thinkers. Although they could not know by what force the sea was set in motion Bede or whoever was responsible for the idea had given an explanation for its rise and fall without introducing some device for altering the volume of its water on which astrological theory as developed by Pliny and medieval thinkers relied.

The knowledge of the Northumbrian people of the tides along their coast was sufficiently accurate for Bede to know that the time of high tide grew gradually later from north to south on the east coast of Britain. In his *History of the English Church and People* he pictured south flowing tidal streams on both sides of the British Isles:

The Isle of Wight lies opposite the boundary between the South Saxons and the Gewissae, and is separated from it by three miles of sea, known as the Solent. In this strait, two ocean tides that flow round Britain from the boundless northern seas meet in daily opposition off the mouth of the River Homelea. This enters the sea after flowing through the lands of the Jutes who live in the Gewissae country; and when the turbulence ceases, they flow back into the ocean whence they spring.[29]

To his other knowledge was joined the realization that high water did not necessarily occur in places with the same longitude as soon as the moon reached the meridian or at an identical interval afterwards but in any one place high water always arrived when the moon was in the same place in the sky.[30] This is the first known exposition of the principle on which knowledge of the establishment of a port depends.[31]

In *De Natura Rerum Liber* Bede seems to have thought that particularly high tides occurred both at the solstices and at the equinoxes but in *De Temporum Ratione* he placed the annual springs correctly at the equinoxes. He again repeated Pliny's idea that tides were smaller in summer than in winter but in place of the eight-year cycle substituted the idea of a nineteen-year cycle of tides, which was put on an empirical basis in the nineteenth century by Sir John Lubbock (1803–1865), to correspond with the nineteen-year lunar cycle on which the ecclesiastical calendar was based.[13]

Bede's work on tides is remarkable for its time and is generally acknowledged as important not only for its contribution to the subject itself but as one of the few pieces of new scientific work to emerge from the long period in Western Europe between the decline of Greek science and the revival of the late Middle Ages.[32] While presumably not making observations himself, Bede showed himself, though almost certainly without knowing it, a successor, in spirit at any rate, of Seleucus and Posidonius in recording the principle of the establishment of the port and in his realization that tides might be due to the transport of water from one place to another and not to sudden additions to the sea or changes of its state. Yet Bede's practical grasp of the subject does not seem to have evolved in isolation. He writes as though it were a subject well known to and discussed by his fellow countrymen. Charles W. Jones considers that his account reveals that the Northumbrian people were developing a spirit of inquiry towards their environment.[33] He goes on to point out the dependence on the tides of the monastic communities, Lindisfarne in particular, and this surely is the key to understanding the background of this competent account. It was the people who used the sea, generally sailors and fishermen, who had the most accurate knowledge of it during the Middle Ages, and later, and such people did not often transfer their accumulated knowledge to paper. The monks of Northumbria, however, combined the practical necessity of a good understanding of tides with the opportunity for recording it in writing and possessed at least one scholar with the ability and wish to correlate the information and set it down.

Bede's writings were widely circulated in Europe during the ensuing centuries and references to his work on tides are to be found as far afield as Iceland and Italy.[34] Commentators constructed circular diagrams and tide tables to show how spring and neap tides alternate during the month. This practice seems to have originated in the late ninth century.[35] The overall influence of Bede's work on tidal theory during the Middle Ages was nevertheless small. Later writers neglected his standard of argument and observation and preferred to concentrate on the far-fetched hypotheses which other writers of the same period put forward to explain tidal phenomena.[31] The fifth-century writer Macrobius revived one of the lesser known Greek theories, the hypothesis of Crates of Mallos (second century B.C.) that the ocean was divided into four branches along equatorial and meridional axes and that the backwash of conflicting currents at the intersection was the cause of tides.[36] Paul the Deacon (A.D. 720–778) helped to popularize the theory, if he did not invent it, that tides were due to a whirlpool alternately sucking in the sea and spewing it out, an idea based on the myth of the Maelstrom.[37] Medieval writers concentrated on reconciling or playing off these ideas with the astrological theory and did not in general bother to ascertain whether they bore more than a superficial resemblance to the facts.

In the Byzantine Empire and the countries surrounding the eastern Mediterranean the break between the old science and the new attitude to learning was not so pronounced. Whereas in Western Europe it was the Roman encyclopaedists who became the authorities for scientific writers in the post-Roman period and few authors referred directly to the works of the Greek scientists, in the east many of the Greek works survived and so too did something of the spirit which produced them. Nevertheless, the overall pattern of development in marine science resembles that of the west with this modification.

Duhem recounts an example of how a spirit of inquiry concerning the sea survived in this part of the world. The replies of the Greek philosopher Priscien of Lydia (*fl. c.* A.D. 529) to the questions of King Chosroes of Persia contains an explanation of the tides which seems to derive from Posidonius's theory and of the saltness of the sea.[38]

The encyclopaedic works, which in the east as in the west formed a large part of scientific output right through the Middle Ages, were based on a much wider selection of sources and discuss in much greater detail subjects like the saltness of the sea which get only a short mention in the comparable works in the west. The Arabic writer El-Mas'údí (*d.* 956) seems to have given a typical treatment of different aspects of the sea in his encyclopaedia *Meadows of Gold and Mines of Gems*.[39] He gives a more extensive geographical description covering not only the Mediterranean but the Indian Ocean as well.[40] The Atlantic, which seemed to inspire a kind of horror, was dismissed in a few sentences.[41] Edrisi (1110–1166) was later to write

no one knows what exists beyond this sea, no one can know anything certain about it because of the difficulties to navigation presented by the depths of the shadows, the height of the waves, the frequency of storms, the large number of monstrous animals and the violence of the winds.[42]

Mas'údí also mentioned the current which flows from the Atlantic into the Mediterranean through the Strait of Gibraltar. Knowledge of this phenomenon had survived both in the west and in the east and references to it or to the Strait's supposed creation by an inrush of water occur in works such as Bede's *De Natura Rerum Liber* and Dicuil's *De Mensura Orbis Terrae*.[43]

In his chapter on tides Mas'údí assembled several different explanations as to why they occur.[44] One idea was that the moon warmed the bottom of the sea. This in turn produced water from the earth which, becoming warm, expanded in volume and raised the level of the sea. The highest tides occurred when the moon was full because it then produced the most heat. Other people pointed out that the sun should therefore cause tides but, since they did not coincide with its passage overhead, suggested that they were produced by vapour in the earth which was discharged into the sea at intervals. Another idea likened the rise and fall of tides to the variations of human temperament. A fourth presupposed a continuous reaction between air and water. The air decomposed the water and increased its volume; the process was then reversed and the sea subsided.

Mas'údí's account of the origin of the sea and its salinity is based on

Aristotle's *Meteorologica*.[45] His summary of opinions on the origin of the sea (he refers readers to his second volume for a fuller discussion) reads very much like Aristotle's quoted on page 4. Among other things, he referred to the idea which Aristotle had attacked, that the sun consumed the fresh water evaporated from the sea, and to the explanation Aristotle preferred which was that the evaporated water returned to the sea after condensation in an unbroken cycle.

The quantity of water remains, therefore, constant, and is neither increased or diminished.

He outlined the idea that salt comes from the earth and Aristotle's description of the properties of salt water.

The arguments and explanations put forward for these phenomena are sometimes common sense, sometimes fantastic as in the passage on water-spouts:

The Tinníns (dragons) are quite unknown in the Abyssinian sea and in its numerous estuaries and bays. They are most frequent near the Atlantic. . . . Different opinions have been advanced as to what the dragon is: some believe that it is a black wind in the bottom of the sea, which rises into the air, that is to say, the atmosphere . . ., as high as the clouds, like a hurricane whirling dust aloft as it rises from the ground, and destroying vegetation. The shape of the dragon becomes longer the higher it ascends in the air.

Some people believe that the dragon is a black serpent which rises into the air, the clouds are at the same time black, all is dark, and this is succeeded by a terrible wind.[46]

Some of the most interesting passages in Mas'údí's work concern the currents of the Indian Ocean:

The Abyssinian sea runs from east to west along the equator; after this line the moveable heavenly bodies and those fixed stars which stand vertically over it make their daily revolutions.[47]

He goes on to explain that sailors reported that in the greater part of the sea the current changed direction with the monsoon winds—flowing from the south-west in summer and from the north-east in winter. Dr Bruce A. Warren recently suggested that this was the first description of the semi-annual reversal of currents in the Indian Ocean.[48] Dr A. A. Aleem, in reply, showed that this knowledge can be traced back at least a hundred years further to the ninth-century writer, Ibn Khordazbeh.[49] The seasonal reversal of winds must always have been a fact of life in those regions. Like oceanic tides, they were one of the natural hazards encountered by Alexander the Great's fleet in the fourth century B.C.[50] The discovery of the similar behaviour of currents had to await the rise of oceanic as opposed to coastal navigation. Dr Aleem conjectures that the Arabs came to know of them during the eighth century when their sailors penetrated to the far east.[49]

This discovery seems to have been the principal practical contribution to physical oceanography made in the eastern world at this time. The standard of information on tides seems to have been rather variable. The geographer Edrisi for example described the Atlantic tides—"which we have seen with our own eyes in the sea of shadows"—without allowing for the daily retardation, which enabled him to suggest that the tides were due to the wind. He also thought that spring tides only occurred at full moon. He wrote:

The reason for that [the rise and fall of the tides] is the wind which stirs up the sea at the beginning of the third hour of the day. As soon as the sun rises above the horizon the flood increases with the wind. Before the day ends the wind falls because the sun is setting and the ebb takes place. In the same way at nightfall the wind rises again and calm is not restored until the night draws to an end. The high tides occur during the 13th, 14th, 15th and 16th nights of the [lunar] month; then the waters rise unusually high, reaching a level which they do not attain again until the corresponding days of subsequent months.[51]

Other writers were better informed and described such features as the bi-monthly springs and the daily retardation.[49] Many different theories were put forward to explain tides, such as those of Mas'údí referred to. The work which, translated into Latin early in the twelfth century, had most influence on theory in Western Europe during the later Middle Ages was the *Introductorium in Astronomiam* of Albumazar (805–886) which attributed tides to the astrological influence of the moon.[52] Other important influences were the twelfth-century writers Alpetragius (*see* p. 30), Averroës and Maimonides.[53]

In countries where the learning of the Greeks had survived, problems of marine science were discussed on a broader basis than was possible in Western Europe before the twelfth century. Arabic writings on geography and astronomy advanced new arguments to explain the existence of tides but the dominant theory which they transmitted to Europe was the astrological theory of Posidonius. Arab sailors furnished the scholars with information about tides, currents and marine biology.[54] At least one of them, Ibn Magid, in the fifteenth century, wrote his own technical works.[55] His account of navigation in the Indian Ocean shows a similar pre-occupation to that of his western counterparts with those aspects of physical oceanography necessary to the safety of shipping, tides, currents and coastal soundings.

After the time of Bede, science seems to have developed little in any field in Europe until the twelfth century when, stimulated by the translation into Latin of works of the scientists of the Greek world and their Arab successors, hitherto unavailable to western scholars, a new spirit of enquiry emerged, heralding, although in a modest and tentative manner, the revival of interest in science which took place during the later Middle Ages. As a result of the new outlook, writes C. H. Haskins,

As we approach 1200, we find an increasing number of brief treatises which discuss the nature of the universe and its elements and the phenomena of earthquakes and tides and volcanoes. The meteorology of the age is definitely Aristotelian.[56]

Aristotle's *Meteorologica* was one of the works which appeared in Latin during the twelfth century.[57]

The writer most often quoted as an example of the new attitude is the Welsh cleric Gerald of Wales, Giraldus Cambrensis (1146?–?1220), whose *Topographia Hibernica*, written in 1187, contains a description of the tides of the Irish Sea.[58] In compiling the account Gerald must have relied largely on the local experience of sailors, "whose accurate information on such subjects", Haskins remarks, "the student of books is too prone to forget", since the picture which it gives is, as far as it can be verified from modern tide-tables, a true one.

Gerald described how at the time when the tide is half way out at Dublin it is half way in at Milford Haven and right out on the coast beyond Bristol.[59] Similarly, half-flood at Dublin coincides with half-ebb at Milford Haven and high water beyond Bristol. He noted anomalies at Wicklow where the tide comes in while it is going out at neighbouring places and goes out while the flood takes place elsewhere.[60] At Wexford the times of high and low water were closer to those of Milford Haven than to those of the neighbouring port, Dublin.[61] To this extent it is easy to show that Gerald's information was fairly accurate but when he goes on to describe a rock in the sea where the tide comes in on one side while going out on the other it is perhaps time to be a bit sceptical. A shrewd observer himself, Gerald was nevertheless inclined to confuse hearsay with fact in his reports of Ireland. Perhaps one should therefore be cautious in accepting his story of a salt stream flowing into the bay at Wicklow but it is quite credible that at Arklow the fresh river water should be detected at some distance out to sea.[62]

Many medieval writers discussed the cause of tides but relatively few of them had any practical knowledge of the phenomena they were trying to explain. Duhem mentions two other authors who show some real knowledge of tides, either from their own observations or from the reports of sailors.[63] The first of these is the unknown author of the *Tractatus de Fluxu et Refluxu Maris*, written some time in the second half of the thirteenth century. He was attempting to explain why there are large semi-diurnal tides on the Channel coasts of England and France but not in the Mediterranean Sea. None of the books he had consulted explained this anomaly and his friends had encouraged him to write down his own views on the subject. The other author is the fourteenth-century French scientist Jean Buridan, who in the second version of the *Questions on Meteors* shows familiarity with the diurnal retardation of tides and the bi-monthly springs.

As a rule tidal theorists were not very well informed. A mistake frequently made, by Gerald of Wales[64] and Roger Bacon[65] among others, was to think that spring tides occurred only once a month. The thirteenth century encyclopaedist, Bartholomew the Englishman, even supposed that there was only one tide every day[66] but he was an exception.

The famous St Albans Abbey tide-table, often printed since Sir John Lubbock published it in 1837,[67] has something of the same dissociation from reality. It dates from about 1250, the time of the chronicler and geographer, Matthew Paris (?1200–1259), and gives times of high water at London Bridge. The late Professor E. G. R. Taylor pointed out that the times given bear little resemblance to the actual times as known since the seventeenth century since they allow for a fixed lunitidal interval of three hours forty-eight minutes and a daily retardation of forty-eight minutes, neither of which accord with the more variable values assigned to these factors today, though the possibility of a change in tidal regime cannot be ruled out.[68]

Tidal theory in the twelfth century was still dominated by the conflicting theories current in the age of Bede (*see* pp. 21–24), the idea of the collision of currents derived by Macrobius from Crates of Mallos, the Maelstrom hypothesis and the astrological theory of the moon's influence on the sea. Alexander Neckham (1157–1217), one of the first western writers to describe the use of the mariner's compass, evidently felt what must have been quite a common sensation of helplessness when faced with such a variety of invention.[69] In his *De Naturis Rerum* he merely lists the alternatives, remarking that it was popularly believed that the cause was the passage of the moon overhead.

It was the task of encyclopaedic writers to describe all current opinions but others could take their choice. The twelfth-century writer Adelard of Bath, whose *Quaestiones Naturales* was one of the earliest products of the new attitude to science, adopted a variation of the Macrobian theory.[70] He would allow, he said, that there was a meeting and retreat of arms of the sea but he did not agree that there was a collision between opposing bodies of water for such a force would soon spend itself. Duhem tells us that the Maelstrom theory remained popular with scholastic philosophers for a long time.[71] Gerald of Wales attempted a synthesis of the three ideas.[72]

He described the sea as swelling under the influence of the moon's rays and rising to its fullest extent at full moon, then subsiding as the moon waned and reverting to its own channels. Similarly after each high water he described the ocean "ad occulta receptacula redisse quas revocans undas."[73] He supposed that the flow of water into and out of the sea might take place at the four extremities of the earth. Tidal streams were more pronounced there both on this account and because there was less land to obstruct them. This was why tides were larger in the Atlantic than they were in the Mediterranean.[74] For a more detailed discussion of these ideas he referred the reader to his work *De Philosophicis Flosculis* but of this book there is no trace today.[75]

During the thirteenth and fourteenth centuries most tidal theories admitted that the moon supplied the motive force, following the lead of Arab science and in particular of Albumazar's *Introductorium in Astronomiam*.[76] As to how the force was transmitted there was less agreement. Some writers, including Robert Grosseteste, Bishop of Lincoln (*d.* 1253), believed that it was the actual rays of light emitted from the moon which caused tides by producing rarefaction in the water of the sea, in a manner similar to the action performed by heat when water boils.[77] Grosseteste supposed that the effect of the moon's rays was greatest when it had risen to the meridian and they were then strong enough to extract and consume the vapour which had accumulated as it rose. As the moon descended from the meridian and its power grew less the ebb set in. The other daily tide, which occurred when the moon was facing the opposite side of the earth, was produced by the reflection of its rays from the sphere of fixed stars, the next to outermost sphere of the Aristotelian universe. This theory was also adopted by Roger Bacon (1214?-1294) in his *Opus Majus*.[78]

One theory which did not receive much support in the thirteenth and fourteenth centuries was that advanced by the twelfth-century astronomer Alpetragius who attributed tides not to the moon but to the attraction of the outermost sphere from which was supposed to come the force which rotated the other celestial spheres, the *primum mobile*. He thought that this force was great enough to pull the sea after it, the flood, to the extent where the backward drag of the water overcame it and the ebb set in. This explanation was adopted by the thirteenth-century writer Giles of Rome.[79] Bacon, while accepting most of the premises, did not think that this force could be responsible for movements as predictable and clearly connected with those of the moon as were tides.[80]

It was not uncommon for writers to prefer, like Jean Buridan,[81] a purely astrological explanation and allied to this was the frequent comparison of the relationship between moon and tides to the equally mysterious phenomenon of magnetic attraction, an analogy which Duhem says can be traced back to William of Auvergne in the thirteenth century.[82] Some on the other hand preferred to think of the effect of the moon's rays or of some other physical cause for tides.[83] A number of individual theories were put forward to this end. The author of the *Tractatus de Fluxu et Refluxu Maris* supposed that tides were caused by the sun evaporating water from the sea at the equator and the moon condensing it at the poles in a combined oceanic-atmospheric circulation.[84] Giacomo de'Dondi (*c.* 1293–1359) attributed tides to the joint effect of the sun and moon and planets.[85]

Although the study of tides was perhaps the aspect of marine science which medieval scientists found most absorbing they frequently discussed other topics. As well as a chapter on tides Adelard of Bath wrote on the saltness of the sea, the origin of springs and the reason why rivers do not make the level of the sea rise.[70] A similar range of subjects is to be found in encyclopaedic writings. The *Summa Philosophiæ*, attributed to a pupil of Robert Grosseteste, contains chapters on tides and the saltness of the sea.[86] As well as his treatise on tides Giacomo de'Dondi wrote a *Tractatus de Causa Salsedinis*.[87] Medieval authors often expressed their ideas in the form of commentaries on classical works. Inevitably the numerous writers who discussed Aristotle's *Meteorologica* must have considered the arguments about the saltness of the sea. One such commentary was written by Walter Burley (*d. c.* 1337) who also wrote *De Fluxu et Refluxu Maris Anglicani*.[88] It would be interesting to know more about the ideas contained in these works though in this aspect even more than for tides, lack of factual knowledge and scientific equipment must have prevented medieval thinkers from making any real advance on the positions of the ancients. They could only agree or disagree with what had already been said, like the author of the *Summa Philosophiæ* who objected to Aristotle's theory on the grounds that on his showing there ought to be a noticeable difference in salinity between tropical and northern seas and that fresh water ought to leave salt behind when it dried up.[89]

Another subject whch aroused a great deal of interest was the problem of how land and sea maintained their equilibrium. The difficulty lay in reconciling the generally accepted system of the universe with the observed pattern of land and sea. According to the belief common at the time the elements should be arranged in order of density with the earth at the centre of the universe, water round the earth forming a concentric sphere and air again as a third sphere. Clearly, however, water did not form such a sphere or there would be no land at all. Duhem describes the many arguments that were put forward to try and get round this problem.[90] Some people even claimed that the surface of the sea was higher than the land. In the fourteenth century Jean Buridan argued that land and water have a continuous surface but that the ocean maintains its position, not because it occupies a hollow in the earth's surface, but because it has collected on that part of the surface nearest to the centre of the earth, following the natural tendency of water to flow towards the centre.[91]

While from the scientific point of view knowledge about the sea had progressed little in this period, sailors had increased their knowledge of navigational aids and were well informed about those features of the sea which were relevant to their profession.[68] They knew the establishment of the ports to which they sailed, that is, the compass bearing of the moon at the time when high water was to be expected. They knew the depth of water and the changes in the character of the bottom in different places on the continental shelf. Gradually this practical knowledge was transferred to paper. Professor Taylor describes, for example, the tide-table of the *Catalan Atlas* of 1375 which gives in the form of a circular diagram the times of high water on the Channel coasts of England and Brittany.[92] There are *Sailing Directions for the Circumnavigation of England* which probably date from the fifteenth century.[92]

This pragmatism contrasts with the static nature of the theoretical debate in learned circles. Throughout the period from the decline of Greek science up to the Renaissance the problems posed by the sea had continued to excite interest and curiosity and were considered by writers of the different cultures, Roman, Byzantine, Anglo-Saxon, Jewish, Arab, Chinese and West European, whenever interest in the natural world was revived. There was however no understanding of the need for making observations and the new facts that were introduced from time to time were invariably derived from the practical experience of sailors and fishermen. Such knowledge played a relatively small part in the deliberation of philosophers whose main energy was spent in dialectical discussion of ideas introduced by the Greeks or by their successors in the first centuries of our era.

2. NOTES

This period, which I have not tried to cover comprehensively, has been dealt with by authorities on the history of science and I have relied a great deal on their work. Much information relative to the development of opinions about the sea is given by the following:

1. Pierre Duhem, *Le Système du Monde: Histoire des Doctrines Cosmologiques de Platon à Copernic*, Paris (1914, 1915, 1958). Vols. **2**, **3**, and **9** respectively. George Sarton, *Introduction to the History of Science*, 3 vols, Washington (1927–1948).

Roberto Almagia, "La dottrina della marea nell' antichita classica e nel Medio Evo. Contributo alla storia della geografia scientifica", *Atti Accad. naz. Lincei Memorie*, 5th series (1904). Vol. **5**, pp. 377–513.

2. William H. Stahl, "Dominant traditions in early medieval Latin science", *Isis* (1959). Vol. **50**, part 2, no. 160, pp. 95–124.

3. Pliny, *The Natural History of Pliny*, translated by J. Bostock and H. T. Riley, 6 vols, London (1855–1857). Vol. **1**, bk 2, ch. 99.

4. *Ibid*. Vol. **1**, bk 2, ch. 104.

5. Pierre Duhem, *op. cit.* Vol. **2**, pp. 286–289; 460–462.

6. J. O. Thomson, *History of Ancient Geography*, Cambridge (1948).

7. Isidore of Seville, *De Natura Rerum Liber, Sancti Isidori Hispalensis Episcopi Opera Omnia, Patrologiæ Latinæ Cursus Completus* (ed. J.-P. Migne), Paris. Vol. **83** (1852), cols 1011–1012.

8. *Ibid*. Vol. **83**, 1011:

> Cur Oceanus in se reciprocis ˜æstibus revertatur, quidam aiunt in profundis Oceani esse quosdam ventorum spiritus, veluti mundi nares per quas emissi anhelitus, vel retracti alterno accessu recessuque, nunc evaporante spiritu efflent maria, nunc retrahente reducant. Quidam autem volunt cum augmento lunari crescere Oceanum, et tanquam ejus quibusdam spirationibus retrorsum trahatur, et iterum ejusdem impulsu ac retractu, in mensuram propriam refundatur.

9. *Ibid*. Vol. **83**, 1013.

10. *Ibid*. Vol. **83**, 1012.

11. Similarly described in his *Etymologiarum Libri* XX, bk 13, ch. 14, *Opera, Patrologiæ Latinæ Cursus Completus* (ed. J.-P. Migne), Paris. Vol. **82**, (1850), 483.

12. Augustin, *De Mirabilibus Sacræ Scripturæ Libri Tres, Sancti Aurelii Augustini Hipponensis Episcopi, Opera Omnia, Patrologiæ Latinæ Cursus Completus* (ed. J.-P. Migne), Paris. Vol. **35** (1845), 2158–2159. William Reeves, "On Augustin, an Irish writer of the seventh century", *Proc. R. Ir. Acad.* (1857–1861). Vol. **7**, pp. 514–522.

13. For the use of these terms *see* Charles W. Jones, *Bedæ Opera de Temporibus*, Cambridge, Mass. (1943), p. 364.

14. Pliny, *The Natural History of Pliny*, *op. cit.* Vol. **1**, bk 2, ch. 105.

15. Dicuil, *Liber de Mensura Orbis Terræ* (ed. G. Parthey), Berolini (1870), p. 76:

> Plinius Secundus in tertio libro: altissimum mare XV stadiorum Fabianus tradit. sed quis credet Fabianum totius profunditatem oceani posse scire?

16. Bede, *De Temporum Ratione*, in *Bedæ Opera de Temporibus* (ed. C. W. Jones) (1943);
The Complete Works of Venerable Bede, in the original Latin, collated with the manuscripts and various printed editions (ed. J. A. Giles), 12 vols London (1843–1844). Vol. **6**, pp. 139–342.

17. Bede, *De Natura Rerum Liber*, in *The Complete Works of Venerable Bede* (ed. J. A. Giles), 12 vols, London (1843–1844). Vol. **6**, pp. 100–122.

18. *Ibid*. p. 116. Cf. Pliny, p. 15.

19. C. W. Jones, *loc. cit.*

20. Bede, *De Temporum Ratione*, in *Bedæ Opera de Temporibus* (ed. C. W. Jones) (1943), p. 128 and note on p. 363.

21. Bede, *De Natura Rerum Liber*, in *The Complete Works of Venerable Bede* (ed. J. A. Giles). Vol. **6,** p. 117.
22. *Ibid.* Vol. **6,** p. 117.

   marinis autem aquis dulces superfundi, utpote leviores: ipsas vero ut gravioris naturæ, magis sustinere superfusas.

23. Bede, *De Temporum Ratione*, in *The Complete Works of Venerable Bede* (ed. J. A. Giles). Vol. **6,** pp. 201–204; p. 201:

   Maxime autem præ omnibus admiranda tanta oceani cum lunæ cursu societas.

24. *Ibid.* Vol. **6,** p. 148.
25. C. W. Jones, *op. cit.* pp. 334–335; pp. 363–364.
26. Bede, *De Natura Rerum Liber*, in *The Complete Works of Venerable Bede* (ed. J. A. Giles). Vol. **6.** Ch. 39, p. 116.
27. Bede, *De Temporum Ratione*, in *The Complete Works of Venerable Bede* (ed. J. A. Giles). Vol. **6,** p. 202.
28. *Ibid.* Vol. **6,** p. 203.
29. Bede, *A History of the English Church and People*, translated by L. Sherley-Price, Penguin Books, Harmondsworth (1955), bk 4, ch. 16, pp. 228–229. Quoted by kind permission of the publishers.
30. Bede, *De Temporum Ratione*, in *The Complete Works of Venerable Bede* (ed. J. A. Giles). Vol. **6,** pp. 203–204:

   Porro aliis in partibus ab ea cœli plaga recessum maris luna, qua hic
   ∗ signat accessum: non solum autem, sedet in uno eodemque littore quo ad Boream mei habitant, multo me citius æstum maris omnem: qui vero ad austrum, multo serius accipere pariter et refundere solent, servante quibusque in regionibus luna semper regulam societatis ad mare quan - cumque semel acceperit.

31. Pierre Duhem, *op. cit.* Vol. **3,** p. 113.
   C. W. Jones, *op. cit.* p. 125.
32. George Sarton, *Introduction to the History of Science.* Vol. **1.** *From Homer to Omar Khayyam* (1927), pp. 510–511.
33. C. W. Jones, *op. cit.* p. 125.
34. *Ibid.* pp. 363–364.
35. Bede, *De Natura Rerum Liber, Patrologiæ Latinæ Cursus Completus* (ed. J.-P. Migne), *Bedæ Opera Omnia.* Paris. Vol. **90** (1850), 258–260. *Vetus Commentarius:*

   Ista rota pertinet ad concordiam maris et lunæ, quæ si concordat, maxima est, ut Beda docet in libro II de Temporum ratione. Nam æstus Oceani quotidie bis venire et remeare perhibetur; in ortu scilicet et occasu lunæ.... Nam interior rotula trium partium mundi habet nomina. Spatium quod extra hanc est, aeris terram undique cingentis, typum gestat: unde et ventorum per aerem flantium nomina habet. Exterior sane rota ætates lunæ habet, a prima usque ad tricesimam. Subter hanc, quæ est linea circularis angustior, continens aquam, significat Oceanum, qui totum orbem circuit. At infra hanc ducta linea numerum continet dierum, quibus accedunt vel recedunt præfati æstus. Unde semper contra primum numerum est foris signatum quota luna incipiat quisque eorumdem accessuum ad malinæ vel lædonæ exortum.

See Charles W. Jones, *Bedae Pseudepigrapha: scientific writings falsely attributed to Bede*, Ithaca (1939), p. 35.

36. Pierre Duhem, *op. cit.* Vol. **3**, p. 116.
37. *Ibid.* Vol. **3**, pp. 113–114.
38. *Ibid.* Vol. **2**, pp. 280–285. It is interesting that these questions and answers survived in a Carolingian manuscript showing that this summary of ancient learning did penetrate to Dark Age Europe.
39. El-Mas'údí, *Meadows of Gold and Mines of Gems*, translated by Aloys Sprenger, Oriental Translation Fund, London (1841). Vol. **1** only.
40. *Ibid.* pp. 260, 281, 285.
41. *Ibid.* p. 282.
42. Edrisi, *Géographie*, translated by P. Amédée Jaubert, *Recueil de Voyages et de Mémoires* publié par la Société de Géographie. Vols. **5** and **6**, Paris (1836–1840). Vol. **6**, p. 2.
43. El-Mas'údí, *op. cit.* p. 283:

> The current from the ocean is so great that it is perceptible.

Dicuil, *Liber de Mensura Orbis Terrae* (ed. G. Parthey) (1870), pp. 72–73, quoting from Solinus.
Bede, *De Natura Rerum Liber*, in *The Complete Works of Venerable Bede* (ed. J. A. Giles). Vol. **6**, pp. 121–122.

> Terrarum orbis universus, oceano cinctus, in tres dividitur partes: Europam, Asiam, Africam. Origo ab occasu solis, et Gaditano freto, qua irrumpens oceanus Atlanticus in maria interiora effunditur.

44. El-Mas'údí, *op. cit.* pp. 272–276.
45. *Ibid.* pp. 300–305.
46. *Ibid.* p. 291.
47. *Ibid.* pp. 274, 277–278.
48. Bruce A. Warren, "Medieval Arab references to the seasonally reversing currents of the North Indian Ocean", *Deep Sea Res.* (1966), Vol. **13**, no. 2, pp. 167–171.
49. Anwar Abdel Aleem, "Concepts of currents, tides and winds among medieval Arab geographers in the Indian Ocean", *Deep Sea Res.* (1967). Vol. **14**, no. 4, pp. 459–463.
50. Arrian, *Anabasis*, Loeb Classical Library (1954). Bk 8, ch. 21.
51. Edrisi, *op. cit.* Vol. **5**, p. 95.
52. Pierre Duhem, *op. cit.* Vol. **2**, pp. 369–386.
53. *Ibid.* Vol. **2**, pp. 386–390.
54. A. A. Aleem, "Concepts of marine biology among Arab writers in the Middle Ages", *Bull. Inst. océanogr. Monaco*, numéro spécial 2 (1968). Vol. **2**, pp. 359–366.
55. A. A. Aleem, "Ahmad Ibn Magid, Arab navigator of the XVth century and his contributions to marine sciences", *Bull. Inst. océanogr. Monaco*, numéro spécial 2 (1968). Vol. **2**, pp. 565–579.

See also:

Historical Introduction, *Report on the Scientific Results of the Voyage of H.M.S. Challenger during the years 1872–1876; A Summary of the Scientific Results:* H.M.S.O., London (1895). Vol. **1**, pp. 31–37.

56. Charles Homer Haskins, *The Renaissance of the Twelfth Century* (1927), re-issue (1957), Meridian Books, New York, pp. 313–314. Quoted by kind permission of the Publishers.

57. Alistair Crombie, *Augustine to Galileo, The History of Science* A.D. *400–1650*, London (1952), pp. 27–28.

58. Giraldus Cambrensis, *Topographia Hibernica et Expugnatio Hibernica* (ed. J. F. Dimock) in *Giraldi Cambrensis Opera* (eds. J. S. Brewer and J. F. * Dimock), Rolls Series, 8 vols (1861–1891). No. 21, part 5 (1867).
Gerald's work on tides is discussed in detail by Duhem, *Le Système du Monde*. Vol. 3, pp. 119–124.

59. Giraldus Cambrensis, *op. cit.* Vol. 5,, p. 77:

> Dubliniæ portum quoties medio refluxu retrogradis undis mare destituit, Britannicum Milverdiæ, navium receptioni sinum optimum, medio influxu redeuntibus aquis jam restituit. Ulteriora vero Bristolli littora fugitivis undis ex toto nudata tunc primo revertens æquor paulatim inserpit.

60. *Ibid.*

> Est et portus apud Wikingelo, eo latere Hiberniæ quo proximius Wallias respicit, qui in generali maris refluxu undas recipit influentes: in reversione vero fluctuum, quas jam recepit emittit et amittit.

61. *Ibid.* p. 78:

> Weisefordiæ namque littora non Hibernicos Dubliniæ, sed Britannicos Milverdiæ fluxus imitantur.

There is a difference of 4 hours 40 minutes between high water at Wexford and at Dublin.

62. *Ibid.* pp. 77–78.

63. Pierre Duhem, *op. cit.* Vol. 9, pp. 41–53; 61–70.

64. Giraldus Cambrensis, *op. cit.* p. 78.

65. Roger Bacon, *Opus Majus* (ed. J. H. Bridges), 3 vols, The Clarendon Press, Oxford (1897–1900). Vol. 1, pp. 139–142. Quoted by kind permission of the Publishers.

66. Pierre Duhem, *op. cit.* Vol. 9, p. 17.

67. Sir John Lubbock, "On the tides", *Phil. Trans.* (1837). Vol. 127, pp. 97–140.

68. Eva G. R. Taylor, *The Haven-Finding Art. A History of Navigation from Odysseus to Captain Cook*, London (1956), pp. 136–137.

69. Alexander Neckam, *De Naturis Rerum* (ed. T. Wright), Rolls Series. Vol. 34 (1863), bk 2, ch. 17.

70. Adelard of Bath, *Die Quaestiones Naturales des Adelardus von Bath* (ed. Martin Müller), *Beiträge zur Geschichte der Philosophie und Theologie des Mittelalters.* Bd. 31, Hft 2, Münster (1934). Ch. 52.
Translated into English by Hermann Gollancz, *Dodi Ve-nechdi of Berachya Hanakdan with Adelard of Bath's Quaestiones Naturales*, Oxford (1920), pp. 140–141.

71. Pierre Duhem, *op. cit.* Vol. 3, p. 125.

72. *Ibid.* pp. 123–125.
Giraldus Cambrensis, *op. cit.* pp. 78–80.

73. Giraldus Cambrensis, *op. cit.* p. 78:

Luna revertentibus radiis cum ultra medietatem jam tumescit, et quasi ventrem facit, occidentis æquora secretis quibusdam naturæ causis exasperari incipiunt et moveri; et usque ad orbicularis perfectionis rotunditatem, undosis fluctuationibus de die in diem amplius intumescunt, longeque trans usuales metas abundantius littora complent. Eadem vero fugitivis ignibus decrescente, et quasi vultum avertente, paulatim tumor ille detumescit; et juxta lunares defectus, tanquam residente derivationis exuberatione, proprios iterum redit in canales.

74. *Ibid*. pp. 79–80.
75. Pierre Duhem, *op. cit.* Vol. **3**, p. 123.
76. *Ibid*. Vol. **9**, ch. 15, pp. 7 ff.＊
    Roger Bacon, *op. cit.* Vol. **1**, p. 140＊

> Et ideo Albumazar in majori introductorio astronomiae determinat omnes differentias fluxus et refluxus, et narrat quod accidunt omni die et nocte secundum quod luna est in diversis partibus sui circuli et respectu solis. Sed non dicit nobis causam, nisi quod luna est causa.

77. Pierre Duhem, *op. cit.* Vol. **9**, pp. 31–33. In this Grosseteste was apparently following the lead of William of Auvergne and Albertus Magnus.
    Ibid. pp. 9–16.
    A. C. Crombie, *Robert Grosseteste and the Origins of Experimental Science, 1100–1700*, Oxford (1953), p. 112.
    Richard C. Dales, "Robert Grosseteste's scientific works", *Isis* (1961). Vol. **52**, pt 3, no. 169, pp. 381–402.
78. Pierre Duhem, *op. cit.* Vol. **9**, p. 34.
    Roger Bacon, *op. cit.* Vol. **1**, pp. 139–142.
79. Pierre Duhem, *op. cit.* Vol. **9**, pp. 55–56.
80. Roger Bacon, *op. cit.* pp. 139–140:

> Alpetragius vero in libro suo de motibus coelestibus aestimat, omnia corpora mundi praeter terram moveri motu coeli primi, et hoc verum est: sed secundum quod magis elongantur tardius moventur, et cum majori impedimento. Unde aqua tardius et irregularius movetur in sphaera sua, quam alia corpora mundi. Addit ergo iste, quod hic motus facit fluxum et refluxum; sed non placet hic, quia fluxus et refluxus sunt determinati et certi, et currunt sicut luna variatur in partibus coeli. Sed motus aquae a motu coeli est confusus, et inordinatus, et irregularis propter hoc, quod virtus coeli primi nimis elongatur ab ejus origine, quando est in aqua, et ideo praevalet virtus aquae propria, scilicet sua gravitas, quia nititur quiescere in loco suo, propter quod non potest hic motus esse ita regularis et distinctus temporibus certis penes accessus et refluxus ut nos videmus in mari.

81. Pierre Duhem, *op. cit.* Vol. **9**, pp. 61–70.
82. *Ibid*. pp. 10, 21.
83. *Ibid*. p. 40.
84. *Ibid*. pp. 45–48 ff.
85. George Sarton, *Introduction to the History of Science*. Vol. **3**, *Science and learning in the fourteenth century* (1947–1948), pp. 1105–1110, 1144.

86. *Die Philosophischen Werke des Robert Grosseteste, Bischofs von Lincoln* (ed. Ludwig Baur), Münster (1912). *Beiträge zur Geschichte der Philosophie des Mittelalters*. Vol. **9**, pp. 622–625.
87. G. Sarton, *op. cit.* Vol. **3**, pp. 1163, 1169–1170.
88. *Ibid.* Vol. **3**, pp. 563–564.
89. *Summa Philosophiæ*, see ref. (86), pp. 623–625.
    Page 624:

    > Vidimus etiam aquas fossarum ab calorem solis virides fieri amaritudini annexas, nec tamen salsas vel salibus faciendis aptas.

90. Pierre Duhem, *op. cit.* Vol. **9**, pp. 79–235.
91. *Ibid.* pp. 200–201.
92. E. G. R. Taylor, *op. cit.* p. 137.
93. *Sailing Directions for the Circumnavigation of England* (ed. J. Gairdner), Hakluyt Society (1889), series 1. Vol. **79**.

Addenda et Corrigenda

p.21, 1.32: *instead* repuation *read* reputation

p.22, 1.2: *instead* alteration *read* alternation

p.29, 1.13: *instead* printed *read* reprinted

p.34, n.30, 1.4: *instead* sedet *read* sed et

p.36, n.58, 1.3: *read* Rolls Series no. 21, 8 vols (1861-1891). Vol. 5 (1867).

p.37, n.76, 1.1: *instead* pp. 7 ff. *read: passim*

p.37, n.76, 1.2: *after* 140 *insert* wrote:

3. THE RENAISSANCE

THE preoccupations of medieval thinkers were not favourable to the environmental sciences and the factual content of essays on tides and other aspects of physical oceanography tended to be less sound than that of their classical models. In the fifteenth and sixteenth centuries some people began to take a more practical interest in the world around them and this showed itself in an empirical approach to problems connected with the sea. In certain branches of the subject the progress of geographical and scientific discovery brought new knowledge and new ideas. Yet, for marine science as a whole, the Renaissance is an age of paradox, for in spite of the stimuli provided by these developments, much of the thinking about the sea was still rooted in the tradition of Aristotle and Pliny which had survived unbroken from the Middle Ages.

One of the most noticeable achievements of Renaissance science was the rise of the idea that knowledge could be put on a new footing by making measurements. One of the first people with this conviction was Cardinal Nicholas of Cusa (1401–1464) whom George Sarton has described as

perhaps the greatest man of the first half of the fifteenth century, as Leonardo was of the second.[1]

In the fourth book of Cusanus's work *The Idiot*, the Idiot, that is, a craftsman, explains to the Orator, a man with a conventional education, how measurement can increase our knowledge, and one of the experiments he describes is a method for measuring the depth of the sea.

The Orator says, in the English version of 1650,

I have heard that some by meanes of a certain instrument, have gone about to finde out the depth of the Sea.[2]

The Idiot replies

It might bee done with a piece of Lead, made after the fashion of the moon of eight dayes old, yet so, that one horn of it be heavier, & the other lighter, and on the lightest horn let an apple, or some other light thing be made fast, with such an instrument, that the lead pulling down the apple after it to the bottom, and first touching the ground with the heaviest part thereof, and so laying itselfe along accordingly, the apple then loosed and freed from the horne, may returne up again to the top of the water, provided that thou have first the knowledge how long such a lead will be sinking, and the apple rising in a water of known depth; for then by the diversity of the weights of the water,* or sand of the hour glass, from the time of the throwing in of the lead, and the apples returne in divers waters, thou mayst finde what thou seekest.

The idea of measuring the depth of the sea with a sounding machine for use without a line was to fascinate scientists for the next four hundred years.[3] Many variations were proposed but the basic principle remained the same: a buoyant object was attached to a weight in such a way that when the device hit the sea floor the float was released and rose to the surface. Timing was an integral part of the method. Cusanus suggested using a clepsydra or an hour glass. Later writers and observers progressed to a pendulum and finally to a clock or chronometer. As Cusanus explained, it was by finding out the ratio between the depth and the time taken by the operation that the method would be made generally useful.

Cusanus does not say why he thought it a good idea to use an instrument of this kind rather than the conventional lead and line but later writers were more explicit. They felt that internal movements in the water would carry a line out of the vertical and so falsify the depth. They did not at this stage recollect that this disadvantage might add some uncertainty to the lineless sounder. Marin Mersenne (1588–1648) argued in his *Cogitata Physico-Mathematica*:

nautæ pluribus modis decipi possunt, exempli gratia, si funis ab aquæ vorticibus & vndis abreptus non rectà, seu perpendiculariter, sed obliquè descendat.[4]

Bernhard Varen made the same argument.[5]

Nicholas of Cusa was not the only fifteenth-century thinker to propose using this method of sounding. His contemporary, the Florentine architect Leone Battista Alberti (1404–1472), described a similar device and the idea has been found to date back at least to the early Middle Ages.[6]

Later writers to propose versions of the sounding machine for use without a line included, in the sixteenth century, Christoff Puehler and Jacques Besson. Puehler (1563) devised a method allowing water to enter the machine during its descent as a measure of time.[7] In *Le Cosmolabe* (1567) Besson described an automatic device for releasing the float from the weight which was triggered off by impact on the sea floor.[8] Reasoning from the still generally accepted Aristotelian theory, that the speed of a falling body accelerates as it approaches the centre of the earth, he supposed that it would be necessary to make a series of observations in order to work out the proportion in which time varied with depth.

The great age of the sounding machine based on this principle was the

* in a clepsydra.

seventeenth century (*see* Ch. 4). Alberti's version was described by Blancanus in his *Sphæra Mundi*.[5, 9] Other accounts are to be found in the works of Mersenne, Varen and Giovanni Battista Riccioli (1598–1671), from whom the Royal Society took its first version of the machine. Before the Society made experiments with the machine it does not seem that anyone had attempted to make use of it. To the authors quoted, and the list might doubtless be extended, it seems to have been no more than a good idea.

Be that as it may, the information available to Renaissance writers on the depth of the sea was no more illuminating than it can have been in previous ages. Olaus Magnus (1490–1558), writing about the steep shelving of the sea floor off the coast of Norway, suggested that the depth of the sea might be proportional to the elevation of the land[10] and Blancanus spoke of this as a principle of general application.[9] Even in 1650 Varen could only say that the depth of the ocean varied and might be as much as a German mile or more.[5] This was no more than William Gilbert (1540–1603) had been able to say, half a century before, in *De Magnete*, even with the benefit of sharing in the close contact that existed between seamen and scientists in England towards the close of the sixteenth century.[11] Discussing the shape of the earth, he wrote

the seas do but fill certain not very deep hollows, having very rarely a depth of a mile, and often not exceeding 100 or 50 fathoms. This appears from the observations of navigators who have with line and sinker explored their bottoms.[12]

The sailors, not unnaturally, limited their efforts to finding out what was immediately necessary for the safety of their ships. Though they made important contributions to physical oceanography in several of its aspects during this period, the depth of the sea was not one of them. Ocean voyagers might put out lines over 300 fathoms long, as did Luke Foxe (1586–1635) in his 1631 voyage,[13] to get warning of approaching land but in general soundings were made only in depths of 100 fathoms or less, on what is now known as the continental shelf. This practice, extended by explorers to newly discovered coasts, was not only designed to warn the sailors of approaching shoals, but, in the coastal waters of Europe, was also an integral part of navigation, developed to the extent where sailors could tell the position of their ships from the depth of the sea and the composition of the sea floor.[14]

It has often been said that Magellan (1480?–1521) was the first person to attempt a deep-sea sounding. This idea appears to be derived from a passage in *Der Ozean* by the German oceanographer Otto Krümmel (1854–1912) who wrote that, in 1521, Magellan tried to measure the depth of the sea between the Pacific islands of St Paul and the Tiburones. He is said to have lowered a line made up of six ordinary deep-sea lines joined together, without discovering the bottom and to have naively concluded that this was the deepest part of the sea.[15] Sir John Murray printed this account in the *Challenger Report* and on this authority it has been generally accepted since.[16]

Krümmel's story, however, is inconsistent with contemporary accounts of the voyage. The different versions of Pigafetta's narrative of the circumnavigation and the log-book of Francisco Albo agree in saying that as they approached these islands the explorers attempted to make soundings in the usual way as a preliminary to anchoring but that, as no bottom could be found, they continued on their way.[17] There is nothing to suggest that any attempt was made to find the depth of the sea in general or that any assumption was made about it; in fact it looks as though a routine precaution has been magnified into a major oceanographic event. The explorers merely noted that they were unable to find bottom near the shore as it was sufficiently unusual, since they must have been unaware of the suddenness with which atolls rise from the depths, to occasion remark.

If Magellan's deep-sea sounding has to be, with regret, accorded the status of a myth, there are other examples in the same century of a new, essentially practical interest in the natural world and, therefore, in the sea. An apparently small but significant number of people endeavoured to throw off the stranglehold of the traditional ideas about the sea which continued to dominate scientific writing on the subject throughout the Renaissance. In this they were not very successful but the fact that these attempts were made is surely of significance in understanding the great overthrow of traditionalist attitudes in the middle decades of the seventeenth century.

Leonardo da Vinci (1452–1519) collected a large amount of material about water in his notebooks.[18] As an artist he described, for example, the stages in the breaking of a wave and he observed the movement of water in rivers and canals from the point of view of an hydraulic engineer.[19] Leonardo is famous for the width of his scientific investigation and a good many of his notes deal with oceanographical subjects. On some occasions he referred to the ideas handed down from classical science. Aristotle had described the Mediterranean as a river, flowing downhill from source to mouth (*see* Ch. 1). Leonardo calculated that if water must have a slope of 6 feet in a mile before it will flow, the Sea of Azov must, according to that idea, be at least 3,500 fathoms higher than the Strait of Gibraltar.[20] He also noted down many of the theories of tides which had originated in the ancient world including the ideas that the sun and moon made impressions on the water, that rivers flowing into the sea caused it to ebb and flow or that the earth breathed the water in and out like a live animal.[21]

The most interesting of these passages, however, are those which show Leonardo considering for himself phenomena presented by the sea. Like some earlier thinkers he was puzzled by the difference between the large tides of the English Channel and their virtual absence in the Mediterranean. He made the memorandum

Write to Bartolomeo the Turk about the ebb and flow of the Black Sea and ask whether he knows if there is the same ebb and flow in the Hercynian or Caspian Sea.[22]

He noticed how waves radiate outwards from the centre of disturbance when a stone is thrown into a pond and how the waves may be reflected from the rim of the pond and pass through each other unchecked.[23] The interest of his recognition of marine fossils in the mountains and his deduction that Italy must once have lain under the sea has long since been recognized.[24]

Because of the haphazard way in which Leonardo jotted down the entries in his notebooks it is often impossible to know which opinions he held himself[25] but there is enough to show that, with the sea, as in other fields of knowledge, he regarded personal observation as an indispensable corrective to received opinion in a way very rarely found in the Middle Ages. Leonardo was by no means unique at the time in taking this view and one might well expect that his contemporaries too touched on these subjects.

The same pragmatism appears some time later in the work of an English writer on navigation and scientific subjects, William Bourne (? 1535–1582).[26] In the fifth book of his work *The Treasure for Travellers*, published in 1578, Bourne writes about what can best be described in the nineteenth century phrase, the physical geography of the sea.[27] The preface to this section is illuminating. In it Bourne apologizes to the reader for presuming to deal with such subjects:

for it is possible, that some people may malice me, for that I am so bolde to deale in these causes, consydering what a great number of so excellent learned menne there are in Englande, bothe in the Vniuersyties, and in diuers other places in this Lande.

He felt this apology necessary

for that my opinion dooth differ from some of the auncient writers in naturall Phylosophy, it is possible that it may be vtterly dislyked of and condemned to be no trueth. But yet notwithstanding they may geue such credit vnto it, as the sequell of the reasons shall support vnto them, for that they bee but my simple opinions wherfore they may beleeue them as they list.

In the first five chapters Bourne described how coastal scenery is modified by the sea and other agencies. He showed how banks and shoals are formed at the point where the current of a river flowing into the sea is checked so that it deposits the silt brought down from the land. Tidal currents wear constantly changing channels in the banks but, where there is little or no movement in the sea, marshes are built up round river mouths and beaches are formed on the sheltered side of spits of land. Bourne goes on to describe how the combined action of the sea, rain and frost have worn away hillsides to produce high cliffs. The force of the waves explained the rounded shape of pebbles and boulders found on the sea-shore. The grinding to which they were subjected soon produced the characteristic appearance no matter what the original stone. He speculated that pinnacles of rock in the sea far from land were the remnants of islands of which the less durable parts had been gradually washed away by the waves.

Bourne turned next to tides. He made what seems to have been a usual distinction between the origin of the diurnal tides and that of the bi-monthly springs. Everyday tides were caused by the pull of the moon which, he supposed, was carried round the earth with the rest of the heavens by the *primum mobile* or outermost sphere of the Aristotelian universe. The bi-monthly springs were due to the moon's astrological influence which rarified the ocean. He supposed that if the sea were able it would follow the moon round the earth in the course of a lunar day but, in the Atlantic, its path was checked by the American continent so that

when the Moone dooth come rounde about, vnto the Southeast, then the powers of the Moone doo tracte or draw the waters vnto the Eastwardes, by whiche meanes the waters hauing a great course or swaye vnto the Eastwardes, are drawen so vehementlye by the powers of the Moone, vntyll such tyme, as the Moone dooth come vnto the Meridian, that it cannot sodaynely reuerse, although the Moone bee paste the Meridian to the Westwarde, as we maye see manye tymes by common experience, that any thing forced to moue violentlye, is not presently stayed, but that it must have a tyme in the staying, as the force of the dryfte dooth decay, which must be by litle and litle.[28]

Like Galileo some years later (*see* p. 51) Bourne compared the movement of water in the ocean once the tidal force was removed to the oscillation of water in a container when it has been shaken.

Bourne made the mistake common at the time of confusing tides and currents. He believed that the westerly movement of the sea observed in the tropics was a tidal current created by the moon's pull on the sea. Apart from the distortions produced by attempting to force what was known into the pattern demanded by this theory, Bourne's description of ocean currents, one of the first full accounts in English, is remarkably accurate and shows how much the explorers of the Renaissance had contributed to this branch of marine science.[29]

Sixteenth and early seventeenth century current theory was based on the idea that there was a perpetual movement of the sea from east to west (*see* p. 47). As Bourne described it, this current rounded the Cape of Good Hope and flowed across the Atlantic. Some of it penetrated the Magellan Strait and continued across the Pacific but the remainder was deflected by the coast of South America and, where this happened north of the Strait, flowed northwards into the Bay of Mexico. From there the current emerged through the Strait of Florida and flowed eastwards across the North Atlantic, which was why ships sailing from America to Europe took a more northerly route than those going in the other direction. In the 1580 edition of *A Regiment for the Sea* Bourne described the final links in the system, the South Equatorial current of the Indian Ocean and its extension southwards, now known as the Agulhas Current.[30]

This far Bourne had been able to draw on experience, his own or other people's, but there was little in either to help him account for the saltness of the sea. The one thing that Renaissance voyages had shown was that, the sea was salt wherever one went, irrespective of latitude. Unlike the author of the *Summa Philosophiae* Bourne had this justification in arguing that Aristotle's theory must be wrong because the sea was not noticeably more salt at the equator than it was near the poles which, if salinity was due to the sun drawing up the "fyne substance of the water", it ought in fact to be. Instead he suggested that the sea had become salt as a result of mixing with dissolved minerals. This explanation was the one most commonly preferred by writers who adopted a critical attitude to former views. Leonardo da Vinci supposed that the sea was saline because rivers dissolved the salt from mines on land and carried it into the sea.[31] Bourne went on to suggest that earthquakes were due to the liquefaction of veins of salt in the earth and that this had been the reason for the disappearance of Atlantis.

Writing at the same time as Bourne and sharing his enthusiasm for the empirical approach was the French craftsman, Bernard Palissy (*c.* 1510–1589). In his *Discours* of 1580 one speaker exclaims

Il faut que je dispute encores contre toy et les Philosophes Latins, parceque tu ne trouves rien de bon s'il ne vient des Latins.[32]

Palissy lacked the experience of the sea itself which Bourne had and his contribution was limited to adopting what seemed to him the most rational of current views. He argued in favour of the evaporation-precipitation cycle as an explanation of the origin of springs and supposed that the salt in the sea was of mineral origin, washed from the land by rivers.[33]

Palissy made a rather involved attempt to explain the bore on the Dordogne.[34] Rejecting the local opinion that it was caused by the river water holding back the tide, he suggested that there was a subterranean channel linking the river with the Garonne. This, he supposed, filled with air at low water; when the tide came in the air rushed out, creating the disturbance.

One of the early exponents of the experimental approach to scientific investigation was William Gilbert.[11] A large section of his work *De Mundo Nostro Sublunari Philosophia Nova* deals with the sea but, like Palissy, when he came to deal with this subject Gilbert had little factual material to work with, except on tides, and was driven back on discussion of existing opinions, for example on the origin of springs.[35] He argued that the magnetic properties of the earth ruled out the possibility of Plato's idea of a vast mass of water in the centre of the globe.[36] Like Bourne, he believed that the Aristotelian theory of salt in the sea was invalidated by recent discoveries and related how explorers searching for the North West Passage and the earlier merchant adventurers who sailed to Russia round North Cape had found the sea to be salt in high latitudes.[37] He put forward his own explanation of salinity based on his idea that there were two, not four, humours, as was commonly supposed. Also, he put forward a new tidal theory (*see* p. 51).

The empirical method of investigation towards which these writers were working found its principal defendant in Sir Francis Bacon (1561–1626). He mentioned several aspects of the marine environment in the list of subjects on which he thought information might profitably be collected, including:

History of Ebbs and Flows of the Sea; Currents, Undulations, and other Motions of the Sea.

History of the other Accidents of the Sea; its Saltness, its various Colours, its Depth; also of Rocks, Mountains and Vallies under the Sea and the like.[38]

Bacon contributed little himself to this formidable task but in *Sylva Sylvarum* he listed several observations including the fact, known also in classical times (*see* Ch. 1), that waves break more readily in shallow than in deep water.[39] He also wrote an essay on the cause of tides, using what information was available to him (*see* p. 50).[40]

Where the sea was concerned the significance of the work of Bacon and the other people mentioned lay in their appreciation of the fact that real understanding of its problems could not be reached without a more accurate knowledge of its behaviour. This realization, rather than their attempts to implement it, was their achievement.

If the good intentions of writers like Bacon remained for the moment unrealized, at the same time developments in other sciences and geographical discoveries did lead to progress in certain aspects of physical oceanography, notably in the knowledge of tides and currents, while ideas on the other subjects remained much as they had been during the Middle Ages.

William Bourne's account (*see* pp. 44–45) shows how rapidly a picture of ocean currents had been built up by explorers during the first century of Renaissance travel. Columbus himself was naturally enough the first to contribute to the knowledge of currents in the Atlantic. During his third voyage he encountered a strong current flowing westwards off the north coast of South America and wrote

the waters of the sea take their course from east to west with the heavens.[41]

The existence of an equatorial current was confirmed by later voyagers and reported in geographical works like Peter Matryr's *Decades of the Ocean*.[42] The generally accepted explanation of this, in the framework of the Aristotelian concept of the universe, was that the spheres of air and water revolved round the stationary earth under the influence of the *primum mobile* together with the celestial spheres.

Early in the sixteenth century Spanish ships encountered the Gulf Stream. Peter Martyr tells us that this was supposed to originate from the Equatorial Current, whose flow was diverted northwards by the American continent.[43] He himself did not agree with this explanation since Cabot had reported a slighter but still westerly movement of the sea further north. He thought that there must be a strait in Central America through which the Equatorial Current flowed into the Pacific, an idea still tenable at the time when he was writing, in the 1520s. The Agulhas Current, discovered by the Portuguese off the south-east coast of Africa, was regarded as the link between the Equatorial Current of the Indian Ocean and that of the Atlantic.

In 1542 the Spanish navigator Bernard de la Torre discovered the North Equatorial Current of the Pacific Ocean. This knowledge was incorporated into the general scheme; the westward movement of the sea in the Atlantic was hindered by the American continent and a current flowed through the Magellan Strait into the Pacific. Sir Humphrey Gilbert (1537?–1583) argued this was too narrow to let all the water through and that there must be a similar strait in North America through which the westward moving water penetrated the Pacific. In his *Discourse of a Discovery for a new Passage to Cataia*, first written in 1566, he gave this as a reason for confidently advocating voyages of discovery to search for a North West Passage.[44] Richard Willes used the same argument in advice he drew up for Martin Frobisher.[45] Their reasoning, of course, proved to be unsound and, instead of finding the mythical Strait of Anian, British sailors commenced the long drawn out exploration of the Canadian Arctic and, instead of a westward current, encountered the meridional Greenland and Labrador Currents.[46]

Although by the late sixteenth century the log and line had come into general use for measuring a ship's speed through the water there was no certain method of measuring the speed of currents so long as inability to determine longitude prevented sailors from fixing their ship's position.[47] Direct current measurements could be made only from a boat at anchor.[48] It was therefore easy to misjudge the rate at which water was moving, particularly if the movement were zonal. This led to disasters and narrow escapes such as that enjoyed in 1593 by Sir Richard Hawkins and his companions who found themselves off the coast of Guinea when they had thought they were 70 leagues from land.[49] Unknown to them their ships had been carried off course by the eastward flowing Equatorial Counter-current.

As the sixteenth century advanced the Copernican system of the universe began to win acceptance among a growing number of thinkers. But some people argued that the earth could not move. If it did, ran one of their arguments, the sea and the air and things in them would get left behind—with disastrous results. In *De Magnete* Gilbert attacked what he termed these "ravings of philosophasters":

More recent writers hold that the Eastern Ocean must needs, in consequence of this motion, so be driven toward the regions to the west that parts of the earth which are dry and waterless would of necessity be daily submerged beneath the waters. But the ocean gets no impulsion from this motion, as there is no resistance, and even the whole atmosphere is carried round also; for this reason, in the rapid revolution of the earth, things in the air are not left behind nor do they have the appearance of moving westward.[50]

In fact both Galileo and Kepler advanced the idea that the westward movement observed in the atmosphere and ocean *was* due to the inability of a fluid body to keep up with the speed of the diurnal rotation of the earth.[51]

The explanation most commonly given for the pattern of ocean currents during the first half of the seventeenth century was derived from the supposed effect of evaporation and precipitation on the ocean. It was argued that the sun moving through the tropics evaporated water from the sea surface in these regions and lowered its overall level while rain fell nearer the poles causing a corresponding rise. Currents, which were by definition movements of water from a higher to a lower level, flowed from the poles towards the tropics and westwards along the equator in order to restore the equilibrium of the ocean.[51] In Fournier's words

La Presence du Soleil sur la Zone Torride, enleuant aussi tres-grande quantité d'eaux en vapeurs peut obliger l'eau à tomber de roideur des autres lieux qui sont sous les Zones froides ou temperées, pour retablir le niueau de la Mer.[52]

Although the resemblance between the wind and current patterns was self-evident no one seems to have thought at this stage that winds might be the cause of major ocean currents, rather that they were responsible only for temporary movements of water. The origin of the winds themselves was obscure for much of the century. Torricelli realized that they must be due to variations in atmospheric pressure but this idea did not come into general use until the time of Halley and Mariotte.[51] William Bourne envisaged wind-generated currents created by the wind's piling up water so that a compensatory movement was necessary to restore the level of the sea to equilibrium.[53] Kircher defined currents as movements of water due to the general motion of the sea to the westwards, to the moon or to wind.[54]

As we have seen in the previous chapter practical knowledge of tides during the Middle Ages had been much more accurate among seamen than among philosophers. Tide-tables were introduced giving the position of the moon at high water in different places and this kind of prediction remained an important part of works on navigation in the sixteenth and seventeenth centuries.[55] For example, William Cuningham (*b. c.* 1531), in *The Cosmographical Glasse*, gave figures for finding the time of high water on any day of the month at different places on the coasts of Britain and Europe.[56] Later writers often gave instructions on how to make tables from which the answer could be read off without calculation. Examples of these are to be found in Edward Wright's *Certain Errors in Navigation* (2nd edition) and in Robert Dudley's *Dell'Arcano del Mare*.[57]

Information on the heights and times of tides was therefore available to people in search of information, such as the Croatian writer Nikola Sagroevic[58] and William Gilbert.[59] The eighteenth-century astronomer Lalande, who wrote a history of tidal studies, refers to several observations made in 1575 by a Frenchman named Candale,[60] but in general it would seem that theoretical writers depended on what they could learn from sailors or at second hand from works on navigation. Galileo's information about tides at Venice seems to have been of this nature.[61] The standard of knowledge shown by writers of all kinds was far higher than it had been during the Middle Ages.

Navigational writers did not often bother themselves much with the causes of tides. Usually they seem to have accepted the idea, which agreed with their practical experience, that the water of the sea was drawn after the moon which itself was moved by the *primum mobile*. This produced the diurnal tides; the bi-monthly variations were attributed to the moon's astrological influence. William Cuningham, for example, described daily tides as a flow of water from one place to another and the monthly springs and neaps as the result of changes in the volume of sea water caused by the light of the moon, quoting Galen (129–199) as his authority.[62] Bourne[63] and Wright[64] speak of the water of the ocean being carried round the world by the moon, attributing tides as well as currents to the westward movement of the sea.

Sir Francis Bacon incorporated the westward movement into his theory of tides.[65] Although he refused to

take refuge either in the violence of the *primum mobile*, which is directly contrary to nature, or in the rotation of the earth

he did suppose that the stars moved round the earth and that the sea shared in this motion. From information already available he knew that high tide occurred at the same time in Florida as on the European side of the Atlantic and that the time of high water got later as one went northwards from Gibraltar to the Strait of Dover. It therefore seemed reasonable to suppose that tides were caused by a progressive movement of the sea and not by oscillations or changes in the volume of its water. He pictured the tidal stream coming up the Atlantic from the Southern Ocean and flowing round Scotland into the North Sea. The meridional direction was enforced by the shape of the continents but the westward tendency was always present and this was why the Mediterranean had little or no tide; because its outlet to the sea faced west the tidal flow did not penetrate it.

Explanations of tides which had been popular in the Middle Ages survived into the sixteenth and even the seventeenth century. In 1528 the Croatian writer Federico Grisogono published a theory close to the ideas of Giacomo de'Dondi[66] and the explanation to be found in the *Verie Necessarie and Profitable Booke concerning Navigation* of Johann Taisnier seems to be derived from the same source, though the immediate authority quoted is Fredericus Delphinus, also of Padua.[67] In the seventeenth century medieval ideas were often used in the scientific works of Catholic writers who were debarred from adopting the Copernican system of the universe and the new explanations of tides based on it. Blancanus and Fournier adopted explanations relying on the light of the moon, like that of Roger Bacon (*see* Ch. 2).[68] Giovanni Battista Riccioli discussed hypotheses ranging from those of the ancient Greeks to Galileo's in his *Almagestum Novum*, published in 1651.[69]

The analogy of magnetic attraction was popular with medieval authors when speaking of the moon's apparent pull on the sea and this comparison continued to be made in Renaissance times. Robert Dudley described it in *Dell'Arcano del Mare*:

la Luna tira, & alza à se l'acqua del Mare con potenza quasi magnetica.[70]

At the same time the concept of gravitational attraction was going through its early stages and Simon Stevin (1548–1620) and Johann Kepler (1571–1630) tried to give it mathematical expression.[71]

In *De Magnete* William Gilbert claimed that the earth was itself a magnet and that magnetic attraction was the reason for the dependence between the moon and the earth, and the cause of tides.[72] In *De Mundo Nostro Sublunari* he elaborated on this simple statement and said that it was not the water that the moon attracted but a subterranean humour:

Quare Luna non tam attrahit mare, quàm humorem & spiritum subterraneum; nec plus resistit interposita terra, quàm mensa, aut quicquam aliud densum, aut crassum, magnetis viribus.[73]

Kepler explained tides as the result of the gravitational attraction exercised by the moon over the water of the ocean in his work *Astronomia Nova seu de Motu Stellae Martis* (1609) which contains a general discussion of the force of gravity.[74] He described how the moon drew the water towards the place where its vertical distance from the earth was least and how the movement was greater in the oceans than in lakes and smaller seas. He realized that the earth also exercised a gravitational pull on the sea; if this were not so the moon would have captured the sea's water altogether. In later years, in the work *Harmonices Mundi*, however, he suggested a conventional astrological explanation of tidal phenomena, giving rise to the suspicion that he might have gone back on his earlier views.[75]

Galileo dismissed Kepler's idea of gravitational attraction as a regrettable concession to medievalism.[76] He himself believed that tides were due to the effect on the sea of the earth's rotation and that their existence constituted proof that the earth moved and therefore of the Copernican system. Apparently he was not the first person to think along these lines. Dr. E. J. Aiton mentions a similar attempt in the *Quæstiones Peripateticarum* of Andreas Caesalpinus, published in 1593.[77] Galileo's theory, according to Stillman Drake, was probably developed by 1595.[78] The final version appeared in 1632 in the *Dialogi sopra i due massimi sistemi del mondo, Tolemaico e Copernicano*.[79]

Galileo began his discussion of tides by criticizing the idea that they were due to changes in the density of sea water caused by the light or heat of the moon. There was no evidence that such changes took place nor could they be reproduced artificially. Natural movement most resembling that of tides could be induced in water by disturbing the container in which it stood. In the barges which carried fresh water to Venice a sudden movement caused an oscillation in the contents so that the level at each end rose and fell alternately with the horizontal movement being more pronounced in the centre. Galileo supposed that the earth moved in an orbit round the sun which it completed in a year and that it simultaneously rotated on its own axis once every twenty-four hours. He argued that at any single point on the earth's surface constant alterations in speed were going on, depending as to whether the orbital and axial motions were acting in the same direction, in which case there would be acceleration relative to the speed of the whole earth in space, or in opposite directions, which would cause relative retardation. The changes in speed of different parts of the earth's surface caused disturbances in the sea bed which, communicated to the water, were the cause of tides.

Galileo explained the observed times and heights of tides, and their variations from place to place, as the result of the limitations imposed on the initial force by the configuration of the sea bed. He knew that oscillations depend for frequency on the depth and also that they do not die down immediately the initial shock is over so that equilibrium is only gradually restored. The monthly variations were, he supposed, due to further irregularities introduced into the earth's movement by the perturbing influence of the moon, which he had to admit was tied in some way to the earth. He thought that the annual high tides occurred at the solstices.

Several years later the French philosopher René Descartes (1596–1650) introduced a completely different hypothesis.[80] He suggested that space is not empty but full of invisible matter or ether. The rotation of the heavenly bodies was due to the vortical motions of the ether. As the moon travelled round the earth it compressed the ether which lay between it and the earth's surface and as it passed over the sea this pressure was communicated to the fluid surface, creating tides.

These three theories of tides, Galileo's, Descartes's, and the early versions of the gravitational theory dominated thought on the subject in the mid-seventeenth century. None of them either then or for some time to come, succeeded in supplanting the others and all had their supporters and their critics. Followers of Galileo echoed his attack on the supposed astrological taint in Kepler's gravitational theory.[81] Galileo's critics attacked the factual basis of his theory on the ground that he did not realize that tides are geared to the lunar, not the solar, day and that the moon therefore must be the principal factor in a genuine explanation.[82] Varen criticized Descartes's theory because, he said, in practice it would produce low water as the moon crossed the meridian and high tide six hours later.[83] In addition to competing with each other these new theories also had to combat revivals of medieval theories by Catholic writers, such as Riccioli, not to mention the flights of imagination produced by amateur theorists and the lunatic fringe.[84]

Another development in the physical sciences during the early part of the seventeenth century which had important consequences for marine science, was the work on the pressure of air. [85]In the Aristotelian theory of the universe the elements of air and water were supposed to have their natural positions in concentric spheres surrounding the earth and to be without weight in their proper places. The principle that fluids exercise vertical and lateral pressure was apparently first stated in the thirteenth century[86] and reasserted by Simon Stevin in the sixteenth[71] but it does not seem to have been generally appreciated that this was so. Taisnier, for example, explained the action of a diving bell by saying that the dryness of the air was capable of resisting the water.[67] Isaac Beeckman (1588–1637) knew that the pressure of water affected divers and deduced from this that air too had weight.[87]

It would seem therefore that the idea of pressure in water was much older than the same concept for air. Nevertheless, it was the work done on the pressure of air by Torricelli and his successors on which later thought about pressure in the sea was based.

In the branches of marine science most closely related to other sciences which were themselves developing, particularly in those dealing with tides and ocean currents, considerable advances were made in theory and in practical understanding during the sixteenth and early seventeenth centuries. In other aspects, thought remained static, though philosophers were beginning to be aware of the scientific challenge they represented. General scientific and geographical works produced during the period bring out the paradox of growth in some directions and stagnation in others and, bearing in mind the reservation that eclectic works rarely reflect the more advanced views of their time, they seem, in this, to give a fair indication of progress or of the lack of it.

Two of the most popular sixteenth century scientific textbooks, judging by the number of references made to them by later authors, were the *De Subtilitate Rerum* of Girolamo Cardano (1501–1576)[88] and the criticism of it by Julius Caesar Scaliger (1484–1558), *Exotericarum Exercitationum ad Cardanum*, both of which were first published in the 1550s.[89] They both discuss the origin of springs, the saltness of the sea and its movements in very much the same terms as those employed by medieval writers.

By the time the standard works of the middle of the seventeenth century, Fournier's *Hydrographie*,[90] Varen's *Geographia Generalis*[91] and Kircher's *Mundus Subterraneus*[92] appeared a change in tone has become apparent. The overall pattern of the topics discussed remains unaltered, what is different is the injection of new information as a result of the geographical discoveries of the preceding 150 years and the weight given to observation, leading to a more vigorous discussion. The way in which these three writers responded to the situation varied with their personalities and circumstances. Fournier and Kircher were Jesuits, living at the height of the Counter-Reformation. Varen lived in the Protestant Netherlands. His

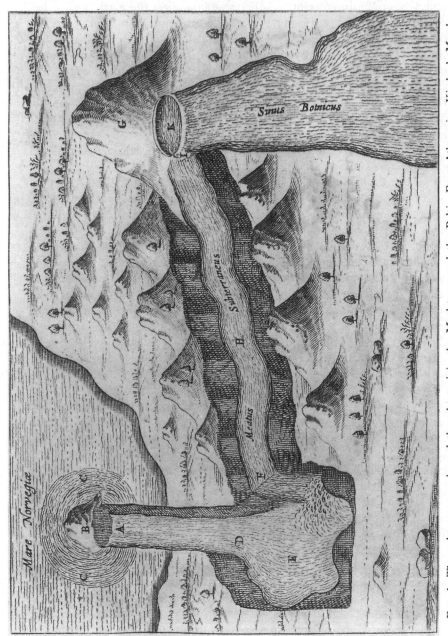

FIG. 1. The subterranean channel thought to join the Maelstrom and the Baltic. From Athanasius Kircher's *Mundus Subterraneus*, 3rd edition (1678). Vol. I, p. 159.

approach was more critical and less dogmatic than theirs. Fournier was inclined to be backward-looking but Kircher was bold and imaginative.

Kircher's speculative faculty is nowhere more marked than in the passages in which he deals with the supposition that there are subterranean tunnels passing under the land and linking the seas together. This idea had affinities with the extremely ancient and then still widely held view of the origin of rivers which had it that the water which emerged on land in springs was not rain water which had collected underground but that it had travelled through the earth from the sea bed. But even Aristotle who did not hold this point of view had supposed that a subterranean link existed between the Caspian and the Black Sea.[93] As a rule, understandably, only a general assertion of the existence of such channels was made but Kircher was serenely unworried by the impossibility of obtaining evidence and, instead, profited by its lack to map out the system as he thought it should be, putting in a link between the Red Sea and the Mediterranean, another between the Gulf of Bothnia and the Maelstrom, and so on.[94]

Kircher argued that the entire ocean was saved from stagnation, and the polar seas from freezing, by circulating continually through the centre of the earth. It disappeared into the earth's interior at the North Pole and eventually came out at the other end—as he expressed it in terms consonant with the vagueness of the concept:

absorptumque per incognitos recessus & inexplorabiles maeandrorum ductus, tortuosis & incomprehensibilibus ambagibus tandem *in Australi Polo denuo emergit.*[95]

It is interesting to compare the opinions of the other two authors on this subject. Fournier was willing to accept the idea of subterranean channels which had a respectable literary pedigree though he was more cautious in going into detail.[96] Varen refused to make any final judgment on the matter; one just could not know whether such links existed and even if one admitted that they might it was another thing altogether to say that any kind of circulation took place through them.[97]

Fournier adopted the explanation of the sea's salinity which was mistakenly ascribed to Aristotle, that is that the salt was produced by the action of the sun on vapours rising from the sea bed and that it was confined to the surface layers.[98] As his authorities he quoted Scaliger[99] and the more recent testimony of the Dutch traveller J. H. van Linschoten who related how he had seen fresh water brought up from the bottom of the sea in Bahrein.[100] Varen realized that there was a difference between Aristotle's opinion and that of the "Other Peripatetics (who also pretend to have *Aristotle* on their side)." He himself had no time for either of them:

Both these Opinions labour under such great Difficulties and Absurdities, that it is a Wonder so many learned Men and Philosophers could be satisfied with them.[101]

The recent geographical discoveries had added little to existing knowledge of these topics. They had on the other hand added enormously to knowledge of the movements of water in the sea and it was in this area of marine science that most new ideas had been forthcoming. As Catholics Fournier and Kircher were obliged to look for concepts which did not involve moving the earth from the centre of the universe, though this did not prevent them from discussing new ideas. Kircher listed three main movements of the sea besides those already described. There was the ebb and flow of the tide which was caused by the moon. Then there was the general movement of the sea from east to west in the tropics. Both he and Fournier ascribed this to the power of the sun which evaporated water from the surface of the sea as it passed across the sky thus creating a current which flowed in from behind to replace the loss.[102] This current in turn drew its resources from regions of the ocean where the evaporated water was restored as rain. Thus one had movements of the sea from north and south towards the equator. Again, the westerly equatorial current divided when it met the eastern shores of the continental masses and branches went north and south. From this pattern of cause and effect Kircher built up a picture of gyratory current movements, clockwise in the northern hemisphere, anti-clockwise in the southern-hemisphere (*see* Fig. 2). He acknowledged that winds too might be a cause of currents.

Varenius attributed both tides and currents to the westward movement of the ocean, which, he said, adopting a modified version of Descartes's hypothesis, was caused by the pressure of the moon, communicated to the sea through the ether and the air.[103] Winds too played an important part in creating currents, for example the monsoon winds of the Indian Ocean. The current along the coasts of Chile and Peru was caused by winds impelling the sea towards the shore.[104] He pointed out that the trade winds and the equatorial currents follow the same general course but thought that this should not be made the ground for supposing, in this case, that the movement of the water was attributable to the wind. Rather, both should be referred back to the overall westerly motion produced by the moon.

* It was much more sensible to suppose that the sea had always been salt or that its salinity was derived from mountains of salt on the sea bed which had been dissolved by its waters over the course of time.

In spite of the new knowledge available to them in the field of marine science the structure of the discussion in the three writers and, in those

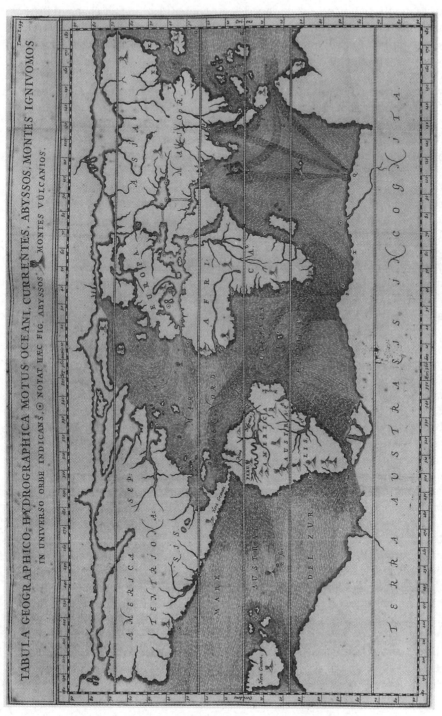

Fig. 2. Chart of ocean currents. From Athanasius Kircher's *Mundus Subterraneus*, 3rd edition (1678). pp. 134–135. *

areas unaffected by recent discoveries, its content had in fact changed little and still remained firmly rooted in the medieval tradition. Yet both Varen and Kircher, for all his credulity, adopted what they conceived of as a strictly empirical standpoint. The difference between their approach and that which was adopted by scientists working in Britain in the years which separated the publication of the *Geographia Generalis* and *Mundus Subterraneus* was largely a methodological one.

The word revolution is applied to the events which transformed scientific activity in Europe in the mid-seventeenth century and it is no less applicable to the changes which took place in the limited sphere of marine science at this time. British scientists working in the 1660s largely forbore to ask questions which were to all intents and purposes unanswerable, a consideration which had rarely deterred previous writers. One hears little about subterranean channels and other necessarily abstruse features. Instead they asked things like: if the sea is really more salt the closer you get to the equator, by how much is it? Or, if the sea gets deeper the further you go from the land, what is its greatest depth? How much does the height of the tides vary from place to place, or in the same place at different times? These were questions to which quantitative answers could be given, provided that someone was prepared to make the necessary observations and that instruments were available when needed.

It would be wrong to assume from this that the people who posed these questions were not interested in the reasons for these happenings or that they had no preconceived notions about them. What had happened was that for the first time since the days of the Greek scientists the sea and its behaviour had become an object of study in its own right, untrammelled by the limited objectives inherent in the observations made by sailors from whom up till now the bulk of new information had come. This did not mean that the people thus engaged had no practical motivation. Their declared aim was twofold: they sought knowledge for its own sake; they also believed that it would give them power to reduce or overcome the hazards encountered at sea.[105] To do this, however, it was necessary to look at underlying causes and not just at the aspects which immediately affected the safety of shipping.

Oceanography is a descriptive and environmental science; as such it depends for its existence on the application of knowledge already gained in the physical and other sciences. Its development has therefore had to wait on advances made elsewhere. It also poses enormous technical problems in the need to measure events taking place in the body of the ocean. The combination of these factors, and others, in particular the immensity of the costs involved, except by the standards of the present day, and the difficulty, or rather impossibility before the perfection of methods of determining longitude at sea, of fixing a ship's position with accuracy, made it easier for men to observe what was going on millions of miles out in space than four miles beneath the surface of the ocean. This must account for the relatively slow and halting progress made by marine science towards full status in the scientific community.

At what point did this recognition occur? Oceanography does not at this day and perhaps by virtue of its very nature never will operate within a single paradigm, every branch of the science having its own. This makes it hard if not impossible to apply a theory of scientific progress like that put forward by Kuhn[106] in its entirety but inasmuch as there is room deliberately left for manoeuvre the following outline has been attempted.

On this theory and from the historical record the decisive step was taken in the closing decades of the nineteenth century. It is then that for the first time you find people seeking to make the study of marine science their life's work and that oceanography acquires both its name and its identity. All this is indisputable and yet if one leaves it here how is one to interpret what went on beforehand?

Between the mid-seventeenth and late nineteenth centuries there were three main periods of activity in the marine sciences. The first of these took shape in the 1660s, the second in the late eighteenth century and the third from the 1860s onwards. In all three periods it can be shown that there existed, admittedly in a limited sense, a body of people with common interests, shared ideas and identity of aims. The principal members of these loosely-knit groups, especially in the 1660s, included people of standing on other accounts in the scientific community which did not question the value of their activities in this direction though the interest and degree of acceptance which they were willing to accord to them does seem to have varied with the general scientific climate, the number of people involved and in some cases with the status of the worker.

There was a degree of cohesion at the times spoken of, albeit restricted in the first two, that make the label of pre-scientific that Kuhn would apply to sciences not yet consolidated by the possession of a single paradigm and a self-perpetuating body of workers seem nevertheless rather less than the truth. Nor is it adequate to describe the work done in these periods as mere data collecting for although there was a good deal of this, which did not of itself lead to anything further, the falling off in activity which ended the first two periods, and in this country to some extent, the third as well, was due to the operation of the limiting factors outlined above, rather than to the lack of ideas for future work.

None of the three epochs here mentioned were entirely self-contained but in their inception they owed little to the one that had gone before. In every instance they took as their starting point the information that was readily to hand, in other words the popular textbooks of the time. This meant that the latter two began with incomplete and sometimes distorted impressions of what had been done before. So too, with greater justification, did the first. The workers of the 1660s revolutionized marine science but their preconceptions were derived from books like the ones already described which represented the final point of a tradition extending back to Pliny and beyond him to Hellenic science.

3. NOTES

1. George Sarton, *Six Wings: Men of Science in the Renaissance*. The Bodley Head, London (1957), p. 15. *See also* pp. 77–78. Quoted by kind permission of the publisher.
2. Nicholas of Cusa, *Idiota; de Sapientia, de Mente, de Staticis Experimentis, Nicolai de Cusa Opera Omnia iussu et auctoritate Academiae Litterarum Heidelbergensis ad codicum fidem edita*, 14 vols (1932–1968). Vol. 5 (ed. L. Baur) Lipsiae (1937), p. 131.
   Nicholas of Cusa, *The Idiot in Four Books*, London (1650), pp. 195–196.
3. Robert P. Multhauf, "The line-less sounder: an episode in the history of scientific instruments", *J. Hist. Med.* (1960). Vol. **15**, pp. 390–398.
   See also:
   "Historical Introduction", *Report on the Scientific Results of the Voyage of H.M.S. Challenger during the Years 1872–1876; A Summary of the Scientific* * *Results*, H.M.S.O., London (1895). Vol. **1**, pp. 56–58.
4. Marin Mersenne, *Cogitata Physico-Mathematica*, Paris (1644), p. 215.
5. Bernhard Varen, *Geographia Generalis*, revised by Isaac Newton, Cambridge (1672), pp. 102–103.
6. Dr. A. G. Keller has kindly allowed me to read an unpublished paper in which he shows that the idea of a lineless sounding machine may be traced back as far as the ninth or tenth century.
7. Robert P. Multhauf, *op. cit.* p. 393.
   Challenger Report, op. cit. pp. 56–57.
8. Jacques Besson, *Le Cosmolabe. Ou Instrument Universel, concernant Toutes Observations qui se peuvent faire par les Sciences Mathematiques, tant au Ciel, en la Terre, comme en la Mer*, Paris (1567), pp. 235–242.
   Besson also invented an odometer for use on land (*op. cit.* pp. 223–226) consisting of a large wheel and an index to record the number of its revolutions and a log for measuring distances at sea (pp. 231–235) which, he hoped, would provide information accurate enough for the calculation of longitude. He described another device for the same purpose in the *Theatre des Instrumens Mathematiques & Mechaniques*, Lyon (1579). *See also:* Eva G. R. Taylor, *Tudor Geography 1485–1583*, London (1930), p. 159.
9. Joseph Blancanus, *Sphæra Mundi, seu Cosmographia Demonstrativa, ac facili* * *methodo tradita*, new edition, *Mutinae* (1635), pp. 53–54.
   Marin Mersenne, *op. cit.* pp. 214–216.
   Giovanni Battista Riccioli, *Almagestum Novum, Astronomiam Veterem Novamque*, 2 vols, Bononiae (1651). Vol. **1**, p. 56; Vol. **2**, p. 397.

10. Olaus Magnus, *Historia de Gentibus Septentrionalibus*, Romae (1555), p. 72:

    Tanta est in plerisɋ montosis littoribus Noruegiæ immensurabilis profunditas, vt funibus quantis repleri possit nauis ingentissima, bolide plumbea infernè demissa, fundus aliquis nequeat inueniri: eaɋ naturæ vis est, vt quantò sublimius montes in excelsum promineant, tantò in eorum radicibus inscrutabilior profunditas apparebit: licet eorum sublimitas respectu cœli minima super terram reputatur. Pedes etiam horum montium ita cauernosi, profundiɋ, & obliqui sunt, vt funibus immissis, quorsum tendat eorum hiatus, difficillimè cognosci poscit.

    It would be interesting to know more about the origin of this idea which persisted well into the nineteenth century.

    Robert P. Multhauf lists Olaus Magnus among the early authors who refer to the instrument for sounding without a line but I have found only a reference to the conventional use of lead and line when (p. 425) he deals with the danger of shoals:

    Verùm his, & similibus occurrentibus malis, periti fidelesɋ nautæ ex industria, & experientia, virtute adhærentis arenæ, bolide in profundum dimissa, cognoscere possunt, an propè, vel procul petendus sit portus, vt aliorsum insidias fugiendo declinent.

11. Edgar Zilsel, "The origins of William Gilbert's scientific method", *J. Hist. Ideas* (1941). Vol. 2, pp. 1–32.

12. William Gilbert, *On the Loadstone and Magnetic Bodies, and on the great Magnet the Earth*, translated by P. Fleury Mottelay, New York and London (1893), p. 65.

13. Luke Foxe, *North-West Fox* in *The Voyages of Captain Luke Foxe and Captain Thomas James, in Search of a North-West Passage, in 1631–32*, Hakluyt Society. Vols 88 and 89, London (1894); Vol. 89, pp. 271 and 273.

    Robert Hooke quotes a sounding of over 500 fathoms made by Sir Francis Drake: Richard Waller, *The Posthumous Works of Robert Hooke*, London (1705), p. 309.

14. David W. Waters, *The Art of Navigation in England in Elizabethan and Early Stuart Times*, London (1958), pp. 18–20.

15. Otto Krümmel, *Der Ozean*, Leipzig and Prague (1886), p. 35; *Handbuch der Ozeanographie*, 2 vols, Stuttgart, (1907–1911). Vol. 1, p. 69.

16. *Challenger Report, op. cit.* pp. 45–46.

17. James Alexander Robertson, *Magellan's Voyage around the World by Antonio Pigafetta*, 3 vols, Cleveland (1906). Vol. 1, pp. 85 and 244–245.

    Lord Stanley of Alderley, *The First Voyage round the World by Magellan*, Hakluyt Society. Vol. 52, London (1874), p. 65.

    Krümmel gives no reference for his version.

18. Edward MacCurdy, *The Notebooks of Leonardo da Vinci*, Jonathan Cape, 2 vols, London (1938).

    Jean Paul Richter, *The Literary Works of Leonardo da Vinci*, 2nd ed. 2 vols, London (1939).

19. J. P. Richter, *op. cit.* Vol. 2, p. 154.

    E. MacCurdy, *op. cit.* Vol. 2, *The Nature of Water*, pp. 11–131.

20. E. MacCurdy, *op. cit.* Vol. 1, pp. 339–342.

21. *Ibid.* Vol. 1, p. 347; Vol. 2, pp. 16–17, 21.

    The idea that the impression of the sun and moon on the water caused tides was suggested by Seleucus (*see* Ch. 1). The idea that they were due to rivers was taken from Plato (*Timaeus*). The Stoics had put forward the idea that the earth resembled a living creature.

22. E. MacCurdy, *op. cit.*, Vol. **1**, pp. 382–390. Quoted by kind permission of the publisher.
23. *Ibid.* Vol. **2**, pp. 11–12.
24. *Ibid.* Vol. **1**, pp. 349–359.
25. G. Sarton, *op. cit.* p. 221.
26. For an account of Bourne's life and work *see:*
    A Regiment for the Sea and other Writings on Navigation, by William Bourne of Gravesend, a Gunner (c. 1535–1582) (ed. E. G. R. Taylor) in the Hakluyt Society Publications, 2nd Series. Vol. **121**, Cambridge University Press (1963).
27. William Bourne, *A Booke called the Treasure for Traveilers*, London (1578).
28. *Ibid.* f. 11.
29. David W. Waters, *op. cit.* pp. 147–8, supposes that Bourne's account of currents was derived from that of Richard Willes (see ref. 45) but Bourne's is fuller.
30. William Bourne, *A Regiment for the Sea and other Writings on Navigation, op. cit.* pp. 306–307.
31. E. MacCurdy, *op. cit.* Vol. **2**, pp. 63–65.
32. Bernard Palissy, *Discours admirables de la nature des eaux et fontaines* in *Les Œuvres de Bernard Palissy* (ed. Anatole France), Paris (1880), p. 199.
33. *Ibid.* pp. 194–202.
    H. R. Thompson, "The geographical and geological observations of Bernard Palissy the potter", *Annls Sci.* (1954). Vol. **10**, pp. 149–165.
34. Bernard Palissy, *Du mascaret qui s'engendre au fleuve de Dourdogne, en la Guienne, op. cit.* pp. 227–229.
35. William Gilbert, *De Mundo Nostro Sublunari Philosophia Nova*, Amstelodami (1651), pp. 277–292. Characteristically he cited the experience of gardeners to make a point against Scaliger (see p. 54).
36. *Ibid.* pp. 293–294.
37. *Ibid.* pp. 294–298.
38. *The Works of Francis Bacon* (ed. J. Spedding, R. L. Ellis and D. D. Heath), 14 vols, London (1857–1874). Vol. **4** (1858), p. 266.
39. Sir Francis Bacon, *Sylva Sylvarum: or a Naturall Historie* (ed. William Rawley), 2nd edition, London (1628), p. 226.
40. Sir Francis Bacon, "On the ebb and flow of the sea", *The Works of Francis Bacon, op. cit.* Vol. **5** (1858), pp. 443–458.
41. Cecil Jane, *Select documents illustrating the four voyages of Columbus*, Hakluyt Society, 2nd Series, Cambridge University Press. Vols **65** and **70** (1929 and 1932); vol. **70**, p. 38. Quoted by kind permission of the publisher.
42. Peter Martyr, *The Decades of the Ocean*, 1st decade, bk 6, in Richard Eden, *The History of Travayle in the West and East Indies, and other Countreys lying eyther way, towards the Fruitfull and Ryche Moluccaes. As Moscovia, Persia, Arabia, Syria, Ægypt, Ethiopia, Guinea, China in Cathayo and Giapan. With a Discourse of the Northwest Passage* (ed. Richard Willes), London (1577), f. 37.
43. *Ibid.* 3rd decade, bk 6; ff. 124–125.
44. Sir Humphrey Gilbert, "A discourse of a discoverie for a new passage to Cataia", *The Voyages and Colonising Enterprises of Sir Humphrey Gilbert* (ed.

David Beers Quinn) Hakluyt Society, 2nd series. Vols **83** and **84,** London (1940); Vol. **83,** pp. 129–164, especially pp. 143–145.

45. Richard Willes, "For M. Captayne Furbisher's passage by the Northwest", *The History of Travayle in the West and East Indies, op. cit.* ff. 230–232.
46. David W. Waters, *op. cit.* pp. 268–269.
47. *Ibid.* p. 122.
48. *Ibid.* p. 576.
49. Sir Clements Markham, *The Hawkins' Voyages during the reigns of Henry VIII, Queen Elizabeth, and James I,* Hakluyt Society. Vol. **57,** London (1878), pp. 133–138.
50. William Gilbert, *On the Loadstone, op. cit.* p. 337.
51. Harold L. Burstyn, "Early explanations of the role of the earth's rotation in the circulation of the atmosphere and the ocean", *Isis* (1966). Vol. **57,** pp. 167–187.
52. Georges Fournier, *Hydrographie contenant la Théorie et la Pratique de Toutes les Parties de la Navigation,* 2nd edition, Paris (1667), p. 362.
53. William Bourne, *A Booke called the Treasure for Traveilers, op. cit.* Bk 5, f. 13.
54. Athanasius Kircher, *Mundus Subterraneus, in XII Libros Digestus,* 3rd edition, 2 vols, Amstelodami (1678). Vol. **1,** p. 135.
55. Désiré Gernez, "Les indications relatives aux marées dans les anciens livres de mer", *Archs int. Hist. Sci.* (1948–1949). Vol. **28,** no. 7, pp. 671–691.
56. William Cuningham, *The Cosmographical Glasse, conteinyng the Pleasant Principles of Cosmographie, Geographie, Hydrographie or Navigation,* London (1559), ff. 145–153.
57. Edward Wright, *Certaine Errors in Navigation,* 2nd edition, London (1610). Appendix pp. 85–92.
    Robert Dudley, *Dell'Arcano del Mare . . . Libri Sei,* Firenze (1646), pp. 66–67. D. W. Waters, *op. cit.* pp. 130–131, gives as his earliest example one described by William Bourne in 1567. See also D. Gernez, *loc. cit.*
58. Žarko Dadić, "The history of the theories of the tide introduced by Yugoslav scientists until the 18th century", *Bull. Inst. océanogr. Monaco,* numéro spécial 2 (1968). Vol **1,** pp. 49–53.
59. William Gilbert, *De Mundo Nostro Sublunari, op. cit.* pp. 299–302.
60. Joseph Jérôme le Français de Lalande, *Astronomie,* 2nd edition, 4 vols, Paris (1771–1781). Vol. **4** (1781), p. 35.
    See also: Georges Fournier, *op. cit.* p. 353, where he speaks of the variations in the annual springs and neaps
        comme autrefois le mesme Seigneur de Candale a pris plaisir d'obseruer exactement en la coste de Medoc, & Emboucheure de Garonne.
61. Galileo Galilei, *Dialogue Concerning the Two Chief World Systems—Ptolemaic and Copernican,* translated by Stillman Drake, Berkeley (1953), p. 417.
62. William Cuningham, *op. cit.* ff. 145–146.
63. William Bourne, *A Booke called the Treasure for Traveilers, op. cit.* Bk 5, f. 10.
64. Edward Wright, *op. cit.* Appendix, pp. 75–76.
65. Sir Francis Bacon, "On the ebb and flow of the sea", *loc. cit.* Vol. **5,** pp. 443–458.
66. Žarko Dadić, *op. cit. See* p. 31.
67. Johann Taisnier, *A verie necessarie and profitable Booke concerning Navigation . . . named a Treatise of continuall Motions,* translated by Richard Eden, London (?1579).

68. J. Blancanus, *op. cit.* pp. 49–51.
    G. Fournier, *op. cit.* pp. 339–341.
69. Giovanni Battista Riccioli, *op. cit.* Vol. 2, pp. 360–380.
    Some authorities doubt whether Riccioli was genuine in his rejection of the Copernican system—J. L. E. Dreyer, *History of the Planetary Systems from Thales to Kepler*, Cambridge (1906), p. 419.
70. Robert Dudley, *op. cit.* p. 64.
71. George Sarton, "Simon Stevin of Bruges", *Isis* (1934). Vol. 21, pp. 241–303. Simon Stevin, "On the theory of ebb and flow", *The Principle Works of Simon Stevin* (ed. E. J. Dijksterhuis *et al.*), 3 vols, Amsterdam (1955–1961). Vol. 3, pp. 324–358.
72. William Gilbert, *On the Loadstone, op. cit.*, p. 136.
73. *Idem. De Mundo Nostro Sublunari, op. cit.* pp. 298–313.
74. Johann Kepler, *Astronomia Nova seu de motu Stellae Martis* in *Joannis Kepleri Astronomi Opera Omnia* (ed. C. Frisch), 8 vols, Frankfurt and Erlanger (1858–1871). Vol. 3 (1860), p. 151.
75. Johann Kepler, *Harmonices Mundi Libri V*, in *Opera Omnia, op. cit.* Vol. 5 (1864), p. 255.
76. Galileo, *op. cit.* p. 462.
77. E. J. Aiton, "Galileo's theory of the tide", *Annls Sci.* (1954). Vol. 10, pp. 44–57.
    H. L. Burstyn, "Galileo's attempt to prove that the earth moves", *Isis* (1962). Vol. 53, pp. 161–185, *see also:* subsequent contributions by both authors in this journal.
78. Stillman Drake, "Galileo Gleanings—X. Origin and fate of Galileo's theory of the tides", *Physis* (1961). Vol. 3, pp. 185–193.
79. Galileo, *op. cit.* pp. 416–465.
80. René Descartes, *Les Principes de la Philosophie*, part 4, sections 49–53, *Œuvres de Descartes* (ed. Charles Adam and Paul Tannery) 11 vols, Paris, (1897–1909). Vol. 9 (1904), pp. 227–230.
    René Dugas, *La Mécanique au XVIIe Siècle*, Neuchâtel (1954), pp. 194–195.
81. Galileo, *op. cit.* p. 462.
82. G. Fournier, *op. cit.* pp. 345–352. *For example*, p. 348:
    > Ce mouuement inegal de la terre qui cause les flux & reflux arriue tous les iours à mesme heure... Donc les flux & reflux ne deuroient tous les iours reculer de 48. minutes, comme nous voyons qu'il se fait ordinairement par tout le monde.... Ne vaut-il donc pas mieux dire que c'est la Lune qui fait non seulement auancer ou reculer les flux, mais encore les produit & les excite.
83. Bernhard Varen, *A Compleat System of General Geography: explaining the Nature and Properties of the Earth* (ed. Newton and Jurin), translated by Dugdale, revised by Peter Shaw, 2 vols, London (1733). Vol. 1, pp. 231–245.
84. *For example*, Ellis Bradshawe, *A New and cleer Discovery, of the true, and proper, natural Cause, of the Ebbing and Flowing of the Main Sea*, London (1649), 10 pp. This repeats the theory, derived from Plato, that tides are caused by water rising from the centre of the earth through chasms in the sea floor.
85. W. E. Knowles Middleton, *The History of the Barometer*, Baltimore (1964).
86. *Ibid.*, p. 5.

87. W. E. Knowles Middleton, *loc. cit.* pp. 5–6.
88. Girolamo Cardano, *Les Livres de Hierome Cardanus Medecin Milannois, Intitulés de la Subtilité, & subtiles inventions ensemble les causes occultes,* ∗ *raisons d'icelles,* translated by Richard le Blanc, Paris (1556). Cardano's *De Subtilitate* was first published in 1550.
89. Julius Caesar Scaliger, *Exotericarum Exercitationum Liber quintus decimus, de Subtilitate, ad Hieronymum Cardanum,* Lutetiae (1557).
90. Georges Fournier, *Hydrographie contentant la Théorie et la Pratique de Toutes les Parties de la Navigation.* First published 1643. Second edition, Paris (1667).
91. Bernhard Varen, *Geographia Generalis, In qua affectiones generales Telluris explicantur,* Amstelodami (1650).
92. Athanasius Kircher, *Mundus Subterraneus, in XII Libros Digestus,* Amstelodami. First published 1665. Third edition 1678.
93. See Chapter 1, p. 11.
94. A. Kircher, *op. cit.* Vol. **1**, pp. 84–89 and 157–163.
95. *Ibid.* Vol. **1**, pp. 169–171.
96. G. Fournier, *op. cit.* pp. 338–339.
97. B. Varen, *A Compleat System of General Geography, op. cit.* Vol. **1**, pp. 198–203.
98. G. Fournier, *op. cit.* pp. 357–358.
99. Julius Caesar Scaliger, *op. cit.* ff. 77–81.
100. J. H. van Linschoten, *Discours of Voyages into the Easte and West Indies,* London (1598), p. 16.
101. B. Varen, *op. cit.* Vol. **1**, pp. 204–209.
102. G. Fournier, *op. cit.* pp. 354–356; A. Kircher, *op. cit.* Vol. **1**, pp. 132–150.
103. B. Varen, *Geographia Generalis, op. cit.* pp. 174–216.
104. *Ibid.* p. 211.
105. See Chapter 4, pp. 70, 88.
106. Thomas H. Kuhn, *The Structure of Scientific Revolutions,* Chicago (1964).

Addenda et Corrigenda

p.56, 11.37-39: These lines should follow quote at head of page

p.57, fig.2, caption: *before* pp. 134-135 *insert* Vol . **1**,

p.60, n.3, 1.6: *after* Vol. **1**, *insert* pp. 1-06E

p.60, n.9, 1.2: *instead: Mutinae read* Mutinae

p.65, n.88, 1.2: *after* occultes *insert* &

MARINE SCIENCE IN THE
SEVENTEENTH CENTURY

4. THE SEVENTEENTH CENTURY MOVEMENT TOWARDS A SCIENCE OF THE SEA

DURING the Renaissance man's knowledge of the world around him expanded as never before and the rise of experimental science opened up new dimensions of understanding. But the disparity between the kind of information which sailors provided on the movements of water in the sea and the requirements of philosophers in search of an explanation of cosmic processes meant that ambitious theoretical developments outpaced the inadequate supply of factual material. As a result of gradual improvement in understanding of the physical properties of fluids, inferences could be made, and sometimes were, about the state of the ocean; for example that the pressure of the ocean at any place on its bed was determined solely by the depth of water there and had nothing to do with the volume of water as a whole, a point brought out by Mersenne in his *Cogitata Physico-Mathematica*.[1] In other respects scientists discussed the sea in terms which had not changed since the days of Aristotle. If this situation was to be altered it was necessary for them to make a first hand examination of actual conditions in the sea. In Britain during the second half of the seventeenth century the broadening of the scientific outlook and the development of instruments led to this being done.

It does not seem possible to point to any one influence as the origin of practical scientific interest in the sea in this country. It must have been due in part to the close co-operation which developed during the early years of the seventeenth century between the mathematicians of Gresham College and the naval officers and ship-builders of Greenwich[2] though this does not seem to have involved research on the sea itself. It is true that explorers were expected to record tides and currents in their logs but there is nothing to show that their observations were regarded as fulfilling more than immediate navigational needs, except in the search for the North West Passage where the direction and force of the current or tidal stream could tell the sailor if open water lay ahead.[3] Nevertheless, there is evidence that some people were aware of the interest and importance of research into the problems which now constitute part of physical oceanography.

In the 1633 edition of his navigational work *The Circles of Proportion* the mathematician William Oughtred (1575–1660) called for organized efforts to collect information which could be used to elucidate problems in navigation and oceanography to the benefit of all those whose livelihood depended on the sea:

If the *Masters of Ships* and *Pilots* will take the paines in the journalls of their voyages dilligently and faithfully to set downe in severall columnes, not only the Rumbe they goe on, and the measure of the Ships way in degrees, and the observations of latitude, and variation of their compasse; but also their conjectures and reasons of the correction they make of the aberrations they shall find, and the quality or condition of their Ship, and the diversities and seasons of the windes, and the secret motions or agitations of the Seas, when they beginne, and how long they continue, how farre they extend, and with what inequallity; and what else they shall observe at Sea worthy consideration, and will be pleased freely to communicate the same with Artists, such as are indeed skilfull in the Mathematicks, and lovers and inquirers of the truth: I doubt not but there shall in convenient time be brought to light many necessary præcepts, which may tend to the perfecting of navigation, and the help and saftie of such, whose vocations doe enforce them to commit their lives and estates in the vast and wide Ocean to the providence of God.[4]

This appeal apparently went unanswered but contemporary instances of growing interest can be found. Luke Foxe, sailor, explorer and friend of Henry Briggs (1561–1630), the first Gresham professor of geometry, although maintaining for the most part a strictly professional attitude to observations at sea, sometimes permitted himself to speculate. When he was discussing the possibility of a North West Passage in the light of Sir Humphrey Gilbert's arguments (*see* Ch. 3) he began to consider why Orkney and Shetland should be free of ice, unlike places in the same latitude on the other side of the Atlantic:

The cause may be the Seas moving about them, their circuits being so small, as the Seas breathing through the Tydes and winds continuall chafing about them, doth evaporate some part of his waremesse into the Ayre, whereby the frost is restrained from the exercise of his power; for the Sea hath a kinde of temperature betwixt too hot and too colde in the hot and cold *Zones*.[5]

A year or two later John Greaves (1602–1652), professor of geometry at Gresham College and later Savilian professor of astronomy at Oxford, travelled to the Mediterranean and was struck by the seeming paradox of an apparently continuous inflow of water through the Strait of Gibraltar. He set down his thoughts on the subject in his study of the pyramids, published in 1646.[6]

From what he had seen in the Strait he

could not so easily be satisfied with that received opinion, that at the streights of *Gibraltar* the sea enters in at the one side, and at the same time passes out at the other.

According to his own observations, with which the captain of the ship in which he was a passenger agreed, there was only one current and this flowed into the Mediterranean Sea. Yet on the face of it, it was impossible that this enclosed sea could absorb all this water, not to mention the rivers of Europe and Africa, without any apparent change of level. By way of explanation Greaves adopted the old idea of subterranean links between seas:

I imagine it to be no absurdity in Philosophy, to say that the earth is tubulous, and that there is a large passage under ground from one sea to another.

He continued

That which gave me occasion of entring into the speculation was this; that in the longitude of eleven degrees, and latitude of forty one degrees, having borrowed the tackling of six ships, and in a calm day sounded with a plummet of almost twenty pounds weight, carefully steering the boat, and keeping the plummet in a just perpendicular, at a thousand forty five *English* fathoms, that is, at above an *English* mile and a quarter in depth, I could find no land or bottom.

This was the deepest sounding known to Robert Hooke (1635–1703) in 1691.[7]

At the same time the possibilities of using instruments for sounding were also envisaged. R. P. Multhauf mentions a patent for a sounding machine taken out by Sir John V. van Berg in 1636.[8] Among the ideas produced by Sir Christopher Wren (1632–1723) during his early years at Wadham College were

Inventions for better making and fortifying Havens, for clearing Sands, and to sound at Sea.[9]

It is not clear whether the primary purpose of these instruments was intended to be for navigational use or scientific enquiry, most likely the former, but the distinction is not perhaps important here.

As one would expect, practical interest in the sea was usually centred on tides because of their relevance to discussions of the system of the universe. In the years preceding 1660 the earliest recorded systematic observations of tides for scientific purposes were those made by the astronomer Jeremiah Horrocks (1617 ?–1641) at Toxteth near Liverpool,[10] the results of which have unfortunately not survived. On 3 October 1640 he wrote to his friend William Crabtree (1610–?1644) of Manchester telling him that he was beginning to study tides.[11] In December he wrote again saying that his observations had been going on for three months and that he hoped that if they could be prolonged for a year he would learn enough about tides to obtain proof from them of the earth's rotation.[12] This was not to be; early in January 1641 Horrocks died and the record of his observations presumably perished, as did the bulk of his papers, in the civil wars and the Fire of London.

In 1669 Joshua Childrey (1623–1670) wrote to Henry Oldenburg (1615?–1677), Secretary of the Royal Society,

I first fell in love with the Lord Bacon's Philosophy in the year 1646.[13]

His letter to the Royal Society and the book *Britannia Baconica*, which he published in 1661, show that he made continuous observations of the weather over some years and was compiling lists of information on natural phenomena. During the 1650s he collected instances of abnormally high tides both from his own experience and from historical records and put forward the suggestion that variations in the moon's distance from the earth were partly responsible for determining the height of tides.[14]

In 1661 Sir Robert Moray (1608–1673) communicated a paper to the Royal Society on unusual tides in the Western Isles of Scotland.[15] His account was based principally on observations made on Berneray in the Outer Hebrides during the month of August some years before. Robertson, his biographer, assigns this work to the period following the collapse of the Glencairn rebellion in July 1654 when Moray became a fugitive, eventually escaping to the continent where he remained until the Restoration. There he passed his time in the study of science.[16] In January 1658 he wrote to his friend Alexander Bruce (1629–1681), later Earl of Kincardine:

I think I may venture to say you are not well enough acquainted with the duration of ebbes and floods yet. I will not now begin to indoctrinate you, the truth is, that is one of the Sciences I find most imperfect. I have sent a list to Kircherus whom I have encouraged to labour to perfect it.[17]

Moray's own observations were sufficiently thorough to enable him to detect a mathematical progression in the varying rates of rise and fall both of the diurnal tides and in the twice monthly cycle of springs and neaps. An entry in the Royal Society minutes for 22 August 1666 reads

Sir ROBERT MORAY relating what he had observed in Scotland concerning a certain and constant proportion of the increase of the tides from the quarter to the spring-tide, and their decrease from the spring-tide to the quarter, as likewise of the ebb's rising and falling constantly after the same manner; he was desired to put the particulars of it in writing, and to draw up directions for observations, to find out in what proportion these increases and decreases, risings and fallings happen to be in regard of one another; which proportion Sir ROBERT conjectured to be that of sines, or something near it.[18]

It was interest in investigating Descartes's theory of tides, and through this the validity of his theory of the universe, that led Sir Christopher

Wren to ask Robert Boyle to construct a barometer and see if the passage of the moon across the meridian was accompanied by compression of the atmosphere. This had unexpected results:

THE Time, when these Observations were made, was about the Year 1658, or 59; at which Time Mr. *Boyle* having a Barometer fixed up, for the observing the Moon's Influence upon the Waters, happened to discover the use of it in relation to the Weather.[19]

Other examples might doubtless be found in the years before 1660 of a growing practical interest in the sea prompted either by the significance of tides in the cosmological debate leading from the ideas of Galileo and Descartes or by the comprehensive curiosity about the natural world, rooted for someone like Childrey in the works of Sir Francis Bacon. Given the greater freedom of travel and more stable conditions after 1660 and the possibilities which better organization and communication provided, particularly through the activities of the Royal Society, the difference between the intermittent interest displayed in marine science before the Restoration and the striking and more easily reconstructed achievements afterwards seems at first sight to bear the interpretation that it may be the quality of the evidence that has changed rather than the underlying activity but though it is certainly to the years before 1660 that we have to look for the origin of the developments which revolutionized marine science during the reign of Charles II, only in a few cases as with Sir Robert Moray, can individual concern be traced back unequivocally into the earlier period. Furthermore, although developments in scientific thought and the growing importance of navigation and seamanship, together with an increasing awareness of the possibilities of scientific investigation, had already aroused British scientists to activity before 1660, their ideas about the sea were still largely dominated by the mixture of traditional thought and modern theory to be found in the scientific works of the time (*see* Ch. 3) and it was in the years after the Restoration that the decisive events occurred which made the science of the sea more forward looking.

Whatever the truth in the debate about the ultimate origins of the Royal Society there seems to be no reason to doubt Birch's account of events immediately preceding its inception:

The greatest part of the Oxford society coming to London about the year 1659, they usually met at Gresham College at the Wednesday's lecture upon astronomy by Mr. Christopher Wren, at the Thursday's upon geometry by Mr. Laurence Rooke; where they were joined by William lord viscount Brouncker, William Brereton, esq; afterwards lord Brereton, Sir Paul Neile, John Evelyn, esq; Thomas Henshaw, esq; Henry Slingesby, esq; Dr. Timothy Clarke, Dr. Ent, William Balle, esq; Abraham Hill, esq; Mr. (afterwards Dr.) William Croune, and divers other gentlemen, whose inclinations lay the same way."[20]

Growing disorder put an end to these meetings for the time being but after the Restoration they were resumed and, in November 1660, put on an organized footing. Membership of the new society was by election and meetings were held once a week. At first presidents were elected monthly and Sir Robert Moray was the first to be chosen, being re-elected on several occasions, but when the Royal Society received its first charter in July 1662 Lord Brouncker was elected president and held office until 1677.[21]

The first indication that the Society was taking a practical interest in marine research occurs in the minutes of the meeting on 14 June 1661 when a document containing *Propositions of some experiments to be made by the Earl of Sandwich in his present voyage* was registered.[22] This was a list of instructions specially prepared, we are not told by whom, for use on the naval expedition to the Mediterranean of 1661–1662 under the command of Edward Montagu, Earl of Sandwich (1625–1672). The six topics of inquiry were to be the depth of the sea, horizontal and vertical variations in its salinity, the pressure of sea water, tides and currents in the Strait of Gibraltar and luminescence (*see* Appendix, pp. 407–408).

To measure the depth of the sea the Society recommended the use of a sounding machine of the type derived from Alberti's writings, though the immediate source of information seems to have been Riccioli's *Almagestum Novum*,[23] a wooden float to be used with a lead shaped like a figure 7. Differences in salinity should be measured firstly by weighing the same volume of water from different latitudes or from different depths and secondly by evaporating samples to dryness and weighing the salt which remained. For bringing up water from below the surface it was proposed to use an instrument working on the same principle as a pump.

These three categories of experiment clearly originate in the literary tradition which, in these fields, was all that would-be observers had to go on. The machine for sounding without a line had been discussed by writers of the fifteenth, sixteenth and early seventeenth centuries (*see* Ch. 3). As seen in earlier chapters the idea that the sea might be salt only at the surface had a long history and was still current in the seventeenth century, as was the idea to be found in medieval writers, that the sea would get more salt towards the equator. Neither of these ideas had been conclusively put to the test. Of the other three topics of inquiry, two seem to have been suggested by sailors' reports of the increase of pressure below the surface and of phosphorescence. The same is probably true of the instruction about observing tides and currents in the Strait of Gibraltar. This is particularly interesting because it contains the earliest reference so far known to the possibility that an undercurrent might exist in the Strait (*see* Ch. 7).

The existence of a programme of research as detailed and as well thought out as this shows how, at an early stage in its life, the Royal Society was already interested in the possibility of improving the standard of knowledge about the sea beyond that to be found in contemporary works on science and had outlined specific problems to be investigated and the methods to be used. This gives the *Propositions* an intrinsic interest besides the distinction of being apparently the first schedule of purely oceanographic research. Unfortunately there is no indication that the Earl of Sandwich ever put these suggestions into practice. Results of astronomical observations made during the voyage are preserved[24] but no specific mention of any oceanographic work has yet come to light. It is quite possible that nothing was done, though later analogies show that this should not be too readily assumed.

It would be interesting to know more about the preparation of these instructions. They may well have been the work of Lawrence Rooke (1622–1662). It has been suggested that Rooke, whose home was at Deptford, derived his interest in the sea from associating with the naval officers and shipbuilders at Greenwich as had the Gresham professors of the early seventeenth century.[2, 25] This is well-founded speculation but it is certain that in January 1662 he drew up *Directions for Seamen bound for far Voyages* for one of the East India Company's captains.[26]

The *Directions* differ considerably from the instructions prepared for the Earl of Sandwich. They were designed to provide a comprehensive programme of research for the scientifically orientated sailor who was asked to record magnetic dip and variation, weather, comets and other phenomena and the topography of coastlines and to make observations of eclipses, as well for oceanographic information. The observer was to discover the times of tides, the direction of tidal streams and the maximum variation of sea level between high and low water, particularly at ports and at oceanic islands like St Helena. He was also "to sound the Depth of the Ocean in severall places" with an instrument like that recommended to the Earl of Sandwich. Finally he was to measure variations in salinity in different latitudes and at different depths by comparing the weight of equal volumes of water. The idea of using a pump for bringing up samples from below the surface was abandoned in favour of a cylinder with a valve at each end:

Take a vessell of mettall made like a pinte pott or a Cilinder and haveing two valvas both opening upwards, one in the bottome, the other on the topp of the vessell, soe that while it descends, both valvas being open, leaves free passage for the water to passe through it, then when it is neere the bottome as soone as it is pulled up the valvas will shutt, and the vessell bring the water that is then in it.

To interpret results obtained with the sounding machine it was necessary to have accurate information on the time taken by the float to return from different depths of water. On 19 March 1662 Lord Brouncker (1620?–1684) gave an account of how a wooden float had been sunk in water and was asked to try it out at sea.[27] On the same day he and Sir Robert Moray made experiments in the Thames and showed that on repeated attempts identical times were obtained in the same depth of water, even when the current was strong.[28] Early in June of the same year Moray visited Portsmouth and while there carried out a much more extensive series of trials with the sounding machine, again apparently with the assistance of Lord Brouncker.[29] Observations were made in depths of up to 100 feet and the times measured in seconds with a pendulum. Most of the observations were checked several times and the results showed, though this conclusion was not expressly drawn at this stage, that, with the apparatus then used, 5 feet of depth was to be allowed for every second of time that the float stayed under water.[30] The only difficulty encountered was that of actually seeing the float among the waves at the precise moment when it came to the surface. A few months later Abraham Hill (1635–1722) reported a similar experiment made by William Ball (1627–1690) but a mistake was found in the results.[31]

In November 1662 Robert Hooke came to London from Oxford as the Society's curator of experiments.[32] In January 1663 he gave an account of how he had constructed a water barometer, in which a column of water 33 feet high was counterbalanced by the pressure of the air.[33] One way in which knowledge acquired through this experiment might be put to use would, he thought, be to

help us to guess at the pressure of the sea-water against air let down to the bottom of it in a diving-engine, by knowing the proportion between the gravity of salt and fresh-water, and the depth, to which the engine is let down: but yet it were very desireable, that such, as have the opportunity of making trials at sea, would be diligent in it. For though there seems to be no doubt, but that the water there does proportionally press according to its perpendicular height, yet it is not easy to predict, how much it may vary from this hypothesis; which deviation may be caused, either by the extreme cold at the bottom of the sea, which may weaken the spring of the air; or from the differing gravity of the upper and lower parts of the salt-water; or from somewhat else, whereof we may be yet ignorant.

He suggested that experiments should be made with a glass jar with a capacity of about a gallon fitted with a brass screw top either with a small hole pierced in it or with a pipe let through and bent so that it opened downwards. By measuring the amount of water brought up in the jar from different depths it would be possible to

give a true account of the pressure of the water at the bottom, without going thither.

At the next meeting Sir Robert Moray suggested that as some of the Society intended to go to the Downs they might try condensing air in this way.[34] Presumably this was the expedition undertaken in order to test the pendulum watches designed by Alexander Bruce for calculating longitude at sea, to which Moray referred in a letter to Christiaan Huygens (1629–1695) written on 19 February:

La semaine prochaine Nous pretendons faire un petit voyage par mer aussi loin qu'aux Dunes, pour essayer les Horologes de Monsieur Bruce qu'il tasche cependant d'adiuster le mieux qu'il se peut.[35]

It was Moray, Bruce and Brouncker who carried out the series of oceanographic experiments "upon the river of Chatham" on 11, 12 and 13 March 1663.[36] Hooke was by his own account present at the experiments with the watches and presumably took part in the oceanographic work as well.[37]

Using a glass pipe which was sealed at one end and bent over at the other they measured the volume of water which entered the apparatus at depths ranging from 8 to 97 feet. The results were in fact illustrative of Boyle's law that the volume of a gas varies inversely in proportion to pressure but this conclusion was not explicitly drawn. Similar experiments were made by lowering upside down a glass bottle fitted with a valve opening inwards in the neck and using a bottle with a bent copper pipe fitted in the neck. They also lowered the instruments to different depths and left them there for some time, attached to a buoy made from a bundle of corks. They attributed slight differences in the results from any one depth to the effect of waves.

The experimenters were not unmindful of Hooke's warning about the effect which changes in temperature and salinity in the water might have on their results. They compared the weight of the water in the Medway with an equal volume of Thames water from Greenwich and found that the Thames water was lighter in the ratio 45 : 46. They also tried to measure variations in temperature between the surface and the bottom of the river with a thermometer, perhaps the first time that this relatively new instrument had been put to such a purpose:

A sealed-up thermometer . . . was let down to the bottom of the water, at the depth of sixteen fathom and a foot, and there suffered to stay a good while, that the coldness of the water might condense the included liquor so far, as to suffer the air to get into the bigger ball, which was therefore placed uppermost. But though the thermometer was suffered to lie a good while at that depth, and then suddenly pulled up, we could not find, that it had any whit more condensed the liquor, than the same would be by being kept a good while under the surface of the water at the top. Whence we judged the temperature of the water, both at the top, in the middle (for by other trials we found the same at other depths) and at the bottom, to be the same.

It was perhaps on this occasion that further experiments with the machine for sounding without a line were made. The second version of the *Directions for Seamen* tells us that experiments were made in the channel at Sheerness over two days by Lord Brouncker, Moray and

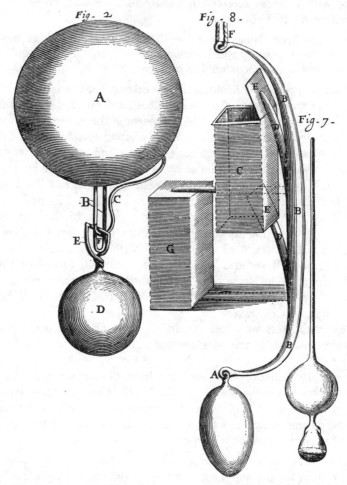

FIG. 3. The instruments for sounding and water sampling as suggested in the *Directions for Seamen* and improved by Robert Hooke, with a hydrometer. Published in *Phil. Trans.* (April 1667). Vol. **2**, No. 24.(Reproduced by permission of the Royal Society.)

Hooke.[38] Between twenty and thirty trials were made with the type of instrument described in the Earl of Sandwich's instructions and in Rooke's *Directions* to see at what angle the two arms of the lead should join to give the best results:

In all these Trials, the greatest difficulty was, in the use of Conical Figures, with Iron Crooks, to bend the Iron, that it might be sure to carry down the Ball with it to the bottom, and when come thither, to let it go: for almost every one of these Leads failed in one of these requisites, till by several Trials they had been adjusted.

With the information provided by the successful attempts they calculated that 5 feet of depth should be allowed for every second that the globe was underwater. This work must have been done before September 1663 when Hooke introduced the new type of sounding machine associated with his name (*see* p. 80) and from the combination of the place and the people taking part it seems likely that it should be regarded as part of the work done in March 1663.

Back in London Lord Brouncker and the others reported on their work to the Society and John Evelyn recorded this in his Diary for March 1663:

24 To Lond: 25. After pub: prayers to our Society, where was an account of severall Experiments made lately at *Sea* by our President & other members a fortnight before.[39]

At the same time the Royal Society was endeavouring to extend its field of research to the ocean itself. One of its members, John Winthrop (1606–1676), had come to London from New England to obtain a royal charter for Connecticut.[40] He was now on the verge of sailing for home and the Society asked him to take a copy of the *Directions for Seamen*, a dozen leads, three or four floats and a cylindrical vessel with valves for bringing up water and to make experiments on the way.[41] Winthrop agreed and the instruments were duly provided.[42] At the same meeting Moray, John Wilkins (1614?–1672) and Hooke were directed to try out two kinds of cylindrical vessels for bringing up water from the bottom of the sea.[42]

On the same occasion that Winthrop was asked to undertake this work Moray suggested that a similar request should be made to Captain Robert Holmes (1622–1692) who was about to set sail for the Straits.[41] On 1 April he was given a copy of the *Directions* and Hooke was instructed to demonstrate the use of the instruments to him.[43] Holmes carried out two sets of experiments in the Bay of Biscay (*see* Appendix, p. 409). On 2 May in a depth of 125 fathoms he made several attempts to use the sounding machine apparently without much success and brought up water from the bottom in the sampler which he found to be lighter and fresher than the water at the surface.[44] The observations were repeated with much the same result on 30 May in 145 fathoms off Cap St Marie.

Winthrop was less successful in his attempts at making observations with the Society's instruments. He wrote reporting that the sounding machine had not worked because there had been too much wind and that the water sampler had leaked.[45] To William Brereton (1631–1680) he wrote

there could be no pfect triall of yᵉ. instrument for depths at sea, the motion of the waves unhookes the lead, &c.[46]

Oldenburg wrote back saying that the Society felt that the experiments should be made in calm weather and that Captain Silas Taylor (1624–1678) who was going to Virginia had offered to repeat the experiments on the way.[47]

On hearing of the failure of Winthrop's apparatus Hooke suggested that better ways of making these observations could be found and the Society asked him to produce some plans. He showed his designs at the following meeting and the operator was told to make models from them.[48] Finally on 30 September Hooke demonstrated his new versions of the instruments for sounding and bringing up water to the Society:*

The way, which I prefer before several other contrivances, which I thought of, for sounding the depth of the sea; and fetching up water from any depth, are these:

The first is with a ball sunk to the bottom of the sea by a weight of lead or stone, the which as soon as it toucheth it, presently returns toward the top of the water, leaving the weight behind, which is thus contrived. Between the long wire staple B, of the ball A, I press in with my fingers a springing wire C, on the bended end F, on which I hang the weight D, by its ring E, and so let them down into the water in this posture; towards the bottom of which they are carried with a considerable swiftness; which the weight D touching first, is thereby stopped; but the ball, by the impetus it acquired in descending, being carried downwards a little after the other is stopped, suffers the springing wire C, to fly back, and thereby sets itself at liberty to re-ascend.

The way for fetching up water from any depth in the sea, is with a square wooden bucket C, whose bottoms EE are so contrived, that, as the weight A, sinks the iron B, (to which the bucket C, is fastened by the two handles DD, on the ends of which are the movable bottoms or valves EE) and consequently draws down the bucket, the resistance of the water to its descending, keeps up the bucket in the posture C, whereby the water has all the while it is descending, a clear passage through; whereas, as soon as the bucket is pulled upwards by the line F, the resistance of the water to that motion beats the bucket downwards, and keeps in the posture G, whereby the included water is preserved from getting out, and the ambient air from getting in.[49]

These are the two instruments most frequently associated with Hooke's contribution to marine research. Descriptions of them were printed in early numbers of the *Philosophical Transactions*—in no. 9, February 1666, and no. 24, April 1667.[50] In May 1666 a French version appeared in the *Journal des Sçavans*[51] where it provoked critical comment from M. Petit,

* See Fig. 3.

Intendant of Fortifications.[52] Petit objected that the instruments were claimed as new inventions and that the descriptions were not clear. He maintained that not enough was known about the behaviour of bodies sinking and rising in water to enable time to be used as a direct indication of depth. If bodies falling in air experienced acceleration it was possible that they might in water too. As for the water-sampler he thought it an unnecessarily complicated device for such work, showing incidentally that, as one might expect, activity in such matters was not confined to Great Britain. He recalled

j'ay fait la même chose autrefois avec une pompe de cuivre d'environ un pied de longueur, à double soupape, que je laissois tomber dans la mer avec une corde, & qui faisoit le même effet que vostre sceau avec son plomb & tout son appareil; car les soupapes s'ouvrant en descandant, se sermoient en montant, & rapportoient de l'eau du fond de la mer.

Mais j'ay toûjours trouvé cette eau salée jusqu'a la profondeur de 5 au 6 brasses, n'ayant point fait d'experiences plus bas. Et certainement si on veut consulter l'experiençe & la bonne Physique, la mer doit estre plus salée au fond qu'en sa superficie, puisque le sel estant plus pesant que l'eau, doit demeurer au bas.

On the face of it there was some truth in Petit's objections. No one of course who was acquainted with the previous work of the Royal Society could have supposed that there was any deliberate intention of claiming originality for the new instruments. That Petit should have supposed that there was, was due to the French version which spoke of Hooke as "l'Auteur de ces deux nouvelles inventions".[53] Yet apparently Robert Boyle felt that insufficient acknowledgment had been made of previous work for Oldenburg wrote to him in March 1666 defending himself and Hooke on the charge of misrepresenting the degree of Hooke's achievement.[54] Oldenburg argued that the passages in the *Philosophical Transactions* could only be interpreted as describing new versions of old ideas. Hooke, he said,

assures me, that that way of sounding with a round leaden or stone ball, he borrowed from no author.[54]

It was unequivocally the improvement of the design of both instruments which was Hooke's contribution; for the sounding machine, as he later said, it was the

peculiar contrivance of the application of the leaden weight to the ball, which he had invented and made use of.[55]

There is no reason to suppose that either he or Oldenburg had any thought of claiming any credit for his work except in this respect. What did give Petit's criticisms their force was that Oldenburg had printed the descriptions of Hooke's instruments with the relevant portions of Rooke's *Directions*[56] without any introduction or explanation and had not therefore given a full picture of the state of knowledge as it then was. He had to rectify these omissions in his reply to Petit's remarks.

Oldenburg defended himself and Hooke against the charge of plagiarism and in a tone verging on the self-righteous argued that the descriptions were perfectly comprehensible to any one conversant with the English language.[57] Hooke's more complicated version of the water-sampler was necessary since

that way, which the *French* Author recommends for this purpose as more simple, *Videl. a Brass-Pump with double Valves*, is not at all unknown in *England*, nor has bin left untried there; but was found inconvenient, in respect that the Valves in descending did not fully open, and give the water a free passage through the Cavity of the Vessel, nor in ascending shut so close, as to hinder the water from coming in at the top.

He denied that the main purpose of this instrument was to satisfy a naive curiosity to see whether the sea were salt at the bottom or not. Its first use was

to know the *degrees of Saltness* of the water according to its nearness to the top or bottom; or rather to know the constitution of the Sea-water in several depths of several *Climats*, which is a matter, much better to be found out by *Triall*, than *Discourse*.

The most important clarification which Oldenburg made was in showing that the discovery that a simple proportion existed between the time given by the sounding machine and the depth of the water in experiments made at sea had been followed up by investigation into the behaviour of objects sinking in water which showed why this was so. The reason was that the resistance of the water counteracted the acceleration due to gravity or, as Oldenburg put it

after it is sunk one or two fathoms into the Water, it has there arrived to its greatest swiftness, and keeps, after that, an equal degree of velocity; the *Resistance* of the water being then found equal to the *Endeavour* of the heavy Body downwards.

This discovery followed work done in 1664. It is difficult to be certain from the context whether Waller was referring to this or to the earlier work at sea when he wrote in his *Life of Hooke* that

About this time many Experiments were made of the Velocity of Bodies sinking and rising in Water, in order to ascertain that Contrivance, which was after made publick, of sounding the Seas depth with the sounding Ball, which is too well known to insist on it.[58]

Unequivocal evidence appears in a letter written by Hooke to Robert Boyle on 21 October 1664:

we did yesterday try the descent of bodies through water.

He expressed the hope that they would as a result

be able to raise a true theory of the resistance of a fluid medium.[59]

It would seem that this work was the basis for the explanation of the theory behind the sounding machine given by Oldenburg and, later on, by Hooke.[60]

The Society directed that Hooke's new sounding machine should be among the exhibits arranged for the visit of Charles II, which was planned in October 1663 but apparently never took place.[61] On a more practical level it issued the new instruments to Robert Holmes who was about to sail for West Africa.[62] Hooke was instructed to try out the instruments in the Thames for Holmes's benefit and "found them to do exceeding well". Whether Holmes was more successful with them than in his earlier attempts can only be conjectured for the document which contained the results of his work with the pendulum watches which was discussed by the Society in 1665,[63] and in which, by analogy with his earlier voyage, one might expect to find any record of oceanographic work, is missing. His journal for the voyage contains no reference to it.[64]

During 1664 a marked lessening of activity in marine research is found as far as the meetings of the Royal Society are concerned though techniques of diving aroused some interest. Sir Robert Moray undertook to ask Prince Rupert to make observations with Hooke's instruments during the naval expedition to Guinea which was being discussed in the autumn of 1664 but never materialized.[65] Moray, Sir Paul Neile (1613–1686) and Dr Thomas Wren (1633–1679) reported on, among other things, irregularities in the tides at Poole observed during a visit.[66] This lull continued until May 1666 when the publication of Wallis's theory of tides again brought marine science back into the forefront of discussion (*see* Ch. 5).

This did not mean that the early work was no longer thought to be important. As already seen experiments leading to an understanding of the theory behind the use of the sounding machine were being made. In 1665 Oldenburg began publishing papers on work already done in the early numbers of the *Philosophical Transactions*. Beginning with the paper on tides which Moray had given to the Society in 1661,[15] he went on to publish Rooke's *Directions for Seamen* together with Hooke's new instruments as an *Appendix* and his own reply to criticism in the *Journal des Sçavans*.[56, 57, 67] In the summer of 1666 he printed Wallis's essay on tides together with some of the discussion and proposals for research which it aroused[68] and a list of work to be done in other areas of marine science, specially compiled by Robert Boyle.[69] Number 24 of the *Philosophical Transactions* was devoted to a revised edition of the *Directions— Directions for Observations and Experiments to be made by Masters of Ships, Pilots, and other fit Persons in their Sea-Voyages*.[70] Apart from incorporating descriptions of Hooke's instruments and the experiments made with the earlier type of sounding machine this new version is principally remarkable for recommending the use of a hydrometer—

improved and first brought into use here divers years ago, by the Noble R. Boyle.

for measuring changes in the specific gravity of sea water.

In November 1666 the Society had adopted proposals put forward by Sir Robert Moray that the *Directions* and enquiries about tides should be printed and the necessary instruments made at the Society's expense and that the Duke of York should be asked to order that all ships should make the observations and record their results in two journals, one for the Society, the other for Trinity House.[71] It was no doubt this which led to the preparation of the new version of the *Directions*.

It was suggested that an additional instruction, to bring up samples of earth from the sea bed, should be added and Hooke was ordered to invent an easy instrument to do this. At the following meetings he produced plans and a model of the instrument but at the end of January he reported that it worked well only in shallow water though he was trying to improve it.[72]

The lessening of the Royal Society's direct involvement in marine science seems to be characteristic of the change in its role which took place after the first few years of its existence. Also members had taken the subject about as far as they could corporately. They had defined what the objects of research should be and had provided instruments, without which little could be done in an element as amorphous as the ocean. It now remained for those individuals who had the opportunity to take up the Society's initiative. They felt that more was to be learned, as Oldenburg put it, "by *Triall*, than *Discourse*" and there is evidence that some attempts were made to put this philosophy into practice. All the notable developments in the knowledge of physical oceanography which took place in Britain during the second half of the seventeenth century owed a great deal to the way in which the Royal Society had stimulated activity throughout a wide and varied circle of people, extending beyond its own membership. In the collection of tidal observations, some of which were used by Newton in the *Principia*, in research into the currents in the Strait of Gibraltar, in the collection of the observations which Boyle used in his oceanographic papers and in other work of different kinds a large number of people were involved whose interest can sometimes be shown to have originated in the days before the foundation of the Society but all of whom participated in the general enthusiasm for acquiring information and many of whom can be shown to have derived an interest in the sea directly from the Society's publications.

It has been rather too readily assumed in the past that the Royal Society's efforts to win co-operation from outsiders through the *Directions for Seamen* and similar instructions were an outright failure. Of the experiments which the Society itself initiated Winthrop's unsuccessful attempts have often been referred to but no one seems to have noted Holmes's results of May 1663. It is not entirely safe to assume that the Earl of Sandwich, Silas Taylor and Holmes on his second voyage did not attempt to carry out the experiments entrusted to them even if there should never be located any record of results. It is more than likely that more attention was paid to the possibility of using Hooke's instruments and their predecessors than would at first sight appear. The reason that we do not hear more about them is the difficulty which observers had in obtaining unequivocal results. Sir Jonas Moore (1615–1679), who went out to Tangier in 1663, told the Royal Society many years later:

that he had made many trials with the ball and weights of lead for the sounding the depth of the sea: and that he had found it exceedingly difficult to determine any thing by them, by reason that it was almost impossible to discover them certainly at their first appearing above water, though they would often leap into the air to a considerable hight; and that was because they would often rise two hundred fathoms from the place, where they were let down into the water. That of twelve, which he had tried at the Straits mouth, not one was found at its first appearance.[73]

In addition to these disadvantages, which were immediately obvious to contemporaries, there was the overall drawback, which they did not appreciate, which was that at great depths the wooden float would become waterlogged as a result of the pressure of the water.

As well as encouraging trials of oceanographic equipment the Royal Society obtained information about the sea through sending out questionnaires on different countries. In November 1662 Colwall suggested that an enquiry about tides should be sent to St Helena, a place particularly mentioned by Rooke in his *Directions*.[74] The following year a reply was received from the governor describing tides and weather conditions.[75] It contained the information that the greatest difference between high and low water was not more than $4\frac{1}{2}$ feet. Early in the same year Oldenburg reported answers to questions on Greenland made by a Mr Grey who described the East and West Greenland currents, tides and the freshness of sea ice—"the cold forcing the saline parts away from the surface of the water"—and thought that the sea there was less salt than further south-wards.[76] Grey believed that falling snow helped to form ice on the surface of the sea and then accumulated on it to form "vast islands of ice". Another informant, writing about Iceland, gave information about tides and attributed the origin of icebergs to the glaciers of Greenland.[77] The Royal Society went on asking for information about the sea and Oldenburg continued to recommend the use of the *Directions* printed in no. 24 of the *Philosophical Transactions* in enquiries drawn up for individual travellers as long as he remained Secretary of the Society.[78]

Outside the immediate records of the Royal Society, in the general literature of the period, one may find further instances of interest in the sea, sometimes explicitly linked with its efforts to stimulate activity. Frederick Martens of Hamburg, who went to Spitsbergen in 1671 and on his return wrote an account of his experiences, was shown a copy of the Royal Society's enquiries for Iceland and Greenland which led him to revise his work and include in it what information he could recollect of scientific interest about the island and the sea around its shores.[79] He described the formation of waves, the colours of the sea and the ice.

Richard Bolland (*d.* 1678) wrote (in his *Mediterranean Journall*) of experiments typical of the kind of work attempted by the imitators of the Royal Society's observations. His account reveals a mixture of enthusiasm and unsound physics which one suspects was characteristic of efforts at this level.

It is well worthy the Curious, to consider the Nature and Quality of Water. April 25 1676, Upon the Ocean, in the Latitude of 38, I made fast a Glass-Bottle to a Dipsidge Lead and Line about 100 Fathoms long; the Bottle was fill'd full of air only, stopt. close with a good Cork well driven down: I lower'd it into 30 Fathom water; after a little while, I haul'd it up again, and found no alteration either in the Bottle or Cork. I took the Cork out, and fill'd the Bottle with Salt Water to the lower part of the Neck, then drove the Cork firmly in as before, leaving 3 inches distance betwixt it and the Salt water: I lower'd it down into 80 Fathom Water, and there let it stay a little time: when I haul'd it up, I found the Cork as firm as it was driven in, but the Vacancy betwixt it and the Salt-water quite filled up. I emptied the Saltwater all out, and cork'd the Bottle still firmly, shouldering the upper part of the Cork; so that there was now nothing in the Bottle but pure Air, which I let down into 70 Fathom Depth: hauling it up, I found the Cork which I had driven so hard in, now drawn into the Bottle, and the Bottle fill'd with Salt-water. The Reason of it I suppose to be this, that, the Bottle being let down into that cold Depth so remote from the influence of the Sun, the air in the Bottle was so condensed, that it was not able to contain it selfe within the Bottle, but forc'd of necessity either to break the Bottle, or find out a more easy way, which was by drawing in the Cork; and by this means it found its freedom, and took its passage to the Superficies of the water. Like this I conceive to be the Cause, why the Balls with Springs for finding Depths never answer'd the end they were design'd for; many of them having been hove overboard, but few or none ever obtain'd their Ressurection to inform those above of what they found below. I have been told by those who have lower'd a Bottle fill'd with air and well cork'd into 150 Fathom (which has reach'd the Bottom), letting the Line run with a heavy Lead so as to fall at once upon the Sand, that, the Cork hath been drawn-in, and the Bottle there filled with Water which has been fresh when halled up aloft. But this is an Information only, of what I never made experiment.[80]

The habit of making observations lasted long after the Royal Society had ceased to take a corporate interest in the sea.[81] Samuel Pepys (1633–1703), whose concern for the sea was as a rule strictly utilitarian, noted the making of such an experiment on the voyage out to Tangier in 1683:

This evening we had our experiments in the sea with a (bottle) let down 120 fathoms.[82]

More examples could be given to show that a quite lively interest in examining the less immediately useful aspects of the sea did exist in the second half of the seventeenth century and to show how the Royal Society had succeeded in creating or furthering enthusiasm. It would of course be exaggerating to assume that more than a small minority of sailors and travellers were involved but there can be no doubt that this minority existed. Their efforts brought them only a very moderate amount of success but this is hardly surprising when one considers the primitive nature of their instruments, the lack of theoretical guidance and background knowledge to direct their researches and the vastness of their field of study together with the slightness and ephemeral nature of the internal changes they were trying to measure.

The efforts of the Royal Society, too, had a limited success in that they did produce a measure of co-operation. The Society's work on the sea took only a small place among the many subjects clamouring for its attention. At best interest was intermittent and after 1666 it slowly died away as far as the majority of members were concerned. Nevertheless in its plans for research, its discussion of new ideas and its testing of apparatus the Society had laid a valuable foundation for the work of others which continued to produce results long after the original impulse had died away.

The aim of all this work seems to have varied very much from person to person. Sometimes, as was not uncommon in the seventeenth century, curiosity about the apparently miraculous was the motive, particularly in studies of the Strait of Gibraltar (*see* Ch. 7). The uniting theme was the dual ideal of expanding knowledge and improving man's environment which inspired the diverse activities of the Royal Society. Thus in the

introductory passages of the *Directions* and in the work of people like
Moray and Boyle, both of whom took an interest in the sea much beyond
the ordinary, research is seen as having a double motive; to know what
goes on in the sea is both interesting for its own sake and is expected to lead
to improvements in methods of seamanship and of deep-sea diving. As
Oldenburg put it, to know how to measure the depth of the sea and to
sample its water "may be of good use, both *Naval* and *Philosophical*".[83]

The successes here outlined seem to owe most to the efforts of three
people in particular. Sir Robert Moray's interest in marine research dates,
as we have seen, to well before 1660. During the early years of the Royal
Society's existence there are few occasions of research at sea or discussion
at home in which he was not involved and often, apparently, in the lead.
Perhaps it is no coincidence that it was when he ceased to take such an
active part in Society affairs that the decline in the level and frequency of
discussion of marine science at meetings set in. The second person whose
influence was clearly decisive at this stage was Henry Oldenburg. Through
his publication in the *Philosophical Transactions* of programmes of oceanographic research, descriptions of apparatus and controversial pieces such
as Wallis's essay on tides, he must have done far more than any other
single person to stimulate the wider interest spoken of earlier. Equally
important was his official work as Secretary of the Royal Society, corresponding with observers both in this country and overseas and sending out
queries addressed to travellers visiting different parts of the world, in both
of which activities many instances of interest in marine research occur.
Possibly of equal significance, but necessarily by the accident of his early
death a more problematic figure, is Lawrence Rooke whose work in
producing the original *Directions* makes it legitimate to suppose that he
may have been at least partially responsible for calling the Society's attention to the science of the sea.

4. NOTES

1. Marin Mersenne, *Cogitata Physico-Mathematica*, Paris (1644). "Ars Navi-
   gandi", bk 1, "Hydrostaticae", p. 228:
   > Prædicta propositio videtur mirabilis, cùm ex ea sequatur libram aquæ
   > super fundum cuiuscumque vasis, tantum, quantum mille libras, imo
   > quantum Oceanum integrum, grauitare. Si enim Oceanum vase includatur,
   > & aquæ libra vas impleat aliud, æquale fundum habens fundo vasis pre-
   > çedentis, tubum verò circa basim affixum tam angustum, ut totum vas
   > vnicam aquæ libram capiat, cuius altitudo æqualis sit altitudini vasis
   > Oceanum concludentis, aquæ libra, sui tubi fundum æquè premet, ac
   > suum Oceanus.

2. F. R. Johnson, "Gresham College: precursor of the Royal Society", *J. Hist. Ideas* (1940). Vol. **1**, pp. 413–438.
E. G. R. Taylor, *The Mathematical Practitioners of Tudor and Stuart England*, Cambridge (1954).

3. For an example of instructions see Prince Henry's instructions to Sir Thomas Button (1612) in *The Voyages of Captain Luke Foxe of Hull, and Captain Thomas James of Bristol, in Search of a North-West Passage in 1631–32* (ed. Miller Christy), Hakluyt Society, Vols. **88** and **89** (1894). Vol. **89**, pp. 636–637; for observations on tides, *ibid.* pp. 296, 299.

4. William Oughtred, *The Circles of Proportion and the Horizontal Instrument*, translated by William Forster, London (1633), part 2, pp. 55–56.

5. Luke Foxe, *North-West Fox* in *The Voyages of Captain Luke Foxe and Captain Thomas James, op. cit.* p. 428. *

6. John Greaves, *Pyramidographia: or, a Description of the Pyramids in Ægypt*, printed in *Miscellaneous Works of Mr. John Greaves* (ed. Thomas Birch) 2 vols, London (1737). Vol. **1**, pp. 137–138.

7. William Derham, *The Philosophical Experiments and Observations of the Late Eminent Dr. Robert Hooke*, London (1726), p. 229.

8. Robert P. Multhauf, "The line-less sounder: an episode in the history of scientific instruments", *J. Hist. Med.* (1960). Vol **15**, pp. 390–398.

9. "A catalogue of New Theories, Inventions, Experiments, and Mechanick Improvements, exhibited by Mr. Wren, at the first Assemblies at Wadham-College in Oxford, for Advancement of Natural and Experimental Knowledge, called then the New Philosophy: Some of which, on the Return of Public Tranquillity, were improved and perfected, and with other useful Discoveries, communicated to the Royal Society", in Christopher Wren jr, *Parentalia*, London (1750), p. 198.

10. Arundell Blount Whatton, *The Transit of Venus across the Sun by the Rev. Jeremiah Horrox*, London (1859), pp. 38–39.
D.N.B. Vol. **27**, pp. 373–375.

11. Jeremiah Horrocks, *Jeremiæ Horroccii, Liverpoliensis Angli, ex Palatinatu Lancastriæ, Opera Posthuma* (ed. John Wallis), London (1673), p. 334, Horrocks to Crabtree, 3 October 1640:
> De Maris fluxu & refluxu novas ego Observationes instituturus sum, ut possim experimentis edoctus, de hujus naturâ aliquid statuere. Parum autem adhuc est quod præstiti; nonnihil tamen reperi quod prius ignorabam.

12. *Ibid.* p. 337, Horrocks to Crabtree, 12 December 1640:
> Observationes meæ de Maris fluxu & refluxu multa mihi rara indicârunt, quæ tibi aliâ occasione impertiam. Est quidem valdè regularis, sed multis motuum varietatibus & inæqualitatibus miris obnoxius, à nullo hactenus notatis. Observationes hactenus nonnisi per tres menses continuavi, spero autem si per annum integrum hîc mansero, multa me detecturum secreta, ut quæ Telluris motum evidenter evincant. Verùm de his posthac.

13. Royal Society Letter Book C. 1, no 9, Childrey to Oldenburg, 12 July 1669.

14. *Ibid.* no. 4, Childrey to Seth Ward, Bishop of Salisbury, 31 March 1669 (1670). Joshua Childrey, *Britannia Baconica: Or, the Natural Rarities of England, Scotland, & Wales*, London (1661), pp. 93–96. See Ch. 5.

15. Royal Society Register Book (Copy) (March 1661). Vol. **1**, pp. 21–24, printed

as "A Relation of some extraordinary Tydes in the West-Isles of Scotland, as it was communicated by Sr. Robert Moray", *Phil. Trans.* (June 1665), no. 4, pp. 53–55.

16. Alexander Robertson, *The Life of Sir Robert Moray*, London (1922), p. 150.
17. *The Kincardine Papers* (MS. copy in the Library of the Royal Society), Moray to Bruce, 8/18 January 1658.
18. Thomas Birch, *The History of the Royal Society of London*, 4 vols, London (1756–1757). Vol. **2**, p. 111.
19. William Derham, *op. cit.* pp. 1–4.
20. Thomas Birch, *History of the Royal Society*. Vol. **1** (1756) p. 3.
21. Sir Henry Lyons, *The Royal Society, 1660–1940*, Cambridge (1944).
22. Thomas Birch, *History of the Royal Society*. Vol. **1** (1756) pp. 29–30.
23. *Ibid.* Vol. **3** (1757) p. 396.
24. *Ibid.* Vol. **1** (1756) p. 106.
    Edward Montagu, Earl of Sandwich, "Observations in his voyage to Portugal", 27 August 1662, *Royal Society Classified Papers*. Vol. **8**(i), no. 5.
25. Thomas Birch, *History of the Royal Society*. Vol. **1** (1756) pp. 68, 69, 74. This suggestion is made by Sir Harold Hartley.
26. Lawrence Rooke, 'Directions for Sea-men bound for farre Voyages", *Royal Society Register Book*. Vol. **1**, pp. 149–152.
27. Thomas Birch, *History of the Royal Society*. Vol. **1** (1756) p. 78.
28. *Ibid.* pp. 78–79. An account of these experiments is also given in *Phil. Trans.* (1667). Vol. **2**, no. 24, pp. 440–441.
29. Thomas Birch, *History of the Royal Society*. Vol. **1** (1756) pp. 86–87.
30. This relationship was explicitly stated later on (see p. 79).
31. Thomas Birch, *History of the Royal Society*. Vol. **1** (1756) p. 110.
32. *Ibid.* Vol. **1** (1756) p. 124.
33. *Ibid.* Vol. **1** (1756) pp. 180–182.
    William Derham, *op. cit.* pp. 96–99.
34. Thomas Birch, *History of the Royal Society*. Vol. **1** (1756) p. 192.
35. *Œuvres Complètes de Christiaan Huygens van Zuylichem*, La Haye, 22 vols (1888–1950). Vol. **4** (1891) p. 318, no. 1102. Moray to Huygens, 1 March 1663 (N.S.). Quoted by kind permission of the Hollandsche Maatschappij der Wetenschappen, Harlem.
36. Thomas Birch, *History of the Royal Society*. Vol. **1** (1756) pp. 208–212; William Derham, *op. cit.* pp. 100–106.
37. Robert Hooke, "The Lord Kingkardine's Observations of the Pendulum Clocks at Sea, in 1662", William Derham, *op. cit.* pp. 4–6. The date is given as 1662 because the custom of beginning the new year from 25 March was still in use.
38. "Directions for Observations and Experiments to be made by Masters of Ships, Pilots, and other fit Persons in their Sea-Voyages", *Phil. Trans.* (April 1667). *Vol. **2**, no. 24, pp. 441–443.
39. *The Diary of John Evelyn* (ed. E. S. de Beer), 6 vols (1955). Vol. **3**, p. 353. Quoted by kind permission of the Clarendon Press, Oxford.
40. Thomas Franklin Waters, *A Sketch of the Life of John Winthrop the Younger, the Founder of Ipswich, Massachusetts in 1633*, Publications of the Ipswich Historical Society (1899). Vol. **7**.
41. Thomas Birch, *History of the Royal Society*. Vol. **1** (1756) p. 207.
42. *Ibid.* p. 212.

43. *Ibid.* p. 215.
44. *Royal Society Classified Papers.* Vol. 3(i), no. 9. (*See* Appendix, p. 409).
45. Thomas Birch, *History of the Royal Society.* Vol. 1 (1756), p. 280.
    A. Rupert Hall and Marie Boas Hall, *The Correspondence of Henry Oldenburg,* 6 vols, Madison, Milwaukee and London, (1965–1969). Vol. 2 (1966) pp. 59–60, no. 274, say that this letter is not to be found.
46. Robert C. Winthrop, "Correspondence of Hartlib, Haak, Oldenburg, and others of the founders of the Royal Society, with Governor Winthrop of Connecticut, 1661–1672", *Proc. Mass. hist. Soc.* (1878). Vol. 16, pp. 219–220, Winthrop to Brereton, 6 November 1663.
47. *Ibid.* pp. 216–218, Oldenburg to Winthrop, 5 August 1663.
    The Correspondence of Henry Oldenburg, op. cit. Vol. 2 (1966), pp. 105–108, no. 289.
    Thomas Birch, *History of the Royal Society.* Vol. 1 (1756) p. 280. There is no record as far as I know that Taylor attempted the observations.
48. Thomas Birch, *op. cit.* pp. 280, 287, 296. See also (47) Oldenburg to Winthrop, 5 August 1663.
49. *Ibid.,* pp. 307–308.
50. "An Appendix to the Directions for Seamen, bound for far Voyages", *Phil. Trans.* (February 1666), no. 9, pp. 147–149.
    "Directions for Observations and Experiments to be made by Masters of Ships, Pilots, and other fit Persons in their Sea-Voyages", *Phil. Trans.* (April 1667). Vol. 2, no 24, pp. 439–443 and 447–448.
51. "Extrait du Journal d'Angleterre, touchant une nouvelle maniere de sonder la profondeur de la mer sans corde, & de reconnoistre la nature de l'eau qui est au fond de la mer", *J. Scavans* (3 May 1666). Vol. 1, no. 18, pp. 419–423.
52. "Extrait d'une Lettre écrite par M. Petit Intendant des Fortifications, à M. Galloys P. touchant la profondeur de la Mer, la nature de l'Eau qui est au fond de la Mer, & quelques autres curiositez", *J. Scavans* (24 May 1666). Vol. 1, no. 21, pp. 457–463.
53. "Extrait du Journal d'Angleterre", *op. cit.* p. 419.
54. *The Works of the Honourable Robert Boyle* (ed. Thomas Birch) (1744). Vol. 5, p. 353;
    The Correspondence of Henry Oldenburg, op. cit. Vol. 3 (1966) pp. 60–63, no. 498; Oldenburg to Boyle, 17 March 1665/6.
55. Birch, *History of the Royal Society* (1757). Vol. 3, p. 397.
56. In "An Appendix to the Directions for Seamen, bound for far Voyages", *Phil. Trans.* (February 1666), no. 9, pp. 147–149.
57. "Some Considerations Touching a Letter in the *Journal des Scavans* of May 24. 1666", in *Phil. Trans.* (June 1666), no. 13, pp. 228–230.
58. Richard Waller, *The Posthumous Works of Robert Hooke* (1705). p. x.
59. *The Works of the Honourable Robert Boyle, op. cit.* Vol. 5, p. 538, Hooke to Boyle, 21 October 1664.
60. Thomas Birch, *History of the Royal Society.* Vol. 3 (1757) pp. 397–398.
61. E. S. de Beer, "King Charles II, Fundator et Patronus", *Notes Rec. R. Soc. Lond.* (1960). Vol. 15, pp. 39–45.
62. Thomas Birch, *History of the Royal Society.* Vol. 1 (1756), pp. 328, 330–331.
63. *Ibid.* Vol. 2 (1756) pp. 23–24.
64. *Capt Robert Holms His Journalls of Two Voyages into Guynea in His Mat'*[s]

Ships the Henrietta and the Jersey in the years 1660/61 and 1663/64, in the Pepysian Library, Magdalene College, Cambridge, MS. no. 2698.

65. Thomas Birch, *History of the Royal Society*. Vol. 1 (1756), p. 467.
66. "Observations of Sr Robert Moray, Sr P. Neil and Dr Wren, made by them in their late excursion into ye Contry", *Royal Society Classified Papers*. Vol. 6, no. 17.
67. "Directions for Sea-men bound for far Voyages", *Phil. Trans.* (January 1666). no. 8, pp. 140–143.
68. John Wallis, "An essay about the flux and reflux of the sea" *Phil. Trans.* (August 1666), no. 16, pp. 263–281.
    See Chapter 5.
69. Robert Boyle, "Other Inquiries concerning the Sea", *Phil. Trans* (October 1666), no. 18, pp. 315–316. *See* Appendix, p. 410 and Chapter 6.
70. *Phil. Trans.* (April 1667). Vol. 2, no. 24, pp. 433–448.
71. Thomas Birch, *History of the Royal Society*. Vol. 2 (1756) p. 122.
72. *Ibid.* pp. 122, 133, 134, 136, 137, 143. The suggestion was originally made by Mr. Hoskyns (Sir John Hoskins, 1634–1705).
73. Thomas Birch, *History of the Royal Society*. Vol. 3 (1757), p. 399.
74. *Ibid.* Vol. 1 (1756) p. 120.
75. *Ibid.* Vol. 1 (1756) p. 296.
    "An Account of ye Tides at St. Helena, sent by ye Governor there, in a letter of April 30th 1663", *Royal Society Classified Papers*. Vol. 6, no. 14.
76. Thomas Birch, *op. cit.* Vol. 1 (1756) pp. 199–202.
77. *Ibid.* Vol. 1 (1756), pp. 491–494.
    Roger Flynt to Lord Brouncker, *Royal Society Letter Book* (Copy). Vol. 1, pp. 239–243, 14 November 1664.
78. These documents are to be found in the Royal Society's *Classified Papers*. Vol. 19.
79. Frederick Martens, *Voyage into Spitzbergen and Greenland*, printed in *A collection of Documents on Spitzbergen and Greenland* (ed. Adam White), Hakluyt Society. Vol. 18 (1855), pp. 26–31, and in *An Account of several late Voyages and Discoveries to the South and North . . . by Sir John Narborough* and others, London (1694).
80. Richard Bolland, *Mediterranean Journall*, pp. 65 and 68, MS. no. 2899 in the Pepysian Library, Magdalene College, Cambridge.
81. This seems to have died away completely by about 1680, *See* Ch. 8.
82. Edwin Chapell, *The Tangier Papers of Samuel Pepys*, Navy Records Society (1935). Vol. 73, p. 13, 8 September 1683. Quoted by kind permission of the Council of the Navy Records Society, London. The editor has supplied the word in brackets but the general sense is plain.
83. *Phil. Trans.* (February 1666), no. 9, p. 147.

Addenda et Corrigenda

p.89, n.5,1.2: *before*: *op cit.* insert Hakluyt Society
p.89, n.5,1.2:*after*: *op cit.* insert Vol **89,**
p.90,n.38,1.3: *after* no. **24,** *insert* pp. 433-438;

5. THEORIES AND OBSERVATIONS OF TIDES

THERE are few indications in the Royal Society minutes during the first five years of its existence that the problem of tides was arousing much interest among members. Questions included in the *Directions for Seamen* and similar guides for research brought in some information about the behaviour of tides in places as diverse as Greenland and St Helena (*see* Ch. 4, pp. 85–86) but the theoretical aspects were not explored at meetings. This was an unusual reversal of the tendency which had persisted since ancient times to discuss tides at the expense of the other characteristics of the sea.

It would, however, be misleading to assume that the question had lost its appeal. During the first half of the seventeenth century several explanations of tides were current; the magnetic or attractive hypothesis of Stevin, Gilbert and Kepler, the argument from the movement of the earth, principally developed by Galileo, and Descartes's theory that the ocean and atmosphere were compressed by the passage of the moon (*see* Ch. 3, pp. 50–52). In Britain the interest aroused by new ideas was linked in the 1640s and 1650s with a growing concern for empirical studies, as seen in the work of people like Horrocks, Childrey, Moray and Wren (*see* Ch. 4, pp. 71–73). Nevertheless the difficulty of establishing a precise relationship between the causes postulated and the appearances observed seems to have deterred most people from taking an active interest in what up to that time had been the most popular branch of marine science, though there were no doubts as to its importance.

Yet some discussion had been going on and out of this came the *Essay about the Flux and Reflux of the Sea*[1] by John Wallis (1616–1703). He sent the essay to the Royal Society in May 1666. By acting as a focus for discussion and observation it provided the necessary incentive for a new attack on tides. For this, he explained, Robert Boyle was responsible and he addressed the essay to him:

You were earnest with me, when you last went from hence, that I would put in writing somewhat of that, which at divers times, these three or four years last past, I have been discoursing with your self and others concerning the

Common Center of Gravity of the Earth and Moon, in order to salving the *Phænomena* as well of the *Seas Ebbing and Flowing*; as of some perplexities in *Astronomical Observations* of the *Places* of the Celestial Bodies.[2]

Wallis's letter was dated 25 April 1666 but a week before this Silas Taylor, who had offered to repeat Winthrop's experiments in 1663 (*see* Ch. 4, p. 80), wrote to Oldenburg from Harwich, apparently in answer to questions on the meeting of tidal streams in the North Sea.[3] In subsequent letters he described how, as he thought, the tide came across the Atlantic from the Gulf of Mexico and divided at the British Isles, one arm flowing round the southern end, partly into the Irish Sea and partly up the Channel and north along the coast of Flanders, the other flowing northwards, part coming down into the Irish Sea, the rest rounding Scotland and flowing down the east coast of England.[4]

Taylor, like Moray in the paper communicated to the Royal Society in 1661 (*see* Ch. 4, p. 72), and most of the contributions earlier, was dealing with the practical side of the science but Wallis who, as he freely admitted, had never made a practical study of tides,[5] was concerned with its theoretical aspect and with improving the theory of Galileo which he regarded as essentially correct but as in need of elaboration:

For that Discourse is to be looked upon onely as an *Essay* of the *general Hypothesis*; which as to *particulars* was to be afterwards adjusted, from a good *General History of Tides*; which it's manifest enough that he had not; and which is in a great measure yet wanting. For were the matter of fact well agreed on, it is not likely, that several Hypotheses should so far differ, as that one should make the Water *then* and *there* at the Highest, *where* and *when* the other makes it at the Lowest; as when the Moon is Vertical to the Place.[6]

Wallis agreed with Galileo in attributing tides to the effect of acceleration and retardation at different points on the earth's surface caused by the combination of its orbital and axial rotations. He quoted Galileo's example of the effect of interrupted movement on water in a container and also illustrated the idea from the behaviour of an object on an irregularly moving surface.

As it stood, however, Galileo's hypothesis would, he argued, account only for high water at noon or midnight. Balianus's hypothesis[7] would account for the necessary progression of the times of high water through twenty four hours every month but it was unlikely that the earth travelled round the moon as this theory entailed. Instead Wallis suggested that it was not the centre of gravity of the earth which made the annual orbit round the sun but a point some distance from it, the common centre of gravity of the earth and moon:

The Earth and Moon being known to be Bodies of so great connexion (whether by any Magnetick, or what other Tye, I will not determine; nor need I, as to this purpose;) as that the motion of the one follows that of the other; (The Moon observing the Earth as the Center of its *periodick* motion:) may well enough be looked upon as *one Body*, or rather *one Aggregate of Bodies*, which have *one common center of Gravity*; which Center (according to the known Laws of *Staticks* is in a streight Line connecting their respective Centers, so divided as * that its parts be in reciprocal proportion to the Gravities of the two Bodies.[8]

In addition to its annual and diurnal motions, therefore, the earth also moved in an epicycle round the common centre of gravity of the earth and moon. It was the combination of this movement with the other two which accounted for the long-established relationship between the moon's passage and the times of high water and for the twice monthly springs and neaps.

Was Wallis original in this idea or was he in fact only repeating a point implicit in Galileo's work? Dr E. J. Aiton and Dr H. L. Burstyn have produced arguments on this point in a recent volume of *Isis*.[9] Whatever the truth of the matter it seems certain that Wallis thought he was introducing a new idea. Discussing the ideas of Pierre Gassendi (1592–1655)[10] in the Appendix to his paper he said

though he would thus have the Earth and Moon looked upon as two parts of the same moved Aggregate, yet he doth still suppose (as *Galilæo* had done before him) that the line of the Mean Motion of this Aggregate (or, as he calls, *motus æquabilis et veluti medius*) is described by the *Center* of the *Earth* (about which Center he supposeth both its own revolution to be made, and an Epicycle described by the Moons motion;) not by another Point, distinct from the Centers of both, about which, as the common Center of Gravity, as well that of the Earth, as that of the Moon, are to describe several Epicycles.[11]

In 1695 he wrote to Newton

I understand you are now about adjusting the Moons Motions; and, amongst the rest, take notice of that of the *Comon Center of Gravity* of the Earth & Moon as a conjunct body: (a notion, which, I think, was first started by me, in my Discourse of the Flux and Reflux of the Sea.)[12]

His contemporaries do not seem to have challenged this assumption.

Wallis ascribed the annual spring tides to an inequality of natural days, caused by variations in the apparent movement of the sun in the ecliptic, and thought that they occurred in February and November:

I do particularly very well remember, that in *November* 1660. (the same year that his Majesty returned) having occasion to go by Coach from the *Strand* to *Westminster*, I found the Water so high in the middle of *King-street*, that it came up, not onely to the Boots, but into the Body of the Coach.[13] *

He thought that it might be possible to justify his ideas from astronomical observations if they enabled the earth's movement in an epicycle to be deduced from its position relative to the stars. The same explanation could also account for perturbations observed in the orbits of Jupiter and Saturn.

Wallis's paper was communicated to the Royal Society on 9 May 1666 and read on 16 May.[14] The principal points raised by members in the discussion which followed were that it seemed to them impossible for two separate bodies to have a common centre of gravity and that the times he assigned to the annual spring tides differed from those generally accepted, at the equinoxes.

Wallis was Savilian professor of geometry at Oxford and rarely attended the meetings of the London society. His defence of his paper was therefore conducted by letter[15] which is fortunate for us. He began by stressing, as he had in the essay itself,[16] that what he had done was to put forward a hypothesis to provoke further discussion and research. He wrote to Oldenburg on 19 May

Sir,

I received yours of May 17. and am very well contented that exceptions are made against my hypothesis concerning the Tydes; being proposed but as a conjecture to be examined, and upon that examination rectified if there be occasion, or rejected if it will not hold water.[17]

In the essay itself Wallis had declared his purpose of giving an explanation of tides without having recourse to the idea that the sea was influenced by "magnetic vertue" or any "occult quality"[18] but his hypothesis necessarily entailed admitting that some form of attraction existed between the sun and the earth and the earth and the moon while denying that attraction in itself had any effect on the water. He now made a much more forceful statement of his belief in some power of this kind. It was much easier, he said, to show that the attraction existed than to explain it:

how the Earth and the Moon are connected, I will not undertake to shew (nor is it necessary to my purpose,) but that there is somewhat that doth connect them (as much as what connects the Loadstone and Iron) is past doubt, to those who allow them to be carried about by the Sun as one aggregate or body whose parts keep a respective position to one another; like as Jupiter with his 4 Satellites, and Saturne with his one. Some ty there is that makes these Satellites attend their Lords, and move in a body, though wee doe not see the tye, or hear the word of command. And so here.[17]

To the objection that annual spring tides occur at the equinoxes he answered that the springs were due to the combined effect of the obliquity of the ecliptic and the apogee and perigee of the sun and repeated his assertion that they occurred in February and November. He himself had often noticed very high tides during November both in London and on Romney Marsh. The difference could only be settled by observation:

a good diary of the hight and time both of high-water and low-water, for a year or two together, even at Chatham, or Greenwich, but rather at some place in the open seas, as at the Point in Cornwall, or the West parts of Ireland; would do more to the resolving of this point; than any verball discours without it.[17]

This letter was read to the Royal Society on 23 May. On the same day Hooke read his paper "concerning the inflection of a direct motion into a curve by a supervening attractive principle",[19] an event of importance in the history of the idea of universal gravitation and very relevant to Wallis's hypothesis. Hooke argued that unless acted upon by external forces the planets would move in straight lines. One possibility of how their observed elliptical or circular paths were maintained was that the universe was filled with ether of varying density, perhaps increasing with distance from the sun so that a planet's natural motion was continually deflected by the greater resistance of the outer layers (an idea he had discussed as early as 1663,[20] in a paper on the effect of heat and cold on the density of water). The second possibility, the one which he preferred, was that the sun was able to attract the planets in the same way as the earth attracted the moon.

A demonstration of this idea was made, followed by an experiment to show what happened when a small globe was joined to and moved round a larger globe which was itself moving round another point:

The intention whereof was to explain the manner of the moon's motion about the earth, it appearing evidently thereby, that neither the bigger ball, which represented the earth, nor the less, which represented the moon, were moved in so perfect a circle or ellipsis, as otherwise they would have moved in, if either of them had been suspended and moved singly; but that a certain point, which seemed to be the center of gravity of these two bodies, howsoever posited (considered as one) seemed to be regularly moved in such a circle or ellipsis, the two balls having other peculiar motions in small epicycles about the said point.

Oldenburg, describing the experiment to Boyle in the same words that were used in the minute, wrote that the intention of the experiment was to throw light on Wallis's hypothesis "which has been pretty well sifted among us" and that Wallis was pleased with the result.[21]

The outcome of the experiment seemed favourable to Wallis's hypothesis about the common centre of gravity of the earth and moon but some members of the Society were not satisfied with his other arguments. Dr Jonathan Goddard (1617?–1675) objected that if Wallis's explanation were true spring tides should occur only once a month. Others pointed out that whereas spring tides occurred two or three days after new and full moon in British waters at some places in the East Indies they arrived when the moon was in quadrature.[22]

Wallis replied that in the absence of precise information it was impossible for him to work out explanations for local variations in tidal behaviour.[23] He thought that geographical situation would have a considerable influence and that the unusual spring tides in the East Indies might be found to occur at places some distance from the ocean, in arms of the sea and rivers, the explanation being that it took longer for the effects to make themselves felt there. To Goddard's objection he replied that both acceleration and retardation had a similar effect on the sea so that spring tides were caused as much by the earth moving in its epicycle contrary to the direction of its annual orbit as when both movements were in the same direction.

Six days later he wrote again. At Oldenburg's suggestion he had been reading the *De Motu Marium et Ventorum Liber* of Isaac Vos (1618–1689) in which tides and currents were explained as the result of the rise in the level of the sea produced when the sun warmed the water at the equator and thereby increased its volume.[24] Wallis did not himself agree with this hypothesis, which went beyond the well-known idea that water was transported from the equator towards the poles as vapour (*see* Ch. 3, p. 48) to suggest that the sea itself moved. He thought that the supposed difference in level, of about a foot, was too small to produce such noticeable movements, nor could he agree to dismiss the connection between the moon and tides as a "casual Synchronism".[25] He thought that the westward movement of the air and sea in the tropics was better explained by Galileo's idea that they were unable to keep up with the rotating earth (*see* Ch. 3, p. 48).

Wallis was present in person at the meeting of the Royal Society on 20 June when the last two letters were read.[26] He later compiled an Appendix to his paper, largely consisting of what he had said in the letters, and this was printed after the essay in the August number of the *Philosophical Transactions*.[11]

Wallis had always emphasized the importance of first-hand observations of tides in proving or disproving his hypothesis and in August he wrote again to the Society suggesting that they should arrange for observations to be made of spring tides during the coming months, near the sea if possible "but any where rather than not at all", to see when the highest springs would arrive.[27] This suggestion was taken up by the Society.[28] Lord Brouncker undertook to get in touch with possible helpers on the Thames and Sir Robert Moray was asked to draw up instructions for making observations, particularly on the varying degrees of rise and fall both in each single tide and in the progression of springs and neaps to see if they were, as he supposed, in the proportion of sines. (*see* Ch. 4, p. 72).

Wallis did not envisage anything very spectacular when he asked for observations; tides, he said,

may be safely observed by a marke made upon any standing Post in the water; by any waterman, or other understanding person who dwells by the water-side.[27,29]

Moray on the other hand had a much more ambitious scheme in mind in his article *Considerations and Enquiries concerning Tides*—nothing less than the construction of a tidal observatory sited where a large tidal range was to be found, perhaps near Bristol or Chepstow, and equipped with a tide-gauge. He wrote:

In some convenient place upon a Wall, Rock, or Bridge, &c. let there be an *Observatory* standing, as neer as may be to the brink of the Sea, or upon some wall; and if it cannot be well placed just where the Low Water is, there may be a Channel cut from the Low water to the bottom of the Wall, Rock, &c. The Observatory is to be raised above the High-water 18. or 20. foot; and a Pump, of any reasonable dimension, placed perpendicularly by the Wall, reaching above the High-water as high as conveniently may be. Upon the top of the Pump a Pulley is to be fastned, for letting down into the Pump a piece of floating wood, which, as the water comes in, may rise and fall with it. And because the rising and falling of the water amounts to 60. or 70. foot, the Counterpoise of the weight, that goes into the Pump, is to hang upon as many Pulleys, as may serve to make it rise & fall within the space, by which the height of the Pump exceeds the height of the Water . . . the first Pulley may have upon it a Wheele or two, to turn *Indexes* at any proportion required, so as to give the minute parts of the motion, and degrees of risings and fallings.[30]

Moray proposed that the observers should make records over months, if not years, of the rate of the rise and fall of the tides and of the heights of high and low water. They were to find out the velocity of the tidal current with log and line and to measure wind speed and strength, temperature, humidity and barometric pressure with the appropriate instruments.[30, 31]

Unfortunately this very advanced plan appears to have remained on paper but at a less ambitious level the Royal Society began to recommend tidal observation as a task to correspondents in different places. In September 1666 Oldenburg wrote to Henry Powle asking him to collect observations on tides, particularly at Bristol or Chepstow.[32] Powle wrote back saying that he would find people willing to make observations and in a further letter reported that he had enlisted the help of a steersman on a ferry boat at Aust.[33] In October Oldenburg wrote to Richard Norwood (1590?–1675) in Bermuda, sending him the *Directions for Seamen* and the *Considerations and Enquiries concerning Tides* by Moray and asking for information on the topics they contained.[34] Similar instructions were included among observations recommended to Sir Peter Wyche (1628–?1699), envoy to Portugal[35], and John Aubrey (1626–1697) gave copies of the inquiries to friends at Chepstow.[36]

Late in October Wallis wrote from Kent to report high tides on Romney Marsh after the last new moon.[37] He thought that their appearance agreed with his hypothesis but the country people attributed them to high winds. The crucial month of November was now approaching and the Royal Society resolved that everyone who could should observe the tides over the whole month and ask their friends to do so.[38] Whether they did so or not the problem seems to have been still unresolved at the end of the month when Wallis attended a meeting and answered, to the suggestion that high tides might be caused by high winds, that he thought the winds and the tides might be due to the same cause.[39]

New light was thrown on these problems in mid-December when Henry Powle gave an account of tides in the Severn.[40] He stated that the annual springs occurred about the beginning of March and the end of September and that winds had the effect of increasing or holding back the tide, according to the direction in which they were blowing[41]:

The greatest tydes that happned this yeare in Autumne were the Springes that followed the new moone that fell upon the 18th of September; at which time the tydes were assisted by a strong gale of wind from some point of the west which brought in the waters in great abundance.

In addition he said that there was a small but regular difference between the heights of the two daily tides, the high water after noon in winter being higher than the tide before noon in winter. In summer the converse was true. In the open sea the highest tides were followed by the lowest ebbs but in the river the ebb took longer and this did not appear. His informants said that spring tides were higher after full moon than after new moon.

At the next meeting Powle's account was supplemented by one from Samuel Colepresse.[42] His information differed rather from Powle's.[43] He had talked to someone living on one of the creeks near Plymouth who told him of a diurnal inequality in the tides which contradicted Powle's account, placing the highest tide before noon in winter and after noon in summer. In addition he said that the highest tide of the year arrived in July.[44] Colepresse promised to make observations himself and to persuade others to do so.

Wallis wrote to Oldenburg in mid-January 1667:

I am well pleased with the care   Mr. Powle hath used in getting observations upon the Severn.[45]

He accepted Powle's timing of the annual spring tides for the Severn, before the vernal and after the autumnal equinox, but repeated his conviction that in Kent they occurred in February and November. He welcomed the information about the diurnal inequality, which, he said, fitted in well with his hypothesis. Later in the month he wrote again, asking for observations of the times of the annual springs to be made along the southern and eastern coasts of England and in Scotland.[46]

Meanwhile Colepresse had returned home to Plympton St Mary and wrote to the Royal Society saying that he was having observations of tides made daily at Lyme and hoped to arrange for further observations in Cornwall.[47] In a later letter he expressed the intention of making observations himself the following summer.[48] Early in March he wrote to report an unusual tide at Cremyll in January and high tides in February:

I must farther add in favour of the worthy Dr. Wallis his Hypothesis, that on myne owne generall observation the Tydes have beene exceeding high about the middle of the last month: and some dayes, when there was noe considerable raine, or winde blowing: unless off att Sea, which often happens, tho'e we perceive it not on the Shoare.[49]

He had not yet had time however to make detailed observations himself.

This information pleased Wallis who took it as support for his views.[50] He thought that the time of annual springs might well vary from place to place since they arose from a combination of astronomical phenomena and were influenced too by the distance they had to travel from the open sea and other "adventitious causes."

Colepresse persevered in finding out about tides, notwithstanding the set-backs that could be encountered in this kind of work, as on one occasion when he sent enquiries to one Mr Warren

who had promis'd me his recommendation of them to some skillfull marriners in his Parish: whereon I promis'd my selfe somewhat, but was fail'd through the sullein humour, and irreconcileable opinions of the Sea-men, as he informs me.[51]

In January 1668 he sent the results to the Society.[52] He repeated what he had already said about the diurnal inequality. The highest spring tides came at the third tide after new moon or full moon, unless the pattern was upset by the winds, and they were followed by the lowest ebbs. This was contrary to the hope expressed by Wallis in 1666.[53] Colepresse said nothing about annual spring tides. He gave examples to show how the rate at which the tide rose and fell gradually increased to a peak at half-flood or half-ebb and then slowed down in the same proportion.

Meanwhile some reports were coming in from overseas. Richard Norwood wrote from Bermuda giving information on the tides there which, he said, never rose more than 5 feet high.[54] Similar information was received from Richard Stafford[55] and Oldenburg wrote to him asking for further details.[56]

John Winthrop wrote to Sir Robert Moray from New England

somthing I should mention concerning the tydes, but, living far up frō the sea side, I have wanted oportunityes to make fitt observations my selfe, and have not yet obteined, after much inquiry, such a satisfactory account of those very great tydes in the Bay of Fundo of Nova Scotia, most seamen that have beene there differing so much in their reports about it that I dare not write any thing of the pticulars of the quantity of the flud & ebb, and swiftnesse of the current of those tydes, till I have had better satisfaction about them, wch I doe indeavour upon all good oportunities, but it is certaine that the water floweth and ebbeth much in that sea, above all the other places of these parts, that I heare of.[57]

Moray was evidently not satisfied and wrote back that of all the information which Winthrop could supply

That of the Tides will be none of the least considerable. You might very well have writ what you hear about them in Nova Scotia. I can hardly think the Ebbes & floods can be greater there than on the Coast of France where the tide rises 14. fathom upright: and you cannot but know that in the Seuerne it flows Ten Fathom. In a word, write what you hear, & enquire further.[58]

In the autumn of 1668 the Royal Society received another collection of tidal observations, this time from Captain Samuel Sturmy of Bristol (1633–1669), author of the *Mariner's Magazine*[59] and an experienced sailor. His information tallied with Colepresse's account in the seasonal variation of the diurnal inequality, the timing of spring tides and the following on of the lowest ebbs.[60] His observations on the rate at which the tide rose and fell differed in giving the greatest velocity at first, followed by a gradual slackening. Oldenburg, writing to thank Sturmy for his work, asked for confirmation of this point[61] and suggested that perhaps the difference between this and what Colepresse had reported was due to Bristol's position, at some distance from the sea. Sturmy also described the Severn bore, which he attributed to the shoaling of the river, and placed the annual spring tides at the equinoxes. This was rather different from what Powle had said and Oldenburg wrote again on Wallis's behalf to ask for more precise information.[62]

This additional evidence on the timing of the annual springs did not shake Wallis's confidence in his theory. He had devised an explanation which would, he thought, account for the difference in time between the highest tides in the west and those on the Kent coast. He suggested in a letter written to the Royal Society in March 1668 that the effect of the causes he had already outlined was to deflect the eddy of the equatorial current, which had a general north-east direction, onto the shores of Europe.[63] When the eddy was deflected eastward high springs occurred on the Kent coast and when it was deflected northwards they occurred in the Severn. This argument enabled him to admit the growing amount of evidence against his original conception without relinquishing it.

This was the position early in 1669 when Joshua Childrey, clergyman, astrologer and amateur scientist, wrote to Oldenburg sending the Society information from Dorset where he was rector of Upwey, a few miles north of Weymouth.[64] Childrey's interest in tides dated back at least to the early 1650s (*see* Ch. 4) and one of the pieces of information which he sent to the Society was an account of unusual tides on 17 July 1666.[64] In his next letter he gave some account of his interest in science and in tides in particular.[65] He recalled that in 1664, when he was a member of the Bishop of Salisbury's household, the Royal Society had sent him a weather-glass but it had got broken on the way "in the Salisbury waggon". He expressed a desire to see Wallis's essay and mentioned his own hypothesis that tides were proportionally higher when the moon was in perigee than when it was in apogee:

this conceit touching the moon in Perigæo, I have had ever since 1653, putting it into an Almanacke I published then.[66]

Oldenburg must have sent Childrey a copy of the essay for in May he wrote to say that he had some criticisms to make of it.[67] Concerning his own hypothesis he asked for observations of any unusual tides in the Thames, which it led him to expect, and said that he would have them observed at Weymouth. He later reported that the sea had ebbed and flowed four times in an hour on 10 July, asking if anything similar had happened in London and whether any thunderstorms had occurred then as at the time of a similar phenomenal tide in July 1666.[68] Oldenburg wrote back thanking Childrey for his information.[69] There were no reports of storms on 10 July but some of the Society supposed that the irregular tides might have been due to a wind blowing at some distance from the shore.

At the end of March 1670 Childrey sent his "Animadversions on Dr. Wallis's Hypothesis of Tides" in a letter to Seth Ward, Bishop of Salisbury.[70] In it he used his ideas on the effect of the moon's distance and of the weather on the tides to argue that in his explanation of the annual spring tides Wallis was confusing phenomena which had no real connection:

My intention is not to argue against that part of the Hypothesis, that relates to the *Common Center of Gravity* of the *Earth and Moon*, and the *Diurnal* and *Menstrual* vicissitudes of the Tydes, the Authors discourse being (in my judgment) so rational and satisfactory as to those, that I cannot see what clear objection can be made against it. But that which I would beg his leave to except against, till better reason convince me, is his opinion concerning the *Annual* vicissitudes, and the true cause thereof, which he supposeth to be quite another thing from the Common center of Gravity, namely the *Inequality* of the *Natural Days.**

---

* Wallis believed that the bi-annual spring tides were due to the same astronomical factors as the inequality of natural days, the eccentricity of the earth's orbit and the obliquity of the ecliptic.

The general opinion among sailors was that the time of year made no difference to the height of tides or, if it did, the highest were at the equinoxes. He did not dispute Wallis's instances of high tides in November but a search of historical records had revealed only one example of a high tide in February. The truth was that other causes than those assigned by Wallis were responsible for the high tides he had noticed.

According to the London watermen, one occasion for high tides in London in rainy weather, and October and November were wet months, was when the incoming tide held back the flood water coming down the Thames. Another thing

notoriously known by all Seamen to be a cause of High or Low Tydes, which I cannot but say, that I wonder, the Author hath taken so little or no notice of it in his Essay, namely the sitting of the *Wind* at such or such a point of compass, and blowing hard.

When he was boy at Rochester he had seen this happen and it was common knowledge that a north-west wind would bring high tides on the Dutch coast and in the Thames estuary by driving the flood tide before it into the North Sea. If the moon were new or full the wind would intensify the effect of the spring tides. At Weymouth the geographical situation of the town was such that tides were increased by a south-south-east wind.

Finally there was the effect of the moon's distance from the earth on the tides:

There is yet another thing, which seems to have (at least) some influence on the Tydes, and to make them swell higher than else they would do, to wit the *Perigæosis* of the Moon. And this hath been my opinion (taken up first upon the consideration of the Moons coming nearer the Earth) ever since 1652, when living at *Feversham* in *Kent* near the Sea, I found by observing the Tydes, (as often as I had leisure) that there might be some truth in my Conjecture; and therefore in a little Pamphlet, publishd in 1653. by the name of *Syzygiasticon instauratum*, I desired, that others would observe that year, whether the Spring-Tydes after those Fulls and Changes, when the Moon was in *Perigæo* (the wind together considered) were not higher than usual. And since that time I have found several high Tydes and Inundations (though I must not say *all*,) to happen upon the Moons being in, or very near her *Perigæum*.

He gave examples of high tides occurring when the moon was near the earth taken both from his own experience in Kent and Gloucestershire and from historical records dating as far back as 1250. The fact, affirmed by seamen, that high spring tides one month were always followed by low springs next month seemed to support his idea since, if the moon were in perigee for one it would be in apogee at the next, but what would make his argument conclusive would be the discovery that neap tides occurring when the moon was in perigee were unusually high since when the moon was in perigee at the quadratures it came closer to the earth than if at new or full moon.

Childrey therefore wished observations to be made, in particular at Bristol, to see if they would bear out his expectations:

I am promised, the observation shall be made here at *Weymouth* for this whole year round; from whence I have already received this account, that this present *February* 1669/70 the Spring-Tydes ran very high after the *Change*, though the weather were pretty calm, and that wind that was not very favourable to the Tydes, and that the Spring-Tydes after the *Full* were very low, and weak, which is exactly according to my conjecture.

It is not clear exactly how Childrey thought the proximity of the moon affected the sea. He agreed with Wallis's hypothesis in general but he was on his own admission "astrologically affected" and may well have envisaged some hypothetical influence of this kind to be at work though he does not explicitly say so in his letters to the Society. In *Syzygiasticon Instauratum* he was less restrained in declaring his belief that natural phenomena were controlled by the stars and that "Astrology wants its History as much as any other part of Philosophie".[66]

A little while before Childrey's comments reached the Society Wallis had received a letter from Henry Hyrne objecting to his hypothesis on the grounds that the causes he described would not produce the known pattern of tides:

no Circular motion of the Earth, as long as the Ambient Air is carried about with it (whatsoever the Hypothesis be,) can at all conduce to the causing of the Flux and Reflux of the sea.[71]

The acceleration and retardation of points on the earth's surface, he argued, would have too small an effect on the sea to produce tides and in any case the known diurnal, monthly and annual tides could not follow from it.

Wallis replied that he thought that the air was as susceptible to movement as the sea.[72] The forces of acceleration and retardation experienced were small but so were the tides they produced in proportion to the size of the earth. The discrepancies of timing to which Hyrne objected between the astronomical factors and the tidal vicissitudes which were supposed to depend on them were due to the time lag between the original impulse on the water and the arrival of the tide which varied from place to place and was controlled by the geographical formation of the sea. The insuperable objection to his own theory would be the production of a better one and he challenged Hyrne to present his own hypothesis, which he did.

Hyrne supposed that the earth's centre of gravity was a point outside the earth, in the middle of its vortex.[73] The earth itself had three movements, the diurnal and annual motions and another alternately from north to south and south to north. As its position varied the water of the sea always moved towards the centre of gravity, causing tides.

The practical contribution which Hyrne made to the discussion was drawn from his personal experience of the effect of storm surges on the east coast of England, which was similar to Childrey's:

I have knowne for a certaine truth ever since the yeare 1653. for having had occasion at that time, to be at the sea side at Warham, about 8 Miles distant from Yarmouth in Norfolk to the Westward, at least twice in a week all summer long, and many times the following Winter, I did constantly observe, that when the wind had been at Northwest, at whatsoever time of the moon it was, the tides were mightily encreased, and I found that the countrey people, who suffered much by the breaking in of the Sea, never thought themselves in danger either at Allhollantide or Candlemas, or any time of the winter unlesse the wind had also been North-west.

The north-west wind caused

the waters in the German Ocean to swell hugely, especially towards the south east end of it, or between England and Holland, and at the outlet of it into the British sea, where Rumney marsh lyeth; which jetting out into the narrow passage between England and France, must of necessity cause the waters to rise there, more than ordinary.

Twelve years experience of weather in the Thames had confirmed him in this view.

Hyrne thought that the monthly variations in the tides were caused by the north-south movement of the earth and that there were no annual variations. He himself admitted that it was a weakness in his hypothesis that it did not account for the relationship between the tides and the moon. His ideas do not seem to have been very widely discussed. Oldenburg wrote to Winthrop summarizing the hypothesis and asking him to find out if high tide occurred on the western side of the Atlantic at the same time as on the east and whether tides were unusually small in the Gulf of Mexico, points which Hyrne had raised.[74]

Replying to Childrey's criticisms, Wallis wrote

I do not find, that he and I are like much to disagree.[75]

He claimed that he had always taken the effect of winds on tides for granted. The idea of the influence of the moon in perigee was not new to him but he had said nothing of it in his *Essay* because he had no evidence of a definite connection and it was in any case subordinate to the main cause of tides. He accepted what Childrey had to say and used it in his reply to Hyrne[76] to argue that winds were not the only causes of unusual high tides. To this he added an example of his own:

in June 1667 it may be remembred by an accident too remarkable that when the Dutch fired our ships at Chatham, they did upon the advantage of a high spring-tide (which then happned presently after the solstice) carry off the Charles (at one tide) to sea, which was then thought to have been impossible, and at ordinary spring-tides would have required 3 spring-tides to do it. Yet was that in summer and in a dry season, and I do not remember that the wind was either N.W. or near that point.[77]

One cannot escape the impression that Wallis was rather disingenuous in dealing with the criticisms of his work. It may have been that his hypothesis would allow variations in the moon's proximity to the earth to affect the tides but as he admitted in his reply to Hyrne and elsewhere he had never made more than casual observations of tides himself and can have had no means of knowing that it did indeed have this effect. He maintained that the theory did not rule out the possibility of wind altering the tides in particular instances but concentrated on the general patterns to be observed but he was willing enough to use particular instances when they supported his argument. He had presented his views as a hypothesis to be criticized and revised but in the event he was unwilling to relinquish his views. He continued to hold the idea that the annual spring tides occurred in Sussex in February and November, no one apparently having the means to check up on this point, and the most he would concede to the circumstantial denials of Hyrne and Childrey was that

since it is not yet (it seemes) agreed, whether such Annual Phænomenon do happen; or, if so, not at what time; (so that, for aught yet appears, it may be at the seasons I design, that is, between the Winter Solstice and the two Equinoxes on either side of it; though, on several coasts, severally remote:) I think it best to let this part of the Hypothesis stand as it is, unrevoked. As that which, when it shall be discovered and agreed on, stands ready enough to give a rational account of it; and, in the mean time, doth no hurt. And, in such a complication of causes so abstruse, scarce any thing, but observation, will determine, which of the causes, and in what degree, is to be judged predominant.[75]

Such remarks were understandably unacceptable to Childrey who wrote to Oldenburg

the Annuall periods of the Tides will not yet downe with me, for a reason which weighs much with me upon second thoughts, and which I shall hereafter give you.[78]

Meanwhile he sent a list of tidal observations made at Weymouth between February 1669 and April 1670 and had arranged with his friend there, "a very able ancient Seamen", to continue the observations for the coming year. The results of the observations so far supported his ideas about the effect of the moon in perigee which pleased him and was no less welcome to the old sailor who had passed on the information to the pilots because he saith (if it hit but as right for the future, as it hath done yet) it will be of good use to them for bringing in, and carrying out of Vessels from that Harbour.

What new objection Childrey had found to Wallis's views remains unknown for he died a few months later, on 26 August 1670. Death had already removed others inclined to argue with Wallis's ideas. Sturmy had died in 1669 after catching a chill exploring a cavern on the banks of the Severn[79] and Colepresse had gone to Leyden where he too presumably died since no more is heard of him.[80]

Wallis's hypothesis seems to have found a wide measure of acceptance as the best solution so far offered but it did not of course lead to the overthrow of the ideas already current but rather took its place with them. On a lower level amateur theorists still came out with ingenious explanations like that put forward by Thomas Philipot (d. 1682) who suggested that the sun and moon compressed the surface of the ocean, releasing a "Vitriolated, Volatile or Armoniack Salt or Spirit" from the depths of the sea,[81] or John Taylor who wrote to R. Pepys, M.P. in 1678 suggesting that the moon lifted the globe as it came above the horizon so that "the ebbing and flowing is nothing but the waters falling from one shore to another".[82] New observations were reported from time to time. Some were mere notices of unusual tides[83] but some were careful studies like Francis Davenport's observations at Tonquin where there was only one high water every twenty-four hours.[84]

Meanwhile Hooke had been developing his ideas on the planetary system and progressed from his position in 1666 (see p. 97) to a statement of the theory of universal gravitation and the inverse square law which eventually led to Newton's completing his own work on the subject.[85] Hooke does not seem to have seen that these principles could be used to explain tides. In 1678, according to Waller, while discussing the discovery of the oval shape of the planet Mercury he said that

all Fluids on the Surface would run into that Shape, and that 'twas not improbable but that the water here about the Earth might do so by the influence of the diurnal Motion of the Earth, which compounded with that of the Moon, he conceiv'd was the cause of the Tides.[86]

Setting aside the intuitive guesses of Gilbert and Kepler the first exposition of the idea that tides are caused by the gravitational attraction of the sun and moon was made by Sir Isaac Newton (1642–1727) in his *Principia*.[87] Applying the principles that the force of attraction decreases as the square of the distance increases and that gravitation is proportional to mass he showed that the diurnal tides were a combination of two separate movements of the water, one produced by the moon and the other, the smaller, by the sun which in spite of its size had less effect on account of being at a much greater distance. On an earth covered entirely with water gravitation would produce a spheroidal shape whose longest axis would be roughly along the line joining the centres of the earth and moon.

The monthly spring tides occurred with the sun and moon in conjunction and opposition when their combined forces acted in the same direction but at the quadratures they acted against each other, producing neap tides. The sun and moon's distance from the earth affected the tides and spring tides occurring near the time when the moon was in perigee were high while those before and after it were low because then the moon was near its apogee (a point made by Childrey in his *Animadversions*). The effects of both sun and moon were greatest when they were on the equator and the highest springs therefore came at the equinoxes.

Tides in any one place also depended upon its latitude for the sea was divided into two hemispherical floods which travelled through all the meridians in twenty-four hours on opposite sides of the equator. It followed that any place north of the equator would have a higher tide when the tidal elevation crossing its meridian was in the same hemisphere than when south of the equator. This was the cause of the diurnal inequality noticed by Colepresse and Sturmy. The seasonal inversion which they described depended on the declination of the moon. Newton explained the anomalous pattern of tides at Tonquin as the result of the arrival of two tidal streams from different directions. In *The System of the World* he also attempted to show why tides at mid-ocean islands were so much smaller than those on the periphery of the ocean.

Newton's solution to the age-old problem of the tides did not win acceptance easily and older theories continued to attract a following, particularly Descartes's hypothesis. The editors of *The Compleat Geographer* offered it to their readers with the remark

There are some very Learned Men, who are of Opinion, That the influence of the Sun, and motion of the Earth ought to be consider'd together with the Moon as concomitant Causes of the Tide; But because these Speculations have something too abstruse and difficult in them, we thought it best to stick to an easie and plainer Hypothesis in this Compendium.[88]

As late as 1740 Descartes's ideas formed the basis of one of the essays awarded prizes by the French Academy.[89]

The difficulty which many people found in grasping Newton's ideas, perhaps because no English translation was available until 1729, was sufficiently acute for Halley's summary of his work on tides, originally written for James II, to be printed in the *Philosophical Transactions* in 1697 because the original was "very little understood by the common

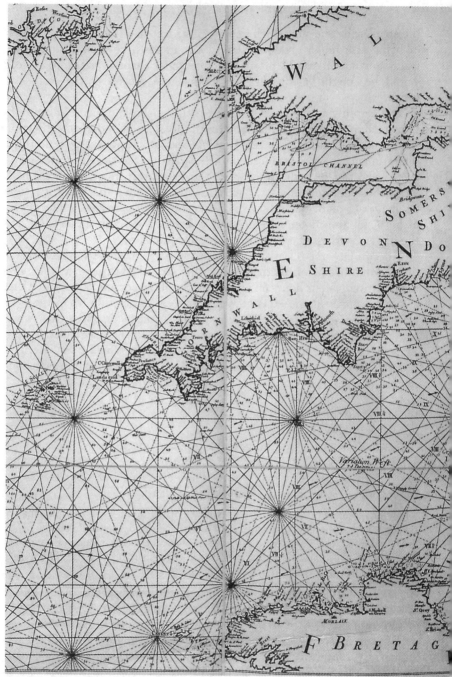

FIG. 4. Chart of the English Channel with tides and currents observed by Edmond Halley. (Reproduced by permission of the trustees of the British Museum.)*

Reader".[94] Halley argued that in fact Newton's theory was easier to understand than its predecessors because it gave a more satisfactory account of what was known to happen:

it is admirable to observe how easily we are enabled to make out very abstruse *and difficult Matters*, when once true and genuine Principles are obtained.

Newton's theory did what Wallis had hoped when he said that the best answer to his hypothesis would be the production of a better one; it gave direct explanations of tidal phenomena which no single earlier idea could comprehend. Yet though he made Wallis's ideas out of date, in using the observations which had been made to test them, Newton gave a permanent value to the work of the 1660s and 1670s.

In addition to the development of tidal theory in Britain at this time some attempts were made to include the study of tides and tidal streams in hydrographic surveys. During the early 1670s Captain Richard Bolland included information on tides in his chart of the Strait of Gibraltar. While collecting his material he had

often cross'd over from the one Shoar to the other, as also anchor'd several Boats, half a League distant from one another, that they have reach'd one third of the Channel over; having on Board each of them, Watches for Time, Logs to inform the turning of the Tide, and several other Conveniences proper for those Observations; by which means, I gain'd some experience how the Tides set, their time and distance from the Shoar.[90]

A remark of John Evelyn's shows that the hydrographic surveys of the British Isles carried out by Captain Greenvile Collins included tidal observations.[91] In 1686 it was proposed that the President of the Royal Society, then Samuel Pepys, should ask Collins for information on tides.[92]

The interest of Edmond Halley in tides dated back at least to 1684 when he discussed Davenport's observations.[93] He was instrumental in persuading Newton to complete his *Principia* and himself made a summary of the passages relating to tides.[94] In November 1687 he read letters to the Royal Society containing accounts of observations which had been made for him on the south coast of England.[95] His most notable contribution in this field was a three month voyage, undertaken during the brief peace, in the summer of 1701, to chart the tides and tidal streams of the English Channel, as a result of which he produced a map which was used throughout the eighteenth century.[96]*

5. NOTES

1. John Wallis, "An Essay of Dr. John Wallis, exhibiting his Hypothesis about the Flux and Reflux of the Sea", *Phil. Trans.* (August 1666), no. 16, pp. 263–281.
2. *Ibid.* p. 264.

3. *The Correspondence of Henry Oldenburg* (ed. A. Rupert Hall and Marie Boas Hall). Vol. **3** (1966) p. 94, no. 510, Taylor to Oldenburg, 17 April 1666.

4. *Ibid.* pp. 105–106, no. 514, 26 April 1666; pp. 116–117, no. 518, 8 May 1666; p. 131, no. 525, 15 May 1666.

5. John Wallis, *op. cit.* pp. 266–267.

6. *Ibid.* p. 265.

7. Giovanni Battista Riccioli, *Almagestum Novum* (1651). Vol. **2**, p. 381.

8. John Wallis, *op. cit.* pp. 271–272.

*9. Dr E. J. Aiton, "On Galileo and the earth-moon system", *Isis* (1963). Vol **54**, pp. 265–266.

* Dr H. L. Burstyn, "Galileo and the earth-moon system: reply to Dr Aiton", *Ibid.*, pp. 400–401.

10. Pierre Gassendi, "Syntagmatis Philosophici", pt 2, bk 1, ch. 4, *Opera Omnia* (1658). Vol. **2**, pp. 27–33, contains a discussion of tides.

11. John Wallis, "An Appendix, written by way of Letter to the Publisher; Being an Answer to some objections, made by several persons, to the precedent discourse", *Phil. Trans.* (August 1666), no. 16, pp. 281–289; pp. 287–288.

12. J. Edleston, *Correspondence of Sir Isaac Newton and Professor Cotes*, London (1850), pp. 300–301, Wallis to Newton, 10 April 1695.

13. John Wallis, "Essay . . . about the Flux and Reflux of the Sea", *op. cit.* p. 276.

14. Thomas Birch, *History of the Royal Society*. Vol. **2** (1756) pp. 88 and 89.

15. The originals or drafts of most of the letters quoted here are preserved in the Letter Books of the Royal Society and those written to or by Henry Oldenburg have been printed in *The Correspondence of Henry Oldenburg* (ed. A. Rupert Hall and Marie Boas Hall). Vol. **3** (1966).

16. John Wallis, "Essay . . . about the Flux and Reflux of the Sea", *op. cit.* p. 266.

17. *Royal Society Letter Book* W.1, no. 21, Wallis to Oldenburg, 19 May 1666.

18. John Wallis, "Essay . . . about the Flux and Reflux of the Sea", *op. cit.* pp. 264–265.

19. Thomas Birch, *History of the Royal Society*. Vol. **2**, (1756), pp. 90–92.

20. Robert Hooke, "An Account of an Experiment touching the different weights of cold and warme water"; printed in Thomas Birch, *History of the Royal Society*. Vol. **1** (1756) pp. 174–176.

21. *The Works of the Honourable Robert Boyle* (ed. Thomas Birch) (1744). Vol. **5**, p. 356, Oldenburg to Boyle, 8 June 1666; reprinted in *The Correspondence of Henry Oldenburg* (ed. A. Rupert Hall and Marie Boas Hall). Vol. **3** (1966) pp. 153–156, no. 537.

22. Thomas Birch, *History of the Royal Society*. Vol. **2** (1756) p. 93.

23. *Royal Society Letter Book*, W.1, no. 23, Wallis to Oldenburg, 2 June 1666.

24. Isaac Voss, *De Motu Marium et Ventorum Liber*, Hagae-Comitis (1663). Translated into English by A. Lovel as *A Treatise concerning the Motion of the Seas and Winds*, London (1677).

25. *Royal Society Letter Book*, W.1, no. 24, Wallis to Oldenburg, 8 June 1666.

26. Thomas Birch, *History of the Royal Society*. Vol. **2** (1756) p. 98.

27. *Royal Society Letter Book*, W.1, no. 28, Wallis to Oldenburg, 18 August 1666.

28. Thomas Birch, *History of the Royal Society*. Vol. **2** (1756) p. 111.

29. Printed as "Some Inquiries and Directions concerning Tides", *Phil. Trans.* (September 1666), no. 17, pp. 297–298.

30. "Considerations and Enquiries concerning Tides, by Sir Robert Moray", *Phil. Trans.* (September 1666), no. 17, pp. 298–301; pp. 299–300.

31. Sir Robert Moray, "Patternes of the Tables proposed to be made for Observing of Tides, promised in the next forgoing Transactions", *Phil. Trans.* (October 1666), no. 18, pp. 311–313 and table between pp. 314 and 315.

32. *The Correspondence of Henry Oldenburg* (ed. A. Rupert Hall and Marie Boas Hall) Vol. 3 (1966), pp. 228–229, no. 567, Oldenburg to Powle, 12 September 1666; Powle is here tentatively identified as Henry Powle, F.R.S. (?1630–1692).

33. *Ibid.* Vol. 3 (1966), pp. 235–236 and 247, nos. 571 and 576, Powle to Oldenburg, 1666.

34. *Royal Society Letter Book*, O.1, no. 35, Oldenburg to Norwood, 24 October 1666.

35. *Royal Society Letter Book* (Copy). Vol. 1, pp. 447–449, observations recommended to Sir Peter Wyche, October 1666.

36. Thomas Birch, *History of the Royal Society*. Vol. 2 (1756), pp. 121–122, 127.

37. *Ibid.* Vol. 2 (1756) p. 119. This letter has been lost: *The Correspondence of Henry Oldenburg* (ed. A. Rupert Hall and Marie Boas Hall). Vol. 3 (1966), p. 275, no. 580, Wallis to ?Oldenburg, 23 October 1666.

38. Thomas Birch, *History of the Royal Society*. Vol. 2 (1756) pp. 119, 121.

39. *Ibid.* Vol. 2 (1756) p. 129.

40. *Ibid.* Vol. 2 (1756) p. 133.

41. Henry Powle, "Observations concerning tydes", *Royal Society Classified Papers*. Vol. 6, no. 18.

42. Thomas Birch, *History of the Royal Society*. Vol. 2 (1756) p. 134.

43. Samuel Colepresse, *Royal Society Classified Papers*. Vol. 6, no. 19.

44. Perhaps the high tide in mid-July which, Colepresse's informant said (43), "this present yeare has risen about 5 foote higher, then has been eyther observed, or remembered these many yeares", was connected with a similar disturbance recorded by Joshua Childrey at Weymouth on 17 July 1666 when the tide suddenly came in and rose and fell several times: *Royal Society Letter Book* C. 1, no. 3, Childrey to Oldenburg, 9 February 1668/9.

45. *Royal Society Letter Book*, W.1, no. 29, Wallis to Oldenburg, 19 January 1666/7.

46. *Ibid.*, no. 30, Wallis to Oldenburg, 31 January 1666/7.

47. *Royal Society Letter Book*, C.1, no. 11, Colepresse to Oldenburg, 8 January 1666/7.

48. *Ibid.*, no. 12, Colepresse to Oldenburg, 1 February 1666/7.

49. *Ibid.*, no. 13, Colepresse to Oldenburg, 6 March 1666/7.

50. *Royal Society Letter Book*, W.1, no. 32, Wallis to Oldenburg, 21 March 1666/7.

51. *Royal Society Letter Book*, C.1, no. 16, Colepresse to Oldenburg, 28 October 1667.

52. Thomas Birch, *History of the Royal Society*. Vol. 2 (1756) p. 240.
Samuel Colepresse, "Of some Observations, made by Mr. Samuel Colepresse at and nigh Plymouth, A. 1667, by way of Answer to some of the Quæries concerning Tydes, propos'd Numb. 17 and 18", *Phil. Trans.* (March 1668). Vol. 3, no. 33, pp. 632–634.

53. John Wallis, "Some Inquiries and Directions Concerning Tides", *Phil. Trans.* (September 1666), no. 17, pp. 297–298.

54. *Royal Society Letter Book* N. 1, no. 26, Norwood to Oldenburg, 18 June 1667.
55. "An Extract of a Letter, written to the Publisher from the Bermudas by Mr. Richard Stafford", *Phil. Trans.* (October 1668). Vol. 3, no. 40, pp. 792–795.
56. *Royal Society Letter Book*, O. 1, no. 89, Oldenburg to Stafford, 16 November 1668.
57. Robert C. Winthrop, "Correspondence of Hartlib, Haak, Oldenburg, and others of the founders of the Royal Society, with Governor Winthrop of Connecticut, 1661–1672", *Proc. Mass. hist. Soc.* (1878). Vol. 16, pp. 232–234, Winthrop to Moray, 18/26 August 1668.
58. *Ibid.* p. 243, Moray to Winthrop, 17 July 1669.
59. Samuel Sturmy, *The Mariner's Magazine; or, Sturmy's mathematical and practical arts*, London (1669). This contains little of interest about tides although mainly devoted to the study of navigation.
60. Samuel Sturmy, "An Account of some Observations, made this present year by Capt. Samuel Sturmy in Hong-road within four miles of Bristol, in Answer to some of the Quaeries concerning the Tydes, in No. 17 & No. 18", *Phil. Trans.* (November 1668). Vol. 3, no. 41, pp. 813–817.
61. *Royal Society Letter Book*, O. 1, no. 80, Oldenburg to Sturmy, 20 October 1668.
62. *Royal Society Letter Book*, O. 1, no. 86a, Oldenburg to Sturmy, 16 November 1668.
63. John Wallis, "A letter . . . concerning the Variety of the Annual High-Tydes", *Phil. Trans.* (April 1668). Vol. 3, no. 34, pp. 652–653.
64. *Royal Society Letter Book*, C. 1, no. 3, Childrey to Oldenburg, 9 February 1668/9.
65. *Royal Society Letter Book*, C. 1, no. 2, Childrey to Oldenburg, 22 March 1668/9.
66. Joshua Childrey, *Syzygiasticon Instauratum. Or, An Ephemeris of the Places and Aspects of the Planets, as they respect the ☉ as Center of their Orbes, Calculated for the Year of the Incarnation of God, 1653*, London (1653). This contains predictions for high and low spring tides in the year 1653 and throws light on Childrey's belief that the weather was controlled by the astrological influence of the heavens.
67. *Royal Society Letter Book*, C. 1, no. 6, Childrey to Oldenburg, 4 May 1669.
68. *Royal Society Letter Book*, C. 1, no. 9, Childrey to Oldenburg, 12 July 1669. MS. partially illegible; see also *Letter Book* (Copy). Vol. 3, pp. 161–164.
69. *Royal Society Letter Book*, O. 2, no. 4, Oldenburg to Childrey, 24 July 1669.
70. *Royal Society Letter Book*, C. 1, no. 4, Childrey to Seth Ward, 31 March 1669 (1670), printed as "A Letter of Mr. Joseph Childrey to the Right Reverend Seth Lord Bishop of Sarum, containing some Animaversions upon the Reverend Dr. John Wallis's Hypothesis about the Flux and Reflux of the Sea, publish't No. 16 of these Tracts", *Phil. Trans.* (October 1670). Vol. 5, no. 64, pp. 2061–2068.
71. *Royal Society Letter Book*, H. 1, no. 107, Hyrne to ?Wallis, 28 February 1669/70. Unlike many people figuring in these pages, Henry Hyrne was not noticeable enough to appear in the D.N.B. and similar works and I have been unable to find out anything about him beyond what he says in the letters. These show that he was living at Parson's Green.
72. *Royal Society Letter Book*, W. 1, no. 102, Wallis to Hyrne, 9 March 1669/70.

73. *Royal Society Letter Book*, H. 1, no. 108, Hyrne to Wallis, 2 April 1669/70.
74. Robert C. Winthrop, *op. cit.* pp. 245–246, Oldenburg to Winthrop, 9 May 1670.
75. *Royal Society Letter Book*, W. 1, no. 104, Wallis to Oldenburg, 19 March 1669/70. Printed as "Dr. Wallis's Answer to the foregoing Animadversions, directed in a Letter to the Publisher", *Phil. Trans.* (October 1670). Vol. **5**, no. 64, pp. 2068–2074.
76. *Royal Society Letter Book*, W. 1, no. 108, Wallis to Hyrne, 4 April 1670.
77. William Laird Clowes' *The Royal Navy. A History from the earliest times to the present*, 7 vols, London (1897–1903), does not have any mention of this circumstance.
78. *Royal Society Letter Book*, C. 1, no. 10, Childrey to Oldenburg, 15 April 1670.
79. E. G. R. Taylor, *The Mathematical Practitioners of Tudor and Stuart England* (1954), p. 242.
80. *The Correspondence of Henry Oldenburg, op. cit.* Vol. **3** (1966), note p. 311.
81. Thomas Philipot, *A Phylosophical Essay, treating of the most probable cause of that grand mystery of nature, the flux and reflux: or flowing and ebbing of the sea*, London (1673).
82. MS. Rawlinson, A. 172, Bodleian Library, John Taylor to R. Pepys, 14 December 1678.
83. For example in the minutes of the Oxford Philosophical Society on 14 April 1685, R. T. Gunther, *Early Science in Oxford*, 14 vols, Oxford, (1921–1945). Vol. **4** (1925) p. 140.
84. "An account of the course of the tides at Tonqueen in a letter from Mr. Francis Davenport July 15. 1678. with the theory of them, at the Barr of Tonqueen, by the learned Edmund Halley Fellow of the Royal Society", *Phil. Trans.* (1684). Vol. **14**, pp. 677–684.
85. Angus Armitage, "'Borell's Hypothesis' and the rise of celestial mechanics", *Annl Sci.* (1948–50). Vol. **6**, pp. 268–282.
86. Richard Waller, *The Posthumous Works of Robert Hooke* (1705), p. xx.
87. Sir Isaac Newton, *Philosophiæ Naturalis Principia Mathematica*, London (1687), pp. 429–434, 463–466; *Sir Isaac Newton's Mathematical Principles of Natural Philosophy and his System of the World*, translated by Motte and Cajori, Berkeley (1934), pp. 435–440, 478–483, 581–589.
88. *The Compleat Geographer*, published by Awnsham and John Churchill and Timothy Childe, London, 3rd edition (1709), p. xli.
89. Daniel Bernoulli, Leonard Euler, Colin Maclaurin and Antoine Cavalleri, *Pièces qui ont remporté le prix de l'Académie Royale des Sciences en 1740*. Paris (1741).*
90. Richard Bolland, "A Draught of the Streights of Gibraltar", *A Collection of Voyages and Travels*, published by Awnsham and John Churchill, 4 vols, London (1704). Vol. **4**, p. 846.
91. Referred to by A. H. W. Robinson, *Marine Cartography in Britain: a History of the Sea Chart to 1855*, Leicester (1962), p. 53.
92. Thomas Birch, *History of the Royal Society*. Vol. **4** (1757) p. 469.
93. "A theory of the tides at the Bar of Tunking by the learned Mr. Edm. Halley, Fellow of the Royal Society", *Phil. Trans.* (1684). Vol. **14**, pp. 685–688.
94. "The true theory of the tides, extracted from that admired treatise of Mr. Isaac Newton, intituled, Philosophiæ Naturalis Principia Mathematica; being a

discourse presented with that book to the late King James, by Mr. Edmund Halley", *Phil. Trans.* (1695–1697). Vol. **19**, pp. 445–457.
95. Thomas Birch, *History of the Royal Society.* Vol. **4** (1757) p. 551.
96. Eugene Fairfield MacPike, *The Correspondence and Papers of Edmond Halley,* Oxford (1932), pp. 117–120.
    See also:
    E. J. Aiton, "Galileo's Theory of the Tide", *Annl. Sci.* (1954). Vol. **10**, pp. 44–57, for Wallis and Childrey.
    Christoph J. Scriba, "A tentative index of the correspondence of John Wallis,
 * F.R.S.", *Notes Rec. R. Soc. Lond.* (1967). Vol. **22**, pp. 58–93.

Addenda et Corrigenda

p.94, 1.17:*instead* practical *read* personal

p.95, 1.5*: after: Staticks insert*)

p.95, 1.39:*instead* Body read: *Body*

p.99, 1.26:*instead* strength *read* direction

p.110, fig.4, caption, 1.2:*instead* trustees of the British Museum *read* British Library

p.111, 1.36:*after* century *insert* (See Fig. 4)

p.112, n.9, 1.2: *delete* Dr

p.112, n.9, 1.3, first word: *delete* Dr

p.115, n.89, 1.3,:*before* Paris *insert:Sur le Flux et Reflux de la Mer*

p.116, n.96, 1.7: *insert* Fig. 4 reproduces part of sheet 1 (western) of the two charts published by Mount and Page of London, c.1702, entitled *A new and correct chart of the Channel between England & France.....shewing the Sands, Shoals depths of Water and Anchorage with ye flowing of the Tydes, and setting of the Current, as observ'd by the learned Dr Halley.* Both sheets of the chart are reproduced, with the chart of magnetic variation derived from observations made on Halley's first two voyages, as the second volume of N.J.W. Thrower's edition of The *Three Voyages of Edmond Halley in the* Paramore, *1698–1701,*Hakluyt Society, Vols **156** & **157** (1981). The journal of Halley's 1701 voyage is published on pp. 220–247 of the first volume. See also Thrower's introductory comments on the voyage, and on the map and its utility, pp. 64–66. Halley's second voyage in the *Paramore* took him far south in the Atlantic and has interesting observations on the appearance of the sea in those latitudes, including accounts of penguins and icebergs, but no mention is made of any attempt to make measurements of depth, salinity, temperature etc. along the lines advocated by the Royal Society. (See Ch. 8,p.168).

6. MARINE SCIENCE IN THE WORKS OF ROBERT BOYLE

THE two preceding chapters have shown something of the extent to which many British scientists and scientific enthusiasts became interested in the investigation of the sea during the seventeenth century. Few, however, produced any very sustained account of their ideas and observations, details of which are to be found diffused among minutes, letters and discussions of sometimes totally unrelated subjects, often published long after they were written and in some cases not at all. Only those articles which found their way into the *Philosophical Transactions* were safe from obscurity both then and since, and it is by taking these alone into consideration that more recent writers have sometimes given a rather unbalanced view of the development of marine science in that age. The only writer to do literary justice at the time to the ideas which were then being put forward was Boyle whose essays on the sea must have been responsible to a great extent for shaping concepts about the sea held in the eighteenth century.

Newton alone excepted, Robert Boyle is acknowledged to be the leading British scientist of his age and, in his breadth of interest and enthusiasm for the advancement of learning, as more typical of it than the author of the *Principia*. It was fortunate for marine science that Boyle's interests ranged so widely that, although he had no particular connection with the sea or ready made opportunity or indeed motivation for studying it, he nevertheless worked on marine problems over a long period. In addition he was a prolific writer and less averse to publication than many of his contemporaries. Aubrey remarked with not much exaggeration that his works would make a library by themselves.[1] Although he professed to be not entirely satisfied with them Boyle published four essays on the sea which, together, form the fullest single account of the ideas and methods of a seventeenth-century student of the sea.

Boyle himself was not directly involved with the experiments and discussions on topics of marine science made in the early 1660s for he did not move to London until 1668 but he was always in close touch with individual members of the Royal Society, some of whom had formerly been his colleagues in Oxford, and through them knew what was going on. His own work on the sea followed much the same lines and was based on a similar framework of knowledge, particularly experimental observations about the physical properties of air and water, and involved a similar preoccupation with measurement and instrumentation. His essays deal with his own work and not with that carried out in the Royal Society group but their closeness both in aims and in activities meant that many of their ideas were alike. Therefore though his essays were very much about his own research Boyle gave an account that is representative of much of the most advanced thinking of his time and unwittingly ensured that it was not entirely lost in the following age when the enthusiasm for improving knowledge of the world around them, which gave the seventeenth-century pioneers their interest in oceanography and other environmental sciences, largely disappeared and the bulk of the work which had been done then was either forgotten or not appreciated.

Boyle's interest in marine science dates back at least as far as 1658-9 when the barometer was constructed in his laboratory, at Wren's suggestion, to enable them to test Descartes's theory of tides.[2] In 1666 it was he who persuaded John Wallis to write down the ideas on tides which they had been discussing and who sent the essay that resulted to Oldenburg for communication to the Royal Society.[3] After the publication of the essay and the discussion and enquiries arising from it, it was Boyle to whom Oldenburg wrote for a supplementary list of questions, knowing that he "had not left unconsidered the Natural History of the *Sea*".[4]

Boyle was not of course the first of the philosophers to draw up a programme of marine research but his *Other Inquiries concerning the Sea* was more comprehensive than anything published hitherto[4] (*see* Appendix, p. 410). It included questions on the variations of salinity and temperature from place to place and at different depths and on the effect of these changes on the density of sea water, on the sea floor and its composition and on currents, waves and tides.

He referred in passing to observations which he had already had made for him on the specific gravity of sea water and which he described more fully in his essay on the saltness of the sea.[5] He had given a hydrometer to a traveller going to the West Indies who found that the specific gravity of the sea increased until they reached a latitude of 30°N and then remained the same. This traveller, whom he does not name, was almost certainly Dr Henry Stubbs (1632–1676) who went out to the West Indies in 1661 and who, although in later years a critic of the Royal Society, made scientific observations during the voyage.[6] He

observ'd at Sea, that though *Glauber* say, the water, as it grows *Salter*, becomes *Greener*, yet that is false. For, after we were out of the Narrow, the Sea grew *darkish*, and after perfect *Azure*, yet it was much more Salt, the further we went; as I tryed by a *Water-poise* of Glass, with Quick-silver at the one end. It rose about half an inch above the Sea-water in the *Downs*; and at 24 *degrees* more, 2 inches; but after that, I never observed any difference unto *Jamaica*, the Sea being probably so impregnated with Salt, as not to imbibe more; which crosses another observation, that the nearer the *Tropiques* and the *Line*, the Salter the Sea.[7]

In *New Experiments and Observations touching Cold* (1665) Boyle discussed evidence from the works of travellers and writers which suggested that the sea below the surface was habitually cold.[8] It was not until 1670, however, with the publication, in the *Tracts about the Cosmical Qualities of Things*, of essays on the temperature and depth of the sea[9] that the full extent of his interest in marine science appeared. Three years after that came *Observations and Experiments about the Saltness of the Sea*.[10] In a preface to this work Boyle explained how he had obtained information about the sea from a wide range of people:

scarce any Writer of Philosophical things having had such opportunities of receiving such Authentick Informations from Sea Captains, Pilots, Planters, and other Travellers to remote parts, as were afforded him by the advantage he had to be many years a member of the Council appointed by the King of *Great Britain* to manage the business of all the *English Colonies* in the Isles and Continent of *America*, and of being for two or three years one of that Court of Committees (as they call it) that has the superintending of all the affairs of the justly famous *East-Indian Company of England*.[10]

To ensure the accuracy of his statements Boyle was, as he said, "very wary in admitting the informations that he imployes".[10] He paid the minimum of attention to previous writers who had merely argued the merits of their respective views. Such fruitless controversies as that over the origin of the salt in the sea were bound to continue unresolved

as long as 'tis argued on both sides but by Dialectical Arguments, which may be probable on both sides, but are not convincing on either.[11]

Instead he relied on experiments made either by himself or at his direction and on first-hand information from those who had been at sea. He did not admit hearsay, nor did he allow even his own unaided memory as evidence without reservation.[12]

In writing about the temperature of the sea below the surface Boyle thought, probably rightly, that he was dealing with quite a new subject, one

of which Classick Authors are so very silent, and about which Philosophers seeme not so much as to have attempted any Experiments (for want of Opportunities and mean to make them.)[13]

He even thought it necessary to define what he meant by the word "submarine" though, apparently, the use of this word was not entirely new, John Wilkins having already employed it in a description of a vessel for making "sub-marine voyages" in his *Mathematical Magick*.[14] Boyle explained that he was using the word to describe the interior of the sea, from the surface downwards, and not the earth which lay beneath the sea.

It seemed to Boyle that in general the temperature of the surface of the sea varied from place to place depending on the weather. Sometimes, though, sudden changes might occur. He found an example of this in the relation of M. de Monts who, during a voyage to North America, had found that after being very warm for three days the sea then turned cold before they reached the Grand Banks. Presumably his ship had crossed from the warm water of the Gulf Stream into the cold Labrador current but Boyle did not realize this. Volcanic activity had been suggested as the cause of such changes but he thought that they might be due to the chemical composition of the water or to the configuration of nearby coasts.

As far as there was any preconceived idea about the temperature of the submarine parts of the sea, it was, said Boyle, that they would be warmer towards the bottom but most of his evidence suggested the opposite conclusion. This appeared from his conversation with a diver, almost certainly the Rochford whose account of attempts to salvage the Swedish ship *Sophia* is preserved in the records of the Royal Society.[15] Rochford found in his diving-bell off the coast of Sweden that though, being June, the surface of the sea was warm, at the bottom the water was as cold as on a wintry day in England. Boyle reported

He told me also, that the upper water did but cool and refresh him; but the deeper he went the Colder he felt it, which is the more considerable, because he had sometimes occasion to stay at 10 fathoms or even 80 foot under water. And I since found that he informed divers Virtuosi, that purposely consulted him, that he found the Coldnesse of the Water encrease with its depth: and gave that for the reason why he could not stay so many hours as otherwise he might, at the bottom of the Sea.[16]

This seemed to be equally true in other parts of the world. In the tropics it was common practice to lower bottles of wine into the sea in order to get cold. Boyle learned of this from a "famous Sea-Commander who had been upon the Affrican coast",[16] and from several other sources. The coldness of sea water in warm regions was also attested to by people who had talked to or swum with divers searching for pearls or coral. Only one related an experience to the contrary, off Cape Cormorin.

The most interesting account which Boyle received was of an observation made in a latitude of approximately 35°S. Having met, he said, an observing Traveller whose affairs or Curiosity had carried him to divers parts both of the East and West Indies, I enquired of him whether he had taken notice of any extraordinary deep soundings in the vaster seas, To which being answered, that some years agoe sailing to the East Indies in a very great ship, over a place on the other side the Line that was suspected to be very deep, they had the Curiosity to let down 400 Fathom of Line, and found they needed no lesse. Whereupon I enquired of him, whether he had taken notice of the Temperature of the sounding Lead as soon as 'twas drawn up: To which he told me, that he, and some others did; and that the Lead which was of the weight of about 30, or 35 1, had received so intense a degree of coldnesse as was very remarkable; insomuch that he thought that if it had been a masse of Ice, it could not have more vehemently refrigerated his hands.[17]

Boyle concluded that as regards temperature the sea should be considered as two layers, the upper layer, of varying depth, having a temperature similar to that of the air above and a lower layer which was always cold. He supposed that

It wil not be irrational to conceive that in reference to Temperature, those two Fluids, *Air* and *Water*, may have this in common, that where their *Surfaces* are contiguous, and in the neighbouring parts, they happen to be sometimes cold, and sometimes hot, as the particles they consist of, chance to be more or less agitated by the variously reflected *Sun-Beams*, or more or lesse affected by other causes of Heat. But that part of the Air which they call the second, & is superior to the first, as also the lower Region of the Sea, being more remote from the operation of those causes, doe retain their naturall or more undisturbed Temperature, which, as to us men, is a considerable degree of coldness.[18]

There was no record of ice being brought up from the sea floor by sounding leads but this did not mean that the cold there was not intense since salt water freezes at a lower temperature than fresh water.

To achieve any greater precision it would have been necessary to make systematic observations at different depths with thermometers. Members of the Royal Society had attempted this in 1663 (*see* Ch. 4) but Boyle was unable apparently to find anyone to do it for him. He wrote

If I had been furnished with opportunity, I would have engaged some ingenious Navigators to examine the Temperature of the Submarine-Regions, both of differing seasons of the year (especially the hottest part of *Summer* and the Coldness of *Winter*,) & with Hermetically seal'd Weatherglasses.[19]

Such experiments would, he expected, show if the temperature of the deep water was as low or lower than the freezing point of water, if it decreased with depth and if this decrease occurred in any recognizable proportion.

Boyle stressed the need to use a hermetically sealed thermometer for making observations at any depth. Some people, he said, would not admit that water had the power to press on mercury but in fact it had and he showed an experiment to prove that this was so. He lowered into water a glass vial full of mercury with a narrow glass tube leading up through the cork into a glass ball full of air. As the apparatus descended

deeper and deeper into the Water, the Mercury was pressed up higher and higher in the stem.[20]

It is interesting to note that Boyle did not find the idea that the sea was coldest at the bottom incompatible with the view that the earth was hottest at the centre. In the companion paper *Of the Temperature of the Subterraneall Regions as to Heat and Cold* he presented evidence which suggested that

in these yet inpenetrated Bowells of the Earth, there are great store-houses of either actuall Fires, or places considerably Hot, or, (in some Regions) of both.[21]

In the essay *Relations about the Bottom of the Sea* Boyle's task of collecting observations was made harder still because of the general lack of interest among seamen, as far as deep water was concerned. One "ancient Sea-Commander" told him

as others had don before, that when they sail'd in the Ocean very far from sight of Land, they did not often put themselves to the trouble of Sounding.[22]

Nevertheless Boyle was able to discover some interesting facts about the sea floor and the movements of the water below the surface of the sea.

It seemed that in general the sea gradually deepened the further one went from the shore. Nevertheless there were exceptions to this rule. The same commander told him that

in the Excavation that makes the Bottom of the Sea, within sight of the *Cape of Good Hope*, where though for the most part, he found the water to deepen more and more as he sailed further from the shore; yet in one place, he and others had met with a Bank (as he conceived it to be) at a considerable distance from the surface of the Water.[22]

Another sailor, "an Ancient Navigator, who passes for the most Experienced Pilote in our Nation for an East Indian voyage", reported that

not far from the mouth of our Channell, he had sometimes found the bottom of the Sea so abrupt, that in sailing twice the Length of the ship he had found the Water deepen from 30 fathom to a hundred, if not also much more.[23]

Boyle concluded that the sea floor must resemble the land in having hills and valleys and plains and precipices.

The idea that water was without weight in its proper position had survived into the seventeenth century, notwithstanding assertions to the contrary by distinguished scientists (*see* Ch. 3). Boyle showed how to demonstrate that the pressure of water increased with depth by lowering an empty glass beaker into water upside down so that the water could be seen to rise further up inside the deeper it went. The same thing happened in diving bells. Nevertheless Boyle wished for experimental proof that pressure increased with depth in the sea. He asked an engineer to do the work for him but he said that he had already done so on his own account. He had lowered a bottle to a depth of 40 fathoms and it had broken and a metal aeolipile had been crushed by the weight of the water.

Boyle had more to say on this subject in *An Hydrostatical Discourse*:[24]

I remember, that a friend* of the learned doctor's and mine, who is so eminent a virtuoso, as to have been once president of the royal society, related a while since to me, that a mathematical friend of his, whom he named, having an opportunity to try an experiment, I have in vain endeavoured to get tried for me, had the curiosity to let down in a deep sea a pewter-bottle, with weight enough to sink it, that he might try, whether any sweet water would strain in at the orifice or any other part; but when he pulled it up again he was much surprized to find the sides of his pewter-bottle very much compressed, and, as it were squeezed inward by the water.[25]

A friend who was accustomed to chill his wine by lowering it into the sea told Boyle that when he brought up his bottle the corks were driven in so hard that it was almost impossible to draw them out again. Someone else who had lowered corked stone bottles to a depth of 100 fathoms to see if any fresh water would strain in had the same experience. Boyle discounted the idea that this might be because the cold in the sea was

condensing the included air, and obliging nature to do the rest for fear of a vacuum.

The temperature of the sea below the surface was comparable to that of a cold day on land where no such effects were observed so that the increase in pressure must be responsible for these phenomena.

Another interesting fact which emerged from Boyle's conversation with the diver Rochford was that the disturbance of the sea by waves decreased with depth. Rochford told him that, once, a storm had blown up while he was at the bottom and that he knew nothing about it until he returned to the surface. He continued that

the Wind being stiffe, so that the waves were manifestly six or seven foot high above the surface of the Water, he found no signe of it at 15 fathom deep; but if the Blasts continued long, then it mov'd the Mudd at the Bottom, and made the water thick and dark.[26]

This seems to be the passage from which originated the idea, widely held in the eighteenth and early nineteenth centuries, and often accepted as true, that Boyle had said that waves could not rise more than 6 feet above the surface of the sea (*see* Ch. 9). This misconception was apparently

* Sir Robert Moray according to a note in the edition cited.

started by Count Luigi Ferdinando Marsigli (1658–1730) in his *Histoire Physique de la Mer*,[27] one presumes because he did not have a copy of Boyle's work by him at the time of writing, and bears no relation to what he was actually talking about.

Boyle also wished to find out if the deeper parts of the sea were subject to tidal streams and currents but he found it difficult

by reason of mens want of Curiosity to obtain satisfaction about a Problem that most Navigators I have conversed with did not seem to have so much as dreamd of.[28]

He was told that it was seamen's practice to keep a small boat in position in a current by lowering the lead into still water below. A naval commander told him that in the Sound the water at the bottom moved in the opposite direction to that at the top[28] (*see* Ch. 7).

Boyle learned from

an Engineer who was curious of Marine Observations, that a famous Sea Commander of his Acquaintance being also a great Mathematician, had affirmed to this Relator, that he had divers times observ'd, that when he let down his Plummet to a great depth but yet not to reach ground, it would be quickly carried by a motion quite cŏtrary to that of the Shallop whence they sounded and very much quicker then it; but I had this only at second hand.[28]

All this was interesting but inconclusive and Boyle had to leave the question open:

how far the inequality of the Soil at the bottom of the Sea, and how far the various depth of the Water, and some other circumstances, may alter the case, and make it hard to determine, what ought to be ascribed to Tides and what to Currents, are things which I will by no means be positive in, till I can meet with further Information.[29]

Boyle's third essay *Observations and Experiments about the Saltness of the Sea*[30] is in many ways the most interesting of the four. Here he started from the unsatisfactory state of affairs prevailing at the time, in which philosophers were challenging the ideas traced back to Aristotle, that the action of the sun on the water was the cause of salt and that the sea was only salt at the surface, but with little factual basis for their arguments. Whether or not one could accept the first premise depended largely on the truth of the second so Boyle wanted first of all to find out if the sea were salt throughout or only at the surface. The experience of divers indicated that it was as salt at the bottom as at the top.*

When he came to have experiments made on his own account Boyle found that he was not alone in seeking this information:

Meting with an inquisitive Engineer, that had frequented the Sea, and had several opportunities to make Observations of other kinds in deep Waters, I

---

* Some people said it was more so. See p. 160.

desir'd him that he would take along with him, a certain Copper Vessel of mine, furnished with two Valves opening upwards, and let it down for me the next time he went to Sea; on which occasion he told me, that (if I pleased) I might save my self the trouble of the intended tryal, for, with a Tin Vessel very little differing from that I had described unto him, he had had the curiosity near the Straight of *Gibraltar's* mouth, (where he had occasion to stay a good while) to fetch up Sea-water from the depth of about forty fathom, and found it to be as salt in taste as the Water near the Surface.[31]

He did not think it right, however, to take the engineer's word without some further proof and got him to obtain some samples of sea water with the apparatus. The engineer sent back specimens from the surface of the sea and from fifteen fathoms depth. Boyle compared their specific gravities by weighing a roll of brimstone first in one and then the other and could find no detectable difference between them.

From these circumstances Boyle felt justified in supposing that the sea was salt throughout and that its salinity was due as many recent writers supposed to the accumulation of dissolved minerals partly washed into the sea from the land by the action of rain and rivers and partly dissolved from the sea bed. Where fresh water occurred at the bottom of the sea, as it appeared, for example by Linschoten's narrative, that it sometimes did, this was probably due to fresh water springs in the sea floor which, as he showed, were perfectly feasible if the head of water were situated higher than the sea bed. But this would be a local phenomenon. It was impossible that fresh water of low density should permanently remain below salt water of high density.

Boyle was interested in measuring the proportion of salt in sea water. He found that evaporating the water and weighing the salt was a rather unreliable method, because the salt was deliquescent. Instead he preferred either to weigh equal volumes of salt and fresh water or to weigh a piece of sulphur in each in turn and to work out the relative densities by this comparison. He had sea water brought for him from the Channel and compared its specific gravity with that of water from the Thames. By the first method the sea water was heavier in a ratio of 1 : 45 parts and by the second in a ratio of 1 : 53 but when he repeated the comparison with distilled water he found that the salt water was heavier by one part in 35.

Boyle had found that water in brine springs might contain as much as one part of salt to eight of water. He reasoned that the sea was capable of holding much more salt than it actually did and tried to find out if the amount it contained varied from place to place. As already mentioned he secured the assistance of Henry Stubbs who made hydrometrical observations on a voyage to the West Indies (*see* p. 118). Stubbs discovered that the specific gravity of the sea increased as they sailed southwards until they reached 30°N latitude and then stayed the same.

This was only one of a number of observations that suggested that the commonly accepted idea that the sea grew more salt the nearer one went to the equator had no basis in fact. In two separate experiments reported to Boyle it had been found that the specific gravities of samples of sea water taken from the equator and from the latitude of the Cape of Good Hope were the same. Sir William Langhorne (1629–1715), factor of the East India Company at Masulipatam, wrote

I did, in order to your command, cause some Water to be saved under the Line, at our first access to it, intending, for want of good scales and weights, (being none to be come at aboard the Ship) to have kept it until it could be weighed, but by the forgetfulness of a servant, it was thrown away. Off the Cape in 37*d*. 00*m*. Southern latitude, I saved some again, and through the same want of weights, was fain to keep it until I came to the Line again; and then made the best shift I could for weights, and compar'd it with the Water there, filling the same Bottle again to the same height by a mark, and found it exactly the same weight. [32]

These results suggested that the salinity of sea water did not vary very much from place to place but Boyle was cautious not to make too sweeping a generalization for, as he observed,

to make a determination with any certainty about the degrees of the Seas Saltness *in general*, a great number of Observations, made in different Climates and in distant parts of the Ocean, would be necessary.[33]

In addition Boyle made some speculations on the nature of sea salt, chemistry not yet being sufficiently developed to enable him to make an analysis. He observed that the crystals of salt found on land and of sea salt looked and tasted similar and concluded that they were the same. Yet sea salt could not be salt alone but was a compound of all the animal, vegetable and mineral substances dissolved by water and washed into the sea. The bitter taste of sea water might further be ascribed, he supposed, to volcanic gases escaping from the sea floor. The most important application which could be expected from a knowledge of how sea water was made up would be the possibility of making it drinkable, by distillation or other means, on long sea voyages.

Boyle's fourth essay, modelled on the other three, dealt with reports about marine plants.[34] This completed his works specifically dealing with the sea but there is evidence that his interest in furthering scientific exploration at sea lasted throughout his life.

At some point in 1677 Boyle obtained from the government that an official returning to Tangier should make experiments for him at sea.[35]

The arrangement was apparently made through the Earl of Danby (1631–1712) and Sir Joseph Williamson (1633–1701) then Secretary of State and President of the Royal Society. The official in question was Captain Richard Bolland who was already actively interested in investigation at sea (*see* Chs. 4 and 7). He carried out the experiments at the mouth of the Strait of Gibraltar from the pinnace of the frigate *St David* in which he was travelling and in the presence of the captain, Sir Richard Munden (1640–1680), and others on 2 January 1678.[35]

Bolland lowered a bottle containing oil of aniseed to a depth of 8 fathoms. After a quarter of an hour they drew up the bottle and found that the oil was congealed which they took as proof of the coldness of the water.[36] They next lowered three bottles on 100 fathoms of line. Two of the bottles were corked with stoppers made from *lignum vitae*, apparently at Danby's suggestion, and after a few minutes these were seen floating on the surface. They hauled in the line and found that the two bottles were broken in pieces. The third bottle, stopped with cork, was full of water which, when tasted, seemed fresher than that on the surface around them.

Bolland sent an account of these experiments to Sir Joseph Williamson and he communicated it to the Royal Society in March 1678.[37] In 1691 Boyle sent the same account to J. C. de la Croze for inclusion in the *History of Learning*, a periodical publication giving, mostly, accounts of newly published books.[38] He wrote

Sir,

I Here send you an Experiment which made a great Noise In the Court of King *Charles* the Second and which will resolve all the Difficulties in the Questions which you propos'd to me, concerning the Coldness of Water. It was made by a Captain of a Ship, a Man of very good Sense, and in the Presence of a great many Persons; insomuch that there can be no manner of Doubt concerning it.[39]

This letter was quoted by Thomas Birch in his *Life of Boyle*, published in 1744.[40]

Another subject which interested Boyle in his later years was some attempts at the desalination of sea water. In 1683 his nephew Robert Fitzgerald (1638–1698) was one of a group of businessmen who applied for a patent for their process of distilling sea water. In November of that year Boyle carried out experiments in the presence of Charles II and his court to show that the water produced by this process was free from salt. His account of these experiments, written as a letter to his friend Dr John Beale (1603–1683), was published with the pamphlet issued by the company to advertise their product.[41]

Boyle did not reveal the nature of the test which he used for the presence of salt in the water. Instead he deposited an account of it with the Royal

Society to be opened after his death. When the papers were made public it appeared that he had used a solution or silver in *aqua fortis* (nitric acid) which when added to water containing, as he said, as little as one part in a thousand of salt produced a white precipitate (silver chloride). Sir Hans Sloane (1660–1753) gave a demonstration of this test at a meeting of the Society.[42] Dr R. E. W. Maddison, who has pieced together the story of Boyle's interest in desalination, points out that since Boyle had already published details of this quantitative test for the presence of salt in 1663, it is hard to see why he became so secretive about it later on.[43]

Dr Maddison describes the long drawn out altercation between Fitzgerald's group and an earlier claimant for the patent, William Walcot (1633–1699), who was finally awarded priority in 1695.[43] Walcot was apparently not the only person who felt a sense of grievance about the success of the company with which Boyle was connected. Dr Charles Leigh (1662–1701) wrote that an aeolipile

gave me the first hint of Dulcifying *Salt-Water*, which Experiment I shew'd to the University of *Oxford*, some Years before Mr. *FitzGerald* had a Patent for it; who Communicated this Experiment to him I know not, but its most certain it was not his own.[44]

It was not, however, the fact that fresh water could be produced by distillation which was contended for this was common knowledge. Dr Maddison shows that Fitzgerald's process involved some form of chemical addition, the nature of which remains a mystery, and that this, while removing the salt, probably made the water unpalatable if not actually poisonous, which was why their projects came to nothing.[43]

If Boyle's interest in marine science did not end with the publication of his essays, they certainly remained his outstanding achievement in this field. They represent more fully than any other work done in this country the new attitudes to scientific discovery as applied to understanding the sea. They succeeded in establishing concepts which have since generally been taken for granted, such as the idea that the entire sea is salt. In addition they recorded, perhaps for the first time, facts which modern oceanography has incorporated such as the diminution of wave activity with depth.

Of course many of the subjects which Boyle dealt with were discussed by his contemporaries if in a more diffuse manner. His essays were and are important because they summed up and digested much of the best of the ideas which were in the air at the time and which would otherwise have had little permanent effect on thinking. Partly because of the ease with which his thought presented in this concise form could be grasped and partly because of his immense scientific reputation, Boyle's essays on the sea were widely quoted, usually with approval. Nor was this confidence undeserved for Boyle gave a much more sober and accurate account of the physical characteristics of the ocean than any one else up to his time. His caution in admitting evidence and stating conclusions can be seen from the fact that while more recent research has explained much that he found mysterious and provided information for lack of which he was obliged to leave questions open there is little in his essays which it has contradicted.

From today's vantage point, exactly three hundred years later, it is possible to see Boyle's essays as an epitome of the much broader revolution which set aside the sterile traditions which had dominated thought about the sea for so long and replaced them with the observational approach from which marine science today has developed. Yet they were also in advance of their time, particularly in the sophisticated understanding they show of the systematic research which would be necessary to develop the subject further, a realization that was slow to dawn on the scientific world as a whole.

From a historical point of view, however, perhaps the most interesting and tantalizing aspect of Boyle's essays is the amount of light thrown by them on the extent to which other people were involved in his researches. Resident in London and Oxford, frail in health and absorbed in many other branches of learning, Boyle was almost entirely dependent on others for his information about the sea. His membership of official committees as well as his influential position both in science and in society enabled him to obtain co-operation over a large field. Professional seamen whose interest in the sea did not extend much beyond the managing of their ships were not often forthcoming but besides them he obtained help from a wide range of people, some of whom had become independently interested in research of this kind. The tantalizing part is that for reasons which are not apparent Boyle scarcely ever mentioned the names of his informants and it is rarely possible to attempt an identification. Nevertheless their undoubted existence strengthens the impression that while the main achievements in marine science during the seventeenth century were the work of comparatively few people, the extent of interest and involvement was very much wider than this (*see* Ch. 4). Certainly without these largely unknown workers and their enthusiasm, however transitory, for scientific research at sea, Boyle's work on marine science would have been largely impossible.

6. NOTES

1. John Aubrey, *Brief Lives* (ed. Oliver Lawson Dick), London (1950), p. 37.
2. Richard Waller, *The Posthumous Works of Robert Hooke* (1705), pp. vii–viii. William Derham, *The Philosophical Experiments and Observations of the late eminent Dr. Robert Hooke* (1726), pp. 1–2.

3. "An essay of Dr. John Wallis, exhibiting his hypothesis about the flux and reflux of the sea", *Phil. Trans.* (September 1666), no. 17, p. 264.

4. Robert Boyle, "Other inquiries concerning the sea", *Phil. Trans.* (October 1666), no. 18, pp. 315–316.

5. Robert Boyle, *Tracts Consisting of Observations About the Saltness of the Sea: An Account of a Statistical Hygroscope And its Uses: Together with an Appendix About the Force of the Air's Moisture: A Fragment about the Natural and Preternatural State of Bodies*, London (1673).

6. "Observations made by a curious and learned person, sailing from England, to the Carib-Islands", *Phil. Trans.* (September 1667). Vol. **2**, no. 27, pp. 494–502.

7. *Ibid.* p. 496.

8. Robert Boyle, *New Experiments and Observations touching Cold* in *The Works of the Honourable Robert Boyle* (ed. Thomas Birch), 5 vols, London (1744). Vol. **2**, pp. 311–312.

9. Robert Boyle, *Tracts Written By the Honourable Robert Boyle. About The Cosmicall Qualities of things. Cosmicall Suspitions. The Temperature of the Submarine Regions. The Temperature of the Subterraneall Regions. The Bottom of the Sea*, Oxford (1671).

10. Robert Boyle, *Observations and Experiments about the Saltness of the Sea* in *Tracts Consisting of Observations about the Saltness of the Sea, op. cit.*, (1673).

11. *Ibid.* pp. 1–2.

12. For example, *Relations about the Bottom of the Sea* in *Tracts about the Cosmicall Qualities of Things* (1671), p. 15, where he says:
    not having committed this Relation to writing, I dare not build much upon it.

13. Robert Boyle, *Of the Temperature of the Submarine Regions as to Heat and Cold* in *Tracts about the Cosmicall Qualities of Things* (1671). Reprinted in *The Works of the Honourable Robert Boyle* (ed. Thomas Birch) (1744). Vol. **3**, pp. 105–109.

14. *Oxford English Dictionary.*

15. "A Relation of M. Rochford's going downe under water at Gothenburg in Sweden", *Royal Society Classified Papers.* Vol. **6**, no. 28.

16. Robert Boyle, *Of the Temperature of the Submarine Regions as to Heat and Cold, op. cit.* p. 10.

17. *Ibid.* pp. 13–14.

18. *Ibid.* pp. 14–15.

19. *Ibid.* pp. 17–18.

20. *Ibid.* p. 19.

21. Robert Boyle, *Of the Temperature of the Subterraneall Regions as to Heat and Cold*, in *Tracts about the Cosmicall Qualities of Things* (1671), p. 28.

22. *Idem.*, *Relations about the Bottom of the Sea*, in *Tracts about the Cosmicall Qualities of Things* (1671), p. 3. Reprinted in *The Works of the Honourable Robert Boyle* (ed. Thomas Birch) (1744). Vol. **3**, pp. 110–113.

23. *Ibid.* pp. 5–6.

24. Robert Boyle, *An Hydrostatical Discourse, occasioned by the objections of the learned Dr. Henry More, against some explications of new experiments made by Mr. Boyle* in *The Works of the Honourable Robert Boyle* (ed. Thomas Birch) (1744). Vol. **3**, pp. 268–289.

25. *Ibid.* p. 286.

26. Robert Boyle, *Relations about the Bottom of the Sea, op. cit.* p. 11.

27. Luigi Ferdinando Marsigli, *Histoire Physique de la Mer*, Amsterdam (1725),

p. 48. Marsigli measured waves seven feet high on the south coast of France. He was under the impression that Boyle had found evidence to show that

le vent le plus fort ne pénetre jamais plus de six pieds, au dessous de l'horizon ordinaire de la Mer.

He supposed that the extra foot of height which he had encountered was due to the shallow sandy beach where his observations were made.

28. Robert Boyle, *Relations about the Bottom of the Sea, op. cit.* p. 14.
29. *Ibid.* pp. 15–16.
30. Robert Boyle, *Observations and Experiments about the Saltness of the Sea.* Reprinted in *The Works of the Honourable Robert Boyle* (ed. Thomas Birch) (1744). Vol. **3**, pp. 378–388.
31. *Ibid.* p. 9.
32. *Ibid.* p. 30.
33. *Ibid.* p. 35.
34. Robert Boyle, *The Fourth Section belonging to the Tract intitul'd Relations about the Bottom of the Sea* in *Tracts Consisting of Observations about the Saltness of the Sea* (1673). Reprinted in *The Works of the Honourable Robert Boyle* (ed. Thomas Birch) (1744). Vol. **3**, pp. 388–389.
35. Richard Bolland to Sir Joseph Williamson, 13 February 1678, *Royal Society Letter Book* (Copy). Vol. **8**, pp. 35–37.
36. Oil of aniseed has a freezing point of —3°C.
37. Thomas Birch, *History of the Royal Society.* Vol. **3** (1757) p. 394.
38. "An account of some observations made in the great congregation of waters, by lowering bottles down into the sea six hundred foot deep from the surface, January 2d, 1677/8", *The History of Learning: or, an abstract of several books lately published, as well abroad, as at home* (ed. J. Cornaud or Cornand de la Croze), London (1691–1692), pp. 58–59.
39. *Ibid.* July 1691, p. 57.
40. Thomas Birch, *The Life of the Honourable Robert Boyle*, London (1744), pp. 281–282.
41. *A letter of Mr. Boyle's to the learned Dr. John Beal, Fellow of the Royal Society, concerning fresh water made out of sea-water, printed at the desire of the patentees, in a tract intitled, Salt water sweetned, by R. Fitzgerald, London, 1683* in *The Works of the Honourable Robert Boyle* (ed. Thomas Birch) (1744). Vol. **4**, pp. 159–160.
42. "An account of the Honourable Robert Boyle's way of examining water as to freshness and saltness", *Phil. Trans.* (1691–1693). Vol. **17**, pp. 627–639.
43. R. E. W. Maddison, "Studies in the life of Robert Boyle F.R.S. Part 2. Salt water freshened", *Notes Rec. R. Soc. Lond.* (1952). Vol. **9**, no. 2, pp. 196–216.
44. Charles Leigh, *The Natural History of Lancashire, Cheshire, and the Peak in Derbyshire*, Oxford (1700), p. 13.

7. THE CURRENTS IN THE STRAIT OF GIBRALTAR

> For want of Experience in the Tides and Currents here, this Age has
> produc'd but too many Examples of the loss both of Men of War, and of
> Merchant-men.
>
> *Richard Bolland*

IN June 1661 the Royal Society approved a list of observations which, it
was hoped, the Earl of Sandwich would carry out during his voyage to the
Mediterranean[1] (*see* Appendix, pp. 407–408). One of the instructions read
as follows:

try whether in the middle of the Straits the surface water flow eastward,
whilst the lower part of it runs westward.

Scientists had at some stage already become aware that the water movements in the Strait of Gibraltar would repay closer study.

The existence of a surface current flowing eastward from the Atlantic
through the Strait of Gibraltar and into the Mediterranean was well
known in ancient times. The author of *De Mundo*, a work attributed to
Aristotle during the Middle Ages but now thought to have come from a
follower of Posidonius, wrote of it in these terms:

at the so-called Pillars of Herakles, the Ocean forms a current into the inner
sea, as into a harbour.[2]

Strabo said that the current resulted from the inrush of the tide from the
ocean, channelled into the Strait by the coasts on either side.[3] El Mas'údí
wrote:

The current from the ocean is so great that it is perceptible.[4]

As time went on and a more questioning attitude arose people began to
wonder how it was that a current of such magnitude could flow per-
petually into an otherwise landlocked sea. The only possible explanation
was that the Mediterranean had some outlet which could not be seen or
that there was some other mechanism at work by which the water escaped
as fast as it went in. Leonardo da Vinci guessed that some might be lost
through evaporation as a result of the joint action of the sun and wind

while the rest, in an analogy with the working of the human body, would, he said,

flow through the bowels of the earth and vivify this terrestrial machine.[5]

John Greaves was forcibly struck by the difficulty of accounting for the surface current during his travels in the Mediterranean[6] (*see* Ch. 4). Since the sea was also supplied by rivers and rainfall he was amazed that it had never become full to overflowing. He discounted the explanation which he had previously come across, that the current flowed in on one side of the Strait and out on the other, since his own experience and that of his ship's captain gave no support to the idea. Instead, prompted by a sounding of over 1,000 fathoms which he had made in the vicinity without finding bottom, he suggested that a subterranean channel opened in the bed of the sea and carried the excess water away. This explanation was to be found in other writers too, Fournier[7] and Kircher[8] included.

The problem continued to fascinate the scientifically inclined and the members of the Royal Society were no exception. Sir Robert Southwell (1635–1702) said in 1675:

I remember, that long since I heard it agitated in this Society as an illustrious problem to give the reason, why the Euxine and ocean both running into the Mediterranean, as also many rivers, why the said sea doth not run over, and by what ways it doth empty itself of what it doth visibly receive.[9]

There was no lack of ideas to choose from. Thomas Smith (1638–1710) listed the alternatives, which included

subterranean vents, cavitys and indraughts, *exhalations* by the *Sun beams*, the running out of the water on the *African* side as if there were a kind of circular motion of the water.

as well as the undercurrent theory which he wished to see adopted.[10]

How the idea of an undercurrent arose and how it came to be considered by the Royal Society in 1661 is not at all clear but Henry Sheeres (*d.* 1710), its most vigorous opponent but a man with considerable local knowledge, gave a clue as to how it may have begun. He wrote:

Mariners, who are most conversant in this Element, are very positive in their Assertions, affirming, that there is a Disemboguing, and that it is performed by a counter Current or invisible Stream some space beneath the Surface running continually back, and think they have the Authority of a Demonstration for this Opinion, from a vulgar Experiment they make by letting fall an Anchor, and veering but two or three Cables; and albeit the Anchor came not near the Bottom; yet they found that the Ship's Way or Motion, became by this means very much retarded, which was evident by their now stemming the Current, which before carried them along with it.[11]

This sounds like the common seamen's practice, described by many writers of the period, such as Sir Jonas Moore,[12] for measuring the speed of a surface current by lowering something that would act as a sea anchor through the current into still water underneath. Dr Henry Stubbs wrote from the West Indies:

To know which way the Current sets, in calm weather, no wind at all stirring, thus they try it. They hoyse out their boat, and having row'd a little from the ship, they let loose their plummet (ours did weigh 40 pounds) and sink it 200 fathom. Then though it never touches the bottom, yet will the boat turn head against the Current (which constantly runs very strongly of it self, since so much of the Sea runs into the Gulf of *Mexico*) and rides as firmly, as if it were fastned by the strongest Cable and Anchor to the Bottom.[13]

Sheeres may have been doing rather less than justice to the seamen for later on there were reports of lines actually being carried outwards by the undercurrent (*see* p. 146). In any case, given that they were originally responsible for the idea, it is tempting to speculate that Lawrence Rooke, who is one of the most likely persons to have composed the instructions for the Earl of Sandwich, perhaps heard of it through seafaring friends (*see* Ch. 4, p. 75) and himself introduced it to the Society.

If this is necessarily rather speculative it is possible to be much more positive as to how the realization came about that an undercurrent existed in the Sound dividing what are now Denmark and Sweden. This knowledge was brought back by sailors and reported to scientific acquaintances as though the events were still quite recent.* The experiences they described may well have been paralleled in the Strait of Gibraltar though as the Sound was both narrower and shallower the undercurrent there was easier to detect and, presumably, well-known to the local inhabitants.

Robert Boyle was told of the undercurrent in the Sound when he was collecting material for his essays on the sea. He wrote:

I was informed by a skilful observer, that commanded many of our English men of war, that he had, near the Sound, observed the upper and lower parts of the water to move with considerable swiftness quite different ways.[14]

Thomas Smith learned of a similar, if not the same occasion, from an able seaman who told him how a pinnace had put out from the ship and been caught in the grip of the surface current. The crew lowered a bucket containing a cannon ball to stop the boat from being swept away. At a "certain depth" it held the boat against the current but when the bucket was lowered deeper still, he reported,

the *boat* was driven a-head to wind-ward against the upper *Current*: the *current*

---

* The naval expedition to the Baltic of 1659?

aloft, as he added, not being above 4 or 5 *fathom* deep, and that the lower the bucket was let fall, they found the *under-Current* the stronger.[15]

The situation discovered in the Sound differed from that in the Strait of Gibraltar in that the direction of the currents was reversed. In the Sound the surface current flowed out of the Baltic into the Atlantic and the undercurrent inwards from the ocean. This is now understood as happening because the Baltic is fresher than the Atlantic so that its water flow outwards is compensated by the inflow of more saline water below. The Mediterranean on the other hand is more saline than the Atlantic so that its water forms an undercurrent while less saline water flows in above. At the time there was no such measure of agreement and people differed very strongly as to the evidence they would accept and the explanation for it.

Smith became interested in the currents in the Strait of Gibraltar when he sailed with a British embassy to Constantinople in 1668. In the journal of the voyage which he published, he argued that the similarity of conditions in the Strait and the Sound made it more than likely that there was an undercurrent in the Strait and that this was how the Mediterranean rid itself of its excess water. He was keen to make observations in the Strait himself but circumstances did not allow it. He wrote:

both times I past, the Easterly wind blew so hard, that there was no putting out the boat with any safety; nor indeed at these times had we any leisure for such a *Curiosity*; which those who liv'd at *Tangier*, might have tryed without any difficulty or danger.[16]

Tangier became a British colony in 1661, part of the dowry of Charles II's Portuguese queen, Catherine of Braganza. It remained in British hands for little over twenty years during which time it was more of a liability than an asset, ceaselessly harassed by the Moroccans and notorious even in that uninhibited age for its riotous living. Yet before the decision to abandon it was taken much time and effort were spent on improvements and one of these was the building of a great breakwater, the Mole, to shelter the anchorage from winter gales. The first contract was given to a committee consisting of Lord Rutherford, Admiral Sir John Lawson (*d.* 1665) and Hugh Cholmley.[17]

One of the engineers working on the Mole in the 1660 s was Henry Sheeres.[18] In 1668 he helped the Earl of Sandwich to make a survey of its progress.[19] Beyond this, nothing seems to be known of his antecedents. Apparently he combined considerable ability as an engineer with a somewhat flamboyant personality and he evidently fancied himself as a polymath. Samuel Pepys who met him during a visit to London in 1667 wrote:

a good, ingenious man, but do talk a little too much of his travels.[20]

Later they became friends and in after years Pepys paid tribute to his competence,[21] an estimate borne out by the durability of his work on the Mole.[19]

Sheeres, like Childrey, was one of these people who while outside the immediate circle of the Royal Society, were influenced by new trends in scientific thought. He seems to have been anxious to contribute to the new learning and may have hoped, perhaps unconsciously, that by doing so he would gain admittance to that *élite*. Whatever his motives, he was resolved not to waste the opportunities which Tangier offered for the study of natural phenomena, of which the current in the Strait of Gibraltar was one. Unfortunately his enthusiasm for research outran his appreciation of the difficulties involved and while his work on the current met with some approval in scientific circles his later endeavours were more or less disastrous.[22]

In 1669 the body responsible for building the Mole was reorganized. Cholmley became surveyor-general and Sheeres was appointed clerk-examiner, one of the chief officials.[23] During the next few years the work suffered a number of vicissitudes. A new construction plan was adopted at Sheeres's instance but things still did not go smoothly. He and Cholmley quarrelled with each other and Cholmley returned to England, leaving Sheeres in charge.

It was presumably while this was going on that Sheeres carried out his study of the Strait of Gibraltar. This clearly occupied him for a considerable length of time. He wrote:

Having therefore kept with much care and exactness, an *Ephemeris* of the Weather, as also of the Current for near four years together during my Abode at *Tangier*, I became both enabled and encouraged to write not only the History of Matter of Fact in both, but upon Mature Debate to make some Offer at the Reason and Causes; for, after having compar'd my Yearly Observations, and finding both the Weather and the Current agreeing in their respective Periods, and their Changes and Resolutions held exact Content and Analogy with the Sun's Motions, I took hence my first Hint for proposing the *Hypothesis* by which *Phænomena* may be resolv'd.[24]

He embodied his conclusions in a pamphlet called *A Discourse touching the Current in the Streight of Gibraltar*.

Sheeres began his *Discourse* with a scathing review of some of the ideas put forward to explain the need for the current flowing into the Mediterranean. The idea of a tunnel leading out of the sea bed seemed to him too "feeble and defective of Argument" to require any refutation further than to observe, that since Nature doth nothing in vain, it would be an idle Supposition to think, so vast a quantity of Water should be hurried into the *Mediterranian* for no other Reason but to be hurried out again.[25]

The idea of an undercurrent in the Strait, he felt, deserved a more detailed criticism though it too was clearly the result of unsound thinking.

Sheeres's reason for dismissing the possibility of an undercurrent was that, as he thought, water can only move from one place to another down a slope or as a result of differences in its own level. When such a disparity

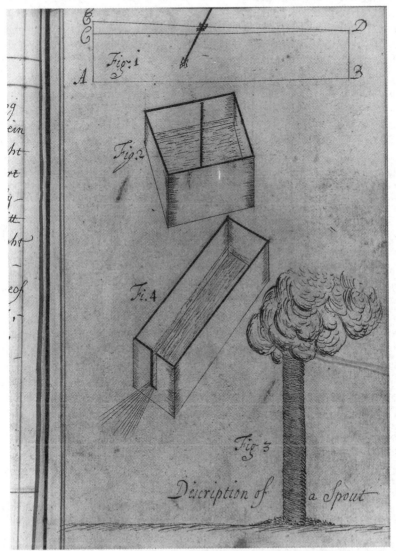

FIG. 5. Sketches illustrating Sir Henry Sheeres's *Discourse touching the Current in the Streight of Gibraltar*. Reproduced by permission of the Master and Fellows of Magdalene * College, Cambridge.

occurs its weight causes it to flow downwards until an even surface is re-stored. He did not go on to consider that water might not be homogeneous and that internal adjustments might take place without any irregularity being present either in the surface of the water or its bed. On his limited premise the only possible cause of the current from the Atlantic was that the surface of the Mediterranean was lower than the level of the ocean out-side. The movement of water was confined to a wedge-shaped layer at the surface, its greatest depth being the same as the disparity between the two bodies of water. By the same argument it was inconceivable that any return flow should take place below.

Sheeres endeavoured to demonstrate the general truth of his assumption by making observations which would show that in any moving water it was only a shallow superficial layer which was actually in motion. He made his observations in the Thames, using a hollow cane with a weight at one end and a cork float fastened in the middle. In still water the cane floated upright but in the current of the river it was seen to bend at an angle in the direction of the current. Sheeres said that this was because the still water beneath the current was acting as a drag on the weighted end below[26] (see Fig. 5).

Having disposed of other theories to his satisfaction, Sheeres proceeded to advance what he thought was the true explanation for the current. This was the evaporation taking place from the Mediterranean, evaporation so rapid that the rivers which flowed into the sea and local rainfall could not keep pace with it. It was a matter of everyday experience that evaporation took place very quickly on land in that part of the world but to ascertain its force at sea he carried out a series of comparative observations. To begin with he prepared a graduated container full of water and left it outside in the mid summer sun for twelve hours.[27] At the end of this time its level had fallen by four inches. Next he repeated the observation with the con-tainer suspended over the mouth of a deep well and found that the water level fell somewhat less. Finally he floated the container in the bay at Tangier for twelve hours. From this result he deduced that

the Mediterranian about that Season of the Year, were it not for the Supplies it receives from the Ocean by the Streight of *Gibralter*, &c. would abate by this violent Effect of the Sun's Heat upon its Surface, at the least three Inches in every four and twenty hours.[28]

This being so, if all the Mediterranean's sources of supply were suddenly cut off, the effect would be dramatic:

it is allmost demonstrable were it not for the Euxin (the Receptacle of many great Rivers) which ever runs and disembogues into the Mediterr: by the Propontis, together with the constant Tribute of many other noble Rivers which discharge themselves directly into this Sea, and the vast floods of rayne that for two and three months together are transported by Southerly winds out of that great Ocean, were it not I say for these Supplyes, and that if we might have liberty to Suppose noe communication with the Ocean but this Sea a vast extended Lake bounded on all Quarters, and then making a Calculation from these Experiments by a rule of meane Proportion it will appeare that by the force and prevalency of exhalation the Mediterr: would abate near 40 foot in a perpendicular line in the revolution of one yeare.[29]

Having established his central hypothesis, Sheeres went on to discuss seasonal variations which, he said, he had observed in the current from the Atlantic and to link them with local weather conditions. He had found, he said, that the current was strongest in summer. In spring and autumn it was less noticeable and in winter it disappeared altogether. According to the Spaniards from Tarifa with whom he had spoken and one of the British commander, Sir John Harman, there was occasionally a current in* the opposite direction at this time of year as well as times at which no current was in evidence and the tidal ebb and flow could be felt right across the Strait.[30]

The explanation which Sheeres gave of these variations was that evaporation took place mostly in summer so that the disparity of level between the Mediterranean and the ocean outside was then at its greatest, causing a strong inflow from the Atlantic. In spring and autumn the sun was less strong and in consequence evaporation less intense and the current slacker. In winter evaporation ceased so that the inflow stopped altogether but this was the time of year when most rain fell in the Mediterranean so that sometimes the disparity of level was reversed and a current flowed out into the Atlantic.

The result, so Sheeres said, was that the current tended to flow in the opposite direction to the wind, since in winter westerly winds prevailed but in summer easterly winds were encountered, often just in the vicinity of the strait. These "levant" winds were, he said, caused by the water vapour rising from the sea surface and escaping through the strait which acted as a funnel. He demonstrated how this happened by heating a bath of water with a gap left in one of the sides to represent the strait[31] (see Fig. 5). The pressure of steam through the gap was sufficient to extinguish a candle. If further proof were needed, the east winds were so damp that at Tangier their watches stood still in their pockets and swords rusted in the scabbard.

Ingenious though it is, Sheeres's exposition of the interaction between the current and the weather and its seasonal changes is not borne out by observations made either at the same time (see p. 144) or since.[32] These rather seem to indicate that easterly winds considerably impede the current whereas Sheeres claimed that it was at its strongest when they were blowing. French oceanographers have shown that there is a relationship between fluctuations in the surface current and undercurrent and variations in barometric pressure over the Mediterranean[33] but these are short term. The possibility of seasonal variations in the currents remains in the realm of probability because observations have to this day never been carried out for more than a few weeks consecutively.[34] Whether evaporation takes place mainly in summer as Sheeres supposed or in winter, as is usual in the ocean,[35] there seems to be no support in fact for his statement that the surface current ceases to flow in winter. He was right in saying that easterly winds prevail there in summer but no one has yet looked to see if they occur directly as the result of evaporation as he thought.[36]

It is therefore still difficult to gauge the precision of Sheeres's observations. There is no doubt however that his arguments were vitiated by his lack of awareness of the most up to date scientific thinking of the day, in which the possibility of internal movements in fluids was admitted (*see* Ch. 5, p. 97, and Ch. 6, p. 125). In addition he never stopped to think what became of the accumulating salt which the evaporation would leave behind in the Mediterranean, but he was not alone in this. All in all the *Discourse*, intended as a piece of good Baconian research, was its very antithesis. Sheeres started with his basic concept and, having made some observations which seemed to support it, imagined that he had satisfactorily solved the problem.

In the winter of 1674–1675 storms breached the Mole and Sheeres and Cholmley submitted rival plans for its repair and continuation to the Lords Commissioners. It was while he was in London for this purpose that Sheeres made his *Discourse* public. In the spring of 1675 he sent a copy to Pepys with a letter,[37] in the fulsome style then approved of, showing amongst other things that he had been talking about it for some time:

Honble Sr

The little Tract touching the Current so long since promised you, and dedicated to you in my thoughts now at length kisses your hands; nor hath it rested all this while through any hopes of a more correct method it could attayne by delay, it being now Borne with the same imperfections it was Conceived: Nor was it reasonable I could think to better my considerations thereupon by study or Delay, since from Bookes I could not hope much service, the Discourse being perfectly new, and Time and Absence would have blotted out the fresh impressions which Observation, Experimt and Warmth of thought upon the Place might suggest, or [word illegible] Notions less apposite then what I finde in my Journall whereof this is allmost a perfect transcript. The Delay then I humbly pray you to beleiue was through a more iust conscience of the Disproportion my utmost study and endeauoure must euer hould with my opinion of your exceeding Merrit, and my owne ambition to offer at something in your Service that might with some sort of Emphasis help me to expresse with what perfect Zeale, Affect. and Obedience I am

Hond Sr Your most Fayth. most Dutifull & most humble Servant
H. Shere

Frō my Lodging 10th Mar. 1674/5.

The *Discourse* was not printed at this stage. Copies were made in manuscript and it was from one of these that the published version was taken in 1703.[38] Even so it is clear that a number of people must have read it. Sir William Petty (1623–1687) mentioned Sheeres's observations at a Royal Society meeting in February 1675, contrasting them with a report from the Sound that wind and current always took the same direction.[39] Two months later Sir Robert Southwell gave a glowing account of the work in his *Discourse on Water*[9] read to the Royal Society in April. In it he welcomed an explanation which accounted for the current in the Strait of Gibraltar without resorting to

subterraneous communication with the Caspian Lake, and without fancying that the water, which comes in at the top, goes out again at the bottom.[40]

Sheeres was elected a fellow not long after. The Society hoped that he would continue his work when he returned to Tangier. It was almost certainly for him that Henry Oldenburg prepared the *Inquiries ffor Tanger, and other parts of Barbary*, dated 22 May 1676.[41] In it the following passage occurs:

The motions of the Mediterranean Sea having been already with much care and ingenuity observ'd by the person, to whom these Inquiries are recommended, 'twill be needlesse to say anything more of that matter here; it being not to be doubted but that his own Curiosity will invite him to adde what Observations he can to those he hath formerly made.

Sheeres's plans for completing the Mole were accepted by the Commissioners and he was appointed surveyor-general in place of Cholmley. When he returned to Tangier in the summer of 1676 his new responsibilities left him little time for scientific pursuits. He wrote to Pepys:

My head is broken with the Cares and Difficultyes I encounter on my Entring upon the Works, though I trust I shall Overcome all, and be shortly more at ease if it please God to send me my health, being at this time very ill in Bedd of a Flux and Feaver, the usuall Welcome Strangers meet with here.[42]

Even this note of optimism had disappeared three years later when he complained of

the unexpected difficulties of my toylsom charge; which to this day render me so little Master of my Resolutions, that the few Minutes I borrow, like broken Slumbers, scarce afford me leave to reflect seriously on any other Subject.[43]

In 1683 Tangier was abandoned and Sheeres had the thankless task of destroying the Mole on which he had spent so many years of his life. Back in England he busied himself in public affairs. He was knighted by James II for his part in the battle of Sedgemoor and after the accession of William and Mary spent several years in disgrace for suspected Jacobite activities. His literary output was considerable and included translations from the classics as well as scientific works but he does not seem to have returned to the subject of the current in the Strait of Gibraltar. Nor was it indeed likely that he would. The question had been satisfactorily settled as far as he was concerned and he was not the kind of person to suffer second thoughts.

Not everyone though was content to accept his solution to the problem and one person who disputed his arguments from an equally good if not better knowledge of local conditions was his subordinate in the Mole Office, Captain Richard Bolland. Bolland is a shadowy figure. He seems to have been in the Navy for he talked of having been with Sir John Lawson on one of his voyages.[44] During the 1660s he came to Tangier and in 1669, at the time of the reorganization, was given a minor official position in the body responsible for work on the Mole.[23] At some stage he became interested in the movement for studying the sea and during a voyage to England in 1676 he made observations of his own (*see* Ch. 4, p. 86). Both these and some of his later ideas show that he was acquainted with the difficulties which were being encountered in this kind of work. On his return voyage, in January 1678, he made further observations, this time on behalf of Robert Boyle (*see* Ch. 6, p. 127).

Bolland was apparently a maritime surveyor by profession. His work at Tangier included making a hydrographic survey of the Strait of Gibraltar and this gave him first-hand knowledge of the water movements going on there. He assembled his results in a chart (Fig. 6) which he presented to Samuel Pepys in a volume of manuscripts called a *Mediterranean Journall*, when he arrived in England in 1676.[44] This was not of course a fortuitous

* gift. Pepys was Secretary to the Navy and Sheeres had provided Bolland with an introduction.[45] In a letter accompanying the *Journall* Bolland modestly expressed the hope that Pepys would

please to accept these imperfect Observations and to pardon the presumption of the Offerer who haveing with some Toyle and time enquired into the various motions and appearances of the Congregation of Waters, the Sphere of your great Comand adventures to lay down before you this Rude and undigested heape of his Triviall remarks.

In notes accompanying the chart Bolland described how he had made

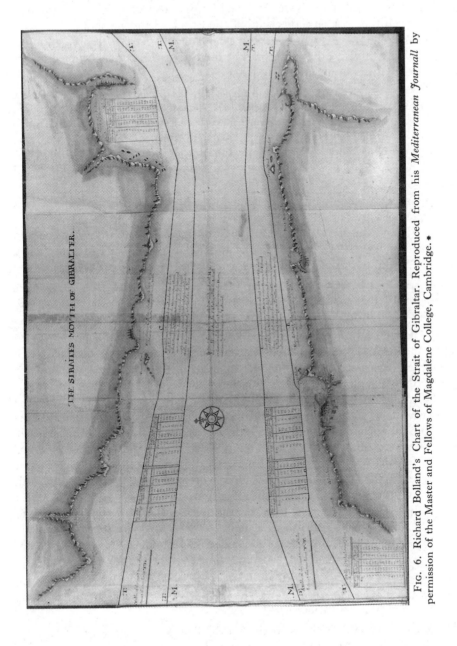

FIG. 6. Richard Bolland's Chart of the Strait of Gibraltar. Reproduced from his *Mediterranean Journall* by permission of the Master and Fellows of Magdalene College, Cambridge. *

his observations of the distribution of surface water movements in the Strait (*see* p. 111). These had shown him that it was possible to distinguish between the areas at either side of the Strait, along the shore, where the movements were predominantly tidal and changed direction with the flood and ebb and the centre part of the Strait which was occupied by the current from the Atlantic. He wrote:

The Current has its continual passage into the *Mediterranean*, if not alter'd by some extream of Weather. And altho' I know some are of a contrary Opinion, yet there is nothing that resembles Truth more, than Demonstration upon Matter of Fact. In Nine Years that I have liv'd and sail'd from *Tangier*, I did never see any Ships in the middle of the *Streights*, happening then to be calm, or little Wind, but was infallibly driven in, if she could not reach the side of Ebb upon neither Shoar.[46]

This was surely intended as a comment on Sheeres's idea of which he must have been well aware.

Bolland did not deny that evaporation must play an important part in disposing of the vast quantities of water flowing into the Mediterranean but he did not think that it necessarily excluded other agencies. He wrote:

it seems most reasonable, that as the *Streights* Mouth of Gibraltar has its continual Indraught aloft, so the superficial part thereof may have its recourse back again below.[47]

Bolland advanced no explanation for the mechanism behind such an undercurrent but suggested that its presence could be detected with special apparatus. He described an instrument resembling the lead for sounding without a line but conical in shape with an interior spring for releasing the float when it hit the bottom. The float would drift with the currents as it came up and if it surfaced ahead of the ship, supposing this to be at anchor and pointing into the surface current, then it would clearly have been affected by a countercurrent (*see* Fig. 7).[48] His other idea was to lower a square canvas sail from a small boat. He thought that when it reached the undercurrent, at a depth of perhaps 100 fathoms, the sail would tow the boat against the surface current.

It seems unlikely that these highly ingenious ideas were ever put into practice. Bolland returned to Tangier early in 1678. On the way he made experiments for Robert Boyle and ended his account of the work, in a letter to Sir Joseph Williamson, with the assurance that he would

Proceed the first convenient opertunity as neare as I can by Experience and Demonstration to resolve you the great Inquiries concerning the Current of the Streights Mouth of Giberaltar.[49]

Six months later Sheeres writing to Sir Palmes Fairborne gave the news that he was dead.[50] Other letters show he had been ill for some time.

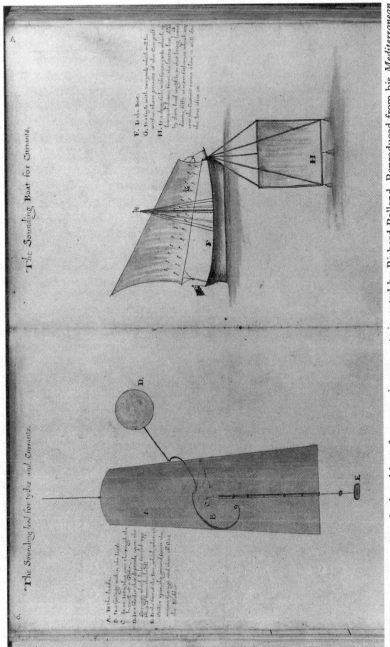

FIG. 7. The sounding lead and boat for measuring currents invented by Richard Bolland. Reproduced from his *Mediterranean Journall* by permission of the Master and Fellows of Magdalene College, Cambridge.*

The undercurrent hypothesis was kept alive by Thomas Smith who in 1683 read a paper to the Oxford Philosophical Society[51] in which he repeated the arguments used in the journal of his voyage to Constantinople (*see* p. 135). It was unfortunate that, like Bolland, Smith was unable to suggest any concrete reason for supposing that the undercurrent really existed. He could only point to similar situations, the currents in the Sound, the conditions off the British coast where, as seamen had long since known, at certain states of the tide the surface water flowed in a different direction from the bottom water, and argue from these that there was a likelihood of the same thing happening in the Strait of Gibraltar. Of the two, Bolland's contribution was the more interesting, on account of his local knowledge, but Smith's paper was published in the *Philosophical Transactions*[10] and gained a currency denied to the other.

There were some interesting repercussions to Smith's paper. In August 1684 a Mr Lee (presumably Charles Leigh) of Brasenose College told the Oxford Society that a friend of his in Lancashire who had lived in Tangier told him that he had investigated the movement of water in the Strait of Gibraltar. He lowered lines with weights on the end and found that whichever way the surface current was going his ropes were always drawn outwards.[52]

Three weeks later, on 26 August 1684, Dr Robert Plot informed the Oxford Society that a Mr Hugh Percy of Weymouth had tried the experiment of lowering a bucket with a weight inside it into the strait and that the bucket had been carried out towards the ocean.[53] Plot introduced this piece of evidence when discussing Smith's ideas and the possibility of the undercurrent in his work *De Origine Fontium* in 1685.[54]

Notwithstanding this favourable evidence, most people seem to have turned against the undercurrent and in Britain the evaporation theory held sway almost unchallenged until the end of the eighteenth century. This preference was presumably due to dislike of an idea which seemed wholly speculative and also to the support given to evaporation by Edmond Halley whose word carried great weight in his own and in succeeding generations. In fact Halley did not discuss whether or not an undercurrent was feasible, people merely assumed from his work that matters could be adequately explained without one. He was primarily interested in finding out how much water was lost from the sea by evaporation (*see* p. 170) and used the Mediterranean as an example but since he did not allow for any loss of water by means of an undercurrent in his calculations their assumption was probably justified.

In order to show how much water could be evaporated from the surface of the sea during an average summer day Halley heated a pan of salt water to an appropriate temperature over a period of two hours and measured the diminution in volume.[55] From the result he calculated that for every 10 cubic inches of the sea's surface one would be evaporated every day in summer. This would, he said,

be found abundantly sufficient to serve for all the Rains, Springs and Dews, and account for the *Caspian* Seas being always at a stand, neither wasting nor overflowing; as likewise for the Current said to set always in, at the Streights of *Gibralter*, tho those Mediterranean Seas receive so many and so considerable Rivers.[56]

Halley used the figure he had obtained and a rough estimate of the area of the Mediterranean to calculate that that sea would lose at least 5,280 million tons of water a day in summer through evaporation, not to mention what would be lost to dry winds blowing over the surface of the sea. Using the only figure available to him, an estimate of the volume of water passing Kingston Bridge on the Thames, he calculated that the rivers flowing into the Mediterranean would replace only 1,827 million tons, or about a third of this. The current from the Atlantic would necessarily supply the remainder.

Given the scanty material he had to work with, Halley's adventurous reasoning was sound as far as it went. Exact measurements of the amount of water evaporated from the Mediterranean are still lacking but Professor G. Wüst has given an average of 10,800 million tons a day and calculates that rivers make good a third of this.[57]

The undercurrent hypothesis was neglected not because there was any barrier of understanding which rendered a theoretical solution inherently impossible in the light of knowledge then available but because its principal champions, Bolland and Smith, were not theoretical men and had no inkling of what lines it would take. That a comprehensive explanation could be achieved at the time is beyond dispute because while the events described were taking place the Italian scientist and engineer Count Luigi Ferdinando Marsigli had studied and explained a similar pattern of currents in the Bosporus—a task which, ironically, had been suggested to him by an Englishman.

Marsigli was born in Bologna[58] and studied under Geminiano Montanari (1632–1687), himself the author in 1684 of a work on the tides and currents of the Adriatic.[59] He went to Constantinople in 1679, when he was 21 years old. There he heard about the undercurrent in the Bosporus from the Turkish fishermen and from the British ambassador to the Sultan, Sir John Finch (1626–1682):

Questo è quel moto da me chiamato col nome di *Corrente Sottana*, opposto al moto superficiale, ò superiore finora descritto, alla cui speculazione mi animarono non solo il pensiere prefissomi della cognizion delle parti interne, ma anchei raconti di molti Pescatori Turchi, e molto più gl'incitamenti del *

Signor Caualier Finchi, Ambasciatore alla Porta per la Maestà del Rè d'Inghil-
terra, e molto intendente degli studij naturali: à cui ciò era stato motivato da un
suo Capitano di Nave, che non ne giunse alla chiarezza con l'esperimento, forsi
per mancanza di tempo.[60]

A current flows through the Bosporus on its way from the Black Sea to
the Mediterranean. Beneath it an undercurrent flows in the opposite
direction. Because the Bosporus is relatively shallow its existence was
known to the local fishermen as also to the ship's captain from whom
Finch had his information.

To make his own observations of the undercurrent Marsigli prepared a
rope to which were fastened pieces of cork painted white so that they
could be seen even at considerable depths in the water. By lowering this
into the Bosporus he observed which way the rope was carried and found
that at a depth of between eight and twelve Turkish feet it changed direction and began to move northwards, in the opposite direction to the surface
water.[61]

Marsigli reasoned that the explanation for the opposing currents was
that, if two liquids of differing densities come in contact with each other,
the heavier will displace the lighter:

La cagione, à mio parere, può esser fondata sul principio, che il più pesante
caccia il più leggiero.[62]

He measured the specific gravity of water from different parts of the sea
with some kind of hydrostatic balance, following the method he had been
taught by Montanari.[63] The measurements showed that the water of the
Black Sea was less dense than that of the Mediterranean. He compared
samples of water taken from the Bosporus, one from the surface and one
from the bottom, and found that the bottom water was ten grains heavier
than that at the surface[64] and must therefore have originated in the Mediterranean. This then was the explanation for the double current. The
water of the Black Sea was relatively fresh, the water of the Mediterranean
relatively saline. Because the two bodies of water were contiguous the
differing specific gravities resulted in mutual instability; in modern terms a
pressure gradient was created. The heavy Mediterranean water flowed
into the Bosporus because of its greater density and a compensating
current of Black Sea water flowed in the opposite direction.

In order to render his arguments indisputable Marsigli made an experimental demonstration of the working of the current system. He divided a tank in two with a partition and filled one half (X) with water of
the same specific gravity as the undercurrent and the other (Z) with water
like that of the Black Sea which he coloured with dye. He made two
openings in the partition, one at the top and one at the bottom. The

heavier water flowed through the hole at the bottom (D) and the lighter water through the hole at the top (E) until the contents had redistributed themselves so that the heavier water formed a continuous layer below the lighter water:

e poi si apra il buco D. che immediatamente si vedrà l'Acqua X. passare in Z. e quella di Z. in X. per il buco E, ove per l'appunto s'incontrano le due frezze, e tal moto durerà fin tanto, che sia fatta l'immistione sufficiente per render omogenee queste due acque.[65]

Marsigli had therefore succeeded in associating the puzzling problem of the currents with the basic principle of fluid mechanics that governed them. His account of these researches was published in 1681 in Rome and dedicated to ex-Queen Christina of Sweden. In 1691 he made another visit to Constantinople and renewed his work on the currents but his results never seem to have been published (*see* Ch. 9).[66]

Marsigli's book did come to England. In January 1684, at the time when Smith's paper was arousing new interest in the subject of under-currents, Hooke mentioned at a Royal Society meeting that there was a recent Italian book dealing with an undercurrent in the Bosporus and Dr Aglionby was asked to read it.[67] So some people must have heard about Marsigli's discovery but it does not seem to have become generally known and had no influence over the controversy about the Strait of Gibraltar which continued as though it had never been made. One has to jump to the early nineteenth century before Marsigli's work began to win the appreciation its ingenuity deserved and its applications elsewhere were realized.

Meanwhile the evaporation theory was almost always preferred and Halley's authority was thought sufficient reason for the choice. Sheeres's work had fallen into oblivion, partly perhaps because of the delay in publication, also, one suspects, because of his unfortunate style of writing which was prolix and slightly pompous as well as being rather involved. Perhaps too, as someone who figures near the end of this book once had occasion to remark, people are willing to accept the *obiter dicta* of great scientists just because they are great and their lesser sayings are given the same prestige as the ideas that made them famous.

It seems to have been largely fortuitous that the efforts of a quarter of a century had this tame and inconclusive ending. Perhaps the most obvious reason for this outcome is that, of the few people who were really interested in the problem, those who had the opportunity to study at first hand conditions in the Strait, that is Sheeres and Bolland, were necessarily both physically and mentally at a distance from the centre of scientific activity. To have carried their ideas any further they would have had to be different people and in addition to have had the leisure to develop their theoretical knowledge which at that time could be done only by obtaining it for oneself or by studying with those who had. The day of the science textbook had not yet arrived. Yet as Marsigli showed, the problem was not an insuperable one. It is tempting to speculate that if someone of the calibre of Boyle or Hooke had had occasion to visit Tangier they would have got to the root of the matter.

Smith too was scarcely in this class and his advocacy of the undercurrent without any attempt at explanation did it almost more harm than good, the more so because he fell into the trap of denying that evaporation had any influence at all. Cautious people therefore came down on the side of the evaporation theory and tended to look on those who were obdurate in supporting the undercurrent as dangerous romanticizers. Bolland alone, it appears, had intuitively foreseen that any complete explanation might comprehend both points of view.

7. NOTES

1. Thomas Birch, *History of the Royal Society*. Vol. **1** (1756) pp. 29–30.
2. Aristotle, *Works* (ed. W. D. Ross). Vol. **3** (1931). *De Mundo*, 393a.
3. Strabo, *Geography*, **3**, ii, 4.
4. El-Mas'údí, *Historical Encyclopaedia entitled Meadows of Gold and Mines of Gems* (translated by Aloys Sprenger) (1841). Vol. **1**, p. 283.
5. Edward MacCurdy, *The Notebooks of Leonardo da Vinci* (1938). Vol. **1**, pp. 339–343, 382.
6. John Greaves, *Pyramidographia* in *Miscellaneous Works of Mr. John Greaves* (ed. Thomas Birch) (1737). Vol. **1**, pp. 137–138.
7. Georges Fournier, *Hydrographie Contenant la Théorie et la Pratique de Toutes les Parties de la Navigation*, 2nd edition (1667), p. 338.
8. Athanasius Kircher, *Mundus Subterraneus*, 3rd edition (1678). Vol. **1**, pp. 161–163.
9. Sir Robert Southwell, "Discourse on Water" in Thomas Birch's *History of the Royal Society*. Vol. **3** (1757). pp. 196–216.
10. Thomas Smith, "A conjecture about an under-current at the Streights-Mouth", *Phil. Trans.* (1684). Vol. **14**, pp. 564–566.
11. Sir Henry Sheeres, "Discourse of the Mediteranian Sea, and the Streights of Gibraltar" in *Miscellanies Historical and Philological: being a Curious Collection of Private Papers found in the Study of a Noble-man, Lately Deceas'd* (Marquis of Halifax), London (1703), p. 2.
12. Sir Jonas Moore, *A New Systeme of the Mathematicks*, 2 vols, London (1681). ∗ Vol. **1**, part 1, pp. 287–288.
13. Henry Stubbs, "An enlargement of the observations, formerly publisht Numb. 27, made and generously imparted by that learn'd and inquisitive physitian, Dr. Stubbes", *Phil. Trans.* (June 1668). Vol. **3**, no. 36, pp. 699–709; p. 707.
14. Robert Boyle, *Relations about the bottom of the sea* in *The Works of the Honourable Robert Boyle* (ed. Thomas Birch) (1744). Vol. **3**, p. 113.

15. Thomas Smith, "A journal of a voyage from England to Constantinople, made in the year 1668", *Miscellanea Curiosa containing a collection of curious travels, voyages, and natural histories of countries, as they have been delivered to the Royal Society*, 2nd edition, 3 vols, London (1727). Vol. 3, pp. 1–31.

16. *Ibid.* p. 13.

17. E. M. G. Routh, *Tangier: England's lost Atlantic Outpost, 1661–1684*, London (1912).

18. Sheeres is the form given by the *Dictionary of National Biography*. The name was also spelt Sheares, Sheres and Shere—the form most commonly used by contemporaries.

19. E. M. G. Routh, *op. cit.* pp. 346, 348.

20. Samuel Pepys, *The Diary of Samuel Pepys* (ed. Henry B. Wheatley), 10 vols., G. Bell & Sons, London (1893–1899). Vol. 7 (1896) p. 119. Quoted by kind permission of the publishers.

21. Edwin Chappell, *The Tangier Papers of Samuel Pepys*, Navy Records Society (1935). Vol. 73, p. 150.

22. Sir Henry Sheeres also published *An Essay on the Certainty and Causes of the Earth's Motion on its Axis, &c.*, London (1698). The late Professor E. G. R. Taylor commented that by the standards of the time its ideas about physics and astronomy were archaic. See *Mathematical Practitioners of Tudor and Stuart England* (1954), p. 261.

23. E. M. G. Routh, *op. cit.* p. 349. Rawlinson MS. A.341.

24. Sir Henry Sheeres, "Discourse of the Mediteranean Sea", *op. cit.* p. 30.

25. *Ibid.* p. 7.

26. *Ibid.* pp. 5–6.

27. *Ibid.* p. 22.

28. *Ibid.* p. 23.

29. Sir Henry Sheeres, *A Discourse touching the current in the Streight of Gibraltar*, Pepysian Library, MS. no. 1476, pp. 69–71. The printed version has "one foot" in error for "40 foot", *op. cit.* p. 24, which makes nonsense of the passage. Professor Georg Wüst has calculated that if a dam were constructed across the Strait of Gibraltar the level of the Mediterranean would fall by rather less than 1 metre a year: "Des Wasserhaushalt des Mittelländischen Meeres und der Ostsee in vergleichender Betrachtung", *Geofisica pura e applicata* (1952). Vol. 21.

30. Sir Henry Sheeres, *Discourse of the Mediteranian Sea*, *op. cit.* pp. 8–9.

31. *Ibid.* p. 39,

32. For example: William B. Carpenter and J. Gwyn Jeffreys, "Report on deep-sea researches carried on during the months of July, August and September 1870 in H.M. surveying-ship *Porcupine*", *Proc. Roy. Soc.* (1870–1871). Vol. 19, pp. 146–221.

33. Henri Lacombe and Jean-Claude Lizeray, "Sur le régime des courants dans le détroit de Gibraltar", *Comptes Rendus* (1959). Vol. 248, pp. 2502–2504.

34. Henri Lacombe and Paul Tchernia, "Quelques traits généraux de l' hydrologie méditerranéenne d'après diverses campagnes hydrologiques récentes en Méditerranée, dans le proche Atlantique et dans le détroit de Gibraltar", *Cahiers Océanographiques* (1960). Vol 12, no. 8, pp. 527–547.

35. D. B. Carter, "The water balance of the Mediterranean and Black Seas", *Publications in Climatology of the Drexel Institute of Technology* (1956). Vol. 9, no. 3.
    Georg Wüst, "Sulle componenti del bilancio idrico fra atmosfera, oceano e

Mediterraneo", *Annale dell'Istituto Universitario Navale di Napoli* (1959), Vol. **28**.

36. *Weather in the Mediterranean*, 2nd edition, 2 vols, H.M.S.O., London (1962, 1964).
37. This letter is attached to the volume of Sheeres's *Discourse* in the Pepysian Library MS. no. 1476. It is printed here by kind permission of the Master and Fellows of Magdalene College, Cambridge.
38. *Miscellanies Historical and Philological: being a curious Collection of Private Papers found in the Study of a Noble-man, Lately Deceas'd*, London (1703).
39. Thomas Birch, *History of the Royal Society*. Vol. **3** (1757) pp. 189–190.
40. *Ibid*. p. 214.
41. Henry Oldenburg, "Inquiries ffor Tanger, and other parts of Barbary", *Royal Society Classified Papers*. Vol. **19**, no. 89.
42. Rawlinson MS. A. 342, Sheeres to Pepys, 14 July 1676.
43. *A Discourse touching Tanger: in a letter to a person of quality*, London (1680). This pamphlet is anonymous but was almost certainly written by Sheeres.
44. Richard Bolland, *Bolland's Mediterranean Journall, containing Descriptions and Draughts relating to severall Ports, Moles and Currents in the Mediterranean, presented to Mr. Pepys Secretary of ye Admiralty of England by ye sayd Capt. Richard Bolland, one of the officers of the Mole at Tangier, 1676*, Pepysian Library, MS. no. 2899, Magdalene College, Cambridge. The first section, dealing with the currents, was printed in 1704 as *A Draught of the Streights of Gibraltar. With some Observations upon the Currents thereunto belonging*, in *A Collection of Voyages and Travels*, Awnsham and John Churchill, London (1704). Vol. **4**, pp. 846–848.
    This naval connection is also attested by references in the minutes of the Navy Board: J. R. Tanner, *A Descriptive Catalogue of Naval Manuscripts in the Pepysian Library*. Vol. **4**. Navy Records Society (1923). Vol. **57**, p. 346.
45. Rawlinson MS. A.342, Sheeres to Bolland, 31 May 1676.
46. Richard Bolland, *A Draught of the Streights of Gibraltar*, *op. cit*. p. 847.
47. *Ibid*. p. 848.
48. *Ibid*. An apparatus on this principle devised by Dr. W. S. Richardson is in use today for measuring the transport of water in the Strait of Florida: *Geo Marine Technology* (1965). Vol. **1**, no. 4, p. 20.
49. *Royal Society Letter Book* (Copy). Vol. **8**, pp. 35–37, Bolland to Williamson, 13 February 1678.
50. Rawlinson MS. A.342, Sheeres to Fairborne, 17 August 1678.
51. R. T. Gunther, *Early Science in Oxford*. Vol. **4** (1925). *The Philosophical Society*, p. 28.
52. *Ibid*., pp. 83–84.
53. *Ibid*. p. 90.
54. Robert Plot, *De Origine Fontium Tentamen Philosophicum*, Oxford (1685), pp. 114–119.
55. Edmond Halley, "An estimate of the quantity of vapour raised out of the sea by the warmth of the sun; derived from an experiment shown before the Royal Society, at one of their late meetings", *Phil. Trans.* (1686–1687). Vol. **16**, pp. 366–370.
56. *Ibid*. pp. 367–368.
57. Georg Wüst, "Der Wasserhaushalt des Mittelländischen Meeres und der Ostsee in vergleichender Betrachtung", *op. cit*.

58. F. C. W. and M. A. Olson, "Luigi Ferdinando Marsigli, the lost father of oceano-graphy", *Qu. J. Florida Acad. Sci.* (1958). Vol. **21**, no. 3, pp. 227–234.
59. Geminiano Montanari, *Il Mare Adriatico e sua Corrente esaminata* in *Raccolta d'Autori Italiani che Trattano del Moto dell'Acque* (ed. Francesco Cardinali), 4th edition, 10 vols, Bologna (1821–1826). Vol. **4** (1822), pp. 461–493.
60. Luigi Ferdinando Marsigli, *Osservazioni intorno al Bosforo Tracio overo Canale* * *di Constantinopli rappresentate in lettera alla Sacra Real Maestà di Cristina* * *Regina di Svezia*, Roma (1681), pp. 52–53.
61. *Ibid.* pp. 55–59.
62. *Ibid.* p. 61.
63. *Ibid.* p. 71.
64. *Ibid.* pp. 72–73.
65. *Ibid.* p. 63.
66. Luigi Ferdinando Marsigli, *Histoire Physique de la Mer*, Amsterdam (1725). Preface.
67. Thomas Birch, *History of the Royal Society*. Vol. **4** (1757) p. 251.

Addenda et Corrigenda

p.137, fig.5, caption, 1.2: *instead* Master and Fellows of *read* Pepys Library,

p.139, 1.15: *instead* commander *read* commanders

p.142, 1.34: *instead* Navy *read* Admiralty

p.143, fig.6, caption, 1.2: *instead* Master and Fellows of *read* Pepys Library,

p.145, fig.7, caption, 1.2: *instead* Master and Fellows of *read* Pepys Library,

p.147, 1.42: *instead* anchei raconti *read* anche i racconti

p.150, n.12, 1.2: *insert* See also below, p. 85.

p.153, n.60. 1.1: *instead* overo *read* o vero

p.153, n.60, 1.2: *instead* Constantinopli *read* Constantinopoli

8. ROBERT HOOKE AND THE VANISHING HARVEST

The Harvest is great, but the Labourers are few

Robert Hooke

THE interest shown by the Royal Society as a corporate body in marine science in general declined after 1663 and in the same way discussion about tides gradually faded out of their meetings in 1667 (*see* Chs 4 and 5). On both occasions the questions which had been raised were taken up by individuals, not always members of the Society or even within its immediate sphere. If one wishes to point to the most productive period of the age as far as interest in the sea is concerned it is perhaps the years just before and after 1670 that were the most fruitful. This period saw Childrey's controversy with Wallis, ended by Childrey's death in August 1670 (*see* Ch. 5, pp. 102–108), the publication of Boyle's four essays on the sea (*see* Ch. 6) and the work on currents at Tangier (*see* Ch. 7).

After this peak had been passed activity declined sharply. Wallis and Boyle both maintained an interest in their respective fields but seem to have added little to their previous work. It is unlikely that Sheeres thought that his arguments about the Strait of Gibraltar needed any revision while Bolland died, presumably before he could put his ideas to the test.

It would be wrong, however, to think that the whole question of marine science passed at once into oblivion. Henry Oldenburg, as Secretary of the Royal Society, continued to recommend the use of *The Directions for Seamen* to travellers as part of his work in compiling inquiries for different parts of the world until his death in 1677.[1] Observations continued to be made at sea (*see* Ch. 4, pp. 86–87), for example those carried out by Sir Dudley North (1641–1691) on pressure at various depths in the Mediterranean and Atlantic in 1680.[2] Nevertheless something of the former spirit was lacking. Sir Robert Moray who had indefatigably promoted the study of marine science during the early years of the Royal Society had died in 1673 and many of those who had been associated with him had died or lost interest.

The one person who seems to have kept intact the old enthusiasm for the scientific investigation of the sea was Robert Hooke. As seen in Chapter 4, very soon after joining the Society in London late in 1662 he had discussed how his experiments on the pressure of air might be extended to discover conditions at sea.[3] As a result of his suggestions observations were made on the pressure, temperature and salinity of water at the mouth of the Thames in March 1663[4] (*see* Ch. 4). In the summer of the same year Hooke produced new designs for instruments for sampling water from different depths and for sounding without a line which, while based on the same idea as those already in use, were supposed to be more reliable in practice[5] (*see* Ch. 4). When the revised edition of the *Directions for Seamen*[6] was being prepared in the autumn of 1666 Hooke invented an instrument for dredging up samples of the sea floor but had to report that it worked well only in shallow water.[7]

After the Society's interest in tides had lessened and in the ten years following, little of significance to marine science was recorded in its minutes, with the exception of the two mentions of Sheeres's essay on the current in the Strait of Gibraltar[8] and a discussion of Vossius's *De Motum Marium et Ventorum*.[9] Then in March 1678 Hooke read out Bolland's account to Sir Joseph Williamson of his experiments for Boyle (*see* Ch. 6) and this provoked discussion about the most accurate ways of making observations in the sea and in deep water.[10]

Hooke said that the pressure of water at any depth could be measured with the aid of a glass tube as had been done near Sheerness (*see* Ch. 4). He said that he

had also other ways for examining the heat and cold of these submarine regions; and to fetch up the water from any depth; as also the earth, sand, &c. from the bottom: that he would give directions for the making of such an apparatus, if there were proper persons appointed to make trial with them.[11]

Other members mentioned the Lake of Geneva and other depths in lakes and the sea which were so great that no one had been able to measure them. Thomas Smith recalled Greaves's deep sounding in the 1630s (*see* Ch. 4). Mr Hill

supposed, with good reason, that in trials of this kind, the lightness and buoyantness of the rope might at length keep the weight from sinking any farther; and so much more line might be taken into the sea than was necessary to measure the depth. It was thought also, that the motion of the under-parts of the water might bend the line very much.[12]

At the next meeting, on 28 March, the subject was resumed. The minutes of the last meeting occasioned discussion about the glass tube which could be used to measure pressure, and therefore depth, in the sea. Sir Christopher Wren objected that the reduction in volume of the air inside the tube might be caused by cold as well and that it would be impossible to know how much importance to assign to this and how much to the effect of pressure. Hooke replied that it was necessary to lower other instruments at the same time which would record the temperature at different depths

and that the said experiment was not less instructive than the other: for the performing of which he alledged that he had a contrivance, by which the same might be certainly examined, and thence the degrees both of the one and the other might be defined.[13]

Someone objected that depth might be measured as well with a sounding line as calculated from pressure but it was again pointed out that for great depths sounding with lead and line might lead to inaccuracy because, firstly, the line might float and, secondly, it might be deflected from the vertical by currents.

Sir Christopher Wren, who was then Vice-President of the Society, said that he had not heard of any real objection to using the wooden balls for sounding. To this it was replied that the method was feasible if the apparaatus was constructed in the way described in the *Philosophical Transactions* (*see* Ch. 4) and care taken to observe the exact time when the float reappeared on the surface but this could be difficult in deep water if the ship or the water were in motion. The form of the apparatus described by Riccioli (*see* Ch. 3) was impracticable; when it had been tried the float had often either come adrift before reaching the bottom or had never been released at all.

On 4 April the reading of the minutes gave rise to renewed discussion. Henshaw said that both the use of the weight and float and of a pipe for sounding were to be found in the writings of Nicholas of Cusa (*see* Ch. 3). Hooke explained the particular way he had invented of attaching the float to the weight (*see* Ch. 4). The President, Sir Joseph Williamson, Henshaw and Hill objected to this method because, among other things, according to Galileo descending bodies accelerated in proportion to the time of their fall, and they could not see how it could be said that the time of the descent and ascent of the float would always be in the same proportion to the depth, in water more than two fathoms deep. Hooke answered that after two fathoms in water the float, both descending and ascending, would reach its maximum velocity.

Williamson observed that Galileo, Gassendi and Mersenne had all said that "descending bodies accelerate their motion in proportion to the squares of the times of their continued descent".[14] Hooke replied that whereas this might be so in a vacuum, in any medium offering resistance, and all mediums did to some extent, it was the difference in specific gravity between the medium and the falling body which governed the speed at which the latter fell. A ball of lead fell to the ground from the top of St Paul's steeple more quickly than a ball of the same size made of wood and the ball of wood fell more quickly than one of cork. He added

farther, that in the thinnest medium, though the acceleration were pretty near what was supposed by the aforesaid authors; yet that it was in none mathematically true, but that there would be in all mediums a certain degree of velocity, which the same descending body would never exceed, though other descending bodies might, and some others would never arrive to: after which degree was attained, the progress of the body would always be made by equal spaces in equal times, though ever so far continued, provided the gravitating powers remained the same.[15]

At the same meeting Hooke showed experimentally that if a glass tube like the one used in 1663 (see Ch. 4) were lowered into water the air inside was compressed in proportion to depth.[16]

The next meeting of the Society was held on 18 April when Sir Jonas Moore, the other Vice-President, was in the chair. He recalled that he had many times attempted to measure the depth of the sea with the weight and float apparatus but had found it extremely hard to make any precise determinations with them. This was because it was so difficult at sea to be certain of the exact time when the float reappeared; it might surface as much as 400 yards away from where it had been sent down. He had tried twelve in the Strait of Gibraltar and not seen one on its first appearance (see Ch. 4). He thought that in lakes this kind of instrument might be useful but saw little future in it for oceanic research. Further queries on the possible acceleration of light bodies brought the series of discussions to a close.

This episode reveals to what extent the efforts of the early 1660s were unknown to or forgotten by almost all the members of the Society active in 1678. Only Hooke was able to remind them of what had been done then and to throw light on the care with which practical and theoretical problems surrounding the use of this type of apparatus had been investigated in the earlier period. It is clear that he was as keenly interested as ever and that he had new instruments which he wished to try out if he could secure the necessary co-operation from other members, but it seems that this was not forthcoming.

Having proceeded as far as they could by discussion the Society relinquished the subject and in the ensuing years references to topics in marine science were as rare again as they had been before. In January 1684 came the news from Oxford of Smith's paper asserting the existence of an undercurrent in the Strait of Gibraltar.[17] Hooke mentioned "an Italian book, lately written to this purpose about the Bosphorus of Thrace" and Dr Aglionby was asked to read it.[18] This seems to be the only indication in the two societies that Marsigli's work was known of and there is nothing to show that his arguments were appreciated. In February, Dr Frederick Slare (1647?–1727) gave an account of experiments made with sea ice from Harwich harbour.[19] Aglionby remarked that the ice might be fresh because the water which froze came from the bottom of the sea which was sometimes found to be fresh. Hooke pointed out that this was exceptional. Captain Knox[20] was about to set out for the Indies and could make observations if one of the instruments previously invented were to be made for him. Martin Lister (1638?–1712) said that in wiches the water grew more salt towards the bottom. Hooke argued that, the ice being partially thawed before they had it, the salt part might have been lost but Lister pointed out that the freshness of sea ice was no new observation.

Hooke's continuing interest in the sea may be seen as clearly in his written works as in his activities with the Royal Society. In his "Account of an experiment touching the different weight of cold and warme water" he speculated on the effect that would be produced in the ocean by heat and cold.[21] Because the sea near the poles would be colder and therefore denser than the sea nearer the equator he supposed that ships coming southwards from the Arctic might need to beware of overloading, unless the greater salinity of the sea in the tropics counteracted the loss in density due to heat. He adopted the view that rivers were dependent on rainfall and therefore on evaporation of water from the sea and its condensation by cold as rain.[22] He had, he said, observed that trees on high hills were damp, particularly on the brow of Box Hill.

In his *Discourse of Earthquakes*, written in 1668, Hooke considered the effect of earthquakes in the sea.[23] It was reasonable to suppose, he thought, that they were as numerous there as on dry land and if earthquakes and volcanic eruptions were responsible for hills and mountains on land presumably they were too for islands and depressions in the sea. He remarked on the volcanic origin of oceanic islands; it was most likely that

most of those Islands that are now appearing, have been either thrown up out of the Sea by Eruptions, such as the *Canaries, Azores, St. Helena, &c.* which the Form of them, and the Vulcanes in them, and the Cinders and Pumice-stones found about them, and the frequent Earthquakes they are troubled with, and the remaining Hills of extinguish'd Vulcanes, do all strongly argue for.[24]

He wondered if they might be relics of Atlantis, for he shared the modern passion for attempting to rationalize the myths of ancient writers, but inclined on the whole to the view that they were of more recent origin since, as today, new islands had been created in living memory.

Hooke incorporated in his views the idea to be found in older writers (*see* Ch. 3) that there must be a compensatory proportion between heights and depths—

An Island cannot be raised in one Place, without leaving an Abyss in another.[24]

He thought that Sir Francis Drake's relation of deep water (over 500 fathoms) in the Magellan Strait, found in proximity to a volcano, was an example of this principle at work.

Hooke realized very clearly that not only the visible face of the earth but the sea floor as well was still in the process of change. Rain and rivers eroded the hills and the sea washed away the coastlines; the sediment carried into the sea would long since have covered the irregularities in the sea floor were it not for renewed disturbances. He speculated: that the deep places in the sea

must have in all Ages been filling with Parts of the Earth, tumbled by the Motion of the Waters, and rowling to the lowest Place, is very probable; and so they would in time have been fill'd up, had not Earthquakes, by their Eruptions and Tumblings, created new Irregularities.[24]

He realized, as did contemporaries like Woodward,[25] that much of England must have been at one time under the sea, and believed that earthquakes had been responsible for raising countries where marine remains were to be found above sea level. Conversely, it was possible that the same cataclysms had sunk whole lands under the sea and, reverting to the Atlantis myth, he speculated on the possibility that a civilization as advanced as their own might have been lost without trace. It was certain that species of plants and animals which had formerly existed no longer did so and though alterations might have been induced by changes in climate and other conditions he supposed that whole species might have been destroyed by natural catastrophes. He also thought that changes might have taken place in the earth's magnetic field and that the poles might have altered their position during the course of time,[26] subjects frequently discussed today.

Hooke continued to take an interest in earthquakes. In July 1690 eyewitness accounts of earthquakes in the Leeward Islands were published in the *London Gazette* and he discussed them in the light of his ideas.[27] One thing that had been noticed was the arrival of tidal waves. He commented

That in an Hour and $\frac{1}{4}$ the Sea Ebbed and Flowed three times in an unusual Degree; which, in probability, were nothing else but Waves propagated from the places where the Ground underneath, and the Sea above, had been by the Concussions of the Earthquake raised upwards.[28]

It is clear that he attributed the movement of the sea to the shock communicated to it by the movement of the earth, much in the same way that Galileo had supposed that tidal forces were generated. It was quite unlike the curious ideas advanced to explain similar phenomena in the mid-eighteenth century and very much antedates the supposed introduction of the idea that wave motion was responsible for the marine disturbances generated by earthquakes, by John Michell, in 1760 (*see* Ch. 10).

In February 1684 Hooke became engaged in a dispute with Dr William Croune (1633–1684) who had shown that fresh water expands before freezing.[29] A further experiment convinced him that Croune was right and that it was not, as he had originally thought, the contraction of the container which produced the effect. In discussing his own experiments on the subject he again turned to the application of this knowledge with reference to the sea. He compared the specific gravities of ice and sea water and deduced

that in the Northern Seas, at least one Eighth Part of the Bulk of any Body of Ice floats above the Water: I say, at least an Eighth; for possibly it may be one Seventh; for first (as it is affirmed by many Voyagers to the Northern Seas) the Ice is found to be pretty fresh, and to have little or no Taste of Brackishness; and so, one Part taken with another, not heavier than this Ice I made use of. Next, the Water, notwithstanding, in which it floats, is salt, and consequently about a 40th Part heavier than common fresh Water. Thirdly, This salt Water, tho' it do not freeze, is yet pretty near the same Degree of Coldness with the Ice that floats in it, and consequently yet more heavy than the same Water when more tepid. For as I shall hereafter prove, Bodies that freeze not, are yet not less cold than other Bodies that do freeze. Fourthly, That the Sea-Water near the Bottom, is yet much more cold, and much more salt, than in the same Place it is near the Top, and consequently must much contribute to the floating of a greater part of the Ice. That the Water is colder at the Bottom, than above, was positively affirmed by Mr. *Roachford*, who try'd it in the *Sound*; and that salt Water is salter at the Bottom, than at the Top, any one may find.[30]

Hooke's interest in the sea extended beyond speculation. As the discussions in 1678 suggest, he had continued his earlier work on oceanographic instruments, producing a whole new range of apparatus, but it was another thirteen years before he made them public. Perhaps the delay occurred because, as his biographers have suggested, some earlier disputes over priority had made Hooke, who suffered from a suspicious and hypersensitive nature, over-secretive about his work. At last, we are told,

In December 1691, he was created doctor of physic, by a warrant from archbishop Tillotson. And in that month he read several lectures, relating to the improvement of instruments for sounding the depths of the sea, which he called *Nuncii inanimati ad fundum abyssi emissarii.*[31]

In 1664 a lectureship had been created by Sir John Cutler (1608?–1693)[32] especially for Hooke who, apart from what the Royal Society could pay him, was then without other means of livelihood. It was the Cutlerian Lectures of December 1691 which Hooke devoted to giving an account of how he had developed oceanographic equipment over the last twenty-five years.[33]

Hooke began by referring to the descriptions of the instrument for

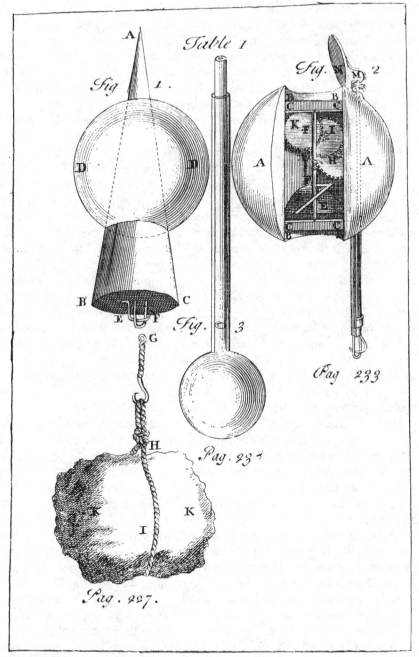

FIG. 8. Robert Hooke's apparatus for measuring depth and deep sea thermometer (1691). Reprinted from William Derham's *Philosophical Experiments and Observations of the Late Eminent Dr Robert Hooke* (1726) (facing p. 227).

sounding given in the *Philosophical Transactions*, nos. 9 and 24 (*see* Ch. 4). This method was perfectly valid but had two disadvantages. Firstly, if the wooden float were to maintain the same velocity on its way up as the combined weight and float on the way down, the proportions of the two parts of the apparatus had to be very carefully adjusted. Secondly, for the experiment to succeed the float had to be sighted at the precise moment it came to the surface. As this was extremely difficult failures were common and the cost of losing, without result, the specially designed leaden weights became prohibitive.

Hooke proceeded to describe a method free from these disadvantages. He had, he said, described it to the Royal Society in 1661 or 1662.[34] Presumably he meant by this that he had described the principle on which his new instrument was based, that pressure in water increases in proportion to depth. The apparatus consisted of a hollow cone, to be made of tin or thin brass, which was to be pierced with a small hole which would let in water as the pressure increased. When the apparatus was brought back to the surface the water was to be weighed and from this the degree of pressure and therefore the depth the apparatus had reached, might be determined. It is not entirely clear if and how this particular instrument worked. If the hole was, as it seems, at the apex it might be expected that all the air would be driven out, and if elsewhere that the water would be lost on the way up. The principle behind it was sound however. Hooke envisaged the cone inserted into a wooden float covered with pitch and carried to the bottom by a weight, if necessary by a stone, and released in the usual way. There would be no need to measure the time the apparatus took to return to the surface and the cost need not be ¼d a time.

Hooke prefaced his second lecture with some remarks on the depth of the sea in general. It would, he said, be a mistake to regard classical and scriptural allusions to bottomless depths as anything more than poetic licence. The greatest depth yet known was that discovered by John Greaves (*see* Ch. 4) but it was impossible to say exactly where it was because Greaves did not state from which meridian his longitude was measured.

The difficulty about using the power of the water to compress air as a measure of depth lay in the fact that the density of water varies according to its temperature and salinity and where any such variations took place it would be impossible to treat the pressure of the column of water as directly proportional to its depth. To overcome this difficulty it would be necessary to measure both the salinity and temperature below the surface.

Another alternative was to measure depth with what Hooke called a "way-wiser", allied to the marine log which he devised to measure a ship's speed and to pedometers and similar instruments for measuring distance on land. This apparatus consisted of a wooden float with a cylindrical hole bored through it. This contained four vanes attached through a central axis to a system of toothed wheels. As the float sank water passing through the central shaft would turn the vanes and the number of rotations would be recorded by the wheels. When the apparatus began its ascent the resistance of water above would depress a lid to cover the top of the cylinder and prevent any alteration in the reading. He explained in his third lecture how it would be possible to arrange it so that a single float could be used to carry two of these way wisers, one to work on the way down, the other on the way up. The whole thing need not cost more than a crown.

Hooke next described a thermometer which he had designed to record the temperature of the deep water. It consisted of a bolt head containing alcohol and a close-fitting inner tube with a valve opening upwards at the bottom. Both tubes were open at the top. Hooke expected that, as the thermometer went down, the pressure of the water in the inner tube would drive it down inside the bolt head as the alcohol contracted with cold. He thought, wrongly, that the pressure would not affect the alcohol, citing some Royal Society experiments as evidence that fluids are not compressible, and that the degree to which the inner tube was driven in would be a measure of temperature only. This was an ingenious attempt to provide a self-registering minimum thermometer. When it came up and the alcohol got warmer and expanded it would be able to rise through the valve into the inner tube without displacing it.

By using the thermometer with the apparatus for measuring the pressure of the water and the way-wiser it would be possible to discover how much the effect of pressure and how much that of cold would contribute to condensing the air in the pressure-gauge. Hooke explained why he used alcohol or spirit of wine in his thermometer. He found in

many Trials, which I purposely made, to perfect that Kind of Thermometers, (of which, I believe, I made the first that were made in *England*, from the Sight of a very small one, brought out of *Italy*, about 30 Years since, by the President) that this Spirit was the most sensible of any Liquor, I could then meet with, of the Degrees of Heat and Cold. And secondly, because this Liquor was capable of enduring the greatest Degree of Cold, I could give it, by the Means of Salt and Ice, and yet remain'd fluid, without Congelation, but did continue to shrink to the last. Now what the Temper of the Sea may be, at those vast Depths, whither this is design'd to be sent, no Man now living, or ever did live upon the Earth, hath experimentally known, (as I am, with good Reason, persuaded). But, by Conjectures, one may be induced to expect, that the Cold should be there very predominant, and, in Probability, such as would congeal, and turn to Ice, a Body of fresh Water. And 'tis, in Probability, one of the Causes that the Sea was made to abound with Salts, by the Divine Providence, who adapted every Thing to its proper Use and End; for 'tis very hard to suppose, that the Heat of the Sun should communicate so powerful an Influence from the Top, or Surface of the Sea, downwards; for the Parts of any uniform Fluid, that are warmer than the rest, are also lighter, and consequently will ascend upwards; but that the heated Particles at the Top, should sink, or descend, 'tis not to be supposed.[35]

The light and heat of the sun might penetrate some way into the sea if the water were clear but could have little or no effect on the deeper parts.

In his final lecture, read on 23 December, Hooke concluded that it should be possible to measure the depth of the sea, particularly with the instrument incorporating way-wisers. This would work even if there were vertical movements up and down in the water as someone had suggested at the previous lecture, though it was hard to see how such movements could be sustained unless one was willing to accept Kircher's dubious system of subterranean tunnels between seas.

Finally Hooke described a release mechanism which could be used to retrieve the apparatus combining the way-wisers with water samplers from any predetermined depth, not necessarily the bottom. He would attach to the wheel recording depth in hundreds of fathoms a "springing round plate" with a notch which could be set against any number. At the determined depth it would slip a catch which in its turn would release the hook on which the weight was hung. In this way water samples and measurements of temperature and pressure could be taken at any depth. One last inquiry which he would have liked made was whether the pressure in the sea was great enough to liquefy air. He thought that this might take place at about 2,200 fathoms.

The range and fertility of invention which these lectures reveal show Hooke to have been outstanding in the oceanographic field as in many others. He anticipated many of the developments which were to take place during the next two hundred years, both in foreseeing the different categories of observation and their interdependence and in forecasting the main patterns of the development of instruments.

It was unfortunate for his ideas and their immediate prospects that they came at a time when the wave of enthusiasm for marine science and similar studies was almost spent. They seem to have aroused no interest at all among contemporaries and, though published by Derham in 1726, have remained comparatively little known ever since.

Hooke himself, it seems, was well aware that this obscurity was likely to be the fate of his suggestions and at one point he made an impassioned plea that the subject should be taken seriously—as also

Thousands of others, which, it were to be wished, this Society would procure Informations of; which, I conceive, is in their Power to effect, if due Means and Methods were made use of, for effecting those Ends. The Harvest is great, but the Labourers are few; and without Hands and Heads too, little can be expected;

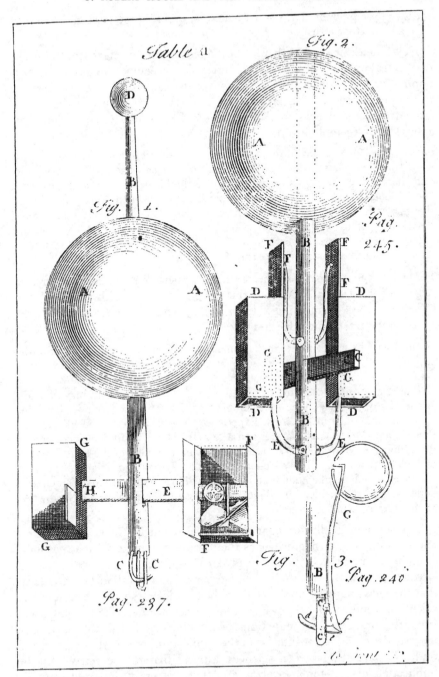

FIG. 9. Robert Hooke's apparatus for measuring depth and water sampling with his device for releasing a weight at any given depth (1691). Reprinted from William Derham's *Philosophical Experiments and Observations of the Late Eminent Dr. Robert Hooke* (1726) (facing p. 237).

and to rely only upon Time and Chance, is, probably the most likely Way to have all our Hopes frustrated.[36]

Nevertheless it is plain that he continued to take an interest in the study of the sea and to look for better things. In December 1696 he was still hoping for opportunities to have experiments made if he lived long enough to see peace restored. Speculating on the possibility of life in the sea he argued that the depths of the sea would be no less well populated by animal and vegetable life than the land

only we are less knowing of them, because they are out of our Element, and we want *Nuntii* or Messengers, to send thither to bring us back Information, and also the Productions and Commodities that this *Terra incognita*, or unknown World, does afford. I have heretofore produced some such *Nuntii*, for this or that particular Design, but when there may be an Opportunity of sending them, I shall be able to produce divers others, for other Purposes, if God spare my Life so long as to see the Seas again free from Rovers, and that the Study of Arts does succeed the Study of Arms.[37]

He had already thirty years before made experiments to see how great a degree of pressure animals and therefore man could withstand and had invented a way of supplying a diver with air and also spectacles to enable him to see under water. He did not admit the objections

as most will be apt to make, that Animals and Vegetables cannot be rationally supposed to live and grow under so great a Pressure, so great a Cold, and at so great a Distance from the Air, as many Parts at the Bottom of very deep Seas are liable and subject to; I say, I think that these Objections may be easily answer'd, by shewing, that they all proceed from wrong Notions that Men have entertain'd, from the small Experience they have had of the Effects, and Powers, and Methods of Nature, and a few Trials will easily convince them of the Erroneousness of them. We have had Instances enough of the Fallaciousness of such immature and hasty Conclusions. The Torrid and Frigid *Zones* were once concluded uninhabitable; and to assert *Antipodes* was thought atheistical, heretical, and damnable; but Time has discover'd the Falsity and Narrowness of those hasty Conclusions.[38]

The sense of disillusionment which is apparent in Hooke's later utterances on marine science provokes the question—why did the atmosphere of enthusiasm of the 1660s wane in the 1670s and 1680s?

It seems that there is no simple answer to this question but it is clear that the vicissitudes of marine science bear a close resemblance to general scientific trends of the time. Historians of science describe a swing away from the practical preoccupations of members of the Royal Society in its early days, with their interest in the applications of science in crafts and trades, towards the abstract sciences, a trend that was reinforced by the publication of Newton's *Principia*.[39] After this event and well into the eighteenth century chemistry, meteorology, oceanography, and similar sciences were neglected in favour of physics, mathematics and astronomy. However, because Newton's achievement was so outstanding only a few people were capable of adding to what he had done in these fields so that the net result was a period of semi-stagnation.

In addition marine science had its own problems which must have acted as a barrier to further progress. The very nature of the sea constituted an almost insuperable difficulty in an age when technology was still in its infancy. The need for instrumental measurements as the foundation for almost all branches of physical oceanography was clearly appreciated and many types of apparatus were devised, some being developed to quite a high standard. Nevertheless without modern materials, such as steel and rubber, and modern techniques it was difficult to achieve the necessary degree of accuracy and reliability. Even when an instrument was apparently working well it was hard to be sure of interpreting its results correctly. It is therefore scarcely surprising that those entrusted with the delicate task of trying them out were sometimes easily discouraged by the apparent impossibility of their task. Research into the physical characteristics of the ocean has always demanded a rare combination of persistence, ingenuity and dedication and never more perhaps than in the seventeenth century. The general uncertainty must have been a powerful factor in causing the decline of interest in research at sea except among a handful of far-sighted people. By 1691 the process had gone too far for Hooke to be able to re-awaken any enthusiasm for his new ideas.

It is possible that by then most people felt, if they thought about it at all, that the problems of marine science had been adequately dealt with. Newton had explained the tides; Halley had established the cause of trade winds and explained, to most people's satisfaction, the current in the Strait of Gibraltar. Boyle had covered most of the other points in his essays. Few people can have shared his interest in the small variations of salinity and temperature at different depths in the sea and other such, to most, inconsequential facts. In the early days of the Royal Society Sir Robert Moray, Oldenburg and others had thought such things significant but by the end of the century neither the intrinsic interest belonging to any aspect of the natural world nor the possible benefit of such work to seamen inspired answering enthusiasm. Hooke was, as he clearly felt, on his own in an intellectual environment which had become unsympathetic. War had for the moment made marine research hazardous but it was indifference which made it impossible.

To appreciate the individualism and perceptiveness shown by Hooke in pursuing his interest in the sea one has only to compare him with Edmond Halley whose early work on meteorology touched on many points of interest common to both sciences. As already described (*see* Ch. 5) Halley took a keen interest in the study of tides and in 1701 made a three-month voyage to map the tides of the English Channel. Neither on this nor on his earlier voyages, however, does he seem to have made any other oceanographical observations of the kind envisaged by Hooke and others.[40]

In 1676 Halley went out to St Helena at his own expense to make astronomical observations. His stay there, lasting until early 1678, also gave him the opportunity to study oceanic winds at first hand. This eventually led, in 1686, to his giving a paper to the Royal Society in which he put forward the since generally accepted explanation of trade winds.[41] European sailors had of course been collecting information about the trade winds of the Atlantic and Pacific and the monsoons of the Indian Ocean throughout the Renaissance but Halley's description of trade winds in the Atlantic was considerably more precise than most written accounts, since these were mainly the work of landsmen.

Halley described how from latitude 28° N to about latitude 10° N in the Atlantic the trade winds blew from the north-east. The complementary south-east trades blew from south of the equator to a latitude of about 4° N and in between lay a belt of calms. He had observed seasonal variations taking place: when the sun was well north of the equator the north-east trades shifted slightly to the east and the south-east trades to the south; when the sun was south of the equator the south-east trades became more easterly and the north-east trades more northerly in direction. During July and August, too, the south-east trades extended further northwards. Along the Guinea Coast, however, the prevailing winds were south-westerly. In the southern part of the Indian Ocean south-east trade winds prevailed but north of about 10° S latitude seasonal monsoons were to be found. As far as information was available to him Halley could see that the pattern of trade winds in the Pacific Ocean was the same as that in the Atlantic.

Discussing the cause of trade winds, Halley defined winds as "the Stream or Current of the Air", a concept which had been implied by the discovery of the variation of barometric pressure but which had not till then been clearly stated. He discussed the view that trade winds were caused by the inability of the atmosphere to keep up with the speed of the earth's rotation. If this were so how could the existence of the south-westerly winds off the coast of Guinea and the calms found at the equator, not to mention monsoons, be explained? It was necessary, he said, to discover a cause

agreeable to the known properties of the Elements of Air and Water, and the laws of the Motion of fluid Bodies. Such a one is, I conceive, the Action of the Suns Beams upon the Air and Water, as he passes every day over the Oceans, considered together with the Nature of the Soyl, and Scituation of the adjoyning Continents: I say therefore, first that according to the Laws of *Staticks*, the Air which is less rarified or expanded by heat, and consequently more ponderous, must have a Motion towards those parts thereof, which are more rarified, and less ponderous, to bring it to an *Æquilibrium*; and secondly, that the presence of the Sun continually shifting to the Westwards, that part towards which the Air tends, by reason of the Rarifaction made by his greatest *Meridian* Heat, is with him carried Westward, and consequently the tendency of the whole Body of the lower Air is that way.[42]

This explanation embodied the principle that wind are caused and their * direction largely determined by the distribution of air masses of differing density, warm air being relatively lighter than cold air. The westward component in the trade winds which Halley attributed to the effect of the sun passing westward over the ocean has since been explained as the effect of the earth's rotation but his general explanation and the importance he attached to the relative situation of land and sea has not been challenged. As the sun warmed the air in the tropics it rose and colder air moved in from higher latitudes, causing "a Kind of Circulation". Halley supposed that winds set on to the Guinea coast from the west because of the extreme rarefaction of the air over the deserts of Africa. Similarly the warmest air was to be found over the Asian continent in summer but in winter it was coldest there, leading to the seasonal reversal of winds in the northern Indian Ocean.

While Halley described how the action of the sun on the air maintains a circulation due to differences in density in the atmosphere which is responsible for prevailing winds, he said nothing about the possibility of a similar circulation in the ocean. Although he stated that the principles he was using applied equally to air and water, he made no reference to ocean currents in his paper. Therefore although such an idea was implicit in his system it would be applying hindsight to regard Halley as the originator of the theory of thermal oceanic circulation.[43]

Halley's unwillingness to follow up his ideas in so far as they affected the sea appears again in his work on the exchange of water between the ocean and the atmosphere. This subject was inseparable from the age old controversy about the origin of springs. In the seventeenth century people held a variety of views, some of which appear in Plot's *De Origine Fontium*, deriving springs directly from the sea by a process of filtration through the earth. Some, like Woodward, believed in the existence of a vast central reservoir of water in the interior of the earth. Such people had no difficulty in, for example, accounting for the disappearance of excess water in the Mediterranean; they said that it merely drained away through the sea bed. Those who opposed these ideas argued that springs and rivers were supplied by rain, water evaporated from the sea. In the years after 1700 this latter view gradually displaced the others, bringing to an end centuries of deadlock. For this profound change Halley seems to have been principally responsible since it is his authority which is invariably given for adopting this particular reasoning.

Following up his experiment to see how much water would be evaporated from the sea in one day,[44] Halley wrote another paper to show that what was true for the Mediterranean was true for the ocean in general.[45] He stated that water vapour from the sea condensed by cold, particularly in mountainous areas, and falling as dew, rain, or snow was the source from which rivers and springs took their origin. In further support of his argument he described his experience in the mountains of St Helena. In the words of *The Compleat Geographer*:

Mr. *Halley* assures us, That during his abode at St. *Helena*, in the Night-time, on the tops of the Hills about 800 yards above the Sea, there was so strange a Condensation, or rather Precipitation of the Vapours, that it was a great impediment to his Celestial Observations; for in the clear Sky the Dew would fall so fast, as to cover each half quarter of an Hour, his Glasses with little drops, so that he was necessitated to wipe them often; and the Paper on which he wrote his Observations would immediately be so wet with Dew, that it would not bear Ink. By which it may be suppos'd how fast the Water gathers in those mighty high Ridges.[46]

He did not however consider what effect evaporation might have on the ocean itself.

Many years later Halley wrote a paper on the saltness of the ocean for presentation to the Royal Society.[47] Adopting the view that the salt in the sea was due to the washing down of minerals from the land by rivers over long periods of time he suggested that if changes in its salinity were to be measured over a number of years it would be possible to estimate the age of the earth:

I recommend it therefore to the *Society*, as opportunity shall offer, to procure the Experiments to be made of the present degree of Saltness of the Ocean, and of as many of these Lakes as can be come at, that they may stand upon Record for the benefit of future ages.[48]

Apart from his work on tides, therefore, Halley's direct contributions to the study of the sea were disappointingly few. His meteorological work was to have important consequences in the future development of marine science but he himself, it seems, had no inkling of this. As time went on he turned from meteorology to pursue his studies of magnetism and astronomy and in his position as Astronomer Royal, which he held from 1721 until his death in 1742, he devoted his energies to attempting to perfect methods of calculating longitude. One area of work at sea which seems to have continued to interest him was deep-sea diving techniques.[49]

Halley's work on trade winds may well be compared with the writings of William Dampier (1652–1715). Dampier was one of the few people to be able to write about the sea from a strictly empirical point of view and in his *Discourse of Winds, Breezes, Storms, Tides and Currents*, published in 1699, he gave an account of conditions at sea based on his own experience.[50] He was not concerned with theoretical discussion and controversy but with what he had himself observed, much of which was very interesting. He related how

In all my Cruisings among the Privateers, I took notice of the Risings of the Tides; because by knowing it, I always knew where we might best haul ashore and clean our Ships.[51]

Among other things he observed how, for example at the Galapagos,

Islands lying afar off at Sea, have seldom such high Tides as those that are near the Main.[52]

He deduced that there must be a strait between New Holland (Australia) and New Guinea because of the large tides setting to the East.[53]

Dampier distinguished between tidal streams which he said flowed near the shore and regularly reversed their directions and ocean currents which were found further out and generally flowed in the same direction all the time. He realized that the region of equatorial currents coincided with that of the trade winds—

in all Places where the Trade blows, we find a Current setting with the Wind.[54]

Indeed he went further than this and suggested that the winds were the cause of the currents.[55] It seems that this was the first time that this connection was explicitly suggested.[56]

In spite of all the efforts of the Royal Society to recommend research into tides and currents to seamen, Dampier was apparently unique, not perhaps in the range of his knowledge, but in his willingness and ability to put it into print. His work and Halley's papers formed the basis for much of what the eighteenth century had to say on the surface of the ocean and its relationship with the movements of the atmosphere. While the interest shown by Boyle and Hooke and others in the interior of the ocean was largely forgotten, Halley's version of the theory deriving rain and rivers from the sea and his theory of trade winds and Dampier's observations on the dependence of ocean currents on prevailing winds came to be regarded as self-evident truths.

The oblivion which overtook most of the seventeenth-century work on marine science was sad but not altogether surprising. As has already been

suggested both outside events in the world of science and inherent difficulties arising from the work itself conspired against its continuance. At
the beginning Sir Robert Moray and the rest had been eager to improve
understanding of the world and certain that closer study would provide
answers to their questions but as far as the sea was concerned they had set
themselves a particularly hard task. Not only was a great deal of time,
effort and expense required to obtain results in the field but there was the
added difficulty of interpreting them once obtained. Especially where
tides were concerned, the issues involved were often too complex to admit
of any simple solution. In the face of such a situation it would not have
been amazing if the original enthusiasm had waned even had there not
been external causes turning people to other things. Even so some people's
interest was maintained but the ultimate obstacle in their way was the
vastness of their task. In many sciences one person could do a great deal.
In marine science, though, as Hooke discovered, an individual of limited
resources could achieve only limited results. No one appreciated this more
than Count Marsigli, the one person to carry something of the old spirit
into the new century.

8. NOTES

1. *Royal Society Classified Papers*, Vol. **19**. For example the *Inquiries ffor Tanger*,
   issued, presumably for Sheeres, in May 1676, no. 89.
2. "Some experiments and observations made of the force of the pressure of the
   water in great depths, made and communicated to the Royal Society by a
   Person of Honour", *Phil. Trans.* (1691–1693). Vol. **17**, pp. 504–506. The author
   of the observations is identified in the original account preserved in the *Royal
   Society Classified Papers*. Vol. **6**, no. 49.
3. Thomas Birch, *History of the Royal Society*. Vol. **1** (1756) pp. 180–182.
4. *Ibid.* pp. 208–211.
5. *Ibid.* pp. 307–308.
6. "Directions for observations and experiments to be made by masters of ships,
   pilots, and other fit persons in their sea-voyages", *Phil. Trans.* (April 1667).
   Vol. **2**, no. 24, pp. 433–448.
7. Thomas Birch, *History of the Royal Society*. Vol. **2** (1756) p. 143.
8. *Ibid.* Vol. **3** (1757) pp. 190 and 213–214.
9. *Ibid.* p. 220.
10. *Ibid.* pp. 394–400.
11. *Ibid.* p. 394.
12. *Ibid.* p. 395.
13. *Ibid.* pp. 395–396.
14. *Ibid.* p. 398.
15. *Ibid.* pp. 398–399.
16. *Ibid.* p. 399. The minute says the experiment demonstrated the compression
    of water in the tube but this is clearly an error.
17. *Ibid.* Vol. **4** (1757)p. 246.

18. Thomas Birch, *History of the Royal Society*. Vol 2 (1756) p. 251.
19. *Ibid.* pp. 258–259.
20. ?Robert Knox.
21. Robert Hooke, "Account of an experiment touching the different weights of cold and warme water", Birch, *op. cit.* Vol. 1 (1756) pp. 174–176.
22. R. T. Gunther, "The Cutler Lectures of Robert Hooke", *Early Science in Oxford*. Vol. 8 (1931), pp. 368–372.
23. Robert Hooke, "Lectures and Discourses of Earthquakes, and Subterraneous Eruptions" in *The Posthumous Works of Robert Hooke* (ed. Richard Waller) (1705), pp. 279–450.
24. *Ibid.* p. 308.
25. John Woodward, *An Essay towards a Natural History of the Earth* (1695). Charles Leigh, *The Natural History of Lancashire, Cheshire, and the Peak in Derbyshire* (1700.) etc.
26. Robert Hooke, *op. cit.* p. 327.
27. *Ibid.* pp. 416–424.
28. *Ibid.* p. 418.
29. Thomas Birch, *History of the Royal Society*. Vol. 4 (1757) pp. 253–254.
30. Robert Hooke, "Experiments on freezing", *Philosophical Experiments and Observations of the Late Eminent Dr. Robert Hooke* (ed. William Derham), (1726), pp. 132–142. Reprinted by R. T. Gunther, *The Life and Work of Robert Hooke*, part 2, in *Early Science in Oxford*. Vol. 7 (1930).
31. John Ward, *The Lives of the Professors of Gresham College*, London (1740), p. 186.
32. Margaret 'Espinasse, *Robert Hooke*, London (1956), p. 4.
33. "Dr. Hooke's Description of some Instruments for Sounding the great Depths of the Sea, and bringing Accounts of several Kinds from the Bottom of it Being the Substance of some of his Lectures, in December, 1691", *Philosophical Experiments, op. cit.* pp. 225–248. Reprinted by R. T. Gunther, *op. cit.* pp. 717–735.
34. Hooke certainly described how to find the relationship between pressure and depth in 1663 but I have found no earlier description of this instrument. Probably the former meaning is the true one.
35. Robert Hooke, *Philosophical Experiments, op. cit.* p. 240.
36. *Ibid.* p. 233.
37. Robert Hooke, "Some farther observations, relating to the Nautilus, and other shell-fish", *Philosophical Experiments, op. cit.* pp. 311–314; p. 313.
38. *Ibid.* p. 314.
39. Margaret 'Espinasse, "The decline and fall of Restoration science", *Past and Present* (1958). Vol. 14, pp. 71–87.
40. Edmond Halley, *A Journall of a Voyage in his Majes[ties] Pink the Paramore intended for the Discovery of the Variation of the Magneticall Compass; A Journal of a Voyage in his Ma[tis] Pink y[e] Paramour intended for the Discovery of y[e] Variation of the Compass . . . anno 1699 & 1700; A Journall of a Voiage in his Ma[tis] Pink the Paramore: for discovery of the Course of the Tides in the Channell of England. Anno 1701*. MSS in the British Museum. *
41. Edmond Halley, "An historical account of the trade winds, and monsoons, observable in the seas between and near the Tropicks, with an attempt to assign the phisical cause of the said winds", *Phil. Trans.* (1686–1687). Vol. 16, pp. 153–168.

42. Edmond Halley, *Phil. Trans.* (1686–1687). Vol **16**, p. 165.
43. In fact Halley was not even the first person to make this assertion about the atmosphere. According to Dr Harold Burstyn a better statement of this theory was made in 1685 by Dr George Garden: H. L. Burstyn, "Early explanations of the role of the earth's rotation in the circulation of the atmosphere and the ocean", *Isis* (1966). Vol. **57**, pp. 167–187.
44. Edmond Halley, "An estimate of the quantity of vapour raised out of the sea by the warmth of the sun", *Phil. Trans.* (1686–1687). Vol. **16**, pp. 366–370.
45. Edmond Halley, "An account of the circulation of the watry vapours of the sea, and of the cause of springs", *Phil. Trans.* (1691–1693). Vol. **17**, pp. 468–473.
46. *The Compleat Geographer*, Awnsham and John Churchill, 3rd edition, London (1709), p. xxxviii.
47. Edmond Halley, "A short account of the cause of the saltness of the ocean, and of the several lakes that emit no rivers; with a proposal, by help thereof, to discover the age of the world", *Phil. Trans.* (1714–1716). Vol. **29**, pp. 296–300.
48. *Ibid.* pp. 299–300.
49. In 1691 he designed a diving bell. For his work on magnetism and astronomy see Sir Edward Bullard, "Edmond Halley (1656–1741)", *Endeavour* (October 1956). Vol. **15**, no. 60, pp. 189–199.
50. William Dampier, "A discourse of winds, breezes, storms, tides, and currents", *A Collection of Voyages*, 7th edition, 4 vols, London, 1729. Vol. **2.**
51. *Ibid.* p. 97.
52. *Ibid.* p. 95.
53. *Ibid.* p. 99.
54. *Ibid.* p. 103.
55. *Ibid.* p. 90.
56. H. L. Burstyn, *op. cit.* p. 182.

Addenda et Corrigenda

p.169, 1,10: *instead* wind *read* winds

p.173, n.40, 1.6: *instead* MSS in the British Museum read British Library, Add. MS. 30368. See Ch.5, n.96.

AN AGE OF PHILOSOPHY
AND CURIOUS NAVIGATION

9. REAWAKENING INTEREST IN THE SEA, 1700–1800

THE interest in studying the science of the sea which had reached its peak in the years 1660–1675 gradually fell away in the later years of the seventeenth century. In the eighteenth century the revival began, intermittently at first, then gathering momentum, until by its end there was a recognized network of research. This was the time when the foundations of modern chemistry, geology, biology and meteorology were laid and all these sciences have affiliations with different aspects of oceanography. In addition to the few people who made a special point of studying the sea there were a growing number who became interested in its problems through their work in other branches of science.

There was little sense of continuity among eighteenth-century contributors to marine science, except in the field of tidal theory where Newton remained pre-eminent. Occasionally mention was made of Boyle's essays or of the instrument designs published by Hooke in the *Philosophical Transactions* but the more obscure aspects of earlier work were completely forgotten. In fact the influence of the seventeenth-century research was present in a more intangible way. Before it took place writers dealt with the sea in concepts and language that had altered little since the days of Pliny. Afterwards, however superficial and incorrect their grasp of the work produced in the seventeenth century, they discussed marine science in terms which are familiar today.

Of the people who had participated in the growth of marine science in the earlier period only a handful survived the first decade of the eighteenth century. Newton lived until 1727 and Halley until 1742 but to both of them the study of the sea as such had always been peripheral to their main interests, notwithstanding the importance of their contributions to it, and neither of them seems to have added to their work in this field during later years. The one person who actively bridged the hiatus between the two centuries was Count Marsigli who as a young man had published an account of the gravitational current system in the Bosporus at a time when British scientists and engineers were puzzling fruitlessly over the same problem in the Strait of Gibraltar[1] (*see* Ch. 7). In 1706 Marsigli turned again to oceanographic research, this time in the south of France.[2] There

he made what must be the first study of a single region and the marine
life to be found in it as opposed to a particular aspect or technique of
oceanography. In this he was partly making a virtue of necessity but
partly too acting on the policy that it was more sensible to attempt certain
limited objectives in a small area than to try and tackle the subject as a
whole as the British scientists had tended to do. From the results which he
obtained he wrote the *Histoire Physique de la Mer*, the first book devoted
entirely to marine science.[3]

Marsigli was first led to this work by his interest in the structure of the
earth and his conviction, formed during a lifetime of travel, that the
mountain chains of southern Europe and the Mediterranean Sea must be
part of the same geological formation. He believed that it was impossible
to understand the processes which had shaped the land without obtaining
first-hand information about the sea.

Marsigli knew Boyle's essays on the saltness of the sea and the sea
floor. The latter he found unhelpful because of the extent to which it
relied on reported information and, in his view, precious little of that. He
even suggested that Boyle must have been accidentally prevented from
carrying his investigation further since he had left it in such an unsatisfactory state:

car on a vû par quantité d'autres ouvrages, qu'il savoit finir parfaitement ce
qu'il se donnoit la peine de commencer.[4]

He was determined not to fall into the same error himself but to rely on
his own observations:

j'ai été obligé de chercher, par moi-même, quelque chose de plus solide, que
la Dissertation de Robert Boyle & de ne me point arrêter à tout ce que me
supposoient les Mariniers. Il m'a falu donc penser à un nombre d'observations,
qui toutes ensemble fissent une compensation à l'impossibilité qu'il y a de
pouvoir, avec les yeux & avec les mains, prendre connoissance sous l'Eau de
cette vérité que l'on recherche.[5]

Marsigli made his headquarters at the little port of Cassis near Marseilles.
From there he put to sea and ran lines of soundings from fourteen different
* places on the shore of the Gulf of Lyons. The results he obtained enabled
him to draw profiles of the sea floor. These revealed a distinctive pattern
that recurred with variations from one profile to another. From the beach,
the sea floor fell away for a few fathoms and then levelled out somewhat.
It gradually deepened to about 60 or 70 fathoms, at varying distances out
to sea, and then fell away sharply to a depth greater than 150 fathoms, the
limit of Marsigli's soundings. In describing these steps Marsigli gave what
must be the earliest account of the formation, found almost universally, of
continental shelf and slope falling to the abyssal regions of the sea.

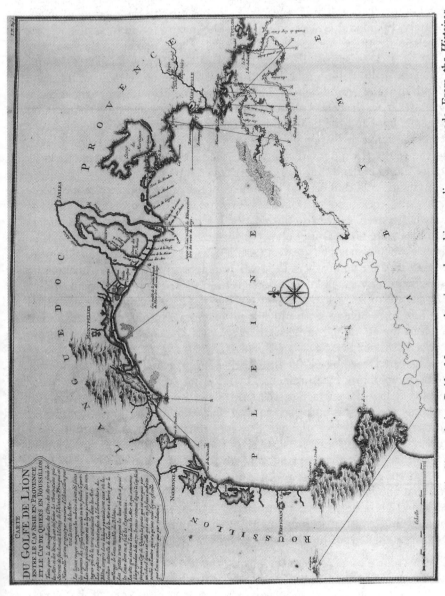

FIG. 10. Marsigli's Chart of the Gulf of Lyons, showing where his soundings were made. From the *Histoire* *Physique de la Mer* (1725), pp. 2–3.

Not surprisingly Marsigli did not recognize what he had found as the place where the continental block gives way to the sea floor. He regarded the hollow of the Mediterranean as compensatory to the mountain ranges of Italy, Spain and Greece and quoted the maxim found in earlier writers that the depth of the sea is proportional to the height of the land (*see* Ch. 3). J. D. Cassini (1625–1712) had calculated the height of Mount Canigou in Roussillon as 1,400 toises and Marsigli asserted that the same depth of water would be found at a comparable distance from the coast, a guess that was recently shown to be surprisingly accurate.[6] His opinion that the land and the bed of the sea formed part of a homogeneous structure was confirmed when he found rock strata dipping down below the sea at the coast. He supposed that the sea bed consisted of the same rocks as those found on land, but more or less covered by sediment.[7]

Marsigli collected several specimens of sea water during these expeditions and measured their specific gravity with a hydrometer.[8] Back at Cassis he used a hydrostatic balance for greater accuracy. Some of his samples were taken from below the surface and these proved to be rather heavier than usual. The greatest variation in surface salinity occurred off the mouth of the Rhône where the river water mixes with the sea, making its specific gravity much lower. Marsigli tried to determine something about the nature of sea salt but chemistry was not as yet sufficiently advanced for him to be able to learn much from his tests. He supposed that the salt present in sea water had been dissolved over the course of time from the rocks of the sea bed.[9]

Between December 1706 and April 1707 Marsigli made a number of serial temperature measurements, by lowering a thermometer to different depths below the surface of the sea.[10] His deepest result was from 120 fathoms and he was surprised to find that whatever the variations which occurred at the surface, the deeper water remained at a constant temperature of $10\frac{1}{2}°$ or $10\frac{3}{4}°$ of his scale. He wondered whether this pattern persisted throughout the year and took advantage of a visit to Cassis in June 1707 to make new observations. He obtained some revealing results, showing that the lower layers of water had warmed up considerably, rising to $15°$ at 120 fathoms.[11] Unfortunately, the appearance of a privateer brought his investigations to an abrupt end and in the ensuing commotion his thermometer got broken:

Il ne manque plus qu'à faire cette meme experience en Eté, car m'étant trouvé encore sur la Côte de Cassis le 30. de Juin, je voulus examiner avec le Thermometre, le degré de Chaleur du fond de la Mer, & après en avoir fait trois observations à 4 h. à 6 h. & à 9 h. du matin, à diverses profondeurs, un brigantin ennemi arrivant sur nous nous fit retirer; dans ce desordre, le Thermometre se cassa, & il ne me fut plus possible de continuer ces observations.

Presumably relying on an inaccurate recollection of *Relations about the Bottom of the Sea*, Marsigli was under the impression that Boyle had laid down that waves never rise more than 6 feet above the general level of the ocean. He wrote "J'ai verifié cette experience dans les plages du Languedoc."[12] In fact, he said, he had found them to be seven feet high but this was because the beach was shallow and sandy. Out at sea they were larger still but this was due to the cumulative effect of waves running into one another.

His observations of tides, made five times a day at Cassis, and of currents left Marsigli little the wiser. He did discover that if the current came either from east or west for some days, wind often followed from the same direction. He concluded that little could be done by an individual working alone in this field:

Je conclus de toutes ces observations differentes, qu'on n'établira jamais rien de solide, touchant les Courans, tant qu'une seule personne travaillera à les observer, & dans un seul endroit comme j'ai fait à Cassis. Il faudroit qu'en même tems, il y eût des Observateurs aux principaux Caps de la Côte & des Isles; lesquels, suivant une méthode, dont on seroit convenu, feroient tous des Journaux exacts, tant à l'égard de la velocité des Courans, que des endroits ou leur cours se tourneroient, sans oublier les courans interieurs oposez à ceux de la superficie, en joignant à cela l'observation des vents, dont ils compareroient la force avec celle des Courans. Mais comme c'est une depense réservée a quelque Prince, amateur, & protecteur des Sciences, je ne dirai autre chose là-dessus.[13]

Marsigli said nothing at this point about his earlier work on the Bosporus, giving only a brief mention of how he came to undertake these researches, which he intended to write up separately, incorporating the work which he did in 1691 with his original account:

Je travaillai pour la premiere fois à cet examen de la Mer, quoique sans une idée si universelle, sur la petite étenduë du Canal de Constantinople, l'an 1680, & mes observations furent communiquées à Christine, Reine de Suede, qui les fit imprimer à Rome. Ensuite un nouveau séjour, que je fis en cette ville Imperiale, l'an 1691. me donna lieu de renouveller mes recherches sur ce sujet, que j'eus toûjours dessein d'unir dans une nouvelle Edition, avec les premieres.[14]

Following his plan of doing what was possible in the limited sphere of activity open to him Marsigli had for the second time in his life scored a remarkable oceanographic success. Eschewing the ambitious aims of some of the earlier workers and concentrating on a more thorough investigation of one area he had learnt a great deal that they had missed. His method had its limitations, as he was quick to acknowledge, particularly when it came to dealing with large scale movements of water, and it was this which led him to call for government support for the study of the oceans. In this he showed foresight for it was not until this help was given that the marine sciences developed their collective identity.

Needless to say, this was far in the future. Marsigli's book was widely read, however, and, being the only work dealing solely with the ocean, was much quoted in the eighteenth and early nineteenth centuries. His influence was undoubtedly strong in promoting the revival of marine science which was going on then in Britain. The more immediate initiative, however, seems to have come from Stephen Hales (1677–1761), rector of Teddington, who was best known for his studies on plant and animal physiology.[15] His work was indicative of a wider movement of renewed interest, which gained in power as the century progressed, in the sciences which had been neglected in the concentration on mathematics and physics after Newton. Chemistry, biology, meteorology, geology and oceanography all began a period of growth.

In 1727 Hales published *Vegetable Staticks* in which he described the use of a pressure gauge for an experiment on fermentation.[16] The apparatus consisted of a glass tube closed at the top and open at the bottom which was immersed in a bath of mercury. Coloured honey on the surface of the mercury in the tube acted as a marker as the column rose and fell. Hales suggested that this contrivance

might probably be of service in finding out unfathomable depths of the Sea, *viz.* by fixing this sea-gage to some buoyant body which should be sunk by a weight fixt to it, which weight might by an easie contrivance be detached from the buoyant body, as soon as it touched the bottom of the sea.

This idea was taken up by John Theophilus Desaguliers (1683–1744) who devised a way of incorporating Hales's apparatus with a weight and float and demonstrated it at a Royal Society meeting in January 1728.[17] As the resulting instrument was made largely of glass one assumes that it would have proved too fragile for use at sea but it was found to work well in a simulated pressure comparable to that which would be experienced in a depth of forty feet of water.

The inspiration for this idea was clearly drawn from accounts of Hooke's version of the machine for sounding without a line, as published in the first and second volumes of the *Philosophical Transactions* (*see* Ch. 4). Desaguliers referred to the difficulty encountered in the previous century of discovering anything definite with these instruments when waves and currents carried the floats away and made it impossible to record the time taken by them accurately.[18] Hales and Desaguliers felt they would obtain a more accurate estimate of depth by measuring pressure. Hooke had of course expressed just such an opinion in his Cutlerian Lectures on oceanography and these had been printed by Derham just over a year before[19] (*see* Ch. 8) but there is nothing to show that either Hales or Desaguliers were aware of them.

In the second part of *Vegetable Staticks*, *Statical Essays*, published in 1733, Hales described a much more practical version of his sounding machine.[20] It was based on the same principle, that the volume of the air in the apparatus would diminish in inverse proportion as the pressure of the water increased. An iron tube or musket barrel 50 inches long was to be attached to a hollow metal container of exactly nine times its volume. In this container was a small hole to let in sea water as the instrument went down. Hales proposed to measure the height to which it rose with coloured oil floating on top of the water. This would leave a trace on a metal or wooden rod fastened in the tube which could be removed for inspection. He imagined that by this method it would be possible to measure accurately depths of as much as two and a half miles. If it were necessary to go to still greater depths the capacity of the reservoir would have to be enlarged. The instrument was to be equipped with a float made of wood, covered with tar to prevent the water from being forced into it by pressure, and a weight which was arranged to detach itself as soon as it struck the sea floor.

This description was published again in 1754, in the *Gentleman's Magazine*,[21] with a note that it was

drawn up about the year 1732, *or* 33, *for the late* Colin Campbell, *Esq*; *who employed the ingenious Mr*. Francis Hawksbee *to make the machine which was tried in various depths of the* Thames, *answered very well, and always returned, leaving the balast behind. It was soon after put aboard the ship in which Mr*. Campbell *sailed for* Jamaica; *and in a clear calm day was by him let down into the sea, not many leagues from* Bermudas, *several other ships being in company, and a good look out ordered from them all; yet it was not seen to return, though they waited for it between three and four hours. This account, and the paper the Communicator had from Mr*. Campbell *himself before his last departure*.[22]

Colin Campbell (*d*. 1752) was a friend of Hales who had proposed his selection to the Royal Society in 1730.[23] His home was in Jamaica. Francis Hawksbee (1687–1763) was a leading instrument maker of the day.[24]

Added to the account in the *Gentleman's Magazine* was a description of a more successful experiment carried out by a Mr Erasmus King in the Baltic.[25] He obtained a measurement of 288 feet which corresponded with the depth measured by lead and line.[26]

Hales accompanied his description of the sounding machine with a few remarks on what the results of such experiments might well be expected to show. The fact that most oceans were interspersed with islands showed that they did not get progressively deeper towards the middle. If the greatest height of the land were equivalent to the greatest depth of the

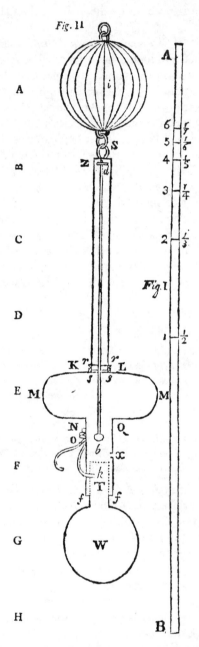

FIG. 11. Stephen Hales's Sea-gage. As described in *The Gentleman's Magazine* (1754). Vol. **24**, p. 216.

sea, he expected that the sea would be found to be 5 or 6 miles deep. If, on the other hand, the volume of water in the sea were equivalent to the amount of earth above sea level then the average depth of the sea would be much less because it covered a so much greater area.[27]

One of Hales's many interests was the design and construction of ventilators for use at sea. Some of them were fitted in slave ships and it was to the captain of one of these, Henry Ellis (1721–1806), of the *Earl of Halifax*, that Hales entrusted the carrying out of experiments on the salinity and temperature of the sea at different depths. He gave him a "bucket sea-gage" which consisted of a covered pail with a Fahrenheit thermometer fastened in it.[28] Valves opening upwards in the top and bottom of the bucket allowed the sea free passage through the apparatus on its way down but remained closed on the way up so that the deepest water was brought to the surface.

In January 1751 Ellis wrote to Hales from Africa to say that he had made several observations with the apparatus in latitude 25°13′ N, longitude 25°12′ W.[29] He lowered the bucket to various depths between 360 and 5,346 feet and brought up specimens of water. He found that the temperature, which was 84° F at the surface, decreased to 53° at 3,900 feet and then stayed the same below that depth. It took three-quarters of an hour to bring up the bucket from the greatest depth but as the temperature of the sample rose only 5° in the same amount of time when left standing in the open air he did not think that it would have altered its original temperature very much during the ascent. From measurements of specific gravity made with a hydrometer he found that the water grew more salt with depth.

Ellis concluded

This experiment, which seem'd at first but mere food for curiosity, became in the interim very useful to us. By its means we supplied our cold bath, and cooled our wines or water at pleasure; which is vastly agreeable to us in this burning climate.

I intend, in our passage to the West Indies, to sound a mile deeper than I have done, having a sufficient quantity of line. But I cannot attempt your method to find the depth of the sea, for want of apparatus. My business at present affords me very little time for speculation.[30]

There is no evidence that Ellis carried out any further experiments at sea. It is certain, however, that Hales continued to take an active interest in the study of marine science. Only a few weeks before his death, in December 1760, he wrote to his friend Swithin Adee, that he was engaged in experimenting on the salinity of sea water from different parts of the world.[31]

Hales led the way for many people of different nationalities who began to take an interest in marine science and as the eighteenth century progressed his work had no small influence. As well as the publications already mentioned a description of his sounding machine appeared in Desaguliers' *Course of Experimental Philosophy*[32] and of Ellis's experiments in *A Description of Ventilators*.[33]

In 1755 the *Gentleman's Magazine* published observations made by Hugh Campbell on the specific gravity of sea water.[34] This work had been carried out during a voyage from England to Bombay. Campbell used a hydrostatic balance to weigh his samples and discovered a state of affairs

contrary to what has been suggested in the *Philosophical Transactions* of the Royal Society, that the nearer you approach the line the greater the weight of sea-water is. For in the latitude of 15° north the sea-water weighed 780½ grains, and at the equator but 779; and in 17° south it weighed exactly the same as at the equator.

Campbell realized that temperature as well as salinity must affect the density of water but as he had no thermometer he was unable to discover what relationship existed between the two. It is plain that he was acquainted with earlier work, most probably the observations made for Boyle by Henry Stubbs (*see* Ch. 6).

Peter Forsskål (1732–1763), naturalist on the Danish expedition to Arabia Felix, made observations of salinity in the Sound and during their voyage to the east in 1761.[35] He attempted to measure salinity at different depths in the Sound, perhaps in the hope of seeing whether Marsigli's ideas could be applied there.

Another student of marine science was the unlucky French astronomer, Jean-Baptiste Chappe d'Auteroche (1728–1769) who was sent to Mexico in 1768 to observe the transit of Venus in 1769, a task that cost him his life.[36] He took with him a hydrometer, supplied by Lavoisier at his request, with which he observed the specific gravity of the sea throughout the voyage.[37] On two occasions he lowered a thermometer wrapped in cloth or canvas to a depth of 100 fathoms and compared the temperature of the sea at that depth with that at the surface.

Antoine Laurent de Lavoisier (1743–1794) compiled a memoir discussing the specific gravity observations which Chappe d'Auteroche had made.[38] In order to use them as an indication of salinity it had been necessary to provide a means of distinguishing the effect of temperature and he had produced a table, based on his own experiments, by which results could be reduced to a uniform temperature. He pointed out that M. de Borda was to use a hydrometer of the same design on a government-sponsored voyage to test ways of measuring longitude and recommended that observations of this kind should be made as a matter of course on all voyages:

Il seroit a souhaiter que les Physiciens s'attachassent, dans les voyages de long cours, à enrichir la Physique de nouveaux faits en ce genre; ils pourroient un jour conduire à des conséquences importantes.[39]

It soon became the rule rather than the exception for observations of this kind to be made as past of the routine on official voyages, not to mention a growing number carried out by private individuals.

The leaders of the mid-eighteenth century voyages of discovery sent out from Britain do not seem to have made any concerted attempts to carry out scientific work. On Anson's voyage round the world they noticed the cold northward flowing Peru current off western South America which

set us to the northward, at the rate of ten or twelve miles each day.[40]

Byron,[41] Carteret[42] and Wallis were instructed to record details of tides and currents but as part of their navigational routine. It was not until the voyages of James Cook (1728–1779) that scientific work in general became an important feature of voyages of discovery from Britain.

Cook's first expedition, 1768–1771, to observe the transit of Venus, was not very productive in terms of physical oceanography. Joseph Banks (1744–1820), though later active in promoting other people's researches (*see* Ch. 11), seems to have done nothing himself in this field.[43] Some observations on tides were made by the astronomer Charles Green (*d.* 1771) and by Cook himself.[44, 45] They revealed, amongst other things, that the tides at Tahiti were very small—

the greatest height scarcely exceeds one foot, in the middle of this wide-extended ocean; which falls far short of what might have been expected from physical principles. The cause of this remarkable difference deserves farther inquiry.[45, 46]

On 10 June 1770 the *Endeavour* struck a reef off the east coast of Australia. It was just after high water and in waiting for an opportunity to refloat his ship Cook discovered that there was a considerable diurnal inequality in the tides, a fact hitherto unsuspected by him. He was hoping to refloat her at the next high water but found that

to our surprize, the tide did not rise high enough to accomplish this by near two feet. We had now no hopes but from the tide at midnight; and these only founded on a notion, very general indeed among seamen, but not confirmed by any thing which had yet fallen under my observation, that the night-tide rises higher than the day-tide. We prepared, however, for the event, which exceeded our most sanguine expectations; for, about 20 minutes after 10 o'clock in the evening, which was a full hour before high-water, the ship floated. At this time the heads of rocks, which on the preceding tide were, at least, a foot above water, were wholly covered.[47]

It was on the second voyage, 1772–1775, that more specific attention was paid to the study of the sea. This was the work of the two astronomers who accompanied the expedition, William Wales (1734?–1798), who sailed with Cook in the *Resolution* and William Bayly (1737–1810), who was with Lieut. Tobias Furneaux in the *Adventure*. Their principal tasks were to make astronomical observations and test chronometers on behalf of the Board of Longitude, the two methods of determining longitude, from measurements of lunar distance and with chronometers, just having been introduced, but they were also instructed to make observations on the saltness of the sea and on the temperature at different depths.[48] The apparatus which they used for measuring temperature below the surface was very like Hales's, which had probably inspired it. It

consisted of a square wooden tube, of about 18 inches long, and three inches square externally. It was fitted with a valve at the bottom, which opened inward, and another at its top, that opened outward, and had a contrivance for suspending the Thermometer exactly in the middle of it.[49]

The obvious precedent for this kind of observation was Ellis's work for Hales (*see* p. 183). Similar observations had also been made in 1769 by Captain Charles Douglas (*d.* 1789) of H.M.S. *Emerald*.[50] On eight separate occasions off the Norwegian coast he compared the temperature of the surface of the sea with that at depths of as much as 260 fathoms. The apparatus he used was a tin cylinder with a thermometer fixed inside it. The tin, filled with sea water, was closed up, lowered on a sounding line and left for half an hour to equalize its temperature with that of the water outside. Annoyed by the time taken to make one observation in this way, Douglas soon turned to lowering the cylinder empty, with holes pierced in it to let the water in as it went down. The idea had been suggested to him by Alexander Wilson (1714–1786), professor of astronomy at Glasgow, and he had provided the thermometer.[51]

Wales and Bayly made their observations from a ship's boat put out over the side to measure the current. They were therefore very much dependent on the wishes of their respective captains though quite to what extent this may have circumscribed their activities is not clear. Certainly on 6 September 1772 Bayly wished to make some deep-sea temperature observations but Furneaux refused to let him have a boat.[52] As it was they made nine observations between them at depths ranging from 80 to 160 fathoms.[53]

One of the objectives of Cook's second voyage was to investigate the possibility of a southern continent, a theme always popular with geographers. Four of the temperature measurements made by Wales and Bayly came during his first attempt to penetrate the Antarctic Ocean, turning back only in latitude 67° S. On one of these occasions, when Wales was out among the ice floes in the *Resolution*'s boat, taking a measurement at 100 fathoms, fog came down, hiding them from the ships. After rowing backwards and forwards for some time "hallowing and listening" they heard the *Adventure*'s bell and were taken on board.[54]

Of the observations made in Antarctic waters, three, all made in December 1772 between latitudes 55° and 58° S, two by Wales at 100 fathoms and one by Bayly at 160 fathoms, had in common the unusual feature that the deep water was slightly warmer than the surface water, the reverse of what they observed elsewhere.[55] Neither of them commented on this phenomenon, caused by the presence of cold but relatively fresh water from melting ice forming a layer on the sea surface above warmer but more saline water below, but commentators like Bishop Watson (1737–1816) were quick to notice the anomaly and to try and explain its cause.[56]

Since to all appearances the temperature observations were made without difficulty it is puzzling to account for the fact that they were soon discontinued. Wales made his last measurement in January 1773, Bayly in March, and neither of them gave any reason for this. Many explanations present themselves. Perhaps it was felt that they had learnt as much as they could from this kind of work and that there was no point in continuing it when there was so much else to be done. Possibly, as on many later voyages, it was due to loss or breakage of their equipment.

Accompanying the expedition as naturalists were Johann Reinhold Forster (1729–1798) and his son George (1754–1794). In their accounts of the voyage the Forsters gave the results of the temperature observations without saying who had made them.[57, 58] Not unnaturally their readers tended to assume that they were themselves responsible for them. This was largely a misconception since, though it was common for one or both to be out in the boat while the observations were being made, it was generally for the purpose of shooting sea-birds for their collection. There can be no doubt that Wales and Bayly made the measurements they individually recorded; on one occasion only is there mention of an observation made by the Forsters and this occurs in Wales's journal for 11 October 1772.[59] Wales relates that his thermometer registered $60\frac{1}{2}$° in the air, 59° in the surface water and 57° at 100 fathoms. The observation was then repeated with a thermometer of Mr Forster's in a tin case and the same results were obtained. This was presumably the cylindrical tin case to which J. R. Forster referred in his *Observations*.[58] There is no indication, however, of any other result obtained with it.

If this one incident were to leave any doubt as to the true authorship of the observations this must be removed by Wales's own words in his *Remarks on Mr. Forster's account of Captain Cook's last voyage*.[60] This pamphlet, written largely in defence of Cook, criticized other aspects of the Forsters' *Voyage round the World*, including their account of temperature measurements:

in relating the experiments which I made to find the difference between the heat of the sea at great depths, and at the surface; he says we were 27½ minutes drawing the thermometer up from the depth of 85 fathoms. These mistakes must continually happen where people will pretend to detail experiments and observations which they know nothing of, but by report. The real circumstances attending those experiments may be seen in the account which I have published for the Board of Longitude.[61]

The instructions issued to Wales and Bayly included a request that they measure the saltness of the sea but no instruments were provided for this and there is no record that anything was done. Neither did the Forsters attempt anything in this direction. J. R. Forster explained

I was obliged to set out upon this expedition almost at a moment's warning and could not therefore provide any apparatus necessary for that purpose.[62]

The expedition was not entirely fruitless in this respect however. From Cape Town the Forsters were accompanied by the Swedish naturalist Andreas Sparrman (1747–1820). On his voyage home from the Cape, in June 1776, he made the experiment of sinking corked bottles to different depths. At 80 fathoms he found that the bottle cracked but at 60 fathoms the cork was pushed in and the bottle filled with water. He subsequently collected numerous samples at this depth and sent them to Torbern Bergman (1735–1784), one of the first chemists to attempt the analysis of sea water[63] (*see* Ch. 10).

One of the other instructions issued to Wales and Bayly was to observe tides and this they did at the places where a stay of some duration was made. They had a tide-gauge which Wales described:

It consists of a square Tube whose side is about 3 inches with a small apperture at the bottom to admit the water. To this Tube is fitted a float of Cork-wood which will just move freely up and down in it. This Float is fixed to the end of a long slender Rod of deal, which is divided into feet and inches from the Float upwards. The buoyancy of the float enabled me to feel the water as soon as it touched it and I then observed what division on the Rod coincided with the top of the Tube. The Tube was placed upright in the water at some distance below low-water mark, and lashed fast to a Tree which grew out of the Bank & hung over the water.[64]

They made observations at Dusky Bay and Queen Charlotte's Sound in New Zealand, at Tahiti and at Tierra del Fuego. At Tahiti they investigated the report made by Green and Cook of a very small tidal range, of about a foot, which surprised most persons who had considered these matters, as being very far short, indeed, of what might have been expected from theory.[65]

They found that at Point Venus, where the observations had been made, the level of the sea was kept up by waves breaking over the reef which then acted as a dam so that the effect of tides was partly obscured. Outside the reef they found a normal rise and fall of about two feet, increasing to three feet at spring tides. Observations were brought abruptly to an end a day before their departure, at the end of August 1773. Wales wrote

In the morning of the 31st when I went to observe the Low water I found that some of the Natives had taken away my Instrument and as Capt. Cook had ordered us to have every thing on board the Next Day there was no time to make a new one.[64]

Less successful in terms of geographical discovery but more interesting for the development of oceanography, was the voyage of Captain Constantine Phipps (1744–1792) in H.M.S. *Racehorse* and *Carcass* in 1773. The voyage was planned by the Admiralty as a result of pressure from the Hon. Daines Barrington (1727–1800) to search for a practicable sea-route to the North Pole.[66] Phipps was keenly interested in scientific observation; he wrote

As a voyage of this kind would probably afford many opportunities of making experiments and observations in matters relative to navigation, I took care to provide myself with all the best instruments hitherto in use, as well as others which had been imperfectly, or never, tried.[67]

He was supplied with instructions by the Royal Society, Joseph Banks and D'Alembert.[68] The Board of Longitude sent Israel Lyons (1739–1775) as astronomer and the expedition's doctor, Dr Irving, also took part in the scientific work.

Until this time although various methods of measuring the depth of the sea had been suggested little had been done to try them out. It seems that Cook on his second voyage made some attempts to sound the depths of the ocean. J. R. Forster wrote

We now and then even out of sight of any land, tried to measure this depth.[69]

On 5 September 1772 they lowered 250 fathoms of line without finding bottom.[70] Phipps went further than this. On 20 June 1773, in a latitude of about 67° N he recorded

Almost calm all day. The water being perfectly smooth, I took this opportunity of trying to get soundings at much greater depths than I believe had ever been attempted before. I sounded with a very heavy lead the depth of 780 fathom, without getting ground.[41]

On the return voyage he sounded again in a calm on 4 September in

FIG. 12. Phipps's expedition to the Arctic in 1773. From a water colour by John Cleveley. Phipps's *Voyage towards the North Pole* (1774), facing p. 68.

latitude 75° N. This time they found bottom in 683 fathoms and the lead came up covered with "a fine soft blue clay".[72]

One of the new instruments which they tried out was a self-registering thermometer designed by Lord Charles Cavendish in 1757.[73] The thermometers which Cavendish had envisaged for use at sea were constructed in the belief that fluids were not compressible and that the effect of pressure could be minimized by leaving them open.[74] In 1762, however, John Canton (1718–1772) had shown that fluids are compressible.[75]

Phipps made four observations with Cavendish's thermometer, including measurements at 780 and 673 fathoms.[76] In order to allow for the effect of compression he applied a correction supplied by Mr Cavendish,[77] presumably Henry Cavendish (1731–1810) the physicist, eldest son of the inventor. The results, however, differed considerably from those obtained by bringing up water from the same depths and measuring its temperature at the surface with a Fahrenheit thermometer. For example, at 683 fathoms the corrected temperature given by Cavendish's thermometer was 32°, but water brought up from the bottom was at 40° F.

The sampler used for bringing up water, none of those sent out having given satisfaction, was devised by Dr. Irving.[78] It was a bottle insulated with a jacket of wool three inches thick encased in a waterproof covering. To close the bottle he used pieces of leather strung on a cord which could be pulled tight into the neck from the inside. With this apparatus he obtained five samples from different depths and measured their temperature and salinity.

Irving also measured the temperature and salinity of surface water. Phipps wrote that during a gale on 12 September

Dr. Irving tried the temperature of the sea in that state of agitation, and found it considerably warmer than that of the atmosphere. This observation is the more interesting, as it agrees with a passage in Plutarch's Natural Questions, not (I believe) before taken notice of, or confirmed by experiment, in which he remarks that the sea becomes warmer by being agitated in waves.[79]

Ice prevented the expedition from penetrating the Arctic Ocean to the north of Spitsbergen and the voyage has been chiefly remembered for Nelson's encounter with a polar bear. It was nevertheless remarkable for the breadth of scientific work attempted and for Phipps's keen personal interest in this side of the expedition which, though he regarded it as subordinate to the main geographical aim, led him, as far as marine science was concerned, to make a critical application and appraisal of new methods.

In 1776 Cook sailed on what was to be his last voyage, an attempt to penetrate the Arctic via the Bering Strait. William Bayly sailed with him in the *Resolution*, the only scientist to accompany the expedition. He took with him a "bucket" to hold a thermometer for measuring the temperature of the sea at different depths, made by Ramsden and a hydrostatic balance with two bottles for weighing sea water, made by Nairne.[80] This time, apparently, he made no temperature measurements, or at least no results are recorded, but made instead about sixty determinations of the salinity of the surface water during the voyage.[81] A formula worked out by Henry Cavendish enabled him to turn measurements of specific gravity into straightforward salinities by converting his results to a standard temperature. Cook and Lieutenant King contributed some measurements of their own.[82] They also measured the surface temperature of the sea almost daily as part of their routine observations.[83]

This concern for using the opportunities provided by long voyages for oceanographic research was not of course restricted to the British. The French were undertaking similar expeditions and on one led by Marion du Fresne in 1773–74, which like Cook's voyage with which it was contemporary, had as its aim the exploration of the Antarctic regions, the naturalist, M. de Pagès, made several observations of salinity.[84] In 1776 he collected further observations during a voyage to the Arctic. Among the scientific equipment taken by the ill-fated Comte de la Pérouse (1741– 1788) when he sailed in 1785 were two instruments for measuring the depth of the sea and one for discovering the temperature and salinity at different depths.[85]

The amount of oceanographic work done on the different voyages varied considerably from one to another. What determined the quantity and quality of the work done was partly the degree to which scientific research in general figured in the aims of the expedition but above all the significance attached to it by the officers in command and their scientists, if any. Although it was rare for anything very outstanding to be achieved it seems to have been equally rare that nothing was attempted. Scientists did not always find life easy and were sometimes frustrated by the indifference of the commander. This was the experience of François Péron (1775–1810), naturalist on the French voyage of circumnavigation sent out by Napoleon in 1800. Péron measured the temperature of the surface of the sea four times daily during the four years' voyage, at midday, midnight, 6 a.m. and 6 p.m.[86] He also wished to measure temperatures at different depths in the sea, a project recommended to him by leading figures in the French scientific world, including the Marquis de Laplace (1749–1827) and Jean-Claude Delamétherie (1743–1817). The best way he could think of for doing this was to insulate a thermometer, send it down to the required depth for as long as was necessary for the temperature there to penetrate the covering and then to draw it up as quickly as possible. He chose a mercury thermometer and encased it in materials known to be bad conductors of heat, glass, charcoal and wood.

In the event this turned out to be the worst method he could have chosen, because of the time needed to obtain results. The expedition's commander, Nicolas Baudin (d. 1803), was apparently unimpressed by the interest of observations of this kind and during the whole voyage Péron made only four, of which two only could be regarded as successful because on one occasion he was not allowed to leave his apparatus down long enough and on another it was brought up too slowly. He sorrowfully compared his lot with that of Irving:

Favorisé par un chef ami des sciences (le capitaine Phipps, aujourd'hui lord Mulgrave), Irving a pu multiplier davantage ses observations; il a pu les faire avec des instrumens plus variés, et par des profondeurs beaucoup plus grandes que je ne le pouvois moi-même, obligé de lutter ici, comme dans tout le reste de mes travaux, contre la mauvaise volonté du chef, ou même contre son opposition directe.[87]

One's sympathy for Péron is somewhat diminished on learning that he used or rather abused the hospitality given to the *Géographe* and *Naturaliste* at Sydney to spy out the land for a report to the French authorities in which he recommended an attack on the British colony.[88] Nevertheless the scientific results he obtained were interesting and useful. He showed that the mean temperature of the sea is higher than that of the air and demonstrated the fallacy behind the idea adopted by Irving and Phipps that the sea grew warmer during a storm. The true explanation, he said, was that the air cooled rapidly as the wind got up while the sea cooled more slowly so that the water became relatively warmer than the air:

Jamais la température absolue des eaux de la mer n'augmente par leur agitation; elle diminue au contraire; elle diminue même d'autant plus, que le vent qui les soulève est plus violent, surtout lorsqu'il est froid; mais dans tous ces cas, elle diminue beaucoup moins rapidement que celle de l'atmosphère.[89]

While they were sailing along the coast of Western Australia in a depth of about 100 fathoms Péron obtained permission, "à force des prières", to put over a dredging net, "une espèce de filet propre à ramener à la surface les substances qui tapissent le fond des mers". With this he brought up quantities of bottom living creatures. To his surprise they were not only phosphorescent but about three degrees warmer in temperature than the water at the surface of the ocean.[90] His observations in the open sea showed, like those of Ellis, Wales, Bayly and Phipps before him, that temperature there decreased with depth.[91]

Off the coast of southern Australia, in April 1802, the *Géographe* and *Naturaliste* encountered H.M.S. *Investigator* under the command of

Matthew Flinders (1774–1814). Flinders had sailed from England in July 1801 to continue his exploration of the Australian coastline. His instructions from the Board of Longitude must have included directions for measuring temperature and salinity since it supplied among his apparatus a "bucket" for bringing up water from different depths.[92] He used this twice to measure temperatures, once at 150 and once at 200 fathoms. He also made measurements of the temperature of the sea surface daily for the first six weeks of the voyage. Then two of his three thermometers got broken and these measurements ceased. A few weeks later the last thermometer was broken bringing all temperature measurements to an end.

Flinders also made tidal observations at King George's Sound and at Port Lincoln, places where they stayed for some time. He explained that as they did not have a proper instrument they were unable to make measurements elsewhere.

The gradual growth of the practice of making oceanographical observations at sea must be seen as part of the development of science in general which took place during the eighteenth century. As interest in astronomy, geophysics, chemistry, biology, geology and meteorology grew on land so they came to play an increasingly important part in the scientific content of voyages of discovery. At the same time, the sea began to arouse more interest among scientists and a growing number of people sought to study its problems either by making observations themselves or by persuading others to do it for them, while instructions of increasing complexity were issued to guide the marine work of official expeditions. They were partly interested in the subject for its own sake but partly too they realized the gains which a study of physical oceanography would give in understanding the other branches of science with which they were concerned. Péron wrote of his work on sea temperatures:

De toutes les expériences de physique, il en est peu dont les résultats soient plus intéressans et plus curieux que celles dont je vais m'occuper ici. Le météorologiste y puisera des données précieuses sur les variations atmosphériques au milieu de l'Océan; elles fourniront au naturaliste des connoissances indispensables relatives à l'habitation des diverse tribus d'animaux marins; le géologiste et le physicien y trouveront l'un et l'autre des faits certains sur la propagation de la chaleur au milieu des mers, et sur l'état physique interieur de ce globe, dont les excavations les plus profondes que l'on ait remarquées peuvent à peine effleurer la superficie; en un mot, il n'est aucune science qui ne puisse avec avantage revendiquer les résultats des expériences de ce genre.[93]

9. NOTES

1. Luigi Ferdinando Marsigli, *Osservazioni intorno al Bosforo Tracio o vero Canale di Constantinopli rappresentate in lettera alla Sacra Real Maestà di* Cristina Regina di Svezia*, Roma (1681).
2. F. C. W. Olson and Mary Ann Olson, "Luigi Ferdinando Marsigli, the lost father of oceanography", *Q. Jl Fla Acad. Sci.* (1958). Vol. **21**, no. 3, pp. 227–234.
3. Luigi Ferdinando Marsigli, *Histoire Physique de la Mer*, Amsterdam (1725). This title is misleading now because the greater part of the book is devoted to marine biology. This section had already been published in Venice in 1711 under the title of *Brieve ristretto del saggio fisico intorno alla storia del mare: see Bull. Inst. océanogr. Monaco*, numéro spécial 2 (1968). Vol. **2**, p. 375.
4. Marsigli, *Histoire Physique de la Mer* (1725), p. 1.
5. *Ibid.* p. 2.
6. Jacques Bourcart, *Géographie du Fond des Mers*, Paris (1949), p. 13. Marsigli estimated the depth at 1,400 toises (2,730 metres). In fact it is 2,785 metres.
7. Marsigli, *Histoire Physique de la Mer* (1725), pp. 2–16.
8. *Ibid.* pp. 18–43.
9. *Ibid.* pp. 11–13.
10. *Ibid.* pp. 16–17.
11. Marsigli had discovered the interesting fact that the temperature of the Mediterranean remains virtually the same, below a surface layer affected by atmospheric changes. He did not know that this is because the Strait of Gibraltar is too shallow to admit an inflow of cold Atlantic bottom water. The rise in temperature which he found in June was caused by the sinking of slightly more saline water produced by evaporation at the surface.
12. *Ibid.* p. 48. Boyle in fact said nothing of the kind. *See* Chapter 6.
13. *Ibid.* p. 47.
14. *Ibid.* Preface. It does not seem that he ever carried out this intention.
15. Hales's life and work has been described in *Stephen Hales, D.D., F.R.S.* by A. E. Clark-Kennedy, Cambridge (1929), who pays special attention to his contributions to oceanography and who has kindly allowed me to make use of his work.
16. Stephen Hales, *Vegetable Staticks*, London (1727), pp. 206–207.
17. J. T. Desaguliers, "An account of a machine for measuring any depth in the sea, with great expedition and certainty", *Phil. Trans.* (1727–1728). Vol. **35**, pp. 559–562.
18. J. T. Desaguliers, *op. cit.* pp. 559–560.
19. William Derham, *The Philosophical Experiments and Observations of the Late Eminent Dr. Robert Hooke* (1726).
20. Stephen Hales, *Statical Essays*, London (1733), pp. 332–355. It is worth noting that Lord Kelvin developed a sounding machine, based on the same principle, which was widely used in the late nineteenth and early twentieth centuries.
21. Stephen Hales, "A description of a sea gage, to measure unfathomable depths", *The Gentleman's Magazine and Historical Chronicle* (1754). Vol. **24**, pp. 215–219.
22. *Ibid.* p. 219.

23. Raymond Phineas Sterns, "Colonial fellows of the Royal Society of London, 1661–1788", *Notes Rec. R. Soc. Lond.* (1951). Vol. **8**, no. 2, pp. 178–246.

24. E. G. R. Taylor, *The Mathematical Practitioners of Hanoverian England, 1714–1840*, Cambridge (1966), p. 128.

25. Stephen Hales, "The description of a sea gage, to measure unfathomable depths", *op. cit.* (1754). Vol. **24**, p. 218.

26. A. E. Clark-Kennedy, *op. cit.* p. 149.

27. Stephen Hales, *op. cit.* p. 218.

28. Stephen Hales, "A letter to the President, from Stephen Hales, D.D. & F.R.S.", *Phil. Trans.* (1750–1751). Vol. **47**, pp. 214–216.

29. Henry Ellis, "A letter to the Rev. Dr. Hales, F.R.S. from Captain Henry Ellis, F.R.S. dated Jan. 7, 1750–51, at Cape Monte Africa, Ship *Earl of Hallifax*", *Phil. Trans.* (1750–1751). Vol. **47**, pp. 211–214.

30. *Ibid.* p. 214.

31. Weeden Butler, *Memoirs of Mark Hildesley, D.D.*, London (1799), p. 371.

32. J. T. Desaguliers, *A Course of Experimental Philosophy*, 2 vols, London, (1744). Vol. **2**, pp. 223–224, 241–247.

33. Stephen Hales, *A Treatise on Ventilators*, part 2 of *A Description of Ventilators* (1743), London (1758), pp. 122–124.

34. Hugh Campbell, "A table of the specific gravity of salt and fresh water, discovered by the hydrostatic balance, in a voyage from England to Bombay in the East Indies", *The Gentleman's Magazine* (1755). Vol. **25**, pp. 260–261.

35. Torbern Wolff, "The Danish expedition to 'Arabia Felix' ", *Bull. Inst. océanogr. Monaco*, numéro spécial 2 (1968). Vol. **2**, pp. 581–600.
Thorkild Hansen, *Arabia Felix* (translated by J. and K. McFarlane), London (1964).

36. Angus Armitage, "Chappe d'Auteroche: a pathfinder for astronomy", *Ann. Sci.* (1954). Vol. **10**, no. 4, pp. 277–293.

37. Jean-Baptiste Chappe d'Auteroche, *Voyage en Californie pour l'Observation du Passage de Vénus sur le disque du Soleil* (ed. Cassini), Paris (1772). An English translation of this work was published in 1778 but both Lavoisier's memoir and the details of Chappe's results were omitted.

38. *Ibid.* pp. 47–52.

39. *Ibid.* p. 52.

40. Richard Walter, *A Voyage round the World, in the years 1740–1744 by George Anson*, London (1748), p. 180.

41. *Byron's Journal of his Circumnavigation, 1764–66* (ed. Robert E. Gallagher), Hakluyt Society (1964), 2nd series. Vol. **122**, pp. 4–5.

42. *Carteret's Voyage round the World 1766–1769* (ed. Helen Wallis), Hakluyt Society (1965), 2nd series. Vols **124** and **125**.

43. Sir Joseph Banks, *The Endeavour Journal of Joseph Banks, 1768–1771* (ed. J. C. Beaglehole), 2 vols, Sydney (1962).

44. Charles Green and James Cook, "Observations made, by appointment of the Royal Society, at King George's Island in the South Sea", *Phil Trans.* (1771). Vol. **61**, pp. 397–421.

45. James Cook, "An account of the flowing of the tides in the South Sea, as observed on board His Majesty's Bark the *Endeavour*, by Lieut. J. Cook, Commander, in a letter to Nevil Maskelyne, Astronomer Royal, and F.R.S.", *Phil. Trans.* (1772). Vol. **62**, pp. 357–358.

46. In fact the smallness of tides on mid-ocean islands was well known in the seventeenth century and Newton had attempted an explanation. (*See* Ch. 5.)

47. James Cook, "Of the tides in the South Seas", *Phil. Trans.* (1776). Vol. **66**, pp. 447–449.

48. *The Journals of Captain James Cook*, Vol. 2, *The Voyage of the Resolution and Adventure, 1772–1775* (ed. J. C. Beaglehole), Hakluyt Society, extra series (1961), no. 35, p. 725.

49. William Wales and William Bayly, *The Original Astronomical Observations, made in the course of a Voyage towards the South Pole, and round the World, in H.M.S. Resolution and Adventure, in the years 1772, 1773, 1774, and 1775* Board of Longitude, 1777, p. liii.*

50. Charles Douglas, "An account of the result of some attempts made to ascertain the temperature of the sea in great depths, near the coasts of Lapland and Norway; as also some anecdotes, collected in the former", *Phil. Trans.* (1770). Vol. **60**, pp. 39–45.

51. Alexander Wilson made Fahrenheit thermometers in London before settling in Glasgow where he became the first professor of astronomy in 1760.

52. *The Journals of Captain Cook*, *op. cit.* Vol. **2**, p. 36.

53. William Wales and William Bayly, *op. cit.* pp. 206, 208, 210, 338, 339, 341, 342.

54. William Wales, *Log Book of the Resolution*, Board of Longitude Papers. Vol. **46**, 14 December 1772.

55. William Wales and William Bayly, *op. cit.* pp. 208, 341.

56. Richard Watson, *Chemical Essays*, 2nd ed., (1782–1787), 5 vols London. Vol. **2**, (1782), pp. 132–137.

57. George Forster, *A Voyage round the World, in His Britannic Majesty's Sloop, Resolution, commanded by Capt. James Cook, during the years 1772, 3, 4 and 5*, London (1777). Vol. **1**, pp. 48, 50, 51, 95, 99, 102.

58. Johann Reinhold Forster, *Observations made during a Voyage round the World, on Physical Geography, Natural History, and Ethic Philosophy*, London (1778), pp. 59–61.

59. William Wales, *Journal*, June 1772–June 1774, MS. Mitchell Library, Sydney. I am grateful to Dr R. I. Currie for providing me with transcripts of the relevant passages.

60. William Wales, *Remarks on Mr. Forster's account of Captain Cook's last Voyage round the World in the Years 1772–5*, London (1778).

61. *Ibid.* p. 21.

62. J. R. Forster, *op. cit.* pp. 56–59.

63. Torbern Bergman, *Physical and Chemical Essays* (translated by Edmund Cullen), 2 vols, London (1784). Vol. **1**, pp. 226–231. See ch. 10.

64. William Wales, *Observations on board the Resolution 1772–1775*, Board of Longitude Papers. Vol. **47**.

65. William Wales and William Bayly, *The Original Astronomical Observations* (1777), p. 95.

66. Daines Barrington, *The Probability of reaching the North Pole discussed*, London (1775).

67. Constantine Phipps, *A Voyage towards the North Pole*, London (1774), p. 13.

68. *Ibid.* p. 12. These have not been located.

69. J. R. Forster, *op. cit.* pp. 53–55.

70. *The Journals of Captain Cook*, *op. cit.* Vol. **2**, p. 35.

71. C. Phipps, *op. cit.* p. 27.

72. *Ibid.* p. 74.
73. Lord Charles Cavendish, "A description of some thermometers for particular uses", *Phil. Trans.* (1757). Vol. **50**, part 1, pp. 300–310.
74. *Ibid.* p. 308.
75. John Canton, "Experiments to prove that water is not incompressible", *Phil. Trans.* (1762). Vol. **52**, part 2, pp. 640–643.
76. C. Phipps, *op. cit.* p. 142.
77. *Ibid.* pp. 145–147.
78. *Ibid.* pp. 142–144.
79. *Ibid.* p. 75.
80. William Bayly, *The original Astronomical Observations made in the course of a Voyage to the Northern Pacific Ocean, for the discovery of a North East or North West Passage . . . in H.M.S. Resolution and Discovery, in the years 1776, 1777, 1778, 1779 and 1780*, London (1782), pp. v, vii.
81. *Ibid.* pp. 345–346.
82. *Ibid.* p. 347.
83. Board of Longitude Papers. Vol. 47*.
84. M. de Pagès, *Voyage autour du monde, et vers les deux poles, par terre et par mer, pendant les années 1767–1776*, 3 vols, Berne (1783). Vol. **3**, pp. 2–3, 208.
85. L. A. Milet-Mureau, *Voyage de La Pérouse autour du Monde*, 4 vols, Paris (1798). Vol. **1**, p. 256.
86. François Péron, *Voyage de découvertes aux terres australes, fait par l'ordre du Gouvernement, sur les corvettes le Géographe, le Naturaliste, et la goelette le Casuarina, pendant les années 1800–1804*, ed. L. de Freycinet, 4 vols, Paris (1824). Vol. **4**, pp. 165–207.
87. *Ibid.* p. 195.
88. Marnie Bassett, *Realms and Islands. The world voyage of Rose de Freycinet in the corvette Uranie, 1817–1820*, London (1962).
89. F. Péron, *op. cit.* p. 171.
90. *Ibid.* pp. 180–181.
91. *Ibid.* pp. 183–189.
92. Board of Longitude Papers. Vol. **51**, "Reduction of the astronomical observations made in the voyage of the *Investigator* 1801–1805".
93. F. Péron, *op. cit.* p. 165.

Addenda et Corrigenda

p.176, 1.33: *instead* Gulf of Lyons *read* Golfe du Lion
p.177, fig.10, caption, 1.1: *instead* Gulf of Lyons *read* Golfe du Lion
p.195, n.1, 1.2: *instead* Constantinopli *read* Constantinopoli
p.197, n.49, 1.4: *instead* 1777 *read* London (1777)

10. WIDENING HORIZONS: THE LAST QUARTER OF THE EIGHTEENTH CENTURY

THE increasing volume of experiments and observations made at sea from the mid-eighteenth century onwards reflect a growing interest in marine science which, favoured by the growing climate of diversity in science and the opportunities provided by the voyages of discovery, soon overtook the work of the seventeenth century. The period between 1750 and the outbreak of the Napoleonic wars was fertile in new ideas and inventions which were to prove very significant. As in the seventeenth century the people involved in these developments included some well-known figures such as Benjamin Franklin (1706–1790), envoy of the nascent United States to the French court, Sir Charles Blagden (1748–1820), Richard Kirwan (1733–1812), who came to the defence of the phlogiston theory, Richard Watson (1737–1816), who by much pulling of strings, in the approved eighteenth-century manner, became successively professor of chemistry and professor of divinity at Cambridge and bishop of Llandaff, and the equally opportunist Benjamin Thompson, Count Rumford (1753?–1814) who progressed from dubious beginnings in America, where he collaborated with the British during the war of independence, to a position of cast-iron respectability as the chief minister of the Elector of Bavaria and the founder of the Royal Institution.

Franklin's interest in the sea and related subjects extended over many years. In 1762 he wrote to his friend Sir John Pringle (1707–1782) describing the internal waves he had observed in a lamp, which he had designed himself, as it hung in his cabin on board ship. The lamp contained a layer of oil floating on water and Franklin saw that while the surface of the oil remained smooth as it followed the movements of the ship, the water at the interface was broken into large irregular waves. Later on, though, when the oil was all used up, the water became calm and untroubled. He found it difficult to explain this phenomenon and so did those to whom he described it. He wrote:

Those who are but slightly acquainted with the principles of hydrostatics, &c. are apt to fancy immediately that they understand it, and readily attempt to

FIG. 13. Bishop Watson. From *Anecdotes of the Life of Richard Watson, edited by his son*, London (1817).

explain it; but their explanations have been different, and to me not very intelligible. Others, more deeply skilled in those principles, seem to wonder at it, and promise to consider it.[1]

Franklin had been interested in discovering the truth in Pliny's account of how oil was poured on waves to calm them ever since a day in 1757,[2] when he had seen how the wakes of two ships were smoother than the others and on asking the captain of his own ship why this was so had been told that it was caused by the greasy water which the cooks had poured down the scuppers. Describing how he had pursued the subject, he wrote to William Brownrigg (1711–1800)

I think with your friend, that it has been of late too much the mode to slight the learning of the antients. The learned, too, are apt to slight too much the knowledge of the vulgar.[3]

He made an experiment to see how this happened, choosing a windy day on Clapham Common, and found that a teaspoonful of oil was sufficient to make about half an acre of the pond "as smooth as a looking-glass".[4] After this he made a point of repeating the observation whenever opportunity arose, carrying the oil around with him in the topmost joint of his bamboo cane. One of his trials was made on Derwent Water with the assistance of Brownrigg and Pringle. As a result of another demonstration, this time in Green Park, the question arose whether it might not be possible to use this knowledge to calm heavy seas breaking on a shore and enable boats to land more safely. In October 1773, at the invitation of Captain Bentinck, Franklin went to Portsmouth and with the assistance of Banks, Solander, Blagden and General Carnac took advantage of a stormy day to see whether this could be done. They found that the oil had no effect on the swell which, generated far out to sea, merely passed through the patch of oil and broke with undiminished force on the shore. What the oil did do was to make the waves less rough and to prevent their crests from breaking in the area it covered. He wrote

Now I imagine that the wind blowing over water thus covered with a film of oil cannot easily *catch* upon it, so as to raise the first wrinkles, but slides over it, and leaves it as smooth as it finds it.

He realized that it would be possible to still the waves at any required place if the oil could be spread over the windward place where they were generated, and that this could seldom if ever be done.

Franklin's best known contribution to oceanography lay in bringing to light the extent of the Gulf Stream. The source of the current in the Strait of Florida had been known since the days of the early Spanish explorers (*see* Ch. 3) but it was not generally realized that it flowed up the American coast and far out into the Atlantic. In 1769 or 1770 Franklin, then connected with the colonial postal service, learned that the mail packets sailing from Falmouth to New York were taking two weeks longer than American merchantmen sailing from London to Rhode Island.[5] He mentioned this to Captain Folger of Nantucket and was told that this was because the packets were unaware that they were sailing against a strong easterly current, the Gulf Stream. American whalers who hunted the whales to either side of the current had done their best to enlighten them but their advice had been disregarded. At Franklin's request Folger marked the course of the current on a chart. Franklin had this printed and distributed but, he said, the packet captains took no notice of him either. With the publication of the chart, however, and of Governor Pownall's *Hydraulic and Nautical Observations on the Currents in the Atlantic Ocean,*[6] which leaned heavily on Franklin's work, people became familiar with the idea that the Gulf Stream extended north-east into the Atlantic far beyond the Newfoundland Banks.

The growing use of the newly developed methods of determining longitude had paved the way for a more precise study of ocean currents, of which little that was new had been learned since Renaissance times, but it was a long time before this possibility was systematically pursued. Meanwhile another way of measuring currents was considered; Franklin and his contemporaries provided themselves not with chronometers but with thermometers.

The challenge of measuring the temperature of the sea below the surface meant that a considerable number of observations had already been made but no one, so it seems, had up till now taken the much more obvious course of making a series of measurements at the surface. Then in 1775 Alexander Dalrymple (1737–1808) made daily observations during the earlier part of a voyage to the East Indies.[7] Cook made a series of similar measurements in 1776.[8] Franklin returned to America in 1775 but came back to Europe in 1776 and on both crossings measured the temperature of the sea surface, several times a day. His observations showed what Folger had presumably suggested to him, that the water in the Gulf Stream was noticeably warmer than the sea to either side.[5] Charles Blagden made similar measurements in 1776 and 1777.[9] The obvious inference from these results was that the thermometer would be generally useful in determining the direction and extent of ocean currents. Blagden went further and suggested that it should be employed as a navigational instrument. If seamen made a habit of using the thermometer to discover when they entered the current and more accurate observations were made on its course, speed and variations in temperature, from being an additional hazard to seamen the Gulf Stream might become "one of the chief means of their preservation upon that dangerous coast".[10]

In general the origin of the Gulf Stream was attributed to the effect of the trade winds which drove the sea westward so that water accumulated in the Gulf of Mexico. Blagden wrote

It seems justly attributed to the effect of the trade-winds, which blowing from the eastern quarter into the great Gulf of Mexico, cause there an accumulation of the water above the common level of the sea; in consequence of which, it is constantly running out by the channel where it finds least resistance, that is, through the Gulf of Florida.[11]

Similar opinions were advanced by Peyssonel,[12] Franklin[13] and Pownall. *

An explanation of the easterly deflection of the Gulf Stream away from the American coast was found by applying to the sea the hypothesis for the easting of the trade winds put forward by George Hadley (1685– 1768). He supposed that currents of air flowing on a meridional course towards the equator appeared to blow from the east because whereas in higher latitudes the air had been moving eastwards at the same speed as the earth, nearer the equator where its circumference was greater the earth was moving faster and the air currents therefore lagged behind.[14] Similarly currents of water moving meridionally away from the equator would have a relative eastward motion faster than that of the sea in higher latitudes and would therefore move ahead of it. This extension of Hadley's ideas to currents was made by Colin Maclaurin (1698–1746) in 1740.[15]

On his return voyage to America in 1785 Franklin repeated his experiments with the assistance of his great nephew, Jonathan Williams (1750– 1815). They also made several observations on the temperature of the water below the surface.[13] Williams was struck by the dramatic fall in temperature as they left the Gulf Stream and came into soundings off the United States coast. As a result of this and further observations made on later voyages he came to the conclusion that shallow water was invariably colder at the surface than the water of the deep ocean. The sailor could therefore use a thermometer to detect the presence of submerged rocks or shoals or the nearness of the shore.[16]

Williams's ideas about "thermometrical navigation" were widely discussed during the early part of the nineteenth century. Humboldt showed that the temperature of the sea did fall over shoals, due, as he said, to the "heaving up of the lower layers of the ocean".[17] Experience demonstrated the practical value of his system in some areas, particularly on the eastern coast of North America.* Captain Andrew Livingston became so convinced of its reliability, he wrote,

* The conditions off the American coast are however exceptional, the result of cold water upwelling on the western boundary of the Gulf Stream, and Williams's predictions were not always found to fit elsewhere.

that when confined below by fever (being totally unable to keep the deck), I caused the thermometer to be regularly examined every two hours, and sometimes much oftener, and the result reported to me below; and the instant it fell two or three degrees, I caused the ship to be tacked, nor did it in a single instance betray me, as it invariably fell before we could find soundings with 100 fathoms. I call it a valuable instrument, and it truly proved so on that occasion to me; for with the wind dead on shore for about twelve or fourteen days, we had only, in a ship of 276 tons, four men and a boy fit for duty, all the rest being sick, officers included, with fever.[18]

If attempts to measure and learn from the temperature of the surface of the sea seem only to have begun about 1775 the list of those who had measured subsurface temperature was already quite respectable by that date and included Marsigli, Ellis, Wales, Bayly, Phipps (see Ch. 9) and the Italian biologist Vitaliano Donati (1713–1763).[19]

Marsigli and Donati worked in the Mediterranean and both discovered that the deeper water had a more or less constant temperature of about 10° Réaumur. Marsigli's results were taken by J. J. de Mairan (1678–1771) in his *Dissertation sur les glaces* and through him by the Comte de Buffon (1707–1788), author of the influential *Histoire Naturelle*, and used in alliance with the hypothesis derived from the philosopher G. W. Leibnitz (1646–1716) who said that the earth was a solid crust round a molten centre. They argued that heat penetrates through the sea floor and warms the water at the bottom of the sea so that it is continually rising, with the result that the sea is maintained at a constant temperature, except for a shallow layer at the surface which is governed by atmospheric conditions.[20, 21, 22] Mairan wrote

les eaux les plus chaudes, & par conséquent, toutes choses d'ailleurs égales, les plus légères, doivent continuellement monter au dessus de celles qui sont le moins. Ce qui donnera à toute cette grande couche liquide du Globe terrestre, une température à peu près égale, conformément aux observations de M. le C. Marsigli; excepté vers la superficie actuellement exposée aux impressions de l'air, & où l'eau se gèle quelquefois, avant que d'avoir eu le temps de descendre par son poids & par son refroidissement.[23]

The rival school of geological thought maintained that the centre of the earth was cold. The Swiss scientist Horace-Bénédict de Saussure (1740–1799) thought that the low temperature which he had measured at the bottom of Alpine lakes was proof of this assertion. Donati's observations of a much higher temperature in the depths of the Mediterranean did not fit into the scheme. De Saussure reasoned that in the sea the temperature ought to decrease with depth because the sun's heat could not penetrate far enough to warm the deeper water and he suspected the accuracy of Donati's measurements, thinking that perhaps he had not insured that the reading of his thermometer would not rise as it passed through warmer water on the way up to the surface. To prevent this from happening to his own he insulated his thermometer with layers of protective material and left it down overnight to acquire the temperature of its surroundings. He made two observations in the Mediterranean, one at 886 feet and one at 1,800 feet, in October 1780, and was surprised to find that at both these depths the temperature was 10·6° R, much as Donati had said.[24]*

British commentators tended to take a less complicated view. Watson in his essay "On the saltness and temperature of the sea",[25] discussed the observations made by Wales, Bayly and Phipps. These showed that in general the temperature decreased with depth. This, said Watson, was what one would expect. In summer the sun heated the surface of the sea but because warm water is less dense than cold water the water which it warmed remained on the surface and had little effect on the layers below. In winter on the other hand water was chilled at the surface and became colder and therefore heavier than the layers below so that it sank through them and chilled them as well. He illustrated the process by describing how this happens if a layer of warmer or colder water is introduced on top of water of a medium temperature in a large container; when warm water was added the temperature was found to decrease from the surface to the bottom. When cold water was added the warmest water was to be found at the bottom but because of the greater density of the cold water cooling took place

not only by the bare communication of cold from the upper water, but by the actual mixture of that water with the rest, so that the difference between the heat of the water at the bottom and the top, will not be so great as it would have been, if the cold water had not mixed itself with the rest. These suppositions of hot and cold water incumbent on the spring water in the cistern, are analogous to the action of the summer and winter atmospheres on the surface of the sea.[26]

In this way Watson accounted for the temperature inversion found in the sea in high latitudes.

Richard Kirwan collected observations of deep-sea temperatures, including in addition to those mentioned by Watson, others made by Douglas (*see* Ch. 9) and the Swedes, Bergman and Bladh.[27] He saw the variations of atmospheric temperature as responsible for the overall distribution of temperature in the sea.

When Péron came to write up his observations made between 1800 and 1804[28] (*see* Ch. 9) he paid more attention to the work of Ellis, Phipps, Wales and Bayly, whose results he wrongly attributed to the Forsters

---

* The deep and bottom water of the Mediterranean Sea is much warmer than the water at the same level in the ocean outside because the deep and bottom currents from polar and sub-polar regions cannot penetrate the relatively shallow Strait of Gibraltar.

(*see* Ch. 9, pp. 187–188), than other writers on the continent had yet done. Their observations, together with his own, proved, he said,

la non existence d'une température uniforme et constante de 10d environ dans les couches les plus profondes des eaux de la mer.[29]

Péron not only supposed that the temperature of the sea decreased with depth but argued that the sea floor was probably covered with ice. This idea appears to have been well received by the commissioners of the Institut National, the revolutionary successor of the Académie Royale des Sciences, though it never gained any widespread measure of acceptance. Jean-Claude Delamétherie, editor of the *Journal de Physique*, commenting on Péron's paper, wrote

Ainsi donc cette théorie ingénieuse d'un feu central intérieur, entretenant une température uniforme de 10° environ dans toute la masse, soit solide, soit liquide de notre globe, éprouve elle-même aujourd 'hui le sort réservé tôt ou tard à presque toutes les théories humaines. Les calculs de Leibnitz qui, le premier, l'imagina; l'éloquence de Buffon qui décida son triomphe, sembloient cependant devoir lui garantir, une existence plus longue et plus paisible.[22]

It was in the 1770s that interest was renewed in the physical properties of sea water, a subject which had not received much attention since the seventeenth century. Edward Nairne (1726–1806) was present at a conversation in which it was suggested that sea ice is not fresh and that if it were the ice in the Arctic must have been formed in rivers and carried by them into the sea. Nairne made experiments which showed that sea water has a freezing point of 28·5°F and that the ice which it forms, when melted separately, gives fresh water.[30]

Sir Charles Blagden made experiments on the alteration of the freezing point of water when various substances are added to it and showed that the freezing point of sea water is controlled by the amount of salt in it.[31] He found too that salt water could be cooled well below its freezing point without solidifying and reduced the temperature of a solution with a freezing point of 28°F to 18·5°F, with it still remaining liquid.[32]

Much of this had of course been quite widely appreciated in the seventeenth century, as had the fact that water contracts in volume as it gets cold only to a certain point and expands again before freezing. This had been noticed by the Florentine Academy[33] and was later demonstrated in the Royal Society.[34] Blagden carried out experiments which showed that fresh water ceases to contract at a temperature of 40°F so that its temperature of maximum density is eight degrees above its freezing point.[31] He went on to see if the same rule applied to salt water using a very strong solution and concluded that it did "as far as one experiment goes". This assumption was to mislead many people who forgot the qualifying parenthesis and the results were far-reaching since sea water in fact follows quite different laws and reaches its point of maximum density at about 22°F, well below its freezing point.

The interest shown in problems of this kind was clearly allied to the new series of attempts to probe the Arctic and Antarctic in the 1770s. The principal obstacle to these voyages was the pack-ice which always eventually turned the explorers back. There was much speculation about its origin and about that of the lone icebergs which were sometimes encountered much farther from the poles. Buffon and some other much read authors supposed that the ice found in the sea had originally been formed in rivers[35] or even that sea water does not freeze at all. Nairne's experiments showed that there was no ground for this belief and, therefore, that arguments that the Arctic Ocean would be free of ice once the initial barrier was passed had no foundation. A similar kind of disagreement existed over the origin of icebergs. Some people, like Johann Forster,[36] argued that since the sea could freeze bergs might be formed by the accumulation of sheets of ice and snow on pack ice. Cook and Wales on the contrary believed that they had their origin on land and, correctly as it happened, saw those they encountered as indirect proof of the existence of the Antarctic continent.[37]

It was beginning to be more generally recognized that differences in density can cause internal movements in water. As already mentioned Watson suggested that in winter water cooled at the surface would tend to sink through the warmer layers beneath.[25] However it was still some time before the consequences of this idea for the sea were fully realized.

The existence of an undercurrent in the Strait of Gibraltar had been reaffirmed early in the century by Dr Hudson.[38] He based his argument on an incident in 1712 when a ship sunk by a privateer in the middle of the Strait had been cast ashore well to the westwards of the point of its disappearance. Buffon, however, asserted that the undercurrent was a physical impossibility and even went so far as to suggest that Marsigli was mistaken over his observations in the Bosporus.[39] He did allow such a contrary movement in the sea off the coast of Guinea, which had been reported by a correspondent, as the result of an onshore wind piling up water against the land.

Disbelief in the Gibraltar undercurrent seems to have been widespread[40] but at least one person grasped the explanation for it during the 1770s. This was Lieutenant, later Admiral, Philip Patton R.N. (1739–1815). While he was serving in H.M.S. *Emerald* an incident when the ship nearly ran aground in the Strait put him in mind of the story of the undercurrent and he set out to prove that differences in density could be responsible for it, reasoning that if the water within the Mediterranean be heavier than the water in the Atlantic, the water of the latter, according to the laws of gravity and fluids, must of course run in above, and at the same rate the water of the Mediterranean, being heaviest, run out below.[41]

He collected samples of sea water from the Mediterranean and the Atlantic and found that the Mediterranean water did indeed weigh more than the same volume of Atlantic water. His brother advanced a similar hypothesis for the Sound, arguing that a strong countercurrent existed there from the discovery, when sounding, that in spite of the surface current his sounding line remained vertical.

At about the same time people were beginning to realize that differences in density might cause more widespread movements in the sea. Richard Kirwan wrote in 1787

As the water in the high northern and southern latitudes, is, by cold, rendered specifically heavier than that in the lower warm latitudes, hence there arises a perpetual current from the poles to the equator, which sometimes carry down large masses of ice, which cool the air, to a great extent.[42]

A similar idea was put forward by Delamétherie in his *Théorie de la Terre* where he suggested that cold but fresh water of low density would flow from the poles towards the equator on the surface while warm but saline water of higher density flowed in the opposite direction in the depths of the sea.[43]*

The modern concept of an ocean circulation sustained by differences in density seems to have had its earliest recognizable expression in the essay "Of the propagation of heat in fluids" by Benjamin Thompson, Count Rumford, first published in 1798.[44] Rumford's experiments led him to assert that water will not conduct heat. He said that heat is distributed through fluids solely by the internal movements of their particles which are set up by the differences in density which inequalities of temperature entail. The specific gravity of fluids varies with temperature and their density increases as the temperature falls. Fresh water, which ceases to contract eight degrees above its freezing point, is an exception to the general rule. As a result of this when water in lakes cools during the winter the colder water floats on top of the deeper layers whose temperature is about 40°F. In the deep Swiss lakes Saussure and Pictet found that the bottom water remained constantly at this temperature.[45]

Rumford realized what too often was overlooked, that sea water behaves in an entirely different way, and he went on to point out the consequences of this important fact in what he called the "economy of Nature":

---

* This sort of circulation actually occurs in high latitudes above the bottom currents flowing towards the equator.

As sea water continues to be condensed as it goes on to cool, even after it has passed the point at which fresh water freezes, the particles at the surface, instead of remaining there after the mass of the water had been cooled to about 40°, and preventing the other warmer particles below from coming in their turns and giving off their Heat to the cold air (as we have seen always happens when fresh, or *pure water* is so cooled), these cooled particles of *salt water* descend as soon as they have parted with their Heat, and in moving downward force other *warmer* particles to move upwards; and in consequence of this continual succession of warm particles, which come to the surface of the sea, a vast deal of Heat is communicated to the air.[46]

The only source of warmth in the sea is the sun and if water which, on being chilled at the surface by cold winds in high latitudes,

descends to the bottom of the sea, cannot be warmed *where it descends*, as its specific gravity is greater than that of water at the same depth in warmer latitudes, it will immediately begin to spread on the bottom of the sea, and to flow towards the equator, and this must necessarily produce a current at the surface in an opposite direction; and there are the most indubitable proofs of the existence of both these currents.[47]

Here we have a clear statement of the pattern of water movements to be expected from differences of temperature and the knowledge that the density of sea water continues to increase until it freezes. As the two causes of this instability—cooling at the poles and the sun's warmth at the equator—operated all the time equilibrium was never regained and the cycle was continuous.

To support his hypothesis Rumford referred to the low temperatures discovered at great depths in the sea by Ellis and Phipps.[48] These were much lower than the mean air temperatures for those latitudes[49] and Rumford argued that the only possible origin for this water was the polar regions. As to the surface return currents, he argued that

What has been called the gulph stream, in the Atlantic Ocean, is no other than one of these currents, that at the surface, which moves from the equator towards the north pole, modified by the trade winds and by the form of the continent cf North America.[50]

Rumford's essay attracted a good deal of critical attention from other scientists but their main concern was to show, in the words of Thomas Charles Hope (1766–1844), that he had "overstrained his conclusions" in saying that water will not conduct heat.[51] They did not follow up what he had said about the difference of behaviour between salt water and fresh water and Hope at least did not realize that this difference existed until many years later.[52] It was to be seventy years before the idea of ocean circulation as Rumford conceived it was generally accepted.

Nevertheless the idea was widely discussed during the early years of the nineteenth century and though there is no reason why it should not have occurred to others about the same time, the terms in which writers later expressed the same idea resemble Rumford's so closely that it seems legitimate to suppose that he was their source. In 1808 Delamétherie described a system of circulation the reverse of one he had put forward a decade earlier. Retaining the idea that currents are responsible for carrying icebergs towards the equator he supposed that in a certain latitude these currents would sink and continue their journey at the bottom of the sea:

Les courans des eaux qui viennent des pôles se font d'abord à la surface des mers jusqu'à une certaine latitude de 60 à 50 degrés, comme le prouvent les masses immenses de glaces qu'ils charient à ces hauteurs; mais rencontrant alors des eaux plus tempérées, ces eaux polaires gagnent les fonds des mers, et se rendent par des courants inférieurs vers les régions equinoxiales.[53]*

Alexander von Humboldt (1769–1859) argued the case for this circulation much as Rumford had done, also pointing out that salinity must be distributed in such a way as not to interfere with the movements due to temperature:

Dans les mers de Tropiques, on trouve qu'à de grandes profondeurs, le thermomètre ne se soutient qu'à 7 ou 8 degrés centésimaux. C'est le résultat des nombreuses expériences du commodore Ellis et de celles de M. Peron. La température de l'air ne baissant jamais dans ces parages au-dessous de 19 à 20 degrés, ce n'est pas à la surface que les eaux peuvent avoir acquis un degré de froid si voisin du point de la congélation et du maximum de la densité de l'eau. L'existence de ces couches froides dans les basses latitudes, prouve par conséquent un courant inférieur qui se porte des pôles vers l'équateur: il prouve aussi que les substances salines qui altèrent la pesanteur spécifique de l'eau, sont distribuées dans l'Océan de manière à ne pas anéantir l'effet produit par les différences de température.[54]

During his travels in South America Humboldt sent reports of his progress to Delamétherie so that it is readily conceivable that either one of them might have suggested the idea to the other but there is no basis for the claim, incautiously made by later writers, that Humboldt invented the idea though he may well have done more than any one else to popularize it.

Delamétherie's interest in the possible factors governing ocean currents was due more than anything to the part assigned to them in the geological theories of the day. One idea put forward by Buffon and earlier writers but principally advocated by the German geologist Abraham Werner (1750–1817) stressed the sedimentary origin of rocks and supposed that the earth

* This is in close agreement with what happens at the Antarctic convergence where in latitude 50°–60°S the Antarctic surface water sinks to form the Antarctic intermediate water and there are similar movements in the Arctic region.

had originally been covered with water, that is by a primitive ocean in which all natural substances were held in solution. During the course of time chemical changes took place which led to the precipitation of the materials from which the rocks were formed and the way in which these were first laid down and the shape of continents decided was thought to have been due to the action of ocean currents.[55]

The eighteenth century saw the first qualitative chemical analyses of sea water. The nature of sea salt had clearly continued to excite interest among chemists and in the middle of the century two French scientists, Gilles-François Boulduc (1675–1742) and Montet, reported that they had found Epsom salt (magnesium sulphate) and Glauber's salt (sodium sulphate) as distinct from crystals of marine salt.[56] In his essay on the distillation of sea water Irving, who sailed with Captain Phipps, wrote

Sea-water contains chiefly a neutral salt, composed of fossil alcali and marine acid. It likewise contains a salt which has magnesia for its basis, and the same acid. These two salts are blended together in our common salt in England, which is prepared by quick boiling down sea water. But when the process is carried on by the sun, or a slow heat, they may be collected separately; that which has the fossil alcali for its basis crystallizing first; and this is of vastly superior quality for preserving meat, and for the other culinary purposes. The mother liquor now remaining, being evaporated, affords a vitriolic magnesia salt, which in England is manufactured in large quantities, under the name of Epsom salt.

Besides these salts, which are objects of trade, sea-water contains a selenitic salt, a little true Glauber's salt, often a little nitre, and always a quantity of gypseous earth suspended by means of fixed air.[57]

In 1772 Lavoisier described how he had analysed sea water collected four leagues off Dieppe.[58] He found that it contained 1·7% of salt (a figure only half that of the average salt content of the sea so that his sample must have been diluted by rain water). The method of analysis he used was to evaporate the sea water and separate the salts by dissolving them in alcohol. He found that of the 1·7% of salt, 1·2% consisted of "sel marin à base d'alkali fixe de la soude" (sodium chloride) and that the rest was composed of a mixture of "marine salt" with Epsom salt and Glauber's salt, "terre calcaire" (calcium carbonate) and selenite (calcium sulphate).[59]

Five years later the Swedish scientist Torbern Bergman published an analysis of sea water giving as the constituents *muria* (common salt), *magnesia salita* (magnesium chloride) and *gypsum*.[60] He observed that sea water turned Brazil-wood paper (*papyrus fernambuco*) blue showing that it is alkaline.[59]

It seems that during the latter years of the eighteenth century sea water analysis became a common exercise for chemists in all countries. They did not necessarily publish their results but among those who did were the French scientists Baumé (1728–1804) and Monnet[61] and the Germans Lichtenberg and Pfaff.[62]

The origin of the salt in the sea continued to be hotly debated. Lavoisier regarded it as the result of the action of water over the entire surface of the earth and predicted that all known substances would be found in it.[63] Watson argued that it was impossible for erosion to have built up the sea's saltness in such a short time.[64] The measured quantity of salt in rivers was far too small to have brought the salinity of the sea to its present level in the period of under 6000 years, which was the figure sanctioned by the church as the age of the world.

Earlier writers had often seen rock salt as a possible cause of the sea's saltness but as geology advanced it became clear that rock salt was itself of marine origin. Benjamin Franklin wrote in 1760

As to the rock salt found in mines, I conceive, that instead of communicating its saltness to the sea, it is itself drawn from the sea, and that of course the sea is now fresher than it was originally.[65]

Kirwan was one of those who pointed out that the horizontal strata of salt deposits and their association with marine remains made this an inescapable conclusion, which he used to argue in favour of the Wernerian hypothesis.[66] He supposed that sea salt was the result of chemical combinations in the primitive ocean in which marine acid had combined with soda and lime to form muriate (chloride) of soda and muriate of lime. Some muriate of lime subsequently decomposed and combined with magnesia and sulphuric acid to form muriate of magnesia and sulphate of lime (selenite). He suggested that at first the ocean must have been twice as salt as it is now.

Thomas Henry (1734–1816), in a passage describing how processes of growth and decay involve a chemical chain reaction, wrote that it could not

be supposed, that the same individual salt has been contained by the ocean from the creation to the present time.[67]

He wrongly supposed that salt was given off in water evaporated from the ocean and suggested the loss might be made good by decaying organic matter which he thought might produce sea salt and magnesia as well as nitre.

Watson called his readers to turn from speculations which he clearly considered to be a waste of time, to the as yet largely undeveloped possibility of learning about the sea's saltness by painstaking observations of its changes from place to place—

how ineffectual soever our attempts may be to explain the cause of the saltness of the sea; yet one might have hoped, that in this age of philosophy and curious navigation, the degree of its saltness in every latitude, and every season of the year, would have been ascertained by accurate experiments. The acquiring knowledge by experiments, is a slow and laborious method, but it is, at the same time, a method within our reach.[68]

Quite a number of observations had of course been made by the end of the eighteenth century (*see* Ch. 9). Both Watson and Kirwan discussed them, Kirwan considering in addition the work of Scandinavian observers, Bladh and Wilke.[69] Watson made use of a table which he had already drawn up for relating specific gravity measurements to the actual salt content.[70] For those without the opportunity of using instruments he suggested that it would be almost as good to weigh a dry towel, dip it in sea water, wring it out, weigh it then and dry it and weigh it again and take the difference as the measure of salt.

As far as one can tell, further experiments were not made with Hales's sounding machine, and ideas about the depth of the sea remained largely speculative, apart from Phipps's observations. Forster called attention to some soundings made by Cook of not more than 250 fathoms and clearly regarded these as exceptional.[71] In fact temperature soundings from the time of Ellis onwards provided the deepest measurements then known.

The possibility of a mechanism which would facilitate measurement of the depth of the sea was not altogether lost sight of and a description of an instrument, much resembling in essentials Hooke's way-wiser of 1691, was published in 1795 by John Charnock (1756–1807), author of several books on naval topics.[72] The instrument had been invented some while before by a man named Greenstreet who worked for the Board of Ordnance. He had submitted the design to the Society for the Encouragement of the Arts but they had refused to back him financially until the apparatus had been proved at sea. Unable to afford this, Greenstreet, in about 1788, sold the design to Charnock who had been trying without success to make one of his own. The instrument consisted of an endless screw joined to a graduated system of notched dials for recording depth, a weight which disengaged itself at the bottom and a wooden float.

In spite of work of Franklin and one or two others the study of sea waves was also comparatively neglected. Mid-eighteenth century writers like Hales believed that waves were caused by fermentation which made the water swell and this was how waves arrived before a storm:*

whereas, it is above observed, that the Sea is for some Days before a Hurricane, agitated with great Surges; this I think may probably be accounted for by the Fermentation of separate Volumes of sulphureous Vapours here and there with the purer Air, whereby the Air in those separate Parts being destroyed, will cause

---

* The systematic study of long swell arriving before a storm had to wait till 1945.

the Sea-water to rise and swell into Waves, which are again instantly repelled downwards by the Force of the Air.[73]

Whatever its origin it does not seem likely that such an idea was taken seriously for long and later writers unequivocally regarded wind as the cause of waves. After his experiments with oil Benjamin Franklin wrote:

air in motion, which is wind, in passing over the smooth surface of the water, may rub, as it were, upon that surface, and raise it into wrinkles, which, if the wind continues, are the elements of future waves.[74]

William Marsden (1754–1836) studied the surf on the coast of Sumatra and though its variations bore no recognizable affinity to local changes in the weather he had no doubt that the action of wind far out in the ocean, perhaps the trade winds, was responsible.[75] Among other things he observed that the forward movement of the water is apparent rather than real and that it is in fact the wave which moves.

Though in the rising and formation of the surf, the water seems to have a quick progressive motion towards the land, yet a light body on the surface is not carried forward, but on the contrary, if the tide is ebbing, will recede from the shore; from which it would follow, that the motion is only propagated in the water, like sound in air, and not the mass of water protruded. A similar species of motion is observed on shaking at one end, a long cord held moderately slack; which is expressed by the word, undulation.[76]

Nicolas Bremontier (1738?–1809), Inspecteur-général des ponts et chaussées, became interested in waves through his work in reclaiming the sand dunes on the coast of the Gulf of Gascony.[77] He suspected that waves could transport sand along the sea floor at a depth of as much as 70 or 80 feet and made experiments with numbered stones to see how material was moved about on beaches. This interest led him to a more general study of waves. Clearly the subject was attracting an increasing amount of attention for during the 1790s the Danish Royal Academy of Sciences asked for a definition of how the height and length of waves depended on the water in which they were formed, but no one was able to give them an answer.[78]

Hales had supposed that his explanation of waves was equally applicable to the marine disturbances which had followed earthquakes at Port Royal and elsewhere.[73] Similar explanations were put forward to account for the waves generated by the Lisbon earthquake on 1 November 1755, the effects of which were seen as far afield as Antigua in the West Indies.[79, 80] The antiquary William Borlase (1695–1772) wrote

it can scarce be imagined, that a shock, so far off as the coast of Spain, could be so immense as to propagate so violent a motion of the water quite home to the shores of Britain in less than five hours; I should rather think that the same cause, diffused in different portions through the intestines of the earth, produced several subsequent rarefactions of the imprisoned vapours; that these rarefied tumid vapours affected the Seas and land above them in proportion to their own power, the dimensions of the caverns they had to extend themselves in, and the superiour or fainter resistance of the incumbent pressure.[81]

John Michell (1724?–1793) gave an alternative explanation in the major paper on earthquakes which he published in 1760.[82] He believed that shocks were caused by the alternate build up and relief of pressure in the earth's interior as subterranean fires turned water into steam which accumulated until it forced its way out. Contrary to ideas such as Borlase held he assumed that disturbances both on land and at sea must be due to waves radiating outwards from the centre of the shock. While he saw the land waves as vapour travelling between the strata of rocks, sea waves, he supposed, were caused when the centre of the earthquake was under the sea. The first escape of steam would make the sea floor subside and the sea flow into the space which was left, causing the initial retreat of water observed on the coasts where the waves arrived. More steam then accumlated so that the sea floor rose again and pushed out the water which had taken its place. The waves that this engendered travelled outwards with a speed governed by the depth of water. This was why they arrived on the other side of the Atlantic in a relatively shorter time than they took to reach the coast of Britain.

This is by no means a full account of the variety of learned interest in the sea during the eighteenth century. The development of the theory and, to a rather less extent, of the observations of tides continued throughout the century and is noticed separately later on (*see* Ch. 12). As early as 1729 Pierre Bouguer (1698–1758) described his optical experiments on the transparency of sea water, using a wooden trough with glass at each end.[83] Luminescence in the sea provided a continuous source of interest and theories as to its cause proliferated. John Walker (1731–1803), professor of natural history at Edinburgh, described three in his lectures,[84] those of Linnaeus, who ascribed it to marine animals, Franklin, who thought of it as an electrical phenomenon, and Canton who said that it was caused by decaying organic matter.[85] This is to say nothing of the general development of marine biology by pioneers like Marsigli, Donati, and others not mentioned here. A picture emerges of all round growth which, in spite of partial interruption due to war, continued well into the nineteenth century.

10. NOTES

1. Benjamin Franklin, *The Complete Works in Philosophy, Politics, and Morals, of the late Dr. Benjamin Franklin*, 3 vols, London (1806). Vol. 2, pp. 142–143, Franklin to Pringle, 1 December 1762.
2. Benjamin Franklin, William Brownrigg and Mr. Farish, "Of the stilling of waves by means of oil", *Phil. Trans.* (1774). Vol. 64, pp. 445–460.
3. *Ibid.* p. 447.
4. *Ibid.* p. 449.
5. Benjamin Franklin, "A letter from Dr. Benjamin Franklin, to Mr. Alphonsus le Roy, member of several academies, at Paris. Containing sundry maritime observations", *Trans. Am. phil. Soc.* (1786). Vol. 2, pp. 294–329. Reprinted by Albert Henry Smyth, *The Writings of Benjamin Franklin*, 10 vols, New York (1905–1907). Vol. 9, (1906), pp. 372–413.
6. Thomas Pownall, *Hydraulic and Nautical Observations on the Currents in the Atlantic Ocean, forming an hypothetical theorem for investigation*, London (1787).
7. Alexander Dalrymple, "Journal of a voyage to the East Indies, in the ship *Grenville*, Captain Burnet Abercrombie, in the year 1775", *Phil. Trans.* (1778). Vol. 68, pt 1, pp. 389–418.
8. Preserved as part of a record of daily observations, July–October 1776, Board of Longitude Papers. Vol. 47*.
9. Charles Blagden, "On the heat of the water in the Gulf-Stream", *Phil. Trans.* (1781). Vol. 71, pp. 334–344.
10. *Ibid.* p. 343.
11. *Ibid.* p. 334.
12. Jean-André Peyssonnel, "Observations upon the currents of the sea, at the Antisles of America", *Phil. Trans.* (1756). Vol. 49, pt 2, pp. 624–639.
13. Benjamin Franklin, "A letter from Dr. Benjamin Franklin to Mr. Alphonsus le Roy", *op. cit.* p. 315.
14. George Hadley, "Concerning the cause of the general trade-winds", *Phil. Trans.* (1735–1736). Vol. 39, pp. 58–62.
15. H. L. Burstyn, "Early explanations of the role of the earth's rotation in the circulation of the atmosphere and the ocean", *Isis* (1966). Vol. 57, pt 2, pp. 167–187.
16. Jonathan Williams, *Thermometrical Navigation*, Philadelphia (1799).
17. Alexander von Humboldt, *Personal Narrative of Travels to the Equinoctial Regions of the New Continent, during the years 1799–1804*, translated by H. M. Williams, 7 vols, London (1814–1829). Vol. 7, (1829). pp. 386–389.
18. Andrew Livingston, "On the thermometer, as an indicator of a ship's approach to land or soundings, with extracts from a thermometric journal kept on board the ship *Asia* of Scarborough, on a voyage from New Orleans to Gibraltar, in August, September and October 1818", *Edinburgh Philosophical Journal* (1820). Vol. 3, pp. 247–252.
19. Horace-Bénédict de Saussure (*see* Ref. 24) discussed Donati's observations but I have not been able to find the original reference. They do not appear to be mentioned in Donati's *Essai sur l'Histoire Naturelle de la Mer Adriatique*, La Haye (1758).

20. George-Louis Leclerc de Buffon, *Histoire Naturelle, genérale et particulière* (ed. C. S. Sonnini) 127 vols. Paris. (1799–1808). Vols 1–3, *Théorie de la Terre* (first published 1749); Vols. 3–4, *Epoques de la Nature* (first published 1773); Vol. 3, p. 172; Vol. 4, p. 45.

21. Jean-Jacques Dortous de Mairan, *Dissertation sur la Glace*, Paris (1749). (First published in 1715).

22. The development of the idea is described in "Extrait d'un mémoire sur la température des eaux de la mer, soit à sa surface, soit à diverses profondeurs, le long des rivages et en pleine mer par M. F. Péron", *Journal de Physique* (1804). Vol. 59, pp. 361–366.

23. Jean-Jacques Dortous de Mairan, *op. cit.* p. 69.

24. Horace-Bénédict de Saussure, *Voyages dans les Alpes*, 4 vols, Neuchâtel (1779–1796). Vol. 3, pp. 153–154, 195–201, 216–218.

25. Richard Watson, "Of the saltness and temperature of the sea", *Chemical Essays*, 2nd edition, London (1782). Vol. 2, pp. 93–139.

26. *Ibid.* pp. 131–132.

27. Richard Kirwan, *An Estimate of the Temperature of Different Latitudes*, London (1787), pp. 35–36.

28. François Péron, *Voyage de découvertes aux terres australes* (ed. Freycinet) (1824). Vol. 4, pp. 165–207.

29. *Ibid.* p. 192.

30. Edward Nairne, "Experiments on water obtained from the melted ice of sea-water, to ascertain whether it be fresh or not; and to determine its specific gravity with respect to other water. Also experiments to find the degree of cold in which sea-water begins to freeze", *Phil. Trans.* (1776). Vol. 66, pp. 249–256.

31. Charles Blagden, "Experiments on the effect of various substances in lowering the point of congelation in water", *Phil. Trans.* (1788). Vol. 78, pp. 277–312.

32. Charles Blagden, "Experiments on the cooling of water below its freezing point", *Phil. Trans.* (1788). Vol. 78, pp. 125–146.

33. Richard Waller, *Essayes of Natural Experiments made in the Academie del Cimento*, London (1684), p. 71.

34. Thomas Birch, *History of the Royal Society*. Vol. 4, (1757) pp. 253–254.

35. George-Louis Leclerc de Buffon, *op. cit.* Vol. 2, pp. 110–118.

36. Johann Reinhold Forster, *Observations made during a voyage round the world* (1778), pp. 69–102.

37. *The Journals of Captain Cook* (ed. J. C. Beaglehole), *The Voyage of the Resolution and Adventure 1772–1775*, Hakluyt Society, extra series no. 35 (1961), pp. 643–646.
William Wales, *Remarks on Mr. Forster's account of Captain Cook's last voyage round the world* (1778), pp. 104–105.

38. Dr Hudson, "Of the currents at the Streights mouth", *Phil. Trans.* (1724–1725). Vol. 33, pp. 191–192.

39. George-Louis Leclerc de Buffon, *op. cit.* Vol. 2, pp. 152–153.

40. For example, Henry More, "Observations on the tides in the Straits of Gibraltar", *Phil. Trans.* (1761–1762). Vol. 52, pp. 447–453.

41. "On the submarine current at the Strait of Gibraltar, and at the Sound near Elsinore", *Edinburgh Philosophical Journal* (1820–1821). Vol. 4, pp. 243–245.

42. Richard Kirwan, *op. cit.* p. 37.

43. Jean-Claude Delamétherie, *Théorie de la Terre*, 2nd edition, 5 vols, Paris (1797). Vol. 4, p. 515 ff.

44. Benjamin Thompson, Count Rumford, *Essays, political, economical, and philosophical*, London, new edition (1800). Vol. **2**, pp. 197–386.
45. *Ibid.* pp. 290–298.
46. *Ibid.* p. 302.
47. *Ibid.* p. 305.
48. *Ibid.* pp. 306–307. See Chapter 9.
49. Calculated by Kirwan—(*see* Ref. 42.)
50. Rumford, *loc. cit.* p. 306.
51. John Dalton, "Experiments and observations on the power of fluids to conduct heat, with reference to Count Rumford's seventh essay on the same subject", *Mem. Proc. Manchr. lit. phil. Soc.* (1802). Vol. **5**, part 2, pp. 373–397.
    Thomas Thomson, "On the supposed currents in hot liquids", *Nicholson's Journal* (1802). Vol. **1**, pp. 81–88.
    Thomas Charles Hope, "Experiments and observations upon the contraction of water by heat at low temperatures", *Trans. R. Soc. Edinb.* (1805). Vol. **5**, pp. 379–405.
52. Thomas Charles Hope, "Inquiry whether sea-water has its maximum density a few degrees *above* its freezing point, as pure water has", *Trans. R. Soc. Edinb.* (1840). Vol. **14**, pp. 242–252.
53. Jean-Claude Delamétherie, "De l'action des courans à la surface du globe terrestre", *Journal de Physique* (1808). Vol. **67**, pp. 81–116.
54. Alexander von Humboldt, *Voyage aux régions équinoxiales du nouveau continent, fait en 1799–1804*, 3 vols, Paris (1814). Vol. **1**, pp. 73–74.
55. Jean-Claude Delamétherie, "Discours préliminaire", *Journal de Physique* (1802). Vol. **56**, pp. 73–76; "De l'action des courans à la surface du globe terrestre" *Journal de Physique* (1808). Vol. **67**, pp. 81–116.
56. Gilles-François Boulduc, "Recherche du sel d'Epsom", *Histoire de l'Académie Royale des Sciences* (1731), pp. 347–357.
    Jacques Montet, "Mémoire sur les salines de Pecais", *Histoire de l'Académie Royale des Sciences* (1763), pp. 441–464.
57. Constantine Phipps, *A Voyage towards the North Pole* (1774), p. 214.
58. Antoine Laurent de Lavoisier, "Mémoire sur l'usage de l'esprit-de-vin dans l'analyse des eaux minérales", *Histoire de l'Académie Royale des Sciences* (1772). Pt 2, pp. 555–563.
59. *Chemical Oceanography* (ed. J. P. Riley and G. Skirrow), 2 vols, London and New York (1965). Vol. **1**, p. 8.
60. First published in the *Transactions of the Royal Swedish Academy of Sciences* (1777).
    Torbern Bergman, *Opuscula Physica et Chemica*, 6 vols (1779–1790). Vol. **1**, Holmiae, Upsaliae and Aboae, (1779), pp. 179–183; *Physical and Chemical Essays*, trans. Edmund Cullen, 2 vols, London (1784).
61. Antoine Baumé, "Examen d'eau de mer, puisée par M. Pagès dans deux parties de l'Ocean très-différentes en latitude & en longitude", *Histoire de l'Académie Royale des Sciences* (1787), pp. 547–549.
    For Monnet *see* Richard Kirwan, *Geological Essays*, London (1799), pp. 360–361.
62. F. D. Lichtenberg, "Chemische Untersuchung des Ostsee-Wassers", *Schweigger's Journal* (1811). Vol. **2**, pp. 252–257.
63. Antoine Laurent de Lavoisier, *op. cit.* p. 560.
64. Richard Watson, *op. cit.* pp. 96–101.

65. Benjamin Franklin, *Complete Works in Philosophy, Politics, and Morals*, *op. cit.* Vol. **2**, p. 91.
66. Richard Kirwan, "Of common salt and its mines", *Geological Essays* (1799), pp. 350–398.
67. Thomas Henry, "On the natural history and origin of magnesian earth, particularly as connected with those of sea salt, and of nitre; with observations on some of the chemical properties of that earth, which have been, hitherto, either unknown, or undetermined", *Mem. Proc. Manchr. lit. phil. Soc.* (1785). Vol. **1**, pp. 448–473.
68. Richard Watson, *op. cit.* p. 110.
69. Richard Kirwan, *op. cit.* pp. 355–356.
70. Richard Watson, "Experiments and observations on various phaenomena attending the solution of salts", *Phil. Trans.* (1770). Vol. **60**, pp. 325–354.
71. Johann Reinhold Forster, *Observations made during a voyage round the world* (1778), pp. 53–55.
72. John Charnock, "Description of a sea gage, for the purpose of sounding in currents and great depths of water", *The Repertory of Arts and Manufactures* (1795). Vol. **2**, pp. 180–184.
73. Stephen Hales, *A Treatise on Ventilators* (1758), pp. 308–309.
74. Benjamin Franklin, William Brownrigg and Mr. Farish, *op. cit.* p. 452.
75. William Marsden, *The History of Sumatra*, London (1783), pp. 28–38.
76. *Ibid.* p. 28.
77. Nicolas Bremontier, *Recherches sur le mouvement des ondes*, Paris (1809).
78. *Ibid.* pp. 1–2.
79. For example, Thomas Heberden, "An account of the earthquake in the Island of Madeira, Nov. 1, 1755", *Phil. Trans.* (1755). Vol. **49**, pt 1, pp. 432–434.
80. "Extract of a letter from the Rev. Mr. Holdsworth, at Dartmouth, relating to the agitation of the waters observed there on the 1st of November, 1755", *Phil. Trans.* (1756). Vol. **49**, pt 2, pp. 643–644.
    Charles Gray, "An account of the agitation of the sea at Antigua, Nov. 1, 1755. By Capt. Affleck of the *Advice* man of war", *ibid.* pp. 668–670.
81. William Borlase, *The Natural History of Cornwall*, Oxford (1758), pp. 54–55.
82. John Michell, "Conjectures concerning the cause, and observations upon the phaenomena of earthquakes; particularly of that great earthquake of the first of November, 1755, which proved so fatal to the city of Lisbon, and whose effects were felt as far as Africa, and more or less throughout almost all Europe", *Phil. Trans.* (1760). Vol. **51**, pt 2, pp. 566–634.
83. Pierre Bouguer, *Traité d'Optique sur la Gradation de la Lumière*, Paris, first published 1729, revised edition 1760.
84. MS. in Edinburgh University Library.
85. John Canton, "Experiments to prove that the luminousness of the sea arises from the putrefaction of its animal substances", *Phil. Trans.* (1769). Vol. **59**, pp. 446–453.
    See: E. Newton Harvey, *A History of Luminescence from the earliest Times until 1900*, Philadelphia (1957). *Mem. Am. phil. Soc.* Vol. **44**.

Corrigenda

p.203, 1.9: *instead* Peyssonel *read* Peyssonnel

11. MARINE SCIENCE IN THE EARLY NINETEENTH CENTURY: A PERIOD OF GROWTH

THE disturbed period of the revolutionary and Napoleonic wars saw some diminution in the study of marine science. Fewer observations were made at sea, partly because oceanic exploration was largely curtailed. Nevertheless the expansion begun in the late eighteenth century was maintained and reached its peak in the years 1815 to 1830.

The events of these fifteen years may well be compared with the happenings of the 1660s in spite of the obvious difference in degree between those early efforts and the, by then, well-established group of studies founded on the sea. Similarities may be seen in the pattern of a long slow build-up, leading to a relatively short period of fairly intense activity and achievement, followed by a sudden loss of interest. The most likely explanation for the commencement of activity seems to be that in both cases, at a time when the scientific horizon was expanding fast and people were looking for new areas to work in there existed a basis of problems and assumptions concerning the sea to which new or untried techniques and knowledge provided by the development of other sciences could profitably be applied. The possibilities were appreciated by a relatively small group of people who had sufficient contact to stimulate each other's interest. Through their efforts to promote the study of the sea they secured the intermittent participation of a much wider body of people.

Though this was largely the work of a new generation one or two people active in the eighteenth century survived to play a leading role in bringing it about. Major James Rennell (1742–1830) had worked as a surveyor first in the navy and then in the East India Company. In 1778 he returned to England and soon afterwards published a chart of the Agulhas bank and current off the southern tip of Africa[1] (*see* Fig. 14). From then on one of his foremost occupations was collecting and correlating information on oceanic winds and currents, taken either from ships' log-books or from the observations made for him by friends. The introduction of chronometers,

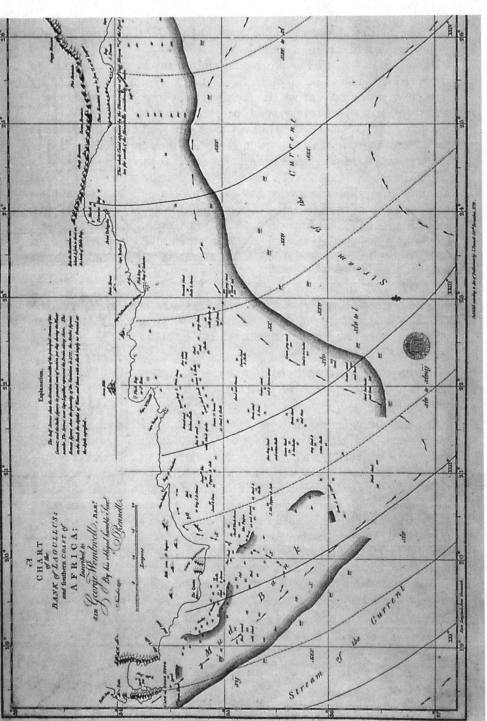

Fig. 14. James Rennell's Chart of the Agulhas Bank and Current, 1778. Reproduced with permission of the Trustees of the British Museum.*

though slow, was making it possible for sailors to establish the difference between their estimated reckoning and actual position and from this the probable effect of a current could be deduced.

It was ironical that Rennell, who did more than anyone before him[2] to improve knowledge of ocean currents, should have come to be principally associated with a current which according to at least one contemporary, and to modern opinion in general, does not exist.[3] A number of ships, including the one in which he himself came home, had found themselves mysteriously arriving to the north and west of their intended position at the mouth of the English Channel. He inferred that there must be a current which flowed into the Bay of Biscay at its southern end, circled northwards up the French coast and ended by flowing back into the main ocean in a westerly direction. This current was to be looked upon as an eddy of another current which he supposed, again mistakenly, flowed southwards along the western margins of Europe. Imperceptible in ordinary conditions it was strongest during westerly gales and might be held responsible for the wreck of Sir Cloudesly Shovell on the Scilly Islands in 1707 and similar disasters.[4]

Only part of Rennell's work on currents was ever published. His daughter Jane brought out the posthumous *Currents of the Atlantic Ocean* which was based on drafts written in the 1820s.[5] He had studied the other oceans too but remarked that

to describe the currents of the *whole circumambient ocean* would have been too great an undertaking for any individual advanced in life, even if proper materials could be found.[6]

Rennell distinguished between drift currents, which were superficial movements of water over a wide area, caused and maintained by prevailing winds and flowing in the same direction, and stream currents which were formed when the water in drift currents met an obstacle in their path, usually the coastline, which caused them to change direction and become more concentrated. Stream currents were relatively narrow, fast and deep. They depended for their impetus not on the wind but on gravity for the wind could raise the level of the sea by piling up water against the land and there must necessarily be some compensating flow away from the area due to the difference in levels.

Rennell's main hypothesis was that the combination of drift and stream currents produced in the Atlantic Ocean

one and the same line of current from the Cape of Good-Hope, north-westward, towards and through the West-Indies and Strait of Florida; and occasionally home to the shores of Europe.[7]

The Agulhas current flowed north into the Atlantic merging with the south-east trade wind drift which in turn became the Equatorial current. The Equatorial current divided once in mid-ocean, one branch flowing northwards into the North Atlantic. The rest subdivided on reaching the coast of South America, one branch flowing southwards and the other north into the Caribbean to form the head of water for the Gulf Stream which flowed into the North Atlantic like, in his own analogy, a river into the plain. Rennell believed that the Gulf Stream eventually turned south-eastwards and petered out near the Azores but that abnormally high sea temperatures in the eastern Atlantic, like those measured by Edward Sabine (1788–1883) in 1822,[8] showed that it might occasionally penetrate as far as the coast of Europe.

This far Rennell had given what is still a recognizable picture of the currents of the Atlantic but his intuition failed him entirely over the eastern part of the ocean. He supposed that the west wind drift and water coming out of the Arctic formed a head of water in the North Atlantic from which a current flowed south past the British Isles. One branch went eastwards to form Rennell's current, another into the Strait of Gibraltar while yet another rounded the bulge of Africa to form the Guinea current while the rest merged with the north east trade wind drift which forms the northern part of the Equatorial current postulating a continuity which was purely imaginary.

In spite of this Rennell's book contained by far the most authoritative treatment yet made of ocean currents. The full significance of some of his points was only apparent much later, for instance he mentioned the existence of cold streaks in the Gulf Stream and of eastward moving water in the Equatorial current.

Rennell was recognized as the leading British geographer of his day and had a wide circle of friends and contacts. This enabled him to enlist the help of sea-goers who made observations of currents and surface temperatures for him. One of these was Captain Edward Sabine of the Royal Artillery who made a voyage to carry out pendulum experiments to determine the figure of the earth. He recalled how

Previously to my leaving England in 1821, I had had the great advantage of much conversation with Major Rennell, on the subject of the currents in the Northern and Southern Atlantic Oceans, and of having my attention directed by him to those points in particular, concerning their velocity, limits, and temperature, on which further inquiries might conduce to the advancement of hydrographical knowledge.[9]

During the voyage he made observations in the Guinea current, the Equatorial current and the Gulf Stream.

Another person whose active life spanned the two centuries, and a friend of Rennell's, was Sir Joseph Banks, President of the Royal Society

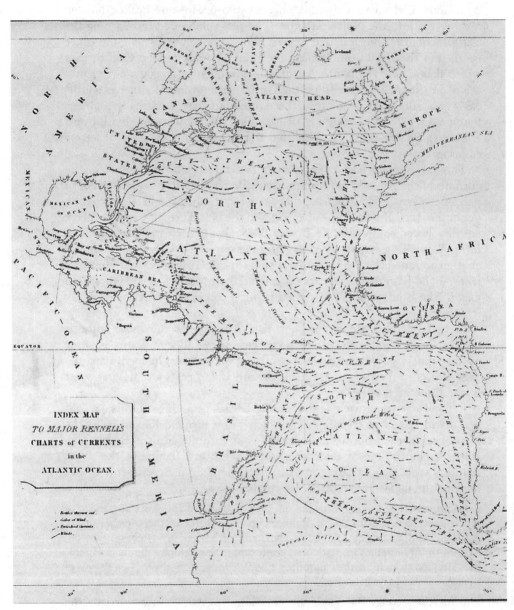

FIG. 15. James Rennell's Chart of the Currents of the Atlantic Ocean. Reproduced from *An Investigation of the Currents of the Atlantic Ocean* (1832).

from 1778 until his death in 1820. Banks showed little interest in the physical aspects of marine science in his early days but in later life, when his scientific role resembled that of a patron in the world of art, he was responsible for inspiring some of the most interesting work of the time.

In 1807 Banks was given some water collected from the Dead Sea. He gave it to Smithson Tennant (1761–1815) who in turn gave it to Alexander Marcet (1770–1822) for analysis. Tennant was a Yorkshireman who had studied medicine at Edinburgh but later concentrated on chemistry. Marcet was Swiss; he too had studied medicine and developed the same predilection, becoming lecturer in chemistry at Guy's Hospital. The two of them had been collaborating for some time on the technique of analysing mineral waters by separating acids and bases with known reagents and calculating their quantities from the scale of chemical equivalents.

While they were discussing the analysis of the Dead Sea water,[10] Marcet said,

it occurred to us that a chemical examination of different seas, in a variety of latitudes and at different depths, might be interesting; and that, however un-likely to be productive of any striking discovery, such an inquiry, conducted with due care and attention, might afford curious results, and throw some light on this obscure subject.[11]

Accordingly they enlisted the help of people with opportunity to collect specimens from different places. The most energetic was Lieutenant, later Captain, Basil Hall R.N. (1788–1844) who supplied them with fourteen samples from the Atlantic and Indian Oceans.

The Strait of Gibraltar held a particular fascination for Tennant who was aware that there might be a current of denser water flowing out beneath the surface current from the Atlantic.[12] In 1811 William Macmichael (1784–1839) collected samples from the surface and 250 fathoms' depth for him to compare their specific gravities but these turned out to be identical. Macmichael used a water sampler which Tennant had invented, a simple box with a spring lid held open by a wedge which could be pulled out at the required depth. The failure of the experiment to produce a positive result illustrates the difficulty they had in finding out what was really going on in the depths of the sea. It was impossible to tell whether the water at the bottom of the Strait really had the same specific gravity as it did at the surface or whether the instrument had not worked properly.

Indirect evidence in favour of Tennant's idea came from Sir Robert Liston (1742–1836), British ambassador to Turkey. He collected samples from the surface and at different depths at the mouths of the Dardanelles and Bosporus. His sampler was designed by Marcet and was very like Hales's bucket though Marcet himself was thinking of one he had seen in a shop window, said to have been used by Irving. He improved upon it by adding a device to lock the flaps which performed as valves so that there should be no possibility of its leaking on the way up. Liston's samples showed the increase of density in the lower layers which Marsigli had accounted for 150 years before but his work in this field was not at all well known in the early 1800s.

What promised to be a fruitful collaboration was brought to an end in 1815 when Tennant was killed by a fall from his horse. Left without further incentive Marcet abandoned the project for several years.

Meanwhile Sir Joseph Banks had been at least partially responsible for encouraging yet another member of the younger generation to take up marine science. This was William Scoresby (1789–1857) who was following his father, William Scoresby senior (1760–1829), in the Arctic whaling industry. Scoresby met Banks in 1807 and it is probably significant that his first published meteorological observations date from that year.[13] Shortly afterwards he began making measurements of temperature and specific gravity at different depths in the sea. At first he used a wooden cask adapted to work like Hales's apparatus but found that under pressure the water penetrated and split the wood.[14]

Meanwhile Sir Joseph Banks was having an apparatus made for him but there was some delay in completing it. In 1810 Banks wrote:

I am sorry to have disappointed you last year in failing to provide for you a proper apparatus for obtaining the temperature of the sea at considerable depths. I myself was disappointed in procuring it by the unexpected death of Mr Cavendish* who had undertaken to superintend the contrivance & afterwards by the deth also of Mr Gilpin who overlooked the execution. The deth of these two admirable men for such they were both of them, made me at the time too negligent & indeed unfit for my usual pursuits I trust however that the instrument is now ready for delivery as I saw it a few days before I left town & gave then the final directions to Mr Carey instrument maker in the Strand to finish it for me. He promised to have it done without delay.[15]

Scoresby took the new apparatus to sea in the spring of 1811. It consisted of a wooden cask, bound with brass, with valves at top and bottom and had a Six self-registering thermometer fastened inside it and glass windows to allow it to be read in position.[14]

The self-registering maximum and minimum thermometer invented by James Six (1731?–1793) was first described in 1782[16] and more fully in 1794 when a version was added designed for use at sea.[17] It consisted of the familiar sealed U-shaped tube with mercury in the bend, one side filled with alcohol, the other partly filled, and indices to mark the highest and lowest temperatures. A. J. Krusenstern (1770–1846) and Johann Caspar Hörner (1774–1834) were apparently the first to use it at sea during the

* Presumably Henry Cavendish.

Russian voyage of circumnavigation of 1802–1806.[18] In spite of disadvantages which gradually became apparent the Six thermometer remained the instrument most widely used for measuring deep sea temperatures until the 1870s.

Scoresby's new apparatus fared no better than its predecessor. He wrote to Banks

It is with some regret I have to inform you, that the instrument, you were so polite as to furnish me with, did not altogether answer the expected purpose ... the *Thermometer* exceeded my expectations, but the substance & workmanship of the apparatus was by no means adequate to resist the various pressures of the water nor the valves so secure as to prevent it passing thro' on the ascent.[19]

To overcome this difficulty he had an apparatus cast in brass which he named his "marine diver" (*see* Fig. 16).

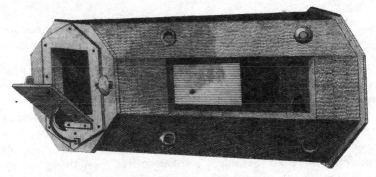

Fig. 16. William Scoresby's Marine Diver. Reproduced from *An Account of the Arctic Regions* (1820). Vol. **2**, plate 2, fig. 2.

Scoresby's scientific career was also closely linked with his studies under Robert Jameson (1774–1854), professor of natural history at Edinburgh. It was to Jameson that Scoresby dedicated his *Account of the Arctic Regions*. Jameson was editor of the *Memoirs* of the Wernerian Natural History Society, which he founded in 1808, and of the *Edinburgh Philosophical Journal*, both of which reflect a keen interest in developments in marine science. He himself encouraged a number of people to make observations. Scoresby corresponded with Jameson, who published much of his work, on more equal terms than with Banks. It was to him that he wrote in lugubrious tones in 1817 when his marine diver was lost because the rope broke after it had been lowered to a depth of 1050 fathoms:

That man is born to disappointments, and where he indulges the highest expectations he is frequently deceived, are truths which I doubt not but you my dear Sir may be disposed to admit.[20]

Scoresby's extensive scientific studies included meteorology, terrestrial magnetism, the formation of ice and the life of the Arctic seas, from the whales down to the microscopic plankton whose blooms streaked the sea and ice with green and yellow, as well as their physical conditions. His temperature measurements showed him that the temperature often increased below the surface and he speculated that a branch of the Gulf Stream might extend into the Arctic, superficially along the Norwegian coast but, further east, sinking below the colder but less dense water of the Greenland Sea.[21]

It was on the 1817 voyage that Scoresby found that the ice which usually encumbered the coast of Greenland had disappeared. Banks came to hear of this and wrote asking for further information.[22] At first he merely welcomed the news as a possible sign of amelioration in the climate after a spell of bad summers but the more he considered Scoresby's report, he wrote,

the more I am convinced that the information given in it to the public for the first time is likely to lead to results highly advantageous to maritime science.[23]

During the eighteenth century legislation had been passed offering financial rewards to the ship which was first to discover the North West Passage or to reach a latitude of 89° north. There had been no response and Banks asked Scoresby how he thought the prospect might be made more attractive.[24] Scoresby replied that few of the whaling captains were equipped to become explorers and none could afford to risk the profit of their catch for a reward that might be unattainable.[25] He thought it would be better to reduce the value of the prizes and make the targets less ambitious. Even if found, it was unlikely that any northerly passage would be open for shipping more than once in ten or twenty years.

Baulked in this hope, Banks approached the Admiralty and found in Sir John Barrow (1764–1848) an enthusiasm for polar discovery equal to his own. From this point the project became a naval one. Two expeditions were planned, one to explore Baffin's Bay and the other to attempt to sail east of Greenland into the Arctic. Captain John Ross (1777–1856) in H.M.S. *Isabella* headed the expedition to Baffin's Bay with Lieutenant William Edward Parry (1790–1855) in H.M.S. *Alexander*. The East Greenland expedition was led by Commander David Buchan in H.M.S. *Dorothea* with Lieutenant John Franklin (1786–1847) in H.M.S. *Trent*. Banks had in vain tried to get one of the commands for Scoresby who, on learning that Greenland captains might be employed as sailing masters or advisers only, left London in a huff.[26] He set out for another whaling voyage, during which he soothed his feelings by exploring Spitsbergen, reiterating his belief that the improvement in the ice was only temporary and that the Greenland expedition would fail to reach a high latitude,[27] in both of which expectations he was proved right.

The instructions for the 1818 polar voyages contained scientific programmes over and above the requirements for exploration.[28] Edward Sabine was loaned to Ross to assist him with the magnetic observations.[29] In the marine field as well as tides, currents and soundings they were expected to record temperature and specific gravity, regularly at the surface and frequently at different depths. To carry out these orders they were provided with a variety of equipment including Six thermometers and apparatus of unspecified design for bringing up samples of the bottom which was "better calculated to bring up substances than the lead usually employed for this purpose".[30] Sir Humphry Davy (1778–1829) provided a water bottle which could be set to open at any depth between 5 and 80 fathoms. He said that this was for examining any southerly currents that might be found in order to learn about the probable state of the Arctic. If, for example, the current was cold and fairly fresh it might be inferred that there was no deep ocean in the polar regions.[31]

Ross found that the bottom sampler did not work satisfactorily and designed and had made on board another one to replace it. This instrument, called a "deep-sea clamm", had a double scoop and brought up several samples of mud from depths of over 1,000 fathoms. These were sizeable enough to have retained their temperature which was recorded and compared with the thermometer readings. It was found that the two agreed well. On one occasion they lowered the clamm to 1,050 fathoms and brought up mud (and a starfish clinging to the line below the 800 fathom mark) with a temperature of $28\frac{3}{4}°F$. Serial thermometer readings showed that the temperature of the sea decreased gradually to this level.[32] This shows that Ross, in all probability unaware of what he was doing, must have been protecting his thermometers from the effect of the pressure of sea water at such depths, presumably by having them enclosed in water-tight cases. Had he not done so the compression of the instrument by the increasing weight of water would have led to readings higher than the real temperature. That this had been so was confirmed by Sabine fifty years later.[29, 33]

Altogether the amount of oceanographic work done by the two expeditions was quite impressive. The Baffin Bay expedition measured a large number of deep-sea temperatures, not all of which were published. Apart from the ones described by Ross in his narrative there were those made by Sabine and Parry, some of which Marcet included in his 1819 paper.[34] They made regular observations on temperature and specific gravity at the surface but only thirteen measurements of specific gravity below the surface. Davy's water bottle was found unreliable.[35]

Meanwhile, on the East Greenland expedition, Franklin, assisted by

Lieutenant Frederick William Beechey (1796–1856), was making observations of surface and subsurface temperatures with a variety of equipment including Marcet's water sampler, a simpler version of Hales's apparatus or just, at times, a corked bottle.[36] Surface temperatures and specific gravities were measured on the *Dorothea* but there is only one record of a serial observation.[37] Like Scoresby, Franklin found that temperature invariably increased slightly with depth in high latitudes.

Both expeditions brought home samples of sea water. Some were given to Jameson who had them analysed, together with samples provided by Scoresby, by Andrew Fyfe (1792–1861), lecturer in chemistry at Edinburgh.[38] They also sent samples to Marcet who was induced to return to his study of comparative salinity and finally published his report in 1819.[11]

Marcet described nearly seventy samples collected from all parts of the world save the Pacific Ocean. They indicated that except in one or two cases the salinity of the sea slightly varies with latitude but not with depth or with longitude. On average it appeared that the South Atlantic was more salt than the North Atlantic, the reverse of the actual situation, but Marcet realized that this might be because a large proportion of his samples from the north were collected in high northern latitudes. As well as comparing specific gravities he had analysed some of the samples and made experiments to fix the point of maximum density of sea water (*see* p. 240). Altogether the paper was one of the most important contributions to oceanographical research during the first half of the nineteenth century.

It was unfortunate that the official voyages which took place after 1818 while being somewhat more successful in their exploratory role failed to live up to the standard of the first as far as oceanography was concerned. Parry received identical instructions when he set out in 1819.[39] He was equipped with the same apparatus except that instead of Davy's water bottle he had a new and improved version of Marcet's sampler. This was still based on the principle of Hales's bucket, in that it allowed the water to pass through freely on the way down and closed on the way up, but it was a far more sophisticated piece of equipment than anything hitherto seen, with brass valves which fell into fitted sockets under their own weight. They were released by the action of a "messenger", a ring-shaped weight which was dropped down the line from the surface when the apparatus had reached the required depth. According to Marcet the instrument maker John Newman was responsible for this invention[40] and it seems to have been the first time anyone had thought of the messenger device which is still widely used today.

Parry had surface temperatures and specific gravities recorded daily while in passage and made some subsurface observations though rarely much below 300 fathoms. On one occasion he found that the index of the self-registering thermometer had stuck and allowed the mercury to rise past it. This seems to have given him some disquiet about the value of his observations and when a value of 27°F was recorded in a 900 fathom sounding he queried it.[41] Nor did he have much luck with his soundings. On two occasions he put over long lengths of line, the second time over 2,000 fathoms, only to find by the mud adhering as it came up that the actual depth was much less. This uncertainty and perhaps too the effort involved in retrieving a clamm or thermometer from this depth—it took the combined crews 1½ hours to get in the 2,000 fathoms of line—decided him that such efforts were wasted until better techniques became available. He clearly lacked the degree of personal enthusiasm that led people like Scoresby to take a chance on success and on his later voyages subsurface observations were rarely undertaken.

While Parry was making his later attacks on the North-West Passage from the eastern end, Beechey was commanding a voyage to the Behring Strait in H.M.S. *Blossom* to try and get through from the west. Beechey had worked with Franklin in 1818 and tackled the task of making oceanographic observations with especial seriousness. He made surface temperature measurements every two or four hours and measured specific gravity regularly. He also made a number of deep-sea temperature observations with self-registering thermometers. Most of them were less than 300 fathoms deep but four were serial measurements with the deepest observation between 650 and 850 fathoms.[42]

Beechey was clearly not protecting his thermometers from the effects of pressure since depth for depth his lower readings are all a good deal higher than the temperatures established by modern work. In addition the four deep serial measurements showed an inversion in the deeper layers, that is the temperature decreased from the surface and then rose again. This was a possible result in the serial observation from the South Atlantic since warm water from the North Atlantic flows south at great depths, but doubtful in the others which came from the Pacific Ocean. It is more likely that the rise in the mercury at these depths was due to the increasing effect of pressure.

Of course these researches were not restricted to the British nation. Marine science increasingly formed a part of the programme of most if not all of the voyages of exploration made in this period. On the *Uranie*, sent out on a voyage of circumnavigation by the French government in 1817, under the command of Louis de Freycinet (1779–1842), surface temperatures were recorded every two hours and fifty-five samples of sea water to be sent home for analysis were collected.[43] On the *Thétis* and *Espérance* under Bougainville and the *Coquille* under Duperrey surface temperatures were measured every six and every four hours respectively.[44]

François Arago (1786–1853), commenting on the scientific work of the *Coquille*, complained that no deep-sea temperature measurements had been made:

Cette recherche, qui se rattache d'une manière si directe à celle de l'existence des courants sous-marins, n'aurait cependant pas retardé d'un quart d'heure le navigation de *la Coquille*.[45]

Compared with Parry's, and other people's, experiences this estimate was a trifle optimistic. However his comments had the desired effect for on the voyages of the *Chevrette*[46] under Fabré and the *Astrolabe*[47] commanded by Jules Dumont d'Urville (1790–1842), deep-sea temperature observations were made. Someone remarked in the *Nautical Magazine* that it was "gratifying" to find the French following the English example.[48]

The Russians had already entered the field. On Admiral Krusenstern's voyage of 1803–1806 the astronomer Johann Caspar Hörner made deep-sea temperature observations with the Six thermometer and Hales's bucket.[18] Hörner's clear appreciation of the interest and value of such work can be well seen in the instructions he prepared for Otto von Kotzebue (1787–1846) who sailed in 1815, and in his discussion of the results collected on that voyage.[49] As well as extensive observations at the surface Kotzebue and his naturalist Adelbert von Chamisso (1781–1838) made over a hundred temperature measurements. These were all at depths of less than 300 save one at 400 fathoms. Kotzebue was lowering one of his precious pair of thermometers, obtained in England by Krusenstern, when

a shark came so close to us that a sailor struck him with an oar, for which he, however, revenged himself by biting through the string of my Six-thermometer, and I lost the instrument in a moment, when I had for the first time, sunk it to five hundred fathoms, and was very anxious for the result.[50]

Bellingshausen's voyage to the Antarctic from 1819 to 1821 saw less of this kind of work but was remarkable for its studies of plankton.[51] The most important of this group of voyages was the second one commanded by Kotzebue, from 1823 to 1826. He had with him the physicist Emil Lenz (1804–1865) who made a series of temperature and specific gravity measurements which were the most extensive and reliable of this period.[52] He used a version of Hales's apparatus designed by Georg Friedrich Parrot (1767–1852), perhaps because they already suspected that, as they were later to demonstrate (*see* p. 242), self-registering thermometers are affected by pressure in the sea.

Marine researches were not confined to the government sponsored voyages. Many observations, ranging from the simple idea of letting a bottle down into the sea, to find out what would happen to it, to quite complicated series of measurements, were still made as the result of individual enthusiasm or curiosity. Scoresby was only one, though one of the most successful, of many who found it fascinating to study the ocean. Surface temperature was the easiest characteristic to observe, particularly if the would-be observer was only a passenger in the ship. A good many such observations were printed by Jameson and quite possibly were made at his request, for example those of Robert Knox in 1817, John Murray (1786?–1851) in 1821 and William Jameson (1796–1873) in 1822.[53] This William was not Robert Jameson's brother but one of his pupils.[54] James Weddell measured surface temperature almost daily during his Antarctic voyage of 1824, until both his thermometers got broken.[55] The intrinsic interest of the observations varied enormously with their frequency and with the area where they happened to be made. Captain Andrew Livingston observed the presence of cold water between the Gulf Stream and the American coast[56] and Captain J. D. Boswall R.N. measured temperatures across the Gulf Stream on passages between Bermuda and Halifax.[57]

A ship's captain had a far better opportunity than anyone else for making observations. It depended entirely on the man himself whether he made use of it but it seems that quite a few did. Captain J. Prescott R.N. made ten serial temperature measurements between 1821 and 1825.[58] Henry Foster (1796–1831) used a Six thermometer and Marcet's water-bottle during his voyage to the South Shetlands.[59] Work of this kind was not yet an integral part of a surveyor's duties but John Frembly R.N., assistant surveyor on H.M.S. *Investigator* working in the North Sea, measured temperatures at and below the surface in 1823–1824 at the instigation of a friend in Leith who lent him the instruments.[60]

As well as supplying Rennell with information on the temperature of the Gulf Stream, Admiral Sir Francis Beaufort (1774–1857) accidentally stumbled upon the effect now ascribed to small changes in the distribution of density with depth in the Mediterranean. While captain of the *Fredericksteen* engaged in surveying the coast of Turkey in 1811–1812 he found a bewildering variety of movements in the water:

in one instance, on sinking the lead, when the sea was calm and clear, with shreds of buntin of various colours attached at every yard to the line, they pointed in different directions all round the compass.[61]

Captain Robert Wauchope (*d.* 1862) made similar observations in the South Atlantic.[62]

Wauchope also collected observations on temperature. He wrote to Robert Jameson

As you are collecting observations on this subject, and expressed a wish to know the results of some of my observations, I now send you the following Table, *viz.* of those made on the surface-water of the sea between St. Helena and England.[63]

These observations were made in 1819. He also described an experiment, made in 1816 in H.M.S. *Eurydice*, to discover the temperature of the sea at great depths in latitude 3°26′ S, longitude 7°59′ E. He lowered a thermometer in a Hales's apparatus made with six cases, one inside the other and with tallow filling the space between the two outermost. They used 1,435 fathoms of line but from the ship's drift estimated the actual depth as around 1,000 fathoms. Wauchope reported that

From the great friction, we found much difficulty in getting it on board again; it took a hundred men just one hour and twenty minutes to do so.[64]

The thermometer registered 42°F, 31° lower than the temperature of the surface water.

The expenditure of time and physical effort required to make observations of this kind must certainly explain why there were so few attempted at this depth, even on voyages especially equipped for research. The great majority of observations were much less ambitious whether single, like those made by the Antarctic explorers George Powell and John Biscoe at 195 and 250 fathoms respectively,[65] or in series like those of Clarke Abel (1780–1826), naturalist and physician to Lord Amherst's embassy to China.[66] Abel, another protégé of Banks, made observations in the Yellow Sea to depths of 40 fathoms but lost all but six of his results in the wreck of H.M.S. *Alceste* in 1817, together with the specimens of marine life collected by Basil Hall and the *Alceste*'s captain, Murray Maxwell.

Throughout the period the same basic types of apparatus were used from one voyage to another. Hales's bucket and the Six thermometer were both products of the eighteenth century. There was nevertheless widespread interest in improving the former and replacing the latter with a more reliable apparatus and new types of equipment were being tried out for other purposes too.

One of those most energetic in this field was Edward Massey of Coventry who, in about 1800, invented a sounding machine designed for use by ships under way in shallow water.[67] It was based on the same idea as that described by Hooke in 1691 (*see* Ch. 8) and recorded the number of turns of a central vane on a dial. Like Hooke, Massey also made a current log on the same principle. He patented the instruments in 1802.[68] In 1807 the Navy Board adopted the sounding machine and ordered 500; Massey was paid £200 by the Board of Longitude. The instrument was found to be inadequate to withstand the pressure in deeper water so Massey strengthened it and in 1811 a thousand more were ordered and Massey * was paid a further £500. In 1818 the Admiralty adopted instead an American device, Burt's buoy and nipper. Massey resented this change and spent a long time trying to prove that his machine was the better of the two. He conducted public trials in the Thames and, when that had no effect, sent a petition to parliament.[69]

He later attempted to adapt the instrument for deep-sea sounding and in 1832 sailed on board H.M.S. *Trinculo* to carry out tests on it.[70] These failed because Massey in spite of the early history of his device, which was not the only one of its kind suggested at the time,[71] relied on wooden floats and a copper globe to bring his instruments to the surface and they failed to withstand the pressure. Nevertheless his machine was used in deep-sea soundings later in the century, on the end of a line, and, like the current log, remained standard navigational equipment for many years (*see* Ch. 13).

Undaunted by his failure to have the monopoly of his sounding machine restored, Massey continued active. In 1823 he wrote to Thomas Young (1773–1829), secretary to the Board of Longitude, describing some new instruments he had been making:

The first is a *Marine Thermometer*, which ascertains the temperature of the water precisely at any depth to which it descends: I paid attention to this instrument at the recommendation of Lieutenant Kotzebue of the Russian Navy. Captain Owen, R. N. was supplied with two of these thermometers previous to his sailing to the coast of Africa; but I have since then improved and simplified it.[72]

According to the minutes of the Board this was a metallic thermometer but of what type they do not say.[73] He was refused financial support to develop it.

Massey's case highlights the ever growing disparity between what the subject required and what the individual could achieve. Even with the sounding machine he complained that the grants made to him had not covered half his expenses.[69] For the thermometer whose value would be purely scientific no support was forthcoming because although it was deemed "ingenious" it was not thought "to be within the sphere of the immediate encouragement of the Board".[73] What Rennell wrote about his own field, currents, was equally true for all branches of oceanographic science at that time:

nothing less than a great number of observations of every kind, and those made through many seasons, in order to embrace all the varieties of cases, can enable the most diligent inquirer to make himself master of the whole subject; *and this can be the work of Government only; for individual inquiry can produce little more than unconnected facts.*[74]

Individual observations were coming to count for less and less as marine science advanced not because they were necessarily any less exact than those made on government sponsored voyages but because they were made randomly and did not provide the theorists with what they were rapidly coming to need, standard observations from season to season spread evenly over the whole surface of the ocean.

Nevertheless some individual work was still very significant. In 1816 John Davy (1790–1868) sailed to Ceylon and measured air and sea surface temperatures and salinity during the voyage. He sent his results in a letter to his brother Humphry because they were, as he said, subjects "in which I know, you are interested".[75] Davy was lucky in being able to win the co-operation of the mates on his ship and with them he recorded air and sea temperatures every two hours for most of the voyage. This gave a much better picture of the diurnal variation of sea temperature than the rather less frequent observations made up to that time. Davy found that the sea varied nearly as much as the air (it was difficult not to exaggerate the similarity, for water pulled out of the sea in a bucket rapidly took on the air's temperature) but its maximum occurred not at noon, but at 3 p.m. Like Wauchope[62] he detected the fall in temperature of the sea approaching Cape Town and attributed it to the general principle advanced by Jonathan Williams (see Ch. 10).*

Contemporary writers often stressed the significance of sea temperature studies in meteorology. Kirwan showed from his theory of specific heats that water takes longer to heat up and cool down than the earth.[76] He recognized five factors on which the temperature of the air at any place might depend, the first being elevation and the second

Vicinity to, or distance from, large tracts of water, particularly from the standard ocean, as its influence is most extensive, and as it is to its temperature that the temperature of all other countries is to be referred, in most cases.[77]

Hörner wrote

A connected series of observations on the temperature of the sea made at the same season of the year, and at the same depth, at the distance of every 5° of latitude from the equator to the pole, would procure us much sooner, and more certainly, general data on the mean warmth of the earth, than the most ingenious theoretical speculations, and the most laborious and tedious observations, on shore, where the mean temperature is changed by so many contingent causes.[78]

Humboldt too appreciated the value of this kind of work and collected sea temperatures during his travels.[79] He instanced the effect of the Peru current on the climate of the west coast of South America:

J'ai observé que, sur toutes les côtes, la température de la mer a une grande influence sur celle du continent voisin: or, la chaleur de la mer ne varie pas seulement selon la latitude, mais aussi selon le nombre des bas-fonds et la rapidité des courans qui amènent des eaux de différens climats. Sur les côtes

---

* In fact it is caused by upwelling off the coast of South Africa.

du Pérou, sous les 8° et 12° de latitude australe, j'ai trouvé la température de la mer du Sud, à sa surface, de 15° à 16° centigrades, tandis que hors du courant qui porte avec force du détroit de Magellan vers le Cap Pariña, le Grand Océan équinoxial a une température de 25° à 26°: aussi le thermomètre a baissé à Lima, en 1801, aux mois de jouillet et d'août, à 13°, 5, et les orangers y viennent à peine.[80]

In later years he collected extensive series of surface temperature measurements, largely unpublished, in the course of working on the distribution of temperature over the globe.[81] Both in synthesizing material gathered by others and in the bent of his researches he had much in common with Rennell and visited him on at least one occasion. Sir Clements Markham prints a letter written by Sabine to Rennell in April 1827 which includes the passage:

I hope that M. de Humboldt, who leaves Paris this day for London, will not be disappointed in the expectation I have given him that he will find you in tolerable health. One of the two principal objects which have induced him to take London on his way to Berlin is to converse with you on the subject of currents and temperatures of the sea, on which he has been latterly thinking and seeking out facts even more diligently than formerly.[82]

Studies of specific gravity required more delicate apparatus and had to be related to standard temperature and these complications may explain why, outside the government sponsored voyages, they were not made very frequently. Marcet's seems to have been the only large-scale independent survey. Thomas Stewart Traill (1781–1862) published a few determinations based on samples collected by naval officers.[83] Gay-Lussac (1778–1850) worked on samples collected by a French naval officer, Lamarche.[84] Andrew Fyfe had studied samples from the Arctic and Scoresby, John Davy and a few others made their own determinations.

Meanwhile major developments were taking place in the chemical analysis of sea water. Bouillon Lagrange and H. A. Vogel published an improved estimate of the quantities of different salts and added carbonates to the list.[85] The major breakthrough came when the new technique which Marcet had applied to the Dead Sea sample (see p. 225) was used for sea water but, because he had delayed finishing the work after Tennant's death, Marcet's own results were anticipated by John Murray (d. 1820), a lecturer at Edinburgh University. Murray first examined the methods previously used in which one evaporated the sea water and simply removed the salts as they crystallized, or made use of their solubility in alcohol.[86] He concluded that the compounds discovered in this way might be formed during the analytical process, and that the carbonates found by Lagrange and Vogel were also formed then. He showed how it was possible to determine every substance separately by causing them to combine with a known quantity of some reagent and in this way obtained values for calcium, magnesium, sodium, sulphuric acid and hydrochloric acid.

Marcet used the same technique and obtained similar results.[11] He was able to add potassium to the list of constituents of sea salt. William Hyde Wollaston (1766–1828) suggested that it might be present and, at Marcet's request, made the experiment using platinum chloride as the reagent, the method which was followed in the determination of potassium until 1939. This led Marcet to suggest in his turn that all soluble substances must be present in sea water. After returning to Switzerland for a short time he resumed his researches in 1821. He detected carbonate of lime and iron oxide in suspension and found ammonia in the bittern but failed to isolate nitric acid, aluminium, silicon, copper and mercury.[87] He intended to go on with the inquiry but died before he could do so, in October 1822.

There was already a considerable literature about the presence of mercury in sea water. Two eighteenth-century chemists, Westrumb and Rouelle, claimed that they had found it and this claim was upheld by J. L. Proust (1761–1826)[88] who recalled that Robert Boyle had discovered mercury in a jar containing lead and common salt (in fact the mercury was in the lead). Marcet concluded that they had been mistaken but other chemists disagreed.[89] In fact the concentration of mercury, 0·00003 mg per litre, was too small to be detected by the techniques in use at that time.

Sir Humphry Davy's discovery of chlorine had settled the debate about the composition of the muriatic compounds and in 1814, with Andrew Fyfe, he discovered the presence of iodine in algae. Early in the 1820s the chemist A. J. Balard (1802–1876) isolated iodine in concentrated sea water from the salt pans of the south of France.[90] At the same time he found very small quantities of a new substance which behaved in very much the same way, bromine. Balard's experiments were repeated in many countries. In Britain Charles Daubeny (1795–1867) succeeded in detecting bromine but failed in his test for iodine.[91]

Marcet published the analysis of 16 of his samples in 1819. He had discovered that all the specimens of sea water

however different in their strength, contain the same ingredients all over the world, these bearing very nearly the same proportions to each other, so that they differ only as to the total amount of their saline contents.[92]

This was only one of the remarkable conclusions in his paper that failed to receive the appreciation it deserved.

The possibilities revealed by a better understanding of the effect of temperature and salinity on density inspired more observations and discussion than any other single train of thought. John Fleming and others showed that, since salinity gave the sea water a greater density than that of river water, the inflowing tide often came upstream underneath the fresh water in estuaries instead of holding it back, as had previously been supposed.[93]

Marcet had continued to take an interest in the current in the Strait of Gibraltar and in 1820 he met Captain W. H. Smyth (1788–1865) who already had many years' experience surveying in the Mediterranean.[94] On hearing of the failure of his previous attempts to obtain decisive information Smyth volunteered to make fresh observations for Marcet. He collected samples of sea water and, in 1824, made a number of soundings in the Strait. Marcet, however, died during his absence and Smyth subsequently gave most of the samples away. In 1827 he met Wollaston who, on hearing the story, asked for the three that remained. Wollaston measured the specific gravity of the samples and found that one, collected at a depth of 670 fathoms inside the Strait, had a salinity of 17·3%, more than four times that of ordinary sea water.[95] The real explanation of this figure must be that the sample had partially evaporated over the years but Wollaston took it as proof that the deep layers of the Mediterranean were of this density.

The most widely discussed implication of density differences was the possibility of general oceanic circulation sustained by differences in temperature. The general idea remained much the same as that proposed by Count Rumford (see Ch. 10) but as time went on the evidence on which it was based grew more substantial. Temperature observations made near the equator confirmed and extended the earlier discovery of cold water not far below the surface. Lenz had shown that salinity increases gradually at the surface as one approaches the equator but reaches its highest concentration a few degrees to either side of the line with an area of decreasing salinity in between.[96]

Davy's results had contradicted Marcet's in showing that the North Atlantic was more salt than the South Atlantic.[75] Lenz discovered that in the North Atlantic the warm, highly saline water extended to a depth of about 1,000 fathoms and then gave way abruptly to colder, less saline water below. It was realized that this might be due to a deep current from the polar regions but only repeated observations could make this certain.[96]

In view of the sometimes highly contradictory results obtained at sea and the number of unknowns it was difficult to discern the outline of Rumford's pattern in a mass of conflicting data. It was possible, for example, that variations in salinity might counteract the effect of differences in temperature although they were so much smaller.[97]

One of the most pervasive causes of confusion was the continued uncertainty about sea water's temperature of maximum density. Some people, Hörner for example,[98] knew and accepted what Rumford had said, that this point was not above the freezing point of sea water. Others quarrelled with this supposition. Scoresby disagreed because his temperature observations consistently showed a slight rise below the surface which seemed logical only if sea water behaved like fresh water and had its point of maximum density well above that of freezing.[99] In fact some of his specific gravity measurements showed that salinity increased slightly with depth as well so that he need not have regarded the overall density structure as unstable. Other people again, like Clarke Abel,[100] had simply not grasped this aspect of Rumford's argument and believed that the similarity of behaviour between fresh and salt water was an established fact.

Yet another achievement of Marcet's paper in 1819 lay in his successful demonstration that sea water does behave differently from fresh water. He showed that it did not expand before freezing and fixed its temperature of maximum density several degrees lower still, at 22°F.[101] This should have settled the point but it is astonishing to see how often this information was overlooked or challenged even after it had been verified independently by other workers.

Before setting out on his voyage in H.M.S. *Pheasant* Sabine had been asked by Sir Humphry Davy to measure the temperature of lakes or "basins of salt water out of the reach of currents from the polar regions".[102] He made one observation, off Cuba, in November 1822, lowering two Six thermometers, one enclosed in an iron cylinder which was supposed to be watertight but leaked, the other in a case through which water could pass freely, on the end of about 1,250 fathoms of line. When they were brought to the surface he found that the first thermometer had registered 49·5°F and the second 45·5°F. He later made a further observation at 650 fathoms, in which the watertight cylinder was used without its leaking, to see if the pressure of the water would have any effect on the unprotected thermometer but as both readings were the same he assumed that it did not.[103]

Sabine regarded his experiment as proof that water from the polar regions was penetrating the Caribbean through deep channels between the islands. This conclusion was perfectly compatible with his view that sea water had its maximum density at 42°F. The temperature structure of the ocean which he envisaged as a result of this differed considerably from that proposed by Rumford and his followers. Sabine wrote

the temperature of 42° may be considered as the mean heat of the surface of the sea in a parallel between the latitudes of 65° and 70°; from whence the influence of external causes renders the surface colder towards the pole, and warmer towards the equator, and in both cases specifically lighter.[104]

The great majority of deep sea temperature measurements agreed with this argument. Few of the deeper ones gave temperatures of less than 40°F and Sir John Ross's low readings were exceptional. The temptation for commentators to put aside his results and, if they knew of it, Marcet's law of maximum density, in favour of the bulk of the evidence was irresistible. It was too easy to argue that there might have been something wrong with Ross's thermometers or that Marcet, now dead, had not allowed for the effect of cold upon his apparatus. In fact, however, Ross's measurements were the only ones which could not be called in question because he had the evidence of the mud brought up by the clamms to support them but this was frequently overlooked.

Lenz's results differed radically from those obtained with unprotected thermometers. He and Parrot had deliberately chosen to use an improved version of Hales's apparatus because it was not subject to the same uncertainties. They worked out the best thickness of rope for supporting the weight while avoiding friction as far as possible and calculated the correction necessary to allow for warming on the way up. Lenz found that temperatures in the sea decreased rapidly at first and then more gradually to about 36°F. The point at which the decrease became insensible rose gradually with latitude.[52]

Lenz had a salutary effect on the work of at least one British writer, H. T. De la Beche (1796–1855). In the first edition of his *Geological Manual*, published in 1830, Marcet and Ross were ignominiously consigned to a footnote and the maximum density fallacy occurred in the text.[105] In the third edition, however, three years later, Lenz's results were added and Marcet and Ross were accorded a place in the text while the paragraph on maximum density was reworded to give the correct view.[106] An intermediate point of view appeared in an article he published in the *Nautical Magazine* in 1832.[107]

Lenz's work nevertheless suffered the same general fate as Marcet's, presumably because Lenz himself was far away in Russia and could not defend or publicize his views. Although a few people realized the significance of what he had said, his work remained largely unappreciated. This was equally true of the extremely important experiments made at Parrot's direction on the effect of pressure on thermometers.

In all the arguments about maximum density and the relative value of results the one aspect which seems to have been totally overlooked was that of the possible effect of pressure on the readings which had been obtained. Everyone knew that pressure increased with depth. Scoresby was only one of several people who experimented on it by lowering blocks of wood into the sea to see how far they would retain their buoyancy.[108] It was found that at great depths wood became waterlogged, a fact that had escaped earlier scientists who had relied on floats to bring their equipment to the surface.

Six had recommended that in a thermometer intended for use at sea the glass should be made thicker than usual[109] but it is not clear whether this suggestion was taken up. Sir John Ross protected his thermometers against pressure but apparently without realizing the significance of what he had done (see p. 229). Sabine must surely have had some inkling of this when he made his second experiment but was content with one result which must have been affected by some other source of error. A great amount of work was done without any consideration of this point and it was extremely unfortunate for the future of marine science in the mid-nineteenth century that the distortion produced was of the right size to give a convincing temperature if one accepted that sea water behaved like fresh water. The two errors combined lent each other a verisimilitude which neither could have maintained on its own.

Parrot actually proved that pressure on a thermometer distorts its reading. With Lenz's help he conducted experiments in a machine of his own construction which was capable of producing a pressure equal to one hundred atmospheres.[110] His apparatus could not take a Six thermometer but his results indubitably showed that they were bound to be affected in the sea and produce readings that were too high. The compression would force the mercury further round in the tube and so push up the minimum index. This discovery was accorded about as much notice as Hooke's marine science lectures had received in 1691. By the time Parrot's paper was published, in 1833, interest in the subject had again suddenly fallen away. The cause was not the passing of a generation or, apparently, a change in the climate of scientific thought but rather the overwhelming attraction of rival fields of discovery. Though Marcet and Rennell had died most of the other people involved had much of their active life still before them but one finds that Humboldt turned more to meteorology, Lenz to other branches of physics and Scoresby and Sabine to studies of terrestrial magnetism. These subjects had in any case constituted the main part of their work and as the relevant sciences expanded they increasingly absorbed their attention. They did not underrate their previous work on the sea but they failed to expound it with sufficient vigour in an age which had lost touch with the spirit of the 1820s. The turn away from marine science was reflected at all levels. Fewer observations were made and less space devoted to the subject, even by Jameson, in scientific journals which, after their sudden proliferation in the early years of the century, were contracting to a more manageable number.

Yet it was natural enough that, having done what they could with the opportunities afforded to them, the scientists should turn to those areas of science in which they could reasonably expect to make progress. Government backing as well as further advances in technology were needed before marine science could advance further and for these the time was not yet ripe. What was more serious was the failure in the coming age to appreciate fully what had been learned in the previous period, a failure that blunted the edge of further progress when it came.

No one had written a reliable appraisal of the work of the 1820s and without such an assessment it was impossible to get a correct idea of developments without going back to the original work. This the mid-nineteenth-century writers were often reluctant to do and they perpetuated the popular errors which had been allowed to survive unchecked. Of these the idea that the sea was full of water of 40°F was only one of the most glaring. Commander James Tuckey (1776–1816) had attempted to fill what he called "this blank in our national literature" with his *Maritime Geography* which was mainly concerned with navigation but contained some physics.[111] Considering that it was written in a French prison camp, the book was surprisingly up to date but it came out in 1815, before much of the important work was done.

Lacking the authoritative treatment it merited, the work of Marcet and his contemporaries languished with scant recognition and the reward of the mid-nineteenth-century indifference was that much energy was to be expended before later scientists got as far as the point where they had left off. There were of course bright intervals in the gloom and the oblivion surrounding marine science was never as great as that which had engulfed it in the decades following the work of the early Royal Society. For the moment however the one aspect of the science to flourish was the study of tides and waves which since the divergence of the late 1660s had developed on a separate course. It is a curious coincidence that, just as in the late 1660s when other aspects of marine science were beginning to decline, so in the late 1820s the tides, till then neglected in this country, began again to dominate the scene.

11. NOTES

1. Sir Clements Markham, *Major James Rennell and the Rise of Modern English * Geography*, London (1895).
2. Since the publication of Franklin's chart of the Gulf Stream (*see* Ch. 10) the literature on ocean currents had expanded somewhat with works like Charles Romme's *Tableaux des vents, des marées et des courans*, 2 vols, Paris (1806), but Rennell seems to have been the first to make a systematic study from original material on this scale.
3. The surveyor Captain Martin White did not share Rennell's belief in this current: *Sailing Directions for the English Channel*, London (1835).
4. James Rennell, "Observations on a current that often prevails to the westward of Scilly; endangering the safety of ships that approach the British Channel", *Phil. Trans.* (1793). Vol. **83**, pp. 182–200.

James Rennell, "Some farther observations, on the current that often prevails, to the westward of the Scilly Islands", *Phil. Trans.* (1815). Vol. **105,** pp. 182–202.

5. James Rennell, *An Investigation of the Currents of the Atlantic Ocean, and of those which prevail between the Indian Ocean and the Atlantic,* London (1832).

6. *Ibid.* p. 5.

7. *Ibid.* p. 20.

8. Edward Sabine, *An Account of Experiments to determine the Figure of the Earth, by means of the Pendulum vibrating Seconds in different Latitudes,* London (1825), p. 429.

9. *Ibid.* p. 426.

10. Alexander Marcet, "An analysis of the waters of the Dead Sea and the River Jordan", *Phil. Trans.* (1807). Vol. **97,** pp. 296–314.

11. Alexander Marcet, "On the specific gravity, and temperature of sea waters, in different parts of the ocean, and in particular seas; with some account of their saline contents", *Phil. Trans.* (1819). Vol. **109,** pp. 161–208.

12. *Ibid.* pp. 175–177.

13. William Scoresby, "Meteorological journals, kept during voyages from Whitby to Greenland, and back again, on board the ship *Resolution,* in the years 1807, 1808 and 1809", *Memoirs of the Wernerian Natural History Society* (1811). Vol. **1,** pp. 249–257.

14. William Scoresby, *An Account of the Arctic Regions, with a history and description of the northern whale-fishery,* 2 vols, Edinburgh (1820). Vol. **1,** pp. 170–203.

15. Manuscript in possession of the Whitby Literary and Philosophical Society, Whitby Museum Library, Whitby, Yorkshire, Banks to Scoresby, 8 September 1810.
    E. G. R. Taylor, *The Mathematical Practitioners of Hanoverian England, 1714–1840* (1966), pp. 262, 306.

16. James Six, "Account of an improved thermometer", *Phil. Trans.* (1782). Vol. **72,** pp. 72–81.

17. James Six, *The Construction and Use of a Thermometer, for shewing the extremes of temperature in the atmosphere, during the observer's absence,* Maidstone *(1794), pp. 59–62.

18. Adam John Krusenstern, *Voyage round the World, in the years 1803, 1804, 1805, and 1806, by order of his Imperial Majesty Alexander I, on board the ships Nadeshda and Neva,* translated by R. B. Hoppner, 2 vols, London (1813).

19. Whitby Literary and Philosophical Society MSS, Scoresby to Banks, 15 September 1811. This is Scoresby's draft of the letter.

20. *Ibid.* Scoresby to Jameson, 27 August 1817.

21. William Scoresby, *An Account of the Arctic Regions, with a history and description of the northern whale-fishery.* Vol. **1,** pp. 203–217.

22. Whitby Literary and Philosophical Society MSS, Banks to Scoresby, 22 September 1817.

23. *Ibid.* Banks to Scoresby, 17 November 1817.

24. *Ibid.* Banks to Scoresby, 26 October 1817.

25. *Ibid.* Scoresby to Banks, 25 November 1817.

26. *Ibid.* Scoresby to Jameson, 20 January 1818.

27. *Ibid.* Scoresby to Banks, 17 April 1818.

28. Sir John Ross, *A voyage of Discovery, made under the Orders of the Admiralty, in H.M.S. Isabella and Alexander, for the purpose of exploring Baffin's Bay, and inquiring into the probability of a North-West Passage*, London (1819).

29. Sabine's record of the voyage is preserved at the Royal Society: *MS Notes Geographical, Magnetical and Meteorological made by Captain Sabine during Ross's Arctic Voyage in 1818.*

30. Sir John Ross, *op. cit.* pp. 10–11.

31. "Instructions for the adjustments and use of the instruments intended for the northern expeditions", *Journal of Science and the Arts* (1818). Vol. **5**, pp. 202–230.
    "Description of the apparatus, alluded to in the foregoing paper, for bringing up water from certain depths in the sea", *ibid.*, pp. 231–233.

32. Sir John Ross, *op. cit.* pp. 192–193, cxxxiii–cxxxvi.

33. Sir Charles Wyville Thomson, *The Depths of the Sea*, 2nd edition, London, (1874), pp. 300–301.

34. Alexander Marcet, *op. cit.* p. 205.

35. Sir John Ross, *op. cit.* p. cxxix.

36. Alexander Marcet, *op. cit.* pp. 168, sheet facing p. 202, 203. See also: "Table of the temperature of the sea, at various depths, made during Captain Franklin's voyage to Spitzbergen with Captain Buchan", *The Edinburgh Philosophical Journal* (1825). Vol. **12**, pp. 233–234.

37. Alexander Marcet, *op. cit.* pp. 203–204.

38. Andrew Fyfe, "On the quantity of saline matter in the water of the north polar seas", *The Edinburgh Philosophical Journal* (1819). Vol. **1**, pp. 160–163.

39. William Edward Parry, *Journal of a Voyage for the Discovery of a North-West Passage from the Atlantic to the Pacific; performed in the years 1819–20, in H.M.S. Hecla and Griper*, 2nd edition, London (1821), pp. xxv–xxvi.

40. Alexander Marcet, *op. cit.* pp. 166, 207. Apparently John Ross had also invented a water sampler to replace Davy's but there is no mention of its use in Parry's narrative.

41. William Edward Parry, *op. cit.* pp. 4, 293. Parry was of course justified in being suspicious. The ease with which the indices could either stick or be shaken out of position was one of the principal drawbacks of the Six thermometer. Also, only the maximum and minimum temperatures were recorded and it need not automatically follow that the minimum temperature was the deepest though this was generally assumed to be so.

42. Frederick William Beechey, *Narrative of a Voyage to the Pacific and Beering's Strait, to co-operate with the Polar Expeditions: performed in H.M.S. Blossom, in the years 1825–1828*, 2 vols, London (1831).

43. François Arago, *Œuvres Completes* (ed. M. J. A. Barral), 17 vols, Paris (1854–1862). Vol. **9**, (1857), p. 164.

44. *Ibid.* pp. 197–202. Hyacinthe de Bougainville, *Journal de la Navigation autour du Globe de la frégate la Thétis et de la corvette l'Espérance pendant les années, 1824–1826*, 2 vols, Paris (1837).

45. François Arago, *op. cit.* p. 201.

46. *Ibid.* p. 228.

47. Jules Dumont d'Urville, *Voyage de la corvette l'Astrolabe executé par ordre du roi, pendant les années 1826–1829*, 5 vols, Paris (1830–1833).

48. "On the temperature of the Mediterranean", *Naut. Mag.* (1832). Vol. **1**, pp. 396–397.

49. Otto von Kotzebue, *A Voyage of Discovery, into the South Sea and Beering's Straits, for the purpose of exploring a north-east passage, undertaken in the years 1815–1818*, translated by H. E. Lloyd, 3 vols, London (1821).

50. *Ibid*. Vol. 2, pp. 186–187.

51. Thaddeus Bellingshausen, *The Voyage of Captain Bellingshausen to the Antarctic Seas 1819–1821* (ed. Frank Debenham) Hakluyt Society, 2nd series (1945). Vols 91 and 92.

52. Kotzebue's account of this voyage, *A new Voyage round the World, 1823–1826*, 2 vols, London (1830) says scarcely anything about Lenz's work which was written up separately in the journal of the St. Petersburg Academy of Sciences E. Lenz, "Physikalische Beobachtungen angestellt auf einer Reise um die Welt unter dem Commando des Capitains Otto von Kotzebue in den Jahren 1823, 1824, 1825 und 1826", *Mémoires de l'Académie Impériale des Sciences de St.- Pétersbourg. 6me Série. Sciences mathématiques, physiques et naturelles* (1831). Vol. 1, pp. 221–341.
An account of Lenz's work, "On the temperature and saltness of the waters of the ocean at different depths", appeared in the *Edinb. J. Sci.* (1832) 2nd series. Vol. 6, pp. 341–344.

53. John Murray, "On the temperature of the German Ocean", *Edinburgh Philosophical Journal* (1821). Vol. 5, p. 220.
R. Knox, "On the climate of southern Africa", *ibid*., pp. 279–287.
G. A. Walker Arnott, "Notice of a 'Journal of a Voyage from Rio de Janeiro to the Coast of Peru, by Mr. William Jameson' ", *Memoirs of the Wernerian Natural History Society* (1823–1824). Vol. 5, part 1, pp. 187–205.

54. *Dictionary of National Biography*. Vol. 29, p. 236.

55. James Weddell, *A Voyage towards the South Pole, performed in the years 1822–24*, 2nd edition, London (1827).

56. Andrew Livingston, "On the thermometer, as an indicator of a ship's approach to land or soundings", *Edinburgh Philosophical Journal* (1820). Vol. 3, pp. 247–252.

57. J. D. Boswall, "Observations on the Gulf-Stream, in crossing it from Halifax to Bermuda, and from Bermuda to Halifax in H.M.S. *Jaseur*, in 1821", *Edinb. J. Sci.* (1825). Vol. 3, pp. 256–261.

58. J. Prescott, "Temperature of the ocean", *Naut. Mag.* (1832). Vol. 1, pp. 172–173.

59. W. H. B. Webster, *Narrative of a voyage to the Southern Atlantic Ocean, in the years 1828, 29, 30, performed in H.M. Sloop Chanticleer under the command of the late Captain Henry Foster*, 2 vols London, (1834).

60. John Frembly, "Results of a series of hydro-thermometrical observations made in the Firth of Forth", *Edinburgh Philosophical Journal* (1823–1824). Vol. 10, pp. 189–190.
John Frembly, "A series of observations on the temperature of the sea at the mouth of the Thames, in the year 1824", *Edinburgh New Philosophical Journal* (1826). Vol. 1, pp. 377–379. It is tempting to guess at the identity of the friend; John Davy was living in Leith at that period.

61. Sir Francis Beaufort, *Karamania, or a brief Description of the South Coast of Asia Minor and of the Remains of Antiquity*, 2nd ed., London (1818), p. 43.

62. Robert Wauchope, "Meteorological and Hydrographical Notes", *Memoirs of the Wernerian Natural History Society* (1821–1822). Vol. 4, part 1, pp. 161–172.

63. *Ibid.* p. 161.
64. *Ibid.* p. 165.
65. George Powell, *Notes on South-Shetland, &c., printed to accompany the chart of these newly discovered lands*, R. H. Laurie, London (1822).
   John Biscoe, *Journal of a voyage towards the South Pole on board the brig Tula* in *The Antarctic Manual* (ed. George Murray), London (1901), p. 316.
66. Clarke Abel, *Narrative of a Journey in the interior of China, and of a voyage to and from that country, in the years 1816 and 1817*, London (1819).
67. Egerton Smith, *Observations on the principle and use of the new patent Sea Log and Sounding Machine, invented by Edward Massey*, 40 pp., Liverpool (1805). (One of many pamphlets describing the instruments.)
68. Robert P. Multhauf, "The line-less sounder: an episode in the history of scientific instruments", *J. Hist. Med.* (1960). Vol. **15**, pp. 390–398; note 12 on p. 395.
69. Edward Massey, *A statement of the case of Mr. Edward Massey, of the city of Coventry, and of Siholes, near Prescot, Lancashire, most respectfully offered to the notice of every Member of Parliament*, Prescot (1820).
70. "Captain Booth's report on Mr. Massey's proposed machine for sounding in hitherto unknown depths", extract from the *Cork Reporter, Nautical Magazine* (1832). Vol. **1**, pp. 498–499.
71. "Depth of the ocean", *Naut. Mag.* (1832). Vol. **1**, p. 174.
72. Board of Longitude Papers. Vol. **25**, Massey to Young, 17 June 1823.
73. Board of Longitude Papers. Vol. **8**, Minutes 1823–1829, 6 November 1823.
74. James Rennell, *An Investigation of the Currents of the Atlantic Ocean* (1832), pp. 264–265.
75. John Davy, "Observations on the temperature of the Ocean and atmosphere, and on the density of sea-water, made during a voyage to Ceylon", *Phil. Trans.* (1817). Vol. **107**, pp. 275–292.
76. Richard Kirwan, *An Estimate of the Temperature of Different Latitudes* (1787).
77. *Ibid.* p. 41.
78. Otto von Kotzebue, *A Voyage of Discovery, into the South Sea* (1821). Vol. **1**, pp. 77–78.
79. Alexander von Humboldt, *Personal Narrative of Travels to the Equinoctial Regions of the New Continent*, translated by H. M. Williams (1814). Vol. **2**, pp. 58–83.
80. Alexander von Humboldt, *Essai politique sur la Royaume de la Nouvelle-Espagne*, 5 vols, Paris (1811). Vol. **4**, pp. 498–499.
81. Alexander von Humboldt, *Personal Narrative*. Vol. **7**, (1829) pp. 386–391.
82. Sir Clements Markham, *op. cit.* p. 146.
83. Thomas Stewart Traill, "Experiments on the specific gravity of sea water drawn in different latitudes, and from various depths in the Atlantic", *Edinburgh Philosophical Journal* (1820–1821). Vol. **4**, pp. 185–188.
84. Louis Joseph Gay-Lussac, "Note sur la salure de l'Océan Atlantique", *Ann. Chim. Phys.* (1817). Vol. **6**, pp. 426–436.
85. E. J. B. Bouillon Lagrange and H. A. Vogel, "Memoir on the sea water of the coasts of France, considered in a chemical and medical point of view", *Thomson's Annals* (1814). Vol. **4**, pp. 200–209.
86. John Murray, "An analysis of sea-water; with observations on the analysis of salt-brines", *Trans. R. Soc. Edinb.* (1818). Vol. **8**, pp. 205–244.

87. Alexander Marcet, "Some experiments and researches on the saline contents of sea-water, undertaken with a view to correct and improve its chemical analysis", *Phil. Trans.* (1822). Vol. **112**, pp. 448–456.

88. Joseph Louis Proust, "Sur le mercure contenu dans le sel marin", *Journal de Physique* (1799). Vol. **49**, pp. 153–155.

89. "Presence of mercury in common salt", *Edinburgh Philosophical Journal* (1825). Vol. **12**, pp. 414–415.

90. Antoine Jérome Balard, "Mémoire sur une substance particulière contenue dans l'eau de la mer", *Annls. Chim. Phys.* (1826). Vol. **32**, pp. 337–381.

91. Charles Daubeny, "Memoir on the occurrence of iodine and bromine in certain mineral waters of South Britain", *Phil. Trans.* (1830). Vol. **120**, pp. 223–237.

92. Alexander Marcet, "On the specific gravity, and temperature of sea waters", *Phil. Trans.* (1819). Vol. **109**, p. 194.

93. John Fleming, "Observations on the junction of the fresh water of rivers with the salt water of the sea", *Trans. R. Soc. Edinb.* (1818). Vol. **8**, pp. 507–513.

94. William Henry Smyth, *The Mediterranean: a Memoir physical, historical and nautical*, London (1854).

95. William Hyde Wollaston, "On the water of the Mediterranean", *Phil. Trans.* (1829). Vol. **119**, pp. 29–31.

96. E. Lenz (*see* ref. 52).

97. As suggested by Humboldt, *Personal Narrative.* Vol. **1**, (1814) p. 63.

98. Otto von Kotzebue, *A Voyage of Discovery, into the South Sea* (1821). Vol. **1**, pp. 70–79.

99. William Scoresby, *An Account of the Arctic Regions* (1820). Vol. **1**, pp. 209–210.

100. Clarke Abel, *op. cit.* p. 345.

101. Alexander Marcet, *op. cit.* p. 188.

102. Edward Sabine, "On the temperature at considerable depths in the Caribbean Sea", *Phil. Trans.* (1823). Vol. **113**, pp. 206–210.

103. Edward Sabine, *An Account of Experiments to determine the Figure of the Earth* (1825), pp. 456–459.

104. *Ibid.* p. 456.

105. Henry T. de la Beche, *A Geological Manual*, London (1831), pp. 20–24.

106. *Ibid.* 3rd edition (1833), pp. 25–26.

107. Henry T. de la Beche, "On the advantages possessed by naval men, in contributing to general science", *Naut. Mag.* (1832). Vol. **1**, pp. 180–185, 299–303.

108. William Scoresby, *op. cit.* pp. 189–203.

109. James Six, *The Construction and Use of a Thermometer, op. cit.* p. 61.

110. G. F. Parrot, "Expériences de forte compression sur divers corps", *Mémoires de l'Académie Impériale des Sciences, op. cit.* (1833). Vol. **2**, pp. 595–630.

111. James Kingston Tuckey, *Maritime Geography and Statistics*, London (1815), 4 vols.

Addenda et Corrigenda

p.221, fig. 14, caption: *instead* with permission of the Trustees of the British Museum *read* by permission of the British Library

p.234, 1.39: *instead* an American device *read* another device made by a rival British instrument maker,

p.234, n.1, 1.1: insert British Library, Maps 188. a. 2(3).

p.244, n.17, 1.2: insert Reprinted, eds J. Austin and A. McConnell, London (1980).

THE UNSATISFIED OCEAN

12. WILD-MEETING OCEANS: THE STUDY OF TIDES

Whare wild-meeting oceans boil Besouth Magellans

Burns

IN CONTRAST with the decline of interest in other branches of marine science, tidal studies remained active during the early eighteenth century but, after Halley's voyage, the initiative passed to the other side of the Channel, particularly to France. The Académie Royale des Sciences had observations made at Dunkirk in 1701–1702 and at Brest in 1714–1716 and the results were published by Jacques Cassini (1677–1756). Observations continued to be made at intervals throughout the century in different places.[1]

In 1738 the mathematicians of the Académie recommended that the prize due to be awarded in 1740 for work on navigation and celestial physics should be given for an essay on tides. In the event the prize was divided among four winning essays. Three of these, by Colin Maclaurin, Daniel Bernoulli (1700–1782) and Leonard Euler (1707–1783), developed Newton's theory. The fourth, by Antoine Cavalleri, was based on the Cartesian hypothesis[2] (*see* Ch. 5).

Maclaurin and Euler put forward proofs to show that under the combined action of the sun and moon an ocean covering the whole surface of the earth would assume the form of a spheroid with its axis approximately along the line joining the centres of the earth and moon. Bernoulli developed this idea and calculated the variations in the tide-raising force due to the varying angular distances of the sun and moon, their distances from the earth and declination from the plane of the equator. He expressed his results in tables which could be used for predicting tides. Euler showed that the attractive force of the moon did not have its maximum effect on the water directly below, because the gravitational pull of the earth outweighed it. It was the horizontal components of the moon's force which caused the tides and these are greatest at an angle of 45° to the line joining the centre of the earth to the centre of the moon. Maclaurin examined the effect of the earth's rotation on meridional currents.[3]

The work of Pierre Simon, Marquis de Laplace, spanned fifty years, the last quarter of the eighteenth century and the first of the nineteenth. He formulated equations to give a dynamic theory of tides on a rotating globe covered with water. This did not enable him to explain the individual variations of tide from one place to another and he enunciated the principle, the basis of future work, that if empirical observations were to be made of the tide produced at a place by any one set of astronomical circumstances it would be possible to predict that an identical tide would be experienced when the same conditions recurred. He had observations reinstituted at Brest in 1806 and after sixteen years analysed the results to show the effect of the altitudes and declinations of the sun and moon.[4]

The difficulty of relating the simple statement of gravitational attraction with the bewildering complexity of local tides was the problem most striking to the layman. Newton's work, said Murdoch Mackenzie the elder (d. 1797),

gave such an easy Solution of some of the most remarkable *Phænomena*, that Mankind seemed to imagine a thorough Knowledge of the Tides might be obtained from an attentive Consideration of the Principles he had established, without the Trouble of further Observations.

In fact the actual movements of the water still remained "as inexplicable, and as little known as ever".[5] Mackenzie's experience of tides had been obtained during his hydrographic surveys of Orkney and Shetland.[6] Later he surveyed the coast of Ireland and the west coast of Scotland for the Admiralty and published information about the tides, giving the interval between the moon's transit and the time of high water at new moon, the direction of tidal streams and the heights of spring and neap tides.[7]

At about the same time Joseph de Lalande (1732–1807) was having observations made by M. de Fourcroy, chief engineer at Calais, which he used to try and establish if the equinoctial spring tides were really larger than the ordinary springs.[8] He compiled tide-tables for Calais and other places and also a history of tidal studies, for which he is principally remembered.[1] Lalande noted the discrepancy between the heights of tides as predicted by theory and those actually observed. In 1772 he wrote to Sir Joseph Banks asking him about the tides of the South Seas.[9] From Banks's reply he learned that the rise and fall of the sea at Tahiti was only 1 foot whereas according to Bernoulli's calculations it should have been 8 feet.[10]

During the late eighteenth and early nineteenth centuries the ideas which prevailed about the movements of the tides in the oceans were contained in the equilibrium theory. This was derived from the work of the mid-eighteenth century mathematicians, Bernoulli in particular. It supposed that the attractive forces of the sun and moon cause the ocean to approach the shape of a spheroid with its major axis approximately aligned so that the greatest elevations of water occur one below the moon and the other on the opposite side of the earth. This was the position of equilibrium but because the earth rotates on its axis the two humps of water appear to travel round the world as the crests of the tide wave, 180° apart, once every 24 hours (*see* diagram, below). For example, this was the explanation given by Tuckey in his *Maritime Geography*.[11]

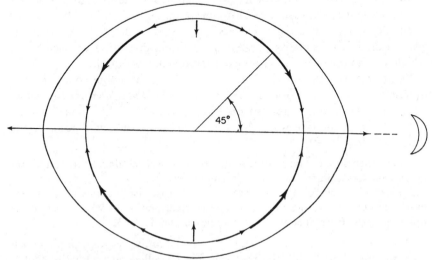

Horizontal and vertical forces exerted in the sea by the moon according to the equilibrium theory. After R. C. H. Russell and D. H. Macmillan, *Waves and Tides*, London (1952), pp. 190–191.

The difficulties in the way of this hypothesis in its simple form were obvious. It failed to take into account the fact that the ocean does not cover the surface of the globe but is divided up by the continental masses. Nor did it allow for friction, inertia or the possible effect of the depth of the sea which, according to the formula of Joseph Louis Lagrange (1736–1813), governed the velocity of waves (*see* p. 264). It could be argued that the modifications produced by these factors in the progress of the tide wave were the cause of the unbridged gap between theory and observation but at an early stage radically new explanations were being offered.

Graeme Spence surveyed the Scilly Islands for the Admiralty between 1789 and 1793.[12] He made tidal observations by having one person on shore recording the height and time of high water and the rate of rise and fall, and a boat anchored in the offing to observe the direction and velocity of the stream and when it turned. From these observations he learnt that the tide was not just a progressive or retrograde movement of the water but also a circular motion so that in any particular place the direction of the stream shifted through every point of the compass once every twelve hours. He suggested that this would be found to be so, too, in the ocean at large.[13]

Dr Thomas Young first published his theory of tides anonymously in 1813.[14] He attempted to improve upon Laplace's efforts to consider what effect the tide-raising forces had upon the sea, allowing for the fact, ignored by the equilibrium theory, that friction and the shape of the oceans would prevent the sea from reaching even an approximation of the shape it would assume on a globe covered with water. He supposed that the gravitational forces acted separately on each ocean, setting up oscillations which obeyed the same laws as the oscillations of a pendulum.

Young commented on the lack of information available about tides in different parts of the world. In an article in the *Encyclopaedia Britannica* he suggested how observations from different places could be used to show the progress of the tide wave.[15] If these were to be tabulated according to time, he wrote,

we might then suppose lines to be drawn on a terrestrial globe, through all the places of observation, in the same order; and these lines would indicate, supposing the places to be sufficiently numerous, so as to furnish a series of tides very nearly contemporary, the directions of the great waves, to which that of the progress of the tides in succession must be perpendicular.[16]

In the existing state of knowledge this could only be attempted for the Atlantic and there it seemed that the tide travelled north up the central part of the ocean, arriving at the British Isles from the south west and flowing part up the English Channel, part round the north of Scotland and down the east coast.

Young's scheme remained on paper, however, and no progress had been made in the practical study he suggested when he died in 1829. In that year the Society for the Diffusion of Useful Knowledge found that the tide-tables published for London were erroneous. It turned out that they had been calculated from the wrong establishment. At the instance of the Society one of its members, John William Lubbock (1803–1865), looked into the matter.[17]

After studying at Trinity College, Cambridge, Lubbock had become a partner in his father's bank but he was also a keen scientist and his chosen subject was physical astronomy. In 1830 he was made Vice-President and treasurer of the Royal Society.

The London tide-tables at this time were not an official publication. They were produced by private individuals who, it appeared, regarded them as private property to be handed down from one generation to another.[18] The method by which they were calculated and the information on which they were based were kept as trade secrets and Lubbock was refused access to them.

As this avenue closed another opened. Lubbock found that high water had been recorded at the site of the London Docks, night and day, since 1801. He obtained the loan of the records and began to analyse them. In the hard work which this involved he was given the help of a naval assistant in the Hydrographic Department, Joseph Dessiou.[19] Sir Francis Beaufort's willing assistance in this and other aspects of the work was to be of crucial importance in the development of tidal studies during the 1830s.

The first fruits of the work of Lubbock and Dessiou appeared in the *British Almanac* for 1830 in the form of tide-tables for London and a historical survey of the development of tidal theory from Kepler to Laplace. Lubbock outlined his proposals for working on the London observations and suggested that a form of tide-gauge should be used so that it was not left for the foreman or night-watchman to look for the highest point of the water, a possible source of error.[20]

What Lubbock was trying to do was to use the record of the heights and times of high water over a long period to calculate the different variations to be detected in the tides, the semi-diurnal rise and fall, the twice monthly springs and neaps, the alterations caused by the variation in the moon's orbit, and to relate them to the astronomical forces which had caused them. When these relationships had been established then he hoped it would be possible to predict future tides as accurately as they could already predict the movements of the heavenly bodies. At his instance tide-tables were introduced into the *Nautical Almanac* but prediction was still largely a thing of the future.

The work which really interested Lubbock was the analysis of records to provide a better understanding of tides in harbours. He seems to have given little thought to how the tides would look in the ocean at large and speaking to the newly formed British Association for the Advancement of Science at Oxford in 1832 he described them in the terms of a modified version of the equilibrium theory. This concept dominated thinking on the subject over the next ten years. It treated the tide travelling round the Southern Ocean, the only stretch of water to encircle the globe, as a forced oscillation, and the tides of the other oceans as free waves propagated northwards by it.

Lubbock wrote

If the ocean were not intersected by continents, the tide-wave would proceed from east to west; and if the luminaries moved in the equator, the *cotidal lines* would be meridians.

The continents of Africa and South America may be considered as immense dams in the course of the tide-wave which completely change its direction, so that it is high water at the same time on the opposite shores of the Atlantic. The rudiments of the cotidal lines which would obtain in the case of a perfect, spheroid probably exist round the south pole, interfered with, as they must be, by the great continent of ice in these regions. Owing to the obstructions I have mentioned, it is high water nearly at the same instant at the Cape of Good Hope, off the Straits of Gibraltar, off the coast of Scotland near the Murray Frith, and in the river Thames. The wave takes six hours in proceeding from the Land's End to the North Foreland, being at the rate of about 70 miles an hour, and in a direction contrary to the course of the luminary. If the ocean completely covered the solid nucleus of the earth, it would only be high water at the same instant at places of which the longitude differed by 180°; and at the equator the tide-wave would travel at the rate of about 500 miles per hour. The motion of the crest of the tide-wave must be carefully distinguished from that of the particles of water themselves, which forms a current, the velocity of which seldom exceeds a few miles per hour.[21]

The task which Lubbock had set himself proved to be more difficult than he had expected. At first he hoped that a comparison of the London observations with those of Laplace from Brest would show that tides could be understood everywhere on the same basis if the allowance to be made for local conditions were established. His work showed that this was not so and convinced him that the work of observation and analysis would have to be repeated for every separate place. At the same time it was learned that there were other factors as well as the astronomical forces to be taken into consideration. Daussy had shown that barometric depressions increased the height of high water on the coast of France while high pressure diminished it and Lubbock learned independently that winds affected the level of tides in the Thames.[22] At first he doubted that barometric variation had any effect at London but further work showed that it did.

It was rapidly becoming clear that to make accurate tide-tables and to improve understanding of tides in general, observations would have to be extended. To this end Lubbock submitted a design for a tide-gauge to the Royal Society, the work of the engineer Henry Palmer.[23] The gauge was to consist of a well let into the side of a harbour and communicating with it by an opening which allowed water to pass in and out freely, maintaining an equal level inside and outside the gauge, but was too small to admit the irregular rise and fall of level due to waves. A float resting on the surface of the water was linked by a system of pulleys to a marker which left a continuous record of its rise and fall on a band of paper. This wound on to a cylinder which was set by a clock to rotate in a fixed time. Except for the fact that it was self-registering this gauge very much resembled the one described by Sir Robert Moray in 1666 (*see* Ch. 5).

The Council of the Royal Society asked the Admiralty to have observations made at naval dockyards and this they agreed to do in August 1831.[24] The first gauge was erected in the dockyard at Sheerness, the following month.[25] It was based on the same principles as Palmer's but the design and execution were specifically credited to the dockyard engineer, Mitchell. At that stage money was needed to complete the gauges at Portsmouth and to build one at Plymouth but observations must have been got under way fairly speedily since results for all three places were published in 1833[26] and in the same year the first volume of Admiralty Tide Tables was published, for London, Sheerness, Portsmouth and Plymouth.

Another gauge of the same kind was erected on the River Avon, four miles below Bristol, by the Bristol Institution.[27] Observations continued in London at the London Docks and the St Katherine Dock but no new gauge was erected and measurements were apparently made in the old way but with rather more attention to accuracy.

Lubbock's determination to rescue the tides from their ignominious position as the most neglected branch of physical astronomy met with a wide response from seamen and scientists alike, so apparent was the need for a better practical understanding of them. Through Beaufort he had the help of Dessiou and later of other members of the staff of the Hydrographic Department. The admiralty as a whole proved sympathetic—as long as the projects put to them did not involve too much time and expense.

On the scientific side the British Association proved an admirable forum for the exchange of ideas and discussion of new results. It set up committees to investigate related problems. Most important of all, from the practical point of view, it was able to provide financial support for new work. The annual budget increased rapidly during the first few years and expenditure on tides and related subjects increased in proportion. During the 1830s it amounted to between a third and a half of the total but fell away in the early 1840s.[28] Although its function here was not to initiate research but to support that already going on, the Association was fulfilling in some measure the need for co-ordination and resources to lift marine science above the purely individual level at which it had so far been pursued and which had been a hindrance to its development.

Among the people whom Lubbock won over to the study of tides was his former tutor William Whewell (1794–1866), Fellow and later Master of Trinity. Whewell co-operated with Lubbock in analysing tidal data but, unlike him, was much more interested in using observations to discover the general pattern of tides throughout the world than in the mere formulation of precise mathematical definitions. In this respect, discussing the general implications of new information and ideas and suggesting and organizing projects, he became more prominent than Lubbock and came near to eclipsing him altogether in some people's minds.[29]

Whewell was aware of Lubbock's preoccupation from an early stage.[30] It was he who provided him with the more convincing phrase "cotidal lines" to replace Young's "contemporary lines" for describing the imaginary line joining points reached simultaneously by the crest of the tide wave.[31] It was not until the beginning of 1833, however, that he began to take an active interest in the work. Then he wrote to Sir John Herschel (1792–1871) "I am going to do something about tides".[32] His first paper—"Essay towards a first approximation to a map of cotidal lines"—was given to the Royal Society in the same year.[33]

Whewell believed that Laplace had been right in treating the tides as a problem of oscillation rather than of the equilibrium of fluids.[34] In 1834 he wrote

the tides, though in the theory to which we refer considered as representing positions of equilibrium of a fluid, are in fact the results of its motion; and it is not at all clear that the elevation which results from the motion will be equal to the elevation which would be requisite for equilibrium.

He continued:

Moreover, the motion of the fluid is of the nature of an oscillation, so that series of increasing and diminishing oscillations at intervals of a half-day, a day, and other intervals, pass through any given part of the ocean. Now it is physically, not only possible but certain, that each oscillation in each series is affected by those which precede it in the same series, and affects those which succeed it, so that their relative magnitude is different from what it would otherwise be. And the effects thus produced will depend upon the depth of the ocean, the form of its shores, and other causes, of which it is impossible to estimate the result *à priori*.[35]

He did not however believe that Laplace's work as it stood offered a better way of explaining the tides at large than did the Newton-Bernoulli equilibrium theory. Apart from his tidal and other original studies Whewell was one of the first historians of science and he understood that a hypothesis which could be examined empirically was likely to be a more rewarding field of inquiry than a theory which he could not develop, even though he felt that the ultimate answers must lie in that direction. The version of the equilibrium theory described by Lubbock in 1832 offered the best immediate framework for correlating information.

Using the information he had been able to glean from documents in the Hydrographic Department and works on navigation Whewell attempted to draw the cotidal lines for the world ocean, Lubbock's efforts having been limited to charting the times of high water. Lack of information made this exercise highly tentative in the Pacific Ocean but in the Atlantic it did seem possible to interpret the times as showing a tide wave moving up from the Southern Ocean. At Cape Frio it appeared to diverge, part flowing south and the rest north. On the opposite side of the Atlantic it seemed that the times of high water became progressively later from south to north and, though between the Cape of Good Hope and the Strait of Gibraltar there was little to go on, from Gibraltar northwards the progression was clearer. Murdoch Mackenzie had said that the tide arrived on the south-west point of Ireland and divided[7] and the existence of a southerly flow on the east coast of England was well known so it seemed likely that part of the tide of the North Sea, or German Ocean as it was then known, came round the north of Scotland while the rest came up the English Channel, causing high water to progress northwards on the coast of the Low Countries. Whewell wrote

We seem to be led therefore to the remarkable conclusion, that a tide-wave which reaches almost or quite to the shores of Denmark, proceeds through the narrow opening of the Straits of Dover, though the main part of the German Ocean is occupied with the tide-wave which enters by the north; and that the tide-wave on the opposite shores of England and Holland runs at the same moment in opposite directions.[36]

He suggested that the interference between the two streams might produce a stationary rather than a progressive wave.

Not all the information fitted neatly into the pattern. There were Spence's rotating tides but these might be explicable as tidal currents meeting or separating.[37] It was lack of positive evidence rather than any obvious contradictions, which rendered the hypothesis doubtful. Whewell wrote

I should regret its publication if I supposed it likely that any intelligent person could consider it otherwise than as an attempt to combine such information as we have, and to point out the want and the use of more.[38]

He suggested that understanding would benefit considerably if the coastguards could make simultaneous observations for, say, a fortnight round the entire coast of Great Britain.

During the summer of 1833 Whewell and Lubbock learned of the existence of a series of tidal observations at Liverpool, already being used as a basis for tide-tables.[39] They were the work of William Hutchinson (1715–1801), harbourmaster, and ran from 1768 to 1793. This unexpected find gave them a valuable source of comparison for the results obtained from the other long term series made at Brest and London.[40]

Meanwhile Whewell was also working on the project he had suggested at the end of his first paper. With Beaufort's help he persuaded the Preventive Service to agree to the plan and arrange for observations to be made for a fortnight by the coastguards. Whewell drew up directions[41] and the scheme was put into operation in June 1834.

The results of the survey showed that it was impossible to draw cotidal lines straight across the North Sea. They seemed to adopt a convex shape, leaving the shore at an acute angle, and Whewell supposed that this was because the tide was freer to travel in the centre of the sea and made less progress at the edges. He concluded that the best way of finding out more about it was to undertake a further series of simultaneous observations, not only in this country but with other countries participating as well.[42]

The idea of international co-operation had a good reception. Beaufort was enthusiastic and when he passed on the proposal to the Admiralty they agreed to approach the Foreign Secretary, the Duke of Wellington. He made the necessary arrangements with foreign governments and the observations were arranged for June 1835. Whewell himself wrote to Lambert Quetelet (1796–1874), director of the Royal Observatory at Brussels, explaining why he wanted them made. The study of tides had been allowed to lag behind the other branches of astronomy and co-operation between nations and government backing were needed to remedy this. It was generally supposed that the tides flowed in opposite directions on the Belgian and English coasts. Only a series of observations from both countries could show exactly how the two tides were connected and how they fitted into the general theory.[43]

Already in 1833 Whewell had hammered home the unpalatable lesson of how much needed to be found out about tides and how little had already been done, with a pointed reference to Sir Francis Bacon's work of over two hundred years before:

We are, perhaps, not even yet able to answer decisively the inquiry which BACON suggests to the philosophers of his time, whether the high water extends across the Atlantic so as to affect contemporaneously the shores of America and Africa, or whether it is high on one side of this ocean, when it is low on the other; at any rate such observations have not been extended and generalized.[44]

Now in 1835 observations were made for a fortnight on both sides of the Atlantic, at twenty-eight or more places on the American and European coasts, between Florida and Nova Scotia and from the Strait of Gibraltar to North Cape, and at over 500 points on the coasts of Great Britain.[45] Whewell wrote to a friend

I shall have such a register of the vagaries of the tide-wave for a fortnight as has never before been collected, and, I have no doubt, I shall get some curious results out of it.[46]

It turned out that his prophecy was fully justified.

The results obtained from the North Sea distorted the cotidal lines still further, until they came to look like the radiating spokes of a wheel, diverging from a central point (*see* chart below). Whewell wrote

It appears that we may best combine all the facts into a consistent scheme, by dividing this ocean into two *rotatory* systems of tide-waves.[47]

one situated in the southern part of the sea between East Anglia and the Netherlands, the other further north. Each revolved round a central area "where there is no tide".

The results for the Atlantic complicated the cotidal lines considerably and introduced a difficulty which was to lead Whewell to abandon the

Whewell's cotidal lines in the North Sea. From *Chart of the Coasts of Europe exhibiting the cotidal lines. To accompany Mr. Whewell's Researches on the Tides. Sixth series* in *Philosophical Transactions* (1836), plate 26 facing page 307. Reproduced with permission * of the Royal Society.

attempt to draw them for the oceans as a whole. It concerned the diurnal inequality, known to tidal theorists since the observations made in the late seventeenth century. The inequality was attributed to the varying declination of the moon and in theory was most pronounced when the moon was furthest from the equator and disappeared when it was nearest to it. The effect was known to follow the cause by an interval and the 1835 results showed that this interval was not the same but varied from place to place. Until now it had been assumed that the tide wave came northwards up the Atlantic reaching places on the same latitude either side at about the same time but the new information made this very doubtful. Whewell wrote

The different epoch of the diurnal inequality in different parts of the world is a very curious fact; and the more so, since it is inconsistent with the mode hitherto adopted of explaining the circumstances of the tides by conceiving a tide-wave to travel to all shores in succession. In accordance with this view the tide on the shores of America had been considered as identical with the tide on the coasts of Spain and Portugal, which occurs about the same moment; nor does it appear easy to imagine the form of the tide-waves so that this shall not be the case. Yet we find that the tides on these two sides of the Atlantic cannot be identical in all respects; for on the 9th, 10th, and 11th of June, when the diurnal inequality was great in America, it was nothing in the West of Europe; and on the 18th and 19th, when this inequality had vanished in America, it was great in Europe. It would seem as if the tidal phenomena on this side of the Atlantic corresponded to an epoch (of the equilibrium-theory) two or three days later than the same phenomena in America; and we may perhaps add, that different kinds of phenomena do not appear to travel at the same rate. And thus the equilibrium-theory, though it may explain the general form of the inequalities, cannot give their epochs and amounts by any possible adjustment of constants.[48]

Whewell developed the idea that the diurnal inequality might be transmitted by its own oscillation travelling at a different rate from those which carried the other components of the tides.[49] Or it could be argued that the tide wave went first to America and then travelled to the coast of Europe, arriving a few days later. The observations made by Sir John Herschel at the Cape of Good Hope in June 1835 put an end to this hypothesis. They showed that the diurnal inequality at a place which, being nearest to the supposed source of tides, should display their characteristics sooner than anywhere else, in fact occurred at the same time as it did in Spain and Portugal where by this reasoning the tide was many days old. Whewell reported this to Herschel, who was apparently unsympathetic to his attempt to explain the tides through the equilibrium theory. He asked him for more observations, though he hoped that this would not entail Herschel's being washed into the sea as had seemingly happened on a previous occasion.[50]

A few months later Whewell wrote to him again, still unable to reconcile facts and theory. He wished that he had more observations in the South Atlantic and confessed

the longer I attend to the subject, the more cautious I become in generalizing.[51]

Lubbock had been awarded the Royal Society's Royal Medal in 1834 and delivered the Bakerian Lecture in 1836.[52] In 1837 his last paper in his series on tides was published in the *Philosophical Transactions*. Meanwhile Whewell was changing his tactics. He had abandoned the attempt to draw cotidal lines for the oceans and embarked on a world-wide study of the diurnal inequality.[53] The East India Company had supplied him with observations from Singapore made from August 1834 to August 1835 and Captain Robert Fitzroy (1805–1865) of H.M.S. *Beagle* had measured the irregular tides of the south-west Pacific. As with cotidal lines a deeper investigation forced Whewell to abandon his earlier ideas. He found that it was impossible to see a pattern of progression in the occurrence of the diurnal inequality in British ports.[54]

In 1838 Whewell read a paper intended to wind up his series in the *Philosophical Transactions*, in which he explained the difficulties that had been encountered in applying the equilibrium theory and called for more observations to be made to see if they could be overcome.[55] Till the subject of tides, he wrote, is

treated in a manner worthy of its scientific importance, and of the promise which it now holds forth, it must be considered as offering a blot in that system of the national cultivation of astronomy, of which our public observatories are, in other departments of science, such effective and magnificent examples.

This was by no means the end of Whewell's work however. He went on studying data from different parts of the world and looking for new sources of information. Early in 1838 he wrote to Mary Somerville (1780–1872)

I inclose a Memorandum respecting Tide Observations to which subject I am desirous of drawing the attention of the Russian government. Nobody knows better than you do how much remains to be done respecting the Tides, and what important results any advance in that subject would have. I hope through your Russian friends you may have the means of bringing this Memorandum to the notice of the Administration of their Navy, so as to lead to some steps being taken, in the way of directing observations to be made. The Russian government has shown so much zeal in promoting science, that I hope it will not be difficult to engage them in a kind of research so easy, so useful practically, and so interesting in its theoretical bearing.[56]

He took a leading part in the British Association's work to establish mean sea level and developed new versions of his tidal theory.

The mathematical theory of waves had been studied by Newton and more recently by Lagrange, Laplace and other French mathematicians.[57] Model studies of waves had been made in Germany by the Weber brothers but few attempts had been made to study waves at sea, phenomena so evanescent and irregular that they defied attempts to assess them with the eye. Lagrange had defined the velocity of a wave as the square root of the product of gravitational acceleration and the depth of water and since the tide was a wave it followed that this and other criteria established for waves should be equally applicable to it. Laplace used the formula to give possible depths for the sea and so did Whewell though he did not think that it was sufficiently well proven to make them reliable.[58] In fact the $\sqrt{gh}$ formula applies to long waves, waves whose length from crest to crest is more than half the depth of the water, and is applicable to tidal and other forced oscillations in the deep ocean. Ordinary surface waves, the ones seen in a storm, behave differently, travelling at speeds proportional to their wave-lengths while in water whose depth is greater than half a wave-length.

In 1834 John Scott Russell (1808–1882) described a solitary wave created by boats in canals, discovered accidentally when a horse drawing a barge on a Scottish canal bolted.[59] The extra speed lifted the boat on to the crest of a long wave created by its own resistance and only a fraction of the energy previously needed to draw it was required.

Russell thought that perhaps the tide was the same as his solitary wave and in 1836 the British Association appointed a committee consisting of himself and John Robison to inquire into the claim. A series of extensive and carefully planned observations were carried out.[60] First Russell measured the progress of the tides in the River Dee, chosen for the regularity of its channel. Then he repeated the observations in the Clyde, chosen for its irregularity, over a stretch of 18 miles with nine tide-gauges erected on a geometric level. Observations of sea waves were made from a yacht lent to the British Association and from steamers crossing the Irish Sea. Finally, he measured induced waves in canals and reservoirs.

Russell concluded that there were two kinds of waves in the sea. The primary wave, of which the only example was the tide, was, he thought, identical with the solitary wave. Its velocity obeyed Lagrange's formula. He called it a great primary wave of translation—believing that the water particles moved horizontally forward as the wave passed over them. He wrote

There is no retrogradation, no oscillation; the motion is all in the same direction, and the extent of the transference is equal throughout the whole depth.

In fact, George Biddell Airy (1801–1892) pointed out, both the solitary wave and the tide wave are long waves and are oscillatory.[61] Their water particles move round ellipses which may be so flattened that the forward and backward movement is almost horizontal.*

Russell classed ordinary waves as secondary waves. He realized that their confused appearance was due to the presence of several conflicting wave trains and that the law which governed their velocity was different from the $\sqrt{gh}$ formula, but was unable to suggest what it might be.

To compare the rise and fall of the tide from one place to another it became necessary to have a universally accepted point of reference from which to measure it. Engineers and surveyors had been accustomed to regard the land as beginning at the low water mark of the lowest ebbs but this varied from place to place as much as 20 feet. Was the mean sea level the same everywhere and if so how could it be defined?

Variations in sea level do occur, due to density differences, wind stress, currents and other factors but they are generally very small. In the eighteenth and early nineteenth centuries when accurate information on the subject was unavailable they were generally either exaggerated or dismissed altogether. John Walker, lecturing at Edinburgh in the 1780s, referred sceptically to the idea that the Pacific Ocean at Panama was some thousands of feet higher than the Atlantic Ocean on the other side of the isthmus.[62] Tuckey wrote

As exceptions to the general level, it has been pretended that the Baltic and Zuyder Zee are higher than the British Sea, the Red Sea than the Mediterranean and that there is a difference in the levels of the Atlantic and Pacific Oceans on the opposite sides of the isthmus of Darien.[63]

From his survey of Panama in 1828 John Augustus Lloyd (1800–1854) determined the difference as $3\frac{1}{2}$ feet, about two times what it really is.[64] French surveyors working in Egypt claimed to have found the level of the Red Sea nine metres higher than the Mediterranean.[65] Opinion in general remained unconvinced, though Rennell's current theory involved differences in the level of the sea and he had shown that they existed in smaller bodies of water, due to the prolonged effect of winds.[66]

The practice of equating mean sea level with half-tide level, the midpoint of the combined range of rise and fall, was apparently adopted during the 1830s by observers such as William Walker at Plymouth and Captain Henry Denham (1800–1887) who made new observations at Liverpool as part of his hydrographic work on the Lancashire coast. Whewell demonstrated with records from Plymouth and Singapore that this point varied little from day to day.[49] Variations in atmospheric pressure and wind were recognizable factors in producing the differences which did occur.[67]

* Also tides are not the only source of long waves in the sea; they are also created by earthquakes and atmospheric disturbances.

It remained to show that the half-tide level was the same everywhere before adopting it as certain. The British Association had first voted money for the project in 1834 but it was not until 1837–1838 that the work was actually done.[68] Levelling was carried out between three points on the coast in the west of England and tidal observations made. The results showed satisfactorily that the mean tide level provided a consistent norm for mean sea level and that the two could be considered as interchangeable.

The man who carried out the work was T. G. Bunt. Bunt was an enthusiastic student of tides and his work on the Bristol observations had attracted the attention of Whewell who obtained grants for him from the British Association.[69] In 1836 he designed, and later erected at Bristol, his own version of the self-registering tide-gauge. He continued to supply Whewell with data for some years and was still active in the 1870s. (*see* Ch. 15).[70]

The information Whewell had collected about the diurnal inequality did nothing to solve the problem of reconciling it with the equilibrium theory. He was more fortunate in the pattern deduced for the tides of the North Sea which received confirmation from the work of Admiralty surveyors. Captain Martin White, working in the English Channel between 1812 and 1829, had found that the tidal streams continually altered their direction:

The motions of the tides throughout the English Channel never continue long in the same direction, or even on a straight line to any considerable distance, except in the immediate draughts of the different channels and passages, and close along the coast, but have a perpetual rotary disposition, making the circuit of the compass in twelve hours, and varying in strength as well as direction in proportion as they approach the land on either side.[71]

In the North Sea surveys verified the existence of a mid-point where as Whewell had predicted there was almost no rise and fall (the amphidrome). Captain William Hewett wrote to Beaufort in August 1840 describing observations made in H.M.S. *Fairy* in latitude 52°27'½ N, longitude 3° 14'½ E, showing a change of about a foot between high and low water.[72] His successor Captain John Washington (1800–1863) repeated the observations from H.M.S. *Shearwater* in July 1842 at a point somewhat further to the south and discovered a variation of 18 inches.[73]

The rotating tides in the North Sea were not an integral part of Whewell's theory; their very existence was taken by some as yet another proof that the simple equilibrium theory was unworkable. Their true significance, as a necessary consequence of the effect of the earth's rotation, escaped detection. At the same time the equilibrium theory was under attack from two further directions, first by Robert Fitzroy as a sailor and secondly by George Biddell Airy, the Astronomer Royal.

Fitzroy's target was Whewell's first paper on cotidal lines which had reached him on board the *Beagle* at the end of 1833. He and his officers had begun making observations with special care and over a period of time whenever they stayed in one place. At the Keeling Islands they erected a simple tide-gauge.[74] As Fitzroy said, it was impossible to make measurements without trying to see how they fitted into the general theory and it soon became apparent that neither the tides of the South Atlantic nor of the Pacific behaved as if they were generated in the Southern Ocean.

When the *Beagle* returned in 1836 Fitzroy wrote in the *Geographical Journal* expressing his doubts:

It may appear presumptious in a plain sailor attempting to offer an idea or two on the difficult subject of 'tides'; yet, with the utmost deference to those who *are* competent to reason upon the subject, I will venture to ask whether the supposition of Atlantic tides being principally caused by a great tide-wave coming from the Southern Ocean, is not a little difficult to reconcile with the facts that there is very little tide upon the coasts of Brazil, Ascension, and Guinea, and that in the mouth of the great river Plata there is little or no tide?[75]

In the appendix to his Narrative of the voyage, he elaborated on these objections.[76] The small tides in the narrowest part of the Atlantic, the south flowing stream on the coast of Brazil and the lack of any noticeable progression along the coast of Africa between the Cape and the Congo, areas for which Whewell had had nothing to go on, all seemed to him to rule out the possibility of the tide travelling up the Atlantic. Instead he asked whether it was not more likely that each ocean had its own tide? A possible explanation which his results suggested was that the sea oscillated to and fro in an east-west direction under the influence of the periodic pull of the moon on the water and the countering force of the earth's gravity as the moon sank below the horizon. He argued that the times of high water would depend on the breadth and depth of the ocean and tides would vary in different zones of the same ocean as a result of these factors. The principal ocean currents too should be seen as the result of the attraction of the sun and moon. Small tides at mid-ocean islands were the result of interference between the tidal oscillations.

Fitzroy dismissed the equilibrium theory because of its empirical shortcomings; Airy was principally concerned with its theoretical inadequacy. In 1842 he published an article on waves and tides in the *Encyclopaedia Metropolitana* in which he argued that tides are forced oscillations set up in each ocean individually.[61] The equilibrium theory had dealt with the problem as though the water were stationary, balanced at each moment by the forces acting on it. Airy went instead to Laplace's work and looked for a dynamic solution.

Airy had advanced the mathematical understanding of waves in canals and he successfully applied his conclusions to explain some aspects of the tides, particularly their behaviour in shallow water and in estuaries.[77] His

* tentative analogy of oceanic tides and progressive waves in canals provided fruitful as a basis for future work. To what extent[78] did he allow for the effect of the rotation of the earth? Hadley's concept of the deflection of winds blowing meridionally, to the right in the northern hemisphere, to the left in the southern hemisphere (*see* Ch. 10), had been extended by Coriolis and Poisson in the 1830s to cover movement in any horizontal direction, though the implication of their work for understanding the circulation of ocean and atmosphere was not spelled out until the 1850s.[78] Whewell's discovery of rotating tides in the North Sea, and the observations of Spence and White in the English Channel might have been interpreted as an example of the working of this principle in practice. Airy, far from admitting any significance for the rotary stream suggested by Whewell for the North Sea, denied its existence and preferred to explain the apparent rotation of tides as the result of interference between progressive waves travelling into the sea round the north and south of the British Isles and the no-tide points as the nodes of the stationary wave they created.[79]

During the early 1840s new hydrographic surveys were carried out in the Irish Sea under the direction of F. W. Beechey. Tidal observations formed part of the programme[80] and Airy believed that the results showed a situation which fitted in well with his previously expressed ideas.[81] The Irish Sea could be regarded as a canal connected with the ocean and its tides as a combination produced by the canal's own natural oscillation and the penetration of the oceanic tide. It seems, he wrote, that there is

a large stationary wave, having a node near Courtown, and making high water simultaneous in all parts of the inland or Irish Sea, and synchronic with low water in the exterior sea; and that there is mingled with it a very small progressive wave.[82]

Whewell felt that Airy had judged the equilibrium theory with unnecessary harshness; it had provided a basis for further understanding equally as good as Laplace's theory. He wrote, early in 1843,

You will perhaps be amused with my defence of the character* of the equilibrium theory; but it has long been my habitual employment to do what I can to prevent people from disprising that* which is really valuable in the history of the past; and your fierce disdain of this most useful step in tidology is a matter which I cannot pass over.[83]

Airy replied

You may refine your equilibrium-theory to any degree that you please, and you are not a whit nearer the truth as regards the moving fluid. A theory of motion, on the contrary, may be imperfect, exceedingly imperfect, but it is right as far as it goes.[84]

* The letters have been bound in such a way as to make these words partially illegible.

Whewell wrote back

Dear Airy,

I see that you stand to your guns very stoutly, as your ancient wont was, but you have not made me think that a theory which has done so much and been put forwards by such men as the equilibrium-theory of tides can properly, in a grave* scientific treatise on the same subject, be called 'contemptible' or 'despicable'. Nor have you persuaded me of any great superiority on the part of Laplace's.[85]

In the Bakerian Lecture which he gave to the Royal Society in December 1847, Whewell outlined the present state of his views.[86] The observations of 1835 and information which had come in since had made it impossible to go on thinking about tidal phenomena in terms of the equilibrium theory. It had turned out that cotidal lines on the ocean boundaries behaved very much like those on the shores of the North Sea, meeting the shore at an oblique angle, so that it was impossible to draw them across the ocean, as the incompatibility of the times of tides at mid-ocean islands with such lines already showed. The tide range at these islands was very small and it seemed reasonable to suppose that in the middle of the oceans there were points of no tide, as in the North Sea. This combination of large littoral tides and small mid-ocean tides could be explained, as by Airy, in terms of a stationary oscillation to either side of a nodal line in the centre of the ocean, turning into a progressive wave at the edges. It could equally well be explained by supposing the tide wave to revolve round a fixed centre. The tides in the North Sea could not be understood in any other way and Whewell believed, contrary to Airy, that the same thing was happening in the Irish Sea.

Whewell was anxious that new information on oceanic tides should be collected. This could better be done by organizing an expedition to concentrate on this subject alone than by relying on observations made incidentally on voyages for other purposes and in 1847 he and Sir James Clark Ross recommended to the British Association that the Admiralty be asked to mount an expedition similar to the voyage to study terrestrial magnetism which Ross had commanded between 1839 and 1843.[87] A two-year voyage would do a great deal to improve the knowledge of tides in the Indian and Pacific Oceans. This project came to nothing and in 1854 Whewell made a renewed plea for an expedition, as he said to "hunt" the tides, when discussing the results obtained by the United States Coastal Survey.[88] According to Admiral Day, Beaufort had put forward the proposal to the Admiralty in 1853 but without success.[89]

Meanwhile Airy's ideas were preferred to Whewell's and for many years the idea of rotating tides was discounted. As a result of further

* The letters have been bound in such a way as to make these words partially illegible.

hydrographic surveys in the 1840s Beechey admitted the existence of rotary streams in the English Channel but denied that they existed in the ocean at large.[90] This attitude seems to have been general over the next fifty years in the work of Samuel Haughton (1821–1896), Sir George Darwin and others. It was not until 1904 that Rollin A. Harris (1863–1918) reinstated the picture given by Whewell for the North Sea when he showed that the effect of the rotation of the earth is to deflect the tidal oscillations so that they appear to rotate round a fixed position, the amphidromic point.[91] When Harris compiled his chart of cotidal lines for the North Sea he found that Whewell's pattern of cotidal lines, based on the 1835 observations, was an accurate representation and that Airy's interpretation had been a retrograde step.[92] He also demonstrated the existence of amphidromic regimes in the oceans but denied that the earth's rotation had any decisive influence on their formation since they seemed adequately explained by interference between standing oscillations and some were centred on or near the equator where the deflecting force would in any case be nil. More recent theories have attempted to take all these factors into account.[93]

The main advance in the second half of the nineteenth century was the introduction of harmonic analysis and tides came to be looked at in quite a different way than had been usual in the 1830s. In the earlier period little had been said about the rise and fall of the water during the individual tide. Whewell had made special observations at Plymouth, Bristol and Liverpool and confirmed Sir Robert Moray's assertion of nearly two hundred years before by showing that the rate of rise and fall could be expressed as a sine curve.[94] Airy had studied observations made at Deptford in a paper which proved to be a forerunner of the analytical methods developed later.[95]

Lubbock and Whewell had succeeded in rescuing the study of tides from oblivion. Observations had multiplied throughout the world (*see* Ch. 13) and tide-tables were being developed and perfected in a process still going on today. They had only partially succeeded in bringing about a better understanding of the tides themselves; the subject remained, and still to some extent remains,[96] as Laplace called it, "le question le plus épineux de l'astronomie moderne".

12. NOTES

1. Joseph le Français de Lalande, *Astronomie*, 2nd ed., 4 vols, Paris (1771–1781). Vol. **4**, (1781), pp. 37, 87, 105.
2. *Ibid.* p. 22.
   Daniel Bernoulli, Leonard Euler, Colin Maclaurin and Antoine Cavalleri, *Pièces* * *qui ont remporté le prix de l'Académie Royale des Sciences en 1740*, Paris (1741). For Descartes's hypothesis, *see* Ch. 5.

3. Rollin A. Harris, *Manual of Tides*. Part I, *Report of the Superintendent of the United States Coast and Geodetic Survey during the year 1897*, Washington (1898). Appendix 8, "Introduction and historical treatment of the subject", pp. 415–421.
E. J. Aiton, "The contributions of Newton, Bernoulli and Euler to the theory of the tides", *Ann. Sci.* (1955). Vol. **11**, pp. 206–223.

4. Rollin A. Harris, *op. cit.* pp. 422–437.
Observations des Marées dans le Port de Brest, 1807–1835, Bureau des Longitudes, Paris (1843).

5. Murdoch Mackenzie, "The state of the tides in Orkney", *Phil. Trans.* (1749–1750). Vol. **46**, pp. 149–160.

6. Llewellyn Styles Dawson, *Memoirs of Hydrography*, Parts 1 and 2, Eastbourne (1885). Part 1, p. 3.

7. Murdoch Mackenzie, *Nautical Descriptions of the Coasts of Ireland, adapted to the several Charts in the Maritim Survey of Ireland*, London (1776).

8. Joseph le Français de Lalande, "Mémoire sur le flux et le reflux de la mer, et spécialement sur les marées des équinoxes", *Histoire de l'Académie Royale des Sciences* (1772). Part 1, pp. 297–324.

9. Warren R. Dawson, *The Banks Letters*, London (1958), p. 517. In fact the rise is slightly greater than Banks thought (*see* Ch. 9).

10. Joseph le Français de Lalande, "Mémoire sur le flux et le reflux de mer", *op. cit.* p. 299.

11. James Kingston Tuckey, *Maritime Geography* (1815). Vol. **1**, pp. 34–36.

12. L. S. Dawson, *op. cit.* pp. 13–15.

13. Graeme Spence, *An Account of the Tides at and about the Scilly Isles, with Tide Tables, 1792*, London (1794).

14. Thomas Young, under the cipher E.F.G.H., "A theory of the tides, including the consideration of resistance", *Nicholson's Journal* (1813). Vol. **35**, pp. 145–159, 217–227.

15. Thomas Young, "Tides", *Supplement to the 4th, 5th, and 6th editions of the Encyclopaedia Britannica*, Edinburgh (1824). Vol. **6**, pp. 658–675. Reprinted in: *Miscellaneous Works of the late Thomas Young, M.D., F.R.S. &c.* (ed. George Peacock and John Leitch), 3 vols, London (1855). Vol. **2**, pp. 291–335.

16. *Ibid.* p. 293.

17. Sir John Lubbock, *An Elementary Treatise on the Tides*, London (1839).

18. William Whewell, "On the empirical laws of the tides in the Port of London; with some reflexions on the theory", *Phil. Trans.* (1834). Vol. **124**, pp. 15–45; p. 16.

19. L. S. Dawson, *op. cit.* p. 84.

20. *British Almanac and Companion* (1830), pp. 5–6, 49–67.

21. Sir John Lubbock, "Report on the Tides", *Report of the first and second Meetings of the British Association for the Advancement of Science* (1835), pp. 189–195.

22. *Ibid.* p. 194.
Sir John Lubbock, "On the tides", *Phil. Trans.* (1832). Vol. **122**, pp. 51–55.

23. Henry R. Palmer, "Description of a graphical registrer of tides and winds", *Phil. Trans.* (1831). Vol. **121**, pp. 209–213.

24. Sir John Lubbock, "Report on the Tides", *op. cit.* p. 192.

25. "The tide gauge at Sheerness", *Naut. Mag.* (1832). Vol. **1**, pp. 401–404.

26. Sir John Lubbock, "Note on the tides", *Phil. Trans.* (1833). Vol. **123**, pp. 19–22.

27. William Whewell, "Directions for tide observations. The diurnal difference of the tides", *Naut. Mag.* (1834). Vol. **3**, pp. 532–537.
28. The cumulative figures are given in the *Report of the seventeenth meeting of the British Association, 1847* (1848), pp. xxii–xxvi.
29. Walter F. Cannon, "William Whewell, F.R.S.: contributions to science and learning", *Notes Rec. R. Soc. Lond.* (1964). Vol. **19**, no. 2, pp. 176–191.
30. Isaac Todhunter, *William Whewell, D.D.*, 2 vols, London (1876). Vol. **2**, *Correspondence*, pp. 134–135, Whewell to Lubbock, 12 November 1831.
31. Sir John Lubbock, "Report on the Tides", *op. cit.* p. 194.
32. Isaac Todhunter, *op. cit.* Vol. **2**, pp. 152–153, Whewell to Herschel, 14 January 1833.
33. William Whewell, "Essay towards a first approximation to a map of cotidal lines", *Phil. Trans.* (1833). Vol. **123**, pp. 147–236.
34. *Ibid.* p. 147.
35. William Whewell, "On the empirical laws of the tide in the Port of London; with some reflexions on the theory", *Phil. Trans.* (1834). Vol. **124**, p. 43.
36. William Whewell, "Essay towards a first approximation to a map of cotidal lines", *op. cit.* p. 187.
37. *Ibid.* pp. 215–217.
38. *Ibid.* pp. 234–235.
39. Isaac Todhunter, *op. cit.* Vol. **2**, pp. 167–168, Whewell to Lubbock, 27 July 1833.
40. Sir John Lubbock, "Discussion of tide observations made at Liverpool", *Phil. Trans.* (1835). Vol. **125**, pp. 275–299.
    William Whewell, "Researches on the tides—fourth series. On the empirical laws of the tides in the Port of Liverpool", *Phil. Trans.* (1836). Vol. **126**, pp. 1–15.
    Sir John Lubbock, "Discussion of tide observations made at Liverpool", *ibid.* pp. 57–73.
    William Whewell, "Researches on the tides—fifth series. On the solar inequality and on the diurnal inequality of the tides at Liverpool", *ibid.* pp. 131–147.
41. William Whewell, "Memoranda and directions for tide observations", *Naut. Mag.* (1833). Vol. **2**, pp. 662–665. Vol. **3** (1834), pp. 98–102, 170–171, 532–537 *See also: Manual of Scientific Enquiry; prepared for the use of Her Majesty's Navy, and adapted for travellers in general*, J. F. W. Herschel and others, London (1849).
42. William Whewell, "On the results of tide observations made in June 1834 at the Coast Guard Stations in Great Britain and Ireland", *Phil. Trans.* (1835). Vol. **125**, pp. 83–90.
43. Isaac Todhunter, *op. cit.* Vol. **2**, pp. 201–202, Whewell to Quetelet, 3 February 1835.
44. William Whewell, "Essay towards a first approximation to a map of cotidal lines", *op. cit.* p. 148.*
45. William Whewell, "Researches on the tides—sixth series. On the results of an extensive system of tide observations made on the coasts of Europe and America in June 1835", *Phil. Trans.* (1836). Vol. **126**, pp. 289–341.
46. Isaac Todhunter, *op. cit.* Vol. **2**, pp. 215–216, Whewell to H. Wilkinson, 2 June 1835.
47. William Whewell, "Researches on the tides—sixth series" *op. cit.* p. 298.
48. *Ibid.* p. 304.

49. William Whewell, "Researches on the tides—seventh series. On the diurnal inequality of the height of the tide, especially at Plymouth and at Singapore; and on the mean level of the sea", *Phil. Trans.* (1837). Vol. **127**, pp. 75–85.
50. Isaac Todhunter, *op. cit.* Vol. **2**, pp. 242–244, Whewell to Herschel, 10 June 1836.
51. *Ibid.* pp. 247–250, Whewell to Herschel, 4 December 1836.
52. Sir John Lubbock, "On the tides at the Port of London", *Phil. Trans.* (1836). Vol. **126**, pp. 217–266.
53. William Whewell, "Researches on the tides—eleventh series. On certain tide observations made in the Indian Seas", *Phil. Trans.* (1839). Vol. **129**, pp. 163–166.
    Idem, "Additional note to the eleventh series of researches on the tides", *Phil. Trans.* (1840). Vol. **130**, pp. 161–174.
54. William Whewell, "Researches on the tides—eighth series. On the progress of the diurnal inequality wave along the coasts of Europe", *Phil. Trans.* (1837). Vol. **127**, pp. 227–244.
55. William Whewell, "Researches on the tides—ninth series. On the determination of the laws of tides from short series of observations", *Phil. Trans.* (1838). Vol. **128**, pp. 231–247.
56. William Whewell to Mary Somerville, 5 January 1838. Letter in the Mary Somerville Papers, Somerville College, Oxford.
57. Hermann Thorade, *Probleme der Wasserwellen*, Hamburg (1931), pp. 1–11.
58. William Whewell, "Essay towards a first approximation to a map of cotidal lines", *op. cit.* pp. 211–213.
    In 1835 Sir Charles Lyell (1797–1875) asked Whewell if Laplace's estimates were reliable. Whewell pointed out that they had been calculated for a sphere covered with water and were not intended to be taken literally. He himself had calculated 50,000 feet as the depth of the mid-Atlantic from information on the velocity of the tide but did not consider the figure reliable since, though velocity certainly depended on depth, he did not regard wave theory as sufficiently developed to give the exact relationship, Isaac Todhunter, *op. cit.* Vol. **2**, pp. 206–209.
59. John Scott Russell, "Experimental researches into the laws of certain hydrodynamical phenomena that accompany the motion of floating bodies", *Trans. R. Soc. Edinb.* (1840). Vol. **14**, pp. 47–109.
60. Report of the committee on waves, appointed by the British Association at Bristol in 1836, and consisting of Sir John Robison, K. H., Secretary of the Royal Society of Edinburgh, and John Scott Russell, Esq., M.A., F.R.S. Edin., *Report on the seventh meeting of the British Association for the Advancement of Science, 1837* (1838). Part 1, pp. 417–496.
61. George Biddell Airy, "Tides and Waves", *Encyclopaedia Metropolitana*, 26 vols (1845). Vol. **5**, pp. 241–396.
62. Quoted by John Walker (*ca.* 1780). Lectures on Natural History, MS. in the Edinburgh University Library.
63. J. K. Tuckey, *Maritime Geography* (1815). Vol. **1**, p. 21.
64. John Augustus Lloyd, "Account of levellings carried across the Isthmus of Panamá, to ascertain the relative height of the Pacific Ocean at Panamá, and of the Atlantic at the mouth of the river Chagres", *Phil. Trans.* (1830). Vol. **120**, pp. 59–68.
65. François Arago, *Sur les phénomènes de la mer* in *Œuvres* (ed. Barral). Vol. **9**, (1857) pp. 585–598.

66. "Permanent difference of level in different parts of the ocean considered", *Naut. Mag.* (1837). Vol. **6**, pp. 306–313, 383–391. Some observations had been made in the British Isles. John Robison had measured the levels on the Forth-Clyde canal and the tides at either end and found the difference in level not more than a foot—"Observations on the difference of level of the east and west seas", *Edinburgh Philosophical Journal* (1821–1822). Vol. **6**, pp. 69–71.

67. H. T. de la Beche, "On the influence of atmospheric pressure on the tidal waters of Cornwall and Devon", *Edinburgh New Philosophical Journal* (1838–1839). Vol. **26**, pp. 415–419.

68. William Whewell, "Account of a level line, measured from the Bristol Channel to the English Channel, during the year 1837–8, by Mr. Bunt", *Report on the eighth meeting of the British Association for the Advancement of Science, 1883* (1839). Part 1, pp. 1–11.
    William Whewell, "Researches on the tides—tenth series. On the laws of low water at the Port of Plymouth, and on the permanency of mean water", *Phil. Trans.* (1839). Vol. **129**, pp. 151–161.

69. Isaac Todhunter, *op. cit.* Vol. **2**, pp. 237–238. Whewell to Rev. W. Vernon Harcourt, 27 May 1836.

70. *Report on the sixth meeting of the British Association for the Advancement of Science, 1836* (1837). Part 2, p. 130; and following reports.
    William Whewell, "Description of a new tide-gauge, constructed by Mr. T. G. Bunt, and erected on the eastern bank of the River Avon, in front of Hotwell House, Bristol, 1837", *Phil. Trans.* (1838). Vol. **128**, pp. 249–251.

71. Martin White, *Sailing Directions for the English Channel*, London (1835), p. 205.

72. "Letter from the late Capt. Hewett to Capt. Beaufort, R.N. (referred to in a communication by Prof. Whewell)", *Report of the eleventh meeting of the British Association for the Advancement of Science, 1841* (1842). Part 2, pp. 32–35.

73. John Washington, "Tide observations—North Sea—Professor Whewell's Theory", *Naut. Mag.* (1842), pp. 566–569.

74. Robert Fitzroy, *Narrative of the Surveying Voyages of H.M.S. Adventure and Beagle, between the years 1826 and 1836, describing their examination of the southern shores of South America, and the Beagle's circumnavigation of the globe*, 3 vols, London (1839). Vol. **2**, p. 629.

75. Robert Fitzroy, "Sketch of the surveying voyages of H.M.S. *Adventure* and *Beagle*, 1825–1836", *Geograph. J.* (1836). Vol. **6**, pp. 311–343.

76. Robert Fitzroy, *Narrative* (1839). Appendix to Vol. **2**, pp. 277–297.

77. R. A. Harris, *Manual of Tides, op. cit.* pp. 444–451.

78. H. L. Burstyn, "The deflecting force and Coriolis", *Bulletin of the American Meteorological Society* (1966). Vol. **47**, no. 11, pp. 890–891. The late Dr A. T. Doodson, however, argued that Laplace and Airy employed the full concept—"Oceanic tides", *Adv. Geophys.* (1958). Vol. **5**, p. 122.

79. G. B. Airy, *op. cit.* paragraphs 525–528.

80. F. W. Beechey, "Report of observations made upon the tides in the Irish Sea, and upon the great similarity of tidal phenomena of the English and Irish Channels, and the importance of extending the experiments round the Land's End and up the English Channel", *Phil. Trans.* (1848). Vol. **138**, pp. 105–116.

81. G. B. Airy, "On the laws of the tides on the coasts of Ireland as inferred from an extensive series of observations made in connection with the Ordnance Survey of Ireland", *Phil. Trans.* (1845). Vol. **135**, pp. 1–124.

82. *Ibid.* p. 121.
83. G. B. Airy MSS, Royal Greenwich Observatory, Whewell to Airy, 18 Jan- *
uary 1843.
Isaac Todhunter, *op. cit.* Vol. **2**, pp. 306–308.
84. G. B. Airy MSS, Royal Greenwich Observatory, Airy to Whewell, 14 Feb- *
ruary 1843.
85. *Ibid.* Whewell to Airy, 22 February 1843. *
Isaac Todhunter, *op. cit.* Vol. **2**, pp. 308–310.
86. William Whewell, "Researches on the tides—thirteenth series. On the tides of
the Pacific, and on the diurnal inequality", *Phil. Trans.* (1848). Vol. **138**, pp.
1–29.
87. "Report by the Rev. W. Whewell, D.D. and Sir James Clark Ross upon the
recommendation of an expedition for the purpose of completing our knowledge
of the tides", *Report of the seventeenth meeting of the British Association for the
Advancement of Science, 1847* (1848). Part 1, pp. 134–135.
88. William Whewell, "On Mr. Superintendent Bache's tide observations",
*Report on the twenty-fourth meeting of the British Assocation for the Advance-
ment of Science, 1854* (1855). Part 2, p. 28.
89. Sir Archibald Day, *The Admiralty Hydrographic Service, 1795–1919*, London
(1967), p. 58.
90. F. W. Beechey, "Report of further observations upon the tidal streams of the
North Sea and English Channel, with remarks upon the laws by which these
streams appear to be governed", *Phil. Trans.* (1851). Vol. **141**, part 2, pp. 703–
718.
91. Rollin A. Harris, *Manual of Tides*—Part IVB, *Report of the Superintendent of
the United States Coast and Geodetic Survey during the year 1904*, Washington
(1904). Appendix 5, "Cotidal lines of the world".
92. *Ibid.* pp. 377–378.
93. Albert Defant, *Physical Oceanography*, 2 vols, London (1961). Vol. **2**, pp. 496–
503.
94. William Whewell, "Researches on the tides—twelfth series. On the laws of
the rise and fall of the sea's surface during each tide", *Phil. Trans.* (1840).
Vol. **130**, pp. 255–272.
95. G. B. Airy, "On the laws of the rise and fall of the tide in the River Thames",
Phil. Trans. (1842). Vol. **132**, pp. 1–8.
96. D. E. Cartwright, "Deep sea tides", *Sci. J.* (1969). Vol. **5**, no. 1, pp. 60–67.

Addenda et Corrigenda

p.261, fig. caption, 1.3: *after* (1836) insert vol. 126

p.268, 1.1: *instead* provided *read* proved

p.270, n,2, 1.2: *after* Paris *insert: Sur le Flux et Reflux de la Mer*

p.272, n.44, 1.2: *insert* (Bacon thought it was the same, see p. 50)

p.275, nn. 83, 84, 85: *The archives of the Royal Greenwich Observatory are
now held in the University Library, Cambridge*

13. THE THRESHOLD OF THE DEEP OCEAN

SETTING aside Lubbock and Whewell's work on tides, the 1830s was not an auspicious decade for marine science. In spite of the existence of specialized works on the physics of the sea, notably by Marcet, Lenz and Parrot, the general standard of writing on the subject did not improve, in fact it declined. No one did for the new oceanography what Lyell had done for the new geology and without the cohesiveness provided by such a recognizable authority past achievements survived only fragmentarily. Scientific effort throughout the middle years of the century was focused on the physical sciences and on biology. With a few exceptions physical oceanography was left to the Victorian scientific sub-culture and the effect was stultifying.

It seems that other environmental sciences, geology and meteorology, shared something of the same malaise but in oceanography the problems were increasingly exacerbated by the wide range of researches involved, still not identified with each other by their common objective. The main problem therefore was one of communication, particularly between specialists in various branches of science and the seamen, surveyors and others who were responsible for most of the new work done at this time. Specialization was becoming more intense and the era was over in which Count Rumford could write in a scientific paper of the heat-retaining propensities of stewed apples. Engineers worked in ignorance of the refinements of mathematical theory and geographers failed to appreciate the work of physicists. As a result much conscientious work at sea failed to give the results it deserved and anachronistic ideas survived long after they ceased to have any validity. This is not to say that no progress was made; after the lean years of the 1830s there was a considerable and increasing extension of knowledge and techniques in some areas but until about 1870 the theoretical framework remained rigid and irresponsive to change to a degree that writers both close to the time and at a hundred years' distance find hard to account for.

The second problem was the old one of the difficulty of organizing marine research on a meaningful basis in the absence of government support. It was not possible for any one person to do for the sea what H. T. de la Beche did for the land when he founded the Geological Survey. Much information was still collected by people with a keen amateur interest in the subject. Wauchope and John Davy repeated the observations they had made in 1816,[1] and there were other instances of the kind[2] but the time had passed when individual effort could have much influence on the development of knowledge. Schemes for co-ordinating scientific material were put forward from time to time but it was long before any of them became effective. The most obvious opportunity for extending oceanographical knowledge in the 1830s and 1840s was through voyages of exploration which reached their apogee at this time, the most important being the French expeditions in the *Vénus*, 1836–1839, under Captain Abel du Petit-Thouars (1793–1864) and the *Astrolabe* and *Zelée*, 1837–1840, commanded by Dumont d'Urville, the American exploring expedition, 1838–1842, led by Charles Wilkes (1798–1877), Sir James Clark Ross's voyage in H.M.S. *Erebus* and *Terror*, 1839–1843, and Sir John Franklin's voyage to the North West Passage and the expeditions sent in search of him. All these ventures, except, understandably, the rescue voyages, devoted a considerable amount of effort to marine research but, largely because of the reasons already hinted at, the observations were not always made on sound premises or their results fully utilized, so that they in some cases actually hindered rather than helped the subject's development.

This was particularly true in the study of deep sea temperatures.[3] The work of Marcet, Lenz and others had not succeeded in eradicating the widely held assumptions that ordinary maximum and minimum thermometers would record accurately at any depth and that sea water had the same point of maximum density as fresh water. The idea sometimes held is that falsehoods contradict each other and that truths can be distinguished by their consistency but in this case it was the falsehoods which were consistent. They received further reinforcement in 1833 with the publication by Dumont d'Urville of the temperature observations made on the first voyage of the *Astrolabe*.[4]

At the time when the voyage was being planned, Dumont d'Urville said, several members of the Academy had expressed the wish that measurements should be made of deep-sea temperature. He therefore went to Arago who gave him instructions and self-registering maximum and minimum thermometers, made by Bunten.[5] During the three-year voyage he made a number of observations at depths of up to almost 1,200 fathoms. The thermometer was encased in a metal cylinder before being lowered and this generally came up with water inside it. The first time it was lowered to 1,000 fathoms both it and the case were broken and a new case had to be made. On another occasion when the cylinder came up full of water from a depth of 1,160 fathoms someone accidentally touched the bulb of the thermometer and it flew to pieces. D'Urville realized that this great pressure might be distorting his results. He wrote

Cet accident me conduisit à penser que la compression de l'eau, introduite dans le cylindre à l'état de rosée très-tenue, était devenue elle-même si forte sur les parois du tube, et particulièrement sur celles du réservoir, qu'elle avait altéré sensiblement sa forme et son volume. Il en était résulté que l'alcohol avait offert une résistance qui avait empêché l'index du *minimum* de monter assez haut, et par conséquent de marquer un degré aussi abaissé qu'il eût dû le faire; au contraire, par suite de cette altération du tube, les deux colonnes de mercure avaient fini par indiquer une température beaucoup trop élevée.[6]

On his return home D'Urville sent the results of his observations to Arago but when two years had elapsed and the scientists had done nothing about them he decided to write them up himself.[5] He was determined to make a thorough job of it and collected information about almost all the important observations hitherto made which he arranged synoptically with regard to depth and latitude but without making any allowance for the pressure effect in deep water. They seemed to show that below a depth of about 600 fathoms the entire ocean was full of water of about 4·4°C. The depth at which this temperature was reached varied with latitude, rising from polar regions to reach the surface between 60° and 40° and then sinking again towards the tropics. D'Urville noticed, as had Hörner,[7] that at the equator cold water rose nearer to the surface than at corresponding depths in the tropics. He reasoned that continual evaporation at the surface must cause the water below to rise towards the surface and that in its turn it would be replaced by water coming in from either side.

Although aware of the work of Erman, who had confirmed Marcet's results,[8] D'Urville reasserted the idea that salt water behaves like fresh water and reaches its maximum density before freezing because, having neglected to take into account what he himself had seen of the effect of pressure on thermometers, it seemed to be the logical way of explaining the results. Like Delamétherie (*see* Ch. 10), he pointed to the region either side of latitude 50° as the place where surface water, whose temperature depended on atmospheric conditions, would reach this point and sink to the bottom of the sea.

D'Urville expounded the 4°C theory with far more thoroughness than anyone before and was often afterwards thought to have invented it. However scientific circles in France were at least partially more enlightened by this time and the observations made by A. Bérard in the Mediterranean in 1831–1832,[9] and on the *Vénus* expedition were obtained with protected thermometers.

Du Petit-Thouars on the *Vénus* was fortunate in having a physicist with the expedition—Urbain Dortet de Tessan (1804–1879). Like Kotzebue's second voyage with Lenz, the voyage of the *Vénus* achieved more in physical oceanography than voyages in which all the physical scientific work devolved on the ships' officers. Tessan took a lively interest in the problems of making observations at sea and in addition to his work with temperatures studied currents, waves, the pressure and transparency of sea water and the possibility of echo-sounding.[10]

The temperature observations recorded on the *Vénus* during her voyage round the world were made with Six thermometers supplied by Bunten. In general they relied on protecting them from pressure with a metal case but a pressure correction of 1·7°C per thousand fathoms had been worked out for one instrument.[11] This enabled results to be obtained down to about 2,000 metres but below that the thermometers and their cases were crushed by the weight of water. After losing one at 3,914 metres Tessan wondered whether Bréguet's bi-metallic thermometer[12] could not be adapted for use at sea. It would still be necessary to work out a pressure correction but this should not be difficult.[13]

With the precautions adopted against the effect of pressure on thermometers the results obtained by the *Vénus* were very different from those of most previous voyages but very similar to those obtained by Lenz (*see* Ch. 11). Many of the deeper observations gave figures well below 4°C and the lowest value in deep water, 2·3°C, was measured in 1,950 metres in latitude 43° 47′ S, the region where according to the 4°C theory the sea was at that temperature from top to bottom. Arago wrote

S'il s'est glissé des erreurs dans ces déterminations, elles ont dû être toutes positives, comme il est facile de s'en convaincre. Les chiffres vrais ne peuvent, en aucun cas, surpasser ceux que nous venons de citer. Il faut donc espérer que le fameux nombre +4°, 4, si étourdiment emprunté aux observations comparatives faites à la surface et au fond des lacs d'*eau douce* de Suisse, cessera de paraître dans des dissertations *ex professo*, comme la limite au-dessous de laquelle la température du fond des mers ne saurait jamais descendre.[14]

In a sense Arago had only himself to blame, on account of his earlier inattention, that far from being expunged from people's minds, the 4°C theory continued to recrudesce not only in popular works like the volume on hydrostatics by Dionysius Lardner (1793–1859) in the *Cabinet Cyclopaedia*[15] and the equivalent works in France[16] but in the writings of very eminent scientists. It is in this respect that the lack of communication between scientists showed itself at its strongest and least explicable. Succeeding investigations continued to improve on Marcet's rough figure of 22°F as the temperature of maximum density of sea water.[8] While it was conceivable that these results might be overlooked by the superficial observer it is almost incredible that the reiterated attacks on the 4°C theory by two of the most influential writers on marine matters of the mid-nineteenth century, Alexander von Humboldt[17] and, rather later, Matthew Fontaine Maury (1806–1873),[18] should have had so little apparent effect. Yet when the three expeditions were sent out almost simultaneously by Great Britain, France and the United States, they were all allowed to fall into the same trap and all put a considerable amount of effort into collecting information with unprotected thermometers, in the firm belief that their results were yet further evidence in favour of a theory of unimpeachable scientific rectitude.[19]

For his voyage in the *Erebus* and *Terror*, Sir James Clark Ross had instructions drawn up by a Royal Society committee on physics and meteorology.[20] The main scientific purpose of the voyage was to measure the earth's magnetic field in the southern hemisphere and to establish the position of the south magnetic pole but apart from this the committee also directed Ross to make meteorological observations, to measure tides and currents and ocean depths, to observe temperatures and to collect samples of water at different depths in the sea.

Apart from giving him a general idea of what was expected in the way of ocean circulation Ross's instructions gave no hint of the vexed state of the subject and one can only assume that those who drew them up had no appreciation of it themselves. Nor did they say anything about the necessity of protecting thermometers, presumably for the same reason. The result was that throughout the three-year voyage Ross conscientiously observed temperatures at depths as great as 1,200 fathoms but, though he had sent out to him during the voyage thermometers specially made to stand up to such pressures without breaking, these were clearly not designed to reduce distortion for he never recorded a temperature lower than 39·5°F at these depths.[21]

Not unnaturally Ross formulated conclusions very like those of Dumont d'Urville. He plotted what he called "the circle of mean temperature" in about latitude 56° S, where, he believed,

the mean temperature of the sea obtains throughout its entire depth, forming a boundary, or kind of neutral ground, between the two great thermic basins of the ocean. To the north of this circle the sea has become warmer than its mean temperature, by reason of the sun's heat, which it has absorbed, elevating its temperature at various depths in different latitudes. So that the line of mean temperature of 39·5°, in latitude 45° S, has descended to the depth of 600 fathoms; and at the equatorial and tropical regions, this mark of the limit of the sun's influence is found at the depth of about 1,200 fathoms; beneath which the ocean maintains its unvarying mean temperature of 39·5°, whilst that of the surface is about 78°.

So likewise to the south of the circle of mean temperature, we find that in the absence of an equal solar supply, the radiation of the heat of the ocean into space occasions the sea to be of a colder temperature as we advance to the south; and near the 70th degree of latitude, we find the line of mean temperature has descended to the depth of 750 fathoms; beneath which again, to the greatest depths, the temperature of 39·5° obtains, whilst that of the surface is 30°.[22]

It is interesting to note that Ross's positions for the circle of mean temperature agree very closely with those for the Antarctic convergence where the cold polar water meets and sinks below the warm water of lower latitudes. Ross was right in believing the area to be significant though wrong in reasoning why. The final touch of incredibility is given to the episode by the existence of a letter, actually printed with the instructions, from Humboldt to the Earl of Minto, First Lord of the Admiralty, calling attention to Lenz's results and to the fallacy of believing that sea water has the same point of maximum density as fresh water.[23]

In general the history of marine biology is outside the scope of this book but at this stage its development shares some of the puzzling features to be found in physical oceanography. The subject advanced rapidly during the early years of the nineteenth century and at the time under discussion one of the principal authorities was Edward Forbes (1815–1854) the Manx naturalist.[24] In 1842 Forbes sailed in H.M.S. *Beacon*, surveying in the eastern Mediterranean, and with the assistance of Lieutenant Thomas Abel Spratt (1811–1888) he studied the distribution of marine animals in the Ægean. He found that the different species were grouped according to depth and defined zones of characteristic fauna between the surface and a depth of 300 fathoms which he considered to be the limit of animal life.[25] He later applied the same kind of classification when studying the littoral fauna in European waters. The same conclusion was arrived at independently by the Swedish zoologist Sven Lovén (1809–1895) though he left open the actual limit of life. [26] This assumption was magnified into a doctrine by their readers. The only justification needed for the idea, they supposed, was the eminently reasonable argument that below this point the pressure, combined with lack of light and heat, must render life untenable. As in the confusion over temperatures evidence to the contrary was generally ignored and, if it became too obtrusive, was argued away, no matter how deviously, so long as the attractive generalization remained intact.[27]

The evidence for the existence of life at great depths was in fact already quite considerable. By a strange coincidence Sir John Ross, whose deep sea temperatures stuck in the gullets of those who had swallowed the 40°F theory, had also found living creatures in his deep soundings but this, like the temperatures, was usually forgotten or discounted.[28] Sir James Clark

Ross was aware of the importance of this particular achievement and had with him in the *Erebus* a deep-sea clamm and dredge with which he obtained creatures in sea floor deposits taken from depths of 300 fathoms and over. He wrote, referring also to his uncle's work,

It was interesting amongst these creatures to recognise several that I had been in the habit of taking in equally high northern latitudes; and although contrary to the general belief of naturalists, I have no doubt that from however great a depth we may be enabled to bring up the mud and stones of the bed of the ocean we shall find them teeming with animal life; the extreme pressure at the greatest depth does not appear to affect these creatures; hitherto we have not been able to determine this point beyond a thousand fathoms, but from that depth several shellfish have been brought up with the mud.[29]

He went on to suggest that these animals might be able to withstand still greater pressures since if they were found in both hemispheres it suggested that they were able to traverse the equatorial regions at great depths.

Another person who found creatures at great depths was the French scientist Georges Aimé (1813–1846) who while sounding off the coast of Algeria in the early 1840s brought up animals of different kinds from depths of up to 1,800 metres.[30] The list could be extended.[31] Spratt himself enlarged Forbes's limit by at least 100 fathoms as a result of further researches on his own.[32]

Unlike the study of temperatures, to which their contribution was sometimes equivocal, the voyages of exploration did provide a positive incentive to marine research by pioneering techniques of deep sea sounding. The *Vénus* made several attempts, putting out up to 4,000 metres of line without finding bottom.[33] Sir James Clark Ross's instructions directed him to make soundings, though they were not very encouraging about the possibilities of lead and line and suggested that he might throw a shell over the side and listen for the noise of its explosion on the bottom.[34] Ross, however, relied on lead and line run out from the ships' boats and after several vain attempts at finding the bottom with a 600 fathoms' line he had one 3,600 fathoms long made on board and on 3 January 1840, in latitude 27° 26′ S, longitude 17° 29′ W, he recorded a depth of 2,425 fathoms.[35] Recently this area was surveyed by the U.S.S.S. *Discoverer* which found the actual depth at the position given by Ross to be 2,100 fathoms.[36]

Most of Ross's soundings were in the 2,000 fathom range but in the Weddell Sea, in March 1843, 4,000 fathoms of line ran off the reel without apparently reaching bottom.[37] This depth—known as the Ross Deep—was accepted by geographers until after the turn of the century but in 1924 Lieutenant-Commander R. T. Gould, using an account of Ross's in the Admiralty archives, showed that although Ross measured the time taken to run out by every 100 fathoms of line, he missed the first slight increase in the regular rate at which it was retarded, and that this was the point at which the weight hit bottom.[38] Ross had not noticed the check because the line continued to be carried out, probably by an undercurrent. Gould gave a depth of 2,200 fathoms for the sounding which was consistent with a sounding of 2,660 fathoms made by the *Scotia* in 1904 a few miles away. Three months later the same thing happened again and this time Ross lost 4,600 fathoms of line in latitude 15° S.

Assessing Ross's contribution to oceanography in general, Gould wrote:

When one considers the enormous amount of oceanographical and other work which Ross, practically unassisted by a scientific staff, and handicapped by his arduous duties and responsibilities as leader of the expedition, undertook and completed in the course of this celebrated voyage, the wonder is not that he made mistakes, but that he did not make more.[39]

This is by and large a fair assessment. Ross had no scientists as such on the voyage and Joseph Dalton Hooker (1817–1911) who went as naturalist had the official post of assistant surgeon to the expedition. As far as oceanographical work was concerned, Ross was poorly advised and can scarcely be blamed himself for not having kept up with research which was so widely neglected by others. On a similar occasion later on he was more fortunate. During the winter of 1848–1849, which he spent ice-bound in H.M.S. *Enterprize* on the way to search for Sir John Franklin, he observed the relation between variations in atmospheric pressure and changes in the level of the ocean.[40] He thought at the time that no one had ever noticed this before but was saved from the embarrassment of repeating it in print by a conversation with Whewell who told him of the work of Daussy and Lubbock (*see* Ch. 12).

As for not recognizing the point when the lead touched the bottom, Ross was by no means alone in this. During the 1840s and early 1850s, before the submarine telegraph cables were thought of, random deep sea sounding enjoyed something of a vogue and Ross's attempts seem to have been influential in setting the fashion. His example was followed by a number of British surveying officers including Sir Edward Belcher (1799–1877) in H.M.S. *Samarang* in 1843,[41] Captain Henry Kellett (1806–1875) in H.M.S. *Herald* in 1845,[42] Captain Owen Stanley (1811–1850) in H.M.S. *Rattlesnake*[43] and Captain Barnett in H.M.S. *Thunder* in 1848–1849.[44] On these attempts either the line ceased to run out at a fairly moderate depth or broke under the strain. Barnett attempted to use wire with the same result.

Meanwhile, American surveying officers had adopted the idea, which they attributed to Sir Francis Beaufort, of using a fairly small lead, of a few pounds' weight as opposed to Ross's several hundred, and a thin line of silk or twine. With this they began to achieve some startling results by allowing the line to run out till it stopped. In 1849 an apparent depth of 5,700 fathoms was measured by the U.S. schooner *Taney*.[45] In 1852 Lieutenant I. P. Parker in the U.S.S. *Congress* reported a sounding of 8,300 fathoms in the South Atlantic. At Rio, the *Congress* encountered H.M.S. *Herald* under the command of Captain Henry Denham and presented her with 15,000 fathoms of line. With this Denham made a sounding of 7,706 fathoms, also in the South Atlantic.[46] A sounding of similar magnitude was reported by an American ship in the Pacific.[47] This curiosity was not confined to the surveyors. When Darwin's co-originator of the theory of evolution, Alfred Russel Wallace (1823–1913), embarked in H.M. brig *Frolic* to sail to the East Indies, he found that her commander had on his own initiative got together equipment for making deep sea soundings.[48]

Depths in the region of 7,000 or 8,000 fathoms were not outrageous in the light of current theory on waves and tides; the Rev. Samuel Haughton for instance spoke in terms of water 11 miles deep in mid-Atlantic.[49] In fact the results were greatly exaggerated. Depths over about 3,500 fathoms make up only a small part of the ocean floor and are mainly confined to the oceanic trenches whose existence was not yet suspected and even here the greatest depth only just exceeds 6,000 fathoms.

The uncertainty and time-consuming nature of soundings, even when the line and weight were not hauled in, gave a new urgency to the search for a reliable sounding machine and many more or less novel ways of measuring depth were suggested.[50] John Ericsson (1803–1889) had invented a way of trapping water in a glass tube as pressure increased.[51] F. H. Walferdin (1795–1880) suggested, and successfully tried, an unprotected thermometer as a pressure gauge.[52] Maxwell Lyte proposed using the effect of pressure on a piston.[53] In practice, a strengthened version of Massey's sounding machine was usually used in this country and in France a similar device invented by the engineer Le Coëntre.[54]

In 1848 F. W. Beechey corresponded with Sir John Herschel over the problem.[55] Beechey was concerned to find an accurate way of measuring depths of up to 100 fathoms. He found Ericsson's lead unreliable under 20 and over 40 fathoms. They discussed a number of valid ways of measuring depth indirectly by pressure; the difficulty lay in adapting an instrument to be able to stand up to use at sea without sacrificing precision.

A possibility often discussed at this time was of using sound waves to measure depth, by exploding a shell either on the sea floor and listening for the sound, or near the surface and listening for the echo.[56] The common source of these ideas was a series of experiments made in 1826 in Lake Geneva. In this instance sound was propagated horizontally by ringing a bell under water and detected through a listening tube held in the water nine miles away.[57] In 1833 Henry Fox Talbot (1800–1877) suggested using an exploding shell to propagate sound from the floor of the sea to the surface.[58]

Following Talbot's article in the *Philosophical Magazine* there were some rather ineffectual criticisms, including the strange idea, found only in works on the periphery of marine science, that pressure at great depths greatly increased the density of the water. The author believed that

Mr. Talbot's shell would *float* long before it could reach the bottom, as it is now pretty well ascertained that at a certain depth the sea is specifically heavier than any body which we are acquainted with, consequently a cast-iron shell could not penetrate it.[59]

Wyville Thomson (1830–1882) remembered, in a characteristically striking passage,

There was a curious popular notion, in which I well remember sharing when a boy, that, in going down, the sea-water became gradually under the pressure heavier and heavier, and that all the loose things in the sea floated at different levels, according to their specific weight: skeletons of men, anchors and shot and cannon, and last of all broad gold pieces wrecked in the loss of many a galleon on the Spanish Main . . . beneath which there lay all the depth of clear still water, which was heavier than molten gold.[60]

In 1836 Tessan suggested the use of echo-sounding in the survey of the Algerian coast[61] and experiments were tried in the United States by Charles Bonnycastle but he found it impossible to hear the echo with the devices at his disposal.[62] Nothing much could be done in this direction until the invention of hydrophones and electronic amplifying apparatus.

Another subject which now came to the fore for the first time was the study of ocean waves. The early dimensional measurements were apparently of speed. Tuckey records that Wollaston measured velocities of 60 m.p.h. on the east coast of Britain[63] and Captain David Thomson made several observations of waves travelling at about 30 knots.[64]

The range of wave heights was very conjectural and it was still possible to find people repeating what Boyle was supposed to have said about waves never rising more than 6 feet above the surface of the sea.[65] At the other extreme Dumont d'Urville reported that he had encountered waves 100 feet high on his voyages. As on other occasions when there was little definite evidence opinions tended to polarize towards the opposite ends of the scale.[66] As more measurements were made a more rational view prevailed. Scientists then, as now, distrusted the ability of sailors to make objective observations in a raging storm and welcomed a more moderate estimate. Arago wrote that by the observations of the *Bonite* and *Vénus*

de prétendues hauteurs de 33 mètres ont été réduites aux proportions modestes de 6 à 8 mètres.[67]

Fitzroy on the other hand was amused by the complacency of landlubbers who set 30 feet as the maximum height of storm waves; he himself had encountered waves twice that high.[68] In the end it was generally admitted that it was unwise to be too dogmatic and that 40- or 50-foot waves in storms were not unlikely. William Scoresby measured waves of this size during his voyage to Australia in 1856.[69]

During the early part of the century it was not generally appreciated that deep water waves, that is, waves whose length was less than half the depth of water, travelled with speeds proportional to their length. This relationship, which had been indicated by Newton, was demonstrated by George Green (1793-1841) in 1839.[70] The difficulty of actually measuring waves at sea was complicated by the presence of numerous separate wave trains superimposed upon one another. In a letter read to the British Association in 1848, Owen Stanley described how he measured the length and velocity of a wave by veering a spar at the end of the lead line until it was a wavelength behind the ship and seeing how long it took for the wave crests to pass from the spar to the ship. He measured height by climbing up the rigging until his eye, the wave crests and the horizon were in line. This method had been suggested to him by Mary Somerville ten years before.[71]

Lyell discussed the geological effects of wave and current action on coasts in the *Principles of Geology*[72] and the engineering aspects were studied by the Stevenson family. Thomas Stevenson (1818-1887) invented an instrument which he called the marine dynamometer to measure the changes in pressure in breaking waves and the force which they exerted.[73] William Walker, the Plymouth harbour master who recorded tidal data for Whewell, also made observations of waves.[74] Aimé devised experiments to show to what depth wave action could be felt in the sea.[75]

In his study of earthquakes the Irish engineer Robert Mallet (1810-1881) gave an improved account of their effect on the sea.[76] Using Darwin's observations in South America to illustrate his account, Mallet described the arrival of forced waves due to earth tremors under the sea, followed sooner or later by the damaging "tidal waves". These, as he correctly explained, were long waves which travelled with a speed relative to the depth of the ocean until they reached shallow water when they became unstable and assumed the catastrophic proportions experienced on shore. Alexander Dallas Bache (1806-1867), Superintendent of the United States Coast Survey, used the record of such waves on the tide gauges of the western coast, following an earthquake in Japan, to calculate the average depth of the Pacific.[77] He arrived at a figure of just over 2,000 fathoms which was much more accurate than the vast depths suggested by some soundings and tidal theory.

Marine chemistry meanwhile continued its largely separate development unaffected by the vicissitudes experienced by other aspects of the subject.[78] A growing number of substances were being identified in sea water in very small quantities and chemists working on a particular element turned to the sea as one of the places where it might occur; for example George Wilson (1818–1859) studied the fluorine in sea water,[79] Daubrée, the arsenic,[80] and silver, copper and lead were identified by Malaguti, Durocher and Sarzeaud,[80] the last two concentrated in seaweed.

There was a growing interest in studying the dissolved gases which sea water contains and their variation with depth, place and time. The French scientists Jean-Baptiste Biot (1774–1862) suggested that on the *Bonite* expedition samples of sea water should be collected at great depths and the gases they contained examined.[81] He designed an apparatus based on one which he had used himself in the Mediterranean in 1808. The samples brought back by the *Bonite* were analysed by Darondeau and Frémy who measured both the saline content and the quantities of dissolved oxygen, nitrogen and carbon dioxide.[82] A more extended study of the gases in sea water was made by Morren who looked to see if they varied with the time of day or from season to season.[83] Charles Daubeny also invented an apparatus for bringing up samples of sea water from different depths; it was successfully tested at Margate and exhibited at the British Association meeting in 1836.[84]

There were some analyses of sea water from different regions such as the English Channel[85] and the Mediterranean[86] and specific gravities were measured regularly both on the big expeditions and by individual travellers but the outstanding study of the saline contents of sea water and their distribution made during the mid-nineteenth century was the work of the Dane, Georg Forchhammer (1794–1865).[87]

Forchhammer began working on sea water in 1843 when an English friend sent him a specimen from the Mediterranean. He proceeded like Marcet in having samples collected for him in different parts of the world by naval officers so that he could see how the component parts of sea salt varied from place to place. By the time he came to publish his results, over twenty years after beginning the project, he, and other chemists working independently, had established the existence of twenty-seven elements in sea water, either directly or by finding them in a concentrated form in marine plants and animals or in the deposits which formed inside the boilers of steam ships.

Like Marcet, Forchhammer found that the proportion of the elements to one another in any sample was constant within narrow limits although the total salinity differed considerably from place to place, from geographical and other causes. He also studied the distribution of salinity at different depths, but did not publish individual analyses of these samples, many of which were the ones collected by Sir James Clark Ross on his Antarctic voyage.

There was not much to equal the thoroughness of Forchhammer's work in the other branches of physical oceanography at this time but one person whose work was outstanding for its range and inventiveness was Georges Aimé.[88] His instruments were comparable to Hooke's in their ingenuity but he was more fortunate in that, in most cases, he was able to put them into use.

Aimé wished to make soundings in the Mediterranean and to measure the temperature and salinity of its deep water. The most immediate difficulty involved was the tendency of the sounding line to break as soon as strain was put upon it to haul it to the surface, with a resulting loss of instruments. He therefore invented a system by which the lead weight on the end of the line could be released, thereby reducing the tension on the line itself. The mechanism was operated by messenger from the surface and could therefore be worked at any depth. Aimé used it in conjunction with an apparatus for bringing up water from intermediate depths which he tested for gaseous contents.

The main problems involved in measuring temperatures at different depths were, firstly, that if an ordinary maximum and minimum thermometer were used only the extreme changes were registered and not necessarily the temperature at the depth intended unless, as in fact usually happens, the temperature decreased continuously with depth. The second problem was the general neglect of the effect of pressure on thermometer readings. Aimé overcame both these difficulties. He established by comparison with protected thermometers the kind of distortion to be found in the readings of unprotected thermometers and recommended that copper tubes be used to prevent the pressure from affecting the delicate part of the instrument. To ensure that the exact temperature at any depth could be measured, Aimé invented separate maximum and minimum thermometers to be reversed, turned upside down, at the required depth, by using a messenger to release a device like the one for disengaging weights. The reversing action trapped the mercury and preserved its level intact to be read at the surface. This method is widely used today but at the time it was revolutionary and over thirty years elapsed before instrument makers adopted it.

Dumont d'Urville and Bérard had made series of measurements of temperature to depths of over 2,000 metres which revealed, as the observations of Marsigli and De Saussure had done (see Chs. 9 and 10) the constant deep water temperature of the Mediterranean of about 12·6°C. Aimé made a much more thorough study of this phenomenon and of the variations in temperature in the upper layers. In conjunction with measurements of air temperatures he showed that the sea temperature varied daily with the atmosphere to a depth of about 17 metres. Seasonal variations extended to about 350 or 400 metres and below that the temperature of the water was constant at 12·6°C. This was the mean air temperature of the region in winter and Aimé reasoned that the bottom water must be formed by water sinking from the surface during the winter months.*

Aimé studied the movements of water in waves and made a series of tidal records; at first (1838–1840), the height was recorded four times a day, then more often. Later a gauge was installed. He found that the lunisolar tide at Algiers had a range of 88 mm. He analysed the effect of changes in atmospheric pressure and showed that the mean sea level had an annual variation of about 20 mm and was highest in the wetter months. Winds blowing over the sea produced seiches—small regular oscillations with a 24-hour period.

With his knowledge of the Mediterranean it is not surprising to find that Aimé was anxious to look for the undercurrent in the Strait of Gibraltar, the existence of which was still conjectural and widely doubted. The relatively high temperature of the deep water in the Mediterranean showed that the shallow sill, revealed by soundings in the Strait, prevented cold ocean bottom water from entering the sea and it was argued that this barrier would equally prevent a movement in the reverse direction. Aimé invented two current meters, one to measure velocity by means of the turns of a propeller, the other to show direction by a device which trapped a compass needle while the apparatus was in the grip of the current. He somehow managed to get a ship but, on account of unforseen circumstances, had to leave before his instruments were ready and reported sadly

j'eus à lutter contre plusieurs difficultés de diverse nature, et je fus forcé, après des tentatives inutiles, de revenir à Alger sans avoir rien pu décider.[89]

A few years later, in 1849, a report was circulated that Admiral Coupvent des Bois had made successful observations of the undercurrent[90] but no details were given and, whatever the merits of his case, the question was still regarded as open. Meanwhile Forchhammer demonstrated the existence of the undercurrent in the Sound by determining the high salinity of its water, as compared to that of the Baltic,[87] and George Buist (1805–1860) argued the likelihood of a similar system at the entrance to the Red Sea.[91]

Aimé clearly suffered from the difficulties which had always dogged enterprises of marine research and which resulted from lack of sufficient means and flexibility of procedure to get the best out of a project. There

* This was the phenomenon being studied at the time of writing by the international oceanographic expedition, MEDOC 1969.

were signs, however, in the mid-nineteenth century of a change of heart by scientific opinion in general though it was a long time before research of the kind Aimé was doing was facilitated, and by then his best ideas had been forgotten and had to be thought up all over again.

The need for some organized means of collecting observations at sea had been appreciated for a long time. The first efforts were concerned with ocean meteorology and the need to find a way of compensating for the lack of fixed stations as on land. William Marsden, who, after his return from the Far East, had become Secretary to the Admiralty, devised the system of dividing the ocean into squares, still named after him, for * correlating data.[92] In 1831 Captain Edward Becher tried to establish the collection and discussion of meteorological observations as part of the work of the Hydrographic Department but had to give it up owing to lack of means.[93] Lieut.-Col. William Reid (1791–1858), who studied the progress of hurricanes, urged the value of synoptical meteorological observations on an international scale. He persuaded the Colonial Office and the East India Company to initiate observations in different parts of the world and corresponded with Krusenstern over the possibility of similar activity in Russia.[94]

As time went on there was also a growing feeling about the need for observations of the sea itself. In 1845 George Buist, who had been editor of the *Bombay Times* until a short time previously, presented a memorial to the Admiralty asking for help in setting up observatories for making tidal and meteorological observations at ten places between Suez and Ceylon. The actual running of the observatories was to be undertaken by the Bombay Geographical Society which, said Buist,

has of late resolved to direct its energies to several branches of research in Physical Geography (greatly in need of elucidation), referring particularly to the direction and velocity of tidal currents; to the epochs and amount of high water; the state of the aqueous and aerial currents along the coasts of Western India, Scinde and Baloochistan, Persia and Arabia, from Bombay to the mouth, or, if possible, to the upper end of the Red Sea.[95]

The winter of 1845–1846 was unusually mild and Edward Sabine recalled that during the previous warm winter of 1821–1822 he had measured high sea temperatures to the southwest of the British Isles which were taken by Rennell to indicate one of his periodic extensions of the Gulf Stream to the coast of Europe (*see* Ch. 11). There was no means of telling whether the present weather was due to the same cause. Sabine wrote

this remarkable phænomenon may take place in any year without our having other knowledge of it than by its effects, although it occurs at so short distance from our ports, from whence so many hundred vessels are continually crossing and recrossing the part of the ocean where a few simple observations with a thermometer would serve to make it known. We have no organized means of learning an occurrence which, whether it be or be not the cause of the present extremely mild winter, cannot fail whenever it does occur to affect materially and for a considerable length of time the climate of an extensive district of the globe including our own islands. History has recorded two instances in which the extension of the Gulf-stream is known to have taken place; and in both we owe our knowledge of it to the casual observations of an accidental voyager. Some one there may be in the present winter whose curiosity may have induced him, in the well-frequented passage between England and Madeira, to dip a thermometer in the sea once or twice a day, and who may therefore, perhaps unconsciously, be in possession of the very facts which it is desirable to know; in such case this communication, should it reach his eye, may be the means of inducing their publication. It is desirable however that we should not be thus altogether dependent on accident for information which may have even greater practical than scientific value.[96]

In 1848 F. W. Beechey who was drawing up a chart of ocean currents for the *Admiralty Manual of Scientific Enquiry* (1849) wrote to Herschel

I have executed it more with a view to excite officers to test it by direct observation and so induce them to attend to such observations, than as a chart pretending to accuracy as yet I believe we know too little of the subject to enable us to offer any thing positive on the subject.[97]

In the United States matters had progressed a little further. The Coast Survey began studying the Gulf Stream in 1844 and under Bache tide-gauges were established on the east and west coasts.[98] Meanwhile Matthew Fontaine Maury, director of the Naval Observatory which was established * in 1844, collected information on winds and ocean currents from the log books deposited at the observatory and in 1847 began publishing a series * of wind and current charts which were designed to enable sailing ships to find better routes at sea.[99] Maury prepared special forms and instructions for recording observations which were issued to naval and merchant ships and he incorporated the information he received in new editions of the charts.

In 1851 Sir John Burgoyne (1782–1871) drew up a plan for co-ordinating meteorological observations made by the Royal Engineers and the British government sent a copy to the United States government suggesting that they should co-operate in this field.[100] Maury suggested that an international conference should be held to co-ordinate observations at sea. The conference was held at Brussels in 1853, under the chairmanship of Quetelet, and resolved that the individual governments concerned be asked to issue their ships with instruments and standard log books for recording not only the meteorological conditions but the temperature and specific gravity of the sea and its temperature at different depths.

In this country the recommendations of F. W. Beechey, one of the delegates at the conference, led to the setting up of the Meteorological Department of the Board of Trade under Fitzroy in 1854.[100] The system for obtaining information was gradually implemented and among the department's publications were tables of the specific gravity and temperature of the ocean and current charts of the North Atlantic.[101]

As Beechey's complaint to Herschel in 1848 indicates, there had been few deliberate attempts to study ocean currents in the years which followed the publication of Rennell's work. When A. G. Findlay reviewed the situation in 1853 he referred principally to the work of the United States Coast Survey in the Atlantic and to that of the *Vénus* expedition in the Pacific.[102] Time had led to the revision of Rennell's picture in some respects, particularly in the north-west Atlantic. It was now generally realized that warm Atlantic water penetrated the Arctic at least as far as North Cape.[103] His south flowing current along the coast of Africa was discredited. Eastward flowing water had been detected in the region of the equator, the equatorial countercurrent, and this was now seen as the origin of the Guinea current.[104]

Little had been done either to elucidate further the theory of ocean currents. Those who followed Rennell looked at the winds as the cause of currents, the view taken by Sir John Herschel in his articles on physical geography.[105] Those who found it necessary to defend the idea instanced the reversal of currents with the monsoons in the Indian Ocean.[106] Not everyone however was content to accept the simple view and William C. Redfield (1789–1857), the American meteorologist, wrote

It is common to ascribe the currents of the ocean wholly to the action of the winds; but, as the waters of the ocean are subject to the same impulses as the superincumbent atmosphere, it is probable that the principal movements of both fluids have their origin in the same causes.[107]

Dortet de Tessan felt that a dynamic theory was needed to explain the presence of currents flowing towards the equator on the western coasts of the continents and toward the poles on the eastern coasts.[108] Some people in the middle of the century were apparently talking of the effect of the earth's rotation as the cause of currents.[87, 106]

There was a similar lack of definition about ideas on general oceanic circulation. The original idea of warm water moving towards the poles at the surface and cold water moving towards the equator at the bottom was quite often quoted by authors in the 1830s but the prevailing belief that the depths of the sea were full of water at 40°F caused the simple idea of the convection cell to be lost sight of. In this view the sinking of the dense water took place between latitude 40° and 60°, and presumably involved some movement towards and away from this area, but this was not clearly specified.

Two people in particular in the middle of the century criticized this point of view and indicated where it was fallacious. The most thorough treatment was in the paper given in 1845 by Emil von Lenz.[109] Lenz recalled his work on Kotzebue's voyage of 1823–1826 and his collaboration shortly afterwards with G. F. Parrot in which they demonstrated the effect of pressure on thermometers. He showed that the results of Dumont d'Urville, Beechey and others made with unprotected Six thermometers were subject to errors small enough in the shallower observations to be masked by the rapid decrease in temperature but increasing with depth, so that in the deeper observations the temperature actually seemed to increase. He concluded that the Six thermometer might still have some use for making comparative observations of horizontal or seasonal variations at the same depth but for any definitive measurements pressure corrections would have to be established.

Lenz used his observations made in the *Rurik* to give a clearer picture of ocean circulation than he had previously permitted himself. He noted the low temperatures to be found not far below the surface in equatorial regions and explained them as the upwelling of water which had come in at great depths from the polar regions to compensate for the outward flow of warm water away from the equator at the surface. This, he said, was the main source of movement in the oceans, influenced by the earth's rotation and altered on the surface by the winds.

Lenz's work was little read in the west and had no apparent effect on contemporary thought. Neither in this respect were people apparently convinced by a very widely read work, Maury's *Physical Geography of the Sea*.[110] This was the first book dealing exclusively with marine science since Marsigli's *Histoire Physique de la Mer*. Maury wrote it in a few months in 1855 in order to secure copyright on material he had already published with his wind and current charts.[111]

Maury's views on currents had already been expressed as early as 1844.[112] In one respect he improved on many of his contemporaries; he realized the value of Marcet's work and the nonsense that was being written in ignorance of it. However, his own account of ocean circulation was confused and contradictory, even in the later editions of the book. He tried to make out that difference in salinity, which he thought might be caused among other things by the presence or absence of marine life, was the principle cause of dynamic movements in the ocean, that saline water sank at the equator and fresher water moved towards it on the surface. At the same time when considering the Gulf Stream he talked of temperature as the disturbing force, with the vivid illustration of what would happen if a body of equatorial water were changed to oil, and cited the Gulf Stream as an instance of warm water moving polewards at the surface.

Maury did not think that the winds played an important role in generating currents, a view that did not cut much ice with leading scientists of the day, any more than did the improbable pattern of atmospheric circulation he devised.[113] Herschel criticized it on the (mistaken) view that for ocean circulation such as Maury envisaged, there would have to be a difference in level great enough for water to flow downhill from the equator towards the poles.[114] He argued that winds were capable of giving a horizontal impulse so that no change of level was involved, a substantial departure from Rennell.

Another point on which Maury was criticized, this time by William Ferrel (1817–1891), was on his failure to adopt the, since 1851, general appreciation of the effect of the earth's rotation on all horizontally moving bodies.[99] Maury had reproduced the old version which allowed for deflection only of bodies moving north or south.

Though in some respects the *Physical Geography of the Sea* characterized the worst kind of superficiality which, while correcting some old errors, introduced a good many new ones, there was a lot of useful information in it, particularly in connection with the exploration of the deep sea floor which was just beginning in the early 1850s and in which Maury had a considerable share.

Maury had cast doubts on the vast depths being reported by surveyors in the early 1850s. He examined the lists of times given for the running out of the line on each occasion and concluded that

when the line ceases to go out at something like a regularly decreasing rate there is no reliance to be put upon the sounding after the change, and that when the rate of going out becomes uniform the plummet has probably ceased to drag the line down, and the force which continues to take the sounding line out is due to the wind, currents, heave of the sea, or drift,—one, some, or all.[115]

Following this argument, the *Congress*'s sounding was reduced from over 8,000 fathoms to about 2,800 fathoms and the *Herald*'s from 7,706 to about 3,200. Maury did however accept the report of a sounding of 6,000 fathoms made by Lieut. O. H. Berryman on the U.S.S. *Dolphin*, in February 1853, because for some reason he could not identify the discontinuity in the times.

Berryman carried out a line of soundings across the North Atlantic in 1853 and from these and others Maury was able to construct the first bathymetric chart of that ocean.[116] The pattern was one of a trough whose greatest depth was about 3,000 fathoms, apart from an area (wrongly) shown by Berryman's survey at about 5,000 fathoms, with what appeared to be a gentle rise in the middle parts of the ocean. Mindful of the schemes already on foot for laying telegraph cables on the sea bed, Maury called the rise the Telegraphic Plateau.

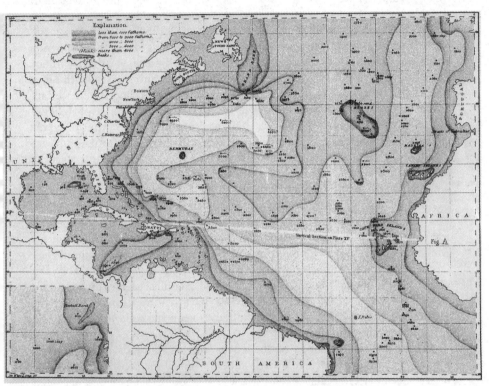

FIG. 17. Maury's chart of the bed of the North Atlantic. Reproduced from *the Physical Geography of the Sea* (1855). Plate 11.

The problem of relieving strain on the sounding line and enabling samples of the sea floor to be brought to the surface was solved in one by one of Maury's assistants at the Observatory, Midshipman Brooke. The apparatus consisted of a cannon ball with a hole bored through the centre in which a tube was inserted. A system of hooks released the cannon ball when it hit the bottom and the tube was brought to the surface with a sample of the sea floor in it. With this apparatus the first specimens of the deep sea floor in the Atlantic and Pacific were obtained in 1855.[117]

In the second half of the 1850s deep sea soundings rapidly multiplied. In 1856 Berryman surveyed the proposed route for the telegraph cable across the North Atlantic and this was repeated the following year by Lieut. Joseph Dayman who made further voyages in 1858 and 1859.[118] In 1860 Sir Leopold McClintock surveyed a route linking Britain, Iceland and Newfoundland.[119] Soundings also featured on hydrographic voyages; Captain T. A. B. Spratt added them to his Mediterranean survey work in 1856,[120] and Captain W. J. S. Pullen sounded in the Indian Ocean in 1858.[121]

The increasing use of steam-powered vessels and steam winches made such voyages a practical possibility. With these aids deep sounding was made possible from the ship and in almost any kind of weather, without need for the vast effort expended on quite modest enterprises in the first half of the century. There was still the problem of bringing the line intact to the surface. On his second voyage Dayman made the habit of deliberately jettisoning it but this was wasteful and meant that no other observations could be attempted at the same time. Rubber accumulators were developed to take the strain on the line as it was drawn to the surface. A strengthened version of Massey's sounding machine was sometimes used in conjunction with the lead and line.[122]

For bottom sampling Brooke's instrument underwent almost as many changes as there were voyages. Spratt found a simple tube good enough for collecting mud samples from the floor of the Mediterranean but on McClintock's voyage where a rough pebbly bottom was encountered they devised a kind of double scoop, rather like Ross's deep sea clamm. Dayman streamlined Brooke's device, giving the lead a conical shape, and Captain Peter Shortland (1815–1888) surveying part of the Indian Ocean in H.M.S. *Hydra* in 1868, had valves added to keep the sediment intact and bring up a water sample as well.[123]

The deep sea soundings of the 1840s and early 1850s and the more systematic surveys which followed, added a new dimension to knowledge of the oceans. They also prompted a few people to challenge accepted views about the conditions of life and temperature in the deep sea. The first steps were taken to try and dislodge the dead weight of the theories which had so taken hold of the imagination of the times.

James Glaisher (1809–1903) warned Admiral Fitzroy at the Board of Trade that pressure would distort the readings of thermometers, as he himself had found by experiments in the Thames in 1844.[124] Accordingly thermometers which had their bulbs protected by a second outer casing were made by the London firm of instrument makers, Negretti and Zambra.[125] The new thermometers were issued to Captain Pullen for his voyage to the Indian Ocean in 1857 and he reported finding a temperature of 35°F at a depth of 2,254 fathoms and at 2,700 in the Atlantic.[121, 126]

Unfortunately the experiment was short-lived; the thermometers turned out to be fragile and their issue ceased.[124] In 1862 Captain Richard Hoskyn was sent in H.M.S. *Porcupine* to sound the sea floor west of Ireland[127] where earlier surveyors had encountered a sudden precipitous drop in the sea bed from the 100 fathom contour to abyssal depths. Hoskyn's task was to locate a less abrupt descent more suitable for cables but he found that the feature extended all the way from latitude 51° to 54° N. He took with him several new instruments, including two pressure gauges, made by Johnson and Hearder, neither of which worked, and a metallic thermometer by Johnson. The thermometer seemed to work satisfactorily, but at a depth of 1,500 fathoms, when a Board of Trade minimum thermometer registered 50°F, it read 31°F. In time, metallic thermometers were shown to be as susceptible to pressure as ordinary ones and were never brought into regular use.[124]

Meanwhile deep sea temperature measurements continued to be made with unprotected thermometers and people like Spratt and George Wallich (1815–1899), an ex-India Army surgeon who sailed with McClintock as naturalist, wrote about the sea in terms of the 40°F theory. Wallich carefully noted when they crossed, in the northern hemisphere, the circle of mean temperature established by Ross.[128]

J. E. Davis later wrote that early in 1868 the attention of the Hydrographer was directed to the need to protect thermometers from pressure.[124] Leading instrument makers, excluding for some unknown reason Negretti and Zambra, supplied instruments and these were sent out with survey ships. Of these one was H.M.S. *Gannet* which, under Commander W. Chimmo (1828–1891), had surveyed the Gulf Stream in the summer of 1868.[129] Captain Shortland of the *Hydra* must have had protected thermometers as his temperature observations between Aden and Bombay showed figures of between 33° and 34°F for depths over 2,000 fathoms.[123, 130]

A new perspective was given to discussion of the supposed azoic zone below 400 fathoms by the work of the surveyors. The sea floor samples obtained with Brooke's sounding machine during the early American surveys were analysed by Jacob Whitman Bailey (1811–1857) and Christian Ehrenberg (1795–1876) who found that they consisted largely of the skeletons of foraminifera and that these were predominantly of one species, globigerina. Bailey took the (correct) view that these creatures lived and died at the surface and Maury in the *Physical Geography of the Sea* described the rain of sediment falling to the ocean floor in characteristically evocative language. Ehrenberg on the other hand thought that the globigerina lived on the bottom and his view was preferred by Thomas Henry Huxley (1825–1895) and William King (1809–1886) who examined samples collected by British ships.[131]

The idea that life was impossible at great depths received a further blow from the observations made on H.M.S. *Bulldog*.[128] Wallich had supposed in advance that Forbes's limit was too restricted and when between the Faroes and Iceland several living creatures were brought to the surface from 682 fathoms he thought that his ideas were amply confirmed. Better things still were in store and on the homeward voyage from Newfoundland thirteen starfish were found, clinging to part of the sounding line which had been lying on the sea bed, which there was 1,260 fathoms deep. Aware of the kind of objections which would be made to the discovery, Wallich was at pains to try and prove that it was impossible for these demersal or bottom-living creatures to have been carried live that far into the ocean by currents or for them to have grasped the line while it was moving through the water.

The situation which existed in the late 1860s was therefore much more promising for new developments in oceanography than at any time since the 1820s. The growth of knowledge and the increasing awareness of the kind of problems involved were beginning to break down the stultifying ideas which, ossified by lack of sufficient opposition, had for too long barred the way to progress. The next few years were to see the whole subject put on a new footing.

Yet the impetus for the new developments did not spring from the events already described. Contributions to marine science in the nineteenth century were largely spasmodic, lacking any clear motive or sequence. It cannot even be said, as has sometimes been done, that they followed as a logical consequence of advances in other branches of science and in technical knowledge. The facile view that the introduction of the submarine telegraph advanced the study of marine science does not take into account the fact that many deep sea soundings were made as much as a decade before surveys for it began. Furthermore, while the surveys greatly increased the knowledge available and new equipment made it far easier than before to obtain, there is little if any sign that this resulted in scientists turning to the study of the sea, except for such isolated instances as when Huxley and others reported on the samples brought up from the sea floor.

The vicissitudes undergone by marine science in the nineteenth century as far as its physical aspects were concerned can only have been due to the fact that the vast majority of people engaged in the physical sciences were completely indifferent to the sea and its problems. The few people who, like Aimé, did become involved in its study worked very much on their own. How long this situation would have gone on, left on its own, is impossible to say since events were precipitated from outside.

In the rapid expansion of marine biology which was taking place in the mid-nineteenth century, work had so far been largely confined to the sea shore and coastal waters. Oceanic work had been done on the voyages of discovery and by individuals such as Huxley, who had sailed on H.M.S. *Rattlesnake*, but this was restricted to the surface layers. By the 1860s attention was beginning to turn to the deeper water and Wallich was not the only person to become increasingly uneasy about the generally accepted idea of the azoic zone. A further incentive to study marine life was provided when Charles Darwin (1809–1882) published his *Origin of Species* in 1859 and it began to look as though the answers to the controversial questions it aroused might lie hidden in the ocean depths.

13. NOTES

1. For example John Davy made observations of the temperature and specific gravity of the Firth of Forth over the period September 1842–April 1843 and also recorded observations during several ocean voyages: John Davy, "On the temperature of the Frith of Forth, and on the specific gravity of its water", *Edinburgh New Philosophical Journal* (1843–1844). Vol. **36**, pp. 1–4. Robert Wauchope reported on the temperature and saline content of a water sample which he obtained from 653 fathoms just north of the equator in 1836 while in command of H.M.S. *Thalia*. He brought it to the surface with an instrument which he had "frequently made use of for this purpose": Robert Wauchope, "Quantity of saline matter in deep and surface sea-water, obtained in lat. 0° 33′ N, and long. 8° 16′ E; also result of three experiments on the temperature of the sea at great depths; and state of the barometer and thermometer during a gale of wind off the Cape of Good Hope", *Edinburgh New Philosophical Journal* (1838–1839). Vol. **26**, pp. 399–401.
2. For example: J. H. Pratt, "Observations on the relative temperature of the sea and air, and on other phaenomena, made during a voyage from England to India", *Phil. Mag.* (1840), 3rd series. Vol. **16**, pp. 176–181.
3. A comprehensive and critical survey of temperature observations and the ideas associated with them was published as long ago as 1875: Joseph Prestwich, "Tables of temperatures of the sea at different depths beneath the surface, reduced and collated from the various observations made between the years 1749 and 1868, discussed" *Phil. Trans.* (1875). Vol. **165**, pp. 587–674.
4. Jules Dumont d'Urville, *Voyage de la corvette l'Astrolabe exécuté par ordre du roi, pendant les années 1826–1829*, 5 vols, Paris (1830–1833).
5. Jules Dumont d'Urville, *Voyage de découvertes de l'Astrolabe pendant les années 1826–1829. Observations nautiques, météorologiques, hydrographiques et de physique*, Paris (1833), pp. 51*–85*: "Notice sur la température de la mer a diverses profondeurs".
6. Jules Dumont d'Urville, *Voyage de la corvette l'Astrolabe, op. cit.* Vol 5, p. 500.
7. J. C. Hörner, "Remarks on the preceding observations on the specific gravity of the sea water in different latitudes, and on the temperature of the ocean at different depths", Kotzebue's *Voyage of Discovery into the South Sea and Beering's Straits*, translated by H. E. Lloyd (1821). Vol. **3**, pp. 425–435.

8. Carl von Neumann, *Ueber das Maximum der Dichtigkeit beim Meerwasser*, Munich (1861).

9. "Résumé des progrès de la géologie pendant l'année 1832", *Bull. Soc. géol. Fr.* (1832–1833). Vol. 3, p. lxxii.

10. Abel du Petit-Thouars, *Voyage autour du monde sur la frégate la Vénus, pendant les années 1836–1839*, 10 vols, Paris (1840–1855). Vols. 1–4 narrative; Vol. 5, zoology; Vols 6–10:
Urbain Dortet de Tessan, *Physique*. Vols 1–5.

11. Urbain Dortet de Tessan, *op. cit.* Vol. 9, 1844, pp. 385–389.

12. Invented *c.* 1817.
W. E. Knowles Middleton, *A History of the Thermometer and its Use in Meteorology*, Baltimore (1966), p. 171.

13. Urbain Dortet de Tessan, *op. cit.* (1844). Vol. 10, pp. 389–396, 120–121.
Metallic thermometers were tried at sea in the 1860s. See p. 297.

14. François Arago, *et al.* "Rapport sur les travaux scientifiques exécutés pendant le voyage de la frégate la Vénus", *C.r. hebd. Séanc. Acad. Sci. Paris* (1840). Vol. 11, pp. 298–343, p. 311.

15. Dionysius Lardner, *A Treatise on Hydrostatics and Pneumatics, The Cabinet Cyclopaedia*, London (1831), pp. 111–112.

16. Jean Jacques Nicolas Huot, *Nouveau Manuel de Géographie Physique*, Paris (1839).

17. Alexander von Humboldt, *Asie Centrale: recherches sur les chaînes de montagnes et la climatologie comparée*, 3 vols, Paris (1843).
Alexander von Humboldt, *Cosmos: a sketch of a physical description of the universe*. Vol. 1, translated by E. C. Otté, London (1848).

18. Matthew Fontaine Maury, *The Physical Geography of the Sea*, London (1855).

19. J. Dumont d'Urville, *Voyage au Pôle Sud et dans l'Océanie sur les corvettes l'Astrolabe et la Zélée, pendant les années 1837–1840*, 11 vols, Paris, (1842–1854).
Charles Wilkes, *Narrative of the United States Exploring Expedition, 1838–1842*, 5 vols, Philadelphia (1845) and "On the depth and saltness of the ocean", *Edinburgh New Philosophical Journal* (1848). Vol. 45, pp. 27–36.

20. *Report of the Committee of Physics and Meteorology of the Royal Society relative to the observations to be made in the Antarctic Expedition and in the Magnetic Observatories*, London (1840).

21. Sir James Clark Ross, *A Voyage of Discovery and Research in the Southern and Antarctic Regions, during the years 1839–1843*, 2 vols, London (1847).

22. *Ibid.* Vol. 2, pp. 375, 378.

23. *Report of the Committee of Physics and Meteorology, op. cit.* p. 93. This letter arrived too late for Ross to have read it before leaving but, if attended to, would have influenced the view taken of his results.

24. Sir William Herdman, *Founders of Oceanography and their Work*, London (1923).

25. T. A. B. Spratt and Edward Forbes, *Travels in Lycia, Milyas, and the Cibyratis*, 2 vols, London (1847). It is in fact true that life in the Mediterranean is sparse below this depth.

26. Edward Forbes, "Report on the Mollusca and Radiata of the Ægean Sea, and on their distribution, considered as bearing on geology", *Report of the 13th*

meeting of the British Association for the Advancement of Science, *1843* (1844). Part 1, pp. 130–193.

Edward Forbes and R. Godwin-Austen, *The Natural History of the European Seas*, London (1859).

Sven Lovén, "On the bathymetrical distribution of submarine life on the northern shores of Scandinavia", *Report of the 14th Meeting of the British Association, 1844* (1845). Part 2, pp. 50–51.

27. The history of this misconception has been outlined by Daniel Merriman who compares it to the reaction to Darwin's *Origin of Species*: Daniel Merriman, "Speculations on life at the depths: a XIXth-century prelude", *Bull. Inst. océanogr. Monaco*, numéro spécial 2 (1968). Vol. **2**, pp. 377–384.

28. Sir John Ross, *A Voyage of Discovery, made under the orders of the Admiralty, in H.M.S. Isabella and Alexander*, London (1819), pp. 178, 193.

29. Sir James Clark Ross, *op. cit.* Vol. **1**, pp. 202–203.

30. Georges Aimé, *Recherches de Physique Générale sur la Méditerranée*. Vol. **1** of *Exploration Scientifique de l'Algérie pendant les années 1840, 1841, 1842: Physique générale*, Paris (1845), pp. 207–208.

31. Charles Wyville Thomson, *The Depths of the Sea*, London (1874), pp. 1–48.

32. T. A. B. Spratt, "On the influence of temperature upon the distribution of the fauna of the Ægean Sea", *Phil. Mag.* (1848), 3rd series. Vol. **33**, pp. 169–174.

33. François Arago, *op cit. C.r. hebd. Séanc. Acad. Sci. Paris* p. 325.

34. *Report of the Committee of Physics and Meteorology, op. cit.* pp. 48–49.

35. Sir James Clark Ross, *op. cit.* Vol. **1**, p. 26.

36. Robert S. Dietz and Harley J. Knebel, "Survey of Ross's deep sea sounding site", *Nature* (Nov. 1968). Vol. **220**, no. 5169, pp. 751–753.

37. Sir James Clark Ross, *op. cit.* Vol. **2**, p. 363.
The line was carried out by strong bottom currents.

38. R. T. Gould, "The Ross Deep", *Geogr. J.* (1924). Vol. **63**, pp. 237–241. The figures were published in the *Nautical Magazine* (1843). Vol. **12**, pp. 471–472.

39. *Ibid.* p. 241.

40. Sir James Clark Ross, "On the effect of the pressure of the atmosphere on the mean level of the ocean", *Phil. Trans.* (1854). Vol. **144**, pp. 285–296.

41. Sir Edward Belcher, *Narrative of the voyage of H.M.S. Samarang, during the years 1843–1846*, London (1848).

42. Berthold Seeman, *Narrative of the voyage of H.M.S. Herald, during the years 1845–1851*, 2 vols, London (1853).

43. John Macgillivray, *Narrative of the voyage of H.M.S. Rattlesnake, 1846–1850*, 2 vols, London (1852).

44. *Nautical Magazine* (1853), pp. 396–400.

45. M. F. Maury, "Ocean soundings: the deepest of the deep sea soundings discussed", *Naut. Mag.* (1853), pp. 394–396.

46. "Deep sea soundings", *ibid.* pp. 98–101.

47. M. F. Maury, *The Physical Geography of the Sea* (1855), p. 207 n.

48. Amabel Williams-Ellis, *Darwin's Moon: a biography of Alfred Russel Wallace*, London (1966), p. 82. The outbreak of the Crimean War prevented the voyage.

49. Samuel Haughton, "On the solar and lunar diurnal tides of the coasts of Ireland", *Phil. Mag.* 4th series (1856). Vol. **11**, pp. 47–64, 262–272, 428–433.

50. See particularly the collection of papers in *C.r. hebd. Séanc. Acad. Sci. Paris* (1851). Vol. **32**, pp. 65–68, *passim*.
51. Ericsson's lead, *Nautical Magazine* (1836). Vol. **5**, pp. 390–394.
52. François Hippolyte Walferdin, "Sur la mesure des plus grandes profondeurs de la mer et sur leur température. Nouvel hydrobaromètre", *Bull. Soc. géol. Fr.* 2nd series (1850–1851). Vol. **8**, pp. 214–217.
53. F. Maxwell Lyte, "On an instrument for taking soundings", *Phil. Mag.* 4th series (1853). Vol. **6**, pp. 344–345.
54. "Plombe de sonde de M. Le Coëntre", *C.r. hebd. Séanc. Acad. Sci. Paris* (1851). Vol. **32**, pp. 551–552.
55. The Royal Society's Herschel Correspondence.
56. As suggested to Ross. See p. 282.
57. J. D. Colladon and J. C. F. Sturm, "Mémoire sur la compression des liquides" *Ann. Chim. Phys.* (1827). Vol. **36**, pp. 113–159 and 225–257.
58. H. F. Talbot, "Proposed method of ascertaining the greatest depth of the ocean", *Phil. Mag.* 3rd series (1833). Vol. **3**, p. 82.
59. "T.R.F." "On Mr. Talbot's proposed method of ascertaining the greatest depth of the ocean", *ibid.* pp. 352–353.
60. Charles Wyville Thomson, *The Depths of the Sea* (1874), pp. 31–32.
61. Urbain Dortet de Tessan, *op. cit.* Vol. **10**, pp. 226–227.
62. H. Drubba and H. H. Rust, "On the first echo-sounding experiment", *Ann. Sci.* (1954). Vol. **10**, pp. 28–32.
63. J. K. Tuckey, *Maritime Geography* (1815). Vol. **1**, p. 31.
64. David Thomson, "On the velocity of the waves of the sea", *Phil. Mag.* (1823). Vol. **61**, pp. 405–407.
65. Robert Schomburgck, "Remarks on the heavy swell along some of the West-India islands", *Geogr. J.* (1835). Vol. **5**, pp. 23–38.
66. For example: M. Coulier, "Hauteur des vagues", *C.r. hebd. Séanc. Acad. Sci. Paris.* (1837). Vol. **4**, pp. 655–666.
67. François Arago, *op. cit. C.r. hebd. Séanc. Acad. Sci. Paris.* (1840). Vol. **11**, p. 326.
68. Robert Fitzroy, *Narrative of the surveying voyages of H.M.S. Adventure and Beagle, between the years 1826 and 1836*, Appendix to Vol. 2 (1839), p. 297.
69. William Scoresby, *Journal of a voyage to Australia and round the world, for magnetical research*, London (1859), p. 123. Modern wave-recording apparatus has measured waves of over 70 feet in the Atlantic.
70. George Green, "Note on the motion of waves in canals", *Trans. Camb. Phil. Soc.* (1842). Vol. **7**, pp. 87–95.
71. Owen Stanley, "On the lengths and velocities of waves", *Report of the 18th meeting of the British Association for the Advancement of Science, 1848* (1849). Part 2, pp. 38–39.
    These methods were incorporated in the *Manual of Scientific Enquiry; prepared for the use of Her Majesty's Navy, and adapted for travellers in general*, J. F. W. Herschel and others, London (1849), pp. 96–96a.
72. Sir Charles Lyell, *Principles of Geology*, 6th ed., 3 vols., London (1840).
73. Thomas Stevenson, "Accounts of experiments upon the force of the waves of the Atlantic and German Oceans", *Trans. R. Soc. Edinb.* (1845–1849). Vol. **16**, pp. 23–32.
74. William Walker, "Oceanic undulations", *Naut. Mag.* (1836). Vol. **5**, pp. 513–518; *ibid.* (1846), pp. 123–126.

75. Georges Aimé, "Recherches expérimentales sur le mouvement des vagues", *Annls. Chim. Phys.* (1842). Vol. 5, pp. 417–427.
76. Robert Mallet, "On the dynamics of earthquakes; being an attempt to reduce their observed phenomena to the known laws of wave motion in solids and fluids", *Trans. R. Ir. Acad.* (1839–1847). Vol. 21, part 1, pp. 51–105.
77. Alexander Dallas Bache, "Notice of earthquake waves on the western coast of the United States, on the 23rd and 25th of December, 1854", in *American Journal of Science and Arts*, 2nd series (1856). Vol. 21, pp. 37–43.
78. J. P. Riley and G. Skirrow, *Chemical Oceanography* (1965). Vol. 1, pp. 13, 23–24.
79. George Wilson, "On the solubility of fluoride of calcium in water, and its relation to the occurrence of fluorine in minerals, and in recent and fossil plants and animals", *Trans. R. Soc. Edinb.* (1845–1849). Vol. 16, pp. 145–164.
80. A Daubrée, "Recherches sur la présence de l'arsenic et de l'antimoine dans les combustibles minéraux, dans diverses roches et dans l'eau de la mer", *Bull. Soc. géol. Fr.* 2nd series (1850–1851). Vol. 8, pp. 350–352.
   F. J. Malaguti, Durocher and Sarzeaud, "Sur la présence du plomb, du cuivre, et de l'argent dans l'eau de la mer, et sur l'existence de ce dernier métal dans les plantes et les êtres organisés", *Annls. Chim. Phys.* (1850). Vol. 28, pp. 129–157.
81. *C.r. hebd. Séanc. Acad. Sci. Paris* (1835). Vol. 1, pp. 410, 416.
82. B. H. Darondeau, "Résultat de l'examen des eaux de mer recueillies pendant le voyage de la Bonite, avec l'appareil imaginé par M. Biot", *C.r. hebd. Séanc. Acad. Sci. Paris* (1838). Vol. 6, pp. 616–620.
83. Auguste Morren, "Recherches sur les gaz que l'eau de mer peut tenir en dissolution en différents moments de la journée, et dans les saisons diverses de l'année", *Annls. Chim. Phys.* (1844). Vol. 12, pp. 5–56.
84. Charles Daubeny, "Reports on the present state of our knowledge with respect to mineral and thermal waters", *Report of the sixth meeting of the British Association for the Advancement of Science, 1836* (1837). Part 1, pp. 1–95.
85. G. Schweitzer, "Analysis of sea-water as it exists in the English Channel near Brighton", *Phil. Mag.* (1839) 3rd series. Vol. 15, pp. 51–60.
86. J. Usiglio, "Analyse de l'eau de la Méditerranée sur les côtes de France", *Annls. Chim. Phys.* (1849). Vol. 27, pp. 92–107.
87. Georg Forchhammer, "On the composition of sea-water in the different parts of the ocean", *Phil. Trans.* (1865). Vol. 155, pp. 203–262.
88. Georges Aimé, *Recherches de Physique Générale sur la Méditerranée, Exploration Scientifique de l'Algérie pendant les années 1840, 1841, 1842.* Vol. 1, Paris (1845).
89. Georges Aimé, "Mémoire sur les courants de la Méditerranée", *Annls. Cim. Phys.* (1845). Vol. 13, pp. 460–477.
90. *The Athenaeum* (18 August 1849). No. 1138, p. 842.
91. George Buist, "On the physical geography of the Red Sea", *Geogr. J.* (1854). Vol. 24, pp. 227–238.
92. Robert Fitzroy, *The Weather Book: a manual of practical meteorology*, 2nd edition, London (1863), p. 49.
93. *Ibid.* pp. 49–50. *

94. Sir William Reid, *An Attempt to Develop the Law of Storms*, London (1838). Reid to Sir John Herschel, 22 May 1839. The Royal Society's Herschel Correspondence.

95. George Buist, *Memoir with Testimonials, &c. of George Buist*, Cupar (1846).

96. Sir Edward Sabine, "On the cause of remarkably mild winters which occasionally occur in England", *Phil. Mag.* 3rd series (1846). Vol. **28**, pp. 317–324.

97. F. W. Beechey to Sir John Herschel, 24 May 1848. The Herschel Correspondence, preserved at the Royal Society.

98. *Report of the Secretary of the Treasury to the Senate on the work of the United States Coast Survey*, Washington (1846). R. F. A. Studds, "The United States Coast and Geodetic Survey: its work and prospects", *Int. hydrogr. Rev.* (1952). Vol. **29**, part 1, pp. 45–66.

* 99. See John Leighly's introduction to the reissue of Maury's *Physical Geography of the Sea and its Meteorology*, Cambridge, Mass. (1963).

100. P. G. Parkhurst, "Ocean meteorology: a century of scientific progress", *Mar. Obsr.* (1955). Vol. **25**, no. 167, pp. 16–21.

101. *Board of Trade Meteorological Papers* (1865). Vol. **12**. *Currents and surface temperature of the North Atlantic Ocean from the equator to 40° North for each month of the year*, London (1872).

102. A. G. Findlay, "Oceanic currents, and their connection with the proposed Central-America channels", *Geogr. J.* (1853). Vol. **23**, pp. 217–240.

103. For example: Lord Dufferin, *Letters from High Latitudes*, London (1857). *See: Papers on the Eastern and Northern Extensions of the Gulf Stream* (ed. E. R. Knorr), Washington (1871).

104. For example: M. Lefebvre, "Note sur les courants de l'Océan Atlantique entre l'équateur et le 10° degré de latitude N", *Annls. Hydrogr.* (1857).

105. Sir John Herschel, *Physical Geography*, Edinburgh (1861), reprinted from *Encyclopaedia Britannica* (1859).

106. T. Hopkins, "On the causes of the great currents of the ocean", *Mem. Proc. Manchr. lit. phil. Soc.* 2nd series (1852). Vol. **10**, pp. 1–15.

107. William C. Redfield, "Summary statements of some of the leading facts in meteorology", *American Journal of Science and Arts* (1834). Vol. **25**, pp. 122–135.

108. André Gougenheim, "Deux ingénieurs hydrographes du XIXe siècle précurseurs en matière de dynamique des mers", *Bull. Inst. océanogr. Monaco*, numéro spécial 2 (1968). Vol. **1**, pp. 87–97.

109. Emil Lenz, "Bemerkungen über die Temperatur des Weltmeeres in verschiedenen Tiefen", *Bulletin de la Classe Physico-Mathématique de l'Académie Impériale des Sciences de St.-Pétersbourg* (1845–1846). Vol. **5**, col. 65–74.

110. Matthew Fontaine Maury, *The Physical Geography of the Sea* (1855).

111. See the introduction by John Leighly to the 1963 reissue of *The Physical * Geography of the Sea, op. cit.*

112. M. F. Maury, "Remarks on the Gulf Stream and currents of the sea", *The American Journal of Science and Arts* (1844). Vol. **47**, pp. 161–181.

113. John Leighly, "M. F. Maury in his time", *Bull. Inst. océanogr. Monaco*, numéro spécial 2 (1968). Vol. **1**, pp. 147–159.

114. Sir John Herschel, *op. cit.* pp. 51–55.

115. M. F. Maury, "Ocean soundings: the deepest of the deep sea soundings discussed", *Naut. Mag.* (1853), pp. 394–396.

116. M. F. Maury, *The Physical Geography of the Sea* (1855). Plate 9.

117. *Ibid.* (1963), pp. 291, 302–303.

118. Joseph Dayman, *Deep Sea Soundings in the North Atlantic Ocean between Ireland and Newfoundland, made in H.M.S. Cyclops, in June and July 1857*, H.M.S.O., London (1858).
    Joseph Dayman, *Deep Sea Soundings in the North Atlantic Ocean between Newfoundland, the Azores, and England, made in H.M.S. Gorgon, in September and October 1858*, H.M.S.O., London (1859).
    Joseph Dayman, *Deep Sea Soundings in the Bay of Biscay and Mediterranean Sea, made in H.M.S. Firebrand, in the summer of 1859*, H.M.S.O., London (1860).

119. Sir Leopold McClintock, *Remarks Illustrative of the Sounding Voyage of H.M.S. Bulldog, in 1860*, H.M.S.O., London (1861).

120. T. A. B. Spratt, *Deep Soundings in the Mediterranean Sea east of Malta: report of deep soundings between Malta and the Archipelago, in 1856 and 1857*, London (1858).

121. W. J. S. Pullen, "Extract of a letter to Admiral Fitzroy, F.R.S., from Captain Pullen of H.M.S. *Cyclops*, dated Aden, March 16, 1858", *Proc. R. Soc.* (1857–1859). Vol. **9**, pp. 189–194.

122. J. E. Davis, *Notes on Deep Sea Sounding*, London (1867).

123. P. F. Shortland, *Sounding voyage of H.M.S. Hydra*, London (1869).

124. J. E. Davis, "On deep-sea thermometers", *Proc. Meterol. Soc.* (1869–1871). Vol. **5**, pp. 305–342.

125. *Board of Trade Meteorological Papers* (1857). Vol. **1**.

126. Joseph Prestwich, *op. cit.* pp. 608–609.

127. R. Hoskyn, *Report of the Deep Sea Soundings West of Ireland made in H.M.S. Porcupine in June, July, and August, 1862*.

128. G. C. Wallich, *The North-Atlantic Sea Bed: comprising a diary of the voyage on board H.M.S. Bulldog, in 1860; and observations on the presence of animal life, and the formation and nature of organic deposits, at great depths in the ocean*, London (1862).

129. W. Chimmo, "Soundings and temperatures in the Gulf Stream", *Proc. R. geogr. Soc.* (1869). Vol. **13**, pp. 92–101. The temperatures in this article seem to have been made with unprotected thermometers and there is nothing about the trial of different types though according to Davis they were ready for cruises in the summer of 1868, *See* Chapter 14.

130. Prestwich, *op. cit.* p. 642.

131. Huxley's report on Dayman's samples of 1857 is in Joseph Dayman, *Deep Sea Soundings in the North Atlantic Ocean . . . in June and July 1857, loc. cit.* King's report on Hoskyn's samples is in R. Hoskyn, *Reports of the Deep Sea Soundings West of Ireland, loc. cit.*

Addenda et Corrigenda

p.290, 1.11: *instead* Edward Becher *read* A.B. Becher (1796–1876)

p.291, 1.27: *instead* director of the Naval Observatory which was established in 1844 *read* head of the Depot of Charts and Instruments, which became the U.S. Naval Observatory in 1854,

p.291, 1.29: *instead* observatory *read* depot

p.303, n.93: *insert* A.Day, *The Admiralty Hydrographic Service*, London (1967), p. 57.

p.304, n.99: See also Frances Leigh Williams, *Matthew Fontaine Maury: scientist of the sea*, New Brunswick, N.J. (1963), pp. 158–194

p.304, n.111,1.2: *instead: op cit.* read 8th (1861) edition, Cambridge, Mass

14. THE MAGNIFICENT GENERALIZATION

IN 1866 Charles Wyville Thomson (1830–1882), professor of Natural History at Queen's College, Belfast, travelled to Norway to visit Michael Sars (1805–1869), one of the leading marine biologists of the time.[1] Sars showed him specimens of marine fauna from Norwegian waters including some which had been dredged by his son, George Ossian Sars, from depths of up to 450 fathoms near the Lofoten Islands.[2] Furthermore, one of them bore a strong resemblance to a creature known otherwise only as a fossil in the chalk and earlier rocks.

At the beginning of his career as a marine biologist Wyville Thomson had dredged in the Firth of Forth with Edward Forbes[3] and had for a long time accepted as a self-evident truth, as had most biologists, Forbes's suggestion, for it had been intended as no more, that no life would be found in the sea at depths greater than 300 fathoms. By the 1860s, however, it was becoming increasingly difficult to sustain the idea of the azoic zone. A decade earlier the analysis of the first samples of the deep sea floor had sparked off a controversy about the skeletons of foraminifera which they contained—did these belong to surface or bottom living creatures? Then there were the star-fishes found by Wallich to be considered (*see* Ch. 13) and new evidence had since come to light, all of it pointing to the conclusion that perhaps, after all, life might be tenable in the depths of the sea. In one case a telegraph engineer Fleeming Jenkin (1833–1885) had found marine animals clinging to a broken cable when it was retrieved for repair from a depth of 1,200 fathoms in the Mediterranean and these had been studied by Professor George Allman (1812–1898) in Edinburgh and Alphonse Milne-Edwards (1835–1900) in Paris.[4]

Wyville Thomson was extremely impressed by the Sars' findings and when in the spring of 1868 he was joined in Ireland by William B. Carpenter (1813–1885) who had been collaborating with him for some time on the study of marine organisms (the Crinoids), he suggested to him that they might undertake some deep sea work on their own account. Carpenter had originally made his name as a biologist with a book, *Principles of General and Comparative Physiology*, published in 1838. His interest in cell structure had led him to study foraminifera and other marine fauna.[5] He was also successful in administration and in the organization of science. Since 1856 he had been Registrar of London University and was at this time * vice-president of the Royal Society[6]; as such he was well placed to arouse interest among leading scientists in a new field of research.

The science of marine biology had been developing in Britain, as elsewhere, since the early years of the nineteenth century. The British Association had given financial support to dredging expeditions in neighbouring seas since the 1840s.[7] However, either because of limitation of funds or because they saw no point in extending operations to deeper waters, or both, the investigators had confined their attention to depths of less than 200 fathoms. Wyville Thomson suggested to Carpenter that the new evidence promised that dredging in deep water would reveal a situation totally different from the accepted view. Carpenter was impressed and urged him to put his ideas in writing so that they could make a formal application for support to the Royal Society. Thomson did so, arguing that the theory of the azoic zone was already untenable and that it could no longer be taken for granted that the diminution of light and decrease in temperature with depth ruled out the possibility of life in the depths of the sea. This fact and the resemblance of some of the Norwegian species to fossil forms of life made it of paramount scientific interest to discover the truth. Dredging would be quite feasible at depths of up to 1,000 fathoms; it was the distances which had to be covered before reaching that depth of water and the labour involved in retrieving the trawls which had put such an undertaking beyond the reach of private enterprise. He hoped that the Royal Society might persuade the Admiralty to use one of its ships for the purpose.[8]

In a covering letter addressed to Edward Sabine, then President of the Royal Society, Carpenter endorsed what Wyville Thomson had said about the importance to science of the proposed research and the necessity of government support. If the Admiralty would allow them both to sail on one of the many ships then stationed to the north and west of the British Isles, they would carry out the scientific work provided the Royal Society would make them a grant to cover the cost of equipment.[9]

The Royal Society agreed to approach the Admiralty and the upshot was that Wyville Thomson and Carpenter sailed from Oban in H.M.S. *Lightning* under Staff-Commander May at the beginning of August 1868.

The first part of the voyage, which took them northwards to the Faroes, was inauspicious. The *Lightning*, said Wyville Thomson, was surely the oldest and most cranky paddle-steamer in the Navy. The weather was atrocious and dredging impossible save in modest depths on the Faroe Bank. It was only on the return voyage, in the intervals between the gales, that they first obtained some surprising results and these concerned not the existence of life in the depths but the distribution of temperature, a subject that no one expected to find illuminating.[10]

Wyville Thomson later wrote

We had adopted the current strange misconception with regard to ocean temperature; and it is perhaps scarcely a valid excuse that the fallacy of a universal and constant temperature of 4°C. below a certain depth and varying according to latitude, was at the time accepted and taught by nearly all the leading authorities in Physical Geography.[11]

In accordance with instructions given by the Hydrographer in the spring of 1868, the *Lightning* was equipped with thermometers of different makes to test how the pressure experienced in deep water affected their performance (*see* Ch. 13). Several of them were attached to the end of the line when the *Lightning* sounded and the mean of the minimum temperatures recorded taken as the temperature of the bottom water. So far in the voyage the temperature at the surface had been consistently over 50°F and at the bottom in the upper 40s, even when the water was 500 fathoms deep.[12] On 29 August they were in lat. 60° 45′ N, long. 4° 49′ W. The surface temperature was normal but on sounding to a depth of 510 fathoms, May found a minimum temperature of 33°F. Next day, in a comparable depth of water, it was only 32°F.

The weather had temporarily improved enough to allow them to use the dredge in deep water for the first time. It came up with a collection of marine animals not numerous but sufficient to show that the premise on which the voyage was based was not mistaken. Results obtained on 3 September gave a similar picture. Life clearly had a foothold at these depths though it seemed to be rather sparse. The alteration in the temperature measurements continued without any apparent reason and they began to doubt the results obtained earlier in the cruise.

The situation altered dramatically a few days later. On 6 September the *Lightning* was in lat. 59° 36′ N, long. 7° 20′ W and in 530 fathoms of water. Here the minimum temperature recorded was 47°F and the dredge came up with a haul which was not only more abundant than the previous ones but composed of quite different species. Some of these were entirely new and some were the same as those identified by the Sars in Norway. Again the resemblance to fossil forms was very marked. The episode, said Carpenter, proved the existence at these depths "not of a degraded or starved out *residuum* of Animal life, but of a rich and varied Fauna".[13]

The investigation was now imbued with a new sense of urgency and excitement. What was the cause of the diversity of temperature in the bottom water? How were the two different climates distributed and was the change in temperature responsible for the complete alteration in the character of the animal life observed between the two areas? Wyville Thomson had other commitments ashore but after landing him at Stornoway, Carpenter and May decided to head for deeper water and repeat their observations there. They sailed north-west until they reached the latitude in which they had first found the colder water and sounded in 650 fathoms. The minimum temperature was 46°F. Sixty miles further on they tried again but this time the depth was only 570 fathoms and the bottom temperature 47°F. Still looking for deeper water and a lower temperature they went yet another 50 miles; the depth increased to 650 fathoms but the sounding line parted and the sinker and three thermometers were lost. May now judged it prudent to turn southwards and they headed for the area between Rockall and the Hebrides where they knew that depths in the region of 1,000 fathoms were to be found, but the weather continued to threaten and in the end they had to return to port.[14]

A month later Carpenter presented their joint report to the Royal Society.[8] He sketched the course of events which had led them to make the voyage, the prolonged acceptance of the azoic theory, and the evidence which should have been enough to modify if not overthrow it. Sabine had supplied him with details of the marine organisms found by Sir John Ross[15] and J. D. Hooker had done the same for Sir James Clark Ross, who had kept the collections made during his voyage but allowed the specimens to decay without having them examined.[16] When they planned the voyage of the *Lightning*, Wyville Thomson and Carpenter had not known of anyone actively interested in deep-sea biology except the Sars but since their return they had heard through Alexander Agassiz (1835–1910) that Count Pourtalès (1823–1880) was dredging with the United States Coast Survey as part of the exploration of the Gulf Stream and that he had already reached a depth of just over 500 fathoms.[17]

In spite of the limited opportunities for dredging, the *Lightning*'s cruise had revealed the existence of a whole new realm of living creatures. Previous studies of material obtained from the sea floor in deep soundings had revealed the existence on the sea bed of the shells of globigerina and other microscopic foraminifera (*see* Ch. 13). These appeared in the *Lightning*'s samples as did the supposed protoplasmic substance *Bathybius* which had been identified and named by Huxley (*see* Ch. 15). Opinion had hitherto been divided as to whether the foraminifera actually lived on the bottom but both Wyville Thomson and Carpenter felt safe in asserting that they did in the light of their other evidence. It was the discovery of the higher forms, the sponges, rhizopods, echinoderms, crustaceans and molluscs, which removed the whole question of life at depth from the sphere of hypothesis and opened the way for further investigation.

The existence of the remains of foraminifera on the sea bed had already caused scientists to speculate that the sea floor would be covered with a substance very similar to chalk deposits on land.[18] The resemblance between the newly discovered marine animals and their fossil counterparts in the chalk gave this idea added weight and led Wyville Thomson to remark "we are still living in the cretaceous epoch".[19]

On balance, however, the voyage had posed as many problems as it solved, particularly the uncertainty which had arisen concerning the accepted but anachronistic notion of submarine temperature. By the time he presented the report of the voyage, Carpenter had hastily revised his ideas. He was able to give some account of how neglect of the discovery that sea water has different properties from fresh water and of the effect of pressure on thermometers had in this field, too, unduly prolonged the existence of a convenient but unsound hypothesis.[20] The temperatures that their thermometers had recorded in the cold area (and it seemed safe to assume that the minimum temperatures they had found were those of the bottom layer of water) showed a degree of cold in the depths of the sea well below the supposed 4°C minimum and if they allowed for some distortion in the reading due to pressure then the real temperature would be lower still.

This still left unsolved the problem of accounting for the marked difference in the submarine temperature of areas not far removed from each other. As a possible explanation Carpenter turned to the idea, which he had read of in books like Humboldt's *Cosmos*, of a general oceanic circulation sustained by differences in density caused by temperature variations. Apart from Lenz's work and the rather confused account given by Maury little had been heard about this theory since the early part of the nineteenth century (*see* Chs. 12 and 13). Carpenter argued that the sudden alteration they had observed between the Faroes and the Shetlands might be due to the presence of two opposing currents, one carrying warm water northwards from the Atlantic and the other bringing cold water from the Arctic.[21] He had before him the measurements made by Captain Peter Shortland in the Arabian Sea which showed the presence there of very cold water at depths of about 2,000 fathoms (*see* Ch. 13). How could it be explained except as water from the Antarctic which had penetrated the lower layers of the Indian Ocean?

There was much here to suggest future lines of research, but for the moment both Wyville Thomson and Carpenter were anxious for an opportunity to dredge at greater depths than had been practicable in the *Lightning* and to experiment on the degree of penetration of light into the sea. Carpenter more particularly was also keen to return to the area they had covered already and get a more detailed picture of the division between the warm and cold water, to see if there were any chemical differences between the two water masses and to observe if possible the actual movements of the deep water for any sign of the currents which he felt were responsible.[22]

The proposal for a new voyage was well received by the Royal Society and in January 1869 a special committee—the Committee on Marine Researches—was set up to make the arrangements.[23] It consisted of the President and officers, with Carpenter and John Gwyn Jeffreys (1809–1885), one of the veterans of shallow water biology. Captain G. H. Richards (1819–1896), the Hydrographer was one of the members. The committee reported on 18 February. It stressed the importance of deep sea exploration to a wide range of sciences, particularly physics, biology and geology, and made it quite clear that "systematic exploration is altogether beyond the reach of private enterprise, requiring means and appliances which can only be furnished by Government". It might well be made a special duty of the Navy but in the meantime they recommended that the Society should ask for the renewed loan of a ship to follow up the work done the previous year.

The Council of the Royal Society adopted the report and made a fresh approach to the Admiralty which agreed to let them have a ship in the summer. The Council also set up a committee to study the subject of scientific instrumentation for the voyage. It had as its members in addition to the President and officers, Richards, the industrialist and inventor Charles William Siemens (1823–1883), the physicist John Tyndall (1820–1893) and Sir Charles Wheatstone (1802–1875).

As soon as he felt certain that a second voyage would be agreed to, Carpenter had consulted the Hydrographer and Casella, head of the firm which made the Admiralty's meteorological instruments, about the need to determine the size of the error due to pressure in deep-sea thermometers.[24] Casella told them that he might be able to protect his thermometers against pressure by strengthening the bulbs. In April the scientific apparatus committee heard from the Royal Society Treasurer, William Allen Miller (1817–1870), who was professor of chemistry at King's College, London, and best known for his contributions to spectrum analysis. He suggested that a Six thermometer might best be protected by using a second bulb added outside the first and partially filled with alcohol to absorb the pressure.[25] Casella made thermometers of both types and constructed a hydraulic press to test them. He found that those with thickened bulbs were after all affected by pressure but the ones constructed at Miller's suggestion showed only a slight rise in the maximum column which Miller explained as the result of heat generated by compression inside the apparatus. This form was therefore adopted and came to be known as the Miller-Casella thermometer.

Wheatstone and Siemens both suggested using electrical thermometers. Siemens's invention, which employed the variations of electrical resistance in a wire with temperature, was made and put aboard the *Porcupine* during the first part of the 1869 voyage but it proved impossible to take readings from it at sea because the galvanometer was so badly affected by the movement of the ship.[26]

The plan this year was much more ambitious. They were being given the use of H.M. survey ship *Porcupine* under the command of Captain Calver for four months. Neither Wyville Thomson nor Carpenter could spare this amount of time from their official duties, so the cruise was divided into three sections and the first, lasting from the middle of May until the beginning of July, was taken by Gwyn Jeffreys. In addition to thermometers of different kinds for comparison and the trawls and dredges they embarked a water bottle to get samples for testing variations in salinity at different depths, and laboratory equipment including hydrometers and apparatus for collecting and analysing the gaseous contents of sea water. It was arranged that on each section of the cruise there should be someone responsible for the chemical work; on the first section this was Carpenter's eldest son, William Lant Carpenter (1841–1890). There were also two assistants to help in sorting the catches.

From the start things went much more smoothly than they had on the previous voyage. The weather was much better and on several occasions they dredged successfully in water over 1,000 fathoms deep off the west coast of Ireland. The greatest depth from which they obtained specimens was 1,476 fathoms. The failure to get results with Siemens's differential thermometer was disappointing but the problem was structural rather than functional and seemed to be nothing that could not be overcome in time. The Miller-Casella thermometers gave no trouble and showed, as expected, results a few degrees lower on the minimum side than those of the unprotected thermometers with which they were compared.[27]

Wyville Thomson was to take over the scientific work on the second leg of the voyage, with an assistant from Queen's College to do the chemical analysis. According to the plan the *Porcupine* was to work in the area between Rockall and the Shetlands but when Thomson heard of the success they already had had with dredging he was eager to see just how deep it would be possible to go. So, after consultation with Calver, he contacted Richards with the request that they might instead make for a position 250 miles west of Ushant, the nearest known piece of deep water and the only one they could reach in the time at their disposal. Richards gave his permission for the change and on 17 July the *Porcupine* sailed from Belfast. Five days later in lat. 47° 38′ N, long. 12° 08′ W, she sounded in 2,435 fathoms. The dredge was put over and, after seven anxious hours of vigilance over the straining line, they succeeded in bringing it to the surface with a haul of mud and marine animals.[28] It was the final nail in the coffin of the azoic hypothesis.

The *Porcupine* remained in the area a day or two longer, making two further attempts at dredging, only one of which was successful, and a series of temperature measurements between the surface and the bottom. Then it was time to return to port to pick up Carpenter who was to take charge of the last part of the voyage.

They now returned to the original plan and sailed northwards back to the area they had worked in the year before so that Carpenter could look at his warm and cold areas. As before, they found the marked separation between the two submarine climates, separated by only a few miles. Depth seemed to have little effect on the distribution; in the warm area the temperature remained warm even at quite considerable depths, whereas in the cold area it was cold even in comparatively shallow water. The immediate mechanism responsible for the demarcation remained obscure (*see* Ch. 16).[28] They found that the marine life in the cold areas was not so sparse as they had thought. The discovery was due to Captain Calver. It so happened that the bottom in the cold area was hard and stony and this had prevented the dredge from working efficiently. Calver suggested that they should attach tangles of stranded hemp to it in such a way that they would be dragged over the sea bed and this proved to be a much more satisfactory way of capturing animals in that kind of environment. The results did not affect the observation that the two populations were very different in character. Carpenter would have liked to extend the cruise as he had the year before but the *Porcupine* was required for survey work and he and Wyville Thomson were put ashore with many questions still unresolved.

The expedition had been a resounding success and with the presentation of its report to the Royal Society in November, accompanied by an exposition of the results by Carpenter at an open meeting, its impact on the scientific world was assured. David Forbes (1828–1876), the younger brother of Edward, wrote in one of the early numbers of *Nature*

it is not too much to say that the results of this expedition must be classed with the most important which of late years have been brought before the notice of the scientific world.[29]

Much of the impetus at this stage was due to Carpenter for whom the dissemination of knowledge was an abiding passion. In February 1870 he lectured at the Royal Institution and, at that part of his talk which described his hypothesis of ocean circulation, gave a demonstration of density currents in a glass tank, using a piece of ice at one end and a steam jet at the other to provide the extremes of temperature and dye to show up the movements of the water.[30] He also lectured to non-scientific audiences and his talk was published in a penny series, Science Lectures for the People.[31]

The effect of this success on Wyville Thomson's career was profound. He was made an F.R.S. in 1869 and in 1870 was appointed Regius Professor of Natural History at Edinburgh, in succession to Allman.

Now that the fact that life exists in the depths of the ocean had been established beyond doubt, Carpenter, who, according to Edwin Ray Lankester (1847–1929), always tended to "seek for large generalizations and the development of philosophical principles,"[6] increasingly turned his attention to studying the possibility of general oceanic circulation. The results of the 1869 cruise had convinced him that this was the cause of the temperature structure they had observed. The serial measurements made from the surface to 2,500 fathoms showed that the temperature in the Atlantic fell rapidly for the first 50 fathoms and then more slowly. At about 400 fathoms the rate of fall increased again and continued till about 1,000 fathoms. After that the decrease was negligible. In the warm area between the Shetlands and the Faroes the fall in temperature followed much the same pattern so that at the bottom the temperature was the same or not much less than it was further south at the same depth. In the cold area serial temperatures showed that the whole of the decrease that occurred over 600 fathoms at intermediate depths in the Atlantic was concentrated between 200 and 300 fathoms and that below this level the temperature hardly fell at all. The minimum in the cold area was about 32°F and in the depths of the Atlantic it was 36°F.

From the theory of oceanic circulation Carpenter deduced that the warmth of the water found in the surface layer in each of these areas and extending in the Atlantic to about 400 fathoms was, except for the first 50 fathoms which were clearly dependent on the atmospheric changes overhead, due to the slow movement northwards of warm water from equatorial regions, a movement of which the Gulf Stream was a local intensification. The very cold water found below 300 fathoms in the cold area was the counter flow from the Arctic. Because of the shallowness of the seas between Iceland, Greenland and the mainland of Europe there were few places where this water could penetrate the Atlantic. Carpenter believed that the cold water in the depths of the North Atlantic had travelled there from the Antarctic, losing some of its frigidity on the way.[32]

Neither Wyville Thomson nor Gwyn Jeffreys, to whom the detail of the new biological studies was now all important, were at all willing to follow Carpenter in embracing what Wyville Thomson called this "magnificent generalization". Both of them asked to be dissociated from the section of the report in which he set out his views.[32]

Further evidence was now desirable on both counts and a new Royal

Society committee was set up which included Carpenter, Gwyn Jeffreys, Richards, Siemens and Tyndall to plan another voyage. It was agreed that this time the *Porcupine* should head for the Mediterranean since it would be useful to study both the physical and biological aspects of a sea partially cut off from the ocean.[33] Gwyn Jeffreys wanted to compare the marine fauna of the Mediterranean with the Tertiary fossils of the area. Carpenter wanted to look for the undercurrent in the Strait of Gibraltar.

The *Porcupine* sailed from Falmouth in July 1870 with Gwyn Jeffreys in charge of the scientific work, a young Swedish zoologist to assist him and William Lant Carpenter to do the chemical work.[33] They sailed southwards along the coasts of Spain and Portugal, concentrating their attention on the biologically rich area between 400 and 800 fathoms deep.

At Gibraltar Carpenter took over the direction of the scientific work. It had been intended that Wyville Thomson should join too but he had been taken ill and had to stay at home. In the harbour at Gibraltar they tried out an apparatus which Siemens had invented to measure the depth to which light rays penetrate the sea. Siemens had intended to send one of his German technicians to look after the instrument and the differential thermometer but the outbreak of the Franco-Prussian war prevented this. Carpenter therefore decided not to use the thermometer; they did test the photometric apparatus but the corrosive action of the sea water affected it so badly that it was impossible to judge its performance.

The *Porcupine*'s first station in the second part of the cruise was chosen in the middle of the narrowest part of the Strait of Gibraltar in water 517 fathoms deep. First they looked at the physical characteristics of the water at different depths. These revealed a quite novel state of affairs. The temperature decreased from 60°F at the surface to 56°F at 50 fathoms. At 100 fathoms it was 55·7° F, at 150, 55·5°F and from there to the bottom there was no change. Specific gravity measurements showed that the water at the bottom was more saline than the surface water but less so than the water at a depth of 250 fathoms which was much more dense than any commonly encountered in the Atlantic. Carpenter was certain that the outflowing undercurrent was located in this intermediate layer.

Captain Calver had had a simple current drag made. It consisted of a wicker basket with two iron bars fixed across it at right angles to each other and sail cloth vanes stretched from them. With this they tried to detect movement in the lower layers of the water. They measured the speed of the surface current from the Atlantic and then attached the drag to a small boat and lowered it to 100 fathoms and observed the boat's movement relative to the surface current. Then they repeated the exercise at 250 fathoms. When the drogue was at 100 fathoms the boat moved with the current but at about half the speed. With the drogue at 250 fathoms it scarcely moved at all. This indicated that at 100 fathoms the water was not moving but that at 250 fathoms there was a current flowing in the opposite direction to the surface current and almost as fast so that the two forces affecting the boat and the drogue virtually cancelled each other out.[34] After a lapse of two centuries Richard Bolland's method had at last demonstrated the existence of the undercurrent in the Strait of Gibraltar (*see* Ch. 7).

The ensuing cruise in the Mediterranean was rather disappointing from the biological point of view. Scanty trawls showed that in fact life was scarce though not extinct in its depths. For Carpenter the time was well spent because the salinity and temperature measurements elucidated the situation in the Strait of Gibraltar. They showed that the density of the intermediate stratum there was characteristic of the bottom water in the shallower parts of the Mediterranean, whereas the less dense water at the bottom of the Strait was similar to the bottom water of the deeper areas in the interior of the sea. The temperature structure inside the Mediterranean presented the same unusual features that measurements in the Strait had revealed. There was scarcely any decrease below about 50 fathoms and the minimum temperature at the bottom was 54·5°F.

On their way home, at the end of September, they repeated the measurements in the Strait of Gibraltar, in the same place. The arrangement of temperature and specific gravity was the same as before, except that the temperatures were slightly lower. This time, though, the surface current was flowing much more sluggishly than it had before and when they lowered the drogue to 250 fathoms they actually saw the boat being towed westwards, against the surface current, at nearly half a mile per hour, thus placing the existence of the undercurrent beyond any doubt.

Carpenter used the results to demonstrate ocean circulation in microcosm. The evaporation of water in the Mediterranean reduced the volume of the water in the sea and increased its density. The fall in level led to an inflow at the surface from the Atlantic to restore equilibrium. At the same time the excess density of the Mediterranean column caused water to be pushed out from the bottom of the column and impelled towards the place where the weight was less, at the foot of the Atlantic column. In this way a continuous vertical circulation was set up.[35]

The same process took place in the ocean but here the motive force was to be found in the cold of the polar regions which had the same effect as the sun in the Mediterranean, reducing the volume of the water and increasing its density. The flow of water from equatorial regions set up by the drop in level at the poles gave the polar columns a weight exceeding that of the equatorial column and led to an outflow from the foot of the polar columns towards the equator. There the polar water would gradually warm up through contact with the water immediately above and slowly rise to the surface to replace the water "draughted off" by the surface current. The result was a rather contrived picture of the movement of water in the ocean. Although Carpenter stated that loss of equilibrium due to differences in density was of equal importance with changes of level in creating the internal instability from which the currents arose, he never seems to have realized that the first cause was on its own sufficient to produce the result he intended. Had he made this step forward in understanding, the arguments which later arose about the second cause could not have assumed such proportions and obscured the real issue.

For the moment, however, the second cruise of the *Porcupine* had consolidated both the achievements of the earlier voyages and the interest felt by the scientific community. Extensive extracts from the report on the 1870 voyage submitted to the Royal Society were printed in *Nature*[36] and the three scientists lectured on their results, at the British Association and elsewhere. The enduring literary monument to the voyages did not appear until 1873 when Wyville Thomson's *Depths of the Sea* was published.[37] This book, which was hailed by reviewers as a literary as well as a scientific masterpiece,[38] still gives an unrivalled picture of the preoccupations of marine science before the *Challenger's* voyage.

Both Wyville Thomson and Gwyn Jeffreys gave papers at the meeting of the British Association at Liverpool in August 1870.[39] The possible implications of Wyville Thomson's remark "we are still living in the Cretaceous Age" was making some geologists uncomfortable and according to *Nature* the venerable Sir Roderick Murchison (1792–1871) told Gwyn Jeffreys that he hoped that he did not intend, like Carpenter, to upset modern geology.[40] On his return from the Mediterranean, Carpenter wrote to rebut, with Murchison's authority, both the remark and the intention it implied[41] but the impression remained that something revolutionary had been said. Lyell referred to it as "a doctrine which has led to much popular delusion as to the bearing of the new facts on geological reasoning and classification".[42] Wyville Thomson and Carpenter protested that they had only intended to convey that the deep sea deposits of the Atlantic strongly resembled chalk and that since it seemed likely that the bed of the Atlantic had remained underwater throughout the intervening period it was reasonable to suppose that the formation had gone on uninterrupted. They had not intended to cast doubts on the existing view of stratigraphical succession.[42]

Some people also sensed an attack on the theory of evolution,* still subject to much criticism, in the emphasis which had been laid on the

* Rightly; Wyville Thomson never accepted Darwin's theory of evolution by means of natural selection.

similarity between some of the deep sea fauna and fossil remains. Wyville Thomson stressed that none of the creatures dredged by the *Lightning* and *Porcupine* had been identical with chalk fossils. He wrote

Accepting, as I believe we are now bound to do, some form of the doctrine of gradual alteration of species through natural causes, one is quite prepared to expect a total absence of identical forms found in the old chalk. The utmost which might be anticipated is such a resemblance between the two faunae as might justify the opinion that the later fauna bears to the earlier the relation of descent with extreme modification.[43]

Nevertheless, if conditions in the abyssal depths had remained virtually unchanged there was no reason why their fauna should have changed either; in his view it was alterations in the environment which led to alterations in species.

However people might argue about the implications of the discovery of life in the depths of the sea, there was no disputing the discovery itself. The whole collection of arguments put forward to sustain Edward Forbes's assumption melted away like a dawn mist. The reversal of opinion was so complete that it was soon hard to recapture the climate of thought before the discovery was made. David Forbes wrote of the evidence existing before 1868

It now appears strange to look back and observe what very little notice was taken of these new data; more especially of the important researches of Dr. Wallich on the North Atlantic sea-bed, which for years, if not all but overlooked, certainly do not appear to have received from zoölogists the full credit which they undoubtedly deserved: geologists and palæontologists were evidently loth to abandon an hypothesis which in many respects suited their requirements.[29]

There was on the other hand a considerable amount of controversy about the physical results. It was not on the whole the measurements which were in question but the interpretation to be put upon them. Many people were reluctant to accept Carpenter's version of the theory of general oceanic circulation and the deductions he made from it.

The biggest single argument raged over the Gulf Stream. Quite a bit was now known about the current itself, thanks to the work of the United States Coast Survey, and scientists in Germany and Scandinavia (Petermann and Mohn) had studied the high surface temperatures to be found in the seas off north-west Europe. It was generally assumed that the one was the cause of the others though there was considerable disagreement as to how the effect was transmitted. A. G. Findlay believed that warm water was carried across the Atlantic by westerly winds.[44] James Croll (1821–1890) thought that the current was large enough to spread its water over the entire surface of the Atlantic.[45] Carpenter's claim that it was the intensification of a much more general movement, and that this was responsible for the warm water in the north-east Atlantic, would, if admitted, strike at the root of these opinions and make much that had recently been written on the subject look rather silly. There was therefore a generally hostile reaction to his suggestions. Even Wyville Thomson preferred the more traditional view and on several occasions quoted the figures published by Croll and by Petermann in the *Geographische Mittheilungen* in an attempt to refute his friend's reasoning.[46]

Carpenter, however, was not prepared to admit that a single current, even the Gulf Stream, could produce the "vast breadth" of warm water, several hundred fathoms deep, which they had found in the Atlantic. A more fundamental cause must be at work—i.e. the general interchange of water between the equator and the poles.[47] But the idea of oceanic circulation was equally repugnant to those who held to the view inherited from Rennell and Herschel, of ocean currents as solely wind driven. One of these was John Knox Laughton (1830–1915), then a lecturer at the Royal Naval College, Portsmouth, who in 1870 published a book called *Physical Geography in its Relation to the prevailing Winds and Currents* (London). Laughton wrote to *Nature* on several occasions in the early months of 1871 attacking a suggestion made in its columns by Keith Johnston that the contiguity of high and low pressure areas in the atmosphere might be a supplementary cause of ocean currents.[48] When Johnston referred to the idea of circulation sustained by differences in density to counter Laughton's claim that wind stress was the one and only cause of currents, Laughton replied with a sweeping dismissal of the whole idea. He refused to accept Carpenter's interpretation of the evidence from the Strait of Gibraltar or to allow that density currents existed in the ocean. Johnston had pointed to the convergence of warm and cold water observed by the German Arctic expeditions as proof but Laughton retorted

the idea is wholly unsupported, and can only be classed as one of those crude speculations which, in every branch of science, do so much harm by tending to unsettle the minds of those who indeed take an interest in the subject, but have not made it a special study.[49]

Carpenter replied with a mildly indignant defence of his ideas and observations and some telling references to Aimé and other authors who had exactly demonstrated the effect of changes in barometric pressure upon sea level[50] by way of administering a damper to Johnston and Laughton who had been crudely speculating on the subject for some months.

Someone who had no intention of allowing his mind to be unsettled was Captain T. A. B. Spratt who in 1857 had made a study of the currents in the Dardanelles and Bosporus as part of his survey work in the Mediterranean.[51] The observations were clearly designed to show if there were an undercurrent travelling counter to the surface current which flowed out of the Black Sea into the Mediterranean. Spratt used floats attached to sinkers by lines of different lengths and measured the speed at which they moved. In one set of observations, made in December 1857, he found that the surface current was flowing at 0·9 m.p.h. The sinkers were lowered into successively deeper layers of water and each time the floats travelled that much more slowly than the surface current until at 40 fathoms, and at all depths below, they were moving at only 0·1 m.p.h. Instead of realizing that this pointed to the existence of a countercurrent moving almost as fast as the surface current, Spratt interpreted his results as showing that all the water was moving in the same direction as the surface current but more slowly with increasing depth. He realized that some salt water must reach the Black Sea but thought that this happened when the surface current reversed during autumn gales.

Naturally Spratt misinterpreted Carpenter's results in the same way and even the result of the one observation which, by his reasoning, should have been counted positive failed to convince him, so great was his repugnance to the whole idea.[52] He still clung to the idea that the bottom of the sea was full of water at 38°F, allowing of course for the pressure correction to thermometers, and that this was the atmospheric mean, and advanced all kinds of arguments, such as the discovery of a sounding line which had been allowed to run out too far and had coiled itself neatly round the lead, to try and maintain the idea of the stillness of the deep oceans.

Carpenter of course pointed out the mistake which Spratt had made in assessing both Carpenter's experiments and his own.[53] The existence of an undercurrent in the Bosporus was confirmed by Commander W. J. L. Wharton (1843–1905) who repeated the observations with H.M.S. *Shearwater* in 1872.[54]

The most serious criticism which Carpenter's ideas had to endure came from James Croll. He interpolated a letter into the Laughton-Johnston controversy in *Nature* which revealed the basis of his objections, though at this stage they seem to have passed unnoticed. He wrote

It is singular that diversity should still exist as to whether ocean currents are due to the impulse of winds, or to difference of specific gravity. That ocean currents are not caused by difference of specific gravity between the waters of the equatorial and polar regions can be proved, as the amount of force from this cause acting on the ocean to produce a current, can be readily calculated.

Assuming, which is not the case, that difference in saltness between the water of equatorial and polar regions does not in any way tend to neutralise the effect resulting from difference of temperature, in other words, that the sea in polar regions is as salt as the sea in equatorial regions, it can be shown that the force resulting from the difference of temperature, tending to produce a current towards the poles, amounts to only $\frac{1}{1820000}$ of that of gravity. For example, the force impelling a cubic foot (64 lb.) of sea water at the surface of the ocean towards the poles is scarcely equal to the weight of one-fourth of a grain. A force so infinitesimal, acting on a fluid even so perfect as water, can produce absolutely no motion. M. Dubuat found by direct experiment that it requires a force four times greater than the above to produce even sensible motion.

Ocean currents are due alone to the impulse of the wind. In the latter half of my paper on the Cause of Ocean Currents, which will shortly appear in the *Philosophical Magazine*, I hope to be able to show that the objections to this theory are founded upon misconceptions regarding the way in which the winds produce the great system of oceanic circulation.[55]

Croll was an unusual and in some ways remarkable person. He had been born into a Perthshire crofting family and left school at fourteen. He was academically ambitious but almost entirely self-taught when, after various occupations, he was appointed Clerk of the Geological Survey in Edinburgh.[56] His success was due to sheer endurance as well as innate ability and he displayed the same dogged refusal to be defeated by adverse circumstances in the dispute which soon followed with Carpenter.

In 1867 Croll had published a paper in the *Philosophical Magazine* on the Ice Age, which as he pointed out was not continuous but broken up into several epochs. The explanation which he favoured for the deterioration of climate was the theory that, at different times in the past, the earth's orbit had varied in its eccentricity. This had not only produced severer winters in the hemisphere away from the sun in aphelion but had led to the deflection of the prevailing winds and of the ocean currents which depended on them and which were responsible for moderating extremes of climate.[57] Croll regarded the wind-driven origin of ocean currents as an essential part of his theory and strenuously denied that the agencies invoked by Carpenter had any effect, though Carpenter in his turn did not deny that the wind was a force in producing currents in the sea.[58]

In a series of articles published in 1870–1871 Croll amplified the views on currents outlined in the earlier paper. He paid special attention to the Gulf Stream and endeavoured to show by calculation that the amount of warm water coming through the Strait of Florida was large enough to produce the high sea temperatures and temperate climate of Northern Europe.[59] In the final section of the paper he turned to discuss the density theory of currents. He wrote

It is difficult to conceive how a theory so manifestly erroneous should have gained such general acceptance.[60]

Croll did not follow Laughton in making an irrational and unconsidered rejection of the whole idea. He acknowledged that differences in density could very well produce currents, if the conditions were right. He wrote

One has no difficulty, for example, in perceiving that if the intertropical waters of the ocean are expanded by heat, and the waters round the poles contracted by cold, the surface of the ocean will stand at a higher level at the equator than at the poles. Equilibrium being thus disturbed, the water at the equator will tend to flow towards the poles as a surface-current, and the water at the poles towards the equator as an undercurrent.[60]

He did deny that in the ocean the difference in level caused by the contraction of water by cold at the poles would be great enough to produce a flow from the equator. He calculated that the difference could not be more than 18 feet at the very most and that if one accepted the experiments on the flow of water over an inclined plane made by Dubuat early in the nineteenth century this was less than half the slope needed to induce flow and overcome the resistance due to friction.

In his insistence on difference of level as the governing factor in creating density currents Croll showed that he too failed to understand the mechanism involved. At one point he wrote

There is an error into which some writers appear to fall to which I may here refer. Suppose that at the equator we have to descend 10,000 feet before water equal in density to that at the poles is reached. We have in this case a plain with a slope of 10,000 feet in 6,200 miles, forming the upper surface of the water of maximum density. Now this slope exercises no influence in the way of producing a current, as some seem to suppose, for this is not a case of disturbed equilibrium, but the reverse. This slope is the condition of static equilibrium when there is a difference between the temperature of the water at the equator and the poles. The only slope that has any tendency to produce motion of the water is the slope formed by the surface of the ocean in the equatorial regions being higher than the surface at the poles; but this is a slope of only 18 feet in 6,200 miles.[61]

Croll had some excuse for his objections since Carpenter's ideas on this point were somewhat confused. When developing them in an address to the Royal Geographical Society early in 1871, Carpenter again made unequivocal references to the effect of the reduction in height of the denser column in producing the inflow from the less dense area. Again, it was the combined weight of the inflow and the denser water which pressed out the water from the bottom of the sea in polar regions. This was what he was thinking of when he laid stress on the importance of polar cold, for the first time as he thought, as the motive force behind ocean circulation.[62] Though he called his conclusions a theory of general oceanic circulation due to differences in density, the theory did not bear much relation in the details of its operation to similar attempts to formulate a theory earlier in the century, insofar as these had attempted detailed considerations of the processes involved[63] or, one presumes, to the further understanding of ocean circulation by the leading physicists who later gave his theory their support. Carpenter's apparent inability at this stage to clarify his ideas meant that when Croll claimed to have calculated that the gravitational force available to do the work involved was insufficient, Carpenter was unable to strike at the root of the misconception and could do no more than dispute Croll's actual figures.[64]

Meanwhile Carpenter's theory had won support from an unexpected quarter. He had sent a copy of his Royal Geographical Society lecture to Sir John Herschel and received a very encouraging reply from the elderly astronomer, written only weeks before his death. Herschel had written

My dear Sir,
    Many thanks for your paper on the Gibraltar Current and Gulf Stream.
    Assuredly, after well considering all you say, as well as the common sense of the matter, and the experience of our hot-water circulation-pipes in our greenhouses, &c., there is no refusing to admit that an oceanic circulation of some sort must arise from mere heat, cold, and evaporation as *verae causae*, and you have brought forward with singular emphasis the more powerful action of the polar cold, or rather the more intense action, as its maximum effect is limited to a much smaller area than that of the maximum of equatorial heat.
    The action of the trade and counter-trade winds in like manner cannot be ignored; and henceforwards the question of ocean-currents will have to be studied under a two-fold point of view. The wind-currents, however, are of easier investigation. All the causes lie on the surface; none of the agencies escape our notice; the configuration of coasts, which mainly determines their direction, is patent to sight. It is otherwise with the other class of movements. They take place in the depths of the ocean; and their movements and directions and channels of concentration are limited by the configuration of the sea-bottom, which has to be studied over its whole extent by the very imperfect method of sounding.
    I am glad you succeeded in getting specimens of Mediterranean water near the place of the presumed 'salt spring' of Smyth and Wollaston, making it clear that the whole affair must have arisen from some accidental substitution of one bottle for another, or from evaporation. I never put any hearty faith in it.
    So, after all, there *is* an under-current in the Straits of Gibraltar.
    Repeating my thanks for this interesting memoir, believe me, Dear Sir,
                                Yours very truly,
                                        J. F. W. Herschel.[65]

It must have been a considerable blow to Wyville Thomson, Croll and Laughton to find that Herschel was now prepared to admit Carpenter's arguments to a place of equal importance since it was on his authority that they had rested much of their case for a causal relationship between winds and currents.[66]

Carpenter also received support from Joseph Prestwich (1812–1896). Twenty years before, Prestwich had collected information for a paper on deep-sea temperatures which he had never written. Now in his presidential address to the Geological Society in February 1871, he outlined the developments which had taken place earlier in the century and the reasons for the recent confusion.[67] He knew about the work of Lenz and other pioneers in the field and was able to give some perspective to the idea of ocean circulation at a time when its historical antecedents were not at all well known. For his own part, he was certain that the water observed in the depths of the Atlantic must be of polar origin though he was not yet prepared to commit himself as to the way it got there. *Nature* was not so cautious. In a leading article in June, commenting on the corroborative evidence which Prestwich had provided and to Herschel's accolade on the general theory, the author concluded "Dr. Carpenter seems to us to have both scientific probability and common sense on his side".[68]

These expressions of support were no doubt very welcome but Carpenter had decided that the one way of clearing up the questions which Croll and others had raised was to lay the whole matter before the leading physicists of the day. If they considered his ideas to be sound then he would be justified in continuing to advance the case for ocean circulation. The British Association provided the best opportunity for open discussion and at the meeting at Edinburgh in August 1871, he read a paper in Section A entitled "On the thermodynamics of ocean circulation."[69] In the discussion which followed Sir William Thomson (1824-1907), later Lord Kelvin, gave it as his opinion that Carpenter had "thoroughly established his case". He believed that there was no question of attributing movements in the depths of the ocean to the effect of wind on the surface. The only contingency in which wind had the power to cause vertical circulation would be when it blew straight into a bay or fjord. This could create a head of water which would escape in a reverse outflow at the bottom. This view was endorsed by G. G. Stokes (1819-1903).

Wyville Thomson and Carpenter were unable to have either the *Lightning* or the *Porcupine* in 1871 but this was not too serious a blow because a much larger expedition was already being talked of.[70] Also, Richards said that Carpenter might sail in H.M.S. *Shearwater* under the command of Captain George Nares (1831-1915), who was being sent on survey duties in the Mediterranean. This gave Carpenter a new opportunity for making observations in the Strait of Gibraltar.[71, 72] The *Shearwater* spent a week in the area repeating the experiments of the previous year in different places. The work showed that the tidal streams had a pronounced influence on both surface and undercurrent and that the undercurrent actually changed direction with the tide. They were nevertheless able to show that the net transport in the lower layers was westwards and observations outside the Strait unmistakably showed the presence of Mediterranean water in the intermediate layers of the Atlantic. Carpenter wrote from Malta: since

an opportunity has recently been afforded me by the Hydrographer to the Admiralty of carrying out, in conjunction with Captain Nares, of H.M.S. *Shearwater*, a series of further researches on the Gibraltar current, which place beyond all doubt the outflow of dense Mediterranean water into the Atlantic, over the 'ridge' or 'marine watershed' between Capes Trafalgar and Spartel, and beneath the surface-inflow of Atlantic water, I would submit (1) whether there must not be some fundamental fallacy in Mr. Croll's computations in regard to the Gibraltar current, and (2) whether this fallacy should not destroy all confidence in the infallibility with which Mr. Croll credits himself in regard to the general oceanic circulation.[73]

He accompanied the *Shearwater* to the Eastern Mediterranean, not reached the year before, and continued his investigation of the physical conditions of the deep water.

In his report Carpenter went into the whole subject of ocean circulation and described his theory with great care. He explained

Mr. Croll's whole manner of treating the subject is so different from that which it appears to me to require, and he has so completely misapprehended my own view of the question, that I feel it requisite to present this in fuller detail, in order that Physicists and Mathematicians, having both sides fully before them, may judge between us: and this must be my apology for dwelling at some length upon considerations so elementary, that I should not otherwise have thought it requisite even to advert to them.

He objected to the arguments that Croll was using against him, particularly those in which he relied on Dubuat's experiments on the resistance in water flowing down a small incline since these had been made over a solid surface and could not very well be applied to the ocean. He attempted too to clarify his own position and stressed that the circulation he envisaged was a continuous process in which the agencies tending to upset equilibrium in the water and the compensatory movements would both be operating at the same time so that there would not even be the few feet of difference between the level of the equator and the poles that Croll allowed. The existence of ocean circulation could equally well be argued from the conditions observed in seas which were cut off wholly or partially from the polar influence. His own observations in the Mediterranean showed this and these had been corroborated by information received from Chimmo in H.M.S. *Nassau*. He had been making temperature measurements in the Far East which showed that in the Sulu Sea, which was cut off from the open ocean below a certain depth, the temperature remained the same from that point to the bottom whereas in the China Sea which was not so cut off the temperature structure was the same as that found in the open ocean.[72]

More and more people were becoming convinced by what Carpenter had to say. One declaration of support came from no less a person than Sir George Airy, now President of the Royal Society, who said in an address to the Society in 1872

I think it right to state, as my opinion, that the flow of surface-water from the places of high temperature, and the return of deep water to the same, are certain in theory and are supported by observation.[74]

Carpenter also received support from H. A. Meyer of the Kiel Commission who had worked on the Baltic undercurrent.[75]

Croll however remained totally unmoved. He wrote

I trust to be able to show that all the principal currents of the globe, the Gibraltar current not excepted, are moving in the exact direction in which they ought to move—assuming the winds to be the sole impelling cause.[76]

He also referred to the effect of the rotation of the earth which, he said, had been greatly exaggerated. The deflecting force depended on the rate of movement and in a current caused by differences in density would be infinitesimal. This caused interventions in the by now routine exchanges between Carpenter and Croll in *Nature*, by J. D. Everett (1831–1904), professor of natural philosophy at Queen's College, Belfast, and William Ferrel, both of whom had contributed to the theoretical treatment of the effect of the earth's rotation. Ferrel emphasized that the force operates only to change the direction in which a body moves and does not accelerate or retard it. He suggested among other things that the tilting caused by eastward deflection in the Gulf Stream might be the cause of the cold water which comes to the surface on the western boundary of the current. He criticized Croll's reliance on Dubuat's figures

As Mr. Croll insists that Dr. Carpenter's experiment, to be applicable to the case, should have been made with a canal 120 feet long, and only one inch deep; so it might be insisted that M. Dubuat's experiment, to be applicable to Mr. Croll's case, should be made with a canal or body of water three of four miles deep. But there is no necessity for us to make any such experiments, for nature is performing the experiment regularly every six hours. . . . If M. Dubuat's experiment were applicable to the ocean, the moon could not cause a tide at all unless its mass were about fifteen times greater.[77]

Ferrel had mistakenly supposed that Croll was using Rennell's version of the wind theory of ocean currents which involved a heaping up of the water by the wind and attacked him on this ground. This brought a swift denial from Croll who then went on to argue that the gravitational force acting on a current caused by differences in density must at least be equal to the deflecting force of the earth's rotation if poleward flow is to be maintained.[78] Ferrel argued that, setting aside resistance, and this was an unknown quantity but in practice small enough to be left out of the calculations, a body would be deflected equally over the same distance irrespective of the kind of motion.[79] Croll tried to introduce a figure for the resistance to deflection and argued that if the large force available for deflection were completely used up in overcoming resistance then the much smaller force supposed to be responsible for the northerly movement would be totally inadequate to overcome the similar resistance to it. He refused to admit the argument from tides made by both Ferrel and Everett and concluded by saying that the poor state of his health now prevented him from continuing the correspondence any further.[80]

Carpenter took the opportunity to point out that at this stage he had the facts on his side.[81] Croll's objections to his theory were purely hypothetical and if he wanted to make them convincing he should say how else he supposed the observations of the past few years were to be accounted for.

Croll by this time was in an isolated position. Many of the leading scientists of the day had pronounced themselves in favour of Carpenter's views. Croll too tried to enlist the support of mathematicians and physicists but obtained on the whole only qualified expressions of sympathy. Professor G. C. Foster agreed with him that Carpenter's Royal Institution experiment was "simply silly" and Osmond Fisher (1817–1914) thought that wind was the major cause of currents but he did not feel that the effect of temperature could be ruled out entirely. Only Samuel Haughton seems to have taken the matter seriously enough to try and produce a mathematical theory of wind-driven circulation.[82]

It was perhaps Croll's general attitude as much as the arguments he was using that did his point of view most harm. The details of the theory of ocean circulation were as yet very vague and no one felt able to say whether his calculations were right or not. Croll had in fact rushed in where others feared to tread. He very much underestimated the difficulty of finding a reliable quantitative solution of the questions he was asking and wrote on one occasion

Dr. Carpenter must be mistaken in supposing that it requires great mathematical skill to determine the value of the forces to which he attributes the circulation of the ocean. The whole subject, when properly viewed, resolves itself into a mechanical problem of such extreme simplicity as not to require for its solution the aid of any mathematics whatever in the ordinary sense of the term.[83]

He was the only person who did regard the problem as a simple one. Carpenter who was conscious of his own lack of knowledge of the physical sciences[84] was far from having an overconfident opinion of his own theory but the fact remained that it fitted in well with what was known of conditions in the sea, conditions which Croll had not even endeavoured to explain, while the theoretical basis of his arguments against Carpenter satisfied few besides himself.

As Carpenter viewed it the wind and density current systems were complementary, the one forming a horizontal, the other a vertical pattern, and there was no question of either one cause or the other being solely responsible. This was far from Croll's position. He had begun by saying that differences in density might produce currents but that they were not great enough in the ocean and ended committed to the view that all major currents were wind-driven, even in the Strait of Gibraltar and similar places. The difficulty of maintaining such a position in the teeth of so much contrary evidence and Carpenter's own difficulty in dislodging him from it while his own theory remained inadequate no doubt account for the note of acerbity which crept into their correspondence from time to time, and even more so when they resumed the argument a year or two later.

There is no doubt that Carpenter was greatly irritated by the tone and content of Croll's criticism which seemed to him both wrongly directed and unconstructive. Perhaps this was at the back of his mind when, in another context, in his presidential address to the British Association in 1872, he attacked

those who set up *their own conceptions* of the Orderly Sequence which they discern in the Phenomena of Nature, as fixed and determinate *Laws*, by which those phenomena not only *are* within all Human experience, but always *have been*, and always *must be*, invariably governed, are really guilty of the Intellectual arrogance they condemn in the Systems of the Ancients, and place themselves in diametrical antagonism to those real Philosophers, by whose comprehensive grasp and penetrating insight that Order has been so far disclosed.[85]

He hoped that the proposed voyage of circumnavigation would produce incontrovertible evidence to support his views and was confident that

within the next few years, a great mass of additional data will be collected, which will afford adequate materials for the construction of a definite Physical Theory, by Mathematicians fully competent to the task.[86]

14. NOTES

1. William A. Herdman, *Founders of Oceanography and their Work: an introduction to the science of the sea*, London (1923), p. 41.
2. Erling Sivertsen, "Michael Sars, a pioneer in marine biology, with some aspects from the early history of biological oceanography in Norway", *Bull. Inst. océanogr. Monaco* (1968). Numéro spécial 2, Vol. **2**, pp. 439–451.

3. Daniel Merriman, "Edward Forbes—Manxman", *Progress in Oceanography* (ed. M. Sears) London and New York (1965). Vol. **3**, pp. 191–206.*

4. Sir Charles Wyville Thomson, *The Depths of the Sea*, 2nd ed., London (1874), pp. 1–30.

5. *Ibid.* pp. 49–50.

6. Edwin Ray Lankester, "Dr Carpenter, C.B., F.R.S.", *Nature* (26 November 1885). Vol. **33**, pp. 83–85.

7. J. Gwyn Jeffreys, "Last report on dredging among the Shetland Isles", *Report of the 38th meeting of the British Association for the Advancement of Science (1868)*, (1869). Pt. 1, pp. 232–247, etc.

8. W. B. Carpenter, "Preliminary report of dredging operations in the seas to the north of the British Islands, carried on in H.M.S. *Lightning*, by Dr. Carpenter and Dr. Wyville Thomson, Professor of Natural History in Queen's College, Belfast", *Proc. R. Soc.* (1868–69). Vol. **17**, pp. 168–200; pp. 198–199.
Also printed in Wyville Thomson, *op. cit.* pp. 50–53.

9. *Ibid.* pp. 197–198.
Wyville Thomson, *op. cit.* pp. 53–54.

10. W. B. Carpenter, *op. cit.* p. 199.

11. Wyville Thomson, *op. cit.* pp. 56–57.

12. W. B. Carpenter, *op. cit.* p. 169 ff.

13. *Ibid.* p. 174.

14. *Ibid.* p. 177.

15. *Ibid.* pp. 177–178.

16. *Ibid.* p. 178.

17. *Ibid.* p. 183.

18. Wyville Thomson, *op. cit.* pp. 470, 496.

19. *Ibid.* pp. 467–501, especially p. 471.

20. W. B. Carpenter, *op. cit.* pp. 185–187. Even though the work of the *Lightning* and subsequent developments finally destroyed any claim it had had to scientific respectability, the idea that the depths of the sea are full of water at 4°C remained and may well still remain part of the popular imagination. It appeared in Parliament as recently as 1961 in the mouth of the then Civil Lord of the Admiralty: *Hansard*, 5th series, (1961). Vol. **638**, 235.

21. W. B. Carpenter, *op. cit.* pp. 187–188.

22. W. B. Carpenter, *op. cit.* pp. 195–196.

23. W. B. Carpenter, J. Gwyn Jeffreys and C. Wyville Thomson, "Preliminary report of the scientific exploration of the deep sea in H.M.S. *Porcupine*, during the summer of 1869", *Proc. R. Soc.* (1869–1870). Vol. **18**, pp. 397–492.

24. *Ibid.* p. 408.
J. E. Davis, "On deep-sea thermometers", (abstract), *Nature* (26 May 1870). Vol. **2**, p. 73.

25. W. A. Miller, "Note upon a self-registering thermometer adapted to deep-sea soundings", *Proc. R. Soc.* (1868–69). Vol. **17**, pp. 482–486.

26. W. B. Carpenter, J. Gwyn Jeffreys and C. Wyville Thomson, *op. cit.* pp. 411–412.

27. *Ibid.* pp. 419–420, 410–411.

28. *Ibid.* pp. 424–429, 430.

29. David Forbes, "The depths of the sea", *Nature* (25 November 1869). Vol. **1**, pp. 100–101.

30. W. B. Carpenter, "On the temperature and animal life of the deep sea", *Nature* (1870). Vol. **1**, 10 March, pp. 488–490; 24 March, pp. 540–542; 31 March, pp. 563–566.
31. *Nature* (23 February 1871). Vol. **3**, p. 332.
32. W. B. Carpenter, J. Gwyn Jeffreys and C. Wyville Thomson, *op. cit.* pp. 453ff.
33. W. B. Carpenter and J. Gwyn Jeffreys, "Report on deep-sea researches carried on during the months of July, August, and September 1870, in H.M.S. *Porcupine*", *Proc. R. Soc.* (1870–1871). Vol. **19**, pp. 146–221.
34. *Ibid.* pp. 162–168.
35. W. B. Carpenter and J. Gwyn Jeffreys, *op. cit.* p. 185 ff.
36. *Nature* (1871). Vol. **3**, 23 February, pp. 334–339; 23 March, pp. 415–417; 6 April, pp. 454–457.
37. Charles Wyville Thomson, *The Depths of the Sea*, London (1873).
38. Daniel Merriman, "A posse ad esse", *J. Mar. Res.* (1948). Vol. **7**, pp. 139–146.
39. "The British Association", *Nature* (1870). Vol. **2**, 22 September, p. 417; 6 October, pp. 464–465; 20 October, p. 503.
40. *Ibid.* p. 503.
41. William B. Carpenter, "The geological bearings of recent deep-sea explorations", *Nature* (27 October), pp. 513–515. But Gwyn Jeffreys stood by his account of the incident: *Nature* (17 November 1870). Vol. **3**, p. 53.
42. Sir Charles Lyell, *The Student's Elements of Geology*, London (1871), p. 263; quoted by Wyville Thomson, "The continuity of the chalk", *Nature* (19 January 1871). Vol. **3**, pp. 225–227.
43. Charles Wyville Thompson, *op. cit.* p. 227.
44. A. G. Findlay, "On the Gulf Stream", *Proc. R. geog. Soc.* (1869). Vol. **13**, pp. 102–108.
45. James Croll, "On ocean-currents I", *Phil. Mag.* (1870) 4th series. Vol. **39**, pp. 81–106.
46. Charles Wyville Thomson, "On deep-sea climates", *Nature* (28 July 1870). Vol. **2**, pp. 257–261; "On the distribution of temperature in the North Atlantic", *Nature* (27 July 1871). Vol. **4**, pp. 251–253.
    A. Petermann, "Der Golfstrom und Standpunkt der thermometrischen Kenntniss des Nord-Atlantischen Oceans und Landgebiets im Jahre 1870", *Geographische Mittheilungen* (1870). Vol. **16**, pp. 201–204.
47. William B. Carpenter, "The Gulf Stream", *Nature* (25 August 1870). Vol. **2**, pp. 334–335.
48. *Nature* (1871). Vol. **3**, 19 January, p. 227; 2 February, p. 265; 9 March, p. 368 (Johnston); 26 January, pp. 246–247; 23 February, p. 326; 6 April, p. 447 (Laughton).
49. *Nature*, 6 April 1871, p. 447.
50. William B. Carpenter, "Influence of barometric pressure on ocean currents", *Nature* (20 April 1871), p. 488.
51. T. A. B. Spratt, *Travels and Researches in Crete*, 2 vols, London (1865). Vol. **2**, pp. 333–351.
52. T. A. B. Spratt, "On the undercurrent theory of the ocean, as propounded by recent explorers", *Proc. R. Soc.* (1870–71). Vol. **19**, pp. 528–556.
53. William B. Carpenter, "Oceanic circulation", *Nature* (23 November 1871). Vol. **5**, pp. 59–60.

54. W. J. L. Wharton, *Report on the Currents of the Dardanelles and Bosporus*, London (1886).
55. James Croll, *Nature* (26 January 1871). Vol. **3**, p. 247.
56. James Campbell Irons, *Autobiographical Sketch of James Croll with Memoir of his Life and Work*, London (1896).
57. James Croll, "On the excentricity of the earth's orbit, and its physical relations to the glacial epoch", *Phil. Mag.* (1867) 4th series. Vol. **33**, pp. 119–131.
58. W. B. Carpenter and J. Gwyn Jeffreys, *op. cit.* p. 219.
59. James Croll, "On ocean-currents", *Phil. Mag.* (1870), 4th series. Vol. **39**, pp. 81–106, 180–194. Vol. **40**, pp. 233–259. Vol. **42**, (1871), pp. 241–280.
60. *Ibid.* Vol. **40**, p. 233.
61. *Ibid.* p. 251.
62. Its significance had in fact been suggested earlier, as in the instructions drawn up by a committee of the Royal Society for Sir James Clark Ross. *See* Ch. 13.
63. For example, George Buist. *See* Ch. 13.
64. W. B. Carpenter, "On the Gibraltar current, the Gulf Stream, and the general oceanic circulation", *Proc. R. geog. Soc.* (1870–1871). Vol. **15**, pp. 54–88.
65. "Sir J. Herschel on ocean currents", *Nature* (25 May 1871). Vol. **4**, p. 71.
66. Wyville Thomson, "On deep-sea climates", *Nature* (28 July 1870). Vol. **2**, p. 260.
67. Joseph Prestwich, Anniversary address, *Q. Jl. geol. Soc. Lond.* (1871). Vol. **27**, pp. xxx–lxxv.
68. "The general oceanic circulation", *Nature* (8 June 1871). Vol. **4**, pp. 97–98.
69. "The British Association meeting at Edinburgh", *Nature* (17 August 1871). Vol. **4**, pp. 315–316. Croll later adopted the argument and said that this kind of circulation could happen in the open sea as well as in bays. *See* Ch. 15.
70. *See* Ch. 15 for the origins of the *Challenger* expedition.
71. G. S. Nares, "Investigations of the currents in the Strait of Gibraltar, made in August 1871", *Proc. R. Soc.* (1871–1872). Vol. **20**, pp. 97–106.
72. W. B. Carpenter, "Report on scientific researches carried on during the months of August, September, and October, 1871, in H.M. Surveying-ship *Shearwater*", *op. cit.*, pp. 535–644.
73. W. B. Carpenter, "The Gibraltar Current", *Nature* (12 October 1871). Vol. **4**, p. 468.
74. G. B. Airy, Address of the President in *Proc. R. Soc.* (1872–1873). Vol. **21**, pp. 23–30.
75. William B. Carpenter, "Oceanic circulation", *Nature* (23 November 1871). Vol. **5**, pp. 59–60.
76. James Croll, "Ocean currents", *Nature* (11 January 1872). Vol. **5**, pp. 201–202.
77. William Ferrel, "Ocean currents", *Nature* (14 March 1872). Vol. **5**, pp. 384–385. Ferrel had summarized his work: "The motions of fluids and solids relative to the earth's surface", *The American Journal of Science and Arts* (1861), 2nd series. Vol. **31**, pp. 27–51.
78. James Croll, "Ocean currents", *Nature* (21 March 1872). Vol. **5**, p. 399; (25 April 1872), pp. 502–503.
79. William Ferrel, "Ocean currents", *Nature* (13 June 1872). Vol. **6**, p. 120.
80. James Croll, "Ocean currents", *Nature* (25 July 1872), pp. 240–241; "Kinetic; energy", 15 August, p. 324; "Oceanic circulation", 3 October, pp. 453–454.

81. William B. Carpenter, "Oceanic circulation", *Nature*, (10 October 1872), p. 473.
82. J. C. Irons, *op. cit.* pp. 283–285, 285–287, 357.
83. James Croll, *loc. cit.*, *Nature*. Vol. 5, p. 202.
84. William B. Carpenter, *loc. cit. Nature*. Vol. 4, p. 468.
85. W. B. Carpenter, Presidential address, *Report of the 42nd Meeeting of the British Association for the Advancement of Science (1872)*, (1837), pp. lxix–lxxxiv.
86. W. B. Carpenter, *op. cit. Nature*, Vol. 5, p. 60.

Addenda et Corrigenda

p.307, 1.2: *instead* was at this time *read* soon to become

p.312, 1.12: *instead* beginning *read* middle

p.329, n.3, 1.2: *instead* London and New York *read* Oxford

15. THE VOYAGE OF H.M.S. *CHALLENGER*

EARLY in the summer of 1871, in a lecture given at the Royal Institution, W. B. Carpenter called on Her Majesty's Government not to allow Britain's present lead in marine science to go by default.[1] News had come from the United States of a projected cruise in the Atlantic and Pacific Oceans to be led jointly by Jean Louis Agassiz (1807–1873) and Count Pourtalès.[2] The Germans were planning an expedition in the Atlantic and Sweden had sent two ships to the Arctic. *Nature* commented that if an opportunity were not found for following up the discoveries already made it would be a blow to national prestige and unfair to the scientists whose efforts had given the country its commanding position.[3]

Carpenter had his own very definite ideas about what the next step should be. As early as 1869 the idea had taken shape in his mind of persuading the government to send out a voyage of circumnavigation which would take the techniques and concepts developed on board the *Lightning* and *Porcupine* and put them to work in the oceans of the world.[4] Now, in June 1871, he wrote to G. G. Stokes, Secretary of the Royal Society, suggesting that the Society should consult with other leading scientific bodies and draw up a joint plan for marine research which could be submitted to parliament.[5] In a further corrrespondence, with George Goschen (1831–1907), First Lord of the Admiralty, he received an assurance that the government would give a favourable consideration to an application with this backing.[6]

The British Association discussed the need for further action at its summer meeting and adopted the resolution that

the President and Council of the British Association be authorised to co-operate with the President and Council of the Royal Society, in whatever manner may seem to them to be best, for the promotion of the circumnavigation expedition specially fitted out for carrying the physical and biological Exploration of the Deep-sea into all the great oceanic centres.[7]

Carpenter, on board H.M.S. *Shearwater*, wrote again to the Royal Society from Malta urging action and revealing the existence of his correspondence with Goschen and its results.[5] At the same time, in a letter to *Nature*, he referred to the

Scientific Circumnavigation Expedition, which (I have every reason to expect) will be fitted out by Her Majesty's Government next year.[8]

If the expedition was to be ready to go in 1872 there was no time to be lost. The Royal Society set up a committee consisting of officers and council members and the people most closely involved in the planning of the previous voyages; it included Carpenter, Wyville Thomson, Gwyn Jeffreys, Captain Richards, T. H. Huxley, Sir William Thomson and J. D. Hooker.[5] On its recommendation the Council asked the government to send out an expedition which would make a scientific study of the oceans.[9] The application was successful, consent being given in April 1872, and preparations for departure began immediately.

The ease and rapidity with which the matter was settled was deceptively simple and gives the impression of open-handedness where science was concerned that was in fact far from true in general. Two factors worked in its favour. One was that the expedition was a single event, one that it reflected favourably upon the country as a whole. In assisting the expeditions sent out to observe the solar eclipses of December 1870 and 1871 the government had already shown itself ready to support specific enterprises of obvious scientific value where there was no question of incurring repeated expenditure.[10] When quite modest financial aid was sought for a long term project the outcome was very different.

In 1867 the British Association had set up a committee, under the leadership of Sir William Thomson, to improve the harmonic analysis of tides.[11] The committee, which consisted of a number of leading scientists and people such as T. G. Bunt who had made special contributions to the study of tides, was financed at a rate of £100 a year. Harmonic analysis represented the greatest advance in this branch of science since Lubbock and Whewell had given it renewed impetus in the 1830s. Briefly, it enabled the complex forces creating tides to be split into simple components whose effects could be individually determined. The new insight which this analysis gave into the complicated structure of the actual tides experienced in any one place enabled the process to be reversed and led a few years later to the construction of Sir William Thomson's tide-calculating machine, which when set with the variables involved, would integrate them to predict the height of tide to be expected at the same point over future periods.[12]

The useful applications of this research were many but in spite of this an application from the British Association to the Treasury in 1871 for a grant to relieve the charge on its annual budget, which was gradually falling off from a peak attained in the late 1860s, was turned down flat.[13] In the letter explaining the decision the Treasury pointed out that if they were to give the £150 a year asked for one kind of scientific work, however deserving, representatives of all the other sciences would feel themselves entitled to similar treatment and an impossible situation would arise.[14] *Nature*'s editorial refrained from commenting on the "narrow stupidity" betrayed by this point of view to

attain the higher object of illustrating, by this pointed example, the present condition of State science in England.[15]

A voyage to consolidate and extend the work done on the *Lightning* and *Porcupine* did not seem likely to open the door to extra commitments and much use was made of the argument that, seeing that a naval vessel would be used, the cost of the expedition would not be very much more than the government would be spending anyway to keep the ship in commission and pay the officers and men.[16] But it is clear that much of the groundwork done by W. B. Carpenter was of crucial importance. Recent research has shown how he was able to use his social contacts with Gladstone and his ministers to get the idea of the voyage accepted with the minimum of delay.[17]

During the summer of 1872 the expedition took shape. The ship chosen was the steam corvette H.M.S. *Challenger* and the Admiralty appointed Captain Nares to take command. Fitting out took place at Sheerness and here the *Challenger*'s guns were removed and laboratories and extra cabins built in the space this set free. Gradually the officers and crew were assembled. Second in command was J. L. P. Maclear (1838–1907) and the lieutenants were Pelham Aldrich (1844–1930), A. C. B. Bromley, G. R. Bethell (1849–1919) and Thomas Henry Tizard (1839–1924).[18]

The task of appointing the civilian scientists fell to the Royal Society. As Carpenter had already declared his intention of not going to sea again, Wyville Thomson was the obvious choice to head the team. He temporarily resigned his professorship and was awarded as compensation a salary of £1,000 a year for the duration of the voyage.[19] Three naturalists were chosen to assist him. Henry Nottidge Moseley (1844–1891) had studied science at Oxford and went on to take medicine at University College, London, but in 1871 he had abandoned the course to go to Ceylon with the eclipse expedition. The second, William Stirling, resigned before they set out and was replaced by a young German biologist who had met Wyville Thomson when he visited Edinburgh with the German North Sea Expedition in 1871. This was Rudolph von Willemöes-Suhm (1847–1875) who died tragically while the *Challenger* was in the Pacific.[20] The last, and ultimately the most important as far as the development of oceanography was concerned, was John Murray (1841–1914). He had been born in Canada but came to Scotland to be educated and eventually entered Edinburgh University, ostensibly to study medicine. Instead, he joined a whaler as surgeon for a seven-month voyage to the Arctic. Like Edward Forbes and Wyville Thomson before him, Murray took no examinations and on his return studied as he pleased. In 1872 he was working under Peter Guthrie Tait (1831–1901), Professor of Natural Philosophy, and it was Tait who recommended him to Wyville Thomson.[21]

Equally individualistic but in a totally different way was John Young Buchanan (1844–1925) who was appointed chemist to the expedition. He came from a well-to-do Scottish family and had studied widely on the continent. In addition he was technically very able, which was a strong reason for his being chosen for a voyage where much would depend on the ability of the scientists to improvise or make do. Unfortunately he also seems to have been a rather hard person to get on with, extremely reserved and impatient with those whose ideas did not keep pace with his own.[22] The team was completed by John James Wild, artist and Wyville Thomson's secretary.

By the beginning of December 1872, the scientists and their equipment had been assembled. The instruments were largely those which had been tried and tested on the earlier voyages. For measuring temperature they had the Miller-Casella thermometers, each with its pressure correction determined individually by Staff-Commander Davis. Unfortunately, bereft of the guidance of W. A. Miller who had died in 1870, Davis had admitted an error into his calibrations by failing to allow for the rise in temperature inside his apparatus and the corrrections were all considerably too large.[23] This led to some confusion as the matter was not finally cleared up until some years after the voyage was over (*see* p. 354). They also took with them Siemens's electrical resistance thermometer and his photometric apparatus[24] and some Johnson's metallic thermometers.[25]

As before they used hemp lines for putting out the nets, trawls and dredges, and for sounding but in June 1872 Sir William Thomson had made a sounding of 2,700 fathoms on board his yacht *Lalla Rookh* using steel piano wire and one of his machines was taken on the *Challenger*.[26] The device was still in its infancy at this stage and when it was tried out the drum collapsed.[27] For sampling the sea floor they used for preference the modification of the *Hydra* sounding machine named after its inventor, Lieutenant C. W. Baillie. The German North Sea Expedition had suggested using a slip water bottle to collect sea water from the bottom when they visited Leith.[28] Buchanan designed and later improved a stopcock water bottle which would bring up samples from intermediate depths and retain the gases dissolved in them.[29]

After the Lords of the Admiralty and the Royal Society committee had inspected the ship, and a farewell dinner party had been held on board,[30] the *Challenger* left for Portsmouth and it was from there that she finally set sail, on 21 December 1872, on a voyage that was to last nearly three and a half years.

It was confidently expected that she would bring back the answers to the questions which the work in the North Atlantic had brought to mind. Would living creatures be found in the greatest depths of the sea? Was the floor of the ocean entirely covered by the modern chalk and by the exciting protoplasmic substance *Bathybius*? Would it be possible to measure by direct and indirect means the vast slow-moving currents which, according to the theory of oceanic circulation, carried the icy water of the polar seas along the sea bed to the equator? These were the possibilities which had been suggested by the discoveries made in the *Lightning* and *Porcupine* (*see* Ch. 14).

During the first weeks of the voyage, as the *Challenger* left the tempestuous seas of the northern winter behind and made for the Canary Islands, her crew of sailors and scientists began to settle down to the routine procedure of scientific stations and tried out their instruments and apparatus. Her officers and men did the actual work of sounding and dredging, current measuring and water sampling. Tizard, who in H.M.S. *Shearwater* eighteen months before had measured the currents in the Strait of Gibraltar for Carpenter, was now in charge of the deep sea temperature measurements made with the Miller-Casella thermometers, in addition to his work as navigating lieutenant. Bethell operated the Siemens thermometer.

As well as bearing the brunt of the oceanographic work, the *Challenger*'s crew were expected to carry out the normal duties of a survey ship, to make meteorological, magnetic and other routine observations, to provide information for improving Admiralty charts and to make soundings on routes for possible submarine telegraph cables.[31]

The naturalists' work was to deal with the contents of the trawls, nets and dredges as they came in, a repetitive task which Moseley came to find frankly boring, much preferring his botanical and anthropological work on shore at their numerous and often exotic ports of call.[32] Buchanan's work was also largely routine. He had to determine the specific gravity of the sea water samples, which he did with a hydrometer, and to extract and analyse the gases which they contained and the carbonic acid content. Samples for full chemical analysis were collected to be sent home. In addition Buchanan had several research projects of his own.[33] Tizard tells us that the after-dinner smoking circle provided the forum for officers and scientists to compare results and discuss their latest ideas.[34]

The voyage proper began when they left Teneriffe, heading for the West Indies. Every two or three days, oftener near land, they hove to, for observations. At every station they sounded and measured the temperature of the surface and bottom water and fairly frequently of the intermediate layers as well. Usually they made one or more hauls with the dredge or trawl and tow-nets and measured the surface current, and on some occasions the subsurface currents also.[35]

They had not been long at sea when a curious change took place in the character of the samples which the sounding machine was bringing up from the sea bed. As the water got deeper the familiar pale grey globigerina ooze which they had thought might cover the entire floor of the ocean, gradually darkened until it became unrecognizable. Examination under a miscroscope showed that the foraminifera remains which constituted the greater part of the ordinary ooze became fewer and fewer.[36] Finally on 26 February 1873 they found themselves in over 3,000 fathoms of water and at the end of what they soon realized had been a transition. Wyville Thomson wrote:

The depth was 3,150 fathoms; the bottom a perfectly smooth red clay, containing scarcely a trace of organic matter.[37]

Thomson's first reaction was not that here was an area too deep for the foraminifera to inhabit but that the red clay was sediment derived from the rivers of South America.[38] He expected it to be a local phenomenon and as the *Challenger* entered the rather shallower area in mid-Atlantic, which Nares called the Dolphin Rise after the U.S. Coast Survey ship which had discovered it, the globigerina ooze returned only to vanish again as they came into deeper water where the red clay reappeared.[39] On 7 March the dredge brought up not only clay but also "a number of very peculiar black oval bodies about an inch long". Thomson thought that perhaps they were fossils but when Buchanan examined them he found that they were composed of almost pure manganese peroxide.[40] The provenance of these mysterious nodules could only be guessed at but a few days later the dredge brought up clay inhabited by marine worms which Willemöes-Suhm identified as tube-building annelids.[41] This was more like what they were looking for. The find showed that living creatures could exist in the greatest depths of the sea—the discovery had been made in nearly 3,000 fathoms depth of water—and since they had sailed over the central parts of the ocean without finding a much greater depth it seemed safe to assume that the greatest depth could not be much more.[42] "It affords, in fact," Thomson wrote

conclusive proof that the conditions of the bottom of the sea to all depths are not only such as to admit of the existence of animal life, but are such as to allow of the unlimited extension of the distribution of animals high in the zoological series, and closely in relation with the characteristic faunae of shallower zones.[42]

After leaving the West Indies, however, he had to revise some of his conclusions. Only 90 miles north of St Thomas they found themselves sounding in water 3,875 fathoms deep and the self-registering thermometers on the end of the line were fractured by the enormous pressure to which they had been subjected.[43] This great depth (in the Puerto Rico Trench) turned out to be exceptional but they had deep water all the way to Bermuda, their next port of call, and the sea bed turned out to be composed almost entirely of red clay. It was no longer possible to think of this as a localized phenomenon [44] and they began to realize that the clay was characteristic of the deeper areas. Though they continued to speak of it as red clay this colouring was in fact local as Wyville Thomson had originally suggested, due to the sediment poured into the sea by the South American rivers, and in other areas darker browns and greys were the general rule.

From Bermuda the *Challenger* sailed for Halifax, Nova Scotia, and on the way made a wide detour to examine the Gulf Stream. The current was already much better known than any of the other ocean currents because of the work of the United States Coast Survey (*see* Ch. 13). The *Challenger* serial temperature measurements showed features which were already familiar to physical geographers—the relatively shallow body of warm water which formed the current and cold water below it which rose to the surface on its western flank and which contrasted sharply with the thick layer of warm water on the eastern side.[45] They also made direct current measurements both at the surface and at different depths below it.

On the Atlantic crossing several attempts had been made to see if subsurface movements of water in a contrary direction to the surface current could be detected. To track the undercurrents they used a drogue of the same construction that Nares and Carpenter had had in H.M.S. *Shearwater*, consisting of four vertical canvas fins stretched on iron bars, the whole thing moored by a line to a buoy or small boat[46] (*see* Ch. 14). On the first few occasions it was used the surface current was superficial and the movement of the lower layers so sluggish as to render the conclusion indeterminate.[47]

Nares had been instructed to use the drogue in the neighbourhood of the equator. His orders ran

There is reason to believe that the depth of the Atlantic equatorial region does not exceed 2000 fathoms, which is easily within reach both of the sounding lead and of the dredge, and it is hoped that by means of anchoring a boat or beacon you will be able to ascertain to what depth the surface current extends, and what are the conditions of the circulation in the lower strata of the ocean.[48]

At station 106, near the equator, they found a westward flowing current of 2 m.p.h. on the surface.[49] At 15 fathoms the westward movement had diminished to three-quarters and at 50 fathoms to half a mile and at 75 fathoms there was no current at all, showing they said, "how very superficial the Equatorial Current is". It was a pity that they did not consider it worthwhile to spend more time on these observations and continue them at greater depths. Had they done so the discovery of the equatorial undercurrent might perhaps have been brought forward by a dozen years (*see* Ch. 16).

As the *Challenger* pursued her crossing from the Cape Verde Islands to Brazil a significant alteration appeared in the pattern of submarine temperature. In the deepest water encountered during the first part of this stage of the cruise the minimum temperature had been 36°F but after passing St Paul's Rocks they began to find 34°F at a comparable depth. In his report to the Hydrographer, Nares speculated that perhaps the Atlantic was divided down the centre by a bank or series of banks extending from the Dolphin Rise in the north to Ascension Island or even St Helena in the south and that this served to separate what he called the "cold stream" on the west from the warmer water to the east.[50] For the moment, however, this speculation about the cause of the change stayed in the realm of hypothesis. When they recrossed the Atlantic further south, from Rio to the Cape of Good Hope, the differentiation had vanished.[51] The exploration of what this implied was left until the *Challenger* returned to the Atlantic in 1876.

During the first few months of the voyage Bethell had made a number of observations on the temperature of sea water at different depths using Siemens's electrical resistance thermometer. He reported that it worked well, giving results which on the whole correlated with those obtained with the self-registering mercury thermometers. However, in the opinion of the heads of the expedition, its disadvantages continued to outweigh its usefulness. It was still ill adapted structurally for use at sea and difficult to read accurately.[52] They felt that though it was potentially a great advance on existing methods for the moment they had done as much with it as was necessary for present purposes. Accordingly when they reached the Cape, late in 1873, Nares had it sent home,[53] a decision which must soon have caused him some annoyance.

On leaving the Cape of Good Hope the *Challenger* sailed along the perimeter of the Indian Ocean calling at the remote and desolate Marion and Prince Edward Islands and the Crozet group before turning southwards to Kerguelen. From there they went on past Heard Island to the edge of the ice pack, reaching a southern latitude of more than 65° before turning north again. In these high latitudes they discovered to their

FIG. 18. H.M.S. *Challenger* off Kerguelen, February, 1874. Sketch by J. J. Wild. Reproduced by kind permission of the *
University of Edinburgh.*

surprise that beneath the cold water on the surface there lay a thick layer of slightly warmer water. At station 153, their furthest south, on 14 February 1874, in 1,675 fathoms of water, the temperature of the surface layer was 29·5°F but at 300 fathoms it was 32°F and at 500 fathoms 32·8F°.[54] This was nothing more than the temperature inversion measured by Wales and Bayly a century before (*see* Ch. 9) but the *Challenger* scientists seem to have been totally unprepared for it. Lieutenant Spry was amused to see their consternation at the find, "putting their whole theory out of gear" as he thought.[55] In fact it was not difficult to understand the probable cause of the inversion. As they saw it two things contributed to keep down the temperature of the surface water, cooling by the air in winter and by the presence of water from the melting ice in summer. Because ice is fresh it would keep down the salinity as well as the temperature of the surface water as it melted so that its density would still be less than that of the warmer layer below. This they identified with the lower layer of the poleward flow from the equator, less affected at this depth by the factors in operation at the surface and therefore still retaining some of its warmth.[56]

The difficulty arose over the remaining 1,300 fathoms of water. Because the Miller-Casella thermometers could only register extremes of temperature they were only satisfactory in conditions where temperature decreased with depth. Their observations showed that the temperature of the bottom layers lay somewhere between the extremes of the cold and warmer layers near the surface and that was all that could be said about it.

Meanwhile an important stage had been reached in the revision of ideas about the deep sea floor. John Murray was in charge of the biological collections made at the surface and at intermediate depths and of the sea floor samples. He used a tow net to catch samples of plankton at depths ranging from 0 to 100 fathoms. His findings threw new light on the diurnal migration of plankton[57] and on the controversy about the habitat of the foraminifera whose remains made up globigerina ooze.

During the 1860s new evidence had been produced by Major Owen to support the view that the relevant species of foraminifera live in the surface layers of the ocean.[58] Gwyn Jeffreys was convinced but Wyville Thomson and Carpenter felt that the instances quoted might have been exceptional and held to their original conviction which was that the creatures lived on the sea bed.[59] Very soon after the *Challenger* set sail Murray had collected enough evidence to show that Owen was in fact right. His catches with the tow net revealed living in the upper layers of the sea just those foraminifera whose remains predominated in the ooze in the sea bed below.[60]

Successive observations, made over the full extent of the ocean, corroborated the theory. Murray found that globigerina live in almost all parts of the ocean but that the distribution and sizes of the different species varied with latitude. These changes and the relative abundance of globigerina and other kinds of foraminifera were faithfully recorded in the varying composition of the globigerina ooze below. For example, south of Kerguelen they found only one species of globigerina, *Globigerina bulloides*, in the tow net and its remains made up the entire foraminifera content of the ooze in this region. As they approached the ice this too disappeared and instead they found diatoms living in the surface water and their remains in the bottom deposit, which they logically named diatom ooze.[61]

Carpenter tried to save his theory by arguing that perhaps the globigerina were pelagic for part of their lives and sank to the bottom as they developed,[62] but Wyville Thomson was completely convinced by Murray's conclusions although they made necessary yet a further revision of his views concerning the clay deposit found in the deepest areas.[59, 63] He had supposed when red clay turned out to be widespread that it was sediment collecting in places too deep for globigerina to survive. Murray's results showed that their remains must fall on all parts of the ocean alike so why was there no sign of their presence in these regions? Examination of samples from different depths showed that in the deeper samples the calcareous skeletons of foraminifera, molluscs and other creatures progressively disappeared. Clearly some chemical reaction took place in these depths which removed the carbonate of lime that made up 98 per cent of the ooze. Thomson supposed that the red clay was the residue of this process. Buchanan pointed to an increase in carbonic acid in sea water at these depths as the cause and attempted to simulate the process in the laboratory. He removed the carbonate of lime from some globigerina ooze and analysed the remainder, finding silica, alumina and red oxide of iron. The substance certainly seemed to look like red clay.

In March 1874 the *Challenger* reached Australia and during a two-month stay at Sydney the members of the expedition enjoyed in their various ways a change from the routine of life on board ship. Wyville Thomson, Murray and Aldrich went to Queensland to study the fresh-water fauna of its rivers. Moseley went on hunting expeditions and returned with the opossums and fruit-eating bats which he shot. For the rest there was a round of balls and excursions culminating in a dredging picnic and farewell party given by the expedition for their hosts.

As the explorers relaxed, on the other side of the world the controversy over the cause of currents had renewed as a result of their unwitting efforts and raged with unabated vigour. As will be remembered the argument had been broken off, though not concluded, in 1871 with W. B. Carpenter unable to see that the motive force lay not exclusively in the superior weight of one column of water over another but in the presence at the same level in the ocean, of water masses of different densities which set up internal pressure gradients, and consequently unable satisfactorily to dispose of James Croll's criticism that the system depended on the difference in level between one part of the ocean and another and that a sufficient difference did not exist (see Ch. 14).

In February 1874 Croll broke his long silence with an article in the *Philosophical Magazine* in which he again attacked the theory of vertical oceanic circulation due to difference in temperature which Carpenter had put forward.[64] This time however Croll did not restrict himself to demonstrating the fallaciousness, as he saw it, of the theory in general. No one could now seriously deny that undercurrents existed in the Strait of Gibraltar and the Bosporus, where Wharton's work in H.M.S. *Shearwater* in 1872 had completely overturned Spratt's earlier conclusions (see Ch. 14).[65] Nor was it possible to deny that in some form water of polar origin was penetrating the depths of the oceans. Some alternative force had to be located to account for these movements if the effect of differences in density were disallowed.

Croll now tried to show that they followed equally well if one took wind stress as the motive power. For example, as he saw it, the system of currents in the Strait of Gibraltar was caused because water drifted eastwards by westerly winds and pouring into the Mediterranean created a head of water there and so set up an undercurrent in the opposite direction.[66] In the ocean the concrete physical barrier of the land which would operate in gulfs and partially enclosed seas would be replaced by the opposition of contrary wind and water movements. Here a current would take the line of least resistance and this might mean dipping below the surface. In this way the polar current which flowed southwards along the coast of Labrador ultimately became an undercurrent below the Gulf Stream and the Gulf Stream itself disappeared below the surface on reaching the Arctic.

Carpenter replied by reiterating his theory that if constant sources of heat and cold are applied to the surface of the sea at different points, disturbance of equilibrium and continual interchange of water must ensue.[67] The *Challenger* temperature observations unequivocally showed the presence of polar water of low salinity not far below the surface of the sea at the equator and this, for him, satisfactorily demonstrated the existence of upwelling polar water at a point where the theory led him to expect it. If Croll were to be believed, the cold deep water in the North Atlantic was attributable to a reflux from the Gulf Stream which would be nowhere near sufficient to put such a large body of water in motion. The *Challenger* observations in the South Atlantic showed that cold water there was much nearer the surface than in the North Atlantic, which accorded well with his theory because, since there was freedom of communication between the

Southern Ocean and the South Atlantic, the density circulation was correspondingly more vigorous. Croll would not be able to account satisfactorily for this activity because there was only a comparatively weak wind-driven surface current flowing southwards from the equator and no land barrier to act as the source of a return current. Croll's arguments attempting to show that the warm water in the surface layers of the Atlantic was derived from the Gulf Stream were equally unsound.[68]

Croll replied that Carpenter had misrepresented his point of view. He had not said that the cold water in the North Atlantic was the reflux of the Gulf Stream, nor was it necessary that the undercurrent of limited extent which he had in mind should keep the whole body of water in motion. A cold current only a fraction of the size of the Gulf Stream would keep the deep water of the Atlantic at Arctic temperatures since the amount of heat gained through the earth's crust had been shown to be negligible.[69] He would not allow that the *Challenger* results favoured Carpenter's views at the expense of his own. Winds and currents prevailing in the Atlantic tended to transport water from south to north so it was logical that cold water came nearer to the surface in the South Atlantic and furthermore since the layer of warm water was so thin at the equator the slope between the equator and the poles must be even smaller than they had supposed and could not exceed $2\frac{1}{2}$ feet.[70] To these points Carpenter found himself unable to make any convincing reply.[71]

Meanwhile the *Challenger* had left Australia to spend the last part of 1874 and the early months of 1875 threading the network of seas between the islands of the East Indies and the mainland of Asia. Many of these seas were cut off from the main ocean below a certain depth by underwater ridges connecting the islands. There they found the phenomenon noticed a year or two before by Chimmo (*see* Ch. 14) who had shown that in each of these basins the temperatures stopped falling at the greatest depth of the surrounding sill and then stayed the same all the way to the bottom. For example the Celebes Sea below 700 fathoms maintained a constant temperature of 39°F and the Sulu Sea of 50·5°F below 400 fathoms although both were more than 2,500 fathoms deep.[72] This illustration of what happened in bodies of water cut off from the influence of polar currents afforded a classic example for the exponents of a general oceanic circulation.

In 1875 the controversy reached its climax. This year saw the publication of two major works, both definitive of their different points of view. Joseph Prestwich's survey of deep-sea temperature observations and theories of ocean circulation appeared in the *Philosophical Transactions*[73] and Croll brought out a book called *Climate and Time* in which he brought together the arguments contained in his earlier papers.[74] Carpenter welcomed the evidence which Prestwich produced to show that previous observations had already induced Lenz and other scientists to adopt a viewpoint similar to his own and to draw the same conclusions over such points as the presence of cold water near the surface at the equator.[75] He was also able to utilize the *Challenger*'s observations in the East Indies and the work of the U.S. Survey Ship *Tuscarora* in the North Pacific in 1874[76] for further corroborative details. Meanwhile, however, Croll was planning to deliver what he confidently expected would be the coup de grâce to Carpenter's theory.

The *Challenger* temperature sections in the North Atlantic had shown the great extent of the unusually deep body of warm water there, about one thousand fathoms in all, which had first been revealed by observations made early in the century. Croll regarded this warm water as the end product of the Gulf Stream but Carpenter cited it as proof of ocean circulation. An independent point of view came from J. Y. Buchanan who explained it as the result of seasonal changes in the ocean. The heat of summer would evaporate the surface water, leaving a layer of warm saline water. As this cooled down in autumn it would sink through the warm but less saline water underneath and distribute its heat to the layers below.[77]

Croll produced his argument to end all arguments at the British Association meeting at Bristol in the summer of 1875.[78] Using the *Challenger* temperatures and tables giving the thermal expansion of sea water he calculated that the vertical extent of the warm water in the North Atlantic must raise its surface above that of the equator where the layer of warm water was shallower. As he understood it the gravitational theory of currents would only work if there were a downhill slope between the equator and the poles so that this discovery showed, as far as he was concerned, that density currents in the ocean were a practical impossibility. Furthermore, he had come to think that the winds performed the very function that Carpenter had ascribed to density differences. By generating the currents which carried water away from the equator to higher latitudes, they indirectly served to build up a head of water which would cause an outflow from the base of the heavier column along the sea bed in the same way that Carpenter had described.[79]

Croll was in fact right in his deductions about the relative height of the North Atlantic and also in that the pattern of winds over the ocean at large could produce differences in water level, but the rest of his arguments were based on a misconceived idea of the theory he was attacking. Yet it was largely due to Carpenter's own misapprehension that the situation had arisen and Carpenter even now could do no more than try and cast doubt on Croll's figures and show that there was in reality a slope favourable to his hypothesis.[80] Not surprisingly Croll was nettled at Carpenter's refusal to concede the victory outright and felt "rather astonished at the nature of the objections which he advances". He wrote in reply to Carpenter's objection that water was so near to being a perfect fluid that the size of the slope did not matter

What possible connection can 'viscosity' have with the crucial test argument? Suppose water to be a perfect fluid and absolutely frictionless: this would not in any way enable it to *flow up-hill*.

The crucial test argument brings the question at issue, in so far as the North Atlantic is concerned, within very narrow limits. The point at issue is now simply this: *Does it follow, or does it not, from the temperature-soundings given in Dr. Carpenter's own section, that the North Atlantic at lat. 38° is above the level of the equator?* If he or anyone else will prove that it does not, I shall at once abandon the crucial test argument and acknowledge my mistake; but if they fail to do this, I submit that they ought at least in all fairness to admit that in so far as the North Atlantic is concerned, the gravitation theory is untenable.

The Atlantic column is lengthened by heat no less than eight feet above what it would otherwise be were the water of the uniform temperature of 32°F., whereas the equatorial column is lengthened only four feet six inches. The expansion of the Atlantic column below the level of the bottom of the equatorial not being, of course, taken into account. How then is it possible that the equatorial column can be above the level of the Atlantic column? And if not, let it be explained how a surface-flow from the equator pole-wards, resulting from gravity, is to be obtained.[81]

But seeing the mounting evidence which still seemed only to be satisfactorily explained by the theory of density currents Carpenter could not let it go because of a mechanical difficulty and tried to find a way round it. He argued that the level of the Atlantic would only be above that of the equator in actuality if the ocean were in a state of equilibrium, but it was not. In any case the low salinity of the water at the equator would tend to neutralize the effect due to temperature further north. And because water was so nearly a perfect fluid very small differences in level would suffice to maintain vertical circulation. He wrote

my position is, that the void created by the slow descent of water chilled by the surface-cold of the Polar area will be so speedily replaced by the inflow of water from the circumpolar area, and this again by inflow from the temperate region, as to produce a continual upper-flow of equatorial water towards the pole, without the gradient which Mr. Croll persistently asserts to be necessary.[82]

Croll agreed that the ocean was not in a state of static equilibrium but this, he argued, had the effect of keeping the equatorial column even lower. He admitted, and this was a considerable departure from his previous statements, that if no other agencies were at work difference in temperature would result in circulation, but as things were, the warm water at the equator was borne away by the winds before it could accumulate sufficiently to set the system going.[83]

It is impossible to escape the conclusion that Croll had managed to appropriate to himself a good deal of the moral superiority which Carpenter's side of the argument had enjoyed in the early days and, while the crew of the *Challenger* and other observers were amassing information which established the existence of density circulation beyond all reasonable doubt, in the context of the private feud Croll was now getting the best of it. The reviewer of *Climate and Time* for the *Philosophical Magazine* wrote

The manner in which Mr. Croll meets and combats Dr. Carpenter's theory of oceanic circulation is very characteristic of the unwearying patience, acuteness, and courage of his investigations. It is not our purpose here to express any opinion on this unfinished controversy, further than to say that Mr. Croll follows Dr. Carpenter into every one of his positions with a resolution and tenacity of purpose which, were it not so really calm and passionless, might almost be looked on as cruel and unmerciful. When, according to his own view, he has completely overthrown any of Dr. Carpenter's arguments by one special line of attack, he opens fire upon it from another point with the same hearty goodwill he might be expected to exhibit in leading a gallant onslaught against any hitherto unassailed position. This he does not do with the intention of thrice slaying the slain, but simply because he has in an eminent degree the faculty of examining a problem from many sides; and he is concerned, not for dialectic triumphs, but for the presentation of the truth in its entirety. No sooner has the active and versatile Doctor marshalled new arguments from new facts in favour of his vast conception, than Mr. Croll is ready to take up his challenge, and show that all the facts can be read off in a light which harmonizes with his adopted wind theory. Mr. Croll has not the literary dexterity and skill which eminently characterize Dr. Carpenter's pen; but he, as much as any man, knows the manifold physical bearings of the vexed question; and while on the one side the exposition of an argument is adorned with literary grace, on the other the real scientific value of facts and observations is more promptly apprehended.[84]

A little while before the currents controversy had become active again there had been a shorter but more acrimonious wrangle in the columns of *Nature* over the naming of the Miller-Casella thermometer. When the *Lightning*'s cruise was under discussion in 1868 leading instrument-makers had been circularized with a view to testing the reaction of their thermometers to the effects of pressure at sea (*see* Ch. 14). One firm, Negretti and Zambra, had not replied. This was the firm which had made protected thermometers for Admiral Fitzroy in 1857 (*see* Ch. 13). Now they complained that the distinction which should rightly have been theirs had been wrongfully pre-empted by Casella in the naming of his thermometer in a way that would never had been sanctioned by W. A. Miller.[85] He had been

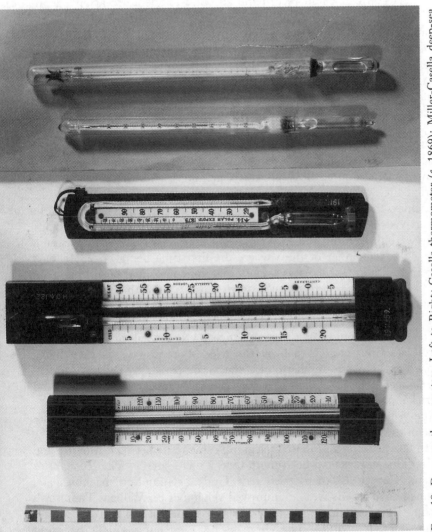

FIG. 19. Deep-sea thermometers. Left to Right: Casella thermometer (*c*. 1869); Miller-Casella deep-sea thermometer (*c*. 1870); Negretti and Zambra reversing thermometer, used on the polar expedition of 1875; Negretti and Zambra reversing thermometer, improved version (1887); Richter's reversing thermometer, Berlin (1902).

Crown copyright. Reproduced by courtesy of the Director of the Royal Scottish Museum.

quick to acknowledge that theirs had priority when he learned of its existence, some time after the appearance of his own.[86]

Having established their case, Negretti and Zambra again turned their attention to the problems of marine instrumentation, this time to the need for a device which could record the absolute temperature at any depth required and so overcome the limitations of the maximum and minimum thermometer. They invented a device which could be used to turn the thermometer upside down as soon as it began to ascend in the water. The thread of mercury then broke and the amount involved in the measurement was trapped in the second arm of the thermometer where it could be read off at the surface.[87] Of course the device immediately became known as the Negretti and Zambra reversing thermometer but no one supposed that they were trying to steal the glory which perhaps belonged to Aimé who had invented a similar device thirty years before (see Ch. 13). Perhaps Casella had after all had a point when he said that the use that was made of an instrument counted for more in its naming than strict considerations of originality.

The new thermometers reached the *Challenger* at Hong Kong where she had arrived in November 1874. They had not been very well packed and many were broken but the survivors were used on a number of occasions during the remainder of the voyage, the first time being on 28 January 1875 in the Sulu Sea.[88] After some initial difficulties had been ironed out they worked well but the results were mostly rather higher than those obtained with the Miller-Casella thermometers and Tizard suspected that they were insufficiently protected against the effects of pressure.[89]

The stay at Hong Kong saw a change in the expedition's leadership. Nares had been chosen to head the expedition which was then being planned to the Arctic and he went home, accompanied by Pelham Aldrich. The *Challenger*'s new commander was Captain Frank Tourle Thomson and Aldrich's place was taken by Lieutenant Alfred Carpenter.[90]

The year 1875 saw the *Challenger* in the Pacific. By now she was not alone in the field. In 1874 the U.S.S. *Tuscarora* had made soundings in the North Pacific along a proposed telegraph cable route between America and Japan. This voyage had been more than a mere survey. The *Tuscarora*'s captain, George Belknap, tried new kinds of sounding machines and obtained good results with an improved version of Sir William Thomson's machine for sounding with wire. He also made surface and subsurface current measurements.[91] The Germans had sent out a round the world expedition of their own in the S.S. *Gazelle* and in 1875 she too was in the Pacific.[92]

The combined efforts of these ships showed the Pacific to differ considerably from the other oceans. Not only did it cover a far greater area but it was uniformly deeper, much of the sea bed being at a depth greater than 2,000 fathoms and covered with the characteristic deep-sea clay. Associated with the clay were larger mineral particles—quartz, mica and pumice in considerable quantities, pieces ranging in size from a pea to a football. This led John Murray to dispute Wyville Thomson's view that the clay was a residue of decayed organic matter and to point instead to volcanic material as its source. The number of volcanoes in the Pacific area, the discovery of pumice associated with them and its ability to float long distances, as they had seen it do, all confirmed him in this belief.[93, 94]

Almost always present with the clay were manganese nodules in far greater quantities than they had found before. The characteristic form which they took was of a concretion round some object which served as a nucleus. This was commonly a shark's tooth or the ear bone of a whale. Such remains were plentiful in the sediment, some only lightly coated with manganese, and showed, said Murray, by their abundance here and scarcity in other types of deposit, how very slowly the clay was being formed in comparison with the oozes in * shallower water. Some of the shark's teeth very were large, one being 4 inches long, and this was later identified as having belonged to a gigantic fossil species, *Carcharodon* * *megalodon*.[95]

It was difficult to account for the presence of the manganese. Murray thought that it too was of volcanic origin and that maganiferous rocks * were decomposed giving carbonate of manganese which was then oxidized by sea water. Buchanan on the other hand suggested that organic remains on the sea bed reacted with the sulphates in sea water to produce sulphides which in turn combined with the iron and manganese which were then changed into oxides by the sea water.[94, 96] Later on the French geologist Dieulafait put forward the idea that manganese was precipitated during a reaction which took place at the surface of the sea between the sea water and the air.[97] But none of these explanations, said their critics, could account for the formation of the nodules.

From time to time the exploring ships came across places in the Pacific which were yet still deeper than the considerable average depth of the ocean as a whole. At one place not far from the coast of Japan the *Tuscarora* had found no bottom in 4,643 fathoms of water.[98] On 23 March 1875, in latitude 11° 24' N, longitude 143° 16' E, the *Challenger* sounded in 4,475 fathoms and again the thermometers broke under a pressure which it had never been expected that they would have to bear.[99]

At depths of this magnitude yet another change came over the character of the bottom deposits. Wyville Thomson announced in a letter written to T. H. Huxley that here the deep-sea clay was replaced by a deposit containing a large proportion of Radiolarians, hence Radiolarian ooze.

Radiolarians lived in all the oceans and at all depths but they were most plentiful in the Pacific. They had siliceous skeletons which did not decay at great depths as did the limey skeletons of foraminifera and so it was easy to see that where there was the greatest depth of water their remains would be most in evidence.[93, 100]

Also in this historic letter, Wyville Thomson announced that the mystery surrounding *Bathybius* had at last been solved. *Bathybius Haeckelii* had been discovered by Huxley in 1868 when he was re-examining the sea bed samples which had been collected by H.M.S. *Cyclops* in 1857 and preserved in spirit. It appeared as a gelatinous substance which had organic properties and Huxley believed that he had lighted upon a form of proto-plasm.[101] The interest of the discovery was enlarged by its possible signi-ficance for arguments current at the time about abiogenesis or spon-taneous generation. One of the foremost exponents of this hypothesis was Ernst Haeckel (1834–1919), hence Huxley's choice of name.[102]

During the first two and a half years of the *Challenger*'s voyage the watery substance from the sea floor samples was examined under the microscope for "hours at a time" without finding any sign of life nor did tests reveal anything resembling the appearances described by Huxley and Haeckel. Then one day someone noticed that a jelly-like substance was to be seen in the samples preserved in spirit but not in the jars containing specimens kept in water.[103] Buchanan examined the mysterious substance and discovered that it did show the chemical appearances they had de-scribed. In subsequent experiments he showed beyond doubt that what had caused so much excitement in the scientific world was nothing more than the result of precipitation of calcium sulphate from the sea water in the deposit by the alcohol in which it had been preserved.[103] Years later he wrote

I had established the mineral nature of *Bathybius* before the *Challenger* arrived at Japan, where she made a stay of nearly two months. Feeling that it would be satisfactory if a chemist at home had a statement from the chemist on board of the method adopted in this demonstration I wrote to my friend and former chief, Professor Crum Brown, in Edinburgh. . . . Professor Crum Brown has related to me how, after receiving my letter, he interested his friends in Edinburgh by showing them how to *make Bathybius*.[104]

On learning of these developments from Wyville Thomson, Huxley freely admitted that he had made a howler.[105] As Buchanan observed, no acknowledgment could have been franker. But Hugh Robert Mill (1861–1950) in his obituary of Buchanan, written fifty years later, tells us that his biological colleagues were very reluctant to believe that Huxley could have been wrong.[106] In an extreme case, fully three years after the return of the expedition, George Allman, speaking through a heavy cold, told the British Association in his presidential address

It is not easy to believe, however, that the very elaborate investigations of Huxley and Haeckel can be thus disposed of. These, moreover, have received strong confirmation from the still more recent observations of the Arctic voyager, Bessels, who was one of the explorers of the ill-fated *Polaris*, and who states that he dredged from the Greenland seas masses of living undifferentiated protoplasm. Bessels assigns to these the name of Protobathybius, but they are apparently indistinguishable from the Bathybius of the *Porcupine*. Further arguments against the reality of Bathybius will therefore be needed before a doctrine founded on observations so carefully conducted shall be relegated to the region of confuted hypotheses.[107]

This unsolicited expression of support put Huxley in an awkward position since he was seconding the vote of thanks but he managed to extricate both himself and the President with a tactful disclaimer which saved both sides from loss of face.[108]

Yet this was far ahead as the expedition sailed on through the Pacific, saddened by the illness and death of Rudolf von Willemöes-Suhm.[109] At last, early in 1876, the *Challenger* passed through the Magellan Straits and regained the Atlantic.

When his routine work permitted, Buchanan had been working on the problems involved in using pressures measured at the sea bed to give an independent source of information on ocean depths. Before the *Challenger* set sail he had made initial observations with an instrument resembling a barometer but recording the pressure of water instead of air, a piezometer. His first task on board ship was to establish the relative compressibility of the fluids to be employed. The hydraulic press which had been sent with them proved unreliable and Buchanan finally adopted the expedient of attaching his instruments to the end of the sounding line along with a deep-sea thermometer and used the measure of depth given by the line to calculate the pressure. In a series of observations made between Tahiti and Valparaiso he collected data on the compressibility of distilled water and then went on to determine the relative compressibility of sea water and mercury. Back in the Atlantic he was at last able to begin getting independent results. He used two instruments, a water piezometer and a mercury piezometer. Mercury alters its volume rapidly in response to changes in temperature but very little as a result of increases in pressure. Buchanan used the depth as given by the sounding line to correct the mercury instrument for pressure, giving the temperature at the bottom. He used this figure to correct the reading of the water piezometer, giving the depth. By reapplying this more accurate figure again to the reading of the mercury he was able to get a yet closer approximation to the true temperature. He realized that the ability which the technique conferred of discovering temperature without the limitations imposed by the self-registering thermometers, would enable them to measure temperatures in a situation like the one encountered in the Southern Ocean, where warm and cold layers of water near the surface had made it impossible for maximum and minimum thermometers to give information about the deeper layers.[110]

Buchanan's independent measurements of temperature made it clear that the pressure corrections which the expedition were applying to the results obtained with the Miller-Casella thermometers were unnecessarily large. When the *Challenger* got home Wyville Thomson turned them over to Professor Tait for a reappraisal of the effects of pressure.[111] In 1877 he wrote to Tizard that the temperature tables would all have to be redone and that it would probably be best to omit corrections altogether since, whatever they turned out to be, they would certainly be very small.[112] Tait had to have a press specially made for the new observations and was not able to start work on them until 1879. He found that Davis had neglected to allow for the increase of heat due to pressure inside his apparatus and that the thermometers were in fact much better able to withstand pressure than they had been given credit for. The true correction varied from instrument to instrument and was not more than $0·14°F$ per mile of depth, very much less than the previous figure of half a degree. Because of the smallness of the changes of temperature in the depths of the sea and their significance in understanding the internal mechanism of ocean circulation, science, said Tait, could not afford to be mistaken about such small but possibly crucial differences.[113]

Back in the Atlantic, the *Challenger* explored more thoroughly the anomalies which had been noticed earlier in the voyage. In 1873 the temperature sections made across the southern parts of the ocean had shown a difference between the eastern and western sides, the bottom temperatures to the east being slightly warmer than the others. Nares had postulated the existence of a ridge in the centre of the ocean keeping the two bodies of water distinct (*see* p. 340). Now, in 1876, as the *Challenger* sailed northwards from Tristan da Cunha to Ascension Island, the soundings showed that she was over an area considerably shallower than was normal for the ocean as a whole.[114] Gradually the daring idea emerged of a continuous mountain range, running parallel to the continental outlines right down the Atlantic from north to south.[115] From the alterations in the deep temperatures on either side of the ridge Tizard deduced the existence of subsidiary ridges branching out from the mid-ocean range and linking it to the continental margins. One of these ran from a point somewhere near Tristan da Cunha to the African mainland (the Walvis Ridge) and prevented the cold Antarctic bottom water from entering the eastern

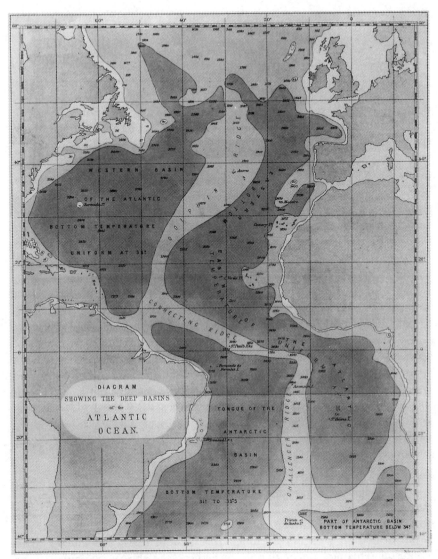

FIG. 20. Diagram showing the Deep Basins of the Atlantic Ocean. Reproduced from the preliminary report of the voyage of H.M.S. *Challenger, Report on Ocean Soundings and Temperatures in the Atlantic Ocean*, H.M.S.O. (1876), plate 6. Reproduced by kind permission of the Hydrographer of the Navy.

basin of the South Atlantic; on the other side but much further north, another one linked the ridge with the coast of South America, keeping the coldest water out of the depths of the North Atlantic.[116]

Far from accepting that this provided proof of the system of general oceanic circulation as proposed by Carpenter, Wyville Thomson now put forward a quite different explanation of his own for the temperature structure which the *Challenger* observations had shown that all the major oceans had in common. He did not deny that cold Antarctic water was moving northwards in the depths of the Atlantic, Pacific and Indian Oceans but he reasoned that it was as compensation for the transport of water vapour by the atmosphere in the opposite direction. Excess of evaporation in the northern hemisphere and of precipitation in the southern created an imbalance in the ocean and it was sensible to think of its movements as part of a combined circulation of ocean and atmosphere produced by water being taken out of the sea in one area and put back in another. There was not, he said,

the slightest ground for supposing that such a thing exists as a general vertical circulation of the water of the ocean depending upon differences of specific gravity.[117]

Carpenter was none too pleased by this new departure and expressed the view that Wyville Thomson should have waited until he got home and had a chance to catch up on recent developments before committing himself to such views.[118] He referred to Froude's paper on friction given at the British Association in 1875 and quoted Sir William Thomson as having said that circulation was a matter "not of opinion but of irrefragable necessity". Wyville Thomson was nevertheless unrepentant. In an address to the British Association in 1878 he reiterated his views. The ocean, he said, might be regarded as consisting of two layers. From the surface to about 500 fathoms its movements were governed by the winds. At this depth

we arrive at a layer of water at a temperature of 40°F., and this may be regarded as a kind of neutral band separating the two layers.[119]

Below this curious survival from the past was the Antarctic underflow.

The incident demonstrated that the *Challenger* had failed in what, in Carpenter's eyes at least, had been its major objective, in that it had not produced incontrovertible proof of the system of ocean circulation which he advocated. It was not so much that people like Croll and Wyville Thomson remained unconvinced since there are always two sides to an argument and their opinions did not alter the convictions of physicists and meteorologists here and overseas. The real difficulty lay in the fact that while basically simple in theory, in practice ocean circulation is a highly complicated process depending upon a large number of variables and resulting in a vast network of interrelated movements which bear only a distant resemblance to the simple pattern of the kind Carpenter used as his model. The picture lay hidden in the vast mass of data on temperature

and specific gravity which the *Challenger* had collected but no one immediately connected with the voyage had the skills necessary for sorting out
the pieces of the puzzle and putting them together. Of all the criticisms
which have been made of the voyage the most telling is that the expedition
ought to have included a physicist who could have paid special attention to
this aspect of the work, which was originally intended to rank equally
with the biological programme (*see* Ch. 16).

As it was, the expedition had been overweighted on the biological side
and most of the physical observations had been left to the ship's officers who
already had plenty to cope with. The result was that apparatus like the
current drogue and the electrical and reversing thermometers were not
used to their full potential. J. Y. Buchanan obtained some interesting
results in the course of his determinations of specific gravity and of the air
dissolved in sea water. He noticed vertical changes in the distribution of
salinity which he found to decrease with depth to about 1,000 fathoms and
then increase slightly towards the bottom.[120] Similarly, the oxygen content
of sea water decreased from the surface to a depth of 300 fathoms and then
increased again. In neither instance does he seem to have considered that
the vertical changes might be due to horizontal movements. He saw the
oxygen deficiency entirely as the result of consumption by animal life,
still plentiful at those depths whereas the oceanic plant life is restricted by
its dependence on sunlight to the first hundred fathoms.[121] Tizard who
was responsible for the temperature observations seems to have had some
interesting ideas about the possibility of a southerly outflow from the
North Atlantic but there is no evidence that he developed them.[122] Apart
from anything else the uncertainty about the size of the pressure correction made it difficult to generalize. The only person who attempted to give
an immediate synthesis of the physical results was Wild who published his
book *Thalassa* in 1877.[123]

In the other main aspects of the voyage's work there was no such
ambiguity and the general results could be better appreciated. The pioneer
work done by Buchanan and Murray on deep-sea deposits during the
voyage had opened up an almost entirely new field which Murray was to
make peculiarly his own in years to come. The biological aims of the
cruise too had been amply fulfilled. The existence of life in the abysses of
the ocean had been established and, though much remained to be done both
as regarded the individual creatures caught and, for the future, in developing more accurate methods of sampling animal populations and
relating them, if free swimming or pelagic, to the actual depths at which
they lived, some generalizations could already be made. The deep sea
fauna had turned out to be remarkably uniform throughout the world. As
for its connection to more ancient forms of life, Wyville Thomson wrote

the relations of the abyssal fauna to the faunae of the older tertiary and the newer mesozoic periods are much closer than are those of the faunae of shallow water; I must admit, however, that these relations are not so close as I expected them to be—that hitherto we have found living only a very few representatives of groups which had been supposed to be extinct.[124]

Before the results of the voyage could be fully assessed the enormous collections of birds, plants, marine animals, rocks, oozes and sea water samples which had been sent home at intervals during the voyage would have to be sorted and sent to the individual scientists best qualified to work on them. Then their findings would have to be published as part of the expedition's report. It was his plans for this undertaking that were uppermost in Wyville Thomson's mind as the *Challenger* headed for home after an absence of three and a half years. No amount of foresight could have enabled him to see how much trouble this was to involve and that the whole procedure was to take five times as long as the voyage itself.

For the moment all was serene. On 24 May 1876 the *Challenger* arrived at Spithead and finally docked at Sheerness where leading British scientists and foreign visitors to the conferences being held in connection with the Loan Exhibition of Scientific Apparatus, then going on in London, came to see her.[125] Queen Victoria conferred a knighthood on Wyville Thomson and by early July he, Buchanan and Murray were back in Edinburgh where their return was celebrated by a civic banquet.[126] The great expedition was over.

15. NOTES

1. *Nature* (8 June 1871). Vol. **4**, p. 107.
2. *Nature* (1 June 1871). Vol. **4**, p. 87.
3. *Nature* (8 June 1871). Vol. **4**, p. 107.
4. Harold L. Burstyn, "Science and government in the nineteenth century: the Challenger expedition and its report", *Bull. Inst. océanogr. Monaco* numéro spécial 2 (1968). Vol. **2**, pp. 603–611.
5. *Report on the Scientific Results of the Voyage of H.M.S. Challenger during the years 1873–1876* (ed. C. Wyville Thomson and John Murray). H.M.S.O., London, *Narrative* (1885). Vol. **1**, part 1, pp. l–li.
6. *Ibid.* p. li.
7. *Nature* (10 August 1871). Vol. **4**, p. 290.
   Nature (17 August 1871). Vol. **4**, p. 313.
8. *Nature* (12 October 1871). Vol. **4**, p. 468.
9. *Challenger Report. op. cit.* pp. li–liii.
10. "The government and the eclipse expedition", *Nature* (22 September 1870). Vol. **2**, pp. 409–410. Also (3 November 1870). Vol. **3**, p. 13 and (17 November 1870). Vol. **3**, p. 52; (24 August 1871). Vol. **4**, p. 324.
11. *Report of the 37th meeting of the British Association for the Advancement of Science (1867)*, (1868), pp. lxi–lxii.

12. Silvanus P. Thompson, *The Life of William Thomson, Baron Kelvin of Largs*, 2 vols, London (1910). Vol. **2**, pp. 729–731.
13. *Report of the 41st meeting of the British Association for the Advancement of Science (1871)*, (1872), p. lxxiii.
    The Association also called for observations to be made on the coast of India, *ibid*. p. lxxiv. This suggestion was taken up.
14. "The Tides and the Treasury", *Nature* (27 June 1872). Vol. **6**, pp. 157–158.
15. *Ibid*. p. 158.
16. Daniel Merriman, "A posse ad esse", *J. Mar. Res.* (1948). Vol. **7**, pp. 139–146.
17. Harold L. Burstyn, *op. cit.* p. 608.
18. *Challenger Report, op. cit. Narrative*. Vol. **1**, part 1, pp. 2–19.
    Charles Wyville Thomson, *The Voyage of the Challenger. The Atlantic. A preliminary account of the general results of the exploring voyage of H.M.S. Challenger during the year 1873 and the early part of the year 1876*, 2 vols, London (1877). Vol. **1**, pp. 9–59.
19. *Challenger Report, op. cit. Narrative*. Vol. **1**, part 1, p. 22.
20. *Ibid*. p. 33.
21. Biographical material about Sir John Murray is to be found in obituary notices in *Proc. R. Soc.*, series B (1915–1916). Vol. **89**, pp. vi–xv; *Proc. R. Soc. of Edinburgh* (1914–1915). Vol. **35**, pp. 305–317, with bibliography; *Nature* (26 March 1914). Vol. **93**, pp. 88–89.
    See also: William A. Herdman, *Founders of Oceanography* (1923), and William N. Boog Watson, "Sir John Murray—a Chronic Student", *University of Edinburgh Journal* (1967–1968). Vol. **23**, pp. 123–138.
    Tait had been a colleague of Wyville Thomson's at Belfast before moving to Edinburgh in 1860.
22. For obituaries of J. Y. Buchanan, *see: Proc. R. Soc.* series A (1926). Vol. **110**, pp. xii–xiii;
    Proc. R. Soc. Edinb. (1924–1925). Vol. **45**, pp. 364–367; *Nature* (14 November 1925). Vol. **116**, pp. 719–720.
    The last two are by H. R. Mill.
23. J. E. Davis, "On deep-sea thermometers", *Proc. Meteorol. Soc.* (1869–1871). Vol. **5**, pp. 305–342. Also in: *Nature* (14 December 1871). Vol. **5**, pp. 124–128.
24. *Challenger Report, op. cit.* pp. 95–97.
25. Preserved in the *Challenger* collection in the British Museum (Natural History).
26. Sir William Thomson, "On deep-sea sounding by piano-forte wire", *Proceedings of the Philosophical Society of Glasgow* (1873–1875). Vol. **9**, pp. 111–117.
    Silvanus P. Thompson, *Life of Lord Kelvin, op. cit.* Vol. **2**, p. 719.
27. *Challenger Report, op. cit.* pp. 70–72.
    John Murray and Johan Hjort, *The Depths of the Ocean. A general account of the modern science of oceanography based largely on the scientific researches of the Norwegian Steamer Michael Sars in the North Atlantic*, London (1912), p. 27.
28. C. Wyville Thomson, *op. cit.* Vol. **1**, pp. 34–37.
29. *Ibid*. pp. 37–40.

30. C. Wyville Thomson, *op. cit.* Vol. **1**, p. 59.
Nature (12 December 1872). Vol. **7**, pp. 109–110.

31. See Nares's instructions from the Hydrographer, *Challenger Report, op. cit.* pp. 34–39. Also, the scientific instructions prepared by the Royal Society, pp. 23–33.

32. Henry Nottidge Moseley, *Notes by a Naturalist. An Account of Observations made during the Voyage of H.M.S. Challenger,* new ed., London (1892), pp. 1, 501–502.

33. John Young Buchanan, "Report on the specific gravity of samples of ocean water, observed on board H.M.S. *Challenger* during the years 1873–76", *Report on the Scientific Results of the Voyage of H.M.S. Challenger. Physics and Chemistry* (1884). Vol. **1**, 46 pp.
John Young Buchanan, "Preliminary Report to Professor Wyville Thomson, F.R.S., director of the civilian scientific staff, on work (chemical and geological) done on board H.M.S. *Challenger*", *Proc. R. Soc.* (1875–1876). Vol. **24**, pp. 593–623.
John Young Buchanan, "On the absorption of carbonic acid by saline solutions", *Proc. R. Soc.* (1873–1874). Vol. **22**, pp. 192–196.
See also: Scientific Papers, Cambridge (1913). Vol. **1** and *Accounts Rendered of Work Done and Things Seen*, Cambridge (1919).

34. Edwin Ray Lankester *et al.*, "The scientific results of the *Challenger* Expedition", *Natural Science* (July 1895). Vol. **7**, no. 41, pp. 7–75.

35. *Challenger Report, Narrative.* Vol. **1**, and *A Summary of the Scientific Results* (1895). Vols **1** and **2**.
Also, "The *Challenger* Collections", *Nature* (18 January 1877). Vol. **15**, pp. 254–256.

36. C. Wyville Thomson, *op. cit.* Vol. **1**, p. 183.

37. *Ibid.* p. 182.

38. *Ibid.* pp. 226–227.
C. Wyville Thomson, "Notes from the *Challenger*", *Nature* (8 May 1873). Vol. **8**, pp. 28–30.

39. C. Wyville Thomson, *The Voyage of the Challenger.* Vol. **1**, pp. 193, 223–225.

40. *Ibid.* pp. 195–196.
C. Wyville Thomson, "Notes from the *Challenger*", *Nature* (15 May 1873). Vol. **8**, pp. 51–53.

41. C. Wyville Thomson, *The Voyage of the Challenger.* Vol. **1**, pp. 201–203.

42. C. Wyville Thomson, "Notes from the *Challenger*", *op. cit.* Vol. **8**, p. 53.

43. *Ibid. Nature* (5 June 1873). Vol. **8**, pp. 109–110.
C. Wyville Thomson, *The Voyage of the Challenger.* Vol. **1**, p. 279.

44. *Nature* (31 July 1873). Vol. **8**, pp. 266–267.

45. C. Wyville Thomson, *The Voyage of the Challenger.* Vol. **1**, pp. 371–375.
Challenger Report, Narrative. Vol. **1**, part 1, pp. 154–158.

46. *Ibid.* pp. 79–82.

47. *Ibid.* pp. 123–124, 154, 157.

48. *Ibid.* p. 36.

49. *Ibid.* p. 193.

50. George S. Nares, *H.M.S. Challenger. Reports of Captain G. S. Nares, R.N. with abstract of soundings and diagrams of ocean temperature in North and South Atlantic Oceans*, Admiralty (1873), pp. 10–12.

51. *Ibid.* p. 13.

52. *Ibid.* p. 2.
    The Voyage of the Challenger. Vol. 1, pp. 242–244.
53. G.S. Nares, *op. cit.* p. 15. He also sent back the photometric device but does not say if it had been tried out.
54. *Challenger Report, Narrative.* Vol. 1, part 1, p. 399; *Summary.* Vol. 1, p. 496.
55. William J. J. Spry, *The Cruise of H.M.S. Challenger*, 10th ed., London (1884), p. 106.
56. George S. Nares, *H.M.S. Challenger. No. 2. Reports on ocean soundings and temperature, Antarctic Sea, Australia, New Zealand* (1874), pp. 10, 15–18.
57. C. Wyville Thomson, "Notes from the *Challenger*", *Nature* (8 May 1873). Vol. **8**, pp. 28–30.
    Diurnal migration was discovered by Bellingshausen. *See* Ch. 11.
58. Samuel Owen, "On the surface-fauna of mid-ocean", *J. Linn. Soc.* (1865). Vol. **8** (Zoology), pp. 202–205. Vol. **9**, Zoology, (1868). pp. 147–157.
59. C. Wyville Thomson, "Preliminary notes on the nature of the sea-bottom procured by the soundings of H.M.S. *Challenger* during her cruise in the 'Southern Sea' in the early part of the year 1874", *Proc. R. Soc.* (1874–1875). Vol. **23**, pp. 32–49; p. 34.
60. *Ibid.* pp. 33–39.
61. *Ibid.* pp. 47–48.
62. William B. Carpenter, "Remarks on Professor Wyville Thomson's preliminary notes on the nature of the sea-bottom procured by the soundings of H.M.S. *Challenger*", *Proc. R. Soc.* (1874–1875). Vol. **23**, pp. 234–245.
63. C. Wyville Thomson "The *Challenger* Expedition", *Nature* (1874–1875). Vol. **11** (3 December 1874) pp. 95–97; (10 December 1874) pp. 116–119.
64. James Croll, "On ocean currents—Part III. On the physical cause of ocean-currents", *Phil. Mag.* (January–June 1874). Series 4. Vol. **47**, pp. 94–122.
65. William J. L. Wharton, "Observations on the currents and undercurrents of the Dardanelles and Bosphorus, made by Commander J. L. Wharton, of H.M. Surveying-Ship *Shearwater*, between the months of June and October, 1872", *Proc. R. Soc.* (1872–1873). Vol. **21**, pp. 387–393. *See* Ch. 14.
66. James Croll, *op. cit.* pp. 168–190.
67. William B. Carpenter, "Ocean currents", *Nature* (2 April 1874). Vol. **9**, pp. 423–424.
68. William B. Carpenter, "On the physical cause of ocean-currents", *Phil. Mag.* (January–June 1874). Series 4. Vol. **47**, pp. 359–362. See also his "Further inquiries on oceanic circulation", *Proc. R. geog. Soc.* (1873–1874). Vol. **18**, pp. 301–407.
69. James Croll, "On the physical cause of ocean currents", *Phil. Mag.* (January–June 1874). Series 4. Vol. **47**, pp. 434–437.
70. James Croll, "Ocean currents", *Nature* (21 May 1874). Vol. **10**, pp. 52–53.
71. William B. Carpenter, "Ocean Circulation", *Nature* (28 May 1874). Vol. **10**, p. 62.
    William B. Carpenter, "Lenz's doctrine of ocean circulation", *Nature* (2 July 1874). pp. 170–171.
    See also: "Ocean circulation—Dr. Carpenter and Mr. Croll", an anonymous letter defending Croll in *Nature* (4 June 1874). Vol. **10**, pp. 83–84.
72. Thomas H. Tizard, *H.M.S. Challenger, No. 3. Reports on ocean soundings and temperature, New Zealand to Torres Strait, Torres Strait to Manila and Hong Kong* (1874), p. 7.

"Remarks on the temperatures of the China, Sulu, Celebes and Banda Seas", *H.M.S. Challenger, No. 4. Report on ocean soundings and temperatures, Pacific Ocean, China and adjacent seas* (1875), pp. 4–9.
Challenger Report, Summary. Vol. **1,** pp. 771, 782.

73. Joseph Prestwich, "Tables of temperatures of the sea at different depths beneath the surface, reduced and collated from the various observations made between the years 1749 and 1868, discussed", *Phil. Trans.* (1875). Vol. **165,** pp. 587–674.

74. James Croll, *Climate and Time in their Geological Relations: a Theory of Secular Changes of the Earth's Climate,* London (1875).

75. William B. Carpenter, "Lenz's doctrine of ocean circulation", *Nature* (2 July 1874) Vol. **10,** pp. 170–171.

76. William B. Carpenter, "Summary of recent observations on ocean temperature made in H.M.S. *Challenger,* and U.S.S. *Tuscarora;* with their bearing on the doctrine of a general oceanic circulation sustained by difference of temperature", *Proc. R. geog. Soc.* (1874–1875). Vol. **19,** pp. 493–514.

77. John Young Buchanan, "Note on the vertical distribution of temperature in the ocean", *Proc. R. Soc.* (1874–1875). Vol. **23,** pp. 123–127.

78. James Croll, "On the *Challenger*'s crucial test of the wind and gravitation theories of oceanic circulation", *Report of the 45th meeting of the British Association (1875)* (1876). Part 2, pp. 191–193.
Ibid., Phil. Mag. (July–December 1875). Series 4. Vol. **50,** pp. 242–250.

79. James Croll, "The wind theory of oceanic circulation.—Objections examined", *Phil. Mag.* (July–December 1875). Series 4. Vol. **50,** pp. 286–290.

80. William B. Carpenter, "Remarks on Mr. Croll's 'crucial-test' argument", *ibid.* pp. 402–404.
William B. Carpenter, "Further remarks on the 'crucial-test' argument", *ibid.* pp. 489–491.
William B. Carpentry, "Ocean circulation", *Nature* (23 September 1875). Vol. **12,** pp. 454–455.

81. James Croll, "Oceanic circulation", *Nature* (7 October 1875). Vol. **12,** p. 494.

82. William B. Carpenter, "Ocean circulation", *Nature* (21 October 1875). Vol. **12,** p. 533.

83. James Croll, "Oceanic circulation", *Nature* (25 November 1875). Vol. **13,** pp. 66–67.

84. Review of *Climate and Time, Phil. Mag.* (July–December 1875) Series 4. Vol. **50,** pp. 322–324.
According to his obituary Croll had "maintained with great force and with general approbation the position for which he contended", *Nature* (25 December 1890). Vol. **43,** pp. 180–181. He was made an F.R.S. in 1876.

85. Henry Negretti and Joseph Warren Zambra, "Deep-sea soundings and deep-sea thermometers", *Nature* (23 October 1873). Vol. **8,** p. 529.

86. See correspondence in *Nature* (1873–1874). Vol. **9** (6 November 1873) p. 5; (20 November 1873) pp. 41–42; (27 November 1873), pp. 62–63; (11 December 1873) p. 102.

87. Henry Negretti and Joseph Warren Zambra, "On a new deep-sea thermometer", *Proc. R. Soc.* (1873–1874). Vol. **22,** pp. 238–241.
"A new thermometer", *Nature* (19 March 1874). Vol. **9,** pp. 387–388.

88. *Challenger Report, Narrative,* Vol. **1,** part 2, p. 655.

89. *Challenger Report, Narrative.* Vol. **1,** part 1, pp. 88–95.

90. *Challenger Report, Narrative.* Vol. **1**, part 2, p. 638.
91. "Deep-sea soundings in the Pacific Ocean", *Nature* (3 September 1874). Vol. **10**, pp. 356–357.
   "Soundings and currents in the North Pacific Ocean", *Nature* (15 October 1874), pp. 484–485.
92. "Temperatures and ocean currents in the South Pacific", *Nature* (11 January 1877). Vol. **15**, p. 237.
93. John Murray, "Preliminary reports to Professor Wyville Thomson, F.R.S., Director of the civilian staff, on work done on board the *Challenger*", *Proc. R. Soc.* (1875–1876). Vol. **24**, pp. 471–544.
94. John Murray, "On the distribution of volcanic débris over the floor of the ocean,—its character, source, and some of the products of its disintegration and decomposition", *Proc. R. Soc. Edinb.* (1875). Vol. **9**, pp. 247–261.
95. John Murray and A. Renard, *Report on Deep-Sea Deposits, Challenger Report* (1891), pp. 268–270.
96. John Young Buchanan, "On the occurrence of sulphur in marine muds and nodules, and its bearing on their mode of formation", *Proc. R. Soc. Edinb.* (1890–1891). Vol. **18**, pp. 17–39.
97. L. Dieulafait, "Le manganèse dans les eaux des mers actuelles et dans certains de leurs dépôts; conséquence relative à la craie blanche de la période secondaire", *C.r. hebd. Séanc. Acad. Sci. Paris* (1883). Vol. **96**, pp. 718–721.
98. "Deep-sea soundings in the Pacific Ocean", *Nature* (3 September 1874). Vol. **10**, pp. 356–357.
99. *Challenger Report, Narrative.* Vol. **1**, part 2, pp. 734–735.
100. T. H. Huxley, "Notes from the *Challenger*", *Nature* (19 August 1875). Vol. **12**, pp. 315–316.
101. T. H. Huxley, "On some organisms living at great depths in the North Atlantic Ocean", *Q. J. microsc. Sci.* (1868). Vol. **8**, pp. 203–212.
102. E(dwin) R(ay) L(ankester), "Ernst Haeckel on the mechanical theory of life and spontaneous generation", *Nature* (2 March 1871). Vol. **3**, pp. 354–356.
103. *Report on the Scientific Results of the Voyage of H.M.S. Challenger, Narrative.* Vol. **1**, part 2, pp. 939–940.
   John Young Buchanan, "Preliminary report to Professor Wyville Thomson, F.R.S., director of the civilian scientific staff, on work (chemical and geological) done on board H.M.S. *Challenger*", *Proc. Roy. Soc.* (1875–1876). Vol. **24**, pp. 593–623; pp. 605–606.
104. John Young Buchanan, *Scientific Papers*, 1913. Vol. **1**, p. ix.
105. T. H. Huxley, "Notes from the *Challenger*", *Nature* (19 August 1875). Vol. **12**, pp. 315–316.
106. Hugh Robert Mill, "Obituary of J. Y. Buchanan", *Nature* (14 November 1925). Vol. **116**, pp. 719–720.
107. George J. Allman, "Presidential address to the British Association", *Nature* (21 August 1879). Vol. **20**, pp. 384–393.
   Report of the 49th meeting of the British Association for the Advancement of Science (1879), (1879). Part 1, pp. 1–30.
108. "The British Association at Sheffield", *Nature* (leader) (28 August 1879). Vol. **20**, pp. 405–407. The writer commented: "Surprise has been expressed in some quarters that Prof. Allman should have ventured to found such momentous speculations, even partly, on so unstable a basis as 'Bathybius'."
109. *Challenger Report, Narrative.* Vol. **1**, part 2, pp. 769–771.

110. John Young Buchanan, "Preliminary note on the use of the piezometer in deep-sea sounding", *Proc. R. Soc.* (1876–1877). Vol. **25,** pp. 161–164.
John Young Buchanan, "Laboratory experiences on board the *Challenger*", *J. Chem. Soc.* (1878). Vol. **33,** pp. 445–469. The *Challenger*'s scientists believed that the maximum and minimum thermometers were incapable of recording temperature inversions but when the final corrections were applied it turned out that in fact they had. This depended on their being reeled out or in quickly enough to avoid being affected by the intervening layers of water.

111. *Challenger Report, Narrative.* Vol. **1,** part 1, pp. 98–102.

112. Daniel and Mary Merriman, "Sir C. Wyville Thomson's letters to Staff-Commander Thomas H. Tizard, 1877–1881", *J. Mar. Res.* (1958). Vol. **17,** pp. 347–374; pp. 354–355.

113. Peter Guthrie Tait, "The pressure errors of the *Challenger* thermometers", *Report on the Scientific Results of the Voyage of H.M.S. Challenger, Narrative* (1882). Vol. **2,** appendix A, 42 pp.

114. C. Wyville Thomson, *The Voyage of the Challenger: The Atlantic* (1877). Vol. **2,** p. 256.

115. *Ibid.* pp. 290.

116. *Ibid.* pp. 291.
Thomas H. Tizard, "Report on temperatures" and "General Summary of Atlantic Ocean Temperature", *H.M.S. Challenger*, No. 7. *Report on ocean soundings and temperatures, Atlantic Ocean* (1876), pp. 5–19.

117. C. Wyville Thomson, "Preliminary report to the Hydrographer of the Admiralty on some of the results of the cruise of H.M.S. *Challenger* between Hawaii and Valparaiso", *Proc. R. Soc.* (1875–1876). Vol. **24,** pp. 463–470; p. 470.

118. William B. Carpenter, "Oceanic circulation", *The Athenaeum* (13 May 1876). No. 2533, pp. 666–667. (Wyville Thomson's views had been reported on 29 April, No. 2531, p. 600.)

119. C. Wyville Thomson, Presidential address to Section E (Geography) of the British Association, 1878, *Nature* (22 August 1878). Vol. **18,** pp. 448–452.

120. John Young Buchanan, "On the distribution of salt in the ocean as indicated by the specific gravity of its waters", *Proc. R. geogr. Soc.* (1876–1877). Vol. **21,** pp. 255–257.

121. *Nature* (26 July 1877). Vol. **16,** p. 255.
J. Y. Buchanan, "Oxygen in seawater", *Nature* (27 December 1877). Vol. **17,** p. 162. The first of these references is a note on Buchanan's paper to the Royal Society of Edinburgh (*see* ref. 122); the second a reply by him to a criticism based on the former made by Wyville Thomson in *The Voyage of the Challenger: The Atlantic*, Vol. **2,** p. 267, in which he said that Buchanan's findings were contrary to experience.

122. John Young Buchanan, "Note on the specific gravity of ocean water", *Proc. R. Soc. Edinb.* (1875–1878). Vol. **9,** pp. 283–287.
Thomas H. Tizard, abstract of paper to the British Association, "On the temperature obtained in the Atlantic Ocean, during the cruise of H.M.S. *Challenger*", *Nature* (28 September 1876). Vol. **14,** pp. 490–491.

123. John James Wild, *Thalassa: an essay on the depth, temperature, and currents of the ocean*, London (1877). Wild also used his drawings, apart from those which appeared in the Report, to write an illustrated account of the voyage:

At Anchor. A narrative of experiences afloat and ashore during the voyage of H.M.S. Challenger from 1872 to 1876, London (1878).
124. C. Wyville Thomson, Presidential address to Section E (Geography) of the British Association, 1878, *Nature, op. cit.* p. 452.
125. *Nature* (1 June 1876). Vol. **14**, pp. 119–120.
126. "Dinner to the *Challenger* Staff", *Nature* (13 July 1876). Vol. **14**, pp. 238–239.

Addenda et Corrigenda

p.335, 1.38: *instead* with the German North Sea Expedition in 1871 *read* with a Danish expedition to the Faroes in 1872

p.341, fig.18, caption, 1.1: *after* off *insert* Cape Challenger

p.341, fig.18, caption, 1.2: *insert* (Edinburgh University Library, MS Gen. 30.3).

p.351, 1.19: *instead* fossil *read* extinct

p.351, 1.22: *instead* maganiferous *read* manganous

16. EDINBURGH AND THE GROWTH OF OCEANOGRAPHY AT THE END OF THE NINETEENTH CENTURY

THE unanimity felt by scientists in their approval of the voyage of the *Challenger* did not long outlast her return. Warned by the fate of scientific collections made on previous voyages, Sir James Clark Ross's to name only one, Wyville Thomson had stipulated before the *Challenger* set sail that the material which they collected should become government property and that funds should be provided on their return for the publication of the results. He also secured an understanding that this should be done under his personal direction. During the voyage he formulated the details of the arrangement in a letter to the Admiralty. When the *Challenger* returned he was to take charge of work on the material they had collected and edit the report with a five-year grant from the Treasury to cover the cost of staff and expenses. The scientific staff of the expedition should be retained until March 1877 to help with sorting the collections of marine fauna but after that he would carry on with Murray and Frederick Pearcey, his assistant during the voyage, and a secretary. The work was to be done in Edinburgh but ultimately the specimens would be sent to the British Museum.[1, 2]

The British Museum hotly contested this arrangement when it became known and attempted to get hold of the entire collection on the expedition's return. Wyville Thomson managed to frustrate their design, with some influential aid, notably from Hooker, now President of the Royal Society, and Huxley, who as Secretary was responsible for much of the background work both before and after the voyage, and the original terms of the arrangement were preserved.[3] The terrestrial items went to the British Museum but the marine collections stayed in Edinburgh, where they had been sent at intervals during the voyage. The Challenger Commission was set up to administer them with Wyville Thomson as Director. The Treasury made a grant of £25,000 to cover the salaries of the permanent staff and the expenses of scientists working on the collections. The reports were to be published by the Stationery Office.

Back in Edinburgh the *Challenger* people were visited by scientists from many different countries who came to see the collections and to help in the work of sorting. One of the first of these was Alexander Agassiz. His friendship with Wyville Thomson dated back to a visit which he had made to Belfast in the autumn of 1869.[4] On that occasion they had agreed that their marine collections should be worked on by the same people either side of the Atlantic.[5] Wyville Thomson now intended to adhere to his* policy and chose scientists to work on the *Challenger* collections irrespective of nationality and purely on the grounds of merit. Among his original selection were Agassiz himself, to work on the Echinoidea, and Theodore Lyman (1833–1897), also of the Museum of Comparative Zoology, Harvard, to do the Ophiuroidea. Some of the sponges were to go to Oscar Schmidt (1823–1886) and the Radiolaria and deep sea Medusae to Haeckel, both in Germany. He himself would do the rest of the sponges and the Crinoids, P. H. Carpenter (1852–1891) the Comatulae, Moseley some species of corals, William C. McIntosh (1838–1931) the Annelids and Albert Günther (1830–1914) the fishes.

Agassiz forwarded this news to the United States where it was printed by the *American Journal of Science and Arts* in February 1877.[6] A month later it re-crossed the Atlantic to appear in the *Annals and Magazine of Natural History*.[7] A violent reaction ensued among certain interested scientists in this country who felt that since the *Challenger* was a British ship they had an indisputable claim to work on the collections first. The problem was that whereas before the *Challenger* set sail relatively few people were interested in deep-sea work, now zoologists were eager to participate in what promised after all to be a rich and rewarding field.

Wyville Thomson received a letter from P. Martin Duncan (1821–1891), a palaeontologist and President of the Geological Society, saying that certain scientists, whom he did not name, had deputed him to request that the *Challenger* specimens should be studied in this country.[8] Thomson replied that he could not alter his decision to please Duncan's anonymous backers. The collections must go to those best equipped to deal with them. In fact, though he had not yet determined the ultimate destination of them all, relatively few would be going abroad. He would have asked Duncan to take over the corals had it not been that Moseley, as a member of the expedition, had priority.[9]

Duncan refused to accept this explanation. Changing his tactics, he wrote to the *Annals and Magazine of Natural History* accusing Wyville Thomson of having "passed over with contemptuous neglect" the claims of promising British scientists. He complained that

For a great nation to send out expensive expeditions and then to distribute the results for determination and description to foreign naturalists, however distinguished, without considering and employing its own naturalists, is rather characteristic of this age of depreciating criticism.[10]

So the belief that the British are overprone to dismiss their achievements is apparently not as new as is often supposed.

The quarrel developed into an unpleasant episode which divided scientific opinion. *Nature* had an editorial endorsing Wyville Thomson's position and printed a letter in his support which included among its signatories Darwin, Huxley, Hooker and Carpenter.[11] On the other side the editors of the *Annals and Magazine of Natural History* took an attitude favourable to Duncan.[12]

Alexander Agassiz had come in for a share of the general opprobrium. He wrote to John Murray

I have a letter from Duncan of the Geological Society who seems to be "howling" mad at the *Challenger* things going out of the country.[13]

Presumably he was behind an article in the *American Journal of Science and Arts* which pointed out that of the sixteen reports on material collected by his father and Count Pourtalès in the *Hassler* twelve had been compiled in Europe.[14]

The affair served to rekindle the smouldering resentment at the British Museum and for a while it looked as though the decision concerning the disposal of *Challenger* collections might be reversed. Ultimately the storm blew over and things went on as before. The bad feeling which had been engendered however persisted for some time. Agassiz believed that certain criticisms of his work on the Echini made by Duncan and F. Jeffrey Bell of the British Museum[15] betrayed a spirit of rancour. He wrote to Wyville Thomson on one of Duncan's articles

The only annoying part of all this is the *tone* of superiority he and Bell and all the english people who think they should have had the Challenger work take, and I only hope they keep clear of you.[16]

But Agassiz enjoyed speaking his mind. Wyville Thomson on the other hand was more sensitive and less resilient and took most seriously the self-imposed task of publishing the results of the *Challenger* in the style he considered fitting. The episode provided an ominous foretaste of the difficulties which lay ahead and were to impose an ever increasing strain upon him.

Whatever may have been the merits or demerits of his adversaries' case, Wyville Thomson's decision to bring in foreign scientists on the *Challenger* had far-reaching results which could scarcely have been foreseen at the time. People have pointed to the *Challenger* expedition as the beginning of modern oceanography but this is rather to misjudge its significance. It neglects the work of earlier scientists and underestimates the strength of the parallel movement in other countries. G. O. Sars and Pourtalès had anticipated Wyville Thomson and Carpenter in moving outwards into the deep sea. By and large too, the *Challenger* did not revolutionize existing knowledge and techniques, it extended them, so that it could equally well be argued that it represents the summit of achievement of an earlier period, the work of John Ross, James Clark Ross, Du Petit-Thouars, Lenz, etc., carried to its logical conclusion. Nor did the voyage usher in an era of government support for marine science. It is true that foreign scientists were able to take advantage of jingoistic tendencies in their own governments who, not to be outdone, sent out expeditions on their own account but of course this particular gambit could not be employed with regard to the British government which, astonished by its generosity over the *Challenger*, assuaged its feelings of guilt by steadfastly refusing financial assistance to any project which could not be shown to have a direct bearing on fisheries research. So that the peculiar situation arose in which, unlike the typical developing science which it is suggested is peopled from the lower ranks of the sciences most closely related to it, most would-be students of oceanography in the late nineteenth century had from economic necessity to go on competing in the disciplines from which they came.[17]

Wyville Thomson's achievement was to create a network of personal relationships which, in the absence of concrete recognition either academic or governmental, served as the first step towards building up an international community of oceanographers. One assumes that this was a quite unpremeditated development. The immense interest generated by the *Challenger* expedition and the material brought back naturally drew scientists from many different countries to visit the team at their Edinburgh headquarters, among them as well as Agassiz, people like Anton Dohrn (1840–1909), Haeckel and Hjalmar Théel. Soon the amount of work being done on the collections exceeded anything that had been anticipated and not a few but many of the leading European marine zoologists were involved, not to mention a large number of contributors from the United Kingdom including Huxley, W. B. Carpenter, Gwyn Jeffreys, Ray* Lankester, Allman, A. M. Norman (1831–1918) and many others.

The visits and correspondence which were entailed in the preparation and editing of the reports served to develop a bond between the scientists and the *Challenger* team which in some cases was life long. In the space of a few years Edinburgh had emerged as the international centre for the marine sciences, and continued to enjoy this position until after the report was completed. This in the end took almost four times as long as Wyville

Thomson had allowed for and during this time the international oceanographic community increased its sense of cohesion in spite of changes
in personalities and emphasis. It is possible that the moves towards
institutionalization which took place on a national and international level
only after the report had been completed were in some measure due to the
vacuum which it left.

Whatever the truth behind the last conjecture, the emergence of Edinburgh as a centre and of Wyville Thomson and his colleagues as arbiters
for the world of marine science is undisputed. From the account given by
contemporaries it is clear that personalities played a major role throughout
and that in the first place it was Wyville Thomson's warmth and charm
of character that served to cement into friendship many of his scientific
contacts. A unique picture of the man and his circle is given in William A.
Herdman's *Founders of Oceanography*. Herdman studied zoology at
Edinburgh and became Wyville Thomson's assistant in 1879. In 1881 he
went to Liverpool as professor of natural history. He was the author of the
Challenger Report on Tunicates.[18]

After the initial year in Edinburgh, Thomson and Murray were left
behind while the other *Challenger* scientists continued their careers.
Moseley became professor of anatomy at Oxford in 1881. Tizard who had
spent a year at the Admiralty went back to sea. They both seem to have
maintained fairly close ties with their former colleagues. The only one
who seems to have dropped out to a certain extent was Buchanan. He
somehow contrived to affront the Treasury so severely that they decreed
that he should not be employed any further on the report.[19] Thomson did
not seem to feel that he was any great loss, perhaps because as someone
once said of Buchanan "I never knew a man who did so much work and
wrote so little about it".[20] Seen as a cold and distant man having no
tendency towards friendship,[20] he was in some respects more clear sighted
than his contemporaries and paid the penalty of detachment. The sever-
ing of his connection with the *Challenger* in no way interrupted his career
as an oceanographer. He was well off and between 1878 and 1882 made
summer cruises on the west coast of Scotland in his own yacht, *Mallard*,
discovering amongst other things that there were manganese nodules on the
bed of Loch Fyne.[21] After that he sailed on cable survey ships and later
still with Prince Albert of Monaco (*see* p. 382).

During the first few years after the *Challenger*'s return everything seemed
to be going well with the actual work on the report though Alexander
Agassiz at one stage wrote to Wyville Thomson "I should die if I had to
undertake a second job of this kind".[22] At the British Association meeting
in 1878 Thomson announced that the only thing materially hindering
progress was that all the suitably qualified artists in Britain were working

on one or another of the monographs so that the rest were being delayed.[23] He expected that the complete report would occupy between fourteen and sixteen volumes.

Serious difficulties were already arising however with regard to the administration of the report. The task of accounting for all the sums of money which had to be paid out to authors for their expenses drove Thomson almost to distraction. As well as quarrelling with the Treasury he also found himself engaged in a battle with the Stationery Office who considered his demands about format exorbitant.[24] Over this Thomson finally had his way but the struggle had caused him to become severely strained and in June 1879 he suffered an attack of paralysis from which he recovered with difficulty.[25]

In the autumn of 1880 the first volume of the *Challenger Report* appeared.[26] Huxley welcomed it as the first in a series of works which would at last reveal some of the

secrets of the busy life which, contrary to all the beliefs of the naturalists of a past generation, blindly toils and moils in the darkness and cold of the marine abysses.[27]

He was somewhat less enthusiastic about some of the conclusions reached in the general introduction. In Wyville Thomson's opinion the overriding lesson of the *Challenger* voyage was that, while evolution of species must be accepted as a fact, there was no need to stipulate natural selection as the cause. He wrote

it seems to me that in this, as in all cases in which it has been possible to bring the question, however remotely, to the test of observation, the character of the abyssal fauna refuses to give the least support to the theory which refers the evolution of species to extreme variation guided only by natural selection.[28]

The dispute was prolonged into further issues of *Nature* and Darwin intervened in defence of his views.[29]

The pleasure felt by the scientific world at the appearance of the *Challenger Reports* was not universally shared. One newspaper took a very disenchanted view of the event

The first volume recording the adventures of the *Challenger* yachting trip is now out, and the other fifty-nine will be ready in less than a century. Everybody knows that Mr. Lowe sent a man-of-war away laden with Professors, and that these learned individuals amused themselves for four years. They played with thermometers, they fished at all depths from two feet to three miles; they brought up bucketfuls of stuff from the deep sea bottom; and they all pottered about and imagined they were furthering the grand Cause of Science. Then the tons of rubbish were brought home, and the genius who bossed the excursion

proceeded to employ a swarm of foreigners to write monographs on the specimens. There were plenty of good scientific men in England, but the true philosopher is nothing if not cosmopolitan; so the tax-payers' money was employed
in feeding a mob of Germans and other aliens. The whole business has cost
two hundred thousand pounds; and in return for this sum we have got one
lumbering volume of statistics, and a complete set of squabbles which are going
on briskly wherever two or three philosophers are gathered together. I believe
the expedition discovered one new species of shrimp, but I am not quite sure.[30]

The official estimate, which Huxley gave, was

that the fifteen or sixteen volumes of which the whole work is to consist may
reasonably be expected to be in the hands of the public by 1884.[31]

Both were wrong, but of the two approximations the former turned out to
be the more accurate.

It was not just the enormous amount of work to be got through and the
inevitable procrastination of some authors which led to the report becoming far larger and longer than anticipated. Wyville Thomson had
enjoined brevity but many of the zoologists, who formed the majority of
people working on the report, found the urge to spread themselves irresistible. Some, instead of confining themselves to the *Challenger* samples of the
creatures on which they were working, dealt as well with those collected
on earlier voyages and, increasingly, on later ones too. Many years later
Alexander Agassiz recalled how, after

scimping in all directions to meet Thomson's request for economy and brief-
ness I often grudged the superb memoirs which came out subsequently.[32]

It soon became clear that the work would never be finished in the
allotted five years but the Treasury gave no hope of a renewal of the grant.
The prospects for the future were so awful that Wyville Thomson, never
fully well after his previous illness, collapsed under the strain. He resigned
his professorship in October 1881 and died on 10 March the following
year.[33]

Thomson's death was regarded as a tragedy, not the less because it
turned out that his suffering had been unnecessary. The Treasury subsequently gave way and appointed John Murray as his successor to the
editorship with a grant for another five years.[34] The situation was saved as
far as the report was concerned but the clock could not be put back and
with Wyville Thomson dead the sense of calamity remained. Agassiz
wrote to Murray

it will be long before we have one who knows so much and says what he knows
in such a charming way.[35]

With Murray in charge there was no longer much doubt of the ultimate success of the report itself. He was a very much more forceful personality. A colleague described him as "a man of tremendous driving power, quick in decision, relentless in carrying out his plans, and sorely incommoded by a very kindly disposition".[36] He was gregarious too and admirably fitted to carry on the informal leadership of the oceanographic community that had begun to group itself around Thomson. During the time the Challenger Commission was in being Edinburgh maintained her position as a centre for marine and other sciences.

One of the unfortunate consequences of Wyville Thomson's death was that the official connection with Edinburgh University ended. Ray Lankester was appointed as his successor to the professorship but on learning that he was actually expected to live in Edinburgh all the year round he speedily decamped to London.[37] The post ultimately went to James Cossar Ewart (1851–1933) who though for some time a member of the Scottish Fisheries Board was primarily interested in other fields and altogether a much more subdued personality. It is impossible not to speculate what might have gone on had Lankester stayed, since later the rivalry between him and Murray was notorious among the younger generation of marine scientists.[38] William Speirs Bruce (1867–1921) later proposed the setting up of a lectureship in oceanography at Edinburgh, but this never came to anything[39] and though links with the university scientists remained strong, marine science after Thomson's death had henceforward to stand on its own feet, which in the long run was probably detrimental.

Before he died Thomson had succeeded in arranging a new expedition to the area between the Faroes and the Shetlands where he and Carpenter had done their first deep sea work (see Ch. 14) in H.M.S. *Lightning*. During the voyage of H.M.S. *Challenger* several anomalies in ocean temperature had been found which Tizard explained as the result of submarine ridges which cut off the deep polar flow from the deeper parts of some ocean basins and marginal seas (see Ch. 15). The tight schedule of the voyage made it impossible to make a thorough investigation of this idea but as Wyville Thomson and Tizard discussed the juxtaposition of warm and cold water in the deeper layers of the Faroe-Shetland Channel, attributed by Carpenter to converging currents (see Ch. 14), it became clear that this might well have an identical explanation. Back at home, Thomson was anxious to put it to the test since if the theory were borne out in this one place it would be legitimate to assume that it held good elsewhere.

It was not until 1880 that the new expedition took place. By this time Tizard had returned to sea and was commanding H.M.S. *Knight Errant* on survey work in home waters and it was his ship which was chosen by the Hydrographer.[40] Wyville Thomson was to be allowed to embark his dredging gear, but with the proviso that it was only to be used when it would not interfere with the routine of survey work.[41] He himself was not well enough to go and remained at Stornoway while Murray took charge of the scientific work. Though the ship was far from adequate for the purpose the voyage was a success in essentials. The outline of a ridge was discovered in the expected position and some dredging work was done.[42]

In the summer of 1882 Murray and Tizard made a further cruise to the area in H.M.S. *Triton*. They charted the ridge more thoroughly than had been possible on the earlier occasion and named it in memory of Wyville Thomson.[43] Afterwards the *Triton* was to make a further cruise from Oban with Professor Chrystal on board, in order to give him the opportunity of making observations in connection with Tait's work on the *Challenger* thermometers.[44]

Meanwhile, the published volumes of the *Challenger Report* began to appear more regularly. Moseley's report on corals was in the second volume and Agassiz's report on the Echini, of which he had written to Wyville Thomson

I felt when I got through that I never wanted to see another sea urchin and hoped they would gradually become extinct[45]

was in the third, both coming out in 1881. By the end of the decade all 32 of the zoological series had appeared.

When Buchanan had to give up his *Challenger* work the sea water samples were taken over by William Dittmar (1833–1892), professor of chemistry at Anderson's College, Glasgow. His report on salinity and the gases dissolved in sea water[46] was compiled in six years but read, according to a reviewer, like the work of a lifetime.[47] It was the first major work on the subject to appear in this country since Forchhammer's paper of 1865 (*see* Ch. 13). Little had been done anywhere in between but new work on the gaseous contents of sea water had come from Jacobsen in Germany, who had passed on his knowledge to Buchanan before the *Challenger* set sail,[48] and Tørnoe, chemist on the Norwegian North Atlantic Expedition.[49]

Dittmar said that his work supplemented Forchhammer's, in that it confirmed his general conclusion that the components of marine salt almost always exist in the same ratio to each other, irrespective of the total salinity, and showed that this is true for water from any depth.[50] But he also introduced direct methods for determining some of the minor constituents which until then had only been assumed to be present because they occurred in marine organisms in a concentrated form.

Murray himself continued work on the marine deposits. From 1878 onwards he had expert help from the Belgian geologist Alphonse F. Renard (1842–1903). W. A. Herdman graphically described how the visitor to the Challenger Office during the 1880s would penetrate the dense cloud of smoke emanating from Renard's cigar and find them both hard at work together with Pearcey and James Chumley, the secretary, in a room "more like an overcrowded scullery than an oceanographic laboratory".[51]

The work developed along the lines which Murray had laid down in his preliminary report (see Ch. 15) and confirmed the conclusions which he had reached during the voyage on the formation of the oozes at moderate depths and of the deep-sea clays. The probability of his theory concerning the origin of red clay was convincingly, if catastrophically, demonstrated by the eruption of Krakatoa in 1883 which left pumice feet thick floating on the surface of the sea and volcanic dust which dispersed right round the world. In 1884 they wrote

Everything seems to show that the formation of the clay is due to the decomposition of fragmentary volcanic products, whose presence can be detected over the whole floor of the ocean.[52]

There was a slight divergence in opinion between the two authors concealed in this statement. Murray ascribed the clay to the decomposition of material from subaerial and submarine eruptions invoking winds and currents as the agencies by which it was transported; Renard believed that submarine volcanoes should be considered the more important of the two.[53]

The report on deep-sea deposits finally appeared in 1891 but it did far more than give an account of the *Challenger* work. Since the *Challenger* returned large numbers of samples had been collected by survey ships from different countries and by the oceanographic expeditions sent out from Norway, Italy, France, Germany and the United States. Most of these had been studied by Murray and Renard.[54] Crates of manganese nodules were shuttled back and forth across the Atlantic, arriving on one occasion minus labels.[55] Alexander Agassiz spent four years persuading A. E. Verrill (1839–1926) to disgorge some specimens that he was anxious Murray should see and gave vent to the remark that "Verrill like hell is paved with good intentions".[56]

Murray and Renard used this information to compile a series of charts of the distribution of marine sediments. They had not only founded the study of submarine geology but established it on such a firm footing that, as the French oceanographer Jules Rouch wrote recently, subsequent * work has only filled in the broad outlines of their picture of the composition of the ocean bed.[57]

The one feature of the *Challenger*'s work which was comparatively neglected was the ocean temperature observations. Carpenter had hoped that they would be used by mathematicians and physicists to construct an authoritative theory of ocean circulation (see Ch. 14) but unfortunately this did not happen. One person who did take great interest in the figures was William Leighton Jordan (1836–1922). He was looking for proof of his theory that ocean currents are caused by conflicting forces of terrestrial and astral gravitation and expected to find evidence of the interweaving of different layers of water. He found that the temperatures printed in the *Challenger Report* proper[58] did not tally with those which he had seen in the preliminary hydrographic reports. The figures were now printed as observed with a small instrumental correction and some showed small increases in temperature with depth whereas the earlier figures given had been overcorrected and fitted into the curve of decreasing temperature. There were also some larger anomalies where the thermometers had apparently registered very sudden changes in temperature.[59] Jordan believed that the original figures had been falsified in a deliberate attempt to suppress his views and to foist what he saw as the arrogantly preconceived notion of the *Challenger* scientists, that temperature always decreases with depth, on a gullible world, with the connivance of the scientific establishment.[60]

It was only after some considerable time had elapsed after the return of the expedition that John Murray turned over the task of producing a report on ocean circulation to Alexander Buchan (1829–1907), who was also doing the meteorological results.[61] Buchan was a meteorologist of the old school, at a time when British meteorology was concerned with little more than statistical studies.[62] He compiled painstaking charts of the distribution of salinity and temperature at different depths but failed to deduce anything from them that was not already fairly well known, still less to provide a qualitative theory of water movements.[63] It was left to physical oceanographers in Germany after 1900 to make use of the material in the way that Carpenter had envisaged.[64] Of course they had the benefit of hindsight but there is no doubt that more could have been learned from them at the time, had there been anyone in this country with a genuine interest and a suitable basis of knowledge.

Important though it was, and Murray was careful to fulfil Wyville Thomson's original intentions, the work on the *Challenger Report* was only a small part of the effort being devoted to marine science in different countries. The science was ongoing and the *Report* to a considerable extent evolved with it, taking into account the new ideas which were coming to the fore.

The attitude of the British government made any further voyages impossible in this country but paradoxically the example of the *Challenger* and preceding voyages had made things easier abroad. Then, as now, an emotional argument based on considerations of national prestige was more effective in swaying the seat of power than a carefully thought out presentation of possible scientific advantages. In Norway G. O. Sars and H. Mohn used the *Challenger* and the voyages leading up to it as precedents in obtaining the summer cruises made in the North Atlantic by the S.S. *Vøringen* in the years 1876–1878.[65] The German North Sea Commission at Kiel, set up in 1870, began its work by studying the Baltic and the North Sea in the S.S. *Pommerania* in 1871 and 1872; this work was followed up by the Hydrographic Department of the German navy with the S.S. *Drache* in 1881, 1882 and 1884.[66] The French government financed three cruises by the *Travailleur* and *Talisman* early in the 1880s in which a team of scientists headed by Alphonse Milne-Edwards took part.[67] In the 1890s the Austrian research ship *Pola* worked in the Mediterranean and the Red Sea[68] and Russian scientists were at work in the Black Sea.[69] All these undertakings were concerned to explore a fairly limited area of the sea, usually adjacent to the country involved, but there were also a number of more ambitious voyages. Germany despatched the S.S. *National* in 1889, the voyage known as the Plankton Expedition because this was its raison d'être, and the *Valdivia* expedition of 1898–1899. Denmark sent an expedition in the *Ingolf* in 1895 and 1896. Several voyages of circumnavigation on the *Challenger* model were made: the *Enterprise* (1883–1886) from the United States, the *Vettor Pisani* from Italy and the *Vitiaz* (1886–1889) commanded by Admiral S. O. Makarov (1849–1904) from Russia.[70]

In all this activity Great Britain was conspicuous only by absence, in spite of repeated appeals by scientists.[71] However, there were various expedients for getting new work done, in spite of the lack of new expeditions, and these were successfully employed by would-be oceanographers in Britain during the 1880s.

It had occurred to marine zoologists by the middle of the nineteenth century[72] that a good way of studying marine life would be to establish small laboratories or field stations at suitable places on the coast, from which they could work without all the expense of running a sizeable ship. Even so organization posed a problem and few attempts had been made to put the idea into practice when Anton Dohrn (1840–1909), a young German zoologist, discussed the prospect with a Russian colleague, N. N. Miklukho-Maklai[73] while they were working together in Sicily.[72] Dohrn decided to try and realize his plan by combining a station and aquarium. He settled on Naples as the site and obtained grants from the governments of Germany and Italy and from scientific institutions in many countries, as well as using his own fortune. The Stazione Zoologica was opened in 1873. It was organized so that interested governments or scientific bodies rented laboratory accommodation and sent out zoologists to work there.[74]

During his travels to arouse support Dohrn had visited the United Kingdom. He addressed the British Association in 1870 and the meeting set up a committee to promote the foundation of marine stations.[75] It was some little time, however, before such a step was taken in this country. The event which finally set things in motion was the International Fisheries Exhibition, held in London in the summer of 1883.[76] It was as a result of ideas then suggested that a meeting of biologists attended by, amongst others, Huxley, Carpenter, Ray Lankester and Moseley, was held in the spring of 1884 to found the Marine Biological Association of the United Kingdom.[77] The Association resolved to set up a permanent marine laboratory and chose Plymouth as the site. Most of the capital cost was met by subscription[78] but the government agreed to make an annual grant provided that the laboratory co-operated with the work of the Scottish Fisheries Board.[79] The Plymouth Laboratory of the Marine Biological Association was opened in June 1888.[80] The first director was the zoologist Gilbert C. Bourne (1861–1933), a pupil of P. H. Carpenter at Eton and of H. N. Moseley at Oxford.[81]

Part of the surplus funds of a fisheries exhibition held in Edinburgh in 1882 was allocated to the Scottish Meteorological Society, which had a fisheries committee of which Murray was the chairman.[82] One of the purposes for which the grant was made was that of setting up a marine station. In August 1883 Murray proposed that the plan be put into effect. He had already seen an ideal site—a flooded quarry on the foreshore at Granton.[83] The plan met with the approval of the Scottish Meteorological Society and the Royal Society of Edinburgh and the fund was made available[84] but the government, when applied to, refused to make any direct grant and the rest of the cost had to be met by subscriptions[85]—which included an anonymous donation of £1,000. A floating laboratory was built on a barge, named the *Ark*. Murray also bought a steam yacht, the *Medusa*, and, later, accommodation on shore was added. The original staff consisted of the zoologist J. T. Cunningham, John Rattray and Hugh Robert Mill as chemist and physicist. The Scottish Marine Station was opened in April 1884.[86]

For the first year of its existence the work of the new station was all on the east coast of Scotland and especially in the Firth of Forth where H. R. Mill studied salinity and temperature changes[87] but in the summer of 1885 Murray took the *Ark* and the *Medusa* to Millport in the Firth of Clyde.[88] Millport was the home of David Robertson (1806–1896), a keen amateur * zoologist.[89] He and Murray apparently got on well and the *Ark* was left there permanently. For the next four or five years the principal work of the Scottish Marine Station was a study of the sea lochs of the west of Scotland, particularly the complex which they named the Clyde Sea

Area.[90] The work was carried on summer and winter and led to a number of unexpected discoveries, notably of a temperature inversion in the waters of Loch Fyne.[91]

To the south, activity in the Irish Sea was centred on Liverpool[92] where W. A. Herdman founded a Marine Biology Committee in 1885.[93] For the first few years the committee's field work was done with a borrowed ship over the Easter or Whitsun weekend. Then they were lent disused telegraph buildings on Puffin Island for a temporary marine station[94] and a few years later (1892) built a permanent laboratory at Port Erin on the Isle of Man.[95]

Parallel developments were going on in many other countries at this time. For example in the United States after the failure of several schemes, including J. L. Agassiz's summer school at Penikese, which he had started in 1872, two laboratories were established at Woods Hole, Massachusetts. The first of these was the laboratory of the United States Fish Commission, in 1885; the second, the Marine Biological Laboratory, was set up in 1888.[96]

Fisheries research was one aspect of marine science which governments were willing to support generously. The dangers of overfishing made it imperative to know about the life-history and movements of food fishes. In the United States the pioneer work of Spencer F. Baird (1823–1887) led to the formation of the United States Fish Commission in 1871.[97] The equivalent organization in the United Kingdom was the Scottish Fisheries Board; originally set up in 1809, it was reconstituted with a research commitment in 1882.[98] In 1898 the Board set up a laboratory at Aberdeen with Thomas Wemyss Fulton (1855–1929) as director.[99] Fisheries research had already been going on under Professor W. C. McIntosh at St. Andrews, in the old fever hospital, and the University's Gatty Marine Laboratory was set up in 1892.[100]

Relations between the Scottish Fisheries Board and the Scottish Marine Station were somewhat ambivalent. Mill relates how the Board felt it beneath their dignity to co-operate with an unofficial body but were obliged to turn to him because the man selected by Cossar Ewart to do their physical and chemical research, John Gibson, disliked work at sea. Murray was reluctant to give official assistance but he allowed Mill to take a "holiday" and do as he pleased. Mill spent a month on the Board's research ship *Garland* in 1886 and in the following year took part in a cruise to the Hebrides in the fishery protection vessel, H.M.S. *Jackal*.[101]

Another development common to most countries at this time was the increasing amount of deep-sea work being done by naval survey ships, often accompanied by specifically oceanographic observations. The Italian government early in the 1880s began using its naval vessel *Washington* under Captain Magnaghi to make observations in the Mediterranean.[102]

The United States Coast Survey continued to make notable contributions through the work of its ship the *Blake*. The *Blake*'s captain, Charles D. Sigsbee (1845–1923), modified the Kelvin sounding machine to enable it to be used in shallow water while the ship was under way.[103] One of the ship's officers, John Elliott Pillsbury (1846–1919) devised a current meter for making surveys of the Gulf Stream which was used when he returned to the *Blake* as captain in 1884.[104] Alexander Agassiz accompanied the *Blake* on three voyages between 1877 and 1880.[105] On the first cruise he and Sigsbee devised, amongst other things, a way of using wire rope for dredging.[103] This had the advantage of saving greatly on storage space and on the time needed for dredging operations and, with wire sounding machines, was soon generally adopted, except by the Scottish Marine Station which clung with rather exaggerated loyalty to hemp lines as used on the *Challenger*.[106] In 1885 Agassiz was invited to become Superintendent of the Coast Survey but he refused, ostensibly because he did not wish to interrupt his own work. On several later occasions he sailed on the Fish Commission's steamer *Albatross* in the Pacific.[4, 107]

A number of the *Challenger*'s officers were by this time in the higher echelons of the British surveying service. Maclear followed Nares in command of H.M.S. *Alert* in South American waters and from 1883–1887 surveyed in the Indian Ocean and far eastern waters in H.M.S. *Flying Fish*. Between 1886 and 1891 Pelham Aldrich captained H.M.S. *Egeria* and H.M.S. *Research* working first in the Indian and Pacific Oceans and then in home waters.[108] The Royal Indian Marine Survey Ship *Investigator* began making deep sea surveys in the Indian Ocean in 1884 under the command of Alfred Carpenter.[109]

The *Challenger* expedition had barely touched the Indian Ocean and in 1887 Murray paid tribute to the amount of work that had been done there since:

It is not many years since we knew little or nothing reliable concerning the depths, contours, and temperature of the deeper waters of this basin; but to all these departments of knowledge we now almost daily receive additions through the present energetic Hydrographer.[110]

This was W. J. L. Wharton whose twenty-year tenure of office began in 1884.

As captain of H.M.S. *Shearwater* Wharton had been responsible for surveying the currents of the Bosporus (*see* Ch. 15). He retained an interest in the subject and one of the projects undertaken by survey ships was the investigation of the similar pattern of water movements in the Strait of Bab-el-Mandeb. The original observations made by Captain W. Usborne Moore in H.M.S. *Penguin* in 1890 were inconclusive. Moore subsequently experimented with the Pillsbury current meter in the Faroe-Shetland Channel and the English Channel and Commander H. J. Gedge used the instrument to make rather more successful observations in H.M.S. *Stork* in January 1898.[111] Observations had already been made there and in the Bosporus and Strait of Gibraltar by Admiral Makarov.[112]

The routine survey work, which included oceanic cable routes, carried out by naval ships contributed enormously to the stock of knowledge about the oceans. By 1889 the Admiralty were publishing annually a *List of Oceanic Depths*. As well as depth, the survey ships observed deep sea temperatures and collected samples of the marine deposits. The medical officers carried on the tradition of the surgeon-naturalists and studied the natural history and geology of the places they visited. All this provided information which gradually helped to fill in the outline picture of the oceans which had been emerging since the *Challenger* began her voyage. Yet it was not wholly a substitute for proper oceanographic cruises. The survey ships scarcely ever carried professional scientists and though some of their personnel became engaged in the subjects under discussion in the scientific world and were allowed some latitude in the work connected with them, the system in which they were working admitted of only limited flexibility and scientific research had ultimately to be subordinated to the service's routine. Mill recalled a visit to Wharton and how

seated at his desk in the Admiralty and fingering absently a basket of odd lengths of red tape at his side—each piece carefully coiled away—he told me plainly, when I spoke of reading deep-sea temperatures to a tenth of a degree Fahrenheit, that no naval officer would ever bother to read any closer than single degrees, any finer approximation being of no significance in hydrography.[113]

Alexander Agassiz complained about material sent to him from the *Albatross* in 1889 when they had made only one haul deeper than 100 fathoms:

It's aggravating but just what I expected from Navy men who are always so anxious to make time.[114]

J. Y. Buchanan solved the problem of going to sea by getting a commercial cable laying concern, the Telegraph Construction and Maintenance Company, to allow him to sail in their ships. In 1883 he sailed from Cadiz to the Canaries in the S.S. *Dacia* on a search for submerged mountain peaks on which a cable had broken the year before.[115] In 1885–1886 he was in the S.S. *Buccaneer*, belonging to the same company, on a voyage from the Cape Verde Islands to equatorial Africa and Ascension Island.[116] When the survey work was over he was allowed to use the ship for making oceanographical observations. In this he was helped by the ship's officers, led by Captain Anthony Thomson. One of their stations early in March

1886 was almost on the equator. There they discovered a strong under-current flowing in an easterly direction below the westerly southern equatorial current and this was found again in the two days following.[117]

Buchanan wrote:

For the double purpose of examining the currents and of obtaining a large specimen of the bottom, the *Buccaneer* was anchored in 1,800 fathoms of water by means of an ordinary light anchor fitted with a canvas bag to receive the mud which would otherwise fall off the flukes on its being weighed. While the ship was lying thus at anchor, the surface water was found to have a very slight westerly set. At a depth of 15 fathoms there was a difference and at 30 fathoms the water was running so strongly to the south-east that it was impossible to make observations of temperature, as the lines, heavily loaded, drifted straight out and could not be sunk by any weight the strain of which they could bear.[118]

The possible importance of this discovery was not lost on Buchanan. He later wrote

During the laying of the submarine cable from Fernando Noronha to Senegal this under current was observed far to the westward, and there is every reason to believe that it is a constant and important factor of oceanic circulation, the heart of which lies in the equatorial belt.[119]

The ideal way of planning one's ocean going research was clearly either to know someone with his own boat or to be rich enough to afford one's own. One or other of these expedients was adopted quite frequently at this stage but among privately organized ventures all others were thrown into the shade by the cruises of Prince Albert I of Monaco (1848–1922). He began his oceanographic work in 1885 in a schooner, the *Hirondelle*, but afterwards graduated to progressively more powerful steamers, the *Princesse Alice I, Princesse Alice II*, and *Hirondelle II*.[120] His first work was to map the surface currents of the North Atlantic which he traced by releasing floats and plotting the course of those that were found and returned.[121] In the larger ships he was able to work more extensively on the conditions and fauna of the deep sea.[122] On one occasion, in 1895, he became involved in a whale hunt off the Azores and grew to be fascinated by the enormous animals and the almost unknown giant squid on which they fed.[123]

On his annual cruises Prince Albert had a team of scientific helpers of which Buchanan became a frequent member. He also built and endowed his own research centre—the Musée Océanographique—at Monaco, opened in 1910.[124]

Much of the work being done at sea and on land in the ways outlined was purely descriptive but several issues were currently being hotly debated and there was also a good deal of evidence hunting in progress by the supporters of rival theories. One such controversy surrounded Alexander Agassiz's view, stoutly maintained in the face of almost universal opposition, that there was no life in the sea between the top and bottom layers.[125] The difficulty in being definitely either for or against this view lay in the factor of doubt which surrounded the functioning of the self-opening and closing nets which were devised to sample the midwater fauna. Agassiz's views were attacked by the German zoologists in particular and this induced in him a state of near xenophobia, so much so that he said he would refuse an invitation to the 1894 meeting of the British Association if Haeckel were also to attend.[126] Murray flew a kite of his own in the theory of bi-polarity in which he held that a resemblance could be distinguished between the deep water fauna of the Arctic and Antarctic oceans.[127]

The controversy which aroused the widest discussion, probably because it came in the interface between oceanography and geology, was over Murray's theory of the origin of coral reefs. Murray had formulated the theory while he was in the *Challenger* but he had not mentioned it in his preliminary report and it was not until 1880 that it was made public. According to the Duke of Argyll (1823–1900), who endeavoured to make it a scandal in 1887, this delay was imposed by Wyville Thomson, apparently because he felt that the *Challenger* work had attacked enough sacred cows for the time being.[128] The sacred cow in this instance was Darwin's theory, put forward as a result of his work in the *Beagle*[129] and substantially endorsed by geologists such as James D. Dana (1813–1895) who defended it against Murray's attacks.[130]

Darwin suggested that atolls were derived from the fringing or barrier reef of an oceanic island. During the course of time the volcanic peak of the original island subsided but this happened so slowly that the reef was able to keep pace with it by growing upwards so that ultimately the central peak entirely disappeared but the encircling reef remained in the form of an atoll. The difficulty was to explain why this subsidence should have taken place. Today it is possible to envisage a mechanism by which this could happen but all Darwin could do was to point to South America where he had found evidence that the land had been progressively elevated above sea level; if it could rise in one place why should it not sink in another?[131] The failure to explain subsidence was the main criticism which Murray and other opponents of Darwin's theory now levelled at it. They also made something of the fact that the *Beagle*'s short stay at the Cocos-Keeling Islands had been his only first hand experience of a atoll. Alexander Agassiz wrote

5 days on a reef at utmost and then nothing but examination of charts!! to build up a theory, absurd.[132]

Murray argued that it was much more likely that a reef occurred where the accumulation of marine sediment on a bank or shoal of volcanic origin had raised it sufficiently close to the surface for coral, which has a limited depth range, to grow upon it.[133] When the reef emerged at the surface it would grow outwards because it could no longer grow upwards. The next stage would be the formation of the shallow central lagoon which would be assisted by the accumulation of sediment killing off the coral and the solvent action of the carbonic acid in sea water.

Seven years after Murray had published his theory the Duke of Argyll accused scientists of a "conspiracy of silence" against it.[134] His opinion was that, unconsciously, scientists tended to adopt an attitude of veneration towards all the ideas put forward by one of their number whom they particularly respected. Darwin's unquestioned greatness had led them to attach weight to all his pronouncements, perhaps uncritically so, hence their unwillingness to accept Murray's theory. There was probably an element of justification in this view but it was not true that Murray's ideas had been in any sense hushed up after the initial delay or that the case in its favour was nearly as clear cut as Argyll supposed. Outraged scientists hastened to defend their integrity and to accuse him of crediting objective scientific opinion with the subjective emotionalism of politics, than which of course nothing could be further removed.[135] Whether or not the Duke achieved his avowed intention of hotting up the debate,[136] it is certain that the next ten years saw a massive amount of research and argument, both in Europe and America.

Because of the impossibility of a scientific cruise Murray was totally reliant on other people for the field-work with which to maintain his position. The survey ships played an important role here, collecting specimens of coral not only from atolls and subsurface reefs but also from the raised reefs to be found in the geological strata of some of the Pacific and Indian Ocean Islands. P. W. Bassett-Smith (1861–1927), surgeon in H.M.S. *Rambler* and then in H.M.S. *Penguin*, studied the zoology of the Macclesfield Bank, a submerged reef in the South China Sea in 1888 and 1892.[137] He completed his work the following year in H.M.S. *Egeria* to which he had been specially transferred for the purpose. Murray's ally among the younger scientists was Henry Brougham Guppy (1854–1926) who, as surgeon in H.M.S. *Lark*, had made a study of the geology and natural history of the Solomon Islands.[138]

The search for evidence by the survey ships had an unlooked for sequel. The samples sent home by H.M.S. *Flying Fish* from Christmas Island in the Indian Ocean turned out to be rich in phosphate. Murray sent Guppy, ostensibly to look at coral reefs, but in fact to investigate this potentially valuable find.[139] People in the area realized that something was afoot and

Guppy was hijacked to the Keeling Islands—where he spent his enforced stay studying the reef and wrote home that he regarded himself as being "very fortunate in being able to examine the only atoll visited by Mr. Darwin—the atoll, in fact, which gave rise to the theory of subsidence."[140] Ultimately Murray was able to persuade the government to annex Christmas Island and obtained a concession to work the deposits.[139]

Of all the people involved in the coral reef controversy by far the most energetic was Alexander Agassiz. His wealth as chairman of a copper mine in Michigan enabled him to travel widely in search of new evidence and within a few years he visited Florida, Hawaii, Bermuda and the West Indies. In 1896 he went to Australia to work on the Great Barrier Reef, where he was largely frustrated by bad weather, and in 1897 had borings made at Fiji.[141] He made several extensive cruises, one through the Pacific in the *Albatross* in 1899–1900, and another to the Maldives in 1901–1902.

Agassiz's work on balance turned him against the Darwinian theory. He wrote

Huxley has always hankered after a Miocene continent in the Pacific and Darwin who has always objected to that kind of juggling with continents could not resist when it came to coral reefs to do just the same thing.[142]

He described his work at Fiji as "the last nail in the coffin of subsidence".[143] He was not, however, emotionally involved, as Murray undoubtedly was, in proving one theory and disproving another. He wanted to look at the facts objectively and then decide, but the trouble was that the facts were always capable of more than one interpretation. In 1896 the Royal Society sent an expedition to Funafuti in order to try and decide the issue by boring right through a reef to see whether the coral extended to any depth or whether it was underlain by marine sediment as Murray predicted. Their work, followed up by two expeditions from Australia in the subsequent years, was claimed by both sides as a vindication of their cause.[144] Agassiz concluded that no one explanation could account for the formation of reefs though he did not think that subsidence had been responsible for any he had seen.[145]

Darwin's theory found plenty of champions and they were not slow to point out weaknesses in Murray's explanation. Their most cogent argument against it was that in one place he was talking about sedimentation taking place, with the skeletons of marine animals building up the basis of a reef, but later on invoked the solvent action of sea water on coral, both being limestone.[146] Much of the work done at the Scottish Marine Station during this period by the chemist W. S. Anderson and Murray's friend Robert Irvine was on the comparative solubility of different types of limestone and other related topics.[147]

Geologists were currently becoming interested too in the shape of the sea bed and how it had been formed. The *Challenger* work on sediments had given a satisfactory outline of which only the details had to be filled in but it was only as the number of soundings began to accumulate that it became clear that the sea bed itself, which till then had been seen as rather featureless, possessed a number of distinctive characteristics. Early cable surveys had encountered the sudden drop from depths of about 100 fathoms to the deep sea floor off the western seaboard of Europe and it gradually appeared that this was an almost universal phenomenon. It was H. R. Mill who coined the term "continental shelf" for the relatively shallow area above the drop[148] and continental slope followed for the fall itself.

As the detail of submarine contours improved it turned out that the slope was not a regular formation but that it was cut in many places by deep canyons which often began far back on the shelf and debouched on the sea bed below. Buchanan and Thomson in the *Buccaneer* discovered the enormous canyon at the mouth of the River Congo.[149] Edward Hull (1829–1917) studied less impressive but still sizeable features of the same kind on the European shelf. He suggested that they were ancient river valleys and had been formed by subaerial erosion.[150] This required that the surface of the Atlantic had at some stage to be 10,000 feet lower than it is today, an idea that people found hard to accept.[151] John Milne (1850–1913), who had made a study of earthquakes in Japan over a number of years, drew attention to the probability that faulting and landslips occurred on the continental slope. Even at this early date he was able to point to the evidence of breaks in submarine telegraph cables due to earthquakes and the vast slumping of sediment.[152]

On the deep-sea bed itself soundings revealed an increasing number of isolated volcanic peaks, rising abruptly from considerable depths to quite near the surface and, where conditions allowed, with coral growing on them. Murray regarded this as a vindication of his theory of reefs.[153] Soundings also showed that the very deep areas of the Pacific stumbled upon by the *Challenger* and the *Tuscarora* were remarkable in other ways than depth alone. It appeared that these great depths were confined to long, narrow gashes in the sea bed which were given the name of trenches. In the course of time others were discovered, mostly in the Pacific. In 1895 Commander A. F. Balfour in H.M.S. *Penguin* made three soundings of over 5,000 fathoms in what is now known as the Kermadec trench.[154] The characteristic form and positioning of the oceanic trenches, near island arcs, soon made them objects of some interest to geologists.[155]

The submarine topography which was being slowly revealed was very different both in form and composition from anything known on land and questions often asked in the 1880s and 1890s were how were the ocean basins formed and had they always been in the same place? Had land and sea ever changed places? G. H. Darwin thought that the moon had once been part of the earth and it was suggested that perhaps the oceans were the gaps left when what was left of the earth's crust fragmented and formed the continents.[156] The *Challenger* biological work had led Wyville Thomson to form the opinion that the oceans must have been in their present position for a very long time[157] and Murray's geological work led him to make the argument still more strongly. He wrote

In the abysmal areas, we find here and there small volcanic islands rising as great cones from the bottom of the sea, sometimes capped with coral, and forming atolls; but we do not find in these areas any traces of continental rocks. Indeed, it is extremely unlikely that any continental land ever existed in these abysmal areas during past ages, and the deposits now forming in these regions, far from our present continental lands, have, so far as we know, no analogues in the geological series of rocks.[158]

Not everyone was willing to accept this argument. Murray himself had shown how slowly the deep-sea clays were deposited. Was it not therefore probable that any that were uplifted would soon have been eroded without trace?[159] The question of the permanence of ocean basins, as well as the coral reef controversy, involved a large number of people during the later years of the nineteenth century.[160]

Work on the *Challenger Report* finally came to an end in 1895 with the publication of two volumes which summarized the work and results of the voyage. When the second term of the Treasury grant expired in 1887 Murray had been granted a further two year extension but was warned that this was the last he could expect. When the time came and the report was still not finished the Treasury remained adamant in refusing renewed aid. They did, however, agree that if Murray continued to produce the report at his own expense they would set aside £1,600 to complete its publication, to be paid when the final volume appeared.[161] On this basis the work continued, surmounting such minor setbacks as the shipwreck of part of the thirty-first zoological volume while on its way to London from the printers. The Stationery Office reported, hopefully, that

It is not impossible that in the eyes of future owners the imperfections of the recovered volumes may be compensated for by the knowledge that the books, like the "Alcyonaria" and "Polyzoa", which are beautifully figured in them, have been drawn from the bottom of the sea.[162]

Throughout this time Edinburgh had retained her dominant position at the head of the oceanographic community. Herdman wrote

for about twenty years Edinburgh was the centre of oceanographic research and the Mecca towards which marine biologists from all over the world turned to inspect the novelties of the wonderful collections and to discuss results.[163]

Her scientific societies flourished, particularly the Royal Society, the Scottish Meteorological Society and the Scottish Geographical Society, all of which published the work of Murray and his colleagues. H. R. Mill spoke of an "intellectual revival".[164] Murray continued Wyville Thomson's tradition of hospitality and entertained many guests from overseas. Abroad there was beginning to be a shift of emphasis away from biology towards the physics of the ocean and his visitors included as well as zoologists like Haeckel and Johan Hjort (1869–1948), people interested also in marine physics like Fridtjof Nansen (1861–1930), Otto Pettersson (1848–1941) and M. J. O. Thoulet (1843–1936).[165]

The aura of prestige which surrounded the *Challenger* work occasionally had comic implications. Mill recalled the visits of Thoulet who, he said,

seemed a rather pathetic figure, looking up hungrily at Murray for guidance in any matter of difficulty.[166]

Mill continued

I remember once when he asked how the water in the great depths of the tropical ocean could be so cold, Murray jestingly said that perhaps it had not had time to warm up since the Great Ice Age. With his characteristic imperviousness to humour, Thoulet solemnly recorded in his book that the deep water of the Pacific still retained the temperature it had acquired in the glacial period.

When the *Challenger Report* had been completed, and the event duly celebrated,[167] the question remained, what to do next? Lack of money was the decisive factor. Without it, it was impossible either to plan new work or to attract new people. A gradual running down of work in Edinburgh and a consequent loss of importance were inevitable. Mill had already left in 1888. He had decided to marry and wrote

As it was impossible to make any sort of a living out of marine research, I turned perforce to the side of education, though the art of teaching was alien to me and the rising generation did not interest me much.[168]

Education did not detain him long and he subsequently became Librarian of the Royal Geographical Society and director of the British Rainfall Association. Murray eventually became quite wealthy through the Christmas Island phosphates. So too did the British government who, by 1914, had made more in taxes than the entire cost of the *Challenger* expedition and its report.[169] This did not however affect the general attitude towards fresh expenditure and Murray had to look for projects consonant with his limitations. In 1898 he applied for the post of director of the Natural History Museum but Ray Lankester was given the appointment.

In 1893–1894 Mill and Edward Heawood had undertaken a bathymetric survey of the English Lakes with a grant from the Royal Geographical Society, bodies such as the Ordnance Survey having declined the task,[170] and shortly afterwards Murray began a similar study of the Scottish lochs.[171] His partner in this project, Frederick Pullar, was drowned in a skating accident in 1901 but his family, who were financing the survey, continued their support.

As early as 1885 Murray had been advocating the renewal of Antarctic exploration.[172] He reasoned rightly that such ventures would have sufficient imaginative appeal to make it possible to obtain support and funds. At the same time he was anxious that any expedition should have a proper scientific programme, in which marine science would have a large share, and not degenerate into a dash for the pole.[173]

J. Y. Buchanan was contemptuous of this expedient. In a lecture at Cambridge he said

for purely marine investigation there are fields nearer home as yet barely scratched, but ready to yield rich harvests for the mere reaping. The warm and pleasant waters of tropical oceans are still almost untouched and teem with objects of interest and in their exploration and investigation there are no difficulties to be overcome, discomforts to be endured or dangers to be faced.[174]

The only difficulty was in getting anyone to back such a voyage so in one way Murray was being realistic, since by making use of a prevailing mood he got some work done instead of none at all.

Murray was involved in the preparations for two Antarctic expeditions, the *Balaena* expedition of 1892–1893 and the Scottish National Antarctic Expedition of 1902–1904. Both of these, particularly the second, made a considerable contribution to oceanographic work.[175] This was not so much the case on the voyages of Scott and Shackleton, though Mill sailed as far as Madeira on the *Discovery* in 1901 to demonstrate the techniques of observation.[176] Many countries sent expeditions south at about this time and most of them contrived to combine discovery and marine science very successfully, notably the *Belgica* expedition with physical studies made by Arctowski, the *Gauss* from Germany, Nordenskjold in the *Antarctic* and Charcot and Rouch in the *Français* and *Pourquoi Pas?* The most outstanding of all polar voyages in this respect was unquestionably Nansen's attempt to drift to the North Pole in the *Fram*. He and his companions made measurements through holes in the ice which showed that the Arctic was a deep ocean basin and not the shallow sea which everyone expected.[177]

These comparisons highlight the changes which people recognized were taking place at the end of the nineteenth century. The initiative in marine science was passing from Great Britain to the other countries of northern Europe. After the *Valdivia* expedition of 1898 someone commented

German physicists, substantially assisted by their Government, are now taking the lead in oceanographical research.[178]

In fact the new headquarters of marine science was Scandinavia, and in particular Sweden. In 1890 Gustaf Ekman and Otto Pettersson began making systematic observations in the Skaggerack and Kattegat.[179] In 1892 following a meeting of Scandinavian scientists they proposed that joint observations should be made at three monthly intervals in the North Atlantic.[180] Sweden and Denmark began the work and were joined by the United Kingdom, Germany and Norway. The British contribution was made by the Scottish Fisheries Board who sent Henry N. Dickson (1866–1922) in H.M.S. *Jackal*.[181] Apparently their part of the enterprise was not wholly successful, bad weather and the failure of the government to make any additional grant for the work being variously held responsible.[182]

Pettersson developed his own theory of ocean circulation in which he held that water from melting ice in polar regions provided the motive force.[183] His colleague at Stockholm, Vilhelm Bjerknes (1862–1951), produced a mathematical theory of circulation which was applied to the ocean by J. W. Sandström, Bjorn Helland-Hansen and Vagn Walfrid Ekman (1874–1954).[184]

In 1897 G. Ekman and Pettersson suggested to the Swedish government that a conference should be held to plan further joint work at sea. Up to this time there had been no international organization representing oceanographers. The term "oceanography" was coming into general usage[185] but the scientists had been content to make contact on a personal basis and to discuss their work at meetings of one or other of the sections or an *ad hoc* sub-section at the British Association annual meetings or at the International Geographical Congresses.[186] The conference now called in 1899 led to the setting up of the International Council for the Exploration of the Sea in 1902.[187] This involved countries at government level and meant that some support for marine science was ensured in member nations. These were Sweden, Norway, Denmark, Finland, Russia, Germany, the United Kingdom and the Netherlands. Belgium joined later.

The new organization ran a laboratory directed by Nansen in Christiania.[188] Here V. W. Ekman did his work on the explanation of the phenomenon of dead water, suggested after the *Fram* had enountered it in the Arctic,[189] and on the increasing deflection of movements in successively deeper layers of fluids, as a result of the effect of the earth's rotation, which came to be known as Ekman spirals.[190] Here too, standard sea water was prepared for use in the chlorine titration method of measuring salinity which became the standard practice.[191] In 1908 the laboratory was closed and its work on sea water was moved to the Council's central bureau in Copenhagen where Martin Knudsen (1871–1949), who had been responsible for the introduction of the chlorine titration method, was hydrographic assistant.[192] Another centre for marine science in Norway was the Bergen Museum which from 1903 to 1914 ran international courses taught by, amongst others, Hjort, Helland-Hansen and H. H. Gran.[193] In Germany the Institut für Meereskunde was set up at Berlin in 1900 and two important cruises were sent out on the *Planet* and the *Deutschland* during the early years of the century.[70]

Elsewhere things were a little different. France, after a promising beginning, had not participated in the development of the marine sciences. In 1895 Thoulet castigated this failure which was leaving other countries to achieve

les travaux, les découvertes—et en même temps—les profits et la gloire.[194]

In 1903 Prince Albert established public lectures in Paris to try and overcome this indifference. Thoulet was the first lecturer. A few years later (1906) Prince Albert founded the Institut Océanographique there.[195]

The situation in Great Britain remained unchanged. Participation in the work of the International Council continued, not without some persuasiveness on the part of British scientists, through the Scottish Fisheries Board and a subsidiary branch of the Plymouth laboratory set up at Lowestoft (1902) for the purpose.[196] Of the other laboratories mentioned, all continued work save the Scottish Marine Station which closed during the early years of the twentieth century. Its place was taken after a short interval by the Scottish Oceanographical Laboratory, set up in 1906 by W. S. Bruce, leader of the Scottish National Antarctic Expedition.[197] This too had only a limited life and was closed in 1920 because of lack of funds, in spite of Bruce's efforts to place it on a permanent footing.

Bruce's expedition was the last from this country to contribute to deep sea work for some considerable time. During the late 1880s and the 1890s G. Herbert Fowler (1861–1940) and other naturalists were given the opportunity to make trips in home waters in H.M.S. *Research*. Fowler was investigating the existence of the mid-water fauna which had been denied by Agassiz.[198] Further projects were however refused by the Admiralty.[199] Possibly Wharton's retirement in 1904 may have had something to do with the change.

Few people were active on the physical side of oceanography. H. N. Dickson, now a geography lecturer at Oxford, made several cruises on a privately owned yacht.[200] At Aberdeen, Wemyss Fulton used drift bottles for current measurements in the North Sea.[201]

Various measures were proposed to try and reverse the trend and to bring about renewed expansion in marine science. W. L. Calderwood, head of the Plymouth Laboratory, suggested that research would do better if it were split off from fisheries investigations.[202] John Murray recommended to the West of Scotland M.B.A. that it should expand its work to include physical studies.[203]

In 1903 the Challenger Society was set up for the "promotion of oceanic zoology and botany".[204] However, when the constitution was discussed its function was changed to the promotion of oceanography, which it has remained ever since. The Challenger Society had, and has, no president because the rivalry between Ray Lankester and Sir John Murray, as he now was, was such that neither could be elected without fear of mortally offending the other.[205]

One of the projects undertaken by the Society was the compilation of a catalogue of publications on marine zoology from 1846 to 1900. This was undertaken by Lancelot Borradaile (1872–1945) with funds made available by Murray.[206] Another was the preparation of a handbook for making observations at sea to be used by yachtsmen, anglers, etc., in the best do-it-yourself tradition of oceanography.[207] One idea, not taken up, was that the Society should publish an international journal of oceanography.[208]

The Sixth International Geographical Congress had set up a committee to rationalize the nomenclature to be applied to forms of sub-oceanic relief. The committee met at Wiesbaden in 1903. Part of its work was to arrange for the preparation of a chart of ocean depths on which the soundings made by ships of different nations would be collated.[209] Prince Albert undertook this work and the *Carte générale bathymetrique des océans* was drawn up at Monaco. Some controversy was aroused by the decision to abandon the personal names given by the *Challenger* and other voyages to features of deep sea topography they had located. Alexander Agassiz wrote

I will never adopt in anything I may publish names which are substituted by the German Committee for the names given to features by pioneers of anglo-saxon race.[210]

At the Ninth Geographical Congress in 1908 Otto Pettersson and Gerhard Schott (1866–1961) called for the shallow seas work of the International Council to be extended to the Atlantic Ocean.[211] Murray wished to participate in this work and achieved his aim by persuading the Norwegian government to lend him their fisheries research vessel, *Michael Sars*, on the understanding that he should pay the expenses of the voyage. He and Johan Hjort made a four month cruise in the Atlantic early in 1910.[212] Had he been able there is no doubt that Murray would have extended his activities much further. In 1913 he wrote to Herdman

Could I afford it at present, I would be off to the Pacific in a Diesel-engined ship!![213]

The sinking of the *Titanic* in 1912 at last galvanized the government into supporting research at sea and in 1913 a voyage was sent out as the first British contribution to the Atlantic Ice Patrol.[214] D. J. Matthews (1873–1956) sailed as oceanographer, L. Crawshay was the biologist, and Sir Geoffrey Taylor the meteorologist. The ship employed was the *Scotia* on which Bruce had sailed to the Antarctic in 1902. The captain had been infuriated by the ineffectual attempts then made to launch kites for making meteorological observations and Taylor had to employ a harmless subterfuge to get his equipment aboard.[215]

The year 1914 was catastrophic for the oceanographic community, as for the world at large. John Murray was proposing to return to Millport, where a permanent station had been opened in 1897,[216] in order to write up the zoological part of his work on the Clyde sea area[217] but in March 1914 he was killed in a motor car accident. W. S. Bruce proposed that his collections should be amalgamated with the Scottish Oceanographical Laboratory to form a Scottish Oceanographical Institute but war intervened.[218]

In 1914 the international community of oceanographers, which Murray had done so much to build up, was disrupted by the outbreak of the First World War. Only Buchanan was now left of the *Challenger* scientists. Appalled by the disaster, which he foresaw but could do nothing to avert, he left Europe for America. He died in 1925, a disillusioned man.

The war did little to change the prospects for marine science in Britain. The foundation of the chair of oceanography and the Tidal Observatory at Liverpool in 1919–20, the work of the Discovery Committee in the 1920s and 1930s and the revival of Millport by the Development Commission were isolated incidents; it was not until after the Second World War that it began to attract government support on a large scale. Meanwhile the pattern of communication between the scientists of different nations had twice been disrupted and had twice re-formed, a tribute to the strength of the ties among those who had established it, and to their successors, in whom man's love of rational enquiry and involvement with the world triumphed over the senselessness and depravity of war.

During the last fifty years oceanography has grown in a manner surpassing the wildest dreams of Bruce and Murray. Yet though the inter-war period saw some important developments, such as the introduction of echo sounding in the 1920s, and notable events, including the German *Meteor* expedition, the founding of the Woods Hole Oceanographic Institution in the United States and the work of the U.K. Discovery Committee, it was during and after the Second World War that the great expansion, which is still going on, began. The realization by governments of the importance of marine problems and their readiness to make money available for research, the growth in the number of scientists at work and the increasing sophistication of scientific equipment, have made it feasible to study the ocean on a scale and to a degree of complexity never attempted and never possible before.

Areas of research, which if not always wholly new, received limited attention before, such as marine geophysics, underwater acoustics and marine optics, have come to rank equally with the older established branches of marine science and these too have undergone revolutionary changes as new techniques of measurement reveal small but significant variations in the movements of the ocean which had hitherto gone unnoticed. As in previous ages marine scientists are taking what the world of science has to offer in the way of innovations and adapting them to their own requirements. Satellite navigation has been brought in to track deep ocean currents, computers to analyse masses of data on waves and tides and advances in biochemistry and biophysics to aid the study of life in the sea.

From being a poor relation of the sciences, oceanography has risen in a mere generation to a position among the foremost. As man increasingly overcrowds and exploits his tiny planet, the significance of the oceans which cover seven tenths of its surface have suddenly become apparent. Their importance as a future source of food and minerals, and perhaps even more so as the great regulator of the world's environment which must be kept free from pollution, ensure that in the foreseeable future this trend is unlikely to be reversed.

16. NOTES

1. C. Wyville Thomson, "Progress of the *Challenger Report*", *Nature* (12 September 1878). Vol. **18**, pp. 534–535.
2. C. Wyville Thomson, "General introduction to the zoological series of reports" in *Report on the Scientific Results of the Voyage of H.M.S. Challenger during the years 1873–76: Zoology* H.M.S.O., London, (1880). Vol. **1**, pp. 1–50; especially pp. 26–28.
3. Harold L. Burstyn, "Science and government in the nineteenth century: the *Challenger* expedition and its report", *Bull. Inst. océanogr. Monaco* (1968). Numéro spécial 2. Vol. **2**, pp. 603–611.
4. G. R. Agassiz, *Letters and Recollections of Alexander Agassiz with a Sketch of his Life and Work*, London, Boston and New York (1913), p. 98.
5. Letters from Alexander Agassiz to Sir Charles Wyville Thomson. MSS in the University Library, Edinburgh: 28 May 1877. Agassiz wrote "as far back as 1869 when Porcupine had just returned we had agreed upon the wisdom of letting the same people work up all the deep sea things from both sides of the Atlantic, as far as practicable."
6. *The American Journal of Science and Arts* (February 1877), 3rd series. Vol. **13**, pp. 165–166.
7. *Ann. Mag. nat. Hist.* (March 1877), 4th series. Vol. **19**, p. 276.
8. The letter was printed in *Nature* (14 June 1877). Vol. **16**, p. 118.

9. Thomson's reply was printed in *Nature* (14 June 1877). Vol. **16**, pp. 118–119.

10. P. Martin Duncan in *Ann. Mag. nat. Hist.* (May 1877), 4th series. Vol. **19**, pp. 429–430.

11. "The *Challenger* collections", *Nature* (14 June 1877). Vol. **16**, pp. 117–119.

12. *Ann. Mag. nat. Hist.* (June 1877). 4th series. Vol. **19**, pp. 508–509.

13. Letters from Alexander Agassiz to John Murray, 21 May 1877. MSS in the University Library, Edinburgh.

14. *The American Journal of Science and Arts* (August 1877), 3rd series. Vol. **14**, pp. 161–162. Agassiz had suggested to Thomson that he should write such a justification in his letter of 28 May 1877. *See* (5) above.

15. P. Martin Duncan, "On the *Salenidae*, Wright", *Ann. Mag. nat. Hist.* (1877) 4th series. Vol. **20**, pp. 70–73, 245–257.
    F. Jeffrey Bell, "Observations on the characters of the Echinoidea", *Proceedings of the Scientific Meetings of the Zoological Society of London* (1879). Vol. **47**, pp. 249–255, 655–662.

16. Alexander Agassiz to Wyville Thomson, 29 December 1879.

17. For example, zoologists like Wyville Thomson, Moseley, McIntosh and Herdman, and geologists such as Hull, Renard and Croll. For some people this does not seem to have been possible—notably the chemists. They had to make a further move. Buchanan, Dickson and Mill changed to geography. Apart from the staff of the marine stations (almost always marine biologists) it was difficult for anyone to become a marine scientist first and foremost. Even Murray and Bruce found the role hard to sustain.

18. William Abbott Herdman, *Founders of Oceanography and their Work*, Edward Arnold (Publishers) Ltd, London (1923), pp. 37–68. Quotations by kind permission of the publishers.
    William Abbott Herdman, "Report on the Tunicata collected during the voyage of H.M.S. *Challenger* during the years 1873–76" in *Report on the Scientific Results of the Voyage of H.M.S. Challenger: Zoology*. Vol. **6**, part 2 (1882). Vol. **14**, part 1 (1886). Vol. **27**, part 4 (1888).

19. Daniel and Mary Merriman, "Sir C. Wyville Thomson's letters to Staff-Commander Thomas H. Tizard, 1877–1881", *J. Mar. Res.* (1958). Vol. **17**, pp. 347–374; pp. 361–362.

20. Hugh Robert Mill, *An Autobiography* (ed. L. Dudley Stamp) London, New York and Toronto (1951), p. 50. Quotations included by kind permission of Geographical Publications Ltd.

21. J. Y. Buchanan, "On the occurrence of sulphur in marine muds and nodules, and its bearing on their mode of formation", *Proc. R. Soc. Edinb.* (1890–1891). Vol. **18**, pp. 17–39; reprinted in *Accounts Rendered of Work Done and Things Seen*, Cambridge (1919), pp. 133–157.

22. Alexander Agassiz to Wyville Thomson, 11 February 1880.

23. C. Wyville Thomson, "Progress of the *Challenger Report*", *Nature* (12 September 1878). Vol. **18**, pp. 534–535.

24. Harold L. Burstyn, *op. cit.* p. 609.

25. Daniel and Mary Merriman, *op. cit.* pp. 360–361.

26. *Report on the Scientific Results of the Voyage of H.M.S. Challenger during the years 1873–76; Zoology* (ed. C. Wyville Thomson). H.M.S.O., London. (1880). Vol. **1**.

27. Thomas H. Huxley, "The first volume of the publications of the *Challenger*", *Nature* (4 November 1880). Vol. **23**, pp. 1–3.

28. *Challenger Report, op. cit.* p. 50.

29. Charles Darwin, "Sir Wyville Thomson and natural selection", *Nature* (11 November 1880). Vol. **23**, p. 32, and Wyville Thomson's reply in *Nature* (18 November 1880), p. 53.

30. P. H. Carpenter kept the cutting from which this quotation was taken in a diary of the voyage of H.M.S. *Valorous* to Greenland in 1875, on which he sailed as naturalist. His son G. J. A. Carpenter found it there and sent it to Sir Alister Hardy as an example of the reaction of the press to the *Challenger* voyage. In fact this very well informed piece of deflation is not typical of the attitude of newspapers such as *The Times* which saw the *Challenger* and the preceding voyages as a notable British achievement:
Daniel Merriman, "A posse ad esse", *J. Mar. Res.* (1948). Vol. **7**, pp. 139–146.

31. T. H. Huxley, *op. cit.* p. 1.

32. Alexander Agassiz to John Murray, 20 September 1895.

33. See obituary, "Sir Charles Wyville Thomson" in *Nature* (16 March 1882). Vol. **25**, pp. 467–468.
For additional biographical material see *Founders of Oceanography, loc. cit.;* a profile of Wyville Thomson in *Nature* (1 June 1876). Vol. **14**, pp. 85–87, and the obituary and bibliography in *Report on the Scientific Results of the Voyage of H.M.S. Challenger: Zoology* (1882). Vol. **4**, pp. i–ix.
W. B. Carpenter did not long survive his colleague. He was in Boston in 1882, lecturing on the deep sea, and Agassiz told Murray "he seems to me much aged and has evidently not kept up to the mark" (Agassiz to Murray, 8 November 1882). He died in November 1885 after an accident at his home: *Nature* (12 November 1885). Vol. **33**, p. 39. See obituary: "Dr. Carpenter, C.B., F.R.S." by E. Ray Lankester, *Nature* (26 November 1885), pp. 83–85.

34. Harold L. Burstyn, *op. cit.* p. 610.

35. Alexander Agassiz to John Murray, 10 March 1882.

36. Hugh Robert Mill, *op. cit.* pp. 43–44.

37. W. Boog Watson, "A missing professor", *University of Edinburgh Journal* (1969). Vol. **24**, No. 1, pp. 55–58. I am grateful to Sir Maurice Yonge for drawing my attention to this article.

38. Hugh Robert Mill, *op. cit.* p. 58.

39. R. N. Rudmose Brown, *A Naturalist at the Poles. The Life, Work and Voyages of Dr. W. S. Bruce the Polar Explorer*, London (1923), p. 256. This was in 1914; *see* p. 393.

40. Daniel and Mary Merriman, "Sir C. Wyville Thomson's letters to Staff-Commander Tizard", *op. cit.* pp. 364–365.

41. C. Wyville Thomson, "The cruise of the *Knight Errant*", *Nature* (2 September 1880). Vol. **22**, pp. 405–407.

42. Thomas H. Tizard and John Murray, "Exploration of the Faroe Channel, during the summer of 1880, in H.M.'s hired ship *Knight Errant*", *Proc. R. Soc. Edinb.* (1880–1882). Vol. **11**, pp. 638–720.

43. Thomas H. Tizard, "Remarks on the soundings and temperatures obtained in the Faroe Channel during the summer of 1882", *Proc. Roy. Soc.* (1883). Vol. **35**, pp. 202–226.

44. *Ibid.* p. 205.
Nature (6 July 1882). Vol. **26**, p. 230.

45. Alexander Agassiz to Wyville Thomson, 8 December 1880.

46. William Dittmar, "Report on researches into the composition of ocean-water collected by H.M.S. *Challenger* during the years 1873–76" in *Report on the Scientific Results of the Voyage of H.M.S. Challenger: Physics and Chemistry* (ed. John Murray) H.M.S.O., London, (1884). Vol. **1**, part 1, 251 pp.

47. Hugh Robert Mill, "The composition of ocean water", *Nature* (24 July 1884). Vol. **30**, pp. 292–294.
Hugh Robert Mill, "The saltness and the temperature of the sea", *Nature* (31 July 1884). Vol. **30**, pp. 313–314.

48. John Young Buchanan, "Laboratory experiences on board the *Challenger*", *J. chem. Soc. (Transactions)* (1878). Vol. **33**, pp. 445–469; *Scientific Papers* (1913). Vol. **1**.

49. Hercules Tornøe, *Chemistry*,
Den Norske Nordhavs-Expedition 1876–1878, Christiania (1880), 76 pp.
See also: J. Y. Buchanan, "The chemistry of the Atlantic", *Nature* (23 February 1882). Vol. **25**, pp. 386–389 and (2 March 1882), pp. 411–413.

50. W. Dittmar, "On the composition of ocean water", *Proceedings of the Philosophical Society of Glasgow* (1884–1885). Vol. **16**, pp. 47–73.

51. W. A. Herdman, *Founders of Oceanography, op. cit.* pp. 85–86.

52. John Murray and A. F. Renard, "On the nomenclature, origin, and distribution of deep-sea deposits", *Proc. Roy. Soc. Edinb.* (1882–1884). Vol. **12**, pp. 495–529; p. 521.

53. John Murray and A. F. Renard, *Report on Deep-Sea Deposits based on the specimens collected during the voyage of H.M.S. Challenger in the years 1872 to 1876* in *Report on the Scientific Results of the Voyage of H.M.S. Challenger during the years 1873–76*, H.M.S.O., London, (1891), p. 190.

54. *Ibid.* p. xxviii.

55. Alexander Agassiz to John Murray, 3 March 1902.

56. *Ibid.* 4 June 1886.

57. J. Rouch, *Les Découvertes Océanographiques Modernes*, Paris (1959), p. 89.

58. "Report on the deep-sea temperature observations obtained by the officers of H.M.S. *Challenger*, during the years 1873–1876", in *Report on the Scientific Results of the Voyage of H.M.S. Challenger during the years 1873–76: Physics and Chemistry* (1884). Vol. **1**, part 3, 2 pp.+258 plates and 7 tables.

59. As Murray pointed out in answering Jordan's points (*see* Ref. 60) there would be the inevitable errors caused by indexes slipping or by misreading.

60. William Leighton Jordan, *The Challenger Explorations*, 15 pp., London (1888).
The Admiralty Falsification of the Challenger Record: Correspondence, 35 pp., London (1890). This information was kindly supplied by Dr H. Stommel and Mrs J. C. Swallow.

61. Alexander Buchan, "Report on atmospheric circulation based on the observations made on board H.M.S. *Challenger* during the years 1873–1876, and other meteorological observations", *Report on the Scientific Results of the Voyage of H.M.S. Challenger: Physics and Chemistry*, London, H.M.S.O. (1889). Vol. **2**, part 2, 78 pp. +263 pp. tables.

62. It remained so up to the time of the First World War. Information from Sir Geoffrey Taylor.

63. Alexander Buchan, "Report on oceanic circulation, based on the observations made on board H.M.S. *Challenger*, and other observations" in *Report on the Scientific Results of the Voyage of H.M.S. Challenger during the years 1872– 76: Summary of the Scientific Results*, H.M.S.O., London, (1895). Vol. **2**, appendix (*Physics and Chemistry*, part 8), 38 pp.+16 maps.

64. Georg Wüst, "History of investigations of the longitudinal deep-sea circulation (1800–1922)", *Bull. Inst. océanogr. Monaco* (1968). Numéro spécial 2. Vol. **1**, pp. 109–120.

65. Memorial presented to the Norwegian Government by Professors H. Mohn and G. O. Sars in March 1874. Printed in: C. Wille, "Historical account", *Den Norske Nordhavs-Expedition 1876–1878*, Christiania (1882), pp. 1–9.

66. *Jahresbericht der Commission zur wissenschaftlichen Untersuchung der deutschen Meere in Kiel für das Jahr 1871*, Berlin (1873). See:
John Gibson, "Report on observations relating to the physics and chemistry of the North Sea during 1888 and 1889, and including a review of the analytical work hitherto undertaken for the Fishery Board for Scotland", *Seventh Annual Report of the Fishery Board for Scotland* (*1888*), Edinburgh, (1889) part 3, pp. 409–472.
Hugh Robert Mill, "Recent physical research in the North Sea", *Scottish Geographical Magazine* (1887). Vol. **3**, pp. 385–398.
John Murray, "Exploration of the North Sea", *Nature* (25 November 1886). Vol. **35**, pp. 73–74.

67. Jacqueline Carpine-Lancre, "Les croisières océanographiques françaises
 * antérieures à 1914"; extended version of a paper given to the 12th International Conference on the History and Philosophy of Science.
Nature (19 April 1883). Vol. **27**, p. 587.
Alphonse Milne-Edwards, "The *Talisman* Expedition", *Nature* (27 December 1883). Vol. **29**, pp. 197–198.
J. Gwyn Jeffreys, "The French deep-sea expedition of 1883", *Nature* (3 January 1884). Vol. **29**, pp. 216–217.

68. K. Natterer, "Oceanographical results of the Austro-Hungarian deep-sea expeditions", *Scottish Geographical Magazine* (1898). Vol. **14**, pp. 636– 642.

69. N. Andrusoff, "Physical exploration of the Black Sea", *Geogr. J.* (1893). Vol. **1**, pp. 49–51.

70. Georg Wüst, "The major deep-sea expeditions and research vessels, 1873– 1960", *Progress in Oceanography* (ed. M. Sears), London and New York (1964). Vol. **2**, pp. 1–52.
John Murray and Johan Hjort, *The Depths of the Ocean: a general account of the modern science of oceanography based largely on the scientific researches of the Norwegian Steamer Michael Sars in the North Atlantic*, London (1912), pp. 11–21.

71. For example, by E. Ray Lankester, "The scientific results of the *Challenger* expedition: Introduction", *Natural Science* (July 1895). Vol. **7**, pp. 7–10.

72. Anton Dohrn, "The foundation of zoological stations", *Nature* (8 February 1872). Vol. **5**, pp. 277–280, describes a plan evolved by Carl Vogt and Henri Milne-Edwards in the 1840s.

73. N. N. Miklukho-Maklai apparently came from a Scottish family. He took a considerable interest in both the physical and biological aspects of marine science: O. I. Mamaev, "N. N. Miklukho-Maklai as an oceanographer",

Izvestiya Vsesoyuznogo Geographicheskogo Obshchestva (1957). Vol. **89**, pp. 255–259.

74. W. A. Herdman, *Founders of Oceanography, op. cit.* pp. 134–144.
    Charles Atwood Kofoid, "The Biological Stations of Europe", *Bulletin of the United States Bureau of Education* (1910). No. 4, whole number 440, pp. 7–32.

75. *Report of the fortieth meeting of the British Association for the Advancement of Science* (*1870*), (1871), p. lxii; part 2, p. 115.

76. "The Fisheries Exhibition", *Nature* (17 May 1883). Vol. **28**, pp. 49–50.

77. "Report of the Foundation Meeting of the Marine Biological Association", *J. Mar. biol. Ass. U.K.* (August 1887). No. 1, pp. 22–39.

78. E. Ray Lankester, "The value of a marine laboratory to the development and regulation of our sea fisheries", *Journal of the Society of Arts* (15 May 1885). Vol. **33**, pp. 749–755.

79. *Nature* (23 July 1885). Vol. **32**, p. 278.

80. Gilbert C. Bourne, "The opening of the marine biological laboratory at Plymouth", *Nature* (28 June 1888). Vol. **38**, pp. 198–201. *See also* (5 July 1888), pp. 236–237.

81. *Nature* (3 May 1888). Vol. **38**, p. 16.

82. "Proposed zoological station at Granton, near Edinburgh", *Nature* (2 August 1883). Vol. **28**, p. 323.

83. James Chumley, *The Fauna of the Clyde Sea Area*, Glasgow (1918), pp. 1–7.

84. "The Edinburgh Biological Station", *Nature* (13 September 1883). Vol. **28**, pp. 467–468.

85. *Nature* (13 March 1884). Vol. **29**, p. 460.

86. "Edinburgh Marine Station", *Nature* (20 March 1884). Vol. **29**, p. 483.
    The Edinburgh Courant (14 April 1884), p. 2.

87. Hugh Robert Mill, "On the periodic variation of temperature in tidal basins", *Proc. R. Soc. Edinb.* (1882–1884). Vol. **12**, pp. 927–932.
    Hugh Robert Mill, "On the salinity of the water in the Firth of Forth", and "On the temperature of the water in the Firth of Forth", *Proc. R. Soc. Edinb.* (1884–1886). Vol. **13**, pp. 29–64 and 157–167.

88. J. T. Cunningham, "The Scottish Marine Station", *Nature* (25 June 1885). Vol. **32**, p. 176.

89. Thomas R. R. Stebbing, *The Naturalist of Cumbrae: a true Story, being the Life of David Robertson*, London (1891).

90. Hugh Robert Mill, "The Clyde Sea Area", *Trans. R. Soc. Edinb.* (1889–1892). Vol. **36**, pp. 641–729, and Vol. **38**, (1894–1896) pp. 1–161.

91. Hugh Robert Mill, *Autobiography*, p. 49.

92. C. A. Kofoid, *op. cit.* pp. 174–184.

93. The Liverpool Marine Biology Committee's work appeared in *Proceedings of the Liverpool Biological Society, Annual Reports* and separate *Memoirs on typical British Marine Plants and Animals* (edited by W. A. Herdman) from 1899.

94. William Abbott Herdman, "The Liverpool Marine Biology Station on Puffin Island", *Nature* (21 July 1887). Vol. **36**, pp. 275–277.

95. Nature (26 May 1892). Vol. **46**, p. 83; (16 June 1892), pp. 155–156: "Opening of the Liverpool Marine Biological Station at Port Erin".

96. Frank R. Lillie, *The Woods Hole Marine Biological Laboratory*, Chicago (1944).

97. A. Hunter Dupree, *Science in the Federal Government: a History of Policies and Activities to 1940*, Cambridge, Mass. (1957), pp. 236–238.
98. *First Annual Report of the Fishery Board for Scotland (1882)*, Edinburgh (1883).
99. *Sixteenth Annual Report of the Fishery Board for Scotland (1897)*, Glasgow (1898). Part 3, p. 12.
100. *Nature* (18 August 1892). Vol. **46**, p. 369. During the first few years of the Board's existence research was carried out at a number of places in Scotland. C. A. Kofoid, *op. cit.* pp. 208–210.
101. H. R. Mill, *Autobiography*, pp. 46–48.
102. Henry Hillyer Giglioli, "Italian deep-sea exploration in the Mediterranean", *Nature* (18 August 1881). Vol. **24**, p. 358; (25 August 1881), pp. 381–382.
103. Charles D. Sigsbee, *Deep-sea Sounding and Dredging*, United States Coast and Geodetic Survey, Washington (1880).
104. John Elliott Pillsbury, *The Gulf Stream. Methods of the investigation and results of the research*, Report of the United States Coast and Geodetic Survey (1890). Appendix no. 10, Washington (1891).
105. Alexander Agassiz, *A contribution to American Thalassography. Three cruises of the U.S.C.G.S. Steamer Blake in the Gulf of Mexico, in the Caribbean Sea, and along the Atlantic Coast of the United States from 1877–1880*, 2 vols, Boston and New York (1888).
106. H. R. Mill, *Autobiography*, p. 44. J. Y. Buchanan later defended the *Challenger*'s use of hemp lines on the grounds that breakages were less: "A retrospect of oceanography in the twenty years before 1895" in *Accounts Rendered*, pp. 28–86 (revised version of his address to the 6th International Geographical Congress, London, 1895).
107. W. A. Herdman, *Founders of Oceanography*, pp. 107–118.
108. Sir Archibald Day, *The Admiralty Hydrographic Service, 1795–1919*, H.M.S.O., London (1967).
109. R. B. Seymour-Sewell, "Oceanographic exploration, 1851–1951", *Sci. Prog., Lond.* (July 1952). Vol. **40**, no. 159, pp. 403–418.
110. John Murray, "On some recent deep-sea observations in the Indian Ocean", *Scottish Geographical Magazine* (1887). Vol. **3**, pp. 553–561.
111. W. J. L. Wharton, "Undercurrents in the Strait of Bab-el-Mandeb", *Nature* (6 October 1898). Vol. **58**, p. 544.
112. S. Makarov, "On some oceanographic problems", *Proc. R. Soc. Edinb.* (1897–1899). Vol. **22**, pp. 391–408.
113. Hugh Robert Mill, *Autobiography*, p. 60.
114. Alexander Agassiz to John Murray, 28 May 1889.
115. John Young Buchanan, "On oceanic shoals discovered in the S.S. *Dacia* in October 1883", *Proc. R. Soc. Edinb.* (1884–1886). Vol. **13**, pp. 428–443. Vol. **13**, pp. 428–443.
116. John Young Buchanan, "The exploration of the Gulf of Guinea", *Scottish Geographical Magazine* (1888). Vol. **4**, pp. 177–200, 233–251.
117. *Ibid.* p. 200. Anthony S. Thomson, "Remarks on ocean currents, and practical hints on the method of their observation", *Report of the Sixth International Geographical Congress* (1895), London (1896), pp. 443–459.
118. John Young Buchanan, "On similarities in the physical geography of the great oceans", *Proc. R. geog. Soc.* (1886). Vol. **8**, pp. 753–769, p. 761.

119. John Young Buchanan, "The Guinea and Equatorial Currents", *Geogr. J.* (1896). Vol. **7**, pp. 267–270.

120. William Abbott Herdman, *Founders of Oceanography*, pp. 119–133. Prince Albert I of Monaco, *La Carrière d'un Navigateur*, reprinted Monaco (1966).

121. Jules Richard, "Les campagnes scientifiques de S.A.S. le Prince Albert 1ᵉʳ de Monaco", *Bull. Inst. océanogr. Monaco* (Fondation Albert 1ᵉʳ, Prince de Monaco), Monaco (February 1910). No. 162, 159 pp. and bibliography.

122. Prince Albert I of Monaco, "Some results of my researches on oceanography", *Nature* (30 June 1898). Vol. **58**, pp. 200–204.
The results of his work were published in the *Résultats des Campagnes Scientifiques accomplies sur son yacht par Albert 1er Prince de Monaco* and the *Bull. Inst. océanogr. Monaco*.

123. John Young Buchanan, "The sperm whale and its food", *Nature* (9 January 1896). Vol. **53**, pp. 223–225.

124. John Young Buchanan, "The Oceanographical Museum at Monaco", *Nature* (3 November 1910). Vol. **85**, pp. 7–11.

125. Alexander Agassiz, *Three Cruises of the U.S.C.G.S. Steamer Blake*, published in the *Bull. Mus. comp. Zool. Harv.* Vols. **14** and **15** (1888). Vol. **14**, p. 202.

126. Alexander Agassiz to John Murray, 22 March 1894.

127. John Murray, "General observations on the distribution of marine organisms" in *Report on the Scientific Results of the Voyage of H.M.S. Challenger during the years 1872–76: A Summary of the Scientific Results obtained at the sounding, dredging, and trawling stations of H.M.S. Challenger* (1895). Vol. **2**, pp. 1431–1462.

128. George Douglas Campbell, 8th Duke of Argyll, "A great lesson", *The Nineteenth Century* (September 1887). Vol. **22**, no. 127, pp. 293–309.
"A conspiracy of silence", *Nature* (17 November 1887). Vol. **37**, pp. 53–54.

129. Charles Darwin, *The Structure and Distribution of Coral Reefs*, 2nd edition, London (1874). First published 1842.

130. James D. Dana, "Origin of coral reefs and islands", *The American Journal of Science and Arts* (1885) 3rd series. Vol. **30**, pp. 89–105 and 169–191.

131. Charles Darwin, *op. cit.* pp. 150–151.

132. Alexander Agassiz to John Murray, 27 January 1890.

133. John Murray, "On the structure and origin of coral islands", *Proc. R. Soc. Edinb.* (1878–1880). Vol. **10**, pp. 505–518.

134. Duke of Argyll, "A great lesson", *The Nineteenth Century*, loc. cit.

135. T. G. Bonney, "A conspiracy of silence", *Nature* (10 November 1887). Vol. **37**, pp. 25–26.
Thomas Henry Huxley, "Science and the bishops", *The Nineteenth Century* (November 1887). Vol. **22**, No. 129, pp. 625–640.

136. See his reply in *Nature* (17 November 1887). Vol. **37**, pp. 53–54.

137. "Survey of the Macclesfield Bank, South China Seas", *Geogr. J.* (1895). Vol. **5**, pp. 73–75.

138. H. B. Guppy, "Observations on the recent calcareous formations of the Solomon Group made during 1882–84", *Trans. R. Soc. Edinb.* (1882–1885). Vol. **32**, pp. 545–581.
H. B. Guppy, "Notes on the characters and mode of formation of the coral

reefs of the Solomon Islands, being the results of observations made in 1882–84 . . . during the surveying cruise of H.M.S. *Lark*", *Proc. Roy. Soc. Edinb.* (1884–1886). Vol. **13,** pp. 857–904.

139. William N. Boog Watson, "Sir John Murray—a chronic student", *University of Edinburgh Journal* (1967–1968). Vol. **23,** pp. 123–138.

140. H. B. Guppy, "Preliminary note on Keeling Atoll, known also as the Cocos Islands", *Nature* (3 January 1889). Vol. **39,** pp. 236–238.

141. G. R. Agassiz, *op. cit.*
Reports of his expeditions appeared in: *Bull. Mus. comp. Zool. Harv.* from Vol. **17** (1889 on).

142. Alexander Agassiz to John Murray, 2 December 1887.

143. *Ibid.* 29 April 1899.

144. W. J. Sollas, "Report to the committee of the Royal Society appointed to investigate the structure of a coral reef by boring", *Proc. R. Soc.* (1896–1897). Vol. **60,** pp. 502–512.
Sollas believed that the results of the expedition gave support to Darwin's hypothesis, if anyone's, but Sydney J. Hickson said that the evidence equally well might be held to support Murray's: "The coral reef at Funafuti", *Nature* (11 March 1897). Vol. **55,** p. 439.
See also Nature (9 December 1897). Vol. **57,** pp. 137–138; (24 March 1898), pp. 494–495.

145. Alexander Agassiz to John Murray, 3 December 1897.

146. For example, T. Mellard Reade, "Coral formations", *Nature* (22 March 1888). Vol. **37,** p. 488.
Charles Darwin, in a letter quoted by T. M. R., "The theories of the origin of coral reefs and islands", *Nature* (17 November 1887), p. 54.

147. W. S. Anderson, "The solubility of carbonate of lime in fresh and sea water", *Proc. R. Soc. Edinb.* (1888–1889). Vol. **16,** pp. 319–324.
John Murray and Robert Irvine, "On coral reefs and other carbonate of lime formations in modern seas", *Proc. R. Soc. Edinb.* (1889–1890). Vol. **17,** pp. 79–109.

148. Hugh Robert Mill, "Sea-temperatures on the Continental Shelf", *Scottish Geographical Magazine* (1888). Vol. **4,** pp. 544–549.
Hugh Robert Mill, *Autobiography,* pp. 48, 53.

149. John Young Buchanan, "On the land slopes separating continents and ocean basins, especially those on the west coast of Africa", *Scottish Geographical Magazine* (1887). Vol. **3,** pp. 217–238.

150. Edward Hull, "The submerged river-valleys and escarpments of the British coast", *Nature* (24 March 1898). Vol. **57,** pp. 484–485.
Edward Hull, "Sub-oceanic terraces and river valleys of the Bay of Biscay", *Nature* (21 April 1898), p. 582.

151. "Geology at the British Association", *Nature* (6 October 1898). Vol. **58,** pp. 558–559, gives a brief account of Hull's paper to the British Association and the discussion on it.

152. John Milne, "Sub-oceanic changes", *Geogr. J.* (1897). Vol. **10,** pp. 129–146, 259–285.

153. John Murray, "Structure, origin, and distribution of coral reefs and islands", *Nature* (28 February 1889). Vol. **39,** pp. 424–428.

154. W. J. L. Wharton, "The deepest sounding yet known", *Nature* (27 February 1896). Vol. **53,** pp. 392–393.

155. James Geikie, "The 'deeps' of the Pacific Ocean and their origin", *Scottish Geographical Magazine* (1912). Vol. **28**, pp. 113–126.

156. Osmond Fisher, "On the physical cause of the ocean basins", *Nature* (12 January 1882). Vol. **25**, pp. 243–244.
Osmond Fisher, *Physics of the Earth's Crust*, London and Cambridge, 1881.

157. C. Wyville Thomson, "General introduction to the zoological series of reports" in *Report on the Scientific Results of the Voyage of H.M.S. Challenger during the years 1873–76; Zoology*, Vol. **1**, (1880), pp. 46, 49.

158. John Murray, "The physical and biological conditions of the seas and estuaries about North Britain", *Scottish Geographical Magazine* (1886). Vol. **2**, pp. 354–357.

159. Henry Alleyne Nicholson, Presidential Address, *Proc. R. phys. Soc. Edinb.* (1894–1897). Vol. **13**, pp. 1–30.

160. See also summary article by Hugh Robert Mill, "The permanence of ocean basins", *Geogr. J.* (1893). Vol. **1**, pp. 230–234. The question was extensively discussed in *Natural Science* during the early 1890s.

161. Harold L. Burstyn, *op. cit.* p. 610. Also Murray's account in the "Editorial Notes" in *Report on the Scientific Results of the Voyage of H.M.S. Challenger during the years 1872–76: Summary of the Scientific Results* (1895). Vol. **1**, pp. vii–xii.

162. A slip bearing this quotation was inserted in the relevant volumes.

163. William Abbott Herdman, *Founders of Oceanography*, *op. cit.* p. 49.

164. Hugh Robert Mill, obituary notice on John Young Buchanan, *Nature* (14 November 1925). Vol. **116**, pp. 719–720.

165. William Abbott Herdman, *op. cit.* pp. 69–98.

166. Hugh Robert Mill, *Autobiography*, pp. 52–53.

167. A Challenger Medal was struck for the occasion, *Nature* (29 August 1895). Vol. **52**, p. 417, and the contributors to the reports presented Murray with a commemorative volume of photographs which is now with the Challenger Collections in the Natural History Museum (W. A. Herdman, *op. cit.* p. 90).

168. Hugh Robert Mill, *op. cit.* p. 85.

169. William Abbott Herdman, *op. cit.* pp. 73–74.

170. Hugh Robert Mill, *op. cit.* p. 51.
Hugh Robert Mill, "Bathymetrical survey of the English lakes", *Geogr. J.* (1895). Vol. **6**, pp. 46–73 and 135–166.
Mill's figures are still used on Ordnance Survey maps, except for Lake Windermere.

171. Sir John Murray and Lawrence Pullar, *Bathymetrical Survey of the Scottish Fresh-Water Lochs. Conducted during the years 1897 to 1909*, 6 vols, Edinburgh (1910).

172. John Murray, "The exploration of the Antarctic regions", *Scottish Geographical Magazine* (1886). Vol. **2**, pp. 527–543.

173. John Murray, "The renewal of Antarctic exploration", *Geogr. J.* (1894). Vol. **3**, pp. 1–37.

174. John Young Buchanan, "Geography. In its physical and economic relations", *Accounts Rendered*, pp. 1–27.

175. William Speirs Bruce and Charles W. Donald, "Cruise of the *Balaena* and the *Active* in the Antarctic Seas, 1892–93", *Geogr. J.* (1896). Vol. **7**, pp. 502–521 and 625–643.
Report on the Scientific Results of the Voyage of S.Y. Scotia during the years

1902, 1903 and 1904, 6 vols (ed. W. S. Bruce), Scottish Oceanographical Laboratory, Edinburgh (1907–1920).

176. Hugh Robert Mill, *Autobiography, op. cit.* pp. 146–147.

177. Fridtjof Nansen, *Farthest North being the record of a voyage of exploration of the ship Fram 1893–96 and of a fifteen months' sleigh journey by Dr. Nansen and Lieut. Johansen*, 2 vols, London (1897).

178. "The German deep-sea expedition", *Scottish Geographical Magazine* (1899). Vol. **15**, pp. 143–145.

179. Otto Pettersson, "A review of Swedish hydrographic research in the Baltic and North Seas", *Scottish Geographical Magazine* (1894). Vol. **10**, pp. 281–302, 352–359, 413–427, 449–462. 525–539, 617–631.

180. Otto Pettersson, "Proposed scheme for an international hydrographic survey of the North Atlantic, the North Sea, and the Baltic", *Scottish Geographical Magazine, op. cit.* pp. 631–635.

181. H. N. Dickson, "Report on physical investigations carried out on board H.M.S. *Jackal*, 1893–94", *Twelfth Annual Report of the Fishery Board for Scotland (1893)*, Edinburgh (1894). Part 3, pp. 336–382.

182. "Hydrographic research to the north of Scotland", *Geogr. J.* (1895). Vol. **5**, pp. 581–583.
    H. N. Dickson, "The movements of the surface waters of the North Sea", *op. cit.* (1896). Vol. **7**, pp. 255–267.

183. Otto Pettersson, "On the influence of ice-melting upon oceanic circulation", *Geogr. J.* (1904). Vol. **24**, pp. 285–333; *Geogr. J.*(1907). Vol. **30**, pp. 273–297.

184. Pierre Welander, "Theoretical oceanography in Sweden 1900–1910", *Bull. Inst. océanogr. Monaco*, numéro spécial 2 (1968). Vol. **1**, pp. 169–173. Welander describes how laboratory experiments made to verify Pettersson's theory were carried out by Sandström and V. W. Ekman before they turned to the mathematical treatment of ocean circulation. He relates the end of this kind of activity among physicists to the rise of quantum mechanics.

185. It was used by Georg von Boguslawski in the title of his *Handbuch der Ozeanographie*, 2 vols, Stuttgart (1884 and 1887) (with O. Krümmel) but only came into general usage slowly. "Thalassography" and "oceanology" were occasional competitors. It had more or less arrived by 1895 when John Murray used it extensively in the Summary volumes of the *Challenger Report*.

186. For example, the British Association meeting of 1894.
    See *Nature* (30 August 1894), "Geography at the British Association". Vol. **50**, pp. 436–437, also Reports of the International Geographical Congresses, especially London (1895) and Berlin (1899).

187. Report of administration for the first year, *Conseil Permanent International pour l'Exploration de la Mer, Rapports et Procès-Verbaux des Réunions, 1902–1903*, Copenhagen (1903). Vol. **1**, p. II.

188. *Ibid.* p. XIV.

189. V. W. Ekman, "On Dead-Water", *Scientific Results of the Norwegian North Polar Expedition, 1893–1896* (ed. F. Nansen), 6 vols, Christiania, London, Leipzig (1900–1906). Vol. **5** (1906), no. 15.

190. V. W. Ekman, "On the influence of the earth's rotation on ocean-currents", *Arkiv för Mathematik, Astronomi och Fysik*, Uppsala and Stockholm (1905). Vol. **2**, no. 11; reprinted 1963.

191. Mieczyslaw Oxner, "Manuel Pratique de l'analyse de l'eau de mer. I.

Chloruration par la méthode de Knudsen", preface by M. Knudsen, *Bull. Comm. int. Explor. scient. Mer Méditerr.* (1920). No. 3, 36 pp.

192. Procès-verbaux de réunions du Conseil: septième réunion, July 1908, *Conseil Permanent International pour l'Exploration de la Mer, Rapports et Procès-Verbaux des Réunions, 1907–1908* (1909). Vol. **11**, pp. 16, 18.

193. Hans Brattström, "The Biological Stations of the Bergens Museum and the University of Bergen 1892–1967", *Sarsia*, Bergen and Oslo (10 September 1967). Vol. **29**, pp. 7–80. Excepting 1910.

194. J. Thoulet, "De l'étude de l'océanographie par les sociétés de géographie ayant leur siège au voisinage de la mer", *Report of the Sixth International Geographical Congress* (1895), London (1896), pp. 475–481.

195. Jules Richard, *L'Océanographie*, Paris (1907), pp. 388–391.

196. C. A. Kofoid, *op. cit.* pp. 163–166.

197. R. N. Rudmose-Brown, *A Naturalist at the Poles*, pp. 249–257, 290–291.

198. G. Herbert Fowler, "Contributions to our knowledge of the plankton of the Faroe Channel—No. 1", *Proceedings of the General Meetings for Scientific Business of the Zoological Society of London for the year 1896*, pp. 991–996, etc.

199. Sir Archibald Day, *The Admiralty Hydrographic Service*, pp. 229–230.

200. Minutes of the Challenger Society, 10 May 1905 and 29 April 1908.

201. T. Wemyss Fulton, "The surface currents of the North Sea", *Scottish Geographical Magazine* (1897). Vol. **13**, pp. 636–645.

202. W. L. Calderwood, "British sea fisheries and fishing areas, in view of recent national advance", *Scottish Geographical Magazine* (1894). Vol. **10**, pp. 69–81.

203. Sir John Murray, address to a conversazione of the W.S.M.B.A., 12 March 1902, *Statement with regard to the Endowment Fund*, Marine Biological Association of the West of Scotland (1903), 33 pp.

204. Challenger Society Minutes, 28 January 1903.

205. Hugh Robert Mill, *Autobiography, op. cit.* p. 58.

206. Challenger Society Minutes, 26 June 1907. The catalogue in the form of a card index is now in the library of the National Institute of Oceanography.

207. *Science of the Sea. An elementary handbook of practical oceanography for travellers, sailors, and yachtsmen* (ed. G. Herbert Fowler, London (1912).

208. Challenger Society Minutes, 3 May and 26 June 1907. The suggestion was made by C. A. Kofoid.

209. "The terminology and nomenclature of the forms of sub-oceanic relief", *Scottish Geographical Magazine* (1903). Vol. **19**, pp. 425–428.

210. Alexander Agassiz to John Murray, 10 April 1903.

211. Otto Pettersson and Gerhard Schott, "On the importance of an international exploration of the Atlantic Ocean in respect to its physical and biological conditions", *Scottish Geographical Magazine* (1909). Vol. **25**, pp. 23–28.

212. John Murray and Johan Hjort, *The Depths of the Ocean, op. cit.*

213. William Abbott Herdman, *Founders of Oceanography, op. cit.* p. 88.

214. Donald J. Matthews, G. I. Taylor and L. R. Crawshay, *Ice Observation, Meteorology and Oceanography in the North Atlantic Ocean. Report on the work carried out by the S.S. Scotia, 1913*, H.M.S.O., London (1914).

215. Sir Geoffrey Ingram Taylor, "Scientific diversions", *Man, Science, Learning and Education* (ed. S. W. Higginbotham). Rice University Semicentennial Publications, (1962), pp. 137–148.

216. William Abbott Herdman, *op. cit.* p. 89.
The Millport station was run by the Marine Biological Association of the

West of Scotland, founded 1901, later (1914) renamed The Scottish Marine Biological Association, both of which published Annual Reports.

217. James Chumley, *The Fauna of the Clyde Sea Area*, Glasgow (1918), pp. 1–7.
218. E. T. Browne to W. T. Calman, 19 June 1914 (letter preserved in the archives of the Challenger Society). Browne wrote:

> You have probably heard that there has been a meeting held in Edinburgh to promote and raise funds for the establishment of a *Scottish Oceanographical Institute*, for the carrying on the work of Murray and Bruce, and to take care of their collections.

* *See also* R. N. Rudmose Brown, *loc. cit.*

Addenda et Corrigenda

p.367, 1.9: *instead* his *read* this

p.369, 1.35: *In fact* Jeffreys, Lankester and Norman *did not contribute directly to the report. Other UK contributors included* George Stewardson Brady, F.R.S. (1832–1921), Henry Bowman Brady, F.R.S. (1835–1891), and George Busk, F. R.S. (1807–1886)

p.375, 1.35: *instead* recently *read* in 1959

p.378, 1.39: *instead* zoologist *read* naturalist

p.398, n.67, 11.2–3: *after* antérieures à 1914; *insert* unpublished manuscript. A shortened version of this paper was presented to the 12 th International Congress of History of Science (*Actes*, Paris [1968], pp.61–65). See also :

p.406, n.218, 1.7: *insert* The Archives of the Challenger Society for Marine Science (also referred to in notes 204, 206, and 208) are now in the National Oceanographic Library, Southampton Oceanography Centre

APPENDIX 1

PROPOSITIONS OF SOME EXPERIMENTS TO BE MADE BY
THE EARL OF SANDWICH IN HIS PRESENT VOYAGE

from Thomas Birch, *History of the Royal Society of London* (1756). Vol. **1**,
pp. 29–30.

1. To sound the depth of the sea in the Bay of Biscay and the Straits, at full sea, or low water, without a line, thus:

Take a globe of some swimming wood, having a hook fastened to it. Then take a lead sufficient to sink it, shaped like the figure of 7; and put the upper part of it into the hook, and as you let it fall into the sea, take notice of the time by a second-watch, and observe how long the globe is submerged in the water; for by that the depth is to be computed. So soon as the lower end of the lead touches the ground, it slips out of the hook, and up comes the globe. The rule of computing the depth of the water by the time of the globe's submersion, is to be made by trying it in a depth of 60, 80, or 100 fathoms; so is another time to another number of fathoms.

2. To sink an empty globe of tin with an addition of lead, fastened to a line, as many hundred fathoms deep as may be, to see what will become of it.

3. In some place of the sea of two or three hundred fathoms deep, or more, draw up some of the water near the bottom, to compare the saltness of it with that next the superfice. It is to be done thus, or some other such way:

Take a cylindrical vessel, and fit a sucker to it, with a shaft or hook to hold a string or small line fastened to it. Put the sucker or stopper down to the bottom of the vessel, which is to have a small hole at the bottom. Then sink and let down the vessel by a long cord into the water, together with a line as long as is fastened at the stopper; and let down so dextrously, as it pluck not up the stopper, till the vessel be at the depth proposed; then pluck out the stopper, and the vessel will bring up the water from the depth that is desired.

4. To take up a glass full of salt-water on the English shore, and weigh it, then evaporate the water, and see what salt it holds; and thus do often; that is at every three or four degrees, as you go southwards.

5. Inquire after a true account of the ebbing and flowing between the Straits; and whether the tide flows always eastward at the shores, and at the middle; and how it varies, if it be not constant. And if you have the opportunity, try whether in the middle of the Straits the surface of the water flow eastward, whilst the lower part of it runs westward.

This is to be done by letting a bucket down 60, 80, or 100 fathoms, and tied to a boat; and then, if there be contrary motions in the water, the boat will stay as at anchor, or move accordingly.

6. Take sea-water in a fit vessel into a dark place, and shake and agitate it so as it may break into drops, to see whether it will sparkle and shine, as when it is in the sea, broken by the wind or otherwise in the night.

APPENDIX 2

EXPERIMENTS MADE BY CAPTAIN ROBERT HOLMES ON 2 AND 30 MAY 1663

From *The Royal Society's Classified Papers*, **3** (i) no. 9.

May 2
Wee tryed the Leades and Balles in the Bay of Biscay in 125 fadam and wee let
ye Lead and Balles goe easilie out of our hands and before the Lead and Ball
was A qter downe the Ball and Lead turninge caused the Ball to turne off Soe
we Lost in the first triall 7 Leades and 3 Balles with that way and another way
that we tryed with the alteracon of the Lead which may bee made knowne.

ditto
When wee lett downe the water pott downe to the bottome being ye same deapth
as Aforesaid and in A qter of A pinte weighing found the water at the Bottome to
bee something fressher and lighter* by : 9 : graines then that of ye superficies.

30
We tryed the Leades and Bales off Capp St Maries in 145 fa and lost 3 leades :
2 : bales, the first lead lost by the former way the other: 2 : Leades and
Balles by the Letter way Invented. Then letting downe Lead and line to find ye
Reason wee found the ground to bee all owsie soe conjecture the Lead stooke
which caused ye Bales to Ascend and goeing downe soe swift A Motion.
Then let downe ye pott to the Bottom for water the forsaid deapth and in A
qter of A pinte weighing found the water at the bottom to be lighter* by 10
graines and fresher then that on ye superficies. Wee would had tryed severall
Times bot opertunities and Calmes did not present which seldome being troubled
with Calmes this is all the Acco^{tt} att present can be given.

* In the manuscript someone has apparently tried to alter "lighter" to "weightier."
In the Bay of Biscay the surface water is in fact more salt than the water beneath.

APPENDIX 3

OTHER INQUIRIES CONCERNING THE SEA

Contributed by Robert Boyle to *Philosophical Transactions* (October 1666).
No. 18, pp. 315–316

What is the Proportion of Salt, that is in the Water of differing Seas; And whether in the same Sea it be always the same? And if it be not, how much it differs?

What is the Gravity of Sea-waters in reference to Fresh Waters and to one another: Whether it vary not in Summer and Winter, and on other Scores? And Whether in the same Season its Gravity proceed *only* from the greater or lesser Proportion of Salt, that is in it, and not sometimes from other Causes? And what are the differing Gravities of the Sea-water, according to the Climats.

What are the Odors, Colours and Tasts, observable in Sea-water?

What is the Depth of the Sea in several places, and the Order of its Increase and Decrements. And whether the Bottom of the Sea does always rise towards the Shore, unless accidentally interrupted?

Of the Bottom of the Sea, and how it differs from the Surface of the Earth, in reference to the Soyl, and Evenness or Roughness of the Superficies; And the Stones. Minerals, and Vegetables to be found there?

What the Figuration of the Seas from North to South, and from East to West, and in several Hemispheres and Climats?

What communication there is of Seas by Streights, and Subterraneal Conveyances?

Of the Motion of the Sea by Winds, and how far Storms reach downwards towards the Bottom of the Sea? Of the grand Motions of the Bulk or Body of the Sea; especially of the Tides: Their History as to their Nature and Differences.

What power the Sea hath to produce or hasten Putrefaction in some Bodies, and to preserve others; as Wood, Cables, and others that are sunk under it?

Of the power ascribed to the Sea to eject Dead Bodies, *Succinum, Ambergris?*

Of the shining of the Sea in the night?

What are the Medical vertues of the Sea, especially against *Hydrophobia?* What is its vertue to Manure Land? And what are the Plants, that thrive best with Sea-water?.

SELECT BIBLIOGRAPHY

As full details of all publications referred to have been given in the notes I have restricted this bibliography to a list of the more important of the manuscript collections, periodicals and books of which I have made use. One or two especially important papers have been individually listed with the latter.

MANUSCRIPT SOURCES

Bodleian Library, Oxford: Rawlinson MSS.
University of Edinburgh Library: Agassiz Correspondence, Walker Lectures.
Magdalene College, Cambridge: Pepysian Library Manuscripts.
Royal Greenwich Observatory, Herstmonceux: Airy Papers, Board of Longitude Papers.
Royal Society of London: Classified Papers, Letter Books, Register Books.
Somerville College, Oxford: Mary Somerville Papers.
Whitby Literary and Philosophical Society: Scoresby Papers.

PERIODICALS

The Royal Society of London—*Philosophical Transactions, Proceedings.*
Annals of Philosophy (*Thomson's Annals*); *A Journal of Natural Philosophy, Chemistry, and the Arts* (*Nicholson's Journal*); *The London and Edinburgh* (*and Dublin*) *Philosophical Magazine and Journal of Science.*
The Royal Society of Edinburgh—*Transactions, Proceedings.*
Memoirs of the Wernerian Natural History Society; The Edinburgh Journal of Science; The Edinburgh Philosophical Journal; The New Edinburgh Philosophical Journal.
The Geographical Journal; The Proceedings of the Royal Geographical Society; The Scottish Geographical Magazine.
Annals and Magazine of Natural History.
Annals of Science.
The British Association—*Reports of Meetings.*
Hakluyt Society Publications.
Memoirs of the Literary and Philosophical Society of Manchester.
Nature.
Nautical Magazine.
The Royal Irish Academy—*Transactions, Proceedings.*
Académie des Sciences—*Comptes Rendus Hebdomadaires.*
Académie Royale des Sciences—*Histoires, Mémoires.*

Annales de Chimie et de Physique.
Annales Hydrographiques.
Journal de Physique.
Bulletin de la Classe Physico-Mathématique de l'Académie Impériale des Sciences de St.-Pétersbourg.
The American Journal of Science and Arts (Silliman's Journal).
Isis.

BOOKS

Agassiz, Alexander, *A Contribution to American Thalassography. Three Cruises of the U.S.C.G.S.S. Blake in the Gulf of Mexico, in the Caribbean Sea, and along the Atlantic Coast of the United States, from 1877 to 1880*, 2 vols, Boston and New York (1888).

Aimé, Georges, *Exploration Scientifique de l'Algérie pendant les années 1840, 1841, 1842: Recherches de Physique Générale sur la Méditerranée*, Paris (1845).

Arago, François, *Œuvres Complètes de François Arago*, ed. M. J. A. Barral, 17 vols, Paris (1854–1862).

Aristotle, *The Works of Aristotle*, ed. W. D. Ross, 12 vols, Oxford (1908–1952).

Bacon, Francis, *The Works of Francis Bacon*, ed. J. Spedding, R. L. Ellis and D. D. Heath, 14 vols, London (1857–1874).

Birch, Thomas, *The History of the Royal Society of London for Improving Natural Knowledge*, 4 vols, London (1756–1757).

Bourne, William, *A Booke called the Treasure for Traveilers*, London (1578).

Boyle, Robert, *The Works of the Honourable Robert Boyle*, ed. Thomas Birch, 5 vols, London (1744).

Buchanan, John Young, *Scientific Papers*, Cambridge (1913).

Idem, Accounts Rendered of Work Done and Things Seen, Cambridge (1919).

Challenger, H.M.S., *Report on the Scientific Results of the Voyage of H.M.S. Challenger during the Years 1873–76*, 50 vols, H.M.S.O., London (1880–1895).

Cook, James, *The Journals of Captain Cook*, ed. J. C. Beaglehole, Hakluyt Society, extra series, no. 35, 4 vols and charts, Cambridge (1955–1967).

Croll, James, *Climate and Time in their Geological Relations: a Theory of Secular Changes of the Earth's Climate*, London (1875).

Darwin, Charles, *The Structure and Distribution of Coral Reefs. The Geology of the Voyage of the Beagle*, part 1, 2nd edition, London (1874).

Dawson, Llewellyn Styles, *Memoirs of Hydrography*, 2 vols, Eastbourne (1885).

Dawson, Warren R., *The Banks Letters: a Calendar of the Manuscript Correspondence of Sir Joseph Banks*, London (1958).

Day, Archibald, *The Admiralty Hydrographic Service*, H.M.S.O., London (1967).

Derham, William, *The Philosophical Experiments and Observations of the late eminent Dr. Robert Hooke*, London (1726).

Descartes, René, *Œuvres de Descartes*, ed. Charles Adam and Paul Tannery, 11 vols, Paris (1897–1909).

Duhem, Pierre, *Le Système du Monde: Histoire des Doctrines Cosmologiques de Platon à Copernic*, 10 vols, Paris (1913–1959).

El-Mas'údí (Ali Ibn Husain), *Historical Encyclopædia, entitled Meadows of Gold and Mines of Gems*, Oriental Translation Fund, vol. 1 only, London (1841).

Fitzroy, Robert, *Narrative of the Surveying Voyages of H.M.S. Adventure and Beagle, between the Years 1826 and 1836, describing their Examination of the*

Southern Shores of South America, and the Beagle's Circumnavigation of the Globe, 3 vols, London (1839).

Fournier, Georges, *Hydrographie Contenant la Théorie et la Pratique de Toutes les Parties de la Navigation*, 2nd edition, Paris (1667).

Franklin, Benjamin, *The Writings of Benjamin Franklin*, ed. Albert Henry Smith, 10 vols, New York (1905–1907).

Galilei, Galileo, *Dialogue concerning the Two Chief World Systems—Ptolemaic and Copernican*, translated by Stillman Drake, Berkeley and Los Angeles (1953).

Gerald of Wales, *Topographia Hibernica, et Expugnatio Hibernica*, ed. J. F. Dimock, Rolls Series, vol. 21, no. 5, London (1867). *

Gilbert, William, *De Mundo Nostro Sublunari Philosophia Nova*, Amstelodami (1651).

Greaves, John, *Miscellaneous Works of Mr. John Greaves*, ed. Thomas Birch, 2 vols, London (1737).

Gunther, R. T., *Early Science in Oxford*, 14 vols, Oxford (1921–1945).

Herdman, William Abbott, *Founders of Oceanography and their Work: an Introduction to the Science of the Sea*, London (1923).

Horrocks, Jeremiah, *Jeremiae Horroccii Opera Posthuma*, ed. John Wallis, London (1673).

Humboldt, Alexander von, *Personal Narrative of Travels to the Equinoctial Regions of the New Continent, during the Years 1799–1804*, translated by H. M. Williams, 7 vols, London (1814–1829).

International Congress on the History of Oceanography, Communications, *Bulletin de l'Institut Océanographique, Fondation Albert Ier, Prince de Monaco*, numéro spécial 2, Monaco (1968).

Jones, Charles W., *Bedæ Opera de Temporibus*, Cambridge, Mass. (1943).

Kepler, Johann, *Joannis Kepleri Astronomi Opera Omnia*, ed. C. Frisch, 8 vols, Frankfurt and Erlanger (1858–1871).

Kircher, Athanasius, *Mundus Subterraneus, in XII Libros Digestus*, 3rd edition, 2 vols, Amstelodami (1678).

Kirwan, Richard, *Geological Essays*, London (1799).

Kofoid, Charles Atwood, "The Biological Stations of Europe", *Bulletin of the U.S. Bureau of Education*, no. 4, whole no. 440 (1910).

Kotzebue, Otto von, *A Voyage of Discovery, into the South Sea and Beering's Straits, for the Purpose of Exploring a North-East Passage, undertaken in the Years 1815–1818*, translated by H. E. Lloyd, 3 vols, London (1821).

Krümmel, Otto, *Handbuch der Ozeanographie*, 2 vols, Stuttgart (1907–1911).

Lalande, Joseph le Français de, *Astronomie*, 2nd edition, 4 vols, Paris (1771–1781).

Lillie, Frank R., *The Woods Hole Marine Biological Laboratory*, Chicago (1944).

Lyell, Charles, *Principles of Geology: or, the Modern Changes of the Earth and its Inhabitants*, 6th edition, 3 vols, London (1840).

MacCurdy, Edward, *The Notebooks of Leonardo da Vinci*, 2 vols, London (1938).

Marcet, Alexander, "On the specific gravity, and temperature of sea waters, in different parts of the ocean, and in particular seas; with some account of their saline contents", *Phil. Trans.* (1819). Vol. **109**, pp. 161–208.

Marsigli, Luigi Ferdinando, *Osservazioni intorno al Bosforo Tracio overo Canale di * *Constantinopli, rappresentate in lettera alla Sacra Real Maesta Cristina Regina * *di Svezia*, Roma (1681).

Idem, Histoire Physique de la Mer, Amsterdam (1725).

Maury, Matthew Fontaine, *The Physical Geography of the Sea*, London (1855); reprinted, ed. John Leighly, Cambridge, Mass. (1963). *

Mill, Hugh Robert, *An Autobiography*, ed. L. Dudley Stamp, London, New York and Toronto (1951).

Murray, John, and Hjort, Johan, *The Depths of the Ocean. A General Account of the Modern Science of Oceanography based largely on the Scientific Researches of the Norwegian Steamer Michael Sars in the North Atlantic*, London (1912).

Newton, Isaac, *Philosophiæ Naturalis Principia Mathematica*, London (1687).

Palissy, Bernard, *Les Œuvres de Bernard Palissy*, ed. Anatole France, Paris (1880).

Péron, François, *Voyage de Découvertes aux Terres Australes, fait par l'ordre du Gouvernement, sur les corvettes le Géographe, le Naturaliste, et la goëlette le Casuarina, pendant les années 1800–1804*, ed. L. de Freycinet, 4 vols, Paris (1824).

Petit-Thouars, Abel du, *Voyage autour du Monde sur la frégate la Vénus, pendant les années 1836–1839*, 10 vols, Paris (1840–1855).

Phipps, Constantine, *A Voyage towards the North Pole undertaken by his Majesty's Command, 1773*, London (1774).

Pliny, *The Natural History of Pliny*, translated by J. Bostock and H. T. Riley, 6 vols, London (1855–1857).

Prestwich, Joseph, "Tables of temperatures of the sea at different depths beneath the surface, reduced and collated from the various observations made between the years 1749 and 1868, discussed", *Phil. Trans.* (1875). Vol. **165**, pp. 587–674.

Rennell, James, *An Investigation of the Currents of the Atlantic Ocean, and of those which prevail between the Indian Ocean and the Atlantic*, London (1832).

Ross, James Clark, *A Voyage of Discovery and Research in the Southern and Antarctic Regions, during the Years 1839–1843*, 2 vols, London (1847).

Ross, John, *A Voyage of Discovery, made under the Orders of the Admiralty, in H.M.S. Isabella and Alexander, for the purpose of exploring Baffin's Bay, and inquiring into the probability of a North West Passage*, London (1819).

Rumford, Benjamin Thompson, Count, *Essays, Political, Economical, and Philosophical*, 4 vols, London (1796–1812).

Sabine, Edward, *An Account of Experiments to determine the Figure of the Earth, by Means of the Pendulum vibrating Seconds in different Latitudes*, London (1825).

Sarton, George, *Introduction to the History of Science*, 3 vols, Washington, (1927–1948).

Scoresby, William, the younger, *An Account of the Arctic Regions, with a History and Description of the Northern Whale-Fishery*, 2 vols, Edinburgh, 1820.

Six, James, *The Construction and Use of a Thermometer, for shewing the Extremes * Of Temperature in the Atmosphere, during the Observer's Absence*, Maidstone (1794).

Smyth, William, *The Mediterranean: a Memoir Physical, Historical and Nautical*, London (1854).

Strabo, *The Geography of Strabo*, translated by H. L. Jones and J. R. S. Sterrett Loeb Classical Library, 8 vols (1917–1932).

Todhunter, Isaac, *William Whewell, D.D.*, 2 vols, London (1876).

Varen, Bernhard, *A Compleat System of General Geography: explaining the Nature and Properties of the Earth*, ed. Newton and Jurin, translated by Dugdale and Shaw, 2 vols, London (1733).

Waller, Richard, *The Posthumous Works of Robert Hooke containing his Cutlerian Lectures, and other Discourses read at the Meetings of the Royal Society*, London (1705).

Wallich, G. C., *The North-Atlantic Sea-Bed: comprising a Diary of the Voyage on Board H.M.S. Bulldog, in 1860; and Observations on the Presence of Animal Life, and the Formation and Nature of Organic Deposits, at Great Depths in the Ocean*, London (1862).

Waters, David W., *The Art of Navigation in England in Elizabethan and Early Stuart Times*, London (1958).

Watson, Richard, *Chemical Essays*, 2nd edition, 5 vols, London and Cambridge (1782–1787).

Wild, J. J., *Thalassa: an Essay on the Depth, Temperature, and Currents of the Ocean*, London (1877).

Williams, Jonathan, *Thermometrical Navigation*, Philadelphia (1799).

Wyville Thomson, Charles, *The Depths of the Sea*, 2nd edition, London (1874).

Idem, The Voyage of the Challenger. The Atlantic. A Preliminary Account of the General Results of the Exploring Voyage of H.M.S. Challenger during the Year 1873 and the early part of the Year 1876, 2 vols, London (1877).

Addenda et Corrigenda

p.413, 1.10: *instead* vol.21, no.5 *read* no.21, vol.5

p.413, 1.46: *instead: overo read: o vero*

p.413, 1.47: *instead: Constantinopli read: Constantinopoli*

p.413, 1.51: *before* reprinted *insert* 8 th U.S. (1861) edition

p.414, 1.37: *insert* reprinted, London: Nimbus Books (1980).

BIBLIOGRAPHY TO SECOND EDITION

INTRODUCTION

Since 1971 the amount of published information on the history of oceanography has increased enormously, as have the resources available for its study. Since 1989 the best way of finding out about new publications, as well as about events taking place in the field, has been the *History of Oceanography Newsletter*. This is at present edited by Eric L. Mills, Professor of the History of Science at Dalhousie University,[1] and appears once a year. Number 1 (1989) contains a Handlist of Source Books for the History of Oceanography (also printed in Mills 1993a). Mills (1993b) also contains a review of literature and a substantial bibliography. Each newsletter up to the present time has contained a bibliography of current items (from 1987 onwards) prepared by Jacqueline Carpine-Lancre, Librarian of the Musée Océanographique at Monaco. The card indexes maintained at the Musée are in themselves a valuable historical resource, as indeed is the library itself, and the museum's archives – not to mention its historic collections of apparatus (Carpine 1987 etc.) and specimens – in particular for the work of its founder, Prince Albert I of Monaco, and for marine science generally, especially in the Francophone world.

For a wider view of the history of science, and for the years up to 1987, the primary source for books and articles on the history of marine science is the annual bibliography published in *Isis*, the journal of the History of Science Society in America. Also useful is the international bibliography published in the *Bulletin signalétique. Histoire de sciences et des techniques, revue trimestrielle*, by the Centre National de la Recherche Scientifique. Particularly for historical articles published in scientific journals or as part of *Festschrift* volumes, scientific bibliographies are useful; an *Oceanographic Literature Review* is published as part of the journal *Deep-Sea Research*.

For scientific papers on the sea published during the nineteenth century, the best source is the printed series of the Royal Society's *Catalogue of Scientific Papers*, though this is arranged by author. This was succeeded by the Royal Society's *International Catalogue of Scientific Literature*, which was organized by subject and ran from 1900 to *c*. 1920.

---

[1] Professor E. L. Mills, Department of Oceanography, Dalhousie University, Halifax, Nova Scotia B3H 4J1, Canada.

A number of bibliographies on specific items have been published. In the Garland series of scientific bibliographies, the volume on *History of Geophysics and Meteorology* (Brush *et al.*, 1985) contains many oceanographic references, and other volumes in the series are also useful. A bibliography on the history of German oceanography (Watermann & Wrzesinski, 1989) was originally prepared for the Fourth International Congress on the History of Oceanography which met in Hamburg in 1987. Bibliographies on related aspects of the history of science and maritime activity include Egerton (1983) (ecology), Porter and Poulton (1978) (geology) and Jenkins (1948) (whaling). As well as lists of expeditions (Defant, 1928; De Buen, 1930, 1934; Bencker, 1944; Roberts, 1958) there are volumes of references to literature on oceanographic expeditions (Fukano & Strickland, 1972; Estok and Boykin, 1976).

For older material, reprints are an increasingly popular method of bringing older texts to a modern audience. One of the pioneers of this is the Hakluyt Society[2] which celebrated its 150th anniversary in 1996; it specializes in printing unpublished accounts of voyages and travels of geographical interest, but also produces critical editions and translations of published works in this field which are otherwise not widely available. Among recent titles of general interest to historians of oceanography, and relevant to passages in this book, are the journals of Halley (1981) on his voyages in the *Paramore* (see p. 111), and Forster's (1982) journal from Cook's second expedition (p. 187). A recent imaginative inclusion in the Maritime History Series of the John Carter Brown Library (for which I contributed the introduction but otherwise take no credit), was to print the original Latin of Vossius' (1993) *De motu marium* in the same volume as a reprint of the English version of 1667. Arno Press unfortunately never got round to an oceanography series, but their ecology and geology series contain useful titles (e.g. Forbes & Godwin-Austen, 1859; reprinted 1977). Two volumes in the Benchmark Papers in Geology series (M. Deacon, 1978; G. Deacon & M. Deacon, 1982) contain reprints of papers of importance in the development of oceanography, and other volumes are relevant, though most contain fairly recent material.

Serious students will want to go further and study the original manuscripts of early oceanographers and the samples they collected and the apparatus they used. To see where these can be found, the first stop is the *Directory of source materials for the history of oceanography* compiled by Anita McConnell (1990). A few guides to specific topics exist, such as

---

[2] For further information, contact The Hakluyt Society, c/o The Map Room, The British Library, Great Russell Street, London WC1B 3DG.

Eileen Brunton's (1994) list of photographs taken during the *Challenger* expedition. Mainly however, it will be necessary to use non-specialist resources in the history of science, such as the guide to manuscripts of British scientists published by the Royal Commission on Historic Manuscripts (1982), and Bridson et al. (1980) on natural history resources in the U.K. Catalogues and guides for specific institutions are helpful, for example the Natural History Museum (Sawyer, 1971) and the British Library (Summers, 1986). To learn more about the instrument makers responsible for apparatus, a directory now exists to British scientific instrument makers (Clifton, 1995). In a few cases we are fortunate to have important surviving manuscript collections of marine scientists, and some of these have printed catalogues; for example St Andrews University has the archives of W. C. McIntosh (Gunther, 1977) and of D'Arcy Thompson (1987) who suceeded him as professor of natural history (their combined tenure of the chair extended for 66 years). Other important collections exist, but where these are in scientific institutions, present-day needs often take precedence over historical material (though the days when this could be seen as lacking in importance have happily long since gone.) A splendid exception to the general rule is the Scripps Institution of Oceanography in California which has had a full archival programme in place for some years.

Exhibitions can also form a permanent as well as an ephemeral resouce where published catalogues exist. Several of these are valuable publications, such as the catalogue of the exhibition celebrating the centenary of the Stazione Zoologica at Naples (Groeben & Müller, 1975) and the exhibit on German oceanography prepared in conjunction with the Fourth International Congress on the History of Oceanography (Watermann, 1989). Of a more ephemeral nature, but still available recently, is a catalogue of an exhibit of books and manuscripts on early oceanography from Edinburgh University Library, which was displayed at the time of the Second International Congress (Deacon, 1972).

Finally, the history of oceanography now has its own multilingual journal. The first volume of the *Historisch-Meereskundliches Jahrbuch* was published in 1992 for the Deutsche Gesellschaft für Meeresforschung[3], and several further volumes have since appeared. Full-length articles on the history of oceanography otherwise appear either in main-stream history of science journals or, more occasionally in oceanographic journals and festschrifts, depending usually on the affiliation of the author. A number of shorter articles (e.g. Adams, 1995) have appeared in *Ocean*

---

[3] Deutsche Gesellschaft für Meeresforschung (DGM) e. V., Bundesstrasse 55, D-2000 Hamburg 13, Germany.

Challenge, the magazine of the Challenger Society for Marine Science.[4] The society was originally founded in 1903 (Deacon, 1984) to promote the science of oceanography in the post-*Challenger* era.

It is impossible in a short summary like this to do anything like justice to the many and varied contributions which have been made to different aspects of the history of marine science in the last twenty-five years, but the following brief bibliography gives an impression of the kind of work being done and lists some of the key items published during that time.

INTERNATIONAL MEETINGS

1963   Colloque international sur l'histoire de la biologie marine, les grandes expéditions scientifiques et la création des laboratoires maritimes, Laboratoire Arago, Banyuls-sur-Mer, 2–6 September 1963, *Vie et Milieu*, supplement 19 (1965).

1966   Premier Congrès international d'Histoire de l'Océanographie, Musée océanographique, Monaco, 12–17 December 1966. Communications, ed. J. Carpine-Lancre, *Bulletin de l'Institut océanographique (Fondation Albert Ier, Prince de Monaco)*, numéro spécial 2, 3 vols (1968).

1972   Second International Congress on the History of Oceanography (*Challenger* Expedition Centenary), Edinburgh, 12–20 September 1972. Proceedings, ed. W.H. Rutherford, *Proceedings of the Royal Society of Edinburgh*, section B, vols 72 and 73 (1972).

1980   Third International Congress on the History of Oceanography, Woods Hole Oceanographic Institution (Fiftieth Anniversary Meeting), 22–26 September 1980. Proceedings, ed. M. Sears & D. Merriman, *Oceanography: the Past*, New York: Springer (1980).

1987   Fourth International Congress on the History of Oceanography, Hamburg, 23–29 September 1987. Proceedings, ed. W. Lenz & M. Deacon, *Ocean Sciences: their History and Relation to Man*, *Deutsche Hydrographische Zeitschrift*, Ergänzungsheft, Reihe B, no. 22 (1990).

1993   Fifth International Congress on the History of Oceanography, Scripps Institution of Oceanography, 7–14 July 1993. Proceedings ed. P. F. Rehbock & K. Benson (in press).

CATALOGUES AND DIRECTORIES

Bridson, G. D. R., Phillips, V. C. & Harvey, A. P., *Natural history manuscript resources in the British Isles*, London: Mansell (1980).

---

[4] Membership is open to anyone interested in the science of the sea, via the Membership Secretary, Challenger Society for Marine Science, c/o Southampton Oceanography Centre, European Way, Southampton SO14 3ZH, U.K.

Brunton, E. V., *The* Challenger *expedition. 1872–1876: a visual index*, London: Natural History Museum (1994).

Carpine, C., "Catalogue des appareils d'océanographie en collection au Musée océanographique de Monaco. 1. Photomètres. 2. Mesureurs de courant". *Bulletin de l'Institut océanographique, Monaco* (1987). Vol. 73 (no. 1437), pp. 1–144.

Carpine, C., "Catalogue des appareils d'océanographie en collection au Musée océanographique de Monaco. 3. Appareils de prélèvement biologique", *Bulletin de l'Institut océanographique, Monaco* (1991). Vol. 74 (no. 1438), pp. 1–159.

Carpine, C., "Catalogue des appareils d'océanographie en collection au Musée océanographique de Monaco. 4. Bouteilles de prélèvement d'eau", *Bulletin de l'Institut océanographique, Monaco*, (1993). Vol. 75 (no. 1440), pp. 1–175.

Carpine, C., "Catalogue des appareils d'océanographie en collection au Musée océanographique de Monaco. 5. Instruments de sondage", *Bulletin de l'Institut océanographique, Monaco* (1996). Vol. 75 (no. 1441), pp. 1–208.

Clifton, G., *Directory of British scientific instrument makers*, London: Zwemmer/National Maritime Museum (1995).

Deacon, M. B., *Marine science in the nineteenth century and the* Challenger *Expedition*. (Catalogue of an exhibition of books and manuscripts arranged for the Second International Congress on the History of Oceanography, Edinburgh: Edinburgh University Library (1972).

Deacon, M. B., "List of the scientific and personal papers of Sir George Deacon, F.R.S.", *Institute of Oceanographic Sciences Deacon Laboratory Report*, vol. 301 (1992).

Groeben, C. & Müller, I., *The Naples Zoological Station at the time of Anton Dohrn*, Paris: Goethe-Institut (1975).

McConnell, A., *Directory of source materials for the history of oceanography*, UNESCO technical papers in marine science, no. 58 (1990).

Royal Commission on Historical Manuscripts, *The manuscript papers of British scientists, 1600–1940*, London: HMSO (1982).

Sawyer, F. C., "A short history of the libraries and list of manuscripts and original drawings in the British Museum (Natural History)", *Bulletin of the British Museum (Natural History), Historical Series* (1971). Vol. 4 (2), pp. 1–204.

Summers, A., *How to find source materials: British Library collections on the history and culture of science, technology and medicine*, London: British Library (1996).

Thompson, D'A. W., *An index to the correspondence and papers of Sir D'Arcy Wentworth Thompson (1860–1948)*, St Andrews University Publications, no. 64. St Andrews: St Andrews University Library (1987).

Watermann, B. (ed.), "Exposition on historical aspects of marine research in Germany", *Deutsche Hydrographische Zeitschrift*, Ergänzungsheft, series B, no. 21 (1989).

BIBLIOGRAPHIES

Brush, S.G., Landsberg, H. E. & Collins, M., *The history of geophysics and meteorology: an annotated bibliography*. New York: Garland (1985).

Egerton, F. N., "The history of ecology: achievements and opportunities", *Journal of the History of Biology* (1983). Vol. 16, pp. 259–310.

Fukano, Y. & Strickland, H., *Selected references to literature on marine expeditions, 1700–1960*, Boston, Mass.: G. K. Hall (1972).

Jenkins, J. T., "Bibliography of whaling", *Journal of the Society for the Bibliography of Natural History* (1948). Vol. 2, pp. 71–166.

Porter, R. & Poulton, K., "Geology in Britain, 1660–1800: a selective bibliography", *Journal for the Society of the Bibliography of Natural History* (1978). Vol. 9, pp. 74–84.

Sarjeant, W. A. S., *Geologists and the history of geology: an international bibliography from the origins to 1978, 5* vols, London: Macmillan (1980).

Watermann, B. & Wrzesinski, O. J., *Bibliographie zur Geschichte der deutschen Meeresforschung. Chronologische Titelaufzählung (1557–1989)*, 2nd edition, Hamburg: Deutsche Gesellschaft für Meeresforschung (1989).

LISTS OF EXPEDITIONS

Bencker, H., "Chronological list of the main maritime discoveries and explorations", *Hydrographic Review* (1944). Vol. 21, pp. 130–174.

De Buen, R., "Lista cronológica de las campañas y navegaciones a las que se deben observaciones cientificas de carácter oceanográfico", *Memorias del Consejo Oceanográfico Ibero-Americano* (1930). Vol. 5, pp. 1–62.

Defant, A., "Die systematische Erforschung des Weltmeeres", *Zeitschrift der Gesellschaft für Erdkunde zu Berlin* (1928). Sonderband, pp. 459–505.

Estok, R. & Boykin, R. E., *A union list of oceanographic expeditions, including results of some major cruise reports*, College Station, Texas: Texas A & M University Libraries (1976).

Headland, R. K., *Chronological list of Antarctic expeditions and related historical events*, Cambridge: Cambridge University Press (1989).

REPRINTS

Deacon, M. B., "The voyage of H.M.S. *Challenger*", [chapter 15 of *Scientists and the Sea*], in R. G. Pirie, *Oceanography: contemporary readings in ocean science*, New York: Oxford University Press (1973), pp. 24–44.

Deacon, M. B. (ed.), *Oceanography: concepts and history*, Benchmark Papers in Geology, vol. 35, Stroudsburg, Penn.: Dowden, Hutchinson & Ross (1978).

Deacon, G. E. R. & Deacon, M. B. (eds), *Modern concepts of oceanography*, Benchmark Papers in Geology, vol. 61, Stroudsburg, Penn.: Hutchinson Ross (1982).

Forbes, E., & Godwin-Austen, R. A. C., *The natural history of European seas*, (First published 1859, London: John Van Voorst), New York: Arno Press(1977).

Murray, J., *Selections from Report on the Scientific Results of the Voyage of H.M.S. Challenger during the years 1872–76*, New York: Arno Press (1977).

Olaus Magnus, *A description of the northern peoples*, part 1, series 2, vol. 182, ed. P. G. Foote (translated by P. Fisher & H. Higgins), London: Hakluyt Society, (1996).

Six, J., *The construction and use of a thermometer, for showing the extremes of temperature in the atmosphere during the observer's absence*, eds J. Austin & A. McConnell, London: Nimbus Books (1980).

Vossius, I., *A treatise concerning the motion of the seas and winds (1677), together with*

De motu marium et ventorum (1663), Delmar, N.Y.: Scholars' Facsimiles and Reprints (1993).

WORK ON THE HISTORY OF OCEANOGRAPHY AND RELATED TOPICS

a) Contributions before 1964

Buchanan, J. Y., "A retrospect of oceanography in the twenty years before 1895", *Accounts rendered of work done and things seen*, Cambridge: Cambridge University Press, pp. xii–xvi, 28–86.

Gudger, E. W., "The five great naturalists of the 16th century: Belon, Rondelet, Salviani, Gesner and Aldrovandi: a chapter in the history of ichthyology", *Isis* (1934). Vol. 22, pp. 21–40.

Harvey, E.N., *A history of luminescence from the earliest times until 1900*, American *Philosophical Society Memoir*, vol. 44, Philadelphia (1957).

Hedgpeth, J.W., "Treatise of maritime ecology and paleoecology", *Geological Society of America Memoir* no. 67 (1957). Vol. 1, pp. 1–16 (Introduction).

Kohl, J. G., *Geschichte des Golfstroms und seiner Erforschung von den ältesten Zeiten bis auf den grossen amerikanischen Bürgerkrieg*, Bremen: Muller (1868).

Legendre, R., *La découverte des mers*, Paris: Presses Universitaires de France (1948). (New edition by J.-M. Pérès published 1965.)

Merriman, D., *A posse ad esse. Journal of Marine Research*, (1948). Vol. 7, pp. 139–146.

Murray, J., "Historical Introduction", *Report on the voyage of H.M.S. Challenger during the years 1872–76. Summary of the scientific results* (1895). Vol. I, pp. 1–106E.

Pécaut, C., "L'oeuvre géologique de Leibniz", *Revue générale des sciences pures et appliquées* (1951). Vol. 58, pp. 282–296.

Seymour Sewell, R. B., "Oceanographic exploration, 1851–1951", *Science Progress* (1952). Vol. 40, pp. 403–418.

Taylor, E. G. R., "The origin of continents and oceans: a seventeenth century controversy", *Geographical Journal* (1950). Vol. 116, pp. 193–198.

Thorndike, L., *A history of magic and experimental science*, 8 vols, New York: Columbia University Press (1923–58).

Yonge, C. M., "Development of marine biological laboratories", *Science Progress* (1956). Vol. 44, pp. 1–15.

b) Contributions to the history of oceanography published 1964 onwards

Adams, J., "Historical studies in the Faroe-Shetland Channel", *Ocean Challenge* (1995), Vol. 6(1), pp. 14–17.

Burstyn, H. L., "The historian of science and oceanography", *Bulletin de l'Institut océanographique, Monaco* (1968). Numéro spécial 2(2), pp. 665–672.

Burstyn, H. L., "Theories of winds and ocean currents from the discoveries to the end of the seventeenth century", *Terrae Incognitae* (1971). Vol. 3, pp. 7–31.

Burstyn, H. L., (1972) "Pioneering in large-scale scientific organization: the *Challenger* expedition and its report. 1. Launching the expedition", *Proceedings of the Royal Society of Edinburgh* (1972). Series B, no. 72, pp. 47–61.

Burstyn, H. L., "Science pays off: Sir John Murray and the Christmas Island phosphate industry, 1886–1914", *Social Studies of Science* (1975). Vol. 5, pp. 5–34.

Carpine-Lancre, J., "La Société d'Océanographie du golfe de Gascogne", *L'aventure maritime, du golfe de Gascogne à Terre-Neuve*, eds J. Bourgoin & J. Carpine-Lancre, Paris: Éditions du CTHS (1995), pp. 31–42.

Carpine-Lancre, J., & Saldanha, L. V. C. *Dom Carlos I, Roi de Portugal, Albert Ier, Prince de Monaco, Souverains océanographes*, Lisbon: Fondation Calouste Gulbenkian (1992).

Deacon, M. B., "Founders of marine science in Britain: the work of the early Fellows of the Royal Society", *Notes and Records of the Royal Society of London* (1965). Vol. 20, pp. 28–50.

Deacon, M. B., (1968) "Some early investigations of the currents in the Strait of Gibraltar", *Bulletin de l'Institut océanographique* (1968). Numéro spécial 2(1), pp. 63–75.

Deacon, M. B., "An early theory of ocean circulation: J. S. von Waitz and his explanation of the currents in the Strait of Gibraltar", *Progress in Oceanography* (1985). Vol. 14, pp. 89–101.

Deacon, M. B., "Crisis and compromise: the foundation of marine stations in Britain during the late 19th century', *Earth Sciences History* (1993). Vol. 12, pp. 19–47.

Deacon, M. B., "British governmental attitudes to marine science", *Man and the maritime environment*, ed. S. Fisher, Exeter: Exeter University Press (1994), pp. 11–35.

Dean, J. D., *Down to the sea: a century of oceanography*, Glasgow: Brown, Son and Ferguson (1966).

De Vorsey Jnr, L., "Pioneer charting of the Gulf Stream: the contributions of Benjamin Franklin and William Gerard de Brahm", *Imago Mundi* (1976). Vol. 28, pp. 105–120.

Frankel, H., "The development, reception, and acceptance of the Vine–Matthews-Morley hypothesis", *Historical Studies in the Physical Sciences* (1982). Vol. 13, pp. 1–39.

Hisard, P., "Mise en évidence du contre-courant équatorial dans l'océan Pacifique et l'océan Atlantique au cours de la première moitié du XIXe siècle", *Océanis* (1993). Vol. 19, pp. 1–68.

Idyll, C. P. (ed.), *Exploring the ocean world: a history of oceanography*, New York: Thomas Y. Crowell (1969). Printed in U.K. as *The science of the sea: a history of oceanography*, London: Thomas Nelson (1970).

Kortum, G., "An unpublished manuscript of Alexander von Humboldt on the Gulf Stream", *Deutsche Hydrographische Zeitschrift* (1990). series B, no. 22, pp. 122–130.

Laird, E. S., "Robert Grosseteste, Albumasar, and medieval tidal theory", *Isis* (1990). Vol. 81, pp. 684–694.

Marvin, U. B., *Continental drift: the evolution of a concept*, Washington: Smithsonian Institution Press (1973, 2nd edition 1981).

McConnell, A., "Historical methods of temperature measurement in Arctic and Antarctic waters", *Polar Record* (1978). Vol. 19, pp. 217–231.

McConnell, A., *No sea too deep. The history of oceanographic instruments*, Bristol: Adam Hilger (1982).

McConnell, A., "The flowers of coral – some unpublished conflicts from Montpellier and Paris during the early 18th century", *History and Philosophy of the Life Sciences* (1990). Vol. 12, pp. 51–66.

Mills, E. L. (ed.), *One hundred years of oceanography: essays commemorating the visit of H.M.S. Challenger to Halifax, May 9–19, 1873*, Halifax, Nova Scotia: Dalhousie University (1975).

Mills, E. L., *Biological oceanography: an early history*, Ithaca, N.Y.: Cornell University Press (1989).

Mills, E. L., "The history of oceanography: introduction", *Earth Sciences History* (1993a). Vol. 12, pp. 1–4.

Mills, E. L., "The historian of science and oceanography after twenty years", *Earth Sciences History*, (1993b). Vol. 12, pp. 5–18.

Mörzer Bruyns, W. F. J., "Matthew Fontaine Maury and the introduction of oceanography to the Netherlands in the second half of the 19th century", *American Neptune*, (1988). Vol. 48, pp. 44–49.

Oreskes, N., "The rejection of continental drift", *Historical Studies in the Physical and Biological Sciences* (1988). Vol. 18, pp. 311–348.

Paffen, K. & Kortum, G., *Die Geographie des Meeres. Disziplingeschichtliche Entwicklung seit 1650 und heutiger methodischer Stand.* Kieler Geographische Schriften, Vol. 60, Kiel: Geographical Institute of Kiel University (1984).

Pfannenstiel, M., "Das Meer in der Geschichte der Geologie", *Geologische Rundschau*, (1970). Vol. 60, pp. 3–72.

Peterson, R. G., Stramma, L. & Kortum, G., "Early concepts and charts of ocean circulation", *Progress in Oceanography* (1996). Vol. 37, pp. 1–115.

Rehbock, P. F., "Huxley, Haeckel, and the oceanographers: the case of *Bathybius haeckelii*", *Isis* (1975). Vol. 66, pp. 504–533.

Rehbock, P. F., "The early dredgers: 'naturalizing' in British seas, 1830–1850", *Journal of the History of Biology* (1979). Vol. 12, pp. 293–368.

Rice, A. L., & Wilson, J. B., (1980) "The British Association Dredging Committee: a brief history", *Oceanography: the past*, eds M. Sears & D. Merriman, New York: Springer (1980), pp. 373–385.

Rozwadowski, H. M., "Small world: forging a scientific maritime culture for oceanography", *Isis*, (1996). Vol. 87, pp. 409–429.

Schlee, S., *The edge of an unfamiliar world. A history of oceanography*, New York: E. P. Dutton (1973). Issued in U. K. as *A history of oceanography. The edge of an unfamiliar world*, London: Robert Hale (1975).

Solis Santos, C., "Captain Henry Sheeres, his currents; o aire y agua en el estrecho de Gibraltar", *Arbor* (1992). Vol. 141, pp. 75–113.

Vanney, J.-R., *Le mystère des abysses: histoire et découvertes des profondeurs océaniques*, Paris: Fayard (1986).

Van Sittert, L. "'The handmaidens of industry': marine science and fisheries development in South Africa, 1895–1939", *Studies in History and Philosophy of Science* (1995). Vol. 26, pp. 531–558.

c) Recent historical writing in related topics

Allen, D. E., *The naturalist in Britain: a social history*, London: Allen Lane (1976).

Alter, P., *The reluctant patron: science and the state in Britain, 1850–1920*, (First published in German [1982] as *Wissenschaft, Staat, Mäzene: Anfänge moderner Wissenschaftspolitik in Grossbritannien, 1850–1920.* Stuttgart: Klett-Kotta), New York: Berg (1987).

Davies, G. L., *The Earth in decay. A history of British geomorphology, 1578–1878*, London: Macdonald (1969).

Fogg, G. E., *A history of Antarctic science*, Cambridge: Cambridge University Press (1992).

Friedman, R. M., *Appropriating the weather: Vilhelm Bjerknes and the construction of a modern meteorology*, Ithaca: Cornell University Press (1989).

Greene, M. T., "History of geology", *Osiris* (1985). Vol. 1, pp. 97–116.

Hamlin, C., "James Geikie, James Croll and the eventful Ice Age", *Annals of Science* (1982). Vol. 39, pp. 565–583.

Hunter, M., *Establishing the new science. The experience of the early Royal Society*, Woodbridge, Suffolk: Boydell & Brewer (1989).

Kutzbach, G., *The thermal theory of cyclones. A history of meteorological thought in the nineteenth century*, Boston: American Meteorological Society (1979).

LeGrand, H., *Drifting continents and shifting theories*, Cambridge: Cambridge University Press (1988).

MacLeod, R. M., (1976) "Science and the Treasury: principles, personalities and policies, 1870–85", *The patronage of science in the 19th century*, ed. G. L'E. Turner, Leiden: Nordhoff (1976), pp. 115–172.

MacLeod, R. M. & Rehbock, P. F., *Nature in its greatest extent: Western science in the Pacific*, Honolulu: University of Hawaii Press (1988).

Oldroyd, D., *Thinking about the earth: a history of ideas in geology*, London: Athlone Press (1996).

Purver, M. S., *The Royal Society: concept and creation*. London: Routledge and Kegan Paul (1967).

Rehbock, P. F., *The philosophical naturalists: themes in early 19th century British biology*, Madison: University of Wisconsin Press (1983).

Ritchie, G. S., *The Admiralty chart: British naval hydrograpphy in the nineteenth century*. (First published [1967] London: Hollis and Carter), Edinburgh: Pentland Press (1995).

Rudwick, M. J. S., *The great Devonian controversy: the shaping of scientific knowledge among gentlemanly specialists*, Chicago: University of Chicago Press (1985).

Winsor, M. P., *Starfish, jellyfish, and the order of life: issues in 19th century science*, New Haven: Yale University Press (1976).

SHIPS AND EXPEDITIONS

Forster, J. R., *The* Resolution *Journal of Johann Reinhold Forster, 1772-1775*, ed. M. E. Hoare, London: Hakluyt Society series 2, vols 152–155 (1982).

Guberlet, M. L., *Explorers of the sea: famous oceanographic expeditions*, New York: Ronald Press (1964).

Halley, E., *The three voyages of Edmond Halley in the* Paramore, *1698-1701*, N. J. W. Thrower, ed. N.J.W. Thrower, London: Hakluyt Society series 2, vols 156–157, (1981).

Hardy, A. C., *Great waters. A voyage of natural history to study whales, plankton and the waters of the Southern Ocean in the old Royal Research Ship* Discovery, London: Collins (1967).

Hsü, K. J., *The Mediterranean was a desert: a voyage of the* Glomar Challenger, Princeton, New Jersey: Princeton University Press (1983).

Levere, T. H., *Science and the Canadian Arctic. A century of exploration, 1818-1918*, Cambridge: Cambridge University Press (1993).

Linklater, E., *The voyage of the* Challenger, London: John Murray (1972).

MacLeod, R. M., "Imperial reflections in the South Seas: the Funafuti expeditions,

1896–1904", *Nature in its greatest extent: western science in the Pacific*, eds R. M. MacLeod & P. F. Rehbock, Honolulu: University of Hawaii Press (1988), pp. 159–191.

Müller, G., *Die Challenger-Expedition. Zum tiefsten Punkt der Weltmeere, 1872–1876*, Stuttgart: Thienemann (1984).

Nelson, S. B., *Oceanographic ships – fore and aft*, Washington, D.C.: Office of the Oceanographer of the Navy (1971).

Rehbock, P. L., *At sea with the scientifics. The* Challenger *letters of Joseph Matkin*, Honolulu: University of Hawaii Press(1992).

Reinke-Kunze, C., *Den Meeren auf den Spur. Geschichte und Aufgaben der deutschen Forschungsschiffe*, Herford: Koehler (1986).

Rice, A. L., "The oceanography of John Ross's Arctic expedition of 1818: a reappraisal", *Journal of the Society for the Bibliography of Natural History* (1975). Vol. 7, pp. 291–319.

Rice, A. L., *British oceanographic vessels, 1800–1950*, London: The Ray Society (1986).

Rice, A. L. (ed.) *Deep-sea challenge: the John Murray/Mabahiss Expedition to the Indian Ocean, 1933–34*, Paris: UNESCO (1986).

Ross, M. J., *Ross in the Antarctic; the voyages of James Clark Ross in Her Majesty's Ships* Erebus *and* Terror, *1839–1843*, Whitby: Caedmon (1982).

Rubin, M. J., "Thaddeus Bellingshausen's scientific programme in the Southern Ocean, 1818–1821", *Polar Record* (1982). Vol. 21, pp. 215–229.

Schlee, S., *On almost any wind. The saga of the oceanographic Research Vessel* Atlantis, Ithaca, N.Y.: Cornell University Press (1978).

Wüst, G., "The major deep-sea expeditions and research vessels, 1873–1960: a contribution to the history of oceanography", *Progress in Oceanography* (1964). Vol. 2, pp. 3–52.

INSTITUTIONS

Allard, D. C., *Spencer Fullerton Baird and the U.S. Fish Commission. A study in the history of American science*, New York: Arno Press (1978).

Benson, K. R., "The Naples Stazione Zoologica and its impact on the emergence of American marine biology", *Journal of the History of Biology*, (1988). Vol. 21, pp. 331–341.

Benson, K. R., "Laboratories on the New England shore: the 'somewhat different direction' of American marine biology", *New England Quarterly*, (1988). Vol. 56, pp. 55–78.

Deacon, M., "British oceanographers and the Challenger Society, 1903–1922', *Deutsche Hydrographische Zeitschrift* (1990). Series B, no. 22, pp. 34–40.

Ehlers, P., Duensing, G. & Heise, G., *Schiffahrt und Meer: 125 Jahre maritime Dienste in Deutschland*, Herford: E. S. Mittler (1993).

Heppel, D. & West, F. M., "Sinel, Hornell, and the Jersey Biological Station", *Société Jersiaise Annual Bulletin*, (1989). Vol. 25, pp. 69–102.

Lee, A. J., *The Ministry of Agriculture, Fisheries and Food's Directorate of Fisheries Research: its origins and development*, Lowestoft: Ministry of Agriculture, Fisheries and Food (1992).

Maienschein, J., *One hundred years exploring life, 1888–1988: the Marine Biological Laboratory at Woods Hole*, Boston: Jones and Bartlett (1988).

Marshall, S. M., "An account of the Marine Station at Millport", ed. J. A. Allen, *Occasional Publication*, no. 4, University Marine Biological Station: Millport (1987).

Metz, C. B. (ed.), "The Naples Zoological Station and the Marine Biological Laboratory [Woods Hole]: one hundred years of biology", *Biological Bulletin* (1985). Vol. 168 (supplement), pp. 1–207.

Morrell, J. & Thackray, A. (eds), *Gentlemen of science. Early correspondence of the British Association for the Advancement of Science*, Camden 4th series, vol. 30. London: Royal Historical Society (1984).

Pinsel, M. I., *150 years of service on the seas: a pictorial history of the U.S. Naval Oceanographic Office from 1830 to 1980*, vol. 1 (1830–1946), Washington, D.C.: Government Printing Office (1981).

Raitt, H., & Moulton, B., *Scripps Institution of Oceanography; the first fifty years*, San Diego: Ward Ritchie Press (1967).

Shor, E. N., *Scripps Institution of Oceanography. Probing the oceans, 1936–1976*, San Diego: Tofua Press (1978).

Southward, A. J. & Roberts, E. K., "One hundred years of marine research at Plymouth", *Journal of the Marine Biological Association of the U.K.* (1987). Vol. 67, pp. 465–506.

BIOGRAPHICAL

Agassiz, G. R., *Letters and recollections of Alexander Agassiz with a sketch of his life and work*, New York: Houghton Mifflin; London: Constable (1913).

Browne, E. J., "The making of the memoir of Edward Forbes", *Archives of Natural History* (1981). Vol. 10, pp. 205–219.

Cohen, E. H. & Ross, J. S., The commonplace book of Edmond Halley. *Notes and Records of the Royal Society of London* (1985). Vol. 40, pp. 1–40.

Deacon, M.B., "G. Herbert Fowler (1861–1940): the forgotten oceanographer", *Notes and Records of the Royal Society of London* (1984). Vol. 38, pp. 261–296.

Desmond, A., *Huxley: the devil's disciple*, London: Michael Joseph (1994).

Groeben, C., *Charles Darwin, 1809–1882; Anton Dohrn, 1840–1909: correspondence*, Naples: Macchiaroli (1982).

Gunther, A. E., *The life of William Carmichael M'Intosh, M.D., F.R.S. of St Andrews (1838–1931). A pioneer in marine biology*, St Andrews University Publications, no. 61, Edinburgh: Scottish Academic Press (1977).

Harrison, A. J., "William Saville-Kent, F.L.S., F.Z.S., F.R.M.S.", *Papers and Proceedings of the Royal Society of Tasmania* (1988). Vol. 122, pp. 165–178.

Heuss, T., *Anton Dohrn: a life for science*, ed. C. Groeben (translated by L. Dieckmann from *Anton Dohrn*, 2nd edition, Tübingen: Rainer Wunderlich [1948]), Berlin: Springer (1991).

Hoare, M. E., *The tactless philosopher: Johann Reinhold Forster (1729–98)*, Melbourne: Hawthorn Press (1976).

Hunter, M. C. W., *Letters and papers of Robert Boyle: a guide to the manuscripts and microfilm*, Bethesda, Md: University Publications of America (1992).

Mill, H. R., *An Autobiography*, ed. L. D. Stamp, London: Longmans Green (1951).

Rice, A. L., Burstyn, H. L. & Jones, A. G. E., "G. C. Wallich M. D. – megalomaniac or mis-used oceanographic genius?", *Journal of the Society for the Bibliography of Natural History* (1976). Vol. 7, pp. 423–450.

Ritchie, G. S., *No day too long. An Hydrographer's tale*, Edinburgh: Pentland Press (1992).

Smith, C. & Wise, M. N., *Energy and empire. A biographical study of Lord Kelvin*, Cambridge: Cambridge University Press (1989).

Speak, P., "William Speirs Bruce: Scottish nationalist and polar explorer", *Polar Record* (1992). Vol. 28, pp. 285–292.

Stamp, T. & Stamp, C., *William Scoresby: Arctic Scientist*, Whitby: Caedmon (*c.* 1975).

Stebbing, T.R.R., *The naturalist of Cumbrae: a true story, being the life of David Robertson*. London: Kegan Paul, Trench, Trübner (1891).

Stoye, J., *Marsigli's Europe, 1680–1730. The life and times of Luigi Ferdinando Marsigli, soldier and virtuoso*, New Haven: Yale University Press (1994).

Williams, F. L., *Matthew Fontaine Maury, scientist of the sea*, New Brunswick, N.J.: Rutgers University Press (1963).

Wilson, G. & Geikie, A., *Memoir of Edward Forbes, F.R.S.*, Cambridge and London: Macmillan (1861).

MODERN OCEANOGRAPHY

Summerhayes, C. P. and Thorpe, S. A., *Oceanography: an illustrated guide*, London: Manson.

INDEX OF PERSONS

A

Abel, Clarke, 234, 240
Adee, Swithin, 183
Adelard *of Bath*, 29, 31
Agassiz, Alexander, 309, 370, 375, 379, 380, 381, 392
  Challenger report, 368, 370
  Challenger Office, visits, 367, 369
  marine life, 374, 383, 391
  coral reefs, 385
Agassiz, Jean Louis, 333, 379
Aglionby, *Dr*, 149, 157, 158
Aimé, Georges, 282, 298, 319, 350
  currents, 298
  marine instruments, 288–290
  temperature observations, 288–289
  wave action, 286, 289
Airy, George Biddell, *Sir*, 264–265, 266, 267–269, 326
Albert, *Prince of Monaco*, 370, 382, 391, 392
Albo, Francisco, 42
Albumazar, 27, 30
Aldrich, Pelham, 335, 343, 350, 380
Alembert, Jean le Rond d' (1717–1783), 189
Alexander *the Great*, 13, 26
Allman, George, 306, 314, 353, 369
Alpetragius, *astronomer* (12th century), 30
Anaxagoras *of Clazomenae*, 5, 6, 10
Anaximander, *Greek scientist*, 4
Anaximenes, *Greek scientist*, 4
Anderson, W. S., 385
Anson, George, 185
Arago, François, 232, 277–279, 285
Archimedes, 12
Arctowski, Henryk (1871–1958), 389
Argyll, *Duke of. See* Campbell, George Douglas, *Duke of Argyll*

Aristarchus *of Samos*, 14
Aristotle, 4, 5–11, 13, 25–26, 28, 31, 124
Aubrey, John, 99, 117
Auteroche, Jean Baptiste Chappe d', 184

B

Bache, Alexander Dallas, 286, 291
Bacon, Francis, *Sir*, 46, 50, 72, 260
Bacon, Roger, 29, 30, 50
Bailey, Jacob Whitman, 297
Baillie, C. W., 336
Baird, Spencer F., 379
Balard, Antoine Jérome, 238
Balfour, A. F., 386
Baliani, Giovanni Battista (1582–1666), 94
Ball, William, 73, 76
Banks, Joseph, *Sir*, 185, 189, 201, 227, 228, 234, 252
  influence on marine science, 223, 225, 226
Barnett, E., *Captain*, 283
Barrington, Daines, 189
Barrow, John, *Sir*, 228
Bartholomew, *the Englishman* (13th century), 29
Bassett-Smith, Percy W., 384
Baudin, Nicolas, 193
Baumé, Antoine, 212
Bayly, William, 186–187, 188, 191–192, 193, 204, 205, 342
Beale, John, *Dr*, 127
Beaufort, Francis, *Sir*, 233, 255, 257, 259, 260, 266, 269, 283
Beche, Henry T. de la. *See* De la Beche, Henry T.
Becher, A. B., 290
Bede, *the Venerable*, 21–24, 25
Beechey, Frederick William, 230, 231, 268, 270, 284, 291, 292, 293

Beeckman, Isaac, 53
Belcher, Edward, *Sir*, 283
Belknap, George, 350
Bell, F. Jeffrey, 368
Bellingshausen, Thaddeus, 232
Bentinck, John Albert (1737–1775), 201
Bérard, Auguste (1796–1852), 278, 288
Berg, John V. van. *See* Van Berg, John V.
Bergman, Torbern, 188, 205, 211
Bernoulli, Daniel, 251, 252, 258
Berryman, H. O., 294–296
Bessels, Emil (1847–1888), 353
Besson, Jacques, 40
Bethell, G. R., 335, 337, 340
Biot, Jean Baptiste, 287
Birch, Thomas (1705–1766), 73, 127
Biscoe, John, 234
Bjerknes, Vilhelm, 390
Bladh, *Swedish observer of sea temperatures*, 205, 213
Blagden, Charles, *Sir*, 199, 201, 202–203, 206
Blancanus, Joseph, 41, 50
Bois, Coupvent des, 289
Bolland, Richard, 10, 86–87, 147, 149, 155, 316
    Strait of Gibraltar, 111, 127, 142–144, 146, 150
Bonnycastle, Charles, 285
Borda, Jean Charles de (1733–1799), 184
Borlase, William, 214–215
Borradaile, Lancelot, 392
Boswall, J. D., 233
Bougainville, Hyacinthe de, 231
Bouguer, Pierre, 215
Boulduc, Gilles François, 211
Bourne, Gilbert C., 378
Bourne, William, 43–45, 46, 47, 49, 50
Boyle, Robert, 117–129, 8, 81, 83, 84–85, 88, 93, 134, 142, 144, 150, 154, 155, 171, 175, 179, 184, 238, 285, 410
    desalination, 271–281
    importance, 128–129
    marine instruments, 118
    marine thermometers, 121–122
    mercury barometers, 73, 118
    effect of pressure, 121–122
    pressure, 122–123

salinity, 124–126, 167, 176
sea, movement at depths, 123–124
temperatures, 120–121
Bréguet, Abraham Louis (1747–1823), 279
Bremontier, Nicolas, 214
Brereton, William, *Lord*, 73, 80
Briggs, Henry, 70
Bromley, Arthur C. B. (d. 1909), 335
Brooke, John Mercer (1826–1906), 295
Brouncker, William, *Viscount*, 73, 74, 76, 78, 79, 98
Brown, Alexander Crum, 352
Brownrigg, William, 201
Bruce, Alexander, *Earl of Kincardine*, 72, 77
Bruce, William Speirs, 373, 391, 393
Buchan, Alexander, 376
Buchan, David, 228
Buchanan, John Young, 336, 337, 338, 358, 370, 374, 381–382, 386, 389, 393
    Bathybius, 352
    Equatorial undercurrent, 382
    gases, dissolved, 357, 364
    pressures at depths, 353–354
    sediments, sea floor, 343, 351
    temperatures, 354
Buffon, *Comte de*. *See* Leclerc, George-Louis, *Comte de Buffon*
Buist, George, 289, 290
Bunt, T. G., 266, 334
Bunten, *instrument maker*, 277, 279
Burgoyne, John, *Sir*, 291
Buridan, Jean, 29, 30, 31–32
Burley, Walter, 31
Burt, *instrument maker*, 234
Byron, John (1723–1786), 185

C

Caesalpinus, Andreas, 51
Calver, Edward Killiwick (1813–1892), 312, 313, 315
Campbell, Colin, 181
Campbell, George Douglas, *8th Duke of Argyll*, 383, 384
Campbell, Hugh, 184
Candale, *Comte de*. *See* Foix, François de, *Comte de Candale*

Calderwood, W. L., 391–392
Canton, John, 191, 215
Cardano, Girolamo, 53
Carnac, John (1716–1800), 201
Carpenter, Alfred, 350, 380
Carpenter, Philip H., 367, 378
Carpenter, William B., 306–328, 333–
  335, 339, 356, 368, 369, 373, 376,
  378, 396
  marine life, 307, 308, 309, 313, 342–
  343
  oceanic circulation, 310, 313–314,
  316–317, 375
    controversy, 318–328, 343–348
  Strait of Gibraltar, 315–316, 319,
  324–325
  transparency, 310
Carpenter, William Lant, 312, 315
Carteret, Philip, 185
Cary, William (1759–1825), 226
Casella, Louis Paschal (1809–1897),
  311, 348–350
Cassini, Jacques (1677–1756), 251
Cassini, Jean Dominique (1625–1712),
  178
Cavalleri, Antoine (1698–1763), 251
Cavendish, Charles, Lord (1703–1783),
  191
Cavendish, Henry (1731–1810), 191,
  192, 226
Chamisso, Adelbert von, 232
Charcot, Jean Baptiste (1867–1936), 389
Charles II, King of England, 73, 83, 127
Charnock, John, 213
Childrey, Joshua, 72, 73, 93, 102, 136,
  154
  tides, 103–108, 109
Chimmo, W., 297, 325, 345
Cholmley, Hugh, 135, 136, 140, 141
Chrystal, George (1851–1911), 374
Chumley, James, 375
Clarke, Timothy, Dr, 73
Coëntre, Le, engineer, 284
Colepresse, Samuel, 100–101, 102, 108
Colladon, Jean Daniel (1802–1893), 302
Collins, Greenvile, 111
Columbus, Christopher (d. 1506), 47
Colwall, Daniel (d. 1690), 85
Cook, James, 185–186, 188, 189, 191–
  192, 202, 207, 213

Coriolis, Gaspard Gustave de (1792–
  1843), 268
Coupvent des Bois. See Bois, Coupvent
  des
Crabtree, William, 71
Crates of Mallos, 24, 29
Crawshay, L., 393
Croll, James, 343, 356
  Gulf stream, 318–319
  oceanic circulation, controversy, 320–
  328, 344–348
Croune, William, 73, 160
Croze, J. C. de la, 127
Cusa, Cardinal. See Nicholas, Cardinal
  of Cusa
Cuningham, William, 49, 50
Cunningham, Joseph Thomas (1859–
  1935), 378
Cutler, John, Sir, 160

D

D'Alembert, Jean. See Alembert, Jean
  le Rond d'
D'Urville, Jules Dumont. See Urville,
  Jules Dumont d'
Da Vinci, Leonardo. See Vinci, Leo-
  nardo da
Dalton, John (1766–1844), 16
Dalrymple, Alexander, 202
Damascene, St John, 14
Dampier, William, 171
Dana, James D., 383
Danby, Earl of. See Osborne, Thomas,
  Earl of Danby
Darondeau, Benoit Henri (1805–1869),
  287
Darwin, Charles, 284, 286, 299, 368,
  371, 383–384
  coral reefs, theory, 383–384
Darwin, George H., Sir, 14, 270, 387
Daubeny, Charles, 238, 287
Daubrée, Gabriel Auguste (1814–1896),
  287
Daussy, Pierre (1792–1860), 256, 283
Davenport, Francis, 108, 111
Davis, J. E., 297, 336, 354
Davy, Humphry, Sir (1778–1829), 229,
  236, 238, 240

Davy, John (1790–1868), 236, 237, 246, 277, 299
Day, Archibald, *Sir*, 269
Dayman, Joseph, 296
De Bougainville, Hyacinthe. *See* Bougainville, Hyacinthe de
De'Dondi, Giacomo. *See* Dondi, Giacomo de'
De Foix, François. *See* Foix, François de
De Fourcroy, Charles René. *See* Fourcroy, Charles René de
De Freycinet, Louis. *See* Freycinet, Louis de
De Galaup, Jean François. *See* Galaup, Jean François de
De la Beche, Henry T., 241, 277
De la Pérouse. *See* Galaup, Jean François de
De Monts, Pierre du Guast. *See* Monts, Pierre du Guast de
De Pagès, *Comte*. *See* Pagès, Pierre Marie François de
De Pourtalès, Louis François. *See* Louis François de
De Saussure, Horace-Bénédict. *See* Saussure, Horace-Bénédict de
De Tessan, Urbain Dortet. *See* Tessan, Urbain Dortet de
Delamétherie, Jean Claude, 192–193, 206, 208, 210, 278
Delphinus, Fredericus, 50
Democritos, *Greek scientist*, 5
Denham, Henry, 265, 284
Des Bois, Coupvent. *See* Bois, Coupvent des
Desaguliers, John Theophilus, 180, 184
Descartes, René, 52, 72, 73, 109
Dessiou, Joseph, 255, 257
Dickson, Henry N., 390, 391
Dicuil, *Irish writer*, 21
Dieulafait, L., 351
Dittmar, William, 374
Dohrn, Anton, 369, 377–378
Donati, Vitaliano, 204, 215
Dondi, Giacomo de' (*ca.* 1293–1359), 31, 50
Dortet de Tessan, Urbain. *See* Tessan, Urbain Dortet de
Douglas, Charles, *Sir*, 186, 205

Drake, Francis, *Sir*, 159
Du Fresne, Marion. *See* Fresne, Marion du
Du Petit-Thouars, Abel. *See* Petit-Thouars, Able du
Dubuat, Pierre Louis Georges (1734–1809), 321, 322, 325, 326
Dudley, Robert, 49, 50
Dumont d'Urville, Jules. *See* Urville, Jules Dumont d'
Duncan, P. Martin, 367–368
Duperrey, Louis Isidore (1786–1865), 231
Durocher, Joseph Marie Elisabeth (1817–1860), 287

E

Edrisi, 25, 27
Ehrenberg, Christian, 297
Ekman, Gustaf, 390
Ekman, Vagn Walfrid, 390
El Mas'údí. *See* Mas'údí, El
Elliot, Gilbert, *2nd Earl of Minto* (1782–1859), 281
Ellis, Henry, 183, 184, 186, 193, 204, 205, 209
Empedocles, *Greek scientist*, 5
Ent, George, *Sir* (1604–1689), 73
Eratosthenes, 11, 12, 13–14
Ericsson, John, 284
Erman, Georg Adolf (1806–1877), 278
Euler, Leonard, 251
Evelyn, John, 73, 79, 111
Everett, Joseph D., 326, 327
Ewart, James Cossar, 373, 379

F

Fabré, *commander of the Chevrette*, 232
Fairborne, Palmes, *Sir*, (1644–1680), 144
Ferrel, William, 294, 326–327
Finch, John, *Sir*, 147–148
Findlay, A. G., 292, 318
Fisher, Osmond, 327
Fitzgerald, Robert, 127, 128
Fitzroy, Robert, 263, 286, 292, 296, 348
tides, 266–267
Fleming, John, 238–239
Flinders, Matthew (1774–1814), 194

Foix, François de, *Comte de Candale* (*d.* 1594), 49
Folger, *captain*, 202
Forbes, David (1828–1876), 313, 318
Forbes, Edward (1815–1854), 281, 282, 298, 306, 318, 336
Forchhammer, Georg, 287–288, 289, 374
Forster, Johann Reinhold, 187–188, 189, 205, 207, 213
Forster, George, 187, 205
Forsskål, Peter, 184
Foster, George Carey (1835–1919), 327
Foster, Henry, 233
Fourcroy, Charles René de (1715–1791), 252
Fournier, Georges, 7, 50, 53, 55, 56, 133
Fowler, G. Herbert, 391
Foxe, Luke, 41, 70
Franklin, Benjamin, 199–202, 203, 212, 213, 214, 215
Franklin, John, *Sir*, 228, 229–230, 231, 277, 283
Frembly, John, 233
Frémy, Edmond (1814–1894), 287
Fresne, Marion du, *French explorer*, 192
Freycinet, Louis de, 231
Frobisher, Martin, 47
Froude, William (1810–1879), 356
Fulton, Thomas Wemyss, 379, 391
Furneaux, Tobias, 186
Fyfe, Andrew, 230, 237, 238

G

Galaup, Jean François de, *Comte de la Pérouse*, 192
Galen, Claudius 50
Galilei, Galileo (1564–1642), 50, 156
   tides, 44, 49, 51–52, 73, 94, 159
   currents, 48
Gassendi, Pierre, 6, 95, 156
Gay-Lussac, Louis Joseph, 237
Gedge, H. J., 381
Gerald *of Wales*, 28, 29–30
Gibson, John, 379
Gilbert, Humphrey, *Sir*, 47, 70
Gilbert, William, 41, 46, 48, 49, 51, 108
Giles *of Rome*, 30
Gilpin, George (*d.* 1810), 226

Gladstone, William Ewart (1809–1898), 335
Glaisher, James, 296
Goddard, Jonathan, 97–98
Goschen, George (1831–1907), 333, 334
Gould, R. T., 282, 283
Gran, H. H., 391
Greaves, John, 70–71, 133, 155, 162
Green, Charles, 185
Green, George, 286
Grisogono, Federico, 50
Grosseteste, Robert, *Bishop of Lincoln*, 30
Günther, Albert, 367
Guppy, Henry Brougham, 384–385

H

Hadley, George, 203, 268
Haeckel, Ernst, 352, 353, 369, 383, 388
Hales, Stephen, 180, 181–184, 186, 213–214, 230, 234, 241
Hall, Basil, 225, 234
Halley, Edmond, 149–150, 171, 175, 251
   trade winds, 49, 167–169
   tides, 109–111
   evaporation and precipitation, 146–147, 169–170
Harman, John, *Sir*, 139
Harris, Rollin A., 270
Haughton, Samuel, 270, 284, 327
Hawkins, Richard, *Sir*, 48
Hawksbee, Francis, 181
Hearder, Jonathan (1810–1876), 297
Heawood, Edward, 389
Helland-Hansen, Bjorn, 390, 391
Henry, Thomas, 212
Henshaw, Thomas (1618–1700), 73, 156
Herdman, William Abbott (1858–1924), 370, 374, 379, 392
Herodotus, 10, 13
Herschel, John, *Sir*, 258, 284, 291, 292
   tides, 262–263
   currents, 292, 294, 319, 323
Hewett, William, 266
Hill, Abraham, 73, 76, 155, 156
Hipparchus, 12
Hjort, Johan, 388, 391, 392
Holmes, Robert, *Sir*, 79, 83, 85, 409

Hooke, Robert, 71, 78, 82, 85, 149, 150, 154, 157, 160–162, 165, 167, 171, 175, 242
  barometers, 76, 77
  density, effect of temperature, 158
  earthquakes, 158–159
  gravitational attraction, 97, 108
  marine life, 166
  sounding machines, 79–83, 155–157, 160–163, 180
  thermometers, 163–164
  water samplers, 80, 155
Hooker, Joseph Dalton, *Sir*, 283, 309, 334, 366, 368
Hope, Thomas Charles, 209
Hörner, Johann Caspar, 226, 232, 236, 239–240, 278
Horrocks, Jeremiah, 71–72, 93
Hoskyn, Richard, 297
Hull, Edward, 386
Humboldt, Alexander von,
  meteorology, 242
  oceanic circulation, 210, 280, 281, 310
  temperatures, 203, 236–237
Hutchinson, William, 259
Huxley, Thomas Henry, 299, 334, 351, 366, 368, 369, 372, 378
  marine life, 371
  Bathybius, 309, 352–353
  habitat, 297
Huygens, Christiaan, 77
Hyrne, Henry, 105–106, 107, 114

I

Ibn Khordazbeh. *See* Khordazbeh, Ibn
Ibn Magid. *See* Magid, Ibn
Irish (the) Augustin, 21
Irvine, Robert, 385
Irving, *Dr*, 189, 191, 193, 211, 225
Isidore *of Seville*, 21, 22

J

Jacobsen, Oscar Georg Friedrich (1840–1889), 374
James II, *King of England*, 84, 109, 142
Jameson, Robert, 227, 230, 233, 242
Jameson, William, 233

Jeffreys, John Gwyn, 311, 312, 314, 315, 317, 334, 342
Jenkin, Fleeming, 306
Johnston, Keith, 319, 320
Jordan, William Leighton, 376

K

Kellett, Henry, 283
Kelvin, *Lord*. *See* Thomson, William, *Lord Kelvin*
Kepler, Johann (1571–1630), 48, 51, 108, 255
Khordazbeh, Ibn, 26
Kincardine, *Earl of. See* Bruce, Alexander, *Earl of Kincardine*
King, Erasmus, 181
King, James (1750–1784), 192
King, William, 297
Kircher, Athanasius, 5, 11, 49, 53, 55, 56, 58, 72, 133, 164
Kirwan, Richard, 199
  oceanic circulation, 208
  salinity, 212–213
  temperatures, 205, 236
Knox, Robert (?1641–1720), 158
Knox, Robert (1791–1862), 233
Knudsen, Martin, 390–391
Kotzebue, Otto von, 323, 279, 293
Krümmel, Otto, 41–42
Krusensturn, A. J., 226, 232, 290

L

La Pérouse, *Comte du. See* Galaup, Jean François de, *Comte de la Pérouse*
Lagrange, E. J. B. Bouillon, 237
Lagrange, Joseph Louis, 253, 264
Lalande, Joseph le Français de, 49, 252
Lamarche, *French naval officer*, 237
Landaff, *Bishop of. See* Watson, Richard, *Bishop of Landaff*
Langhorne, William, *Sir*, 126
Lankester, Edwin Ray, 314, 369, 378, 388, 392
Laplace, *Marquis de. See* Simon, Pierre, *Marquis de Laplace*
Lardner, Dionysius, 279
Laughton, John Knox, 319, 320, 321, 323

Lavoisier, Antoine Laurent de, 184, 211 212
Lawson, John, *Sir*, 135, 142
Le Coëntre. *See* Coëntre, le, *Engineer*
Leclerc, George Louis, *Comte de Buffon*, 204, 207, 210
Leibnitz, G. W., 204
Leigh, Charles, 128, 146
Lenz, Emil, 241, 242, 276, 369
  oceanic circulation, 293
  salinity, 239
  specific gravity, 232
  temperatures, 232, 310, 324, 346
  thermometers, pressure effects, 241, 277, 281
Lichtenberg, F. D., 212
Lincoln, *Bishop of*. *See* Grosseteste, Robert, *Bishop of Lincoln*
Linnaeus, Carl (1707–1778), 215
Linschoten, J. H. van, 55, 125
Lister, Martin, 158
Liston, Robert, *Sir*, 225–226
Livingstone, Andrew, *Captain*, 203–204, 233
Lloyd, John Augustus, 265
Lovén, Sven, 281
Lubbock, John William, *Sir*, 263, 276, 283, 334
  tidal studies, history, 23, 29
  tides, 254–259, 270
Lussac, Louis Joseph Gay. *See* Gay-Lussac, Louis Joseph
Lyell, Charles, *Sir*, 273, 276, 286, 317
Lyman, Theodore, 367
Lyons, Israel, 189

M

McClintock, Leopold, *Sir*, 296, 297
McIntosh, William C., 367, 379
Mackenzie, Murdoch, *the elder* (d. 1797), 252, 259
Maclaurin, Colin, 203, 251
Maclear, John L. P., 335, 380
Macmichael, William, 225
Macrobius, 24, 29
Maddison, R. E. W., 128
Magellan, Ferdinand (?1480–1521), 41–42

Magid, Ibn (15th century), 27
Magnaghi, *captain, Italian navy*, 379
Magnus, Olaus, 41
Mairan, Jean Jacques Dortous de, 204
Makarov, S. O. (1849–1904), *Russian navy, admiral*, 377, 381
Malaguti, F. J. (1802–1878), 287
Mallet, Robert, 286
Marcet, Alexander, 229, 242, 243, 276, 277, 278, 287, 293
  chemical analysis of sea water, 225–226, 237, 238
  salinity, 230, 239
  temperature of maximum density, 240, 241, 279
  water sampler, 229
Mariotte, Edmé (1620–1684), 49
Markham, Clements, *Sir*, 237
Marsden, William, 214, 290
Marsigli, Luigi Ferdinando, *Count*, 124, 172, 184, 215, 293
  currents, Bosporus (Strait), 147–149, 157–158, 175, 179, 207, 226
  Gulf of Lyons, study, 175–180
  temperatures, 204, 288
Martens, Frederick, 86
Martyr, Peter, 47
Massey, Edward, 234–235
Mas'údí, El, 25–26, 132
Matthews, D. J., 393
Maury, Matthew Fontaine, 280, 291, 293–295, 297, 310
Maxwell, Murray, 234
Maxwell Lyte, F., 284
May, (?) Walter William, *Commander* (1830–1896), 307, 309
Mead, Joseph, 5
Mersenne, Marin, 40, 41, 69, 156
Meyer, H. A., 326
Michell, John, 159, 215
Miklukho-Maklai, N. N., 377, 398–399
Mill, Hugh Robert, 352, 381, 388
  expeditions, 378, 379, 389
  continental margin, 386
Miller, William Allen, 311, 336, 348
Milne, John, 386
Milne-Edwards, Alphonse, 306, 377
Minto, *Earl of, 2nd*. *See* Elliot, Gilbert, *2nd Earl of Minto*

Mitchell, *naval engineer*, 257
Mohn, Henrik (1835–1916), 318, 377
Montagu, Edward, *Earl of Sandwich*, 74, 75, 85, 132, 134, 135, 407
Montet, Jacques (1722–1782), 211
Montanari, Geminiano, 147, 148
Monts, Pierre du Guast de (*ca*. 1560–1611), 120
Moore, Jonas, *Sir*, 85, 134, 157
Moore, W. Usborne, 380–381
Moray, Robert, *Sir*, 73, 74, 79, 83, 88, 94, 101, 154, 167, 172
    observations at sea, 77, 99
    soundings, 76, 78
    temperatures, 77
    tides, 72, 84, 93, 98, 102, 256, 270
Moren, Auguste, 287
Moseley, Henry Nottidge, 335, 337, 343, 367, 370, 374, 378
Multhauf, R. P., 71
Munden, Richard, *Sir*, 127
Murchison, Rockerick, *Sir*, 317
Murray, John (*d*. 1820), 237
Murray, John (?1786–1851), 233
Murray, John, *Sir* (1841–1914), 336, 358, 359, 378, 379, 380, 388, 392, 393
    bathymetry, 386–387, 389
    Challenger report, 42, 366, 370, 372–373, 376, 387
    coral reefs, 383–387
    expeditions, 374, 378, 379, 389, 392
    marine life, 342–343, 383–387
    sediments, 351, 357, 375

N

Nairne, Edward, 192, 206, 207
Nansen, Fridtjof, 388, 389, 390
Nares, George, *Sir*, 339, 350, 380
    expeditions, 324, 325, 335
    submarine topography, 338, 340, 354
Neckham, Alexander, 29
Negretti and Zambra, *instrument makers, London*, 296, 297, 348–350
Neile, Paul, *Sir*, 73, 83
Newman, John, *instrument maker*, 230
Newton, Isaac, *Sir*, 84, 95, 117, 166, 167, 175

    tides, 108–111, 252, 258
    waves, 263, 286
Nicholas, *Cardinal of Cusa*, 39—40, 156
Nicholson, Henry Alleyne (1844–1899), 403
Nordenskjold, Otto (1869–1928), 389
North, Dudley, *Sir*, 154
Norwood, Richard, 99, 101

O

Oldenburg, Henry, 72, 80–86 *passim*, 94, 96, 97–99, 100–103, 106, 107, 118, 141, 154, 167
    influence on marine science, 88
Osborne, Thomas, *Earl of Danby*, 127
Oughtred, William, 70
Owen, Samuel, 342

P

Pagès, Pierre Marie François, *Comte de* (1748–1793), 192
Palissy, Bernard, 45–46
Palmer, Henry Robinson (1795–1844), 256–257
Paris, Matthew, 29
Parker, I. P., 284
Parrot, Georg Friedrich, 232, 241, 242, 276, 293
Parry, William Edward, 228, 229, 230, 231, 232
Patton, Philip, 207–208
Paul *the deacon*, 24
Pearcey, Frederick, 366, 375
Pepys, Roger, *M.P.*, 108
Pepys, Samuel, 87, 111, 135–136, 140, 141, 142
Percy, Hugh, 146
Péron, François, 192, 193, 194, 205–206
Pérouse, *Comte de la*. See Galaup, Jean François de, *Comte de la Pérouse*
Petermann, August Heinrich (1822–1876), 318, 319
Petit, Pierre (1598–1677), 80–81
Petit-Thouars, Abel du, 277, 279, 369
Pettersson, Otto, 388, 390, 392

Petty, William, *Sir*, 141
Peyssonel, Jean André, (1694–1759), 203
Pfaff, Christian Heinrich, 212
Philipot, Thomas, 108
Phipps, Constantine, 209, 211
  Arctic expedition, 189–191
  soundings, 189–191, 213
  temperatures, 191, 193, 204, 205
Pigafetta, Francisco Antonio (1491–1535?), 42
Pillsbury, John Elliott, 380
Plato, 5, 6, 8, 13
Pliny, 7, 13, 15, 20, 23, 175, 201
Plot, Robert, 6, 146, 169
Plutarch, 21, 191
Poisson, Siméon Denis (1781–1840), 268
Posidonius, 11, 14–15, 23, 25, 132
Pourtalès, Louis François de, *Count*, 309, 333, 368, 369
Powell, George, 234
Powle, Henry, 99, 100, 113
Pownall, Thomas, 202, 203
Prescott, J., 233
Prestwich, Joseph, 323–324, 345–346
Pringle, John, *Sir*, 199, 201
Priscien *of Lydia*, 25
Proust, Joseph Louis, 238
Ptolemy, 21
Puehler, Christoff, 40
Pullar, Frederick, 389
Pullen, W. J. S., 296
Pytheas *of Marseilles*, 13, 14

Q

Quetelet, Lambert, 260, 291

R

Ramsden, Jesse (1735–1800), 192
Rattray, John, 378
Redfield, William C., 292
Reid, William, 290
Renard, Alphonse F., 374–375
Rennell, James, 220, 222, 233, 237, 242, 292, 319
  currents, 221–224, 235, 265, 290, 294, 326

Riccioli, Giovanni Battista, 41, 50, 52, 74, 156
Richards, George H., *Sir*, 311, 312, 315, 324, 334
Robertson, David, 378
Robison, John, *Sir* (1778–1843), 264, 274
Rochford, *diver* (17th century), 120, 123
Romme, Charles (1744–1805), 243
Rooke, Lawrence, 73, 75–76, 88, 134
Ross, James Clark, *Sir*, 269, 277, 280, 288, 309, 366, 369
  marine life, 282
  soundings, 282–283
  temperatures, 281, 297
Ross, John, *Sir*, 228, 229, 241, 242, 281, 309, 369
  clamm, 229, 282, 296
Rouch, Jules, 375, 389
Rouelle, Hilaire (1718–1779), 238
Rumford, *Count*. *See* Thompson, Benjamin, *Count Rumford*
Rupert, *Prince* (1619–1682), 83
Russell, John Scott, 264–265
Rutherford, Andrew, *Lord*, 135

S

Sabine, Edward, 223, 229, 237, 240, 307, 309
  temperatures, 242, 290–291
  magnetism, 242
Sagroevic, Nikola, 49
St Ambrose, 21
St Augustine, 21
Sandström, J. W., 390
Sandwich, *Earl of*. *See* Montagu, Edward
Sars, George Ossian, 306, 308, 309, 369, 377
Sars, Michael, 306, 308, 309
Saussure, Horace-Bénédict de, 204–205, 288
Scaliger, Julius Caesar, 53, 55
Schmidt, Oscar, 367
Schott, Gerhard, 392
Scoresby, William (1760–1829), 226
Scoresby, William (1789–1857), 226, 230, 231, 233, 237, 286
  explorations, 227–229

Scoresby, William (1789–1857), *cont.*
  temperatures, 228, 240
  effect of pressure on wood, 241
  magnetism, 242
Scott, Robert Falcon, 389
Seleucus *of Babylon*, 12, 14, 23
Shackleton, Ernest, 389
Sheeres, Henry, 133, 134, 135–142, 144, 149, 155
Shortland, Peter, 296, 297, 310
Shovell, Cloudesly, *Sir*, 222
Siemens, Charles William, *Sir*, 311, 312, 315
Sigsbee, Charles D., 380
Simon, Pierre, *Marquis de Laplace*, 192, 267, 268, 270
  tides, 252, 254, 255, 256, 258
  waves, 263–264
Six, James, 226, 242
Slare, Frederick, 158
Slingesby, Henry, 73
Sloane, Hans, *Sir*, 128
Smith, P. W. Bassett. *See* Bassett-Smith, P. W.
Smith, Thomas, 133, 134, 146, 155, 157
Smyth, William Henry, 239, 323
Solander, Daniel (1736–1782), 201
Solinus, Gaius Julius, 21
Somerville, Mary, 263, 286
Southwell, Robert, *Sir*, 133, 141
Sparrman, Andreas, 188
Spence, Graeme, 253–254, 259, 268
Spratt, Thomas Abel B., 281, 282, 296, 297, 319–320, 344
Spry, William J. J., 342
Stafford, Richard, 101
Stanley, Owen, 283, 286
Stevenson, Thomas, 286
Stevin, Simon, 51, 53
Stirling, William, 335
Stokes, George G., 324, 333
Strabo, 10, 11–12, 13, 132
Stuart, James, *See* James II, 84
Stubbs, Henry, 118, 125, 134, 184
Sturm, Jacques Charles François (1803–1855), 302
Sturmy, Samuel, 102, 108
Suhm, Rudolph von Willemöes. *See* Willemöes-Suhm, Rudolph von

T

Taisnier, Johann, 50, 53
Tait, Peter Guthrie, 336, 354
Talbot, Henry Fox, 284–285
Taylor, Geoffrey, *Sir*, 393
Taylor, John, 108
Taylor, Silas, 80, 85, 94
Tennant, Smithson, 225–226, 237
Tessan, Urbain Dortet de, 279, 285, 292
Théel, Hjalmar, 369
Thompson, Benjamin, *Count Rumford*, 199, 276
  oceanic circulation, 208–210, 239–240
Thomson, Anthony, 381, 386
Thomson, Charles Wyville, 306, 312, 317, 324, 343, 372–373, 383, 388, 396
  Challenger expedition, 334
  Challenger report, 354, 366–370
  density, effect of pressure, 285
  evolution, 317, 372, 376
  marine life, 306–308, 309–310, 317–318, 338–339, 342–343, 351–352, 357–358, 373–374
  ocean basins, 387
  oceanic circulation, 312–315, 318–319, 323, 356
  sediments, 338–339, 351
  temperatures, 308–309, 310, 354, 373
Thomson, David, 285
Thomson, Frank Tourle, 350
Thomson, William, *Lord Kelvin*, 324, 334, 336, 356
Thouars, Abel du Petit. *See* Petit-Thouars, Abel du
Thoulet, Marie Julien Olivier, 388, 391
Tizard, Thomas Henry, 335, 337, 350, 354, 357, 370, 373, 374
Tørnoe, David Hercules (1856–1907), 374
Torre, Bernard de la, 47
Torricelli, Evangelista, 49, 53
Traill, Thomas Stewart, 237
Tuckey, James Kingston, 243, 253, 265, 285
Tyndall, John, 311, 315

U

Urville, Jules Dumont d', 232, 277–278, 280, 285, 288, 293

V

van Berg, John V., 71
van Linschoten, J. H. *See* Linschoten, J. H. van
Varen, Bernhard, 7, 40, 41, 52, 53, 55–58
Verril, Addison Emery, 375
Victoria, *Queen of England*, 358
Vinci, Leonardo da, 42–43, 45, 132
Vogel, H. A., 237
von Chamisso, Adelbert. *See* Chamisso, Adelbert von
von Lenz, Emil. *See* Lenz, Emil von
von Humboldt, Alexander. *See* Humboldt, Alexander von
von Willemöes-Suhm, Rudolph. *See* Willemöes-Suhm, Rudolph von
Voss, Isaac, 98, 155

W

Walcot, William, 128
Wales, William, 186–188, 193, 204, 205, 207, 342
Walferdin, François Hippolyte, 284
Walker, John, 215, 265
Walker, William, 265, 286
Wallace, Alfred Russel, 284
Waller, Richard, 82, 108
Wallich, George, 297, 298, 299, 306, 318
Wallis, John, 154
    tides, 83, 93–98, 100–103, 106–108, 111
Ward, Seth (1617–1689), *Bishop of Salisbury*, 103
Washington, John, 266
Watson, Richard, *Bishop of Llandaff*, 187, 199, 205, 207, 212–213
Wauchope, Robert, 233–234, 236, 277
Weber, Ernst Heinrich (1795–1878), 264
Weber, Wilhelm Eduard (1804–1891), 264
Weddell, James, 233
Wellesley, Arthur, *Duke of Wellington*, 260

Werner, Abraham, 210–211
Westrumb, Johann Friedrich (1751–1819), 238
Wharton, William J. L., *Sir*, 320, 344, 380, 381, 391
Wheatstone, Charles, *Sir*, 311, 312
Whewell, William, 266, 283, 286
    tides, 257–264, 266, 268–269, 270, 276, 334
    mean sea level, 265
White, Martin, 266, 268
Wild, John James, 336, 357
Wilke, Johann Karl (1732–1796), 213
Wilkes, Charles, 277
Wilkins, John, 79, 120
Willemöes-Suhm, Rudolph von, 335, 338, 353
Willes, Richard, 47
William *of Auvergne*, 31
William and Mary, *King and Queen of England*, 142
Williams, Jonathan, 203, 236
Williamson, Joseph, *Sir*, 127, 144, 155, 156
Wilson, Alexander, 186, 197
Wilson, George, 287
Winthrop, John, 79–80, 85, 94, 101–102, 106
Wollaston, William Hyde, 238, 239, 285, 323
Woodward, John, 5, 159, 169
Wren, Christopher, *Sir*, 71, 72–73, 93, 118, 155, 156
Wren, Thomas, 83
Wright, Edward, 49, 50
Wüst, Georg, 147
Wyche, Peter, 99

X

Xenophanes, *Greek scientist*, 5, 6

Y

York, *Duke of. See* James II, *King of England*
Young, Thomas, 235, 254

SUBJECT INDEX

A

Academie del Cimento, Florence, 206
Académie Royale des Sciences, Paris, 206, 251, 277
Acceleration of sounding machines, 81–83, 150–157
Account of an experiment touching the different weight of cold and warme water (Hooke), 97, 158
Account of the Arctic Regions (Scoresby), 227
Accumulators, rubber, for use in soundings, 296
Admiralty, United Kingdom. *See* United Kingdom. Admiralty
Admiralty Manual of Scientific Enquiry (1849), 291
Adventure, H.M.S., 186, 187
Agulhas Current, 45, 222
  chart, 220, 221
  discovery, 47
Albatross, U.S.S., 380, 385
Alceste, H.M.S., 234
Alert, H.M.S., 380
Alexander, H.M.S., 228
Almagestum Novum (Riccioli), 50, 74
Amateurs, observations at sea, 232–233
American Journal of Science and Arts, 367
Amphidromes, 270. *See also* Tides, rotary systems
Animadversions on Dr. Wallis's Hypothesis of Tides (Childrey), 103, 109
Annals and Magazine of Natural History, 367, 368
Annelids, 338, 367
Antarctic Convergence, 281
Antarctic expeditions, 389
  Bellingshausen (1819–1821), 232
  French, 192

Antarctic Ocean. *See* Salinity; Specific gravity; Temperatures
Arab science, 24–27
Arcano (Dell') del Mare (Dudley), 49, 50
Arctic Convergence, 319
Arctic expedition, 350, 389
Arctic Ocean. *See* Currents; Salinity; Soundings; Specific gravity; Temperatures; Water samples
Aristotelian influence, 29, 39
Ark (barge), 378
Astrolabe (French ship), 232, 277
Astronomia Nova Seu de Motu Stellae Martis (Kepler), 51
Atlantic Ice Patrol, 393
Atlantic Ocean. *See* Currents; Equatorial Current; Temperatures; Tides
Atlantis, 45, 158
Atmosphere
  circulation, 169
  pressure, 49, 52–53
    effect on tides, 256
    measurement, 99
    variations, cause, Halley, 168
Atolls. *See* Coral reefs
Azoic zone, theory of, 281–282, 297–298, 299, 306, 307–309, 313. *See also* Marine life, theories

B

Balaena expedition (1892–1893), 389
Barometers, 73
  Boyle, 118
  water, Hooke, 76
Barometric pressure. *See* Atmosphere, pressure
Bathybius, 309, 337, 352–353
Bathymetric charts, 295, 355, 392
  Maury, 294–295

Bathymetric surveys, freshwater, 389
Bay of Biscay. *See* Soundings
Beacon, H.M.S., 281
Beagle, H.M.S., 263, 266, 267, 383
Belgica expedition, 389
Belgium, marine science in, 260, 291, 389, 390
Bergen Museum, Norway, 391
Bering Strait expedition (1825), 231
Black Sea. *See* Depths; Subterranean channels
Blake U.S. survey ship, 380
Blossom, H.M.S., 231
Board of Longitude, United Kingdom, 186, 189, 194, 234, 235
Board of Ordnance, United Kingdom, 213
Board of Trade, United Kingdom, 296, 297
    Meteorological Department, 292, 296
Bombay Geographical Society, 290
Bombay Times, 290
Bonite (French ship), 285, 287
Bores,
    Dordogne River, 45–46
    Severn River, 102
Bosporus (Strait). *See* Currents; Density
Bristol Institution, 257
Britain. *See* United Kingdom
Britannia Baconica, 72
British Almanac (1830), 255
British Association for the Advancement of Science, 255, 264, 269, 286, 287, 317, 324, 328, 333, 334–335, 346, 353, 356, 370, 378, 383
    marine science forum, 257, 324, 390
    sea level studies, 263, 266
    support for work, 257, 307, 334
British Museum, Natural History, London, 366, 368, 388
British Rainfall Association, 388
Bromine, 238
Buccaneer, S.S., 381, 382
Bulldog, H.M.S., 298
Buoyancy, 8
Burt's buoy and nipper, 234. *See also* Sounding machines
Byzantine Empire, 24

C

Cabinet Cyclopaedia, 279
Calcium Sulphate. *See Bathybius*
Canyons, continental shelf, 386
Carbonic acid, 337, 343, 384
Carte générale bathymetrique des océans, 392
Catalan Atlas (1375), 32
Centre of gravity of earth and moon, 95–97
Certain Errors in Navigation (2nd ed.) (Wright), 49
Challenger Commission, 366, 373
Challenger expedition (1872–1876), 317, 333–358, 388
    collections, 366, 369, 372
    importance, 368–369, 377
    marine biology, contributions to, 357
    marine science programme, 337–338
    shortcomings, 356–357
Challenger, H.M.S., 335–358 *passim*, 366, 368, 373, 374, 375, 376, 377, 380, 381, 383, 386, 387
Challenger Office, Edinburgh, 374–375
Challenger Report, 42, 370–376, 387, 388
Challenger Society, 392
Chemical analysis of sea water, 211–212, 237–238, 286–288, 374
    Dead Sea, 225. *See also* Salinity; Chlorine titration
Chevrette (French ship), 232
Chlorine titration, 390–391
Chronometers, 40, 220–222
    tests, 186
Circle of mean temperature, Ross, 280–281. *See also* Temperatures, depths, theories
Circles (The) of Proportion (Oughtred), 70
Clamms, deep sea, 282, 296
    invented by Ross, 229
Clays, deep sea, 338–339, 343, 351, 387
    minerals in, 351
    origin, 375
Climate and Time (Croll), 345, 348
Clyde Sea Area, 378–379
Coast Survey, United States. *See* United States Coast Survey

Coasts, effect of currents and waves, 44, 286
Cogitata Physico-Mathematica (Mersenne), 40, 69
Colonial Office, United Kingdom, 290
Committee on Marine Researches. *See* Royal Society. Committee on Marine Researches
Compleat (The) Geographer, 109, 170
Congress, U.S.S., 284, 294
Considerations and Enquiries Concerning Tides (Moray), 99
Continental shelf, 176
  canyons, 386
  emergence of term, 386
  off Norway, 41
Continental slope, 176, 297, 386
Convection cell, 293. *See also* Oceanic circulation
Copernican system, 48, 50
Coquille (French ship), 231, 232
Coral reefs
  experimental borings, Royal Society, 385
  theories
    Darwin, 383–387
    Murray, 383–387. *See also* Great Barrier Reef
Cosmographical (The) Glasse (Cuningham), 49
Cosmolabe (Le) (Besson), 40
Cosmos (Humboldt), 310
Cotidal lines, 254–256, 258–262, 266, 269
  North Sea, 260–261
Course of Experimental Philosophy (Desaguliers), 184
Crinoids, 306, 367
Current drogues, 339–340, 357
Current logs, Massey, 234
Current meters
  Aimé, 289
  Pillsbury, 380, 381. *See also* Drift bottles
Currents of the Atlantic Ocean (Rennell), 222
Currents
  Atlantic Ocean
    Columbus, 47
    Rennell, 222–224
    United States Coast Survey, 292

Arctic Ocean, 229
Bay of Biscay
  Rennell, 222, 223
Bosporus (Strait), 11, 12, 147–149, 225–226, 319–320, 380
  Marsigli, 148–149
Boyle, 118
charts, Agulhas current, 220–221
  Atlantic Ocean, 224, 291–292
  world ocean, 57
correlation of information, 220
density differences as cause of. *See* Oceanic circulation
depth, 124, 134, 339
earth's rotation, effect, 203, 294, 326, 390. *See also* Ekman spirals
Indian Ocean, 26
mapping, Atlantic Ocean, 382
monsoons, effect, 26, 292
North Sea, 391
observations, *Challenger* expedition, 337, 338
  methods, 48
  Ross, 280
  Tessan, 279. *See also* Drift bottles
reversals, monsoons, 26, 292
speed, measurement, 134
Strait of Bab-el-Mandeb, 380, 381
Strait of Gibraltar, 12, 25, 70–71, 74, 84, 132–150, 223, 225, 239, 289
  Observations, 315–316, 324–325
  Sandwich's expedition, 407–408
  seasonal variations, 139–140
  theories, 48
  early ideas, 132–133
  evaporation, 146–147, 149–150
  Greaves, 133
  Sheeres, 136–142
  subterranean channels, 133. *See also* Undercurrents
theories
  17th century, 48
  19th century, 292–294
  Bourne, 44–45
  earth's rotation, 49, 292
  evaporation–precipitation cycle, 48
  gravitation, W. L. Jordan, 376
  Kircher, Varen, 56
  wind, 56, 171, 222. *See also* Oceanic circulation

Currents (*cont.*)
　Thermometers for measurement, 202–204. *See also* Agulhas Current; Antarctic Convergence; Arctic Convergence; Equatorial current, counter-current *and* undercurrent; Gulf Stream; Guinea Current; Greenland currents; Labrador Current; Oceanic circulation; Peru Current; Undercurrents
Cyclops, H.M.S., 352

D

Dacia, S.S., 381
Dead water, 390
Decades of the Ocean (Martyr), 47
Deep sea soundings. *See* Soundings
Deep water waves. *See* Waves, deep-water
Denmark, marine science in, 184, 287–288, 377, 390–391
Density, 8–9, 162
　depths
　　Bosporus, 226
　　observations, Holmes, 410
　pressure, supposed effect on, 285
　salinity, effect on, 118, 238–239
　temperature, effect on, 118, 158, 238–239
　temperature of maximum, fresh-water, 160, 206
　　sea water, 207, 230, 239–242, 277, 279, 281. *See also* Specific gravity
Density currents, demonstrations, Carpenter, 148–149, 313–314; *See also* Oceanic circulation
Deposits. *See* Sea floor; Sediments
Depths, measurement by pressure, 155–156, 297
　Hooke, 162–163. *See also* Soundings
Depths of the Sea (C. W. Thomson), 317
Desalination, 127–128
Description (A) of Ventilators (Hales), 184
Deutschland (German ship), 391
Dialogi sopra i due massimi sistemi del mondo, Tolemaico e Coperniciano (Galileo), 51
Diatoms, 343

Directions for Observations and Experiments to be made by Masters of Ships, Pilots, and other Fit Persons in their Sea-Voyages (Royal Society), 78, 84, 86, 154
Directions for Seamen Bound for far Voyages (Rooke), 75–76, 78, 79, 82, 83, 85, 88, 93, 99, 154, 155
Discours admirable de la nature des eaux et fontaines (Palissy), 45
Discourse of a discovery for a new Passage to Cataia (Gilbert), 47
Discourse of Earthquakes (Hooke), 158
Discourse of Winds, Breezes, Storms, Tides and Currents (Dampier), 171
Discourse (A) touching the Current in the Streight of Gibraltar (Sheeres), 136–140, 141
Discoverer, U.S.S., 282
Discovery, H.M.S., 389
Discovery Committee, 393
Dissertation sur les glaces (Mairan), 204
Dolphin, U.S.S., 294
Dorothea, H.M.S., 228, 230
Drache, S.S., 377
Dredges, 282, 312
　Challenger expedition, 337, 338
　wire rope, 380
　Hooke, 155
Drift bottles, 382, 391
Drogues. *See* Current drogues

E

Earl of Halifax (ship), 183
Earth and moon, common centre of gravity, 95–97
Earthquakes, 45, 158–159, 214–215, 286. *See also* Tidal waves
Earth's interior, temperatures, 204
East Greenland Expedition (1818), 228–230. *See also* North West Passage
East India Company, 75, 119, 126, 220, 263, 290
Echo-sounding, 279, 282, 284–285
　experiments, 285, 393
Edinburgh Philosophical Journal (ed. by Jameson), 227
Egeria, H.M.S., 380, 384

Ekman spirals, 390
Elements in sea water, 211, 287. *See also* Chemical analysis; Minerals
Emerald, H.M.S., 186, 207–208
Encyclopaedia Britannica, 254
Encyclopaedia Metropolitana, 267
Encyclopaedic writers, Middle Ages, 20–28
Endeavour, H.M.S., 185
English Channel. *See* Tide tables; Tides
Enterprise, U.S.S., 377
Enterprize, H.M.S., 283
Equatorial Current, 47, 223, 339–340
Equatorial Countercurrent, 48, 292
Equatorial Undercurrent, 339–340, 381–382
Equilibrium of land and sea, 31–32, 158–159, 178, 182–183
Equilibrium theory of tides. *See* Tides, theories, equilibrium
Equinoxes. *See* Tides
Erebus, H.M.S., 277, 282
Espérance (French ship), 231
Essay about the Flux and Reflux of the Sea (Wallis), 93–96
Essay on Currents at Sea (Mead), 5
Essay towards a first approximation to a map of cotidal lines (Whewell), 258
Essay towards a Natural History of the Earth (Woodward), 5
Eurydice, H.M.S., 234
Evaporation, 7, 21, 170
    Mediterranean Sea, 132–133, 138–139
Evaporation–precipitation cycle, 5–6, 45
Evolution, theory of, 317–318, 371
Exotericarum Exercitationum ad Cardanum (Scaliger), 53
Expeditions. *See* Oceanographic expeditions; Voyages

F

Fairy, H.M.S., 266
Fish Commission, United States, 379, 380
Fisheries research, government support, 379
Florentine Academy. *See* Academie del Cimento, Florence

Fluorine, 287
Fluxu (De) et Refluxu Maris Anglicani (Burley), 31
Flying Fish, H.M.S., 380, 384
Foraminifera, 297, 306, 309, 338, 342–343. *See also* Globigerina; Diatoms; Radiolarians
Fossils, marine, 11, 43, 159, 306, 315, 351
Founders of Oceanography (Herdman), 370
Fram expedition, 389, 390
Français (French ship), 389
France, marine science in, 80–81, 175–179, 184–185, 192–194, 210, 214, 215, 231–232, 238, 251–252, 277–279, 282, 287, 288–290, 377, 391
Fredericksteen, H.M.S., 233
Freezing point of sea water, 206
Frolic, H.M. brig, 284

G

Gannet, H.M.S., 297
Garland (ship), 379
Gases, in sea water, 287, 288, 337, 357, 374
Gatty Marine Laboratory, Aberdeen, 379
Gauss expedition, 389
Gazelle, S.S., 350
Gentleman's Magazine, 181, 184
Géographe (French ship), 193
Geographia Generalis (Varen), 53
Geographical Journal, 267
Geographische Mittheilungen (Pettermann), 319
Geography (Strabo), 10
Geological Manual (De la Beche), 241
Geological Society, 324, 367, 368
Geological Survey, Edinburgh, 321
Geological Survey, United Kingdom, 277
German expeditions, 390, 391
German North Sea Commission, Kiel, 326, 377
German North Sea Expedition (1871), 335, 336
Germany, Navy. Hydrographic Department, 377

Germany, marine science in, 350, 367, 377, 389, 390, 391, 393
Globigerina, 297, 309, 338
   distribution, 342–343
Gravitation, inverse square law, 108–109
Great Barrier Reef, 385
Great Britain. *See* United Kingdom
Greek scientists, 4–16
Greenland currents, 48, 85–86
Guinea current, 223, 292
Gulf Stream, 47, 223, 290–291, 323
   caused by trade winds, 203, 318
   observations, 201–203, 297
      Challenger expedition, 339
      United States Coast Survey, 309, 339
   temperature as cause, 294, 319
   upwelling, 326
   volume of flow, Strait of Florida, 321, 344–345

H

Handbook for observations by amateurs, 392
Harmonices Mundi (Kepler), 51
Hassler, U.S.S., 368
Herald, H.M.S., 283, 284, 294
Hirondelle, S.S., 382
Historia Naturalis (Pliny), 15, 20
Histoire Naturelle générale et particulière (Buffon), 204
Histoire Physique de la Mer (Marsigli), 176–180, 293
History of Learning (ed. by de la Croze), 127
Hour glasses, 39. *See also* Pendulums. Chronometers
Humboldt current. *See* Peru current
Humidity, measurement, 99
Hydra, H.M.S., 296, 297
Hydraulic and Nautical Observations on the Currents in the Atlantic Ocean (Pownall), 202
Hydrographic Department, U.K. *See* United Kingdom Hydrographic Department
Hydrographic surveys, 111, 142, 252, 253, 294–297, 380, 384

Hydrographie contentant la Théorie et la Pratique de Toutes les Parties de le Navigation (Fournier), 53
Hydrometers, 84, 118, 178, 312, 337
Hydrophones, 285
Hydrostatic balances, 184, 192
Hydrostatical Discourse (Boyle), 123

I

Icebergs, origin, 86, 207
Indian Ocean. *See* Currents; Salinity; Temperatures; Tides
Ingolf (Danish ship), 377
Inquiries ffor Tanger and other parts of Barbary (Oldenberg), 141
Institut für Meereskunde, Berlin, 391
Institut National, Paris, 206
Institut Océanographique, Paris, 391
Instruments
   Boyle, 118
   Challenger expedition, 336–337
   Hooke, 160–165
   Porcupine expedition, 311–312
   Specific gravity, difficulties of determination, 237. *See also* Clamms; Current drogues; Dredges; Hydrometers; Hydrophones; Lead and line; Log and line; Messenger devices; Pendulums; Piezometers; Pressure gauges; Sounding machines; Thermometers; Tide gauges; Trawls
International co-operation, tidal observations (1835), 260–261; 390. *See also* Scientific Co-operation
International Council for the Exploration of the Sea, 390–391
   area of research, 392
   Laboratory, Christiania, Norway, 390
International Fisheries Exhibition, London (1883), 378
International Geographical Congress
   6th, 392
   9th, 392
   forum for marine science, 390
Introductorium in Astronomiam (Albumazar), 27, 30
Investigator, H.M.S., 193–194, 233

Investigator (Royal Indian Marine Survey Ship), 380
Iodine, 238
Isabella, H.M.S., 228
Islands, volcanic, 158, 387
Italy, marine science in, 147, 204, 377, 379
Jackal, H.M.S., 379, 390
Journal de Physique (ed. by Delamétherie), 206
Journal des Sçavans, 80, 83

K

Kermadec Trench, 386
Kiel Commission. *See* German North Sea Commission, Kiel
Knight Errant, H.M.S., 373

L

Labrador current, 48
Lalla Rookh (yacht), 336
Lark, H.M.S., 384
Lead and line, 10, 41, 42, 155, 156
Life of Boyle (Birch), 127
Life of Hooke (Waller), 82
Lightning, H.M.S., 307–310 *passim*, 318, 324, 333, 335, 337, 373
Lindisfarne, monastery, 24
List of Oceanic Depths (Admiralty), 381
Liverpool Marine Biology Committee, 379
Liverpool Tidal Observatory, 393
Loan Exhibition of Scientific Apparatus, London (1876), 358
Log and line, 48
London Gazette, 159
Long waves. *See* Waves, long
Longitude, determination, 58–59
  effect on study of currents, 202
  Halley, 170–171
Luminescence, 74, 215, 408, 410

M

Machines. *See* Instruments
Magellan Strait, 45, 47
Magnete (*De*), Gilbert, 41, 48, 51

Magnetic field, Southern Hemisphere, 280
Magnetic observations, *Challenger* expedition, 337
Magnetic variations, 170
Maelstrom, 24
  hypothesis of tides, 29
Mallard (yacht), 370
Manganese nodules, 338, 351, 370
Marine acoustics, 394
Marine Biological Association of the United Kingdom, 378
  Plymouth Laboratory, 378, 391
Marine biology, 215
  19th century, 281–282, 298–299, 307, 388
  Aristotle, 8
  Challenger expedition, 357
  government support, 19th century, 307
  Porcupine expedition (1870), 315, 316
  See also Marine life
Marine chemistry, 19th century, 286–288. *See* Chemical analysis
"Marine Diver", Scoresby, 227
Marine dynamometer, 286
Marine fossils. *See* Fossils, Marine
Marine geophysics, 394
Marine life, 306–313
  at great depths, 166, 229, 281–282, 297–298, 309, 315, 318, 337, 357
  characteristics, 338–339
  theories of distribution
    bi-polarity, Murray, 383. *See also* Azoic zone; Diatoms; Foraminifera; Marine Biology; Plankton
    Agassiz, 383
Marine optics, 215, 394
Marine science
  Bourne, 43–45
  British Association for the Advancement of Science, influence, 257
  Centres, Edinburgh, 369, 387–388
    Scandinavia, 390–391
  17th century, 69, 73
  18th century, exploratory voyages, 183–194
  19th century, 220, 242–243, 276–277, 298, 389–394

Marine science (*cont.*)
    co-operation, international conference
        (1853), 260–261, 291, 390
    co-ordination of observations, 291–
        292
    description, 58
    discipline, 3–4, 59–60
    East Greenland expedition, 229
    Edinburgh, 19th century, 369–370,
        373
    effect of exploratory voyages, 277
    government support, 376–378, 391
    need for, 179–180, 235
    measurement in, 3, 39, 167, 236
        Boyle, 118
        instruments, 234–235
        World Wars I and II, 393
    naval surveys, 379–380
    North West Passage expedition
        (1818), 229
    regional studies
        Clyde Sea Area, 378–379
        Gulf of Lyons, 175–180
    research
        government support, 311, 333–335
        naval survey ships, 19th century,
            295–298, 381
        scientific co-operation, 19th century,
            260–261, 290, 291–292
    submarine telegraph cables, influence
        on, 298
    Titanic disaster, influence on, 393
Marine scientists, international com-
    munity, 369–370, 390–393
Marine Stations, development of, 377–
    379
Marine zoology, catalogue of publica-
    tions, 392. *See also* Marine life
Mariners' Magazine, 102
Maritime Geography (Tuckey), 243,
    253
Marsden squares, data co-ordination,
    290
Mathematical Magick (Wilkins), 120
Meadows of Gold and Mines of Gems
    (Mas'údí), 25, 26
Mean sea level. *See* Sea level, mean
Measurements
    importance, 3
    Renaissance science, 39

Mediterranean Journall (Bolland), 86,
    142, 144
Mediterranean Sea
    Aristotle's description, 11
    origin, Strato, 11–12. *See also* Evapo-
        ration; Soundings; Strait of
        Gibraltar; Subterranean chan-
        nels; Temperatures; Tides
Medusa (yacht), 378
Mensura (De) Orbis Terrae (Dicuil), 25
Mercury, 238
Messenger devices, 230, 288
Meteor expedition, 393
Meteorologica (Aristotle), 4, 5, 7, 8, 9,
    10, 28, 31
Meteorological Office, United King-
    dom. *See* United Kingdom,
    Board of Trade, Meteorological
    Office
Meteorology
    Halley, 167–168
    observations, 280, 337, 376, 393
    observatories, planned, 99, 290
    scientific co-operation in, 290, 291
Michael Sars (Norwegian ship), 392
Mid-Atlantic Ridge, 340, 354–355
Milesian philosophers, 4–5
Minerals
    deep sea deposits, 351
    relative concentrations, sea water,
        374. *See also* Elements
Monaco, marine science in, 382, 392
Monsoons, 26, 168
Moon, effect on tides, 13, 14, 30. *See
    also* Tides, theories
Motu (De) Marium et Ventorum Liber
    (Voss), 98, 155
*Mundo (De) Nostro Sublunari Philoso-
    phia Nova* (Gilbert), 46, 51
Mundus Subterraneus (Kircher), 5, 53
Musée Océanographique, Monaco, 382
Museum of Comparative Zoology,
    Harvard, 367

N

Nassau, H.M.S., 325
National, S.S., 377
Natura (De) Rerum Liber (Bede), 21,
    22, 23, 25

Natura (De) Rerum Liber (Isidore of Seville), 21
Naturaliste (French ship), 193
Nature (journal), 313, 317, 319, 320, 324, 326, 333, 335, 348, 368, 371
Naturis (De) Rerum (Neckham), 29
Nautical Almanac, 255
Nautical Magazine, 241
Navy Board, U.K., 234
New Experiments and Observations touching Cold (Boyle), 119
North Sea. *See* Currents; Temperatures; Tides
North West Passage expeditions, 46, 47, 69, 70, 228, 231, 277
Norway, marine science in, 306, 377, 390, 391, 392

O

Observations and Experiments about the Saltness of the Sea (Boyle), 8, 119, 124–126
Observations made during a voyage around the World (Forster), 187–188
Ocean basins, 386–387
  permanence of, theory, 387
Oceanic circulation
  Bjerknes, mathematical theory, 390
  Bourne, 44–45
  controversy between Carpenter and Croll, 318–328, 345–348
  density differences, cause, 207–211, 293, 310, 313–317, 328, 343–348, 355–357
  Pettersson, 390
  Rumford, 208–210
  salinity, variations, cause, Maury, 293–294
  temperature, variations, cause, 239
    Maury, 294. *See also* Oceanic circulation, density differences
  Thomson, C. W., 356
  wind, 319–328, 343–348
  See also Currents
Oceanographic expeditions, 324–325, 336, 350, 351, 373–374, 375, 377, 379–383, 389–390, 393

Blake, U.S.S., voyages, 380
Buccaneer, S.S., cruises, 381–382
Challenger, H.M.S., 337–358
Fram expedition, 389
German North Sea expedition (1871), 335, 336
Knight Errant, H.M.S., voyage, 373–374
Lightning, H.M.S., 307–309
Porcupine expedition (1869), 311–314; (1870), 315–317
Sandwich's, *Earl of*, expedition, 74–75
  instructions, 407–408
Scottish National Antarctic Expedition (1902–1904), 389, 391
Valdivia expedition (1898), 389–390
Oceanography, use of term, 390, 404. *See also* Marine Science
Oil, effect on waves, 199, 201
On the Saltness and Temperature of the Sea (Watson), 205
On the thermodynamics of ocean circulation (Carpenter), 324
Opus Majus (Roger Bacon), 30
Ordnance Survey, United Kingdom, 389
Origin of Species (Darwin), 299
Origine (De) Fontium (Plot), 146, 169
Other inquiries concerning the Sea (Boyle), 118, 410
Oxford Philosophical Society, 146
Ozean (Der) (Krümmel), 41

P

Pacific Ocean
  average depth, calculation from tidal waves, 286
  characteristics, 350–353. *See also* Soundings; Tides
Pack-ice, origin, 207
Pendulum experiments, determination of earth's shape, 223
Pendulums, 39, 76, 83
Penguin, H.M.S., 380, 384, 386
Peru current, 56, 185, 236
Phaedo (Plato), 5
Pheasant, H.M.S., 240
Philosophical Magazine, 285, 321, 344, 348

Philosophical Transactions (Royal Society), 80, 81, 83, 84, 88, 98, 109, 117, 146, 156, 162, 175, 180, 184, 263, 345

Philosophicis (De) Flosculis (Gerald of Wales), 30

Physical Geography in its Relation to the Prevailing Winds and Currents (Laughton), 319

Physical Geography of the Sea (Maury), 293, 294, 297

Piezometers, 353

Plankton, 232
　diurnal migration, 342
　distribution, 297, 342–343. *See also* Diatoms; Foraminifera, Globerina; Radiolarians

Plankton Expedition (1899), 377

Planet (German ship), 391

Pola (Austrian ship), 377

Polaris (ship), 353

Pommerania, S.S., 377

Porcupine expedition (1869), 311–314; (1870), 315–317

Porcupine, H.M. survey ship, 297, 312, 313, 315, 318, 324, 333, 335, 337, 353

Potassium, 238

Pourquoi Pas? (French ship), 389

Pressure as an indication of depth, Hooke, 155–157, 162–163

Pressure gauges, 76, 180–181, 197
　effect of temperature, 155–156

Pressure in the sea, 53, 74, 154, 155–156
　demonstration, Boyle, 122–123
　measurements, Tessan, 279. *See also* Piezometers

Preventive Service, United Kingdom, 259

Princesse Alice I, S.S., 382

Princesse Alice II, S.S., 382

Principia Mathematica (Newton), 84, 108, 111, 117, 166

Principles of General and Comparative Physiology (Carpenter), 306

Principles of Geology (Lyell), 286

Problemata (Aristotle), 8

Propositions of some experiments to be made by the Earl of Sandwich in his present voyage, 74, 75, 407–408

Q

Quaestiones Naturales (Adelard of Bath), 29

Quaestiones Peripateticarum (Caesalpinus), 51

Questions on Meteors (Buridan), 29

R

Racehorse, H.M.S., 189

Radiolarian ooze, 351–352

Rambler, H.M.S., 384

Rattlesnake, H.M.S., 283, 299

Regiment for the Sea (Bourne), 45

Relations about the bottom of the Sea (Boyle), 122–124, 179

Remarks on Mr. Forster's account of Captain Cook's last voyage (Wales), 187

Research, H.M.S., 380, 391

Resolution, H.M.S., 186, 187, 192

Ross Deep, Weddell Sea, 282–283

Royal Academy of Sciences, Denmark, 214

Royal Artillery, 223

Royal Geographical Society, 322, 389

Royal Institution of Great Britain, 199, 313, 327, 333

Royal Naval College, Portsmouth, 319

Royal Navy. *See* United Kingdom. Admiralty

Royal Observatory, Brussels, 260

Royal Society of London, 72, 76–77, 85, 96, 97, 117–118, 127–128, 136, 156, 158, 162, 170, 180, 181, 223, 254, 258, 263, 269, 307, 309, 313, 326, 334, 366
　Committee on Marine Researches, 311
　coral reefs, studies, 385
　currents, Strait of Gibraltar, 133–134, 141, 149
　experiments on fluids, 163
　instructions for voyages, 86, 132, 189, 280, 314–315, 337, 407–408
　marine science, co-ordination of, 333, 335
　influence on, 73–74, 84–88
　interest in, 83, 154, 166–167
　research, 79, 80, 81

Royal Society of London (*cont.*)
  observations by, 77–79
  scientific co-operation efforts, 87
  sounding machines, 41
    discussion of, 155–157
  tidal observations, 98–101, 102, 103,
    111, 155, 171, 256–257
Royal Society of Edinburgh, 378, 388
Rurik (ship), 293
Russia, marine science in, 232, 241–242,
  263, 293, 377, 381, 390

S

*Sailing Directions for the Circumnaviga-
  tion of England*, 32
Saint Albans Abbey tide table, 29
  retardation value, 22
Saint David, H.M.S., 127
Saint Helena, tides at, 85
Salinity, 45, 158, 186, 188
  analysis, 287–288. *See also* Chemical
    analysis
  Antarctic Ocean, 192
  Arctic Ocean, 192, 240
  Aristotle, 6–8, 55
  Baltic (Sound), 184
  Boyle on, 118, 124–126, 127
  Challenger Report, 374, 376
  conversion of specific gravities to, 192
  distribution, 209, 225, 230, 239, 357
    Forchhammer, 287–288
    Dittmar, 374
  effect on density, 162, 163–164, 238–
    239
  Fournier, 55
  Indian Ocean, 236
  Mas'údí, 26
  measurement, 74. *See also* Chemical
    analysis; Chlorine titration
  Middle Ages, theories, 21, 31
  observations, 74, 75, 378
    Mediterranean Sea, 288, 315–316,
      323, 324
    planned, Earl of Sandwich's ex-
      pedition, 74, 75, 407
  origin, 212–213
    Aristotle, 6–8, 46
    Boyle, 125
    Halley, 170

  surface, 7–8, 178, 184, 192
  Thames estuary, 77, 155
  Varen, 55–56. *See* Water samplers
Samarang, H.M.S., 283
Scientific communication, 276, 279, 393
Scientific co-operation, 69, 70, 290–292
  Boyle's efforts, 121, 124, 128
  Marsden squares, 290
  Royal Society's efforts, 86–87
Scientific Revolution, 58
Scotia, H.M.S., 283, 393
Scottish Fisheries Board, 378, 379, 390,
  391
Scottish Geographical Society, 388
Scottish Marine Station, Edinburgh,
  378–379, 380, 385, 391
Scottish Meteorological Society, 378
Scottish National Antarctic Expedition
  (1902–1904), 389, 391
Scottish Oceanographical Laboratory,
  391, 393
Sea, depths, 41–42, 182. *See* Soundings
  Boyle, 119
  equilibrium of land and sea, 178
Sea, origin, Greek theories, 4–5
  Mas'údí, 26
Sea floor
  composition
    Boyle, 118
    C. W. Thomson, 317
    theories of, 297, 309–310
    Challenger expedition, 337, 375
  exploration, 19th century, 294–298.
    See also Soundings
  oozes, 279, 309, 338, 342–343, 351–352
  samplers, 84
    Brooke, 295, 296. *See also* Clamms;
    Dredges
  topography
    17th century, 122
    19th century, 386–387. *See also*
    Sediments; Clays
Sea level
  atmospheric pressure, effect on, 283,
    319
  Greek scientists, 12
  mean, 263, 265–266, 289
Sea lochs, studies, Scotland, 378–379
Sea salt, characteristics, 126. *See also*
  Salinity

Sea water
  freezing point, 206
  physical properties, 206–211, 239–
    240. *See also* Salinity
Sediments, 338–339, 351–352, 375, 386
  distribution, charts, 374. *See also*
    Clays; Sea floor, oozes
Seiches, 289
Shearwater, H.M.S., 266, 320, 324, 325,
  333, 337, 380
Siemens differential thermometer. *See*
  Thermometers, electrical
Six thermometers, 229, 232, 233, 234,
  240, 293
  invention, 226–227
  pressure effects, 242–279
  protection, 311
Society for the Diffusion of Useful
  Knowledge, 254
Society for the Encouragement of the
  Arts, 213
Solstices. *See* Tides
Sounding machines, 39–41, 71; 17th
  century, 40–41; 18th century,
  213; 19th century, 284
  acceleration due to gravity, 81–83,
    156–157
  Baillie, 336
  Brooke, 295, 296
  difficulties, 85, 86–87, 157
  experiments on, 76, 85
  Hales, 180–184
  Hooke, 74–83, 155, 160–164
  Hydra, 296, 336
  Kelvin, 336, 350, 380
  Massey, 234–235, 296
  pressure, effect on floats, 85
  release mechanism, Hooke, 164
  Sandwich, *Earl of*, expedition, 407
  timing, 39. *See also* Pendulums;
    Hour glasses; Chronometers
  wire, 380. *See also* Burt's buoy and
    nipper; Echo-sounding; "Way
    Wiser"
Sounding wire, 283, 336, 350
Soundings, Renaissance, 39–41; 18th
  century, 189, 191; 19th century,
  282–284, 294, 295–297
  accumulators, introduction of, 296
  Arctic Ocean, 229, 389

Atlantic Ocean, 181, 284, 294–296,
  297
Bay of Biscay, 410
Challenger expedition, 337, 338, 351
Gulf of Lyons, 176
Mediterranean Sea, 10–11, 71, 296
navigation, Renaissance, 41–42
Pacific Ocean, 41–42, 284, 351
Ross, 280, 282–283
steam winches, effect, 296
Strait of Gibraltar, 85, 157, 239
Sandwich, *Earl of*, expedition, 407
techniques, 74, 282–285
  discussion of, 155–157. *See also*
    Echo-sounding; Lead and line
South-east wind drift, 223
Specific gravity
  Antarctic Ocean, 342
  Arctic Ocean, 226, 229, 230, 231
  comparison of ice and sea water, 160
  conversion to salinities, 192, 213
  observations, 125–126, 178, 184, 237,
    337
    instruments and difficulties, 237.
      See also Hydrometers
  Strait of Gibraltar, 207–208, 315–316
  tables, 292
  temperature effects, 184
  See also Density
Sphaera Mundi (Blancanus), 41
Springs, origin, 5–6
  16th century, 45, 46
  17th century, 169–170
  Halley, 169–170
Statical Essays (Hales), 181
Statione Zoologica, Naples, 377–378
Stationery Office, H.M., 367, 371, 387
Stork, H.M.S., 381
Strait of Gibraltar. *See* Currents;
  Soundings; Tides
Submarine geology, 374–375. *See also*
  Sea floor
Submarine ridges, 340, 354–355
  effect on temperature distribution,
    373–374
Subsurface temperatures. *See* Tem-
  peratures, depths
Subterranean channels (supposed), 11,
  21, 46, 54
  Fournier, 55

Subterranean channels (*cont.*)
   Kircher, 55
   Varen, 55
   Greaves, 71, 133. *See also* Currents;
      Strait of Gibraltar; Bosporus
Subtilitate (*De*) *Rerum* (Cardano), 53
Summa Philosophiae, 31, 45
Sweden, marine science in, 205, 211,
   390, 392
Sylva Sylvarum: or a Naturall Historie
   (F. Bacon), 46
System of the World (Newton), 109
Syzygiasticon Instauratum (Childrey),
   105

                    T

Talisman (French ship), 377
Taney, U.S. Schooner, 284
Telegraph Construction and Main-
   tenance Company, 381
Telegraphic Plateau, 295
Temperature, effect on density, 158,
   162, 163–164, 238–239
Temperature differences, cause of
   oceanic circulation. *See* Oceanic
   circulation, theories, density
Temperatures, observations
   Antarctic Ocean, 186, 232
   Arctic Ocean, 229, 230, 231, 226–227
   atmosphere, measurement, 99
      Indian Ocean, 236
   Boyle, 119–120
   Challenger expedition, 338, 375–376
   depths, 183, 186, 192, 194, 204–207,
      232, 240–241, 277, 278
      Antarctic Ocean, 187, 342
      Atlantic Ocean, 184, 191, 231–234,
         296, 314, 340. 346, 354–355
      Boyle, 120–121
      charts, *Challenger Report*, 376
      China Sea, 325–326
      constant, supposed, 204, 206
      correlation, Prestwich, 323–324, 345
      distribution,   308–310,   373–374;
         theories. *See* Oceanic circulation,
         theories, density
      Indian Ocean, 297, 310, 380
      Mediterranean Sea, 178, 204–205,
         288

   problems of measurement, 231
   Ross, 280
   serial observations, 229, 231, 314,
      338, 339
   Sulu Sea, 325, 350
   theories, 4°C., 240, 278–281, 292–
      293, 297, 308, 310, 320, 356. *See
      also* Circle of mean temperature
   Yellow Sea, 234
   Gulf Stream, 202–203, 233, 297
   Hales's apparatus, 183, 186, 232, 234,
      241. *See also* Thermometers;
      Marine Diver
   inversions, 187, 342, 379
   North Sea, 233
Surface observations, 187, 192, 194,
   202, 231–232, 233, 236
   diurnal variations, 192, 236, 289
   relative to atmosphere, 191, 193, 314
   tables, 292
   variations, seasonal, 178, 289, 378
   Thames estuary, 77, 155
Temporum (*De*) *Ratione* (Bede), 21–23
Terror, H.M.S., 277, 281
Textbooks, 16th and 17th centuries, 53
Thalassa (Wild), 357
Thames estuary. *See* Salinity; Temperatures
Théorie de la Terre (Delamétherie), 208
Thermometers, 77, 186, 349
   bi-metallic, Bréguet, 279
   Cavendish, C., 191
   electrical, 312, 315, 337, 340, 357
   insulated, 192–193, 205
   maximum and minimum, 288. *See
      also* Six thermometers
   measurement of currents with, 202–
      204
   metallic
      Johnson, 297, 336
      Massey, 235
      pressure, effects on, 297
   Miller-Casella, 311, 312, 336, 337
      controversy, 348, 350
      limitations, 342
      pressure corrections, 354
   minimum, self-registering, Hooke, 163
      Board of Trade, 297
      pressure corrections, *Challenger* ex-
         pedition, 374

Thermometers (*cont.*)
  pressure effects on, 121, 240–242, 277–
    278, 293, 296, 308, 310, 311, 339
    Aimé, 288
  protection, 229, 279, 296–297
  reversing, 288, 357
    Negretti and Zambra, 350
  self-registering, 226–227
    pressure effects, 232
"Thermometrical navigation", Wil-
    liams, 203–204
Thétis (French ship), 231
Thunder, H.M.S., 283
Tidal establishments, Bede, 22
Tidal observatories, 99, 290, 393
Tidal streams, North Sea, 24, 94
  distinction from currents, 44, 171
Tidal waves, 159, 214–215, 286
  calculation of ocean depth, 286
Tide gauges, 99, 255, 256, 257, 266
Tide tables, 24, 32, 49, 252, 254–255, 257
  prediction, 234, 252
Tides, 49–50, 71–73, 93–111, 251–270
  Arctic Ocean, 229
  Atlantic Ocean, 13, 14–15, 27, 260–267
  atmospheric pressure, effect on, 256
  Australia, 185, 194
  Bay of Fundy, 102
  British Isles, 111, 252
  Cadiz, Spain, 14–15
  calculating machines, 334
  charts, English Channel, 110
    Strait of Gibraltar, 143
  Clyde estuary, 264
  current, 51, 94, 254, 259
  cycles, 15
    Bede, 23
    diurnal inequality, 100, 102, 109,
      262–263, 266
    Australia, 185
    Indian Ocean, 14
    oscillation, Whewell, 262
  diurnal retardation, 22, 29
  earth's rotation, effect on, 268, 270
  English Channel, 28–29, 83, 96, 100–
    101, 111, 168, 266
  Europe, 50, 260–262
  factors affecting, 253, 258
  France, 50, 102, 179, 251–252
  harmonic analysis, 270, 334–335

  height, measurement, 99
    theories, Childrey, 72
    See: Tide gauges; Theories
  hydrographic surveys, 111
  Indian Ocean, 12–13, 290
  Indus River, 13
  Irish Sea, 28, 259, 268
  lunitidal interval, 15
  Mediterranean Sea, 28–29, 43, 179, 289
  moon's effect, 13, 14, 15, 30, 104
  North Sea, 94, 106, 260, 266
  observations, 75, 98–102, 263
    Aristotle, Euripus, 9, 10
    comparisons, 256, 259
    East India Company, 263
    Greeks, 8–10, 13–16
    importance, 98, 252, 259
    international co-operation (1835),
      260–261
    Ross, 280
  oscillations, effect of earth's rotation,
    270. *See also* Tides, rotary systems
  Pacific Ocean, 188–189, 263, 267
  Persian Gulf, 14
  Pliny, 15–16
  rate of rise and fall, 72, 99, 102,
    270
  records, harbours, 255, 257, 259
  research, (government support, 334–
    335
  River Dee, 264
  rotary systems, 253–254, 266
    North Sea, 261, 268, 269–270
  St Helena, 85
  Scilly Islands, 253–254
  Scotland, Western Isles, 72
  semi-diurnal, 13–14, 21, 28–29
  springs, 21, 23, 29, 95, 96, 97, 98
    cause, 100, 109
    equinoxes, 252
    occurrence, 102–109
  Severn River, 100, 102, 266
  Strait of Gibraltar, 74, 111, 144, 324
  studies, history (Lalande), 252
  Tahiti, 185
  Thames Estuary, 29, 103; effect of
    wind, 104, 256
  theories, 215; Middle Ages, 21, 24–
    25; 12th century, 29–31; 16th
    century, 49, 53

Tides (*cont.*)
theories
Adelard of Bath, 29
astrological, 24, 29
Bacon, Francis, 50
Balianus, 94
Bede, 21–24
Bourne, 44
Boyle, 118
Catholics, Renaissance, 52
Childrey, 104–105
collision of currents, 29
compression by moon, 14, 93. *See
also* Tides, theories, Descartes
Descartes, 52, 72, 109, 251
earth's rotation, 51, 72, 93. *See also*
Tides, theories, Galileo
equilibrium, 252–253, 255–256,
258, 262, 263, 266–269
Galileo, 52–53, 94–95
Gerald of Wales, 30
gravitational attraction (Kepler),
51, 52
history, Lubbock, 255
Hyrne, 105–106
Kircher, 56
magnetic attraction, 30–31, 50–51,
93, 94
Maelstrom hypothesis, 24, 29
Mas'údí, 25
navigators, 16th century, 49
Newton, 108–111, 251
oscillations, 254, 258, 267–269
Voss, 98
Wallis, 83, 93–103, 106–108
Whewell, 258–259, 261–263, 269
Toxteth, near Liverpool, 71
velocity, measurement, 99
Venice, 49
Weymouth, 107
wind effects, 22, 103, 106
Thames estuary. *See also* Cotidal
lines; Tide gauges; Waves
Titanic, S.S., disaster, influence on
marine science, 393
*Topographia Hibernica et Expugnatio
Hibernica* (Gerald of Wales), 28
Topography
submarine, 122, 386–387
17th century, 122

19th century, 386–387
nomenclature, 392. *See also* Bathy-
metric charts; Canyons; Con-
tinental shelf and slope; Mid-
ocean ridges; Submarine ridges;
Trenches
Tractatus de Causa Salsedinis (Dondi), 31
Tractatus de Fluxu et Refluxu Maris, 28,
31
*Tracts about the Cosmical Qualities of
Things* (Boyle), 119
Trade winds, Halley, 168–169
Transparency, sea water, 215, 279, 310
instruments, 315, 336
Travailleur (French ship), 377
Trawls, 312, 336
Treasure for Travellers (Bourne), 43
Treasury, U.K. *See* United Kingdom.
Treasury
Trenches, deep sea, 386
Trent, H.M.S., 228
Trinculo, H.M.S., 235
Triton, H.M.S., 374
Tsunami. *See* Tidal waves
Tuscarora, U.S. Survey ship, 346, 350,
351, 386

U

Undercurrents, 124, 232
Bosporus, 147–149, 175, 179, 207,
320, 344
detection, machines, 144. *See also*
Current drogues and metres
equatorial regions, 339, 382
Sound, 134–135, 146, 208, 326
Forchhammer, 289
Strait of Gibraltar, 74, 133, 135, 144–
146, 157, 175, 207–208, 225, 289,
315–316, 319, 323, 344
See also Currents
United Kingdom. Admiralty, 189, 228,
234, 252, 253, 256–257, 260, 266,
269, 307, 311, 325, 333, 334, 366,
370, 381
tide tables, 257
Board of Longitude, 186, 189, 194,
234, 235
Board of Ordnance, 213
Board of Trade, 296, 297
Meteorological Department, 292

United Kingdom (*cont.*)
  Colonial Office, 290
  Geological Survey, 277
  Hydrographic Department, Admir-
    alty, 255, 257, 258, 290, 296–298,
    380–381
  Navy Board, 234
  Ordnance Survey, 389
  Preventive Service, 259
  Royal Artillery, 223
  Stationery Office, H.M., 367, 371, 387
  Treasury, 370, 371, 372, 387
    grant for *Challenger Report*, 366
United States of America. Coast Survey,
    269, 286, 380
  currents, 292
  Gulf Stream studies, 291, 309, 339
  temperatures, Atlantic Ocean, 318
USA Fish Commission, 379, 380
USA Naval Observatory, 291
United States of America, marine
    science in, 202, 203, 277, 286,
    291, 293–296, 297, 309, 350, 351,
    367, 377, 379, 380, 385, 393
Upwelling, Atlantic Ocean, 233, 236
Uranie (French ship), 231

                    V

Vegetable Staticks (Hales), 180, 181
Valdivia expedition (1898), 389–390
Valdivia, S.S., 377
Volcanic activity, effect on submarine
    topography, 158–159, 387
  as source of deep sea clays, 351, 375
Vénus (French ship), 277, 278–279, 282,
    285, 292
*Verie Necessarie and Profitable Booke
    Concerning Navigation* (Tais-
    nier), 50
Vettor Pisani (Italian ship), 377
Vitiaz (Russian ship), 377
Volcanoes, supposed effect on tem-
    peratures, 120
Vøringen, S.S., 377
Voyages of exploration, 231–232, 277
  British, 185–192, 194, 228
  French, 192–193, 231–232
  contributions to marine science, 185–
    194, 228–232, 277–281

                    W

Walvis Ridge, 354
Washington (Italian ship), 379
Water bottles. *See* Water samplers
Water samples, 230, 231, 407
  Arctic Ocean, 230
  Bosporus, 225
  depths, Ross, 280
  Mediterranean Sea, 239
Water samplers, 79–81, 312; 19th
    century, 225–227
  Daubeny, 287
  Davy, 229, 230
  Hales, 183, 186, 232, 234
  Hooke, 155
  Marcet, 225–226, 230, 233
  stop-cock, Buchanan, 336
  See also "Marine Diver"
Waterspouts, Mas'údí, 26
Waves, 285–286
  Aristotle, 9
  Boyle, 118
  breaking, measurement of force ex-
    erted, 286
    Leonardo da Vinci's studies, 42
  deep water, behaviour in, 286
  effect of oil, 199, 201
  effect on coasts, 214, 286
  experienced at depths, 123, 286
  heights, 179, 285
    measurement, Stanley, 286
  induced, 264
  length, measurement, 286
  long, 264–265
  model studies, 264
  movement of water in, 214, 289
  observations, 264
    Tessan, 279
  origin, fermentation, 213–214
    wind, 214
  theories, 263–265
    Newton, 263
  translation, wave of, 264–265
  velocity, 253, 285
    definition, Lagrange, 264
    measurement, Stanley, 286
  water movements in, Aimé, 289
  See also Seiches; Tides; Tidal waves
"Way-Wiser", Hooke, 162–163

Wernerian Natural History Society Memoirs, 227

West of Scotland Marine Biological Association, 392

West wind drift current, 223

Winches, steam, effect on soundings, 296

Wind and current patterns, 49

Winds, 50, 168, 203
  charts, Maury, 291
  correlation of information, 290
  speed, measurement, 99

Wire rope, 380

Wood floats, effect of pressure on, 241

Woods Hole Marine Biological Laboratory, U.S.A., 379

Woods Hole Oceanographic Institution, U.S.A., 393

World wars I and II, effect on marine science community, 393

Z

Zelée (French ship), 277